RESEARCH HANDBOOK ON PARTNERSHIPS, LLCs AND ALTERNATIVE FORMS OF BUSINESS ORGANIZATIONS

RESEARCH HANDBOOKS IN CORPORATE LAW AND GOVERNANCE

Elgar *Research Handbooks* are original reference works designed to provide a broad overview of research in a given field while at the same time creating a forum for more challenging, critical examination of complex and often under-explored issues within that field. Chapters by international teams of contributors are specially commissioned by editors who carefully balance breadth and depth. Often widely cited, individual chapters present expert scholarly analysis and offer a vital reference point for advanced research. Taken as a whole they achieve a wide-ranging picture of the state-of-the-art.

Making a major scholarly contribution to the field of corporate law and governance, the volumes in this series explore topics of current concern from a range of jurisdictions and perspectives, offering a comprehensive analysis that will inform researchers, practitioners and students alike. The *Research Handbooks* cover the fundamental aspects of corporate law, such as insolvency governance structures, as well as hot button areas such as executive compensation, insider trading, and directors' duties. The *Handbooks*, each edited by leading scholars in their respective fields, offer far-reaching examinations of current issues in corporate law and governance that are unrivalled in their blend of critical, substantive analysis, and in their synthesis of contemporary research.

Each *Handbook* stands alone as an invaluable source of reference for all scholars of corporate law, as well as for practicing lawyers who wish to engage with the discussion of ideas within the field. Whether used as an information resource on key topics or as a platform for advanced study, volumes in this series will become definitive scholarly reference works in the field.

Titles in this series include:

Research Handbook on Executive Pay
Edited by Randall S. Thomas and Jennifer G. Hill

Research Handbook on Insider Trading
Edited by Stephen M. Bainbridge

Research Handbook on Directors' Duties
Edited by Adolfo Paolini

Research Handbook on Shareholder Power
Edited by Jennifer G. Hill and Randall S. Thomas

Research Handbook on Partnerships, LLCs and Alternative Forms of Business Organizations
Edited by Robert W. Hillman and Mark J. Loewenstein

Research Handbook on Partnerships, LLCs and Alternative Forms of Business Organizations

Edited by

Robert W. Hillman

FBP Distinguished Professor of Law, University of California, Davis School of Law, USA

Mark J. Loewenstein

Monfort Professor of Commercial Law, University of Colorado Law School, USA

RESEARCH HANDBOOKS IN CORPORATE LAW AND GOVERNANCE

Cheltenham, UK • Northampton, MA, USA

© The Editors and Contributors Severally 2015

All rights reserved. No part of this publication may be reproduced, stored in a retrieval system or transmitted in any form or by any means, electronic, mechanical or photocopying, recording, or otherwise without the prior permission of the publisher.

Published by
Edward Elgar Publishing Limited
The Lypiatts
15 Lansdown Road
Cheltenham
Glos GL50 2JA
UK

Edward Elgar Publishing, Inc.
William Pratt House
9 Dewey Court
Northampton
Massachusetts 01060
USA

A catalogue record for this book
is available from the British Library

Library of Congress Control Number: 2015935890

This book is available electronically in the Elgaronline
Law subject collection
DOI 10.4337/9781783474400

ISBN 978 1 78347 439 4 (cased)
ISBN 978 1 78347 440 0 (eBook)

Typeset by Servis Filmsetting Ltd, Stockport, Cheshire
Printed and bound in Great Britain by T.J. International Ltd, Padstow

Contents

List of contributors		viii
Introduction		1

PART 1   CONTRACTUAL FREEDOM

1	The siren song of unlimited contractual freedom *Leo E. Strine, Jr. and J. Travis Laster*	11
2	Freedom of contract for alternative entities in Delaware: myth or reality? *Mark J. Loewenstein*	28
3	Contractual freedom and family business *Benjamin Means*	40

PART 2   INTERNAL RELATIONSHIPS

4	Alternative entities in Delaware—re-introduction of fiduciary concepts by the backdoor? *Douglas M. Branson*	55
5	*Achaian* and interest transfers among existing partners and members *J. William Callison*	70
6	Agency in the alternatives: common-law perspectives on binding the firm *Deborah A. DeMott*	81

PART 3   RELATIONSHIPS WITH THIRD PARTIES

7	Is the liability of limited liability entities really limited? *Allan G. Donn*	99
8	Mitigating the impact of a counterparty LLC's financial distress *Jennifer Ivey-Crickenberger and Michelle M. Harner*	116
9	Attacking asset protection LLCs *Franklin A. Gevurtz*	129

PART 4   TAX AND ACCOUNTING

10	Tax aspects of partnerships, LLCs, and alternative forms of business organizations *Bradley T. Borden*	147

vi   *Partnerships, LLCs and alternative forms of business organizations*

| 11 | Capital accounts in LLCs and in partnerships
Donald J. Weidner | 168 |

PART 5   DISSOLUTION AND FUNDAMENTAL CHANGES

| 12 | Fundamental changes in the LLC: a study in path-divergence and convergence
Joan MacLeod Heminway | 189 |
| 13 | Care and loyalty after the dissociation from or dissolution of an unincorporated entity
Thomas E. Rutledge | 206 |

PART 6   SPECIALIZED ENTITIES

14	Nonprofit and charitable uses of LLCs *Cassady V. "Cass" Brewer*	227
15	State laboratories and social enterprise law *J. Haskell Murray*	252
16	Business trusts *Peter B. Oh*	268
17	The law firm as an industry model for entity choice and management *Allison Martin Rhodes and Robyn Axberg*	280

PART 7   JUDICIAL AND LEGISLATIVE RESPONSES

18	Harmonization, rationalization, and uniformity *Robert R. Keatinge*	299
19	Casual convergence in unincorporated entity law *Nadelle Grossman*	319
20	Dictum in alternative entity jurisprudence and the expansion of judicial power in Delaware *Mohsen Manesh*	336

PART 8   INTERNATIONAL PERSPECTIVES ON ALTERNATIVE FORMS

| 21 | Partnership options in the UK: good things come in threes
Elspeth Berry | 357 |
| 22 | Legislative policy of alternative forms of business organization: the case of Japanese LLCs
Zenichi Shishido | 374 |

23	Return of the prodigal form? Partnerships and partnership law in the People's Republic of China *Nicholas Calcina Howson*	390
24	Alternatives to capital-oriented corporations under Russian law *Vladimir Orlov*	412
25	The advent of the LLP in India *Afra Afsharipour*	429
26	The evolution of non-corporate forms of business in Taiwan—introducing the LLP as an alternative business form *Andrew Jen-Guang Lin*	447
27	Brazilian alternatives to the corporate form of organization *André Antunes Soares de Camargo*	471

Index   481

Contributors

Afra Afsharipour, University of California, Davis, School of Law

Robyn Axberg, Holland & Knight LLP

Elspeth Berry, Nottingham Law School, Nottingham Trent University

Bradley T. Borden, Brooklyn Law School

Douglas M. Branson, University of Pittsburgh School of Law

Cassady V. "Cass" Brewer, Georgia State University College of Law

J. William Callison, Faegre Baker Daniels LLP

André Antunes Soares de Camargo, Insper, São Paulo, Brazil

Deborah A. DeMott, Duke University School of Law

Allan G. Donn, Willcox & Savage, PC

Franklin A. Gevurtz, University of the Pacific, McGeorge School of Law

Nadelle Grossman, Marquette University Law School

Michelle M. Harner, University of Maryland Francis King Carey School of Law

Joan MacLeod Heminway, The University of Tennessee College of Law

Nicholas Calcina Howson, University of Michigan Law School

Jennifer Ivey-Crickenberger, University of Maryland Francis King Carey School of Law

Robert R. Keatinge, Holland & Hart LLP

Hon. J. Travis Laster, Delaware Court of Chancery

Andrew Jen-Guang Lin, National Taiwan University College of Law

Mark J. Loewenstein, University of Colorado Law School

Mohsen Manesh, University of Oregon School of Law

Allison Martin Rhodes, Holland & Knight LLP

Benjamin Means, University of South Carolina School of Law

J. Haskell Murray, Belmont University

Peter B. Oh, University of Pittsburgh School of Law

Vladimir Orlov, University of Helsinki

Thomas E. Rutledge, Stoll Keenon Ogden PLLC

Zenichi Shishido, Hitotsubashi University, Graduate School of International Corporate Strategy

Hon. Leo E. Strine, Jr., Delaware Supreme Court

Donald J. Weidner, Florida State University College of Law

Introduction

This book is devoted to alternative entities—primarily partnerships and limited liability companies. The partnership has been a viable form of association for centuries. The much more recent limited liability company (LLC), which traces its origins to a statute drafted by a group of Wyoming lawyers in 1977, has increasingly become the business organization of choice for new businesses in the United States. Modeled after partnership law, the purpose of the Wyoming statute was to develop a limited liability entity that would qualify for partnership taxation. Prior to the LLC, the entity of choice to achieve those goals was the limited partnership (LP). The LP was less than ideal for these purposes, however, as the general partner retained unlimited liability and the Internal Revenue Service (IRS) could scrutinize the LP's agreements to determine whether the entity had more corporate-like characteristics than partnership-like characteristics. If it did, the IRS took the position that the entity should be taxed like a corporation; if not, the entity would be taxed like a partnership, with pass-through taxation. This IRS practice generated significant transactions costs for LPs, as promoters had to carefully craft their partnership agreements to meet the IRS tests and, to assure limited partners of pass-through taxation, retain a lawyer to render a legal opinion that the entity would be taxed as a partnership.

The Wyoming LLC was successful in achieving its twin goals. It simply provided that no member of the entity would be vicariously liable for the entity's debts or obligations merely by being a member. And as to the tax question, the statute provided certain partnership-like characteristics were "hard wired;" that is, those statutory provisions could not be altered by agreement, thus assuring that the entity would be treated as a partnership for tax purposes. Except for such provisions, the parties were free to craft their relationship as they chose.

The post-1977 preference for the LLC accelerated with a change in the federal income law in 1997, when the IRS abandoned its decades-long practice of scrutinizing whether an alternative entity should be taxed like a corporation and, instead, let alternative entities, regardless of the terms of their governance documents, elect to be taxed as a corporation or partnership. This new regulation is widely known as the "check-the-box" rule. The hard-wired provisions in the Wyoming statute and those that followed its lead were no longer necessary and, rather quickly, statutes were amended to delete such provisions. Somewhat belatedly, the National Conference of Commissioners Uniform State Laws (NCCUSL) proposed a uniform LLC act in 1995 (ULLCA, amended in 1996 to accommodate the check-the-box rules). ULLCA was substantially revised in 2006 (RULLCA). Although these uniform acts have not been widely adopted by the states without substantial amendment, each has influenced the drafters of state LLC laws.

With the development of attractive alternatives to corporations, there has been a growing body of case law and scholarly commentary. A good deal of this litigation and scholarship has focused on the extent to which there might be limits on the contractual freedom afforded to parties under the applicable statute. This volume presents three chapters devoted to the topic. Internal relations, that is, the law and policy as they relate to the relationship among the parties to a partnership or LLC, as well as the relationship of these actors to outsiders, are considered in six chapters. Tax and accounting issues are represented in two chapters, as are dissolution and fundamental changes.

Alternatives to corporations have been used in many specialized settings and for a variety of purposes, not just as vehicles for commercial enterprises. Four chapters are devoted to this phenomenon. This volume also includes three chapters considering the ways in which the courts and legislatures have responded to the growth of alternative entity law. It concludes with seven chapters offering international perspectives, drawing on the law of the United Kingdom, Japan, China, Russia, India, Taiwan and Brazil.

A summary of the chapters follows.

Chapter 1, by two distinguished jurists from the Delaware judiciary—Leo Strine Jr., the Chief Justice of the Delaware Supreme Court, and J. Travis Laster, the Vice-Chancellor of the Court of Chancery—challenges the conventional wisdom of allowing virtually unlimited contractual freedom in alternative entity agreements. In their experience, arms-length bargaining between sponsors and investors over the terms of the governing instruments of alternative entities does not take place. Moreover, when investors try to evaluate contract terms, the expansive contractual freedom authorized by the alternative entity statutes hampers rather than helps. A lack of standardization prevails in the alternative entity arena, imposing material transaction costs on investors with corresponding effects for the cost of capital borne by sponsors, without generating offsetting benefits. Because contractual drafting is a difficult task, it is also not clear that even alternative entity managers are always well served by situational deviations from predictable defaults. In light of these problems, the authors propose that a sensible set of standard fiduciary defaults might benefit all constituents of alternative entities.

Chapter 2, by Professor Mark Loewenstein, explores whether, in fact, the Delaware courts consistently honor the contractual freedom enshrined in the Delaware alternative entity statutes. He finds that a number of Delaware cases can give one pause about the commitment of the Delaware judiciary to freedom of contract, either because the language of the opinion seems less than absolute or the result can be characterized as an implicit rejection of freedom of contract. The latter are relatively rare, he concludes, but extant, while the former are abundant.

In Chapter 3, Professor Benjamin Means considers the wisdom of contractual freedom in family businesses, concluding that a contractarian framework is typically insufficient to support the expectations of family participants. As is true of any closely held business, contracts in family businesses establish relationships rather than the terms of specific, bargained-for exchanges, and the parties cannot be expected to anticipate and adequately address all eventualities that may occur over time. For family businesses, relational aspects are particularly significant: the time horizon stretches across generations, objectives often include more than simple profit maximization, and business dealings involve emotional consequences for the participants that also need to be acknowledged. Instead of adhering to a false assumption that the parties to a business venture are capable of negotiating adequate protections for themselves and likely to do so, Professor Means concludes that contract law should offer a resource—a set of principles that credit the parties' negotiated bargain in full context but that also compensate for what they cannot anticipate or adequately address.

Chapter 4, by Professor Douglas Branson, considers the importance of the implied covenant of good faith and fair dealing in interpreting agreements that govern alternative entities (e.g., operating agreements for LLCs and partnership agreements for LPs). The implied covenant is a part of every contract and, despite statutory freedom of contract provisions in Delaware alternative entity statutes, may serve as a way courts can impose fiduciary duties on those who manage and control alternative entities. His chapter explores the question of how application of the implied covenant results in the application of fiduciary-like concepts, if not fiduciary duties themselves.

In Chapter 5, William Callison examines the case of *Achaian v. Leemon Family LLC*, where the Delaware Court of Chancery held that the terms of an LLC agreement permitted the transfer of voting and other non-economic interests among existing members without member consent. The Court supported its decision with substantial dictum to the effect that the so-called "pick-your-partner" rule of partnership and LLC law provides the same result. His chapter discusses the pick-your-partner concept, criticizes the *Achaian* decision, and considers whether allowing inter-member transfers of both economic rights and managerial and voting power without member consent should be the default rule.

In Chapter 6, Professor Deborah DeMott explores the external aspects of agency law in the context of unincorporated firms, that is, the capacity to bind the firm to the legal consequences of interactions with third parties. She focuses in particular on the impact of acts done by a representative of the firm for which the representative lacked actual authority. She differentiates the terminology and concepts associated with partnership law from the common law of agency, and she argues that basic agency issues in the context of LLCs are muddled, in part due to a historically explicable overhang of partnership concepts and terminology—since obviated by changes in tax law—and that the muddle most significantly affects LLCs organized under the Delaware LLC statute. Her chapter demonstrates that such confusion is not inevitable and that, short of formal changes in statutory text, judicial decisions and an arguable consensus among expert lawyers may mitigate the confusion.

In Chapter 7, Allan G. Donn explores the liability "shield" that owners and affiliates assume will protect them from third-party claims arising out of the property or activities of the entity. Many exceptions have developed, however, to the anticipated liability protection. He categorizes the exceptions into three types: first, explicit exceptions in the entity's organization statute or judicial interpretations of that statute; second, judicial concepts, such as piercing the corporate veil and successor liability; and third, a statutory override of the entity act's general liability shield. The chapter demonstrates that erosion of the liability shield continues not only with the application of judicial concepts, such as piercing the veil and successor liability, but by the proliferation of statutes that impose liability directly on owners and affiliates of an entity.

In Chapter 8, Jennifer Ivery-Crickenberger and Professor Michelle Harner consider the law as it relates to the rights of a counter-party to an LLC when that LLC experiences financial distress. They note how the law governing creditors' rights against LLCs continues to evolve and is often called upon to reconcile federal bankruptcy law, applicable state entity law, any operating agreement governing the LLC, and the parties' contract. This chapter summarizes certain key issues facing creditors of alternative entities, including: the enforceability of waivers and ipso facto (bankruptcy termination) clauses in prepetition operating and partnership agreements; the impact of the automatic stay and plan injunction provisions on creditors' rights against the members or partners of a bankrupt entity; and the effect of charging orders in the bankruptcy context.

In Chapter 9, Professor Franklin A. Gevurtz addresses LLCs set up to protect property personally used by the LLC's owner from seizure by the owner's creditors (asset protection LLCs). He notes that the normal remedy available to creditors of owners of an LLC is a charging order commanding the company to pay to the creditor, instead of the debtor, the debtor's share of any distributions the company makes. This does not work when the LLC is set up to hold assets personally used by a solitary owner rather than to operate a business. The chapter examines the creditor's remedies based upon creative use of charging orders, bankruptcy law, fraudulent transfer statutes, and reverse piercing. It challenges existing scholarship in the area and argues that, properly understood and aggressively applied, these remedies are sufficient to prevent abuse.

In Chapter 10, Professor Bradley T. Borden explores taxation, an important part of any discussion of alternative entities. He provides an overview of U.S. partnership tax (the most complex and perhaps prevalent form of flow-through taxation) and introduces other forms of flow-through taxation. He observes that although alternatives offer tax advantages that explain a large part of their popularity, choosing between corporate and non-corporate entities can be complicated for many businesses, and he explains why some partnerships and LLCs elect to be taxed as corporations. The chapter also identifies some basic cross-border uses of such entities in tax planning.

In Chapter 11, Dean Donald J. Weidner elucidates the significance and use of capital accounts (separate equity accounts) in both partnerships (where they normally are required) and LLCs (where they are not required). He explains why a fundamental understanding of capital accounts analysis is important for understanding accounting practice, potential state default rules, and federal income tax compliance. He also demonstrates how capital accounts analysis is a powerful analytic tool to sharpen the understanding of the economic arrangement of the owners, particularly with respect to how and to what extent they have agreed to share different items of loss.

Chapter 12, by Professor Joan MacLeod Heminway, explores how LLC law deals with fundamental changes, including amendments to LLC organizational documents, organic transactions (merger, conversions, and domestications), and dissolutions. Noting that LLC law originally derived principally from partnership law and emphasized co-equal consent and private ordering among business venturers, she observes that in the courts and in state legislatures corporate law norms have come to play a stronger role in LLC law and emphasis on freedom of contract has intensified. As a result, current LLC law generally does not treat ownership interests in LLCs as property in which members have vested rights that require their individual consent, along with that of all other members, to actions taken by the LLC. Finally, changes to LLC law consistent with these trends have provoked changes to the structure of LLC statutes and entity law statutes more generally. This chapter reviews the current state of fundamental change doctrine in the LLC form in the United States, maps elements of that doctrine to key developments in LLC law, and draws related summary conclusions.

Chapter 13, by Thomas Rutledge, considers fiduciary duties in the context of an event of dissociation or the dissolution of the alternative entity. He notes that both the dissociation of a participant from, and the dissolution of, an unincorporated venture are occasions on which the existing relationship and the resultant fiduciary obligations are subject to either modification or termination. The existing statutory laws are inconsistent in acknowledging the impact of dissociation and dissolution upon fiduciary obligations and as well in providing guidance thereon, even as the most famous partnership case, *Meinhard v. Salmon*, arose out of allegations that the fiduciary bond between partners continued as to activities post the partnership's purpose. This chapter discusses the manner in which uniform and model unincorporated entity statutes do or do not address the impact of dissociation and dissolution, the confusing case law guidance that has been handed down, the manner in which these disputes should be initially analyzed, and the important of a priori drafting to address potential problems.

In Chapter 14, Professor Cass Brewer explores the use of LLCs in nonprofit and charitable ventures, including the use of LLCs in hybrid for-profit/nonprofit arrangements. This chapter provides necessary background information on the nonprofit and charitable sector, surveys the relatively common use of LLCs as nonprofit subsidiaries or affiliates, and examines how LLCs are used to facilitate certain charitable or quasi-charitable activities, including program-related investments and social enterprise. He concludes with some very recent, innovative uses of LLCs by donors to charities.

In Chapter 15, Professor Haskell Murray, explores the use of LLCs in the growing field of social enterprises. Social enterprise legal forms first emerged in the United States in 2008 and now a majority of states have passed one or more social enterprise statutes. These social enterprise forms include low-profit limited liability companies ("L3Cs"), benefit corporations, benefit limited liability companies, flexible purpose corporations, social purpose corporations, and public benefit corporations. Social enterprises, also called hybrid firms, have attracted increasing academic attention, but little has been written on if and how states are competing for these entities. This chapter attempts to fill that void, while also providing an overview of the different entity types and highlighting some of the variations within each type.

In Chapter 16, Professor Peter B. Oh challenges the common view that the business trust is an obscure and unimportant form of business association and argues the importance of the business trust today. He traces the development of business trusts over the past two centuries as the form has evolved from a creature of common law into modern statutory and contractarian forms. Not surprisingly, Delaware again takes the lead by allowing statutory business trusts with unquestioned limited liability (for beneficiaries and trustees) and by embracing a *laissez faire* approach allowing contractual flexibility. The chapter discusses contemporary uses of business trusts in such diverse settings as holding real estate, asset securitization, risk management, and pooled asset management (most notably, pension plans). Although the chapter suggests business trusts should be used to an even greater extent than they are today, it recognizes that to unlock the true potential of this alternative, more empirical and other information on the use of business trusts is required.

In Chapter 17, Allison Martin Rhodes and Robyn Axberg discuss why law firms are distinct from typical business entities and how the notion of the law partnership has evolved and will continue to evolve to serve the profession. The chapter explores the unique regulatory, cultural, and historical forces affecting law firms, which drive entity selection, governing agreements, and management. Partnership law is the beginning of the story, but ethics rules that govern lawyer conduct and order relationships among lawyers and with clients play a pervasive role. State regulation of the law firm and the high stakes of personal and professional liability also drive the business model. The chapter evaluates how law firms struggle to select structures that both ensure compliance with the ethics rules and promote stability and flexibility in firm management.

In Chapter 18, Robert Keatinge explores the phenomena of harmonization, rationalization, and uniformity in business entity legislation. The number of business entities from which an entrepreneur may choose has increased dramatically in the past 40 years. This change has been reflected in modification of the traditional forms of business organization (such as partnerships, corporations, and LPs), the introduction of variants on the traditional forms (such as the LLP and limited liability limited partnership) and the introduction of entirely new forms (the best example of which is the LLC). Each form may be considered as a collection of "characteristics." The proliferation and changes in the forms of business organization have resulted in a corresponding change and increase in the characteristics of the forms and fostered a desire to bring some order and consistency to the statutes under which the organizations exist. This desire has been reflected in three statutory movements: harmonization (the attempt to eliminate unintentional distinctions among the characteristics), rationalization (a desire to eliminate intentional distinctions among the forms seeking to select the "best" characteristics from among the traditional and new forms and impose that characteristic on all forms), and pursuit of uniformity (the movement to conform the statutes of the various jurisdictions governing a particular form to each other). This chapter compares and contrasts these three movements, providing insights into how the law might efficiently evolve.

In Chapter 19, Professor Nadelle Grossman focuses on uniformity as a goal in alternative entity law, analyzing the debate between supporters of uniformity, including NCCUSL, who argue that uniformity among state LLC acts generates administrative and cost savings, and its critics, who argue that uniformity undermines state experimentation to achieve more efficient LLC laws. She argues in the chapter that these debates about uniformity are misguided. She demonstrates, through a qualitative study of the LLC acts of the first seven adopters of RULLCA, that states diverge frequently, often extensively, from RULLCA. Relying on her interviews of practitioners on the committees that ushered through these new LLC acts, she concluded that uniformity was not a primary goal sought by most of these LLC act committees. She argues that a framework of casual convergence, rather than uniformity, better captures the posture of LLC law. By reformulating LLC law as casually convergent, she suggests that commentators and policy makers can turn their debate to the advantages and disadvantages of such loose convergence, and whether it achieves the right balance between uniformity and state experimentation.

Chapter 20, by Professor Mohsen Manesh, explores the use of dictum by Delaware courts to shape the law of alternative entities. He notes that the liberal use of dictum by the Delaware courts to address matters unnecessary to the resolution of the disputes with which they are presented is a celebrated facet of the state's rich corporate law tradition. Indeed, academics, practitioners, and jurists alike have praised the judicial practice as a distinctive and invaluable feature of Delaware corporate law—a vital reason for the state's success in attracting corporate charters. Less noticed, however, is dictum's role in Delaware's burgeoning unincorporated alternative entity jurisprudence. As this chapter shows, when one probes Delaware's LP and LLC decisions, one sees the same judicial hallmarks of dictum familiar to the state's corporate law precedents. This use of dictum, in both the corporate and alternative entity contexts, in turn represents only one facet of

Introduction 7

a larger legal system that has evolved in Delaware to empower the state bench to act as the chief regulator of all Delaware businesses.

In Chapter 21, Professor Elspeth Berry evaluates the three types of partnership which the UK offers as alternatives to a company as a business vehicle. These are the general partnership, the LP and the limited liability partnership (LLP). She observes that of the three, the general partnership, enshrined in statute in the 19th century, offers the most flexibility, informality, and privacy. It is governed by one short piece of legislation, much of which is subject to contrary agreement. The LP, which was established shortly afterwards, is a variation on the general partnership and offers limited liability to some of the partners in return for registration and the non-engagement of those partners in management. In contrast, the more recent LLP is actually a body corporate and offers features of both partnership and company law, including limited liability for all its members in return for registration and disclosure of its accounts. The author notes that the LLP legislation has yet to be fully tested by the courts, so that considerable areas of uncertainty remain, particularly as to whether members can also be employees, and their mutual duties and their enforcement. She also comments that it suffers from the modern disease of excessive legislative governance with over 30 enactments to date.

In Chapter 22, Professor Zenichi Shishido examines choice of legal form by closely held business organizations in Japan, with a primary focus on the Stock Company and LLC forms. These two forms provide firms with varying degrees of contractual freedom, particularly relating to order-made membership rights, exit options, and fiduciary duties. But demand for contractual freedom varies depending on the needs of a given firm. By analyzing the incentive structures of family firms, partnership-type firms, and venture capital-backed firms, the chapter elucidates the advantages and disadvantages of the Stock Company and LLC forms for firms with different appetites for contractual freedom. It discusses implications for the legislative policy surrounding choice of legal form, and it offers a proposed solution allowing firms to choose complementary "sets" of fiduciary duties and exit options depending on the dynamics of the bargaining situation they face.

Chapter 23, by Professor Nicholas Calcina Howson, provides a broad introduction to the partnership form of business organization in the People's Republic of China (PRC). It considers historical antecedents of the law-based partnership form in China's imperial, Republican, and Communist post-1949 but pre-reform periods; critical aspects of the PRC's current partnership law and applied partnership norms (including those designed for foreign-invested but China-domiciled partnership vehicles); and the ways in which China's judicial institutions presently engage with both formal partnership establishments and other law-based and non-law-based alternative enterprise forms in contemporary China (including holdovers from an entirely different ideological and political economic context). Of particular note is the chapter's discussion of the judiciary's aggressive efforts to apply statutory or apparently equitable partnership law principles ex post with respect to capital aggregating arrangements that are not ex ante registered as formal partnerships under PRC law or subject to explicit partnership agreements, and indeed arrangements that are registered or self-declared as something else entirely.

In Chapter 24, Professor Vladimir Orlov explores the legal forms of business activity in Russia that are distinct from capital-oriented corporations because of the personal participation of owners. These forms include partnerships, cooperatives, and limited liability companies. He discusses the recently updated business law in the context of a legal culture that traditionally is highly prescriptive in nature. He concludes that in contrast with large companies, smaller enterprises based on owners' personal participation need simple and flexible rules. They are not well served by inflexible legislative solutions and a business law that is becoming ever more prescriptive in nature.

Chapter 25, by Professor Afra Afsharipour, evaluates India's 2008 legislative adoption of the Limited Liability Partnership Act. The chapter discusses how the legislation, which was a long time coming, was prompted by the pleas of entrepreneurs and professionals for a more flexible associational form offering limited liability and reduced regulatory compliance costs when compared with the existing company option. But despite the initial fanfare, the new LLP option has fallen short of its potential. Professor Afsharipour discusses the reasons for the lukewarm reception, including regulatory uncertainties concerning the use of the LLP form by law firms and continuing obstacles to foreign direct investment in LLPs. She concludes that the LLP experience demonstrates that the success of future legislative reforms will key on comprehensive reform of the legislative process and a more complete buy-in from powerful constituencies.

In Chapter 26, Professor Andrew Jen-Guang Lin discusses the fundamentals of partnership law in Taiwan as well as existing options of Silent Partnerships under the Civil Code and Unlimited Companies with Limited Liability Shareholders set forth in the Company Act. He notes that the special needs of venture capital, accounting, and law firms have prompted efforts, supported by the government, to introduce yet another form of business association, the LP, to Taiwan. Although the Proposed Limited Partnership Act has not been enacted into law, its favorable prospects prompt him to offer a detailed analysis of how the new LP will differ from existing associational forms.

In Chapter 27, Professor André Antunes Soares de Camargo presents a broad view of the Brazilian alternatives to the corporate form of organization, starting with the main characteristics of doing business in Brazil, then analyzing the most important contractual forms that an investor may take into account as a first move into the Brazilian market. The chapter discusses the main business association forms under Brazilian laws and considers investor options in establishing a different and separate legal entity, which leads to different rules (rights and obligations) and possible reduction of autonomy but synergy gains as well. The chapter also evaluates the main changes that two Bills of law currently under discussion by the Brazilian Congress will possibly cause to this subject matter.

PART 1

CONTRACTUAL FREEDOM

1. The siren song of unlimited contractual freedom
Leo E. Strine, Jr. and J. Travis Laster

One frequently cited distinction between alternative entities—such as limited liability companies (LLC) and limited partnerships (LP)—and their corporate counterparts is the greater contractual freedom accorded alternative entities. Eschewing the supposedly rigid mandatory default rules that characterize American corporate law statutes, the statutes that authorize alternative entities declare as public policy the goal of granting the broadest contractual freedom possible,[1] and permit the parties to the governing instrument to waive any of the statutory or common law default principles of law and to shape their own relationships.

Consistent with this vision, discussions of alternative entities tend to conjure up images of bargaining similar to what occurs between sophisticated parties bargaining over a commercial agreement, such as a joint venture or licensing agreement, with the parties tailoring a contract to the unique features of their relationship. As judges who collectively have over 20 years of experience deciding disputes involving alternative entities, we use this chapter to surface some questions regarding the extent to which this common understanding of alternative entities is sound. In particular, we question whether this understanding diverges from reality in precisely the context in which it is most important: namely, when alternative entities are used as vehicles to raise capital, either directly from ordinary investors or from accredited investors such as pension funds, universities, or foundations.

Based on the cases we have decided and our reading of many other cases decided by our judicial colleagues, we do not discern evidence of arms-length bargaining between the sponsors of the alternative entities and the investors in the governing instruments of alternative entities that raise capital from diverse investors. Rather, these governing instruments seem to be drafted unilaterally by the sponsors and proposed on a take-it-or-leave-it

---

[1] *See* 6 *Del. C.* § 17-1101(c) ("It is the policy of [the Limited Partnership Act] to give maximum effect to the principle of freedom of contract and to the enforceability of partnership agreements."); 6 *Del. C.* § 18-1101(b) ("It is the policy of [the LLC Act] to give the maximum effect to the principle of freedom of contract and to the enforceability of limited liability company agreements."); *see also* 12 *Del. C.* § 3825(b) ("It is the policy of [the Trust Act] to give the maximum effect to the principle of freedom of contract and to the enforceability of governing instruments."); *PHL Variable Ins. Co. v. Price Dawe Ins. Trust*, 28 A.3d 1059, 1077 (Del. 2011) ("The policy of the Delaware Statutory Trust Act is to give maximum effect to freedom of contract . . . ."); *Olson v. Halvorsen*, 986 A.2d 1150, 1160 (Del. 2009) ("The Delaware LLC Act seeks to give maximum effect to the principle of freedom of contract . . . ." (internal quotation marks omitted)); *Elf Atochem N. Am. v. Jaffari*, 727 A.2d 286, 290 (Del. 1998) ("The Delaware [LLC] Act has been modeled on the popular Delaware LP Act. . . . The policy of freedom of contract underlies both the [LLC] Act and the LP Act."). *See generally* Martin I. Lubaroff & Paul M. Altman, Lubaroff & Altman on Delaware Limited Partnerships § 1.2 (1995 & 2010 Supp.).

11

basis to the investors.[2] Furthermore, these governing instruments—which contain unique provisions that lead to *ad hoc* judicial decisions interpreting specific provisions that provide no predictability in future cases—are often poorly drafted and unclear, leading to increased litigation costs and inefficiencies for all parties.

Among the hallmarks of these agreements are broad waivers of all fiduciary duties, including the duty of loyalty.[3] Traditionally, the duty of loyalty provided the most meaningful protection to passive investors in corporations and partnerships. Yet at the same time the alternative entity agreements eliminate this bedrock protection, they also fully utilize the expansive contractual freedom authorized by alternative entity statutes to grant managerial discretion.[4] In approaching these entities, investors therefore cannot rely on their understandings of default principles of law. Instead, they must evaluate entity-specific provisions, ostensibly bargained for on an investment-by-investment basis to protect their interests, and then practice *caveat emptor* by foregoing entities whose governing instruments are too unfavorable. But because bargaining, at best, occurs only sometimes, and because it is difficult to participate in certain sectors other than through alternative entities, the practical alternatives for a skeptical investor are often stark: invest without adequate protection against self-dealing or avoid the asset class altogether.

Ironically, when investors try to evaluate contract terms, the expansive contractual freedom authorized by the alternative entity statutes hampers rather than helps. Precisely because the statutes lack mandatory terms and permit great flexibility, a profusion of provisions abounds. Unlike corporate certificates of incorporation and bylaws, which are relatively short, alternative entity agreements typically contain 90-plus pages of dense, complex, and heavily cross-referenced legalese. To digest the contractual prose, the reader

---

[2] Our anecdotal impressions on the limited extent of actual bargaining correspond to the results of a literature survey. *See* Sandra K. Miller, *The Best of Both Worlds: Default Fiduciary Duties and Contractual Freedom in Alternative Business Entities*, 39 J. Corp. L. 295, 317, 323 (2014) (surveying empirical literature on the extent of actual bargaining and finding at best mixed evidence with strong indications of a lack of bargaining in publicly traded alternative entities).

[3] Our anecdotal experience corresponds to the results of two empirical studies of the governing agreements of publicly traded Delaware alternative entities. *See* Brent J. Horton, *The Going-Private Freeze-Out: A Unique Danger for Investors in Delaware Non-Corporate Entities*, 38 J. Corp. L. 53 (2013); Mohsen Manesh, *Contractual Freedom Under Delaware Alternative Entity Law: Evidence from Publicly Traded LPs and LLCs*, 37 J. Corp. L. 555 (2012) [hereinafter *Evidence*]. Professor Horton finds that 29.41% of LLCs and 57.97% of LPs, representing cumulatively 52.32% of the publicly available agreements reviewed, eliminate all fiduciary duties. Horton, *supra*, at 94. He finds that 47.06% of LLCs and 94.20% of LPs, representing cumulatively 84.88% of the publicly available agreements reviewed, use a contractual "Special Approval" mechanism as the primary protection for interested transactions. *Id.* We discuss the Special Approval mechanism below. Professor Manesh reaches similar results. *Evidence*, *supra*, at 558 ("Of the 85 firms studied, 75 (or 88%) either totally waive the fiduciary duties of managers or eliminate liability arising from the breach of fiduciary duties."). He concludes that "the use of fiduciary waiver and exculpation provisions among publicly traded Delaware alternative entities is widespread." *Id.* at 556. He also finds that "publicly traded alternative entities have either not adopted uncorporate substitutes [for fiduciary protections] or adopted uncorporate substitutes that only trivially constrain managerial discretion." *Id.* Like us, he infers that sponsors "have largely utilized the freedom of contract to reduce managerial accountability to investors without committing to significant offsetting constraints on managerial discretion." *Id.*

[4] *See Evidence*, *supra* note 3, at 558.

must decode multi-layered sentences, incorporate the meaning of defined terms, and be constantly on the watch for more specific provisions elsewhere in the agreement or language that applies "notwithstanding anything to the contrary." Even when language appears familiar, it often departs subtly from the precise terms interpreted in earlier judicial opinions—and intentionally so. Alternative entity drafters are sophisticated, and they respond quickly to judicial constructions by tweaking or rewriting their provisions. Judicial decisions on alternative entity agreements therefore tend to be *ad hoc* interpretations of specific provisions that do little to advance the development of common understandings among market participants. Because they turn on contractual clauses that frequently differ from case to case, the decisions produce few general principles that could lead to predictable and reliable practices.

Interestingly, because contractual drafting is a difficult task, it is also not clear that alternative entity managers are always well served by situational deviations from predictable defaults. Different language sets up the possibility of a different result, creating opportunities for litigation that otherwise might not exist. Greater complexity also increases the possibility for human error, conflicting contractual provisions, and ambiguity, all of which can leave alternative entity managers potentially exposed. The difficulties drafters have in substituting their own bespoke provisions for the equitable principles that have been forged by cases over centuries should not be surprising. After all, these equitable principles emerged in large measure to address the situations involving the exercise of authority by one person over another's property that could not be effectively addressed by contracting.

In light of these problems, it seems to us that a sensible set of standard fiduciary defaults might benefit all constituents of alternative entities. Under this framework, the governing agreement would presumptively waive the investors' ability to hold managers liable for money damages for breaches of the duty of care, while presumptively retaining the traditional fiduciary duty of loyalty. For publicly traded entities, the duty of loyalty would be non-waivable.[5] The requirement of a non-waivable duty of loyalty in these settings would promote investor confidence, create a predictable body of case law, and enable contract drafters to simplify the tangled web of provisions that currently attempts to substitute for traditional duty-of-loyalty analysis. The framework would not threaten the two key benefits that motivated the rise of LPs and LLCs as alternatives to corporations: (i) the elimination of double taxation at the entity level and (ii) the ability to contract out of the corporate opportunity doctrine. For managers, it would provide more predictable rules of governance and a more reliable roadmap to fulfilling their duties in conflict-of-interest situations. The result arguably would be both fairer and more efficient than the current patchwork yielded by the unilateral drafting efforts of entity sponsors.

---

[5] Perhaps it would also be beneficial if the duty of loyalty were non-waivable for private entities with a diverse set of investors, in a manner akin to the way that the Securities Exchange Act imposes registration requirements on an issuer whose securities are held by certain number of persons and whose total assets have crossed a certain threshold amount. *Cf.* 15 U.S.C.A. § 78l(g) (requiring issuers with assets exceeding $10,000,000 and a class of equity security held by either 500 persons who are not accredited investors or 2,000 persons to register that security with the SEC).

1. THE MOTIVATIONS FOR FORMING ALTERNATIVE ENTITIES

To many familiar with the traditional form of American business entity—the corporation—it is likely not apparent why there would be a market demand for alternative entity statutes authorizing complete freedom of contract. After all, American corporate law statutes have few mandatory requirements, particularly when compared to other nations' corporate law statutes. The Delaware General Corporation Law (DGCL), which has emerged as the market leader, is "broadly enabling"[6] and designed to facilitate individual tailoring rather than "one-size-fits-all" solutions. Thus, the notion that American corporate statutes contain burdensome and non-waivable provisions that hamper managerial effectiveness is not an intuitively obvious one. To the contrary, the DGCL and its counterparts predominantly offer default rules that can be altered through private ordering via the corporation's certificate of incorporation and bylaws.

Indeed, the primary justification for alternative entity statutes had nothing at all to do with avoiding corporate statutory requirements. Rather, the primary justification for the development of alternative entity statutes was (and remains) minimizing taxes.[7] Because the federal tax code taxes corporate earnings at both the entity and investor level, but does not impose taxes at the entity level for pass-through entities like traditional general partnerships, the latter have a huge advantage when delivering cash flows to investors. Once it became settled that LPs and LLCs could receive pass-through tax treatment, alternative entities began their meteoric rise in popularity.[8] Differential tax treatment cannot be blamed on poorly drafted corporate statutes, because none of the mandatory provisions in the corporate codes gives rise to the differential tax regime. The distinction is merely an artifact of federal tax policy.

Of course, there is one important secondary reason why some managers have preferred alternative entities that can be traced to an aspect of corporate law: a desire to limit the

---

[6] *Williams v. Geier*, 671 A.2d 1368, 1381 (Del. 1996) ("At its core, the Delaware General Corporation Law is a broadly enabling act which leaves latitude for substantial private ordering . . . ."); *see also* Leo E. Strine, Jr., *Delaware's Corporate Law System*, 86 Cornell L. Rev. 1257, 1260 (2001) (describing the DGCL as "largely enabling" and as creating "a wide realm for private ordering").

[7] *See* Rodney D. Chrisman, *LLCs Are the New King of the Hill: An Empirical Study of the Number of New LLCs, Corporations, and LPs Formed in the United States Between 2004–2007 and How LLCs Were Taxed for Tax Years 2002–2006*, 15 Fordham J. Corp. & Fin. L. 459, 465–66 (2010) (describing tax-driven origins of alternative entity statutes); *accord* SYMONDS & O'TOOLE ON DELAWARE LIMITED LIABILITY COMPANIES § 1.01 (2012) (explaining that the 1998 IRS ruling clarifying that limited liability companies qualified for the favorable "pass-through" income taxation given to partnerships spurred the enactment of the Delaware Limited Liability Company Act and the popularity of limited liability companies) (*citing* Rev. Rul. 88-76, 1988–2 C.B. 360); *Evidence*, *supra* note 3, at 573 ("Firms utilizing the alternative entity form, over the corporate form, do so chiefly because of the favorable 'pass-through' partnership tax treatment that is afforded to alternative entities."). At present, the only meaningful restriction on further increases in the number of publicly traded alternative entities is a continuing limitation of pass-through tax treatment to entities whose income is purely passive, usually firms operating in the oil and gas industry. Horton, *supra* note 3, at 94–95.

[8] Chrisman, *supra* note 7, at 466.

risks posed by the corporate opportunity doctrine.[9] The corporate opportunity doctrine was something sponsors wished to avoid because it was seen as inhibiting to the ability of entity sponsors. The idea, as we understand it, went like this. A sponsor operating in a particular industry, such as the energy arena, wishes to raise capital from investors for a particular project, such as exploiting a natural gas field. The sponsor wishes to form an entity for that particular project. The sponsor does not want the entity to have a claim to all future opportunities in the natural gas industry that might come to the sponsor's attention. The sponsor fears that if the project were pursued using a corporation, and the sponsor then identified other natural gas opportunities, such as fields in the same region, the corporation's stockholders could sue the sponsor for breach of the duty of loyalty under the theory that the corporate opportunity doctrine required the sponsor to pursue the other opportunities through the corporation. To address this concern, the drafters of alternative entity statutes decided that it would be prudent to permit the entity's governing agreement to restrict or limit the fiduciary duties that the managers of the entity might otherwise owe.[10]

As a policy basis for using alternative entities, this does not seem to us to be all that substantial. The case law under the corporate opportunity doctrine hardly suggested that the doctrine provided a genuine basis for fear for any entity manager that proceeded in a careful and thoughtful manner. But for present purposes, what is most important is that this policy basis was rapidly addressed by corporate drafters themselves. In 2000, for example, the DGCL was amended specifically to provide a safe harbor against corporate opportunity claims through the inclusion of a provision in the certificate of incorporation renouncing any interest of the corporation in any business opportunities that are presented to the corporation's officers or directors.[11] Thus, to the extent the corporate opportunity doctrine might once have tipped the scales in favor of alternative entities, it no longer should.

Another argument often made in favor of alternative entity statutes is that they allow for the elimination of fiduciary duties and the establishment of a purely contractual

---

[9] See Miller, *supra* note 2, at 306 (explaining the need in some businesses for corporate opportunity protection). For the classic statement of the corporate opportunity doctrine, see *Guth v. Loft, Inc.*, 5 A.2d 503, 272–73 (1939) ("[I]f there is presented to a corporate officer or director a business opportunity which the corporation is financially able to undertake, is, from its nature, in the line of the corporation's business and is of practical advantage to it, is one in which the corporation has an interest or a reasonable expectancy, and, by embracing the opportunity, the self-interest of the officer or director will be brought into conflict with that of his corporation, the law will not permit him to seize the opportunity for himself."); Eric Talley, *Turning Servile Opportunities to Gold: A Strategic Analysis of the Corporate Opportunities Doctrine*, 108 Yale L. J. 277, 279 (1998) ("[The corporate opportunity doctrine is] the law's attempt to regulate circumstances in which a corporate officer or director may usurp new business prospects for her own account without first offering them to the firm. The doctrine—a subspecies of the fiduciary duty of loyalty—has been a mainstay in the corporations law of virtually every state for well over a century.").

[10] See, e.g., 6 *Del. C.* § 18-1101(c) ("To the extent that, at law or in equity, a member or manager or other person has duties (including fiduciary duties) to a limited liability company or to another member or manager or to another person that is a party to or is otherwise bound by a limited liability company agreement, the member's or manager's or other person's duties may be expanded or restricted or eliminated by provisions in the limited liability company agreement.").

[11] 8 *Del. C.* § 122(17).

relationship between entity managers and investors.[12] As judges who have seen our fair share of alternative entity disputes, we do not immediately grasp why this would be seen as a compelling advantage. Fiduciary duties emerged as a non-waivable common law overlay in the corporate area because the statutory drafters recognized the difficulty of developing provisions that would provide an efficient and fair path forward in all of the diverse circumstances that businesses confront. Wishing to avoid the prescriptive codes common in civil law nations, American corporate law drafters took an enabling approach with relatively few, albeit very important, statutory requirements and relied upon the judicial enforcement of fiduciary duties to ensure fairness. Moreover, through the business judgment rule, equity itself was mindful of the need for managers to have the flexibility to innovate and the incentives to take good faith risks in the pursuit of profit, and thus of efficiency concerns.

Delaware's experience in the 1960s with a comprehensive revision of the DGCL illustrates this approach. That revision was undertaken with the guidance of one of America's leading corporate law scholars, Ernest Folk of the University of Virginia, and with input from prominent corporate lawyers from across the nation. At the time, American courts and corporate practitioners had nearly a century of experience working with the combination of general corporation statutes and the equitable overlay of fiduciary duties. The distinguished group of experts who carefully examined and rewrote the DGCL, section by section, had the opportunity to craft statutory language that, if followed, would conclusively resolve the competing interests of managers and investors and foreclose any judicial inquiry under equitable principles. They declined to take that approach, recognizing that a rigid set of statutory rules could not properly balance the interests of managers and investors and achieve both efficiency and fairness across the diverse and ever-changing circumstances that corporations face in a dynamic economy. They opted instead to maintain corporate law's twofold tradition: first, a broadly enabling statute that nevertheless contains important and fairness-enhancing mandatory rules, such as requirements for the regular election of directors, stockholder votes on major transactions like mergers and sales of substantially all assets, and a stockholder right to access corporate books and records for a proper purpose; and second, an equitable overlay of fiduciary duties, enforced primarily by the ability of stockholders to sue directors in the courts for breach of their duty of loyalty.[13]

To date, the best minds in corporate law continue to think this policy balance is the sensible one, because it remains difficult to craft more specific statutory language that will balance efficiency and fairness concerns as effectively as an approach that uses

---

[12] *See generally Evidence*, *supra* note 3, at 562–63 (summarizing and contrasting the positions of the "fiduciary traditionalists" with the "contractarians," who argue that private parties should be able to contractually modify and fully eliminate fiduciary duties).

[13] *See Schnell v. Chris-Craft Indus., Inc.*, 285 A.2d 437, 439 (Del. 1971) ("[I]nequitable action does not become permissible simply because it is legally possible."); Adolf A. Berle, Jr., *Corporate Powers as Powers in Trust*, 44 Harv. L. Rev. 1049 (1931) ("[I]n every case, corporate action must be twice tested: first, by the technical rules having to do with the existence and proper exercise of the power; second, by equitable rules somewhat analogous to those which apply in favor of a *cestui que trust* to the trustee's exercise of wide powers granted to him in the instrument making him a fiduciary.").

an equitable overlay of fiduciary duties in combination with a more flexible enabling statute. The corporate bar is diligent, savvy, and market sensitive. The corporate bar regularly proposes statutory changes when a consensus emerges on a more effective method for authorizing corporate action or when a judicial decision or other development focuses attention on a new area. Yet despite decades of effort, the corporate bar has yet to propose, much less achieve, an all-encompassing statute that obviates the need for fiduciary duties. Given the diligence and expertise of the corporate bar, it hardly seems likely that some obvious solution is waiting to be found. Nor does it seem likely that a perfectly anticipatory code could be drafted if only we had a better class of scriveners.

The corporate experience makes us skeptical that the drafters of the governing instruments of alternative entities are likely to have greater success in attempting to provide contractually for all reasonably conceivable circumstances. It takes only a moderate degree of self-awareness and modesty to recognize that the human mind cannot foresee every potential situation that could arise after contracting. All contracts necessarily will be incomplete. But assuming that drafters could anticipate all future states of the world, a fully complete contract still would be beyond the parties' power. After all, contracting is costly. Trying to identify, negotiate, and draft language to address every eventuality would take so much time and require such a large investment of resources that the deal itself would never happen. To top it off, language is an inexact instrument. No matter how carefully the drafters draft, complex provisions in commercial agreements inevitably produce degrees of vagueness and areas of ambiguity, and the potentially different interpretations are particularly likely to be found by lawyers who are reading purposefully for arguments to make for their clients in the context of a specific dispute. By definition, the cases that are litigated will be those where skilled advocates can argue plausibly for competing interpretations; otherwise the case would not be brought. And we have not yet introduced the simple possibility of human error, either by the drafters, the party-interpreters, or the judge deciding the case. Sadly, the normative ideal of rational parties contracting efficiently to allocate risks is just that—an ideal.[14]

It seems to us, therefore, that of the three major motivations for preferring alternative entities to corporations, two are canards. The overarching dream of a complete contract cannot be realized in a world of human frailty, and the specific manifestation of contracting around the corporate opportunity doctrine can be readily achieved in the corporate form. Only the tax code remains as a meaningful advantage, and achieving favorable tax treatment does not require complete freedom of contract. Therefore we will not run afoul of a core purpose of the alternative entity vehicle by positing that some degree of standardization could well be desirable.

---

[14] An extensive scholarly literature discusses the impossibility of complete contracting. For an accessible introduction to the area that focuses on Delaware alternative entities, see Mohsen Manesh, *Express Contract Terms and the Implied Contractual Covenant of Delaware Law*, 38 J. Corp. L. 1 (2013).

2. THE CONTRADICTORY COMPLEXITY OF THE "MARKET STANDARD" FOR CONFLICT-OF-INTEREST TRANSACTIONS

To suggest that entities designed to raise capital from diverse investors benefit from a degree of standardization is hardly heretical. Standardization reduces transaction costs and facilitates trading in liquid markets.[15] Although we do not pretend to have done a comprehensive review of the alternative entity cases, much less of the key provisions of the governing instruments of a statistically significant sample of alternative entities, our profession requires us to read a large number of decisions in which we and our judicial colleagues undertake the daunting task of deciphering alternative entity agreements that routinely run for 90-plus pages. It appears to us that lack of standardization prevails in the alternative entity arena, imposing material transaction costs on investors with corresponding effects for the cost of capital borne by sponsors. And it is not clear to us that contractual freedom has generated offsetting benefits.[16] To illustrate the problem we see, we will focus on the provisions used to simultaneously empower and constrain decision making by the general partner of an LP or its LLC analog, the managing member. For simplicity, we use the language of the LP, where most litigation has occurred to date, even though LLCs now predominate.[17]

A major difficulty facing alternative entity investors is the illusion of familiarity and the reality of divergence. A degree of surface-level standardization has begun to occur, with alternative entity agreements coalescing around particular features and concepts. At present, however, this superficial standardization is overwhelmed by diversity in implementation, which limits the efficacy of precedent and creates fertile opportunities for future litigation. Moreover, as exemplified by the decision-making provisions in publicly traded master LPs (MLPs), the contractual provisions that drafters use are mind-numbingly complex. Having repeatedly engaged in the head-hurting task of parsing these provisions, we believe that to the extent a "market standard" exists for conflict transactions in the alternative entity space, it is an odd and arguably ineffective one.[18]

---

[15] See E. ALLAN FARNSWORTH, CONTRACTS § 4.26 (3d ed. 2004) (noting that standardization in contracts reduces costs and risks); see also Marcel Kahan & Michael Klausner, *Standardization and Innovation in Corporate Contracting (Or "The Economics of Boilerplate")*, 83 Va. L. Rev. 713, passim & 763 (1997) (discussing the benefits of standard contract terms and explaining that "[w]hen a firm incorporates in a particular state, it adopts that state's mandatory corporate law rules, and it adopts any or all of that state's default terms by choosing not to customize an alternative term. In effect, these rules operate as standard contract terms: they are the same for all firms that adopt them, and many firms do in fact adopt them.").

[16] Professor Horton reports that Moody's raised the risk profile for 26 publicly traded LPs that it monitors, relative to public corporations with comparable financial metrics, because of the ability of alternative entity agreements to waive or limit fiduciary protections and the widespread use of such provisions. Horton, *supra* note 3, at 59.

[17] See Chrisman, *supra* note 7 (documenting explosive growth of LLCs and their prevalence relative to other alternative entities and corporations).

[18] Professor Horton remarks on the complicated nature of operating agreements and the fact that "[a] provision often takes on a different meaning once the reader considers cross-references and defined terms." Horton, *supra* note 3, at 83. He notes that "[s]imilar provisions in two agreements can lead to different results, and it would be a work of folly to

The following provisions roughly illustrate the pattern we see. The agreement starts by broadly eliminating all duties other than contractual duties.[19] A typical provision states:

> Except as expressly set forth in this Agreement, neither the General Partner nor any other Indemnitee shall have any duties or liabilities, including fiduciary duties, to the Partnership or any Limited Partner or Assignee and the provisions of this Agreement, to the extent that they restrict, eliminate or otherwise modify the duties and liabilities, including fiduciary duties, of the General Partner or any other Indemnitee otherwise existing at law or in equity, are agreed by the Partners to replace such other duties and liabilities of the General Partner or such other Indemnitee.

The term "Indemnitee" is usually defined broadly to include the general partner, "any Person who is or was an Affiliate of the General Partner," and "any Person who is or was a . . . director . . . of . . . the General Partner," thereby covering all potential defendants.[20]

This provision has a few notable features. Most importantly, it purports to replace all duties that otherwise would be owed to investors with contractually specified duties. The agreements tend to preserve only portions of the traditional duty of loyalty. In traditional corporate law, one of the common law duties is the duty that a self-dealing transaction be fair to the corporation. Although a great deal of complexity has been introduced over the years into that doctrine—e.g., procedural means such as a majority of the minority vote that can have an effect on the doctrine's application—in its pure form, the doctrine subjected an interested fiduciary to liability even if the fiduciary acted in good faith unless the transaction was substantively fair to the corporation.[21]

Most LP agreements now eliminate this scienter-free aspect of the duty of loyalty and leave in its place a liability standard that exposes LP managers and others who would traditionally be considered fiduciaries to the LP to liability only if they act in subjective bad faith.[22] In fact, these agreements often go further and cut off any inquiry into the

---

attempt to explain every possible permutation." *Id.* Like us, he also notes that the agreements "are remarkably similar in structure and language. By way of example, the fiduciary elimination provision (to the extent there is one) is almost always contained in Section 7.9 . . ., regardless of the law firm that drafts it, and the agreements use language that is remarkably similar . . . ." *Id.*

[19] Professor Manesh found that out of 85 publicly traded Delaware alternative entities in existence in June 2011, 42 (49%) fully eliminated fiduciary duties. *Evidence, supra* note 3, at 575.

[20] There are agreements, however, that omit particular parties, leaving them exposed to traditional fiduciary duty claims. We suspect these omissions are examples of the human errors that inevitably creep in during any lengthy drafting assignment (including the preparation of judicial opinions). Other agreements do not clearly and explicitly eliminate fiduciary duties but rather rely on detailed contractual provisions to displace fiduciary standards. *See* Horton, *supra* note 3, at 74 (discussing cases in which provisions failed to include particular defendants or claimants); *Evidence, supra* note 3, at 576 (finding that 43 out of 85 firms do not eliminate fiduciary duties but provide broad exculpation for all fiduciary duty claims).

[21] *Weinberger v. UOP, Inc.*, 457 A.2d 701, 710 (Del. 1983) ("The requirement of fairness is unflinching in its demand that where one stands on both sides of a transaction, he has the burden of establishing its entire fairness, sufficient to pass the test of careful scrutiny by the courts.") (citing *Sterling v. Mayflower Hotel Corp.*, 93 A.2d 107, 110 (Del. 1952)).

[22] *See, e.g., Brinckerhoff v. Enbridge Energy Co.*, 2011 WL 4599654, at *8 (Del. Ch. Sept. 30, 2011) (interpreting an LP agreement that included a provision stating: "[n]otwithstanding anything to the contrary set forth in this Agreement, no Indemnitee shall be liable for monetary damages

good faith of an interested fiduciary by stating that the use of certain procedures or the existence of certain conditions dispositively resolves any question about the validity or fairness of a transaction and immunizes the interested fiduciary from liability.[23]

Another feature of this provision is that it fails to define exactly who owes these contractual duties and to whom they are owed. Presumably, the duty to carry out a contractual obligation is owed in the first instance by the party whom the contract designates to carry out the obligation.[24] But in an alternative entity, the manager of the LLC or the general partner of the LP, as the case may be, ultimately is responsible for ensuring that the entity carries out its obligations. In other words, the contractual standard does not address the concept of oversight, which is a familiar one in corporate law. The duty to carry out a contractual obligation is likewise presumably owed to the counterparties under the contract, who can therefore sue for breach. The contractual standard does not address whether the appropriate enforcer of contractual duties is the entity itself or the diverse limited partners and their assignees. Put differently, the contractual standard does not address the distinction between direct and derivative actions, also familiar in corporate law and one which alternative entity defendants regularly raise.

At the same time that the standard provision eliminates all but contractual duties, the agreements often contain indemnification and exculpation provisions that suggest the duties may continue. For example, in a case where the defendants argued vigorously that they owed no duties other than contractual duties, the indemnification provision stated:

> The General Partner, [the manager of the General Partner], each of their respective directors, members, partners, shareholders, officers, employees, agents and affiliates . . . (each an "Indemnitee") shall be indemnified and held harmless by the Partnership to the fullest extent legally permissible under and by virtue of the laws of the State of Delaware, as amended from time to time, from and against any and all loss, liability and expense (including, without limitation, losses due to trade errors caused by such persons, judgments, fines, amounts paid or to

---

to the Partnership, the Limited Partners, the Assignees or any other Persons who have acquired interests in the Units, for losses sustained or liabilities incurred as a result of any act or omission if such Indemnitee acted in good faith.").

[23] For example, the LLC agreement at issue in *In re Atlas Energy Resources, LLC* included a provision which provided that:

> [W]henever a potential conflict of interest exists or arises between any Affiliate of the Company, on the one hand, and the Company or any Group Member, on the other, any resolution or course of action by the Board of Directors in respect of such conflict of interest shall be permitted and deemed approved by all Members, and shall not constitute a breach of this Agreement . . . or of any duty existing at law, in equity or otherwise, including any fiduciary duty, if the resolution or course of action in respect of such conflict of interest is (i) approved by Special Approval, (ii) approved by the vote of holders of a majority of the Outstanding Common Units (excluding Common Units held by interested parties), (iii) on terms no less favorable to the Company than those being generally available to or available from unrelated third parties or (iv) fair and reasonable to the Company, taking into account the totality of the relationships between the parties involved (including other transactions that may be particularly favorable to the Company).

2010 WL 4273122, at *7 (Del. Ch. Oct. 28, 2010).

[24] *Gotham Partners, L.P. v. Hallwood Realty Partners, L.P.*, 817 A.2d 160, 172 (Del. 2002) ("It is a general principle of contract law that only a party to a contract may be sued for breach of that contract.").

be paid in settlement and reasonable attorney's fees and expenses) incurred, or suffered by the Indemnitee in connection with the good faith performance by the Indemnitee of his, her or its responsibilities to the Partnership *provided, however, that an Indemnitee shall not be indemnified for losses resulting from his, her or its gross negligence, willful misconduct or violation of applicable laws* . . . .[25]

In the corporate context, gross negligence is the traditional standard for pleading and later proving a breach of the fiduciary duty of care when the standard of review is the business judgment rule.[26] To include the concept of gross negligence as a basis for indemnification suggests that common law fiduciary duties persist.[27] In other words, the inclusion of such a provision provides a basis for arguing that the manager of the entity can be sued for a breach of the duty of care, notwithstanding the otherwise broad waiver of fiduciary duties in the governing agreement, which typically includes severe limitations on the traditional duty of loyalty. As might be expected, the decisions generated when provisions of this type have come into play in real world challenges by investors of conflict transactions implemented by alternative entity managers yield little in the way of general principles of sound governance.

For starters, the structure of alternative entities and the provisions in their governing agreements have led to a particularly odd pattern of routine veil piercing. Most alternative entities have no human fiduciary. Rather, most LPs have a general partner that is another business entity.[28] Likewise, most LLCs have a managing member that is another business entity.[29] These governing fiduciaries are often corporations, and often have human beings who serve as directors.[30] Under traditional principles of entity law,

---

[25] *Paige Capital Mgmt., LLC v. Lerner Master Fund LLC*, 2011 WL 3505355, at *42 (Del. Ch. Aug. 8, 2011) (emphasis added); *accord Lazard Debt Recovery GP, LLC. v. Weinstock*, 864 A.2d 955, 975–76 (Del. Ch. 2004) (discussing an alternative entity agreement that eliminated fiduciary duties but contained a carve-out to exculpation for loss or damage "due to willful misconduct, bad faith, or gross negligence of the General Partner").

[26] *See Smith v. Van Gorkom*, 488 A.2d 858, 873 (Del. 1985); *Aronson v. Lewis*, 473 A.2d 805, 812 (Del. 1984).

[27] Professor Manesh catalogs the various formulations of exculpatory provisions that he found in alternative entity agreements, including three that failed to exculpate for breaches of the duty of care and five that denied exculpation for conduct constituting gross negligence. *See Evidence, supra* note 3, at 576–78.

[28] *See* 6 *Del. C.* § 17-101(5) ("'General partner' means a person who is named as a general partner in the certificate of limited partnership or similar instrument . . . and who is admitted to the limited partnership as a general partner . . . ."); *id.* § 17-101(14) ("'Person' means a natural person, partnership (whether general or limited), limited liability company, trust . . ., estate, association . . ., corporation . . . or any other individual or entity (or series thereof) . . . ."). *See generally* Robert W. Hamilton, *Corporate General Partners of Limited Partnerships*, 1 J. Small & Emerging Bus. L. 73 (1997) (discussing the origins and implications of corporate general partners).

[29] *See* 6 *Del. C.* § 18-101(10) ("'Manager' means a person who is named as a manager of a limited liability company in, or designated as a manager of a limited liability company pursuant to, a limited liability company agreement or similar instrument under which the limited liability company is formed."); *id.* § 18-101(12) ("'Person' means a natural person, partnership (whether general or limited), limited liability company, trust . . ., estate, association . . ., corporation, . . . or any other individual or entity (or series thereof) . . . .").

[30] Hamilton, *supra* note 28, at 85 ("[W]here limited partnerships are used today, it is the norm to use a corporation as the sole general partner.").

so long as the governing fiduciary was well-capitalized and not a sham, it and it alone should owe fiduciary and contractual duties to the alternative entity and its investors. The governing fiduciary's own directors and investors should bear no direct liability to the alternative entity's investors unless those investors can satisfy the difficult task of piercing the governing fiduciary's corporate veil. But, those traditional principles of corporate law have been put to the side in the contractual world of alternative entities. Under *USACafes*[31] and its progeny, it has become routine in Delaware and other states to treat the directors of the governing entity of an alternative entity as owing contractual and fiduciary duties directly to the alternative entity and its investors.[32] The governing instruments of alternative entities do little to address this situation. Instead, they seem to assume that the individual fiduciaries of the governing entity will owe default fiduciary duties directly to the alternative entity and its investors and then tailor those duties in the governing instrument.[33]

Consistent with this analogy, the governing instruments tend to accord the so-called independent directors of the governing entity with a status similar to the status of corporate directors in the traditional public company corporate context. Thus, a corporate managing member's independent directors are often called on to approve conflict transactions between the managing member and the alternative entity, and that approval is given liability-limiting effect. But, of course, there is a fundamental difference that is elided. An independent director of a corporation is accorded that status precisely because she has no conflict of interest and is not subject to any material influence that would prevent her from acting solely in the best interests of the corporation and its stockholders *qua* stockholders and thus is well positioned to act to protect against any unfair proposals from managers who do suffer from conflicts of interests. But an independent director of a corporation that is a managing member of an LLC owes a fiduciary duty to act in that corporation's best interest, and is not in a direct fiduciary position as to the alternative entity and its

---

[31] *In re USACafes, L.P. Litig.*, 600 A.2d 43 (Del. Ch. 1991).

[32] *See, e.g., Wallace v. Wood*, 752 A.2d 1175, 1180–81 (Del. Ch. 1999) (citing *USACafes* and finding that the directors of a corporate general partner owed fiduciary duties to the partnership and its limited partners); *Bigelow/Diversified Secondary P'ship Fund 1990 v. Damson/Birtcher Partners*, 2001 WL 1641239, at *8 (Del. Ch. Dec. 4, 2001) (holding that the affiliates of a general partner who exercise control over the LP's assets may owe fiduciary duties to both the partnership and the limited partners).

[33] For example, in *In re Encore Energy Partners LP Unitholder Litigation*, 2012 WL 3792997, at *7–8 (Del. Ch. Aug. 31, 2012), the Court of Chancery examined an LP agreement which provided that "[e]xcept as expressly set forth in this Agreement, neither the General Partner nor any other Indemnitee shall have any duties or liabilities, including fiduciary duties, to the Partnership or any Limited Partner . . . ." The agreement defined Indemnitee to include any "Affiliate of the General Partner." Affiliate was, in turn, defined to include any person, including both natural persons and business entities, who had the power to direct or cause the direction of the management and policies of any other person. The Court of Chancery explained that construing the definition of affiliate in accordance with its literal terms meant that the directors of the General Partner were affiliates, and were therefore Indemnitees under the partnership agreement who owed those duties "expressly set forth in [the limited partnership agreement]" and "whatever nonwaivable default obligations the implied covenant of good faith and fair dealing imposes." *See also Gerber v. EPE Holdings, LLC*, 2013 WL 209658, at *6 (Del. Ch. Jan. 18, 2013) (interpreting similar provisions in the same manner).

investors.[34] Thus, the independent directors of a managing member of an LLC are placed in a conflict situation when they are employed to act to ensure that the managing member does not benefit itself at the unfair expense of the alternative entity.

We suppose that more imaginative minds than ours could connect this inherently conflicted status to the liability standards of the kind we have highlighted, and contend that the provisions that can be plausibly read as exposing these directors to the possibility of monetary damages liability for breaching their duty of care is a response to the inherent conflict they face. Perhaps an argument could be made that, by exposing them to liability against which most corporate directors are exculpated by use of a Section 102(b)(7) provision, alternative entity governing instruments provide a countervailing contractual fairness guarantee that corrects for the conflict faced by these fiduciaries. Likewise, by conditioning any liability-immunizing effect of the employment of certain procedural protections on their good faith use, alternative entity agreements could be providing a similar contractual check on this inherent conflict.

The cases, however, cast doubt on the idea that the liability standards in alternative entity governing instruments reflect such a high-minded, careful consideration of the unusual role of the human beings who serve as fiduciaries of general partners and managing members. Nor do the cases suggest that these standards are the result of bargaining between entity managers who wish to limit their own liability and investors who want to be able to hold them and their human fiduciaries accountable.

The record in actual cases rarely, if ever, reflects that any bargaining at all occurred over the governing instrument. Instead, it is almost always the case that the manager or general partner's counsel drafted the governing instrument and investors were only given the choice to sign up or not, but not to bargain over its terms. Consistent with this pattern, the cases almost always involve the managers and their human directors arguing that the governing instrument eliminated or severely constricted the fiduciary duties owed to the alternative entity and that if the procedures in the instrument were literally followed, that investors had their full contractual expectations satisfied and could not press a claim that a conflict transaction was unfair to the alternative entity and unjustly enriched the manager.[35] Put simply, there is no hint that the arguable retention of due care liability

---

[34] See *Gotham Partners, L.P. v. Hallwood Realty Partners, L.P.*, 2000 WL 1476663, at *19–20 (Del. Ch. Sept. 27, 2000) (explaining the structural conflict that exists when the directors of a corporate general parent owe fiduciary duties both to the corporate general parent and its owners and to the LP and its unitholders); *see also* LUBAROFF & ALTMAN, *supra* note 1, § 11.2.11 ("[After *USACafes*,] a director of a corporate general partner [is] in a position of having to deal with potentially conflicting and irreconcilable fiduciary duties (the director's traditional fiduciary duty to the stockholders of the corporation of which it is a director, and the director's new partnership fiduciary duty)."); *id.* (explaining that before *USACafes*, many practitioners believed that the limited partners did not have a claim against the directors of the corporate general partner but only against the corporate general partner itself and that an advantage of that approach was that it "would avoid putting directors in the situation of having potentially conflicting and irreconcilable fiduciary duties to stockholders of the corporation and to limited partners of the limited partnership").

[35] See, e.g., *In re Atlas Energy Resources, LLC*, 2010 WL 4273122, at *6 (Del. Ch. Oct. 28, 2010) ("[T]he defendants argued] that the LLC Agreement completely eliminated [the general partner's] directors' and officers' fiduciary duties and replaced them with a contractually defined duty of good faith that Plaintiffs have not adequately alleged was breached."); *Brickwell Partners v. Wise*,

to the investors or the proscription of bad faith conduct was in fact intended to provide genuine protection to investors.

What has resulted from these exercises in unilateral drafting are cases that turn on the unique and often seemingly contradictory terms of specific governing instruments. Admittedly, some drafters have taken a very stark and straightforward approach to drafting contractual procedures that, if followed, are dispositive of any investor challenge to an interested transaction. For example, in *Kahn v. Icahn*, the court held that a provision in an LP agreement that provided that "[a]ny Partner, Record Holder or Affiliate thereof ... may compete, directly or indirectly, with the business of the Partnership .... [A]nd neither the Partnership nor any of the Partners or Record Holders shall have any right to participate in such other business interests or ventures or to receive or share in any income derived therefrom" was a provision that clearly allowed the LP's general partner to make investments without first presenting the opportunities to the LP.[36] But in the more typical situation, although the defendants argue that the contract provides a dispositive procedural standard that immunizes the defendants from liability and that requires dismissal of the complaint, the contractual language purporting to waive fiduciary duties is laden with scienter-based qualifiers that invite a consideration of whether the humans involved in the entity's governing process have acted in good faith.[37] Unsurprisingly, the ensuing judicial decisions have results that yield few general principles.

In situations where a key party—such as a managing member selling or buying assets from an LLC—has a self-interest, then freighting procedural safe harbors with scienter-based qualifiers necessarily tends to generate issues of fact that cannot be resolved on the face of a pleading.[38] Similarly, because the governing instruments often can be rationally read as contemplating liability for gross negligence,[39] it is often possible to craft a dismissal-proof complaint against alternative entity managers by focusing on arguable

---

794 A.2d 1, 2 (Del. Ch. 2001) ("According to the defendants, the [Limited Partnership Agreement] precludes the plaintiff's claims for breach of fiduciary duty."); *Bay Ctr. Apartments Owner, LLC v. Emery Bay PKI, LLC*, 2009 WL 1124451, at *8 (Del. Ch. Apr. 20, 2009) ("The defendants claim that the parties took full advantage of [the statutory] flexibility by eliminating all fiduciary duties in the LLC Agreement.")

[36] *Kahn v. Icahn*, 1998 WL 832629, at *2–4 (Del. Ch. Nov. 12, 1998).

[37] As Adolf Berle recognized, "The moment ... that 'good faith' is introduced in the picture the fiduciary principle is raised. The phrase implies good faith towards someone, arising out of some previous relation." Adolf Berle, *Corporate Powers as Powers in Trust*, 44 Harv. L. Rev. 1049, 1054 (1931).

[38] *See, e.g., Kelly v. Blum*, 2010 WL 629850, at *11 (Del. Ch. Nov. 10, 2009) (denying a motion to dismiss in a case where the LLC agreement exculpated managers for all conduct except "willful or fraudulent misconduct or willful breach of ... contractual or fiduciary duties under this Agreement" because the plaintiff had alleged facts that, if true, indicated that the managers acted willfully); *Cont'l Ins. Co. v. Rutledge & Co., Inc.*, 750 A.2d 1219 (Del. Ch. 2000) (declining to enter summary judgment where a factual question existed as to whether the behavior that the general partner engaged in was covered by the provisions in the LP agreement that modified the general partner's duty of loyalty to the limited partners).

[39] LUBAROFF & ALTMAN, *supra* note 1, § 11.2.4 (noting that exculpation provisions in LP agreements "typically provide[] that there is liability ... if such loss or liability is attributable to the general partner's gross negligence or willful misconduct").

process deficiencies when such a complaint against corporate directors would not survive judicial review because of the existence of an exculpatory charter provision.[40]

Aside from often resulting in a need for discovery and thus larger litigation costs, these contractual liability standards have generated mixed substantive results. In a number of cases, managing members, general partners, and their human fiduciaries have suffered damage awards for failing to comply with their duties.[41] But it is also the case that contractual liability standards have generated judicial decisions that leave investors with no remedy because of the court's need to be faithful to the contract, even in circumstances when the court itself harbored serious doubt that the alternative entity had gotten a fair shake.[42]

There is another profound danger that this adventure in attempting in one generation to master a contractual approach to issues that for centuries our forebears have been unable to tackle by contracting presents—and that is for contract law itself. When situations arise when the managers of alternative entities have appeared to act in ways that are grossly unfair to investors but in literal compliance with the explicit safe harbor provisions of the agreement, plaintiffs can be expected to latch on to the statutorily required bottom line of the implied covenant of good faith and fair dealing.[43] In traditional contract law, the

---

[40] Compare *Forsythe v. ESC Fund Mgmt Co.*, 2007 WL 2982247, at *7–9 (Del. Ch. Oct. 9, 2007) (denying the defendant's motion to dismiss in a case where the general partner was only liable under the partnership agreement for "acts or omissions resulting from bad faith, willful misconduct, gross negligence, or a material breach of the Partnership Agreement" and finding that the plaintiffs had stated a claim that the general partner acted with gross negligence because the general partner had not exercised oversight over the partnership activities), *and Albert v. Alex Brown Mgmt Servs., Inc.*, 2005 WL 2130607, at *5–8 (Del. Ch. Aug. 26, 2005) (finding that the plaintiffs, limited partners in an investment fund, had alleged facts sufficient to survive a motion to dismiss in a case where the partnership agreement exculpated the general partner unless its conduct constituted "gross negligence or intentional misconduct" when the plaintiffs had alleged that the general partner breached its duty of care to the LP by devoting inadequate time and attention to the management of the funds), *with Malpiede v. Townson*, 780 A.2d 1075, 1095 n.71 (Del. 2001) ("[P]roving the existence of a valid exculpatory provision in the corporate charter entitles directors to dismissal of any claims for money damages against them that are based solely on alleged breaches of the board's duty of care.").

[41] See, e.g., *Gelfman v. Weeden Investors, L.P.*, 859 A.2d 89 (Del. Ch. 2004); *Auriga Capital Corp. v. Gatz Props., LLC*, 40 A.3d 839 (Del. Ch. 2012), *aff'd Gatz Props., LLC v. Auriga Capital Corp.*, 59 A.3d 1206 (Del. 2012); *Gotham Partners, L.P. v. Hallwood Realty Partners, L.P.*, 855 A.2d 1059 (Del. Ch. 2003).

[42] See, e.g., *Norton v. K-Sea Transp. Partners L.P.*, 67 A.3d 354, 366–67 (Del. 2013) (finding that, although the plaintiff had pled facts that indicated that the general partner "used its position to extract an excessive amount of compensation" and that would permit the court to infer that the general partner may not have acted in good faith, the general partner had followed the requirements of the LP and the plaintiff's claims could not survive a motion to dismiss).

[43] See 6 *Del. C.* § 18-1101(e) ("A limited liability company agreement may provide for the limitation or elimination of any and all liabilities for breach of contract and breach of duties (including fiduciary duties) . . . provided, that *a limited liability company agreement may not limit or eliminate liability for any act or omission that constitutes a bad faith violation of the implied contractual covenant of good faith and fair dealing.*") (emphasis added); 6 *Del. C.* § 17-1101(e) ("A partnership agreement may provide for the limitation or elimination of any and all liabilities for breach of contract and breach of duties (including fiduciary duties) . . . provided, that *a partnership agreement may not limit or eliminate liability for any act or omission that constitutes a bad faith violation of the implied contractual covenant of good faith and fair dealing.*") (emphasis added).

implied covenant is a carefully interpreted one that only applies "when the express terms of the contract indicate that the parties would have agreed to the obligation had they negotiated the issue."[44] When the contract specifically covers the situation, the implied covenant cannot be used to vary its meaning.[45] As important, the contractual use of the term good faith in that context is far different from the use of good faith by cases in equity addressing the duties of fiduciaries. In that contractual context, good faith is a confined concept dealing with the requirement that a party not take action to defeat the expectations clearly implied by the explicit terms of the agreement.[46] In the corporate fiduciary context, good faith is the state of mind of a loyal fiduciary bound to advance the best interests of the stockholders.[47]

We fear that judges faced with cases where faithful adherence to the broad exculpatory and safe harbor provisions of alternative entity agreements would seem to excuse unfair self-interested behavior—for example, because the explicit procedural steps were taken that immunized a transaction from scrutiny even under a bad faith standard—will be tempted to wield the implied covenant as a substitute for the very fiduciary duties that the agreements explicitly eliminated. If the implied covenant begins to take on this role, the predictability of the law will suffer in two important ways. Not only will the well-understood default principles of fiduciary duty be rendered less dependable as a method for investors and managers to form relationships and run businesses, but the potential expansion in the role of the implied covenant could render contractual expectations less predictable, thereby raising the cost of contracting and deterring the formation of some relationships.

It is not clear to us that this patchwork of outcomes provides systemic benefits to investors, or even managers. For investors, the detriments are obvious. Because there

---

[44] *Nemec v. Shrader*, 991 A.2d 1120, 1127 n.20 (Del. 2010) (quoting *Fitzgerald v. Cantor*, 1998 WL 842316, at *1 (Del. Ch. Nov. 10, 1998); *see also Auriga Capital Corp. v. Gatz Properties*, 40 A.3d 839, 853–54 (Del. Ch. 2012) ("The implied covenant is to be used cautiously and does not apply to situations that could be anticipated, which is a real problem in the business context, because fiduciary duty review typically addresses actions that are anticipated and permissible under the express terms of the contract, but where there is a potential for managerial abuse. For these reasons, the implied covenant is not a tool that is designed to provide a framework to govern the discretionary actions of business managers acting under a broad enabling framework like a barebones LLC agreement.") (internal citations omitted), *aff'd* 59 A.3d 1206 (Del. 2012).

[45] *Allied Capital Corp. v. GC-SUN Holdings, L.P.*, 910 A.2d 1020, 1032–33 (Del. Ch. 2006) ("[I]mplied covenant analysis will only be applied when the contract is truly silent with respect to the matter at hand, and only when the court finds that the expectations of the parties were so fundamental that it is clear that they did not feel a need to negotiate about them.").

[46] 23 WILLISTON ON CONTRACTS § 63:22 (4th ed. 2002) ("As a general principle, there can be no breach of the implied promise or covenant of good faith and fair dealing where the contract expressly permits the actions being challenged, and the defendant acts in accordance with the express terms of the contract.").

[47] *See In re Walt Disney Co. Derivative Litig.*, 907 A.2d 693, 755 (Del. Ch. 2005) ("To act in good faith, a director must act at all times with an honesty of purpose and in the best interests and welfare of the corporation.") *aff'd*, 906 A.2d 27 (Del. 2006); *see also* Leo E. Strine, Jr., Lawrence A. Hamermesh, R. Franklin Balotti, & Jeffrey M. Gorris, *Loyalty's Core Demand: The Defining Role of Good Faith in Corporation Law*, 98 Geo. L. J. 629, 644 (2010) ("[G]ood faith is the defining term that Delaware Courts employing the business judgment rule standard of review use to articulate the state of mind required of a loyal fiduciary exercising corporate powers.").

are no reliable defaults, investors are either required to become diligent and expert readers of alternative entity agreements, which may involve the expenditure of material costs for legal advice, or to blindly accept the risks of investing in asset classes where no dependable protection against self-dealing and other conflicts of interest exists. Because those detriments are unrelated to the primary reason alternative entities are attractive to investors—the tax benefits—it is not clear why investors should wish or need to incur them. Given the reality that many of the accredited investors who invest in non-public alternative entities are themselves fiduciaries, such as pension funds who invest on behalf of ordinary Americans who depend on those investments to pay for their retirement, these detriments cannot be shrugged off as something only incurred by the affluent and thus not a public policy concern.

For managers, the freedom to impose one's own draft has been a decidedly mixed blessing, as many managers have found themselves exposed to liability as a result of their own infelicitous drafting.[48] Rather than being able to draw on market experiences and practices that have been generalized from other cases, managers implementing their own playbook have often been flagged for violations by courts or had to pay to settle cases more expensively than might have been the case if they had simply been operating under general default principles of corporate law.

For all these reasons, it remains unclear to us that the common understanding of alternative entity governance as intensely contractual and as reflecting efficient situational-specific bargaining is an apt one, at least as it applies to alternative entities raising capital from diverse investors. Rather, the experience with litigated cases suggests that alternative entity governing instruments are not the products of negotiation, but are drafted solely by entity managers. Those governing instruments seem to achieve little in terms of wealth-creating efficiency beyond what can be achieved under current "broadly enabling" corporate law statutes, which already provide for the ability to avoid liability under the corporate opportunity doctrine. In fact, if alternative entity statutes were amended to (1) provide for a default standard that no liability exists for breach of the duty of care absent a contractual provision imposing such liability; and (2) provide that where a governing instrument of a managing member or general partner specifies that certain directors have a duty solely to consider the best interests of the alternative entity and its investors, their actions will be entitled to the same deference as would be given to independent directors of a corporation, then it is not clear why, as a matter of systemic efficiency, much less fairness, the fiduciary duty principles of loyalty that apply in the corporate context should be subject to elimination.

---

[48] *See, e.g., Kahn v. Portnoy*, 2008 WL 5197164, at *13 (Del. Ch. Dec. 11, 2008) (declining to grant the defendants' motion to dismiss in a case where the provisions of the LLC agreement were ambiguous and noting that, with the broad discretion given to parties to craft an LLC agreement "comes the risk—for both the parties and this Court—that the resulting LLC agreement will be incomplete, unclear, or even incoherent.").

2. Freedom of contract for alternative entities in Delaware: myth or reality?
Mark J. Loewenstein

The idea that contractual commitments of competent adults are enforceable against those adults is an accepted, indeed revered, concept of American jurisprudence. The concept is sometimes referred to as freedom of contract, a term that enhances its appeal: we are a nation that prizes individual freedoms and the freedom to make enforceable contracts is among those freedoms. As any lawyer knows, and most non-lawyers would intuit, there are limits to the freedom of contract.[1] Courts will not enforce a promise that violates public policy (e.g., a promise to commit a crime) or one that is unconscionable (whatever that means). But what of a contract that does not meet either of those limitations, such as a contract that appears to be terribly unfair to the party against whom enforcement is sought? These are often the "hard cases" that make "bad law," as courts often find ways to ameliorate or avoid the adverse consequences of enforcement of bad bargains, sometimes stretching the concept of public policy or equitable principles to achieve a "just" result.

Delaware, however, purports to eschew such judicial shenanigans, at least for alternative entities. By contrast, neither the Delaware courts nor the Delaware legislature has embraced the notion of contractual freedom for corporations. Corporate officers and

---

[1] In a 2013 opinion, then Vice Chancellor Strine provided the most extensive definition of the concept that I have found:

> Delaware is a state that respects the freedom of contract. Thus, when two parties have a contract on which a payment must be made, they are free to determine the basis for that payment. For example, if parties determined that a contractual payout would be determined in part by rainfall on a particular day in a particular location, they could stipulate that the rainfall would be as reported by the National Weather Service. In such a case, however arbitrary the input, the court could not second-guess the rainfall measurement of the National Weather Service by hearing expert testimony on how much rain actually fell in that particular location on that particular date. Rather, the contractual input would be respected as the ones chosen by the parties. This is not to say that the court would uphold an unjust result. But injustice would not be based on an argument and a resulting judicial inquiry into the possibility that the National Weather Service in good faith made a measurement error. Such a substantive judicial reconsideration of the National Weather Service's measurement would be entirely inconsistent with the parties' own contract, which included as an input to a key formula the reported measurement of the National Weather Service, not the measurement of the National Weather Service subject to a de novo judicial re-examination. No, the only injustice that would be relevant in contractual terms would be if a party to the contract had tainted the National Weather Service measurement by giving a large bribe to the local official charged with reporting rainfall to the NWS. In that (unthinkable) case, the party suffering from that breach of contract would, of course, have the right to relief because the contractual input had been tainted by a breach of the implied covenant of good faith and fair dealing.

Senior Housing Capital, LLC v. SHP Senior Housing Fund, LLC, 2013 WL 1955012 at *24 (Del. Ch. May 13, 2013).

directors are bound by a well-developed jurisprudence recognizing a duty of loyalty to the corporation; the ability of corporate fiduciaries to contract around that duty is virtually nonexistent. For alternative entities, Delaware privileges freedom of contract, enshrining the concept in its statutes and judicial opinions. But is the judiciary really true to the concept? What does it do when faced with a really hard case—will it toe the freedom-of-contract line?

A number of Delaware cases can give one pause about the commitment of the Delaware judiciary to freedom of contract, either because the language of the opinion seems less than absolute or the result can be characterized as an implicit rejection of freedom of contract. The latter are relatively rare, but extant, while the former are abundant. In this chapter, I explore the extent to which the Delaware courts embrace the freedom of contract in light of the statutory and common law mandates requiring that they do.

As a starting point, the Delaware statutes, particularly those dealing with alternative entities, state the concept with clarity and in nearly identical language across the alternative entities statutes. For instance, § 18-1101(b) of the Delaware Limited Liability Company Act provides: "It is the policy of this chapter to give the maximum effect to the principle of freedom of contract and to the enforceability of limited liability company agreements." The statute does not describe what "maximum effect" means and the cases do not either. Arguably, it means that the courts should honor the intent of the parties even if the result is painful to one of the parties. But that is also a description of the broad concept of contractual freedom without the "maximum effect" modifier. Another possible interpretation is that the courts should enforce a contract without regard to public policy or the concept of unconscionability. But the Delaware courts have eschewed that approach, clearly carving out these limits on contractual freedom.[2]

The concept of maximum effect is also undercut by occasional pronouncements from members of the Chancery Court. For instance, Vice Chancellor Glasscock recently expressed the possibility that equitable considerations might play a role in the context of an LLC operating agreement that limited access to judicial dissolution. In *Huatuco v. Satellite Healthcare*,[3] the plaintiff sought judicial dissolution on the basis that the members were deadlocked in the conduct of the business. The operating agreement expressly limited the availability of dissolution and rejected the default provisions of the Delaware code, including, by implication, judicial dissolution. For those reasons, the court dismissed the complaint.

Interestingly, the court addressed the plaintiff's equitable arguments as to why judicial dissolution should be available. These arguments were that without judicial dissolution, the plaintiff would have no exit options and would be exposed to additional liability. Among other things, the court noted that the plaintiff could withdraw from the LLC and observed: "there is no absolute prohibition on withdrawal, and the Plaintiff's argument that the LLC is insolvent and may require him to undertake further liability is equitably

---

[2] See, e.g., Abry Partners V, L.P. v. F & W Acquisition LLC, 891 A.2d 1032 (Del.Ch. 2006) (contractual provision relieving a party of liability for intentional misrepresentations would be unenforceable as contrary to public policy); Ryan v. Weiner, 610 A.2d 1377 (Del.Ch. 1992) (unconscionable contract subject to rescission).

[3] 2013 WL 6460898 (Del.Ch. 2013).

deficient."[4] Tellingly, the court noted that the plaintiff may have a claim for breach of contract, which, if successful, would give him the relief that he sought. By addressing the plaintiff's equity claims and noting alternative possibilities for relief, the court hedged a bit on a full-throated endorsement of freedom of contract, despite citing the principle several times. Early in the opinion, the court foreshadowed the role that equity could play, albeit not in this fact scenario. Footnote 2 to the opinion reads:

> Whether the parties may, by contract, divest this Court of its authority to order a dissolution in all circumstances, even where it appears manifest that equity so requires—leaving, for instance, irreconcilable members locked away together forever like some alternative entity version of Sartre's Huis Clos—is an issue I need not resolve in this Memorandum Opinion. As I find below, considerations fundamental to equity are absent here.[5]

Were freedom of contract given its maximum effect, why would equity have any role to play? Put differently, this footnote suggests that equitable considerations are at least a possibility in the right fact situation.

This tendency to hedge, at least a bit, is common in many recent Delaware cases and might give one doubts about the judiciary's commitment to freedom of contract. In an earlier case considering the enforceability of an operating agreement that precluded judicial dissolution, *R & R Capital, LLC v. Buck & Doe Run Valley Farms, LLC*,[6] Chancellor Chandler supported his opinion in part by explaining why there may be "legitimate business reasons why members of a limited liability company may wish to waive their right to seek dissolution...."[7] He noted that lenders to an LLC may deem the filing of a petition for judicial dissolution as a noncurable event of default. Thus, "a disgruntled member could push the limited liability company into default on all of its outstanding loans simply by filing a petition with this Court."[8]

Chancellor Chandler also addressed the role of equity, noting that the plaintiffs appeared to have a claim under the implied covenant of good faith and fair dealing, but they failed to name the breaching party in their complaint. I will discuss the implied covenant below, but suffice it to say that the *R & R Capital* opinion is noteworthy because Chancellor Chandler apparently felt it necessary to counter a perception that the agreement was unduly one-sided and that the plaintiffs were without a remedy. If freedom of contract was as strong a principle as judicial dictum sometimes suggests, this would be unnecessary.

Other hedges are evident in Chancery Court opinions. For instance, then Vice Chancellor Strine (now Chief Justice of the Delaware Supreme Court), faced a challenge to a related party transaction in *Brickell Partners v. Wise*.[9] The partnership agreement provided that the resolution of a conflict of interest "shall be conclusively deemed fair and reasonable to the Partnership if such conflict of interest or resolution is approved by Special Approval...." In this case, such approval was obtained and, per the agreement,

---

[4] Id. at *6.
[5] Id. at *1, n.2.
[6] 2008 WL 3846318 (Del.Ch. 2008).
[7] Id. at *7.
[8] Id.
[9] 794 A.2d 1 (2001).

that should have been the end of the matter. But Vice Chancellor Strine did not let the matter rest there. Instead, he analyzed the composition of the Special Committee that approved the acquisition, noted that the plaintiff did not allege facts impugning their objectivity and, in a footnote, said that "[t]he complaint is also devoid of even a conclusory allegation that DeepTech or any other defendant tainted the Special Approval process by defrauding or otherwise tainting the work of the Conflicts and Audit Committee."[10] These "reservations" in the opinion, of course, provide a basis for setting aside future "special approvals."

Two other common hedges are worth noting as well—whether the approval of a related party transaction includes the trappings of a good faith negotiation and whether the equity holders had an opportunity to vote on the deal. Both of these hedges were present in the extensive litigation involving Encore Energy Partners, L.P. The applicable limited partnership agreement (LPA) for Encore was typical of many in Delaware litigation—related party transactions were permitted and the general partner was afforded considerable leeway and protection in approving them. Consistent with the LPA, this deal obtained "special approval" from a conflicts committee, which was only required to act in subjective good faith, defined as the belief that the transaction was in the best interests of the partnership. The Chancery Court, in an opinion by Vice Chancellor Parsons, dismissed the complaint challenging the transaction.[11] His opinion made reference to freedom of contract and admonished investors who challenge transactions that are approved in the manner set forth in their partnership agreement. His stern language is similar to that found in many other Delaware cases:

> The near absence under the LPA of any duties whatsoever to Encore's public equity holders presumably would discourage risk averse investors unwilling to take a leap of faith from investing their money in an enterprise controlled by the General Partner and its Affiliates ... Investors apprehensive about the risks inherent in waiving the fiduciary duties of those with whom they entrust their investments may be well advised to avoid master limited partnerships like Encore ... Delaware law "give[s] maximum effect to the principle of freedom of contract and to the enforceability of partnership agreements." The parties to the partnership agreement at issue here plainly intended to give the General Partner and its Affiliates maximum flexibility. Under these circumstances, an inference that the concededly modest protections afforded to Plaintiffs by the LPA frustrated their legitimate expectations would be unreasonable even on a motion to dismiss. Accordingly, in this case, there does not appear to be any reasonably conceivable set of circumstances susceptible of proof under which Plaintiffs could recover on a claim to that effect.[12]

This robust endorsement of freedom of contract should, however, be read in context. The opinion notes that the deal was put to a vote of the unitholders and overwhelmingly approved by them. Moreover, the court carefully set out the actions of the committee, describing how the committee was constituted (independent members), its two sets of legal advisors (one an expert in oil and gas exploration and the other on the duties of the committee under Delaware law), its retention of an independent investment banker, its due diligence, and its negotiation efforts with the general partner to improve the terms

---

[10] Id. at 5, n.9.
[11] In re Encore Energy Partners LP Unitholders Litigation, 2012 WL 3792997 at * 13 (Del.Ch. Aug. 31, 2012).
[12] Id. at *13 (footnotes omitted).

of the deal. To the extent that the price was questionable in that it represented a small premium over market, the court seemed to credit the defendants' explanation—that the price depended on the distributable post-merger cash flow that the acquirer could anticipate and that the market price of the units already reflected the market's anticipation of a merger. As in other cases, the court did not avoid a consideration of the substance of the deal or the extent to which the procedural protections actually provided in the applicable agreement were, in some sense, adequate.

Eventual appeals to the Delaware Supreme Court were unsuccessful.[13] The High Court focused on the plaintiffs' argument that to determine whether the Special Committee in fact acted in subjective good faith, the court should consider objective evidence of the fairness of the deal. While the court said that such evidence was "neither necessary nor sufficient to justify a reasonable inference that the Conflicts Committee did not act with subjective good faith," in some extreme cases, such evidence may suggest bad faith.[14] The court also conceded that allegations in a complaint that the defendants knew of facts indicating that a transaction approved by them was not in the best interests of the partnership may be sufficient to withstand a motion to dismiss, but such allegations were not present here. *Allen* has been characterized as an example of the courts' confirmation "that clear, express and unambiguous language modifying fiduciary duties will be enforced."[15] This is not an unfair characterization, as the Supreme Court, like the lower court, made a point of emphasizing the pre-eminence of freedom of contract, but, again, in the factual context of this case it was not particularly difficult to enforce the contract of the parties.[16]

To this point, I have highlighted cases where the Delaware courts have enforced operating agreements and LPAs that provided a process to approve related party transactions that would not have met the standards under corporate law. In each of these cases, however, the Delaware courts have noted facts that soften the impact of enforcement while, at the same time, stating the importance of contractual freedom. But, one might ask, have the Delaware courts actually refused to enforce contracts? Though not a frequent occurrence, the answer is yes. In short, the Delaware courts will apply principles of equity in rare situations and, increasingly, are turning to the implied covenant of good faith and fair dealing to provide relief where no other avenue exists.

The most prominent case in which equitable considerations determined the outcome may be *VGS, Inc. v. Castiel*,[17] a 2000 opinion of then Vice Chancellor Steele. The case involved an LLC that was, indirectly, owned by two individuals, Castiel and Sahagen. Castiel indirectly owned 75 percent and had the right to appoint two of the three managers. He appointed himself and Quinn. Sahagen indirectly owned the balance and appointed himself as the third manager. Due to differences with Castiel, Sahagen devised a strategy to oust Castiel—he would cause the LLC to merge into a corporation that he controlled. He persuaded Quinn to go along with this scheme and to keep it a secret from Castiel. Since the operating agreement authorized the managers to approve a merger on

---

[13] Allen v. Encore Energy Partners, L.P., 72 A.3d 93 (Del. 2013).
[14] Id. at 108.
[15] Richards Layton & Finger client letter dated July 23, 2013.
[16] See, also, Sonet v. Timber Co., L.P., 722 A.2d 319, 326 (Del.Ch. 1998) (merger transaction subject to supermajority vote of limited partners, which general partner could not control).
[17] 2000 WL 1277372, 27, Del. J. Corp. L. 454 (Del.Ch. Aug. 31, 2000).

behalf of the LLC, Castiel and Quinn had the authority to approve the merger. Using a Delaware statute that permitted managers of an LLC to act by majority written consent without prior notice (assuming they were otherwise authorized to act by majority vote), Quinn and Sahagen accomplished the merger and squeezed Castiel out of control. Castiel sued, claiming that the merger required unanimous approval of the managers (rejected by the court) and that Sahagen and Quinn violated their fiduciary duties to him (accepted by the court).

The Vice Chancellor never cited the principle of contractual freedom and never explained why one manager of an LLC would owe a fiduciary duty directly to a co-manager. That concept is without precedent as far as I have been able to determine. The outcome of the case is reminiscent of a 1971 corporate law case, *Schnell v. Chris-Craft Industries, Inc.*,[18] where, similarly, the directors of a corporation engineered a course of action that was permitted under the corporation's bylaws but had the effect of unfairly disadvantaging a dissident faction of shareholders seeking board representation. To justify the relief to the dissidents, the Delaware Supreme Court said, "[I]nequitable action does not become permissible simply because it is legally possible." That is, essentially, the principle that best explains the outcome in the *VGS* case. Were the *VGS* case to come before the Delaware courts today, however, it is likely that the case would turn on the implied covenant of good faith and fair dealing, as explained below.

A second example, arising from a similar fact situation, can be found in *Twin Bridges Ltd. Partnership v. Draper*,[19] which, interestingly, did cite *Schnell*. *Twin Bridges* involved an amendment to an LLC operating agreement that, in turn, facilitated a merger between the LLC and another entity. The ultimate result was that the surviving LLC had three general partners instead of two and the resulting operating agreement (unlike the original operating agreement) disclaimed fiduciary duties of the general partners. The controlling group filed a declaratory judgment action seeking an order that the multi-step transaction was valid, while the minority defendants counterclaimed that the transaction was invalid and amounted to a breach by the plaintiffs of their fiduciary duties. The court ruled that the amendment to the operating agreement and the merger were valid, but refused to grant summary judgment to the plaintiffs on the defendants' counterclaim that in approving the operating agreement that disclaimed fiduciary duties, the plaintiffs acted in breach of their fiduciary duties. As in the *VGS* decision, the court here did not articulate the duty that was breached. Together with the earlier citation to *Schnell*, the inescapable conclusion is that equitable considerations drove the decision.[20]

A different approach—narrow construction of an agreement—is evident in a number of Delaware cases and *Miller v. American Real Estate Partners, L.P.*[21] provides a good example. In this case the plaintiffs challenged a number of actions by the general partner, including related party transactions, claiming, among other things, that the general

---

[18] 285 A.2d 437, 439 (Del. 1971).
[19] 2007 WL 2744609 (Del.Ch. Sept. 14, 2007).
[20] Schnell has been cited with approval in other cases involving alternative entities. See, e.g., Alpine Investment Partners v. LJM2 Capital Management, L.P., 794 A.2d 1276, 1284 n.13 (Del.Ch. 2002); Juran v. Bron, 2000 WL 1521478, at *19–20 (Del.Ch. Oct. 6, 2000).
[21] 2001 WL 1045643 (Del.Ch. Aug. 2, 2001). See, also, In re Atlas Energy Resources, LLC, 2010 WL 4273122 (Del.Ch. Oct. 28, 2010).

partner breached its fiduciary duty of loyalty. The defense rested on the partnership agreement, which included a now common clause giving the general partner broad discretion:

> Whenever in this Agreement the General Partner is permitted or required to make a decision (i) in its "sole discretion" or "discretion", with "absolute discretion" or under a grant of similar authority or latitude, the General Partner shall be entitled to consider only such interests and factors as it desires and shall have no duty or obligation to give any consideration to any interest of or factors affecting the Partnership, the Operating Partnership or the Record Holders, or (ii) in its "good faith" or under another express standard, the General Partner shall act under such express standard and shall not be subject to any other or different standards imposed by this Agreement or any other agreement contemplated herein.[22]

The defendants argued that this provision, combined with another that delegated to the general partner "full, exclusive and complete discretion to manage and control the business and affairs of the Partnership," precluded a claim that the general partner breached its duty of loyalty.[23] Vice Chancellor Strine did not agree, ruling that the sole discretion standard set forth in the agreement "does not expressly state that default provisions of law must give way if they hinder the General Partner's ability to act under the sole discretion standard."[24] The court thus rejected the notion that a sole discretion standard renders the actions of the general partner nonreviewable, although that is certainly a plausible construction of the provision. Less plausible is the standard that the court suggested might apply here—a fairness standard.[25] In any case, Vice Chancellor Strine sent a message to lawyers who seek to limit the fiduciary obligations of their clients:

> In view of the great freedom afforded to such drafters and the reality that most publicly traded limited partnerships are governed by agreements drafted exclusively by the original general partner, it is fair to expect that restrictions on fiduciary duties be set forth clearly and unambiguously. A topic as important as this should not be addressed coyly.[26]

Plaintiffs seeking relief from one-sided agreements are less likely to rely on *Schnell* or equitable principles or on some form of strict construction as the Delaware courts have developed a robust jurisprudence around the implied covenant of good faith and fair dealing. The implied covenant, which is a part of every contract and cannot be disclaimed under Delaware law, provides the courts with a tool to police harsh bargains. A recent Chancery Court decision describes the implied covenant:

> The implied covenant is a limited gap-filling tool to infer contractual terms to which the parties would have agreed had they anticipated a situation they failed to address; it is not a "free-floating duty" or "a substitute for fiduciary duty analysis." Put differently,
>
>> "[f]air dealing" is not akin to the fair process component of entire fairness, i.e., whether the fiduciary acted fairly when engaging in the challenged transaction as measured by duties of loyalty and care ... It is rather a commitment to deal "fairly" in the sense of consistently

---

[22] Id. at *6.
[23] Id. at *7.
[24] Id. at *8.
[25] Id. at *10–11. (The court left the question open as it ultimately dismissed the complaint but, with respect to certain claims, without prejudice.)
[26] Id. at *8.

with the terms of the parties' agreement and its purpose. Likewise "good faith" does not envision loyalty to the contractual counterparty, but rather faithfulness to the scope, purpose, and terms of the parties' contract. Both necessarily turn on the contract itself and what the parties would have agreed upon had the issue arisen when they were bargaining originally.

Additionally, when a contract confers discretionary rights on a party, the implied covenant requires that party to exercise its discretion reasonably. And "what is 'arbitrary' or 'unreasonable'—or conversely 'reasonable'—depends on the parties' original contractual obligations" and "reasonable expectations at the time of contracting." Fundamentally, therefore, "[t]he implied covenant cannot be invoked to override the express terms of the contract."[27]

The implied covenant of good faith and fair dealing is considered in greater detail in Chapter 4 of this book. My purpose here is to describe the interplay between the implied covenant and the concept of freedom of contract. That interplay is perhaps best demonstrated in *Gerber v. Enterprise Products Holdings, LLC*,[28] an important 2013 precedent decided by the Delaware Supreme Court.

Gerber, like so many other recent Delaware cases, involved a challenge to a related party transaction against a background of an LPA that gave considerable leeway to the general partner. The complexity of the transactions led the Supreme Court to include three charts in its opinion to illustrate them, but, from a doctrinal perspective, those transactions can be briefly summarized. Essentially, two transactions were the source of plaintiff Gerber's complaint. As the court dealt with each transaction in a virtually identical fashion, we need only consider one of the transactions (which the court refers to as the "2009 Sale") to understand how the court employed the implied covenant of good faith and fair dealing. In the 2009 Sale, Enterprise Products GP, the general partner of EPE, a limited partnership, sold a partnership asset, Teppco GP, to an affiliate of the general partner for, allegedly, a fraction of its value. On the same date, the general partner caused EPE to sell Teppco LP to that same affiliate in a separate but related transaction (the Teppco LP Sale). Gerber was a limited partner in EPE and filed a damage action against the general partner and its affiliates (Affiliates) (the defendants) involved in the transactions. The general partner's defense was that the LPA disclaimed all fiduciary duties and that the general partner fully complied with each of the contract provisions.

The following provisions of the LPA were of particular importance in the case:

- Section 7.9(b) of the LPA expressly provided that the conduct of the general partner or any of its "Affiliates" must be in "good faith," defined as a "belie[f] that the determination or other action is in the best interests of the Partnership":

    > Whenever the General Partner makes a determination or takes or declines to take any other action, or any of its Affiliates causes it to do so, ... then unless another express standard is provided for in this Agreement, the General Partner, or such Affiliates causing it to do so, shall make such determination or take or decline to take such other action in good faith, and shall not be subject to any other or different standards imposed by this

---

[27] In re Encore Energy Partners LP Unitholder Litigation, 2012 WL 3792997 at *13 (Del.Ch. Aug. 31, 2012) (footnotes omitted).
[28] 67 A.3d 400, overruled on other grounds, Winshall v. Viacom Intern., Inc., 76 A.3d 808 (Del. Sup.Ct. 2013).

Agreement, any other agreement contemplated hereby or under the Delaware Act or any other law, rule or regulation or at equity. In order for a determination or other action to be in "good faith" for purposes of this Agreement, the Person or Persons making such determination or taking or declining to take such other action must believe that the determination or other action is in the best interests of the Partnership.

- In addition to defining the duties of the general partner, the LPA also created two separate layers of protection designed to insulate the defendants from judicial review of whether they had satisfied their contractual duty. The first layer of insulation was Section 7.9(a) of the LPA, which covered "conflict of interest" transactions. That provision created four "safe harbors" within which the general partner and its Affiliates could effectuate a conflict of interest transaction free of any claim that they breached "any duty stated or implied by law or equity." Section 7.9(a) relevantly provided:

    Unless otherwise expressly provided in this Agreement, whenever a potential conflict of interest exists or arises between the General Partner or any of its Affiliates, on the one hand, and the Partnership or any Partner, on the other hand, any resolution or course of action by the General Partner or its Affiliates in respect of such conflict of interest shall be permitted and deemed approved by all Partners, and shall not constitute a breach of this Agreement . . ., or of any duty stated or implied by law or equity, if the resolution or course of action in respect of such conflict of interest is[:]

    (i) approved by Special Approval,
    (ii) approved by the vote of a majority of the Units excluding Units owned by the General Partner and its Affiliates,
    (iii) on terms no less favorable to the Partnership than those generally being provided to or available from unrelated third parties, or
    (iv) fair and reasonable to the Partnership, taking into account the totality of the relationships between the parties involved (including other transactions that may be particularly favorable or advantageous to the Partnership).

"Special Approval" was defined in the LPA as "approval by a majority of the members of the Audit, Conflict, and Governance Committee (the ACG Committee)." The layer of insulation afforded by Section 7.9(a) purported to preclude judicial review of any conflict transaction that is the subject of "Special Approval."

- The second layer of insulation from judicial review was afforded by Section 7.10(b) of the LPA, which applied more broadly and was not limited to conflict of interest transactions. Section 7.10(b) created a "conclusive presumption" that the general partner acts in "good faith" where the following condition is satisfied:

    The General Partner may consult with . . . [experts or] investment bankers . . ., and any act taken or omitted to be taken in reliance upon the opinion . . . of such Persons as to matters that the General Partner reasonably believes to be within such Person's professional or expert competence shall be conclusively presumed to have been done or omitted in good faith and in accordance with such opinion.

In the 2009 Sale, the general partner sought and obtained Special Approval; that is, the deal was approved by the ACG Committee which, in turn, relied on a fairness opinion that the general partner obtained from Morgan Stanley & Co., a well-known investment banker. That opinion, however, opined on the fairness of the total consideration paid for both the 2009 Sale and the Teppco LP Sale. Morgan Stanley did *not* opine, however, on the fairness of the portion of the total consideration specifically allocable to the 2009 Sale, which Gerber challenged in this lawsuit. The general partner defended the plaintiff's claim on the basis of the contract provisions set forth above. In response, the plaintiff argued that while the general partner may not have violated those express contractual provisions, it did violate the implied covenant.

The Chancery Court held that the implied covenant was not implicated in this case.[29] The Vice Chancellor framed the issue as follows: "can a plaintiff plead that a defendant breached the implied covenant when the defendant is conclusively presumed by the terms of a contract to have acted in good faith?"[30] He concluded that the plaintiff could not. The Vice Chancellor reasoned that because the general partner may, under the terms of the LPA, rely on the opinion of Morgan Stanley, so too could the ACG Committee. As the LPA provided that such reliance establishes, conclusively, the Committee's good faith, the implied covenant was inapplicable. Critically, the Vice Chancellor wrote:

> Under the plain terms of the LPA, if Section 7.10(b) applies to an action taken by [the general partner], then [the general partner] is protected from any claims asserting that the action was taken other than in good faith. *That would include good faith claims arising under the duty of loyalty, the implied covenant, and any other doctrine.* In contrast to Section 7.10(b)'s broad pronouncement, our Supreme Court has determined that the implied covenant is a "limited and extraordinary legal remedy." It is a gap-filler, and may not be used to "infer language that contradicts a clear exercise of an express contractual right." Moreover, our Supreme Court has repeatedly stated that "one generally cannot base a claim for breach of the implied covenant on conduct authorized by the agreement."[31]

The Vice Chancellor was troubled by this transaction, writing that the "facts of this case take the reader *and* writer to the outer reaches of conduct allowable under [Delaware law]."[32] As he viewed the case, however, the general partner complied with the LPA and those were all of the protections for which the limited partners contracted. This opinion is as strong an endorsement for freedom of contract as one can find in Delaware jurisprudence. (Interestingly, the Vice Chancellor did not mention the terms "freedom of contract" or "contractual freedom" in his lengthy opinion.)

The Delaware Supreme Court, however, reversed this holding of the lower court, concluding that Section 7.10(b)'s conclusive presumption of good faith does not preclude a claim based on the implied covenant.[33] To reach this result, the Supreme Court first distinguished between the concept of good faith in the implied covenant and what it called the contractual fiduciary duty of good faith. The latter concept was reflected in Section 7.9(b) of the LPA and, as a contractual fiduciary duty, this provision required the general partner to act in the best interests of the partnership at the time it made a

---

[29] Gerber v. Enterprise Products Holdings, LLC, 2012 WL 34442 (Del.Ch. June 10, 2013).
[30] Id. at 12.
[31] Id. at 13 (footnotes omitted; emphasis added).
[32] Id. (emphasis supplied).
[33] Gerber v. Enterprise Products Holdings, LLC, 67 A.3d 400 (Del. 2013).

business decision for the partnership. The general partner satisfied this obligation under Section 7.10(b) if it relied on the opinion of a qualified expert, which it did. However, as the court read the LPA, "[n]othing in Section 7.10(b) pertains to or addresses the implied covenant."[34] This was the key move by the court, allowing it to conclude that the general partner's "attempt to take advantage of Section 7.10(b) may itself be subject to a claim that it was arbitrary and unreasonable and in violation of the implied covenant."[35] The Supreme Court framed the issue as "whether an implied covenant claim is stated where the defendant allegedly has attempted to satisfy its contractual obligations by relying on a fairness opinion that did not value the consideration that the LP unitholders actually received,"[36] and concluded that a claim was stated.

The essence of the opinion is that the implied covenant can survive in agreements that define what constitutes good faith. This case was an especially strong endorsement of that idea because Section 7.09(a) of the LPA expressly provided that if any one of the four options for approving a related party transaction was obtained, the transaction was deemed approved by all partners and could not constitute a breach of the LPA "or of any agreement contemplated . . . therein, or of any duty stated or implied by law or equity . . . ." In other words, the LPA seemed to have anticipated an attack based on the process chosen and provided a defense to such an attack. It is difficult to articulate what additional language the LPA could have included to avoid the applicability of the implied covenant. Would the case have turned out differently if Section 7.09(a) had said, additionally: "The general partner shall have no obligation to evaluate any opinion rendered by a reputable investment banker and the general partner's reliance thereon shall be conclusively presumed to be in good faith"? Perhaps that additional language would have altered the outcome, but perhaps not. The court painted with a broad brush, asking whether the plaintiff could have anticipated that the "ACG Committee would grant Special Approval based on their reliance on such a flawed opinion."[37] The hypothetical addition to Section 7.09(a) might not clue the plaintiff into that possibility.

As noted above, the *VGS* case relied on equitable considerations in deciding that two managers of a limited liability company, holding a minority interest in the company, could not squeeze out the third member. Note how easily *VGS* would fit into an implied covenant analysis. The court could have reasoned that the majority member could not have anticipated that his co-members would approve a merger by written consent without so informing him and their actions thus constituted a violation of the implied covenant. *Twin Bridges* lends itself to a similar analysis. In short, the implied covenant is a powerful tool to police bargains.

While the concept of the implied covenant of good faith and fair dealing is an old one, it is an increasingly important part of the jurisprudence involving related party transactions in alternative entities. This is so because the contractual freedom in alternative entities, which includes the ability to disclaim fiduciary duties, has exposed investors

---

[34] Id. at 420.
[35] Id.
[36] Id. at 422.
[37] Id. at 424.

to potential abuse and, consequently, the Delaware courts have employed it to address abuse in a number of cases. But it is unclear whether that jurisprudence has also eroded the freedom of contract. It may be that what freedom of contract means in Delaware, at least in alternative entity law, is the freedom parties have to shape their relationship as they desire, with one caveat: if a party alleges that he or she has been treated with gross unfairness, the Delaware courts will scrutinize the operative agreement and will be amenable to arguments based on the implied covenant of good faith and fair dealing. Nevertheless, although in comparison to other jurisdictions, the Delaware courts do embrace a relatively strong adherence to contractual freedom, that embrace may not be absolute.[38]

---

[38] Compare, e.g., R & R Capital, LLC, supra note 6, with Holdeman, Executor v. Epperson, 857 N.E.2d 583 (Oh. 2006) (contractual provision limiting rights of successor to member not honored).

3. Contractual freedom and family business*
Benjamin Means

1. INTRODUCTION

Although the parties to a prospective business venture should clarify key points before investing—for instance, when capital contributions may be required, how business decisions will be made, how earnings (or losses) will be distributed, and what types of opportunities belong to the business—the resources of contract are limited. The parties cannot anticipate every contingency that might arise in a long-term business relationship. Also, because bargaining is expensive, the costs of negotiating a more complete contract will eventually outweigh the benefits. Moreover, the participants in a closely held business may rely upon trust, even as to matters that could have been specified in advance.

In the corporate context, most jurisdictions recognize a need for judicial monitoring of the parties' relationship to prevent the opportunistic exploitation of gaps in the contractual bargain.[1] For instance, even when they have not negotiated specific protections, minority shareholders can seek relief for oppression, often premised on the notion that controlling shareholders owe fiduciary duties and must honor the minority's reasonable expectations. While courts will not rescue investors from the consequences of entering a one-sided bargain, neither will courts stand by and allow controlling shareholders to deprive minority shareholders of any return on their investment.

In recent years, however, small-business investors have flocked to the LLC instead of the corporation,[2] and the extent to which courts will play a similar role in policing LLC bargains remains unclear. While the popularity of LLCs can largely be explained by tax considerations, the LLC is also distinctive in its emphasis on the freedom of contract.[3] As long as it is written down in the operating agreement, almost anything goes. Courts, therefore, expect that the parties will draft the provisions they want and may be reluctant to invoke equitable principles to rectify oversights.[4] In some jurisdictions, the operating agreement trumps the LLC statute and even a blanket waiver of fiduciary protection is permissible.[5]

---

* Portions of this chapter draw significantly from Means (2014, 2013, 2010). I thank Jim Burkhard for reviewing a draft of this chapter and providing helpful comments.

[1] *See* Thompson at 394.

[2] *See* Friedman at 35 (noting, a decade ago, that the LLC "has become the dominant form for newly-created small businesses in a clear majority of the states").

[3] *See, e.g.*, Sutherland v. Sutherland, No. 2399, 2009 WL 857468, at *4 (Del. Ch. Mar. 23, 2009) (distinguishing freedom of contract in LLC from more limited freedom in corporate context).

[4] *See, e.g.*, Willie Gary LLC v. James & Jackson LLC, 2006 WL 75309, at *2 (Del. Ch. Jan. 10, 2006) ("With the contractual freedom granted by the LLC Act comes the duty to scriven with precision.").

[5] O'NEAL & THOMPSON at § 6:23 ("LLCs differ from close corporations to the extent that participants may be able to sometimes use their operating agreement to waive statutory provisions. . . .").

Yet, in corporations and LLCs alike, gaps in the parties' negotiated bargain often leave room for opportunism, either because the parties have failed to address significant issues, or because their agreement lacks clarity.[6] Even when the parties are sophisticated and engage in arm's-length bargaining, it is no easy task to foresee all the ways other members might seek to evade contractual constraints to obtain an unfair advantage over the course of a long-term relationship.[7] Thus, a maximalist insistence upon the priority of contract sometimes makes it harder for the parties to establish a business venture that reflects their mutual expectations.

Other chapters in this volume explore the boundaries of the contractarian ideal, identifying limits even in Delaware, whose set policy for unincorporated businesses, if not state motto, is to "give the maximum effect to the principle of freedom of contract."[8] Professor Branson observes that contractual waivers of fiduciary duty are never comprehensive because the implied covenant of good faith and fair dealing remains part of every contract.[9] As a practical matter, contractual good faith can import something like a fiduciary duty by the backdoor, regardless of the parties' operating agreement.[10] Chief Justice Strine and Vice Chancellor Laster dismiss unlimited contractual freedom as a "siren song" and argue that a more fixed statutory structure would improve upon impenetrable, *ad hoc* bargains that too often fail to reflect a true arm's-length negotiation.[11]

This chapter builds on the points made by Professor Branson, Chief Justice Strine and Vice Chancellor Laster, and argues in favor of a different conception of contractual freedom, one that places renewed emphasis on the importance of default rules and background equitable principles as tools for facilitating the parties' business relationship. In other words, contractarianism should not be seen as synonymous with contract; a meaningful freedom of contract is broader and more complex than the proverbial blank sheet of paper on which to draft and a deferential court willing to enforce the results, however nonsensical. Rather, to facilitate the underlying contractual values of personal autonomy and welfare maximization, it may be better to guide the parties' relationship with well-crafted default rules and reasonable equitable constraints.

In a family business, for instance, a contractarian framework is typically insufficient to support the expectations of family participants. As is true of any closely held business, contracts in family businesses establish relationships rather than the terms of

---

[6] *See, e.g.*, Moll at 885; O'NEAL & THOMPSON at § 2:10 ("Many shareholders in small, incorporated businesses apparently do not understand fully the consequences that flow from incorporation, and in particular they do not realize that in the absence of special arrangement, ultimate and near-absolute control of a corporation rests in holders of a majority of its voting shares.").

[7] *See, e.g.*, VGS v. Castiel, No. C.A. 17995, 2000 WL 1277372 (Del. Ch. Aug. 31, 2000), discussed *infra* Section 2.

[8] 6 Del. C. § 17-1101(c) (partnership agreements); 6 Del. C. § 18-1101(b) (limited liability company agreements); 12 Del. C. § 3825(b) (trust instruments).

[9] Branson, Chapter 4.

[10] *Id.*

[11] Strine & Laster, Chapter 1. They worry that, under a fully contractarian approach, the implied covenant of good faith may be used not just to ensure that the parties live up to their negotiated agreement, but also to enforce more general equitable good faith obligations. *Id.* Better, in other words, to include fiduciary duties up front than to bring them in by the backdoor Professor Branson identifies.

specific, bargained-for exchanges, and the parties cannot be expected to anticipate and adequately address all eventualities that may occur over time. For family businesses, relational aspects are particularly significant: the time horizon stretches across generations, objectives often include more than simple profit maximization, and business dealings involve emotional consequences for the participants that also need to be acknowledged.[12] Instead of adhering to a false assumption that the parties to a business venture are capable of negotiating adequate protections for themselves and likely to do so, contract law should offer a resource—a set of principles that credit the parties' negotiated bargain in full context but that also compensate for what they cannot anticipate or adequately address.

The argument proceeds as follows. Section 2 describes the contractarian precepts of LLC law and offers some general reasons to be skeptical of the parties' ability to craft a complete bargain sufficient to govern their long-term business relationship. Section 3 uses family businesses to illustrate the challenges of defining and protecting the parties' expectations. Section 4 argues that a broader understanding of contract, informed by the parties' actual relationships and sensitive to the practical limits of arm's-length bargaining, would provide a more reliable mechanism for coordinating the parties' rights and obligations.

2. DISCORDANT NOTES IN THE SIREN SONG

The LLC form of business organization offers substantial advantages for privately owned businesses.[13] No longer must investors choose between the managerial flexibility and flow-through tax features of partnership law on the one hand and the stability and limited liability of the corporate form on the other; the LLC provides the attractive aspects of both without restriction.[14] Also, for investors concerned about vague fiduciary norms, the LLC's more explicitly contract-oriented format may be preferable.[15] Accordingly, one scholar contends that the close corporation was "a misbegotten compromise"[16] and has proved to be an "evolutionary dead end."[17]

---

[12] Judicial monitoring remains important as a backstop to prevent opportunism and oppression when relationships falter and one party is in a position to exercise its power over another. *See* Thompson at 394 ("A fully contingent contract cannot be drafted, so some *ex post* settling up by courts is used to support these [unstated] assumptions.").

[13] *See* Miller, at 1609–10 (noting that "entrepreneurs have an unparalleled range of choices for structuring LLC relationships, and LLC participants have access to the twin benefits of corporate limited liability and flow-through partnership tax status.").

[14] *See* RIBSTEIN, at 119.

[15] *See* Miller at 1610 (citing Dale A. Oesterle, *Subcurrents in LLC Statutes: Limiting the Discretion of State Courts to Restructure the Internal Affairs of Small Business*, 66 U. COLO. L. REV. 881, 881 (1995); Donald J. Weidner, *Three Policy Decisions Animate Revision of Uniform Partnership Act*, 46 BUS. LAW. 427, 428 (1991)). Although the LLC statutes contain default terms, and some, unlike Delaware, include mandatory fiduciary duties, "[t]he statutes typically assume that the individual owners will develop their own LLC operating agreements that define their respective rights, responsibilities, and remedies." *Id.* at 1610–11.

[16] RIBSTEIN at 252.

[17] *Id.* at 102.

However, the LLC's contractual flexibility does not provide a panacea for oppression.[18] Investors are expected to bargain for governance terms, and the task of creating an LLC operating agreement that deals appropriately with all relevant contingencies is substantially the same as negotiating articles of incorporation, by-laws, and shareholder agreements in a close corporation.[19] Also, access to the LLC form is not restricted to those who have taken the trouble to negotiate their own operating agreement, and LLCs resemble close corporations in that an aggrieved party has no automatic right to exit the investment under the default rules.[20] Thus, absent careful bargaining, minority investors in an LLC are vulnerable to mistreatment by the majority, just as they would be in a close corporation.[21]

Given these striking parallels, it is hard to see why an added degree of contractual flexibility should make a difference. That is, even before the advent of the LLC, prospective investors already had the ability to negotiate protections contractually. As one treatise explains, "shareholder agreements, supermajority requirements, and buy-sell provisions are only some of the contractual tools that shareholders can use to strengthen their employment, dividend, exit, and other rights."[22] However, "[d]espite this apparent opportunity for ex ante contracting, it is widely recognized that investors in closely held corporations typically fail to engage in such contracting."[23] Declaring contract king does not establish that it is actually capable of governing its realm.

Nor would it solve the problem if LLC statutes took the contractarian approach to its logical conclusion, implementing "a forced contracting system . . . that would allow the parties to participate in an activity or enterprise only if they actively choose their own terms."[24] Setting aside the costs of such a scheme, arm's-length deals frequently fail to anticipate all relevant contingencies. Therefore, courts adjudicating LLC disputes must either apply equitable principles akin to those applicable to corporate shareholder disputes or else accept serious injustice in individual cases when the terms of an agreement fail to reflect the parties' intent.

For instance, in *VGS, Inc. v. Castiel*,[25] despite having bargained for the right to appoint two of the three members of the Board of Managers, a founding member lost control of the LLC.[26] Although the sequence of events leading up to the founding member's

---

[18] *See* Miller at 1612 (finding that "classic 'squeeze-out techniques,' which have a long history in the close corporation setting of the past fifty years, are now surfacing in the context of the LLC").

[19] For an argument that courts should apply a full panoply of contract principles, including unconscionability, when parties waive fiduciary obligations in an LLC agreement, see DiMatteo at 279.

[20] *See* RIBSTEIN at 179–80.

[21] *Id.* at 180 ("Removal of buyout rights from LLCs has the perverse secondary effect of forcing lawmakers to provide a backup exit right. Therefore, judicial dissolution, which had brought so much unpredictability to close corporations, now haunts the LLCs that replaced them.").

[22] MOLL & RAGAZZO at § 7.01[E][1].

[23] *Id.*

[24] DAGAN at 179 (arguing that forced contracting would not correct for underlying disparities of power and would have an unequal, unjust impact).

[25] No. C.A. 17995, 2000 WL 1277372 (Del. Ch. Aug. 31, 2000).

[26] Ironically, this bargained-for protection left him more exposed than he would have been had he relied on "the statutorily sanctioned mechanism of approval by members owning a majority of the LLC's equity interests." *Id.* at *4. If the court chose to apply a formalistic

unfortunate predicament violated none of the literal terms of the parties' bargain, the Delaware Court of Chancery applied equitable principles to avoid an untoward result.

In *Castiel*, the independent member of the Board, who held a minority interest in the LLC, convinced an appointed member to defect and to effectuate a merger of the LLC into a corporation, relegating the founding member to a minority position.[27] The court observed that while the founding member would certainly have removed the faithless member of the Board, if given notice of the proposed merger, "the LLC Act, read literally, does not require notice . . . ."[28] Yet the court further reasoned that the lack of a notice requirement was to enable "LLC managers to take quick, efficient action in situations where a minority of managers could not block or adversely affect the course set by the majority even if they were notified . . . ."[29] That statutory purpose was not implicated, because the founding member "had the power to prevent any Board decision with which he disagreed."[30] The court rescinded the merger, relying on "a classic maxim of equity—'equity looks to the intent rather than to the form.'"[31]

As *Castiel* illustrates, it is difficult to address all varieties of possible opportunism through contractual provisions. Strine and Laster further observe that such efforts can become counterproductive, because "[u]nlike corporate certificates of incorporation and bylaws, which are relatively short, alternative entity agreements typically contain ninety-plus pages of dense, complex, and heavily cross-referenced legalese."[32] In agreements of that length, just keeping definitions and usage consistent can be a challenge.[33] Also, because each agreement contains unique provisions, judicial interpretations "produce few general principles that could lead to predictable and reliable practices."[34] As discussed in the next section, the lack of general principles is a particular problem for family businesses, both because heavily negotiated bargains are uncommon, and because the parties need a predictable, reliable investment vehicle in order to successfully combine business and family interests.

---

contract interpretation, the express decision to reject the default protection would be presumed deliberate and informed, and the court would have no reason to consider evidence of overall intent.

[27] See id. at *2. The founding member of the LLC was also excluded from the board of directors of the newly formed corporation. *See id.*
[28] *Id.* at *4.
[29] *Id.*
[30] *Id.* at *1.
[31] *Id.* at *4 (citations omitted). The court described its holding in terms of the "duty of loyalty" members owe to the LLC and one another and to a general obligation of "good faith." *Id.* The connection the court intended to draw between fiduciary obligations and the equitable interpretation of contract is not entirely clear. For further discussion, see Loewenstein at 450 (arguing that *Castiel* is best understood as an example of contractual good faith analysis).
[32] Strine and Laster, Chapter 1.
[33] *Id.*
[34] *Id.*

3. CONTRACTUAL CHALLENGES FOR FAMILY BUSINESS

In family businesses—defined broadly as businesses in which a family has the ability to control business decisions and at least two family members have a stake in the business[35]—private ordering is complicated by the presence of business and family considerations. For instance, the fate of a business co-owned by a married couple that divorces may turn on a prenuptial agreement (or the absence of such an agreement) as much as any business bargain. Also, in family businesses that survive into a second, third, or fourth generation, it can become increasingly difficult to accommodate the diverging interests of active and passive owners. Nor are these niche concerns. According to some estimates, "[f]amily dominated businesses comprise more than 80 percent of U.S. enterprises, employ more than 50 percent of the nation's workforce, and account for the bulk . . . of America's gross domestic product."[36]

Overlapping Values

Family businesses present distinctive challenges for private ordering because they combine the values and expectations of the workplace with more intimate family bonds. Even if it were realistic to suppose that the parties would engage in arm's-length contracting to define their mutual expectations, those expectations are complex and difficult to specify within the four corners of an operating agreement. Moreover, to the extent that arm's-length negotiation reflects the values of the workplace, and may be an affront to the informal norms that characterize family life, it cannot provide a neutral method for finding an appropriate reconciliation between the two sets of values.

According to social identity theory, people use social roles to "categorize themselves and others as a means of ordering the social environment and locating themselves and others within it."[37] Thus, "[s]ocial role differentiation, in enabling people to occupy different roles at different times and places, enables them to establish different priorities in different parts of their lives."[38] These roles are not casually adopted: "[e]xperiences are constrained and filtered through institutionalized structures such that the very sense of self in many situations is derived largely from the role one is enacting."[39]

However, although "roles are typically associated with differentiated social domains" and "differentiated audiences,"[40] family businesses conflate family and workplace categories. An employer–employee relationship may also be a parent–child relationship. Thus,

---

[35] Note that there is no single agreed-upon definition for family business. For present purposes, precise boundaries are less important than the participants' own understanding that a business is family owned.

[36] DRAKE at 274.

[37] ASHFORTH at 25 (stating that "[b]y identifying, individuals perceive themselves as psychologically intertwined with the fate of the social category or role, sharing its common destiny, and experiencing its successes and failures").

[38] ANDERSON at 25.

[39] ASHFORTH at 27.

[40] Id.

it may be unclear which role should take precedence in any given situation. The expectations that we have of members of our family—that we will put the family's interests first, that we will take care of each other—may conflict with the goal of maximizing economic return in a business.[41] To the extent the social roles are incompatible, family business has a built-in conflict.

Also, because the social identities of work and family are linked, it can be difficult for one generation to cede control to the next—stepping down as CEO may feel like a surrender of status as a family patriarch or matriarch. Or, alternatively, the power structure of the family system may work at odds with any changes of control contemplated in the business. Tension associated with role transitions helps explain why family businesses are often most vulnerable to internal dissension when control must be transferred across generations.[42]

To be clear, the point is not that business and family values cannot be combined successfully, or that advance contractual planning is useless. In fact, effective private ordering is essential to define expectations regarding the basis for family participation in a shared venture. For a contract regime to be successful, however, it must recognize that the parties are interdependent, and that they define their economic objectives within a context of business and family values.[43] This context may affect the matters relevant to the business bargain, the extent to which arm's-length bargaining is feasible, and the default rules that would best support the venture.

Overlapping Doctrine

In addition to the problems caused by conflicting social roles, private ordering in family businesses is complicated by the need to account for legal rules applicable to family relationships. Indeed, family law's influence runs through the essential questions of business organization law: who the members are, what obligations they owe to one another, and how the assets of the firm will be controlled and distributed.

The impact of divorce law on family businesses co-owned by married couples illustrates the entanglement of family law and business law. Not only must the parties exit the marital relationship, but their separation will also in most cases involve the exit of one or both parties from the co-owned business. Just as a practical matter, the simultaneous winding up of two different legal entities creates problems of coordination. Further, the parties' rights are not identical in each context and equitable principles of divorce law often trump conflicting business law rules. Moreover, the threat posed by divorce continues if a family business survives long enough to include children and grandchildren, as their spouses may also be entitled to a share of business assets as marital property. Since nearly half of all marriages fail, the legal complications of divorce should be seen as a predictable, recurring feature of family business ownership.[44]

---

[41] *See, e.g.*, Lansberg at 2 (noting that, regardless of merit, "it is assumed that in allocations among siblings, each individual is entitled to an equal share of resources and opportunities").
[42] ASHFORTH at 3.
[43] *Cf.* NEDELSKY at 130 (arguing that our core understanding of property as an extension of individual autonomy fails to capture the essential interdependence of a modern economy).
[44] *See* Long & Sissel at *1 ("In a mature family-owned business, one that has been in existence long before the marriage of one of its young shareholders, the founders should have

Family law can also affect business outcomes when control of a family business passes to the next generation. As one commentator observes, "succession law is characterized by a need to manage multiple sets of legal rules from different subject matter areas that converge on the nexus of a business succession."[45] For example, the family owners might create a trust to effectuate a transition, because it is possible to allocate company stock and managerial control to one or more members of the family without depriving other family members of business profits.[46] Technically, the trust owns the stock and the children, who are beneficiaries of the trust, are not themselves owners.[47] Thus, a more capable child or an outside manager could be selected to serve as trustee while the remaining offspring receive some measure of economic security through their beneficial trust interest.[48] Alternatively, parents might give children a stake in a business, even a majority share, without relinquishing their own control.[49] In trust-controlled businesses, the law of trusts can supersede otherwise applicable business law.

4. PROTECTING THE PARTIES' EXPECTATIONS

A contract law that includes well-considered default rules and background equitable principles can play a constructive role in facilitating business relationships. For example, rather than abdicating responsibility to family members who may be disinclined to bargain with each other, or unable to do so effectively, the law can provide a useful mechanism for mediating the intersections of business and family systems in a family business. If done appropriately, these interventions should not be seen as limitations of the freedom of contract. Instead, the law expands the freedom of contract by taking an active role in identifying and protecting the parties' expectations.

For instance, when family obligations introduce uncertainty, as when co-owners of a business divorce, contract offers an explanatory resource for resolving disputes consistent with the parties' expectations.[50] Family members' agreements regarding business and

---

engaged in business-succession planning that contemplates the possibility of a shareholder's divorce.").

[45] Rosen at 405.

[46] *See* BORK at 42 ("As a general principle, countless problems can be avoided if family members who do not intend to be active in the business are not left stock in it.").

[47] The trust creates "a fiduciary relationship with respect to property, subjecting the person by whom the title to the property is held to equitable duties to deal with the property for the benefit of another person . . . ." RESTATEMENT (SECOND) OF TRUSTS § 2 (1959).

[48] *See, e.g.*, Boxx at 234–35 (describing the estate plan of the jeweler, Harry Winston). As Professor Boxx notes, "Mr. Winston had the same instincts as most parents in this situation: he wanted to treat his sons equally financially but also wanted his business-oriented son in charge of the company." *Id.* at 235.

[49] *See* Sherman at 1273; Sitkoff at 646 n.122 (observing that this control can, in some cases, become oppressive when settlors seek "to maintain dominance over their family after death").

[50] Family objectives are not necessarily what a rational actor would formulate and appreciating them may "force us to reckon with the role of far less rational emotions—particularly, love—in guiding the familial structures." Dubler at 2292.

family matters interrelate and should not be read in isolation.[51] Thus, if corporate assets are at issue in a divorce, the enforceability of a prenuptial agreement specifying what counts as marital property may be as crucial to the business as any shareholder agreement.

When applied in this spirit, the principles of private ordering help to make sense of the parties' intersecting relationships. Though their formal legal doctrines diverge, businesses and families are both institutions that facilitate cooperative relationships designed, in important part, to achieve economic objectives.[52] Business organization laws permit the entry of individuals into long-term relationships to achieve shared purposes, partly defined by the state and subject to its regulation. Similarly, the institution of marriage gives legal recognition to the voluntary union of two people, and, if needed, judicial monitoring of their rights and obligations. In each context, the parties' relationship is said to be contractual,[53] even if some aspects are mandatory or subject to fiduciary constraint.[54]

As a practical matter, therefore, private ordering in family businesses extends beyond the traditional subject matter of business contracts. This is as it should be. After all, the central insights of the contractual conception of the firm are that "shareholders' rights and duties are (or should be) defined by contract . . . that corporate law should be 'enabling' rather than mandatory . . . [and] that no particular set of outcomes is best for all firms."[55] Rather than adhering to a formalistic and narrow conception of business law that would limit the parties' ability to integrate their business and family objectives, the boundaries of contract should encompass all agreements that relate to the family business.[56]

However, perceiving a family business in contractual terms does not entail a narrow approach to the interpretation and enforcement of relevant bargains. To the contrary, a contractual approach informed by evidence of the choices families make, including common mistakes, could serve as a resource—a best-practices synthesis of business law and family law. In some cases, as when a child is given a beneficial interest in a trust or shares of a corporation, there is no literal bargain.[57] Nevertheless, envisioning a broad set

---

[51] *See* Gulati et al. at 894 (arguing for a conception of "connected contracts" in which the boundaries of a firm are constantly undermined by "a fluid, nonlinear, nonhierarchical set of interactions and interrelationships").

[52] *See* Alchian & Demsetz at 777 ("The mark of a capitalistic society is that resources are owned and allocated by such nongovernmental organizations as firms, households, and markets.").

[53] Courts treat questions of governance and distribution largely as default matters subject to modification by the parties. *See* Case at 1779; Singer at 1567 ("A preference for private over public ordering has characterized the development of family law over the past quarter century.").

[54] *See* Lifshitz at 1597 ("Traditionally, legal regulation of marriage expressed and supported shared moral principles and interests of society as a whole, sometimes even at the cost of limiting the couple's freedoms." (citation omitted)); Eisenberg (observing that the characterization of corporate law as a series of default rules ignores important mandatory provisions that cannot be abrogated by the parties).

[55] *See* Macey at 1269.

[56] To erect a barrier to voluntary contracting when family relationships are at issue would be inconsistent with the more general recognition that the parties themselves are in the best position to establish the rules for their business venture. *See* DEL. CODE ANN. tit. 6, § 18-1101(b) ("It is the policy of this chapter to give the maximum effect to the principle of freedom of contract and to the enforceability of limited liability company agreements.").

[57] *See* Sitkoff at 639 (contending, in the context of trust law, that "even if the beneficiaries do not literally contract with the other principal parties . . . contractarian principal-agent modeling

of voluntary business and family relationships makes it possible to catalogue options so that default rules broadly match expectations. Indeed, "contract supposes and depends on a rich background of social norms to stabilize the parties' expectations and to guide legal interpretations of their obligations."[58]

In sum, a contractual approach does not require courts to abandon minority investors, family or otherwise, to the explicit terms of their bargain, regardless of whether those terms are consistent with the parties' reasonable expectations. If the business is a contract, it is a relational contract intended to endure over time and not a discrete, bargained-for exchange. Judicial protection of vulnerable minority investors conflicts with private ordering only if we assume the artificially rational world of neoclassical economics. But LLC members and corporate shareholders live in the real world, not in the pages of a game theory treatise, and the ties of family and friendship, the social norms of business, and the constraints imposed by transaction costs all impact the likelihood that the parties will negotiate adequate protections against possible future discord.

5. CONCLUSION

Admittedly, it is counterintuitive to suggest that greater intervention into the parties' relationship can enhance their freedom of contract. Indeed, the natural response—consonant with the rational-choice assumptions of traditional law and economics, as well as the strictures of Delaware law—is that the best method for protecting the parties' contractual freedom is to invite the parties, ideally with the assistance of counsel, to reduce their intentions to writing and then to enforce the agreement as written. This chapter's goal is not to diminish the value of tailored contractual bargaining, but to show that the parties' expectations reflect all aspects of their mutual relationships. By expanding the scope of contractual analysis, courts can better assess the parties' bargain in full context.

In family businesses, for instance, contract is more than just a tool for interpreting and synthesizing explicit bargains in particular cases. Honoring the parties' intentions can be difficult because the communal aspects of family life color individual choices and the self-interest attributed to a rational actor does not always provide a reliable guide to intentions.[59] Moreover, family members may not have addressed key issues in advance because actual bargaining can undermine trust.[60] Properly informed, contract law could serve as a resource for the parties, generating a set of preferred outcomes and facilitating more

---

nonetheless illuminates the problems of governance relevant to the beneficiaries' welfare"). Therefore, according to Professor Sitkoff, "greater insight into the nature and function of trust law will come from a conception of the trust as a de facto entity that serves as the organizing construct for an aggregation of contractarian relationships." *Id.*

[58] Gilson et al. at 1446 (2010) (citing EMILE DURKHEIM, THE DIVISION OF LABOR IN SOCIETY 211–16 (George Simpson trans., MacMillan & Co. 1933) (1893)).

[59] *See* BORK at 26 (arguing that "what is going on in the individual [is] inseparable from the family network of relationships in which the individual is embedded, [and] the emotional processes in that system."). Ayres & Gertner (1989) (exploring the role of courts in defining contractual obligations in the absence of explicit terms based on assumptions regarding the parties' intentions).

[60] *See* Blair & Stout at 1805 (noting that parties may avoid explicit bargains in order to preserve trust).

particular bargaining.[61] By overlaying simultaneously relevant business and family considerations, a contractual approach makes it possible to appreciate what is truly at stake.

REFERENCES

Alchian, Armen A. & Harold Demsetz, *Production, Information Costs, and Economic Organization*, 62 AM. ECON. REV. 777 (1972).
ANDERSON, ELIZABETH, VALUE IN ETHICS AND ECONOMICS (1993).
ASHFORTH, BLAKE E., ROLE TRANSITIONS IN ORGANIZATIONAL LIFE: AN IDENTITY-BASED PERSPECTIVE (2001).
Ayres, Ian & Robert Gertner, *Filling Gaps in Incomplete Contracts: An Economic Theory of Default Rules*, 99 YALE L.J. 87 (1989).
Ayres, Ian & Robert Gertner, *Majoritarian vs. Minoritarian Defaults*, 51 STAN. L. REV. 1591, 1598 (1999).
Blair, Margaret M. & Lynn A. Stout, *Trust, Trustworthiness, and the Behavioral Foundations of Corporate Law*, 149 U. PA. L. REV. 1735, 1805 (2001).
BORK, DAVID, FAMILY BUSINESS, RISKY BUSINESS 26 (1986).
Boxx, Karen E., *Too Many Tiaras: Conflicting Fiduciary Duties in the Family-Owned Business Context*, 49 HOUS. L. REV. 233, 234–35 (2012).
Case, Mary Anne, *Marriage Licenses*, 89 MINN. L. REV. 1758, 1779 (2005).
DAGAN, HANOCH, RECONSTRUCTING AMERICAN LEGAL REALISM & RETHINKING PRIVATE LAW THEORY (2013).
DiMatteo, Larry A., *Policing Limited Liability Companies Under Contract Law*, 46 AM. BUS. L.J. 279 (2009).
DRAKE, DWIGHT, BUSINESS PLANNING: CLOSELY HELD ENTERPRISES (2d ed. 2008).
Dubler, Ariela R., *All Unhappy Families: Tales of Old Age, Rational Actors, and the Disordered Life*, 126 HARV. L. REV. 2289 (2013) (reviewing HENDRIK HARTOG, SOMEDAY ALL THIS WILL BE YOURS: A HISTORY OF INHERITANCE AND OLD AGE (2012)).
Eisenberg, Melvin A., *The Structure of Corporation Law*, 89 COLUM. L. REV. 1461 (1989).
Friedman, Howard, *The Silent LLC Revolution—The Social Cost of Academic Neglect*, 38 CREIGHTON L. REV. 35 (2004).
Gilson, Ronald J., et al., *Braiding: The Interaction of Formal and Informal Contracting in Theory, Practice, and Doctrine*, 110 COLUM. L. REV. 1377, 1446 (2010).
Gulati, G. Mitu, et al., *Connected Contracts*, 47 U.C.L.A. L. REV. 887 (2000).
Hirsch, Adam J., *Default Rules in Inheritance Law: A Problem in Search of Its Context*, 73 FORDHAM L. REV. 1031, 1101 n.52 (2004).
Lansberg, Ivan, *Managing Human Resources in Family Firms: The Problem of Institutional Overlap*, 12 ORGANIZATIONAL DYNAMICS 39 (Summer 1983).
Lifshitz, Shahar, *Married Against Their Will? Toward a Pluralist Regulation of Spousal Relationships*, 66 WASH. & LEE L. REV. 1565, 1597 (2009).
Loewenstein, Mark J., *The Diverging Meaning of Good Faith*, 34 DEL. J. CORP. L. 433 (2009).
Long, William M. & Scott A. Sissel, *Divorce and the Family Business—What are the Options?*, 9 BUS. ENTITIES 30 (2007).
Macey, Jonathan R., *Fiduciary Duties as Residual Claims: Obligations to Non-shareholder Constituencies from a Theory of the Firm Perspective*, 84 CORNELL L. REV. 1266 (1999).
Means, Benjamin, *A Contractual Approach to Shareholder Oppression Law*, 79 FORDHAM L. REV. 1161 (2010).
Means, Benjamin, *Nonmarket Values in Family Businesses*, 54 WM. & MARY L. REV. 1185 (2013).
Means, Benjamin, *The Contractual Foundation of Family-Business Law*, 75 OHIO ST. L.J. 675 (2014).
Miller, Sandra K., *The Role of the Court in Balancing Contractual Freedom with the Need for Mandatory Constraints on Opportunistic and Abusive Conduct in the LLC*, 152 U. PA. L. REV. 1609 (2004).
Moll, Douglas K., *Minority Oppression & the Limited Liability Company: Learning (or Not) from Close Corporation History*, 40 WAKE FOREST L. REV. 883 (2005).
MOLL, DOUGLAS K. & ROBERT A. RAGAZZO, CLOSELY HELD CORPORATIONS § 7.01[E][1] (2015).
NEDELSKY, JENNIFER, LAW'S RELATIONS: A RELATIONAL THEORY OF SELF, AUTONOMY, AND LAW (2011).
O'NEAL, F. HODGE & ROBERT B. THOMPSON, OPPRESSION OF MINORITY SHAREHOLDERS AND LLC MEMBERS (rev. 2d ed. 2004 & supp. 2012).

---

[61] See Hirsch at 1101 n.52 ("[t]he tendency of parties to accede to default rules in order to avoid the cost of contracting around them renders them 'sticky.'") (citing Ayres & Gertner (1999) at 1598).

RIBSTEIN, LARRY E., THE RISE OF THE UNCORPORATION (2010).
Rosen, Kenneth M., *Company Law and the Law of Succession*, 62 AM. J. COMP. L. 387, 405 (Supp. Summer 2014).
Sherman, Jeffrey G., *Posthumous Meddling: An Instrumentalist Theory of Testamentary Restraints on Conjugal and Religious Choices*, 1999 U. ILL. L. REV. 1273 (1999).
Singer, Jana B., *The Privatization of Family Law*, 1992 WIS. L. REV. 1443 (1992).
Sitkoff, Robert H., *An Agency Costs Theory of Trust Law*, 89 CORNELL L. REV. 621, 671–72 (2004).
Thompson, Robert B., *The Law's Limits on Contracts in a Corporation*, 15 J. CORP. L. 377 (1990).

PART 2

INTERNAL RELATIONSHIPS

4. Alternative entities in Delaware—re-introduction of fiduciary concepts by the backdoor?
Douglas M. Branson

1. INTRODUCTION

In the 1980s, styling themselves "contractarians," law and economics scholars advocated that corporate law has no role to play other than approximation of an "off-the-rack" contract. That contract would approximate the bargain parties to a business venture would reach on their own, were they to be free of transaction costs (lawyers' fees, communication costs, travel).

A corollary of that proposition was that the parties would be free to opt out of any provision that the off-the-rack contract contained, including even the fiduciary duties of care and loyalty. Those duties, which exist in the brooding omnipresence overhanging all of corporate and partnership law, once were thought to be universal and unwaivable, or nearly so. The duties were powerful, omnipresent gap fillers the common law had always superimposed on express statutory obligations and used to fill gaps in instances in which the statute had been silent.

Seemingly, Mr. Chief Justice Veasey of the Supreme Court of Delaware put paid to the notion that contract and self-ordering could trump common law fiduciary duties, as the economics scholars and more specifically the contractarians had advocated. In *Paramount Communications, Inc. v. QVC Network, Inc.*,[1] the court, per Justice Veasey, expressly rejected contractarians' contentions to the contrary: "To the extent that a contract, or a provision of it, purports to require a board to act or not act in such a fashion as to limit the exercise of fiduciary duties, it is invalid and unenforceable." He added that "Paramount directors could not contract away their fiduciary obligations."

Early in this century the Delaware Legislature began reversing *Paramount*, at least insofar as it applied to fiduciary duties incumbent upon those who control non-corporate entities such as limited partnerships (LPs) or limited liability companies (LLCs). In a series of pronouncements applicable to what are termed "alternative entities," the Legislature made clear that members or partners may opt out of the applicability of fiduciary duties to LLC managers, or managing partners, or members or partners, either in part or completely, by provisions in the operating agreement or the limited partnership agreement.

In those sorts of entities, to paraphrase Chancellor William Chandler, "For Shakespeare, it may have been the play, but for a Delaware limited liability company, *the contract's the thing*."[2] In Delaware alternative entities, then, contract, indeed, seems in all instances supreme, as the contractarians wished it to be.

---

[1] 637 A.2d 34, 51 (1994).
[2] Quoting *Hamlet* in R & R Capital LLC v. Buck & Doe Run Valley Farms, LLC, 2008 Lexis 115 (Aug. 19, 2008).

Holding that contract is in all instances supreme, contrary to the situation involving an incorporated entity, does not end the question. On the face of things, a complete or near-complete opt-out gives license to overreaching and extreme self-dealing in those types of alternative entities. Those types of censorious conduct might especially occur in situations in which those in control of the entity possess a high level of sophistication and experience while rank-and-file members or partners do not.

Yet in Delaware, as in a number of other states, an implied term of any contract is the implied covenant of good faith and fair dealing. Opting out of fiduciary duty then in Delaware brings to the fore the implied covenant, the covenant of good faith and fair dealing. In recent cases, the manner in which Delaware Chancellors and Justices have applied the covenant appears, arguably, in certain instances to bring back into the picture duties very similar to fiduciary duties.

In fact, a further proposition is that Delaware judges are utilizing the covenant, as well as express contractual provisions, in certain instances at least, to re-introduce fiduciary concepts of the high-minded, aspirational sort, making them applicable to LLC managers or managing partners. This chapter intends to trace these developments, unpacking some of the implications.

2. *PARAMOUNT COMMUNICATIONS, INC. v. QVC NETWORK, INC.*

The case involves what merger and acquisitions (M & A) lawyers call deal protection measures. How do a takeover target and a favored offeror bullet proof the transaction they have agreed upon, for instance in the case in which a hostile second bidder later comes in with a higher offer? The answer is that they don't, or can't, bulletproof it, at least not completely. If target and offeror attempt to do so, they may very well find their deal without any protection at all, at least if a court has struck down as extreme or draconian deal protections measures.

That, though, is today's answer, albeit in simplified form. Twenty years ago the answer was not so clear.

Twenty years ago, more or less, the entertainment company Viacom had agreed to a friendly tender offer, followed by a second step merger, with Paramount, Inc., the film and theme park company. To seal the deal, the stock purchase agreement provided that Paramount agreed to a "no shop clause," a generous stock option to Viacom of Paramount shares, and extremely generous payment terms should Viacom exercise the option. Those were deal protection or perhaps even "lockup" provisions.

Along came a second suitor for Paramount, QVC, the television shopping channel, in a hostile overture, offering Paramount shareholders clearly superior terms. As the Supreme Court of Delaware was poised to affirm a finding that the Paramount directors had violated their fiduciary duties, Viacom intervened. "Wait a minute, we had a contract," that is, Viacom had a contract with Paramount, said Viacom's attorneys. That contract contained the deal protection measures (no shop, options grant).

Nothing in a contract can override the fiduciary duties applicable to corporate officers and directors, in this instance the *Revlon* duties, the court held. Those duties require that, once the sale or breakup of the corporation is inevitable, the directors cease being "defenders of the corporate bastion" and must seek out the best offer for the target. Deal protection measures of the sort involved would seriously inhibit Paramount directors from comporting with those duties.

Opposite the contractarians stood the so-called constitutionalists school, members of which maintained that law, in particular corporate law, does have a role to play. There exists an irreducible minimum or core which the parties cannot take away, whether by contract or otherwise. These constitutionalist scholars cheered, writing pieces in praise of the *Paramount v. QVC* decision.

3. BEGINNING EROSION OF THE PARAMOUNT PRINCIPLE

In 2004, the Delaware Legislature played a trump card by enacting an additional provision to the Delaware Limited Liability Company Act. Section 18-1101(e) allows an LLC to "provide for the limitation or elimination of any and all liabilities for breach of duties (including fiduciary duties)." The amendment to the Delaware statute applicable to another "alternative entity," the limited partnership, is identical (Del. Title 6, §17-110).

Prior judicial precedents, most recently in 2002, *Gotham Partners, LP v. Hollywood Realty Partners, LLC*,[3] had held that while through private ordering parties to an agreement (LP or LLC agreement) could expand or limit fiduciary duties, they could not, by contract, eliminate those duties altogether. The court emphasized the doctrinal centrality and importance of fiduciary duties in Delaware jurisprudence. The 2004 legislative enactments made clear that in alternative entities from henceforth you could do so, that is, eliminate fiduciary duties altogether, in effect reversing *Gotham Partners*.

Without discussion, in *Wood v. Baum*,[4] the Supreme Court of Delaware confronted such a contractual opt-out of fiduciary duty. There, members had accused directors, or a substantial subgroup of them, of having engaged in related party transactions and of having cooked the books.[5] The latter involved overvaluing non-performing assets to make the LLC appear to be performing better than it was.

In a derivative action, which this was, under most states' laws demand on the board of directors may be excused, though, if it would be futile. It would be futile if a critical group of the directors, even though less than all, or even less than a majority, faced a "substantial likelihood of personal liability" and not merely "the mere threat of personal liability." Here the opt-out in the LLC's operating agreement held that directors would not be held personally liable, at least if the actions complained of did not constitute fraud or illegality. No substantial threat of liability therefore existed, meaning that demand was not excused as futile. Plaintiffs had made no demand. The Chancery dismissed the case; the Supreme Court affirmed.

---

[3] 817 A.2d160, at 167 (Del. 2002).
[4] 953 A.2d 136 (2008).
[5] In the typical case, LLCs have managers or are managed directly by the members. But that is not a legal requirement. If the draftsperson wishes to denominate those in charge of the LLC and its affairs as directors, or as anything else, she is free to do so. LLC statutes permit a maximum, or near maximum, of flexibility.

That was not all, though. The plaintiffs made a second argument. The same provision of the Delaware LLC Act quoted above continues, stating that although an operating agreement may eliminate liability for violation of duties, including fiduciary duties, the LLC "may not limit or eliminate liability for any act or omission that constitutes a bad faith violation of the implied contractual covenant of good faith and fair dealing." The Legislature, and the Supreme Court, had left the backdoor open, at least a bit, possibly more.

In the case at bar, though, Mr. Justice Jacobs dismissed the implied covenant argument out of hand. "The implied covenant is a creature of contract, distinct from fiduciary duties . . . . The implied covenant functions to protect stockholders' expectations that the company and its board will properly perform the *contractual* obligations they have under the operative organizational agreements."

Seeming to shut the door, Mr. Justice Jacobs's comment does not, for many lawyers and certain judges believe that those contractual duties include fiduciary-type duties. Can we determine how much the door remains open?

4. DELAWARE JUDICIAL ATTITUDES

An important recent case is *Auriga Capital v. Gatz Properties, LLC*.[6] The Gatz family owned a large parcel of land on Long Island, holding it in an LLC. Together with minority investors, the Gatz family LLC formed a second LLC, which constructed a high-end golf course (Peconic Bay) on the property, which it then leased to a golf course operator.

The venture was not a success. Expiration of the 10-year management contract was looming. While pretending to be a seller, Gatz, the family patriarch and the LLC manager, sandbagged the search for strategic opportunities as well as for potential sales of the property. He was only pretending to be a seller when his secret desire was to be a buyer, at the lowest price possible.

Chancellor Strine was contemptuous of such actions and their effect on minority members, finding them to constitute a course of dealing amounting to a complete abnegation of fiduciary duty: "[G]atz described [his] tactic as his attempt to play 'hardball' with the Minority Members. His choice of the word 'hardball' reveals in plain terms how he viewed the Minority Members: as competitors, not teammates. A fiduciary may not play 'hardball' with those to whom he owes fiduciary duties . . . ." Further, the Chancellor took the extraordinary step of awarding attorney's fees to the plaintiff LLC members. "In cases of serious loyalty breaches," Chancellor Strine found, "equity demands that the remedy take the reality of litigation costs into account as part of the overall remedy, lest the plaintiffs be left with merely symbolic victory."

Auriga has become a focal point for a larger debate within not only the Delaware bar, but also the Delaware judiciary. Led by Chancellor Strine, some Delaware judges are of the opinion that if an LLC operating agreement is silent, fiduciary duties exist. So an agreement must speak to "opt out" of such duties.

---

[6] 40 A.3rd 389 (Del. Ch. 2012) (Strine, CH.).

Others, led by now former Chief Justice Steele, believe that contract rules all. If an operating agreement is silent, such duties do not exist. So an agreement must speak to "opt into" such duties.[7]

As the debate heated up (opt out or opt in?), *Auriga* came before the Supreme Court of Delaware, which affirmed the Chancery decision down the line, including the award to plaintiff of attorney's fees. The court's opinion, however, was both *en banc* (all five justices rather than the usual three) and *per curiam*, which often means that no individual justice wished to take ownership of the reported decision. The probable reason? The court used the latter pages of its opinion to administer a wrist slap to Chancellor Leo Strine for unnecessarily making findings which would foreclose the larger debate. Strine went on to hold that unless an express opt-out exists in an LLC operating agreement, fiduciary duties (default fiduciary duties) exist. "[I]t was improvident and unnecessary for the trial court to reach out and decide, *sua sponte*, the default duty issue as a matter of statutory construction."

Instead, the entire dispute could have been, and should have been, resolved solely by reference to the terms of the LLC operating agreement. Section 15 of that agreement provided that neither a member nor a manager (Gatz here) could "enter into any additional agreements with affiliates on terms and conditions which are less favorable to the Company than the terms and conditions of similar agreements which could then be entered into with arms-length third parties, without the consent of a majority of the non-affiliated members."

The court found fiduciary duties to exist, but as a result of contract and not brought down from some brooding omnipresence. "[T]here is no requirement in Delaware that an LLC operating agreement use magic words, such as 'entire fairness' or 'fiduciary duties.' . . . [W]e construe the operative language . . . [as] subjecting the manager and other members to obtain a fair price . . . Viewed functionally, the quoted [operating agreement] language is the contractual equivalent of the entire fairness standard of conduct," found in fiduciary duty cases.

5. DEFAULT RULES OR NO DEFAULT RULES—OPT OUT OR OPT IN

In *Gatz*, the Supreme Court of Delaware went to some length to "stick the needle" into Chancellor Strine, albeit in the gentlemanly, collegial way of Delaware courts. The opinion begins with a summary: "We hold that the manager violated *a contracted-for fiduciary duty*" (emphasis added). Later on in its opinion, the court states "the pivotal legal issue . . . [is] whether Gatz owed *contractually-agreed to-fiduciary duties* to Peconic Bay" (emphasis supplied).

Chancellor Strine though may have the last laugh, at least insofar as these matters are capable of provoking mirth at all. Late in 2012, Chief Justice Myron Steele, who has acted as the strongest advocate of contract *über alles* and contract and contract alone (no

---

[7] *See generally*, Note, *Opt-in Versus Opt-out: Settling the Debate Over Default Fiduciary Duties in Delaware LLCs*, 37 Del. J. Corp. L. 531 (2012).

default duties), announced his retirement. In January, 2014, the Governor of Delaware announced his appointment of 49-year-old Leo Strine as the new Chief Justice of the Supreme Court of Delaware.

But, in reality, Chancellor Strine did not have the last laugh; the Delaware Legislature did. In between Justice Steele's resignation and Chancellor Strine's appointment, the Legislature amended the LLC statute to adopt the opt-out choice. Fiduciary duties exist as a default unless the LLC operating or LP agreement expressly modifies or eliminates them. "In any case not provided for in this chapter, the rules of law and equity relating to fiduciary duties . . . shall govern," the 2013 enactment reads.

The Legislature's 2013 enactment merely makes express what the original 2004 enactment implicitly contained. A statute providing for "the limitation or elimination" of duties and liabilities based upon violation thereof, the 2004 statute, presumes or implies that if nothing is done those duties (default duties) will remain. In other words, Strine was right all along; Justice Steele was misguided.

6. THE IMPLIED COVENANT OF GOOD FAITH AND FAIR DEALING—GENERALLY

In *Bleak House*, Charles Dickens said of English Chancery courts, "Fog everywhere." The covenant of good faith and fair dealing is a bit like that.

Consulting the oracles, Samuel Williston and Arthur Corbin, Williston's treatise, *Williston on Contracts*, has a middling amount to say, while *Corbin on Contracts* has very little to say. Professor Williston, and the reviser, Professor Richard Lord, frame the covenant as "a term implied in the parties' bargain that each will, at a minimum, act in good faith and deal fairly with the other party, and will do nothing that will prevent the other party from enjoying the fruits of the contract." Put another way, "[t]he duty embraces . . . an implied obligation that neither party shall do anything to injure or destroy the right of the other party to receive the benefits of the contract."

Of course, at first blush, the benefit of the contract such as an operating or partnership agreement is to generate revenues and profits. Yet none of those in control of an alternative or any other business entity, be they the managing member or the general partner, is a guarantor of the enterprise's success. So, as applied to business entities, the implied term must be modified to mean something else, perhaps not to do anything to deprive the entity and the other parties to the contract of *the opportunity to make revenues and profits*.

Williston states that "bad faith [the inverse of good faith] cannot be inferred from the expected course of business." The expected course is usually (not always) to make revenues and profits.[8] So what Professor Williston's statement must mean is that, from the failure to make revenues and profits, one cannot infer bad faith or less than good faith and, therefore, a violation of the covenant of good faith and fair dealing.

What the covenant requires may ratchet up, depending upon the circumstances. "Indeed," says Williston, "where the dependence [of one party on the other] is especially

---

[8] In some instances, the goal of a partnership or LLC (strategic alliances) is to get access to the technology or other information, not revenues or profits.

great, a court may even imply . . . promises or terms imposing fiduciary or quasi-fiduciary duties." So when the LLC members are highly dependent upon the skill of the managing member, or limited partners on the general partner, fiduciary duty may come back into the picture, by the back door, so to speak, by virtue of the implied covenant of good faith and fair dealing. As examples, Williston cites a retainer agreement between an attorney and her client, or a property settlement contract between divorcing spouses.

The reader may find it helpful to have adumbrated (partially—an exhaustive list is impossible, for what the covenant requires in all sorts of circumstances is indeterminate) what sorts of actions would violate the implied covenant of good faith and fair dealing. First, though, perhaps a list of sorts of conduct that *never* are breaches of the covenant might also be useful.

Actions for breach of the conduct will not lie for:

- Conduct which is merely negligent. Compare this standard to the fiduciary standard in corporate law. There an action will lie for violation of the fiduciary duty of care, at least the old-fashioned duty of care, for negligent conduct, particularly of non-action as opposed to when directors or officers have made a decision and judgment. In the latter case, of course, the business judgment rule may intervene to shield the directors from liability.
- Conduct which is pursuant to some express term of the contract or express language in the contract.
- Failure to carry out an obligation or responsibility that is not ancillary to the basic duties imposed by the contract. In other words, courts will not use the covenant to make a contract for the parties.

Breaches which can be held to be violations of the covenant:

- Fraud or inequitable conduct (not particularly helpful—fog?);
- Acting in a commercially unreasonable manner while exercising some discretionary power conferred by the contract's express or implied terms;
- Acting in a manner which was intentionally malicious, the traditional paradigm of "bad faith;"
- Acting with conscious disregard of any potential harm to the plaintiff, also an example of bad faith and frequently denominated as recklessness of a high sort;
- Dishonesty.

The RESTATEMENT [SECOND] CONTRACTS adds little. In black letter, section 205 opines that the covenant is universal: "*Every contract* imposes upon each party a duty of good faith and fair dealing in its performance and its enforcement." In commentary, the RESTATEMENT adds that:

> Subterfuges and evasions violate the obligation of good faith . . . even though the actor believes his conduct is justified. But the obligation [imposed by the covenant] goes further: bad faith may be overt or may consist of inaction, and fair dealing may require more than honesty. . . . [T]he following types [of conduct] are among those which have been recognized in judicial decisions:
> - Evasion of the spirit of the bargain.
> - Lack of diligence and slacking off.

- Willful rendering of imperfect performance.
- Abuse of a power to specify [further] terms.
- Interference or failure to cooperate in the other party's performance [bullet points added].

As a test, application of these general concepts to *Auriga Capital v. Gatz* is easy. Managing member Gatz had in the wings a seriously interested, ready, willing and able purchaser for the golf course property which was the subject of the LLC. By means of "subterfuge and evasion," Gatz led the other LLC members to believe that no other willing and able purchasers existed. He violated his fiduciary duty, whether viewed as emanating from the contract or from the implied covenant of good faith and fair dealing.

In Professor Williston's terms, Gatz engaged in fraud and inequitable conduct. He acted with malicious intent. Last of all he was dishonest. He intentionally hired an appraiser who had no knowledge of golf course operations, who, predictably, submitted a low-ball appraisal. He misled the potential third party purchaser as well as his fellow LLC members. He did all this to put himself in a position to bid in the property as a foreclosure sale, which he did. *Gatz* is an easy test case for application of the covenant.

7. THE IMPLIED COVENANT OF GOOD FAITH AND FAIR DEALING—DELAWARE

Stewart v. Bolthouse Holdco, LLC,[9] contains as good as any other explanation of how Delaware and other courts interpret the covenant. "When considering an implied covenant claim, a court must ask whether it is clear [that the parties] . . . would have agreed to proscribe the act later complained of as a breach of the implied covenant of good faith—had they thought to negotiate with respect to the matter" (internal quotation marks omitted) in the first place. In other words, there must be a "gap" in the contract the parties negotiated.

If an express provision deals with the matter, then the claim is for violation of it, that is, for breach of contract rather than for breach of the implied covenant of good faith and fair dealing. There is not space in which the implied covenant can operate.

Bolthouse involved managerial employees who purchased 7,611 common B units, for $25 per unit. The purchase agreement granted the employer LLC a 120-day option to re-purchase the units if for any reason employment was terminated. A 2010 email from the CFO, nearly contemporaneous with the cessation of employment, which occurred in the same month of February, valued the B units at $200 (8.5 X EBITDA) which quickly could turn into $2,340 per unit if forecasts predicting a rosy future were met.

Within the 120 days, Bolthouse exercised the option, saying the units were worthless (a value of $0). Two years later Bolthouse resumed negotiations it had discontinued two and one-half years earlier, concluding a sale to Campbell's Soup for $1.55 billion, or $1,200 per common unit.

The Bolthouse purchase agreement provided that fair market value of the shares was to "be determined by the Board in good faith after taking into account all factors

---

[9] 2013 WL 5210220 (Del. Ch. 2013) (Parsons VC).

determinative of value . . . but without regard to minority discounts." The modifier "good faith" left two possibilities: one, if the board had acted in good faith, no case would exist; and, two, if the board had acted in bad faith or less than good faith, the board would have breached the contractual good faith requirement. Under that scenario, not only was there no room for the implied covenant to operate; its use was unnecessary. Breach of contract was sufficient to do the job, or not do the job, as the case might be.

Vice Chancellor Parsons therefore upheld the motion to dismiss those portions of the plaintiffs' case based upon breach of the covenant of good faith and fair dealing. He turned away, however, motions to dismiss based upon breach of the express contractual provision that valuation of the securities be undertaken in good faith. Both the Purchase Agreement and the LLC Agreement contained such express good faith requirements.

In certain cases, the contract involved is a lengthy, detailed one, say, in a stock purchase agreement (SPA) or merger situation in which the contract's express terms attempt to deal with every kind of contingency that may eventuate. Typically, such agreements run to 60 or 70 single-spaced typewritten pages. In *Oram Sylvania, Inc., v. Townsend Ventures, LLC*,[10] Sylvania bought a post-closing action against the sellers of a company (Encelium), alleging material adverse changes (MACs), channel stuffing and other improper revenue recognition practices, failures to disclose and disclosures in misleading ways, all of which violated numerous representations and warranties as well as other express provisions of the SPA. For good measure, Sylvania threw a breach of the implied covenant claim into its complaint. The court, though, saw the breach of the implied covenant for what is was—a meaningless catchall. "To state a claim [for breach of the implied covenant] a plaintiff must at a minimum allege a specific implied contractual obligation."

Although not impossible, stating an added implied obligation is unlikely in the case of a lengthy, detailed and well-thought-out contract. Chancellor Parsons said as much when he wrote:

> Nearly all of the alleged misconduct by Sellers is governed by express provisions of the SPA. For example, Sellers' alleged efforts to inflate revenues by shipping excess product [channel stuffing] [and] holding payment invoices . . . were proscribed by its obligations to operate the Company in the ordinary course of its business. Relatedly, Seller's alleged manipulation of sales results . . . was prohibited by Sellers' warranty of Encelium's financial statement.

Chancellor Parsons concluded his recitation of such examples with the observation that "express contractual provisions always supersede the implied covenant."

Winshall v. Viacom Int'l Inc.[11] is a non-LLC or LP (alternative entity) case that sheds further light on use of the covenant. Viacom acquired Harmonix, a manufacturer of music-oriented video games. Viacom paid $175 million in cash plus agreed to an earn-out provision. Under the earn-out provision, Harmonix shareholders such as Mr. Winshall might receive future payments depending upon Harmonix's performance going forward.

Subsequently, Viacom received an offer by a music game distributor to reduce its fees, which would have increased Harmonix's earnings and therefore the additional sums due

---

[10] 2013 WL 61995544 (Del. Ch.) (Parsons, VC).
[11] 76 A.3rd 808 (Del. Supr. 2013).

its former shareholders. Viacom would have had to agree to certain things in return for the discount so Viacom decided to leave the distribution fee level unchanged.

Harmonix shareholders sued for, *inter alia*, violation of the implied covenant of good faith and fair dealing. Mr. Justice Jacobs described another frequently encountered occasion to which the implied covenant often applies: "[W]hen a contract confers discretion on one party, the implied covenant of good faith and fair dealing requires that the discretion . . . be exercised reasonably and in good faith." Looking carefully at the contract at issue in the case, Justice Jacobs concluded that "no such obligation [to exercise discretion] can be implied under the Viacom-Harmonix Merger Agreement."

If Viacom considered the distributor's offer, that consideration was out of the goodness of Viacom's heart. If Harmonix had wanted Viacom to be required to examine such offers and in good faith exercise Viacom's discretion, Harmonix could easily have so provided. "The implied covenant is not a license to rewrite contractual language to negotiate for protection that, in hindsight, would have made the contract a better deal."

Two or three gleanings may be taken then from the judicial writing on the implied covenant. One is that if contract language exists, the claim is not breach of the implied covenant but a simple breach of contract action. Only when a gap exists in the original contract, and contract breach action would not lie does breach of the implied covenant come into play.

Two is an exception to one. If, though, by its terms the contract grants discretion to the opposite party with regard to certain matters that may arise in the future, in exercising such discretion the obligor must act reasonably and in good faith. If they do not do so, the proper action may be one for breach of the implied covenant of good faith and fair dealing.

Three, claims for breach of the implied covenant should not be used as a catchall or for what appears to be an afterthought: the more detailed, lengthy and carefully crafted the agreement purported to bind the opposite party, the more likely implied covenant claims will be viewed in that way (as an afterthought).[12]

8. THE UPSHOT? FANCY AND DETAILED DRAFTING IN LP AND LLC AGREEMENTS

Master Limited Partnerships (MLPs) have become the vehicle whereby vast amounts of pipeline, oil and gas, timber and other resources are held by deep and wide swaths of the public. Such MLPs have hundreds of millions of units and 10,000, 20,000 or greater numbers of unit holders.

The Delaware limited partnership has become the vehicle of choice for the 7,000–8,000 hedge funds (private wealth funds) which exist and numerous private equity firms as well, partly due to the express statutory authority Delaware has for limiting or eliminating fiduciary duties. There are 90–95 publicly held LLCs: with one exception, all are Delaware

---

[12] Two similar cases are Eurofins Panlabs, Inc. v. Ricera Biosciences, LLC, 2014 WL 2457515 (Del. Ch. May 30, 2014) (Noble, VC) (Stock and Asset Purchase Agreement (SAPA)), and Deere & C. v. Excelon Acquisitions, LLC, 2014 WL 904251 (Del. Superior 2014) (SPA).

LLCs, because of alternative entity opt-out statutory provisions and because of the primacy overall Delaware and its courts give to contract and self-ordering.

Needless to say, the dollars involved and the sophistication of the managers and promoters lead to the employment of extremely capable, highly specialized attorneys. The complexity of the legal tableau and the twists and turns it has taken also attract high-powered transactional attorneys, much as bears are attracted to honey. In turn, these elements lead to fancy, artful drafting and provisions in LP and LLC operating agreements.

First, let's review the twists and turns. In 2004, Delaware adopted statutory provision making clear the ability of LPs and LLCs to limit or eliminate fiduciary duties. Subsequent developments made clear, however, that if an agreement does not expressly opt out of fiduciary duty, duties of loyalty and care very similar to those which exist in the corporate setting apply.

On the other hand, if the draftsperson has eliminated fiduciary duties, nonetheless she is not home free. The implied covenant of good faith and fair dealing may creep in through the side door, or the backdoor, bringing with it obligations similar to but not co-extensive with common law fiduciary duties. It is this partial re-entry of fiduciary-like obligations which drafters seek to box in or contain by additional provisions in LP or LLC operating agreements.

Two recent Delaware Supreme Court opinions deal with the subject. *Allen v. Encore Energy Partners, L.P.*[13] is the latest in a series of cases involving conflicted transactions in the MLP context. Vanguard Resources, LLC sought to force the buyout of the 54 percent of the Encore units Vanguard did not already own. Vanguard already had four of its employees on the Encore managing board, two of whom were the Encore CEO and CFO.

Preceding announcement of its offer, Vanguard made some "value depressing disclosures": namely, that Vanguard could cause the distributions to Encore unit holders to be cut. Unit values promptly fell 5.3 percent. Vanguard then waited for further market declines. Finally, Vanguard made its offer: a merger in which the consideration would be .72 Vanguard unit for 1.0 of each Encore unit.

Because of conflicts of interest (several Encore board members were Vanguard employees), the full Encore board delegated the matter to a committee (the Conflicts Committee), which bargained some but not very hard and which finally approved an offer which its financial advisor, Jefferies & Co., opined had been below the midpoint of the average valuation range Jefferies had set out in its fairness opinion. To twist the knife more, because Vanguard units' market price had declined, Encore unit holders received even less in money's worth than the original Vanguard offer had portended, even though the ratio had improved a bit, .72 to .75.

Needless to say, Encore unit holders sued. The first item the plaintiff unit holders encountered was a provision in the Encore LP Agreement that "neither [the Encore GP (General Partner)] nor any other Indemnitee shall have any duties or liabilities, including fiduciary duties, to the Partnership or any Limited Partner."

The complaining unit holders were not without hope, though. Deeper down, the Encore LP Agreement had imposed a contractual duty (not a fiduciary one) on the Encore GP and further required that GPs consent before Encore could merge with any

---

[13] 72 A.2d 93 (Del. 2013).

other entity. In giving or withholding its consent, the Encore GP had to act in accordance with a contractual duty of good faith. Even without the latter contractual provisions, however, a fair guess is that the covenant of good faith and fair dealing would supply the good faith requirement.

The solution for the draftsperson is simple: define good faith, or compliance with a good faith requirement, in a manner which makes clear the roadmap to follow in reviewing the transaction.

Thus, the Encore LP Agreement established "four safe harbors" that defendants could use to comply with their contractual good faith duty:

> [A]ny resolution or course of action by [the Encore GP] or its Affiliates in respect of [a] conflict of interest shall be permitted and approved by all Partners, and shall not constitute a breach of this agreement . . . or of any duty stated or implied by law or equity, if such resolution or course of action in respect of such interest is (i) approved by Special Approval, (ii) approved by a vote of a majority of the [disinterested] Common units . . . ., (iii) on terms no less favorable to the Partnership than those generally being provided by or available from unrelated parties, or (iv) fair and reasonable to the Partnership.

The agreement defined special approval as approval by the Conflicts Committee. The agreement further provided that "if Special Approval is sought, then it shall be presumed that, in making its decision, the Conflicts Committee acted in good faith."

The Court of Chancery dismissed plaintiff Allen's complaint. Per Mr. Chief Justice Steele, the Supreme Court of Delaware affirmed.

The other recent Delaware case, *Gerber v. Enterprise Holdings, LLC*,[14] decided a few months before *Allen*, both describes a similar drafting technique and sheds more light on the implied covenant of good faith and fair dealing. Gerber held units in an MLP, Enterprise GP Holdings, LP (EPE), a Delaware LP. EPE sat atop a complex multilevel structure of LPs and LLCs, not relevant here. Gerber's complaint was that EPE acquired a pipeline company for $1.1 billion in 2007 but two years later caused the pipeline to be sold to a related party for $100 million, only 9 percent of EPE's original purchase price.

Defendants scurried to invoke, one, the opt-out of fiduciary duty which the DRULPA (Delaware Revised Uniform Limited Partnership Act) permitted and which they had implemented; two, the substitution of a contractual duty of good faith; and three, satisfaction of that good faith requirement through pursuance of four safe harbors identical to those in the Encore Limited Partnership Agreement, *supra*, and actions taken to come squarely within a safe harbor. By so doing, defendants provoked a learned digression by Mr. Justice Jacobs on the implied covenant of good faith and fair dealing.

A contractual provision for a duty of good faith does not oust the implied duty of good faith, as the Chancellor below had opined. The contractual duty is separate from the implied duty. The reason why is that "the temporal focus is critical." A fiduciary or contractual duty "examines the parties as situated at the time of the wrong." By contrast,

> An implied covenant claim . . . looks to the past. It is not a free-floating duty unattached to the underlying legal documents. It does not ask what duty the law should impose on the parties

---

[14] 67 A.3rd 400 (Jacobs, J.) (en banc).

given their relationship at the time of the wrong, but rather what the parties would have agreed to themselves had they considered the issue in their original bargaining positions at the time of contracting.

So the two duties can co-exist or, in the absence of a contractual substitute, the implied covenant would still exist.

The Delaware opt-out provisions permit an alternative entity to limit or eliminate fiduciary duty. But the same statute "explicitly prohibits any partnership [or LLC] agreement provision that eliminates the implied covenant." Insofar as fancy drafting techniques, their spelling out of safe harbors and their erection of a "conclusive presumption" attempt to negate also the good faith component of the implied covenant, they violate the statute's prohibition and are void.

So, despite the careful drafting and the thinking behind it, it did not neutralize the good faith component of the implied covenant, which still exists, compliance with the contractual procedure regardless. The final question for the court then was whether the implied covenant good faith component would do Gerber and his case any good.

The court held that it would, reversing the Vice Chancellor's decision and remanding the case to the court below. Had they thought about it at the time of contracting, the parties would have bargained and agreed that any fairness opinion (a standard-type third party review by a reputable investment banking or similar financial firm that the terms are within the range of reasonableness) had to address whether the consideration of the sale of the pipeline subsidiary was fair. Plaintiff Gerber had pled that defendant EPE had procured and relied upon an unresponsive fairness opinion. "That is the type of arbitrary, unreasonable conduct that the covenant prohibits." Concluding, the court found that "the general partner selected the Special Approval process in bad faith in breach of its duties under the implied covenant."

9. CONCLUSION

A cynic would conclude that the Delaware Legislature, the Delaware courts and smart transaction lawyers have concocted a scheme whereby, by the use of alternative entities and heads-up drafting, managers and others in control can sanitize mediocre deals, less than mediocre deals and sharp dealing, as in *Allen*. On the other hand, the Legislature and the courts will not allow really lousy or rotten deals, such as the demonstrably unfair asset sale the limited partnership in *Gerber* attempted to accomplish. If a reviewer adopted a legal realist perspective, reasoning backward from her gut reaction, she might arrive at such a cynical appraisal.

One may also wonder how in this day of MLP and publicly held LLCs, the Delaware Legislature and courts can apply to millions of investors, who have little or no bargaining power and no ability to review the organic documents, room for pro-management contractual freedom and flexibility originally designed to facilitate self-ordering among the members of small, consensual groups. It seems a recipe for no good. Nonetheless, to state that MLP promoters, putative hedge fund GPs, and attorneys forming LLCs are flocking to Delaware is an understatement.

Delaware courts do have a bully pulpit, which they have not been hesitant to use in the past. In *Schnell v. Chris-Craft Indus.*,[15] catching wind of a possible forthcoming proxy contest, Chris-Craft directors advanced the annual meeting date by seven to eight weeks. They also moved the site of the meeting to Courtland, New York, where Chris-Craft had a facility and where winter snows were likely to make it difficult for shareholders to attend. Both actions not only were permissible but expressly authorized by the corporation's bylaws.

Overall, though, the effect of the board's actions was pernicious: the would-be insurgents would no longer have time to file proxy material with the SEC and solicit votes for the meeting. "Inequitable action does not become permissible merely because it is legally permissible," the court held in enjoining the Chris-Craft actions and the advanced annual meeting. Similarly, a court of equity could intervene if the individual actions by LP or LLC promoters, even though individually permissive, resulted in widespread fraud or obvious unfairness.

A similar Delaware bully pulpit case is *Fliegler v. Lawrence*.[16] Similar to corporate statutes in every state, Delaware's statute contains an interested director transaction safe harbor. By full disclosure and a vote of the disinterested directors, a director may sanitize a transaction such as a sale of a parcel of land to the corporation. But what if after disclosure, and a vote by truly disinterested directors, a lopsided or very smelly transaction threatens to go forward? That was the situation in *Fliegler*. Despite compliance with the interested director statute by the parties, the court intervened. The effect of such statutes only is "to remove an interested director cloud." Nothing in the statute or in Delaware jurisprudence sanctions "obvious unfairness to the corporation."

It is no stretch to say that nothing in Delaware jurisprudence sanctions obvious unfairness to an LLC member or to a limited partner in a Delaware alterative entity. Hopefully, this chapter has lifted some of the fog surrounding opting out of fiduciary duties in alternative entities and the re-entry, in certain cases, of the implied covenant of good faith and fair dealing

BIBLIOGRAPHY

Altman, Paul M. & Raju, Srinivas M., Delaware Alternative Entities and the Implied Covenant of Good Faith and Fair Dealing Under Delaware Law, 60 Bus. Lawyer 1469 (2005).
American Law Institute, Restatement (Second) Contracts §2.05 (1962) (Supp. 2013).
Branson, Douglas M., Assault on Another Citadel: Elimination of Fiduciary Standards Applicable to Corporate Officers and Directors, 57 Fordham L. Rev. 401 (1989).
Branson, Douglas M., Corporate Governance §2.04, at 80 & §7.16 at 373 (1993).
Branson, Douglas M., The Death of Contractarianism and the Vindication of Structure and Authority in Corporate Governance and in Corporate Law, in Progressive Corporate Law at 93 (1995) (L. Mitchell ed.).
Branson, Douglas M. & Pinto, Arthur R., Understanding Corporate Law §11.08 at 369 (4th ed. 2013).
Diamond, Thomas A. & Foss, Howard, Proposed Standards for Evaluating When the Covenant of Good Faith and Fair Dealing Has Been Violated: A Framework for Resolving the Mystery, 47 Hastings L. J. 585 (1996).
Lewis, Winnifred A., Waiving Fiduciary Duties in Delaware Limited Partnerships and Limited Liability Companies, 82 Fordham L. Rev. 1017 (2013).
Perillo, Joseph M. & Bender, Helen H., Corbin on Contracts §5.27 at 134–39 (1995).

---

[15] 285 A.2d 437 (Del. 1971).
[16] 361 A.2d 218 (Del. 1976).

Steele, Myron T., Judicial Scrutiny of Fiduciary Duties in Delaware Limited Partnerships and Limited Liability Companies, 32 Del J. Corp. L. 1 (2007).

Steele, Myron T., Freedom of Contract and Default Contractual Duties in Delaware Limited Partnerships and Limited Liability Companies, 46 Am. Bus. L. J. 221 (2009).

White, Monica, "Package Deal": The Curious Relationship Between Fiduciary Duties and the Implied Covenant of Good Faith and Fair Dealing in Delaware Limited Liability Companies, 21 Miami Bus. L. Rev. 111 (2013).

Williston, Samuel, 23 Williston on Contracts, §63.21, at 497; §63.22, 506–08 & 511–20 (2002).

5. *Achaian* and interest transfers among existing partners and members
J. William Callison

1. INTRODUCTION

Under most general partnership, limited partnership and limited liability company statutes, in the absence of contrary contractual provisions partners or members can freely transfer their economic interests, but the transferee is not admitted as a member of the entity unless the other members consent to the admission.[1] Thus, without member consent, the transferee is entitled only to receive the share of profits or other distributions and the return of contributions to which the transferor would otherwise be entitled, and has no right to participate in the management of the entity's business or to become a member. In addition to an inability to participate in member voting or management, it is probable that the transferee has no record inspection or disclosure rights and that no fiduciary responsibilities run to him or her.[2] This hybrid arrangement, in which economic interests can be freely transferred but non-economic interests cannot, has been justified as part of the "pick-your-partner" ("PYP") rule.[3] PYP generally works well, or at least it is well understood and easily applied, when the transferee is not already a member of the entity.[4] However, the partner having been "picked," the result is less certain when the transferee is already a member of the entity and is acquiring an interest from another member. *Achaian, Inc. v. Leemon Family LLC* addresses this issue, but leaves the result uncertain in situations where the partnership agreement or operating agreement does not provide an answer.[5] This chapter discusses PYP principles in the context of *Achaian*, highlights various issues involved with inter-member membership interest transfers, and provides some thoughts concerning appropriate results.

---

[1] Rules that apply in the absence of alternative contractual provisions are referred to as "default rules."

[2] *See* Cordts-Auth v. Crunk, LLC, 815 F.Supp.2d 778 (S.D. N.Y. 2011) (assignee cannot bring member derivative claim, accounting action or action to inspect LLC books and records). *See also* Bauer v. Blomfield/Holden Joint Ventures, 849 P.2d 1365 (Alaska 1993) (partners do not owe a duty of good faith and fair dealing to the assignee of a partner's interest).

[3] *See* Goldberg v. Goldberg, 375 Pa. 78, 99 A.2d 474 (Pa. 1953) (under Uniform Partnership Act §25(2)(b) a general partner may assign interest in specific partnership property to a co-partner without consent. Reasons for nonassignability to non-partners include prevention of outsider interference in conduct of partnership business and nature of partnership as voluntary relationship).

[4] However, the PYP rule raises significant questions in single-member limited liability companies when it is the member's creditor who seeks control. *See* J. William Callison, *Charging Order Exclusivity: A Pragmatic Approach to Olmstead v. Federal Trade Commission*, 66 BUS. LAW. 339 (2011) (arguing that PYP limitations make little sense in charging order cases involving single-member LLCs).

[5] Achaian, Inc. v. Leemon Family LLC, 25 A.3d 800 (Del. Ch. 2011).

2. THE *ACHAIAN* CASE

In *Achaian*, the entity in question, Omniglow LLC, had three members—Leemon Family LLC ("Leemon") owned a 50 percent interest, a family trust ("Trust") owned a 30 percent interest, and Achaian, Inc. ("Achaian") owned a 20 percent interest. After several years in which Leemon and Trust, collectively owning 80 percent of the LLC, managed Omniglow's business, Leemon allegedly took sole control of Omniglow over the objections of Trust and Achaian. Trust then sold its entire 30 percent interest to Achaian, which previously had been a passive investor, and Achaian filed for judicial dissolution alleging a 50/50 deadlock among the members and that it was no longer reasonably practicable to carry on Omniglow's business in conformity with Omniglow's LLC agreement.[6]

Leemon moved to dismiss Achaian's judicial dissolution complaint, arguing that Achaian did not own the 50 percent membership interest in Omniglow required for a deadlock to exist. Instead, in Leemon's view, Achaian maintained its initial 20 percent interest but had not been admitted as a member in connection with Trust's transfer of its 30 percent interest. Stated differently, Leemon alleged with respect to the 30 percent transfer that Achaian obtained Trust's economic interest only but did not succeed to Trust's non-economic interests, including the management powers needed to create a 50/50 deadlock. The court addressed this one question, stating that a single issue *of law* was presented.[7]

After stating the "mundane notion" that conflicts between statutory default rules and the members' operating agreement are resolved in favor of the agreement, the court considered Omniglow's operating agreement.[8] Notwithstanding its conclusion that the agreement governs, the court provided dictum concerning the default rule for membership interest assignments in the absence of the members' agreement to the contrary. It indicated that the default rule is that

---

[6] *See* Vila v. BV WebTies LLC, 2010 WL 3866098 (Del. Ch. 2010) (LLC judicial dissolution warranted when two co-equal owners and managers deadlocked as to future direction and management of enterprise and operating agreement provided no mechanism for breaking deadlock).

[7] 25 A.3d at 802. The court stated, "The case therefore presents a single question of law: may one member of a Delaware limited liability company assign its entire membership interest, including that interest's voting rights, to another existing member, notwithstanding the fact that the limited liability company agreement requires the affirmative consent of all members upon the admission of a new member, or, must the existing member assignee be readmitted with respect to each additional interest it acquires after its additional admission as a member." It should be noted that the court called this a "single issue *of law*," but proceeded to hold that Omniglow's LLC agreement resolved the issue. Thus, it appears incorrect for the *Achaian* court to state the issue as one of law, rather than one of contract and, perhaps, a better issue statement would have been, "Although there could be an issue of law in this case, the initial question is a contractual one: does the Omniglow limited liability company agreement permit one member to assign its entire membership interest, including the interest's voting rights, to another existing member without the other member's consent to the substitution." Appropriate delimitation of the issue might have led to a clearer holding.

[8] *Id.* at 802–03. *See* Elf Atochem N. Am., Inc. v. Jaffari, 727 A.2d 286, 290 (Del. 1990). In most or all other states, the limited liability company agreement is termed an "operating agreement." For simplicity's sake, this chapter refers to the members' agreement as an "operating agreement."

assignment of a limited liability company interest does not entitle the assignee to become or exercise any rights or powers of a member [and instead only] entitles the assignee to share in such profits and losses, to receive such distribution or distributions, and to receive such allocation[s]. . . to which the assignor was entitled, to the extent assigned. . . .

Instead, the assignee is admitted as a member, as a default rule, only with the consent of all LLC members. The court noted that "there are likely two motivations for the statutory default rules." The first motivation is an outdated approach to obtaining partnership tax classification. The second motivation, according to the *Achaian* court, "may rest on the notion that one generally is entitled to select his or her own business associates in a closely-held business enterprise," and that "it is far more tolerable to have to suffer a new passive co-investor [i.e., owner of an economic interest] one did not choose than to endure a new co-manager without consent."[9] This is, in short, the PYP principle. The court did not attempt to determine how "tolerable" enduring a new co-manager without consent would be or the boundaries of "tolerance," since it then held that the Omniglow operating agreement superseded statutory default rules.[10]

In reaching its decision, the court considered three provisions of the Omniglow operating agreement. First, the agreement defined the term "Interest" as "the *entire* ownership interest of the Member" in Omniglow.[11] Second, the operating agreement provided that "[A] Member may transfer all or any portion of its Interest to any Person at any time."[12] Third, the operating agreement provided that "No Person shall be admitted as a Member without the written consent of the [other Members]."[13] Without conceding its argument that member consent is not required under the default rule for an interest transfer from one member to another, Achaian argued that Omniglow's operating agreement specifically permitted transfer of the entire interest, including management powers, without Leemon's consent, and that consent was necessary only to "admit" a person who is not already a member as a member. The court agreed and held that the written

---

[9] *Id.* at 804, note 14 (citing to Milford Power Co., LLC v. PDC Milford Power, LLC, 866 A.2d 738, 760 (Del. Ch. 2004)).

[10] The court did state, "[I]t is clear that the default rule under the Act is that an assignment of an LLC interest, by itself, does not entitle the assignee to become a member of the LLC; rather an assignee only receives the assigning member's economic interest in the LLC to the extent assigned." *Id.* at 804–05. It also noted that these rules "might" lead to a different result in the absence of agreement. *Id.* at 805.

[11] *Id.* The Delaware LLC Act defines "limited liability company interest" as a member's share of LLC profits and losses and a member's right to receive distributions of LLC assets. §18-101(8). The court did not analyze a distinction between "ownership interest" under the contract and "LLC interest" under the statute.

[12] *Id.*

[13] *Id.* The operating agreement was written while Omniglow was owned by a single member, which then sold its interest to Achaian, Leemon and Trust, and it referred to member in the singular. The agreement also provided that it would be amended if Omniglow were to have two or more members. That amendment never occurred, and Omniglow continued to operate under its earlier operating agreement. The court made little mention of this situation, and presumably afforded it little weight. One might argue that this unusual fact pattern meant that there was no agreement between Achaian, Trust and Leemon on some matters, perhaps including member interest transfers, and therefore that application of default rules was needed to resolve the question.

consent requirement was "a limited proviso that requires the written consent of the existing members in order to confer the status of Member on a person who, at the time of the transfer, was not already a Member."[14]

To reach this conclusion, the court first ruled that the agreement's definition of "Interest" as the "entire ownership interest" meant that a member could transfer the whole of what he or she owns.[15] However, the transferor's power to transfer all of what he or she owns does not necessarily mean that the transferee is admitted as a member, with all rights and powers of a member. To reach that conclusion, the court considered the effect of the operating agreement's provision that "No Person shall be admitted as a Member ... without the written consent of the [Members]." The court stated that nothing in this provision suggests that once a person has been admitted as a member, he or she must be admitted again in order to acquire additional voting rights when acquiring additional interests.[16] Why? The court held that the *reason* for the consent check on free transferability "is most naturally read as a manifestation of the unremarkable idea that one gets to choose one's own business partners (or in the case of an LLC, one's co-members)."[17] Leemon's argument that an existing member continues to hold a veto power over how much additional voting power his or her co-members may acquire was held "a strained extension of the traditional idea underlying partnerships and limited liability companies, and is not supported rationally by the operating agreement's text *or its context*."[18] Since Leemon had already agreed to become a co-member with Achaian and the Trust, knowing that its co-members collectively owned a 50 percent interest which, when voting together, could "stymie Leemon from acting unilaterally," Leemon had already "picked-its-partners" and could not object to a transfer of full ownership rights among its co-partners.[19] Thus, the court held that, by its plain terms, the consent requirement is directed at, and applies only to, a person who is not yet "admitted as a Member." Further, the court noted that Leemon failed to cite to any authority "in the [Delaware] LLC Act, the Uniform LLC Act, or learned commentaries and treatises on alternative entities suggesting that a serial admission scheme is standard practice."[20]

---

[14] *Id.* at 807.
[15] *Id.*
[16] *Id.* at 810.
[17] *Id.*
[18] *Id.*
[19] In fact, it is likely that Leemon picked neither Achaian nor the Trust as co-members. Instead, it is probable that the original, founding member transferred its interest to Leemon and the Trust simultaneously and was the one to admit all three transferees as members. A better description is that Achaian bought into an LLC with three members. I suspect that would lead to the same result.
[20] *Id.* at 811. One wonders whether Achaian cited any similar authority suggesting that a serial admission scheme is not standard practice, or whether this was a judicial rhetorical flourish. The court did recognize that the Eighth Circuit Court of Appeals held in *Ault v. Brady* that consent was needed for intra-member transfers of voting and other, non-economic, rights. 37 Fed. Appx. 222 (8th Cir. 2002). However, the court ruled that the operating agreement in *Ault* provided a blanket restriction on the transfer of a membership interest's voting rights since it provided that "[a]ny person acquiring rights with respect to any interest in the Company ... shall not be deemed a substituted member" and shall be restricted to the right to receive distributions. *Id.* at 225. The court seems to be dancing on a narrow line when it distinguishes the *Ault* language from Omniglow's operating agreement provision that "[n]o person shall be admitted as a member ...

74 *Partnerships, LLCs and alternative forms of business organizations*

It is possible to take a narrow, contract-based reading of the court's analysis. Under this approach, the court held only that Omniglow's particular operating agreement required member consent for assignments of non-economic rights to persons who were not already LLC members. Such a holding, although arguably incorrect as a matter of contract interpretation, would have limited effect. However, the court's broader, dictum-based, deviation into PYP principles, which it held to be the contextual "reason" for the operating agreement's provisions allowing free transferability of non-economic rights and powers among existing members is more problematic since it indicates the court's belief that PYP concepts are limited to third-party assignments.

3. BACKGROUND OF "PICK YOUR PARTNER" AND ITS INCORPORATION INTO MODERN UNINCORPORATED BUSINESS ORGANIZATION STATUTES

Some Historical Background on PYP

In the 1790s, Lord Kenyon wrote, "It is an imprudent thing for a man to enter into a partnership with any person, unless he has the most implicit confidence in his integrity."[21] The thrust of this declaration is that a partnership is not only a legal and financial relationship, but is also a personal relationship. More than that, a partnership is a fiduciary relationship, which requires good faith on the part of each partner to the other partners.[22]

The PYP rule is rooted in ancient partnership law, which stems from Roman law and Italian merchant law.[23] In his 1916 treatise on partnership law, Burdick noted an unnamed early writer who iterated an ancient form of the rule:

> Societie is a contract by consent about a thing to be had or used in common on both sides . . . . But that only is properly called Societie, which by mutual consent is applied to that end, that there may be partnership or fellowship among the persons contracting; wherein so soon as they are fully agreed, the one is properly called the other's fellow.[24]

Roman law was the first to be associated with this doctrine of contractual consent.[25] The Roman system grew out of the code of Justinian, and, in some respects, was similar to later Anglo-American partnership law.[26]

---

without the written consent of the Member[s]." Perhaps the main difference between the cases in that *Ault* did not deviate into general statements of PYP principles. However, it is significant that the *Ault* court stated that the requirement of member consent to inter-member transfers "is also dictated by Arkansas's Limited Liability Company statute." *Id.* at 226, note 8. Although this statement was not recognized in *Achaian*, it does state a default rule different from that espoused in *Achaian*.

[21] FRANCIS M. BURDICK, THE LAW OF PARTNERSHIP INCLUDING LIMITED PARTNERSHIPS, 8 (1917) (citing *Wells v. Masterman*, 2 Esp. 731 (1799); *Baker v. Charlston*, Peake, 80 (1791)).
[22] SCOTT ROWLEY, MODERN LAW OF PARTNERSHIP, 118 (1916).
[23] BURDICK, *supra* note 21, at 2.
[24] *Id.* at 5, *quoting* West's Symboleography (1590), § 26.
[25] *Id.* at 5.
[26] ROWLEY, *supra* note 22, at 5.

In the Middle Ages, Italian merchants incorporated Roman doctrine into their mercantile law.[27] During this period there was significant commercial activity and partnerships were commonplace; thus the Italians modified Roman law to conform to their needs.[28] From the law of merchants grew two different types of partnerships: "commenda" and "societas."[29] "Commenda" was an early form of a limited partnership where the partner who provided the capital was the only member to withstand a risk of loss and take the largest share of profits.[30] "Societas" involved partnership members sharing equal rights, remaining individually liable for their actions, and contractually binding the other members.[31] These two forms of partnership developed during the thirteenth century and eventually made their way to England.[32] The Italian merchants traded in England, so it is likely the early English laws on partnership were adopted from the Italian mercantile customs.[33]

No printed English decisions regarding partnership were produced until the mid-seventeenth century.[34] Most of the cases written during this period dealt with either a partner's right to an accounting[35] or denied the right of survivorship upon the death of a partner.[36] By denying survivorship rights, the courts were effectively prohibiting a personal representative of a deceased partner from taking the decedent's place in the firm without the consent of the other partners, thus echoing the personal nature of the partnership contract and, thereby, PYP principles.[37]

In 1890, the English Partnership Act was enacted.[38] This Act codified the PYP principle by stating "No person may be introduced as a partner without the consent of all existing partners."[39] It was not long before American law followed suit and codified the PYP rule in the Uniform Partnership Act ("UPA") in 1914.[40]

Embodiment of PYP Principles in Uniform Partnership Act and Revised Uniform Partnership Act

The Uniform Partnership Act expresses the PYP (*delectus personae*, or "choice of person") principle in several places, most notably in the UPA §27 partnership interest assignment rules:

---

[27] BURDICK, *supra* note 21, at 5.
[28] *See* ROWLEY, *supra* note 22, at 6–7.
[29] *Id.* at 7.
[30] *Id.*
[31] *Id.*
[32] *Id.* at 8.
[33] *Id.* at 7.
[34] *Id.* at 9.
[35] *Id.* (*citing* Y. B. 30 Edw. L. Account 127; Y.B. 38 Edw. III Account 7; Fitzherbert Nat. Brev. Account 267 (D)).
[36] *Id.* (*citing Hamond v. Jethro*, 2 Brownl. & G. 97n; *Jeffereys v. Small*, 1 Vern. Ch. 217, 23 Eng. Reprint 424. *See also Bellasis v. Hester*, 1 Ld. Raym. 280).
[37] BURDICK, *supra* note 21, at 8 (*citing Pearce v. Chamberlain*, 2 Ves. Sr. 33 (1750)).
[38] ROWLEY, *supra* note 22, at 10.
[39] BURDICK, *supra* note 21, at 8 (*quoting* Partnership Act, 53 & 54 Vict. C. 39, § 24(7); *Setzer v. Beale*, 19 W. Va. 274, 288 (1882)).
[40] UNIF. PARTNERSHIP ACT ("UPA") § 18(g) (1914).

A conveyance by a partner of his interest in the partnership does not of itself dissolve the partnership, nor, as against the other partners in the absence of an agreement, entitle the assignee ... to interfere in the management or administration of the partnership business or affairs, or to require any information or account of partnership transactions, or to inspect the partnership books; but it merely entitles the assignee to receive in accordance with his contract the profits to which the assigning partner would otherwise be entitled.[41]

The PYP principle makes sense against the backdrop of historical general partnership law in which all partners have equal rights in partnership management,[42] all partners have apparent agency authority to act on behalf of the partnership,[43] all partners have personal liability for partnership debts and obligations,[44] and any partner can cause the partnership's dissolution.[45] By preventing assignees (both voluntary and involuntary) from participating in partnership business, the PYP principle avoids undue and unbargained-for risk to the partnership business and the other partners posed by the admission of a stranger to the partnership.

Many of the UPA's concepts were continued in the Revised Uniform Partnership Act ("RUPA"), including the PYP principle. Thus, RUPA §503 states that a transfer of a partner's "transferable interest" is permissible, but that a transfer does not entitle the transferee to participate in the management and conduct of the partnership business or obtain record inspection rights.[46] A "transferable interest" is that partner's share of the partnership's profits and losses and the partner's right to receive distributions; that is, the partner's financial rights.[47] As with the UPA, the incorporation of PYP principles in RUPA makes sense since, as default rules, each partner has an equal right in partnership management,[48] all partners have apparent agency authority to bind the partnership,[49] and, except in the case of limited liability partnerships, each partner is jointly and severally liable for partnership debts and obligations.[50]

Pick-Your-Partner Principles in Limited Partnerships

Limited partnership law also embeds PYP principles. The 2001 iteration of the Uniform Limited Partnership Act provides generally that general partners and limited partners are admitted only with the consent of all partners.[51] General and limited partners may freely transfer only their transferable interest which, as with RUPA, is defined as "a partner's right to receive distributions."[52]

---

[41] UPA §27(1).
[42] UPA §18(e).
[43] UPA §9(1).
[44] UPA §15.
[45] UPA §29.
[46] RUPA §503.
[47] RUPA §502.
[48] RUPA §401(f).
[49] RUPA §301.
[50] RUPA §306.
[51] UNIF. LIMITED PARTNERSHIP ACT (2001) ("ULPA") §301 (limited partners), ULPA §401 (general partners).
[52] ULPA §§701, 702 (transferability); ULPA §102(22) (definition of transferable interest).

Notwithstanding the application of the PYP rule to both general partnership interests and limited partnership interests, one can argue that the basis for the rule's application weakens in the case of limited partnership interests. Limited partners generally do not participate in management of the partnership's business and lack agency authority to bind the partnership and thereby to create personal liability exposure for any other partner, specifically the general partner.[53] Thus, at least in my experience, limited partnership agreements frequently deviate from the default rule and permit limited partners to freely transfer both economic and, to the extent they exist, non-economic rights and powers to third parties without any partner consent. Stated differently, with respect to limited partner interests, PYP remains as a default rule. It is often not followed in practice.

Pick-Your-Partner Principles in Limited Liability Companies

Using the latest iteration of the Uniform Limited Liability Company Act ("RULLCA") as a template, the PYP rule is alive and well in the LLC context.[54] First, RULLCA states generally that after the LLC is formed, a person becomes a member only with the consent of the other members. The transfer of a "transferable interest," again defined as the economic rights of membership, is permissible without consent, and the transferee is entitled to receive distributions but not to participate in LLC management.[55]

Although the RULLCA drafters do not appear to have stated a rationale for applying the historical general partnership-based PYP principle to modern LLCs, it is not difficult to develop such a rationale, at least in the case of LLCs formed under statutes that are not based on RULLCA.[56] In most LLC statutes, LLCs are either member-managed or manager-managed, with member-management as the default rule. Stated differently, in most states, LLCs are member-managed unless the LLC's articles of organization provide that the LLC shall be managed by one or more managers. In member-managed LLCs, as a default rule under most state statutes, all members participate in management and each member has the apparent agency authority to bind the LLC. Thus, even though members are not liable for LLC debts and obligations, it makes sense that members care about who their co-members are, since they are actively in business together.

This rationale may fade in manager-managed LLCs, where the default rule is that managers, and not members in their capacities as members, manage and control the LLC business. There, since members are similar to passive limited partners, the basis for the PYP rule weakens. However, the default rule is that LLCs are member-managed and, if there is to be a single rule, PYP application makes sense.

The same analysis probably follows in RULLCA, although it is somewhat more

---

[53] Further, historical income tax entity classification rules, in which lack of free transferability of interests was significant to partnership tax classification, changed with the advent of the "check-the-box regulations" in 1997.

[54] The official comment to Revised Uniform Limited Liability Company Act ("RULLCA") §502 states: "[o]ne of the most fundamental concepts of LLC law is its fidelity to the "pick your partner" principle. There is no discussion of why the PYP principle is "reflected and protected."

[55] RULLCA §502 (transfer); RULLCA §101.

[56] Very few state LLC acts are RULLCA-based.

difficult. RULLCA separates LLCs into two categories—member-managed and manager-managed—and provides that LLCs are member-managed as a default rule.[57] In a member-managed LLC, RULLCA states that the LLC's management is vested in the members and that each member has an equal right to participate in management and conduct of the LLC's activities.[58] In a manager-managed LLC, RULLCA provides that managers exclusively manage the LLC's business.[59] In each case, RULLCA demurs from statements, common in other LLC statutes, concerning member and manager agency authority. It leaves agency questions to common law principles, and states that application of agency law "depends fundamentally on the contents of the operating agreement and any separate management contract between the LLC and its members or managers."[60] Although little or no case law has developed in this regard, it is likely in most cases that members in member-managed LLCs and managers in manager-managed LLCs will have general agency authority to bind the LLC. Again, since RULLCA's default rule is member-management and since member-management entails member participation in management and control and probable agency authority, a default PYP principle makes sense in RULLCA-based LLCs.

Summary

Because, in my view, PYP principles are grounded in management and agency rules, it is necessary to consider entity management structures when deciding whether PYP principles should apply to particular entities. Partnership and LLC law does a decent job of this. General partnerships, in which partners possess management and agency powers and in which they share personal liability, most strongly require PYP applications to protect partners. For the same reasons, limited partnerships require PYP applications on a general partner level, but less so on a limited partner level. However, it makes sense for there to be one rule for all partners in a limited partnership, particularly because limited partnership agreements can, and frequently do, establish transfer rules for limited partnership interests that deviate from the default rule. The advent of limited liability partnerships and limited liability limited partnerships, in which partners do not have personal liability for partnership obligations, reduced the stakes somewhat, but did not change management and agency rules. Thus, PYP principles remain significant.

Limited liability companies add additional wrinkles. Management and agency rules are at least bi-modal, depending on whether the LLC is member-managed or manager-managed. However, the default rule in most state LLC acts is member-management with members having agency authority to bind the LLC. Again, particularly if one desires a simple rule of general application that can be varied by agreement, it makes sense for PYP principles to apply to multi-member LLCs.

---

[57] RULLCA §407(a).
[58] RULLCA §407(b).
[59] RULLCA §407(c).
[60] *Comment*, RULLCA §407.

4. HOW SHOULD PYP PRINCIPLES BE APPLIED—PICK YOUR PARTNER OR PICK YOUR POWER AND RISK?

At least through its liberal use of dictum, *Achaian* stands for the proposition that once a person is a member of an LLC, the person's interest in both LLC economics and management can increase without the consent of the other members. Presumably, as with other default rules, this is because there is a belief (which is not expressed by the *Achaian* court) that people, acting without a written agreement and without transaction costs, would adopt this as the rule.[61] I question whether this is indeed the case.

For example, assume XYZ LLC, formed with X and Y each owning a 45 percent interest and Z holding a 10 percent interest. XYZ LLC is member-managed, as was apparently the case with the Omniglow LLC. Thus, under most LLC statutes, each member would have power to participate in the management and control of LLC business, would generally have agency authority to bind the LLC, and, in the event of disagreement among the members, members owning a majority of the interests control the LLC business. To add spice to the blend, assume XYZ LLC is profitable and that it historically has made cash distributions to members in an amount at least sufficient to cover the members' tax liabilities. All is peaceable in this kingdom.

Now, assume that X and Y begin to have some disagreement concerning whether the XYZ LLC should expand into a riskier line of business. If status quo were to remain, Z would have the deciding vote since neither X nor Y has a majority of the LLC's voting power. X, who is wealthy, decides to take matters into her own hands, approaches Z and offers a decent price premium to acquire Z's interest in XYZ LLC. Z, being a prudent homos economicus and recognizing a premium when he sees one, sells to X. Z would have sold to Y on the same deal if Y had made the offer. X, now armed with *Achaian* and a 55 percent interest in XYZ LLC causes the LLC to commence the new line of business, which is capital intensive and uses the cash flow from the original business. Distributions, even to pay taxes on the continuing taxable income from the existing business, cease. Pleasure, at least to Y, turns into pain.

Y complains, alleging that X did not succeed to Z's 10 percent control interest and therefore that he and X are equal owners of management and control attributes. There being no member with voting control to change the LLC business, Y argues that the status quo remains and that expansion cannot occur. X responds that she is acting in good faith and in the LLC's best interest in expanding the business, and that she acquired not only Z's economic interest, but also Z's management rights.

Who wins? Under an *Achaian*-like analysis, X presumably wins because she already is an LLC member. But assuming that XYZ LLC is not a Delaware LLC, judges are not bound by *Achaian*'s dictum.[62] Thus, the question becomes who should win? In my view, Y has a very strong argument that he bought into an LLC in which no member had supreme authority, thereby forcing at least two of the members to agree in order for there to be

---

[61] *See generally* FRANK H. EASTERBROOK & DANIEL R. FISCHEL, THE ECONOMIC STRUCTURE OF CORPORATE LAW 1–39 (1991); Frank H. Easterbrook & Daniel R. Fischel, *Contract and Fiduciary Duty*, 36 J. L. & ECON. 425 (1993).

[62] Even in Delaware, the Chancery Court could refuse to follow its dictum.

changes to the status quo. Stated differently, although Y did pick his partners, he also picked a particular power arrangement that cannot be upset without his consent. In my view, Y has the better case, despite *Achaian*.

CONCLUSION

Achaian, in part because it is replete with unanalyzed dictum, is not the final word on the application of PYP principles to intra-membership transfers. Policy-makers, in state legislatures and on legislative drafting committees, would be well-advised to consider the rationale for applying PYP principles to unincorporated business organizations and, having made such determinations, should be more precise in applying PYP concepts. Otherwise, it is quite possible that *Achaian*-like analyses will become commonplace or, alternatively, that there will be no consistent approach from one state to another as the question is decided on an ad hoc, judicial, basis. Arkansas is not Delaware. It is my belief that the decision should be that members pick an overall power structure, and not just the persons who generally participate in that power structure, and therefore that the PYP principle should apply to transfers among members as well as transfers to outsiders. If the policy determination is that PYP means partner-picking and not deal-picking, then so be it. In either case, clear enunciation of a rule allows members to prepare their own agreements against a clear default rule background.

In the meantime, lawyers who draft LLC operating agreements and partnership agreements should take great care to discuss the potential application of PYP principles with their clients, particularly in light of *Achaian*. To the extent clients seek more nuanced approaches, then careful drafting should begin.

6. Agency in the alternatives: common-law perspectives on binding the firm
*Deborah A. DeMott**

1. INTRODUCTION

Although agency is not itself a form of business entity, the implications of agency doctrine are inescapable in explaining how entities "get things done"[1] with concrete or legal consequences, in particular in interactions with persons situated externally to the entity. More broadly, agency law is foundational to any entity, furnishing as it does the bases on which the law ascribes consequences to conferrals of power and authority within any organization.[2] This chapter focuses more narrowly on agency law's external aspects, that is, the bases on which an actor's conduct has legally salient consequences for a firm that the actor represents in dealing with third parties. Principals often argue, after the fact, that an agent acted without authority and that the agent's action should not carry legal consequences for the principal. Across legal systems, agency law addresses these arguments through doctrines that bear some similarities but also differ in significant respects.[3] All systems, though, draw a fundamental distinction between binding the principal on the basis that the agent acted with actual authority, consistently with a reasonable interpretation of the principal's expressed or known wishes, as opposed to other bases for attribution, such as apparent authority. This chapter uses the perspective afforded by the common law of agency to assess issues about external agency in connection with alternative business entities, in particular general and limited partnerships and limited liability companies (LLCs). Although partnerships and partnership statutes are not recent phenomena, ongoing controversies and confusion surround the bases for external agency within LLCs. Focusing on common-law agency can add clarity in understanding the underlying concepts and terminology as well as in specifying the relationships between statutory provisions and the general law.

The chapter begins by examining long-established elements of general partnership law through which partners are able to take action with legal consequences for the partnership. The agency concept uniquely characteristic of partnership law—termed by the chapter the "positional power" held by partners concerning matters within the partnership's ordinary business—is related to but distinct from the doctrinal fundamentals of common-law agency, in particular, the robust doctrine of apparent authority. The chapter next turns to the bases under LLC statutes through which an LLC member or manager may bind

---

* I served as the Reporter for the Restatement (Third) of Agency (2006) but this Chapter, unlike the Restatement, is not a publication of the American Law Institute.
[1] Ribstein et al. at 8.
[2] Orts at 54.
[3] Busch & Macgregor at 386 et seq.

the LLC. LLC statutes vary markedly among jurisdictions—contrasting sharply with common-law agency and partnership law—and agency-related doctrines are unsettled in some jurisdictions, in particular, Delaware. This confusion surprises some observers, who "thought this was so simple . . . ."[4] At least some of the muddle may stem from statutory terminology, as well as from confusion about foundational common-law concepts. The chapter demonstrates that statutory confusion is not inevitable and, additionally, may be mitigated by judicial opinions as well as by expert consensus among legal advisors.

2. GENERAL PARTNERSHIP AND A GENERAL PARTNER'S POSITIONAL POWER

General Partnership

Partnership statutes define a partner's capacity to bind the partnership, using the language of successive uniform acts. Under section 9 of the original Uniform Partnership Act (1914) (UPA), every partner "is an agent of the partnership for the purpose of its business . . ." This delimits the scope of a partner's agency position to actions that serve the partnership's "purpose" and its "business," and, additionally under section 9, by whether the partner's act was "for apparently carrying on in the usual way the business of the partnership . . ."[5] If so, the partner's act "binds the partnership . . ." However, section 9 also recognizes that a partner may, as to any particular act, lack "authority" conferred by fellow partners (just as any agent may lack actual authority conferred by the principal), for example as a consequence of a restriction or limit imposed by the partnership agreement. Section 9 reconciles the possibility that a partner may deal with a third party by acting without actual authority but by also "apparently carrying on in the usual way the business of the partnership" by looking to the state of knowledge of the party with whom the partner dealt: the partnership is bound unless the third party "has knowledge of the fact that" the partner lacks authority. Thus, as to third parties who lack such knowledge, a partner's unauthorized act binds the partnership when the act and the partner's manner of acting satisfy the criteria prescribed in section 9. By acting without authority the partner acted wrongfully toward the partnership and, like any agent whose unauthorized conduct binds the principal, the partner would be subject to liability to the partnership.[6]

Eighty years on, the 1997 successor to the original Uniform Partnership Act changed little of relevance. Section 301 of the 1997 statute ("RUPA") replaces "the usual way" limitation with "in the ordinary course," and, more substantively, provides that a partnership is not bound by a partner's unauthorized act when the third party "knew or had received a notification that" the partner lacked authority to bind the partnership through

---

[4] Frost at 47.

[5] A corollary of this limit is the implication stemming from section 18(e) that a unanimous vote of all partners is necessary to authorize a non-ordinary transaction. Ribstein et al. at 129.

[6] Restatement (Third) of Agency § 8.09 cmt. b. If a partner purports to have authority to bind the partnership but the partner's act does not bind it, the partner may be subject to liability to the third party for breaching an implied warranty of authority. See id. § 6.10.

the act.[7] More significantly, although a partnership may file in public records a statement of authority concerning some or all of the partners, persons who are not partners are deemed to know of limits on a partner's authority only when the limits concern authority to transfer real property held in partnership name, and then only when a certified copy of the filed statement is on record "in the office for recording transfers of real property."[8] Filed therein, the statement is likely to come to the attention of the transferee or the transferee's lawyer. Thus, apart from transfers of real property, third parties dealing with a partner are not deemed to know of privately imposed or otherwise unknown limits imposed on the partner's authority.

Positional Power

Although the statutory treatment of partners as agents resembles aspects of the common law of agency, the common law is not identical to partnership law. As a consequence, the terminology of "power" better captures the capacity to bind the firm conferred by statute on partners than does the terminology of "authority." "Power," a broader term, encompasses in this context the possibility that it may be exercised without the right to do so.[9] Partnership statutes, like the common law, recognize that actual authority (and ratification, which creates actual authority after the fact) is not the sole basis for attributing the legal consequences of an agent's act to the principal.[10] When a partner acts without actual authority, by statute a third party may bind the partnership when the partner appeared to act in the ordinary course of partnership business and the third party did not know and had not received a notification that the partner lacked authority. The basis for binding the partnership, in other words, derives from the partner's status or position as a partner, subject to stated limits, including the third party's knowledge, and not from communications or other manifestations about authority made by the partnership, whether to the partner, a particular third party, or a broader audience, including manifestations made

---

[7] As RUPA defines the term, a notification is given by "taking steps reasonably required to inform another person in ordinary course," and is received when the notification comes to the recipient's attention or is "duly delivered" either to the recipient's place of business or to another place held out by that person to receive communications. RUPA § 102(c) & (d). RUPA also drops the specification of acts that are presumptively unauthorized contained in UPA section 9(3). The list may have been helpful, although admittedly some of its items were outdated, such as the power to "[s]ubmit a partnership claim or liability to reference in arbitration." Unif. Partnership Act § 9(3)(e). The other presumptively unauthorized acts were assigning partnership property "in trust for creditors or on the assignee's promise to pay the debts of the partnership;" disposing of the partnership's business good will; doing any other act "which would make it impossible to carry on the ordinary business" of the partnership; and confessing a judgment. For the proposition that the list added predictability, which was helpful, see Ribstein et al. at 130.
[8] *Id.* § 303(d)(e).
[9] Bishop & Kleinberger ¶ 7.05[1] at 7–41.
[10] Formally defined, "[a]n agent acts with actual authority when, at the time of taking action that has legal consequences for the principal, the agent reasonably believes, in accordance with the principal's manifestations to the agent, that the principal wishes the agent so to act." Restatement (Third) of Agency § 2.01.

through a title assigned to the partner that is generally understood to encompass authority of a particular type and scope.

The analysis is not the same within common-law agency. Unless the principal has ratified an agent's unauthorized act, a third party seeking to hold the principal to the act's legal consequences would turn to the doctrine of apparent authority. An agent's apparent authority stems from a manifestation made by the principal; the principal is bound when the third party reasonably believes the agent (or other actor) has authority to act on behalf of the principal and that belief is traceable to a manifestation of the principal.[11] Apparent authority looks outward, to the principal's manifestations, their connection to the third party, and the reasonableness (or not) of the third party's belief. Apparent authority is not an inward-focused doctrine grounded in the principal's relationship to the agent, as is a partner's statutory power to bind the partnership.

To be sure, it is understandable that a partner's statutory power to bind might be characterized as an instance of "apparent authority"[12] when it diverges from actual authority. The statutory language itself refers to "apparently" carrying on partnership business in the usual way, and a third party with knowledge or on notice that a partner lacks authority may not bind the partnership (unless it ratifies the partner's act), just as a third party on notice that an agent lacks authority may not rely on apparent authority to bind the principal. But a third party seeking to hold a partnership need show no manifestation made by the partnership that underpinned the third party's belief that the partner had authority. More narrowly (and more theoretically), a partner may have actual authority on the basis of the partner's status as a partner plus the absence of any relevant restriction or limitation in the partnership agreement, but with no separate or discrete manifestation conferring authority from the partnership to that partner.

Of course, a partnership may act through agents who are not its partners. Non-partner agents may be situated internally as firm employees, such as a business manager or an associate lawyer in a law firm that is organized as a partnership, or externally, such as an external investment manager or broker. Whether the acts of a non-partner agent bind the partnership is not resolved by partnership law, but by general common-law agency. However, partnership law itself, and the partnership agreement, determine whether a partner binds the partnership by engaging a particular actor as an agent. For example, if an individual partner, acting contrary to the partnership agreement, engaged the "agent," UPA section 9 and RUPA section 301 require inquiry into whether the partner's action constituted "apparently carrying on in the usual way" (or the ordinary course of) the partnership's business, and whether the "agent" knew or had

---

[11] Restatement (Third) of Agency § 2.03 ("[a]pparent authority is the power held by an agent or other actor to affect a principal's legal relations with third parties when a third party reasonably believes the actor has authority to act on behalf of the principal and that belief is traceable to the principal's manifestations.").

[12] For this usage, see Ribstein et al. at 127 (referring to "the scope of the partners' *apparent* authority, at least to the extent that third parties are not notified of any limitation on the partners' power"). More guardedly, RULLCA's drafters state that UPA (1914) "codified a particular form of apparent authority by position . . ." RULLCA, Prefatory Note at 3 & § 301, cmt. a (UPA "codifies the common law notion of apparent authority by position . . . ").

received a notification that the partner lacked authority to engage her on behalf of the partnership.[13]

Inherent Agency Power

For these reasons, the terminology of "positional power" more cleanly specifies partners' position as agents and differentiates them from common-law agency.[14] For some scholars, the closest point of comparison within general agency law is likely to be the doctrine of inherent agency power,[15] introduced as a formal proposition in Restatement (Second) of Agency but jettisoned by Restatement (Third). Intended to protect third parties from the unfairness that would result if an enterprise "could have the benefit of the work of its agents without making it responsible to some extent for their excesses and failures to act carefully,"[16] inherent agency power applied when no other basis for attribution sufficed to hold the principal.[17] It cut across a broad and variegated swath—encompassing the liability of principals (whether disclosed or undisclosed[18]) when agents with general managerial responsibility overstep privately imposed limits on authority, as well as an employer's liability for torts of employees committed within the scope of employment—and was formulated at a level of generality that did not identify the normative principle that justified the principal's liability. As one scholar summarized, inherent agency power was an ontological concept, not a normative principle.[19]

Viewed more instrumentally, inherent agency power for the most part responded to the narrowness with which Restatement Second formulated other agency doctrines, in particular apparent authority. In more historical or theoretical terms, as I have written elsewhere, inherent agency power may have represented an interim response to early challenges to the intellectual merit of agency as a "proper title in the law."[20] As a freestanding doctrine, inherent agency power risked outcomes in transactional contexts in which a third party on notice of limits on an agent's authority would nevertheless be able to bind a disclosed principal.[21] In any event, as a doctrinal formulation, inherent agency

---

[13] Agency law is also relevant to defining supervisory authority an entity's employees. See RULLCA, Prefatory Note at 4.

[14] Referring to the power as "positional" is clearer than "partnership power;" an agent who acts with apparent authority but not actual authority exercises a power but one stemming from manifestations made by the principal, not the agent's status or relationship to the principal.

[15] See Bishop & Kleinberger ¶ 7.05[2] at 7–43.

[16] Restatement (Second) of Agency §8A, cmt. a.

[17] *Id.* § 8A ("the power of an agent which is derived not from authority, actual authority or estoppel, but solely for the agency relation and exists for the protection of persons harmed by or dealing with a servant or other agent").

[18] When a principal is undisclosed, a third party has no notice that the agent is acting for a principal. Restatement (Third) of Agency § 1.04 (2)(b). A principal is "unidentified" when the third party has notice that the agent acts for a principal but does not have notice of the principal's identity. *Id.* § 1.04(2)(c). In earlier terminology, an unidentified principal was a "partially disclosed" principal. Restatement (Second) of Agency § 4(2) (criticizing term as less accurate than "unidentified principal").

[19] For this critique, see McMeel.

[20] DeMott at 1818–19 (quoting doubts of Oliver Wendell Holmes).

[21] The theoretical possibility was realized in Menard, Inc. v. Dage-MTI, Inc., 726 N.E.2d 1206, 1208 (Ind. 2000).

power operated only one way, that is, to bind the principal at the behest of a third party. A partner's statutory or positional power, in contrast, operates bilaterally, to bind both the partnership and the third party with whom the partner dealt. And neither the text of Restatement (Second), nor the available history, relies on partnership law for an instance of inherent agency power.[22]

3. AGENCY AND THE LIMITED LIABILITY COMPANY

Within the menagerie of business forms, the LLC is "a relatively new, hybrid form of business entity that combines the liability shield of a corporation with the federal tax classification of a partnership."[23] LLCs (like corporations) are formed under state law; unlike general partnership law, LLC law is far from uniform.[24] LLC statutes vary in many ways, including the circumstances under which the LLC is bound by the unauthorized act of a member or manager of the LLC. LLC statutes also vary in the clarity with which they address agency-related issues, including the statute's relationship to the common law; at times some statutes have been explicitly disconnected from the common law in basic respects, while some statutory formulations are confused.

The confusion may stem from the history of LLC legislation and from drafters' reliance on partnership statutes. From early days, LLCs could elect to be managed by their members (resembling in this respect a general partnership) or centrally by managers. LLCs from early days also contemplated the execution of two documents: (1) an organizational form to be submitted for filing with the secretary of state or another official designated by the state, like the document and filing requisite for a corporation or a limited partnership; and (2) an internal agreement, not filed with the state, often termed an operating agreement or LLC agreement (which many statutes do not require to be reduced to writing) and which resembles a partnership agreement.[25] Early concerns centered on achieving tax classification for LLCs as partnerships, likely prompting some of the agency-related provisions in LLC statutes. The tax concerns were obviated in 1997 by a "check-the-box" regime for unincorporated domestic entities that do not issue publicly traded interests, which enables each entity to choose its own tax treatment. Regardless, and returning to the metaphor of the menagerie of business forms, viewed from the perspective of agency-related characteristics, many LLC statutes house the new entity either in close proximity

---

[22] For an account of that history, see DeMott. The drafter of the original UPA, exploring its history, did not examine specifics of the fit between partners' agency powers and common-law agency but did discuss the impact of a partner's death on the agency capacity of the surviving partners plus whether partners were to be viewed as agents of a legal entity or as co-principals (and agents) on an aggregate account of partnership. Lewis at 638, 639. Partnership makes a brief appearance in Restatement (Second) of Agency, in which § 8A repeats the definition in UPA § 6 ("an association of two or more persons to carry on as co-owners a business for profit").

[23] Bishop & Kleinberger ¶ 1.01[1] at 1–7 (footnotes omitted).

[24] As of late summer 2014, seven states plus the Virgin Islands had adopted the Uniform Limited Liability Company Act (1996). Seven states plus the District of Columbia had adopted the Revised Uniform Limited Liability Company Act (2006).

[25] And the Delaware statute now excludes the applicability of the state's general statute of frauds. See Del. Code Ann., tit. 18-101(7).

Positional Powers under LLC Statutes

In some LLC statutes, provisions comparable to the language in partnership statutes specify the position of members and managers as agents. For example, under section 301 of the Uniform LLC Act (ULLCA) (1996), "each member is an agent of the limited liability company for the purpose of its business" and the member's act "for apparently carrying on in the ordinary course the company's business" binds the LLC, unless the member lacked authority so to act for the LLC and the third party "knew or had notice" that the member lacked authority. But—and in contrast to a default-rule general partnership—centralized management is an express and formal statutory option for LLC structures. Under ULLCA, when an LLC is manager-managed, "a member is not an agent of the company for the purpose of its business solely by reason of being a member."[26] Each manager is an agent for the purpose of the LLC's business, subject to the same limitations applicable to a member's agency power in a member-managed LLC.[27] ULLCA requires that the articles for an LLC specify whether it is to be manager-managed,[28] which could enable third parties to make this basic determination about any LLC with which they may deal. Along the same lines, when an entity is a limited, not a general partnership, only the general partner holds the positional powers of an agent;[29] a limited partner, in the terminology of the most recent uniform act, "does not have the right or power as a limited partner to act for or bind the entity."[30] Reasonable third parties, that is, who know they deal with a limited partnership or a manager-managed LLC, are assumed to be aware that other members or partners are not positioned as agents simply through their status in the firm. However, to determine whether an LLC is manager-managed may require inquiry into the public record of the firm's filed articles of association because LLC law does not require that the firm use a name that would reveal its management structure,[31] in contrast to limited partnership law.[32]

The Impact of Restrictions on Authority in Operating Agreements

Unlike ULLCA and partnership statutes, some LLC statutes may create the possibility that provisions in LLC agreements that limit the authority of members or managers could be operative as against third parties who do not know or have notice of the restrictions. If so, LLC law clashes with common-law agency doctrine. The doctrine of apparent authority protects third parties who act reasonably on the basis of principals' manifestations

---

[26] ULLCA § 301(b)(1).
[27] ULLCA § 301 (b)(1).
[28] ULLCA § 203 (a)(6).
[29] Uniform Limited Partnership Act (2001) (ULPA) § 402.
[30] Id. § 302.
[31] Revised Limited Liability Company Act (2006) (RULLCA) § 301, cmt. at 49 (2011).
[32] ULPA § 108 (c).This requirement has a counterpart in corporate law. See, e.g., Del. Code Ann., tit. 8, § 102(a)(1).

about their agents; the underlying point is that "[a] principal may not choose to act through agents whom it has clothed with the trappings of authority and then determine at a later time whether the consequences of their acts offer an advantage."[33] Apparent authority enables third parties to proceed on the basis of principals' manifestations about agents' authority unless reasonably under the circumstances the third party should inquire further. Many cases apply the elements of apparent authority to determine whether incorporated principals are bound by acts taken purportedly on their behalves by agents of all sorts, including their officers.[34] In contrast, giving operative effect to restrictions in a document—an operating agreement—that is not a matter of public record requires third parties to seek formal confirmation of authority in circumstances well beyond the operation of common-law agency doctrines.[35] Separately, some LLC statutes decouple the power of members or managers to bind the firm from limitations comparable to those imposed by ULLCA and partnership statutes, thereby creating the possibility that the LLC would be bound by an unauthorized act that was wrongful, or not in the ordinary course of the LLC's business, or effected through means not typical of the LLC.[36] These outcomes, too, are at odds with common-law agency because each scenario makes it likely that the third party did not act reasonably, as apparent authority requires.

As it happens, the Delaware LLC statute may pose both of these problems, providing as it does in section 18-402 that "[u]nless otherwise provided in a limited liability company agreement, each member and manager has the authority to bind the limited liability company."[37] As many LLCs organize under Delaware law but have their principal places of business elsewhere,[38] arguable ambiguities in statutory language affecting basic issues are significant. For starters, in what sense would a member or manager have "authority" to bind the firm if the LLC agreement provides otherwise? "Authority" here must mean positional power, as discussed above, to avoid inconsistency within the same sentence. But notice the power's breadth, unrestricted as it is by partnership-like statutory limitations.[39]

Perhaps to mitigate the risks of a statutorily uncabined power to bind an LLC, section 18-402 couples the conferral of power with the "unless otherwise provided" prelude, which makes the conferred powers subject to the LLC's limited liability company agreement, a private document not filed with the state. Read literally, "unless otherwise provided" detaches Delaware LLCs from the operation of apparent authority, creating the possibility that an LLC may deal with third parties through members and managers who bear titles or are otherwise placed in positions that would lead a reasonable third party to believe that the member or manager's actual authority matches the manifestation made

---

[33] Restatement (Third) of Agency § 2.03, cmt. c.
[34] See Restatement (Third) of Agency §§ 3.03 cmts. c–e & rep. notes.
[35] Moreover, if an LLC lacks an equivalent for the secretarial function customary in corporations, obtaining formal confirmation of authority may be more difficult. On the customary authority of corporate secretaries to certify the due adoption of resolutions and to certify officers' signatures, see Restatement (Third) of Agency § 3.03, cmt. e(5). A functional solution for LLCs is filing a statement of authority. See RULLCA § 302(a)(2), discussed infra.
[36] Bishop & Kleinberger ¶ 14.04[3][a] at 14–115–16.
[37] Del. Code Ann., tit. 6, § 18-402.
[38] Gevurtz at 67.
[39] Bishop & Kleinberger ¶ 14.04[3][a] at 14–115.

by the LLC through the title or placement, subject to being confounded by restrictions in the LLC agreement of which the third party had no notice.

Experts—lawyers who attended a 2006 meeting of the ABA's Business Section Partnership Committee—reportedly exhibited "significant confusion" about the meaning of this portion of the Delaware statute.[40] A few read the sentence to address only actual authority, to be governed by the operating agreement, with the consequence that the statute itself confers no apparent authority "but regular principles of agency law apply" and make apparent authority available to third parties to bind the LLC.[41] Reading further into the statute, its final provision may support this reading because it makes applicable "the rules of law and equity" to "any case not provided for in this chapter . . . ."[42] On the other hand, Delaware's statute does not explicitly make the common law of agency applicable,[43] and arguably "the case" is "provided for" by section 18-402. Reportedly, many Delaware lawyers treat section 18-402 to mean "that third parties may not assume that a member or manager of a Delaware LLC ever has apparent authority . . . the statute specifically provides the operating agreement governs authority, period."[44] Scholarly authority acknowledges that section 18-402 could be read both ways.[45]

Separately, policy commitments explicitly articulated in the statute weigh in favor of confining section 18-402 and the impact of an LLC's operating agreement to actual authority. Delaware's LLC statute expressly states that "[i]t is the policy of this chapter to give the maximum effect to the principle of freedom of contract and to the enforceability of limited liability company agreements."[46] Basic contract law limits a contract's legal consequences to the parties to the contract and to a limited cast of further characters, in particular third parties who have enforceable rights to benefit from performance of the contract. A commitment to "the principle of freedom of contract" implicitly demarcates parties to a contract from non-parties; the principle is not equivalent to deeming the world at large to know the contract's terms.[47] Even more startling than the confused state of Delaware LLC law, some states' statutes explicitly provided that an LLC is not bound by the act of a member or manager that contravenes the operating agreement although the third party is unaware of the restriction and acts reasonably.[48] Less extreme language elsewhere still deems third parties to have knowledge of restrictions on a member or

---

[40] Frost at 11.
[41] *Id.* at 47.
[42] Del. Code Ann., tit. 6, § 18-1104.
[43] As does N.C. Gen. Stat. § 57D-2-30(e), discussed *infra*.
[44] Frost at 47.
[45] Ribstein et al. at 161 (statute "arguably makes the operating agreement control both actual and apparent authority of members and managers, but it could also be argued that the default rule conferring on each member and manager authority to bind the LLC confers apparent authority on one who does not know of a contrary provision in the operating agreement"); Bishop & Kleinberger ¶ 14.04[3][a] at 14–115 (characterizing "authority" as ambiguous).
[46] Del. Code Ann., tit. 6, §18-1101(b).
[47] For an example of statutory language accepting this point, see N.C. Gen. Stat. § 57D-2-30(b)(2)(LLC's operating agreement not applicable to persons not party to agreement or otherwise bound by it).
[48] To this effect were Colo. Rev. Stat. Ann. § 7-80-406(4), and Iowa Code § 490A.702(3)(b), both since repealed.

manager's authority when the LLC's articles of organization—filed with the state—state that the operating agreement contains restrictions.[49]

More generally, it is not evident what policy objective is furthered by holding third parties who deal reasonably to the consequences of contractual terms of which they had no notice. Many dealings by LLCs, like those of businesses more generally, are "quotidian" and do not reasonably invite inquiry beyond the generally understood manifestations about its representatives made by the entity with which third parties deal.[50] Proceeding on the basis that "the operating agreement governs authority, period"[51] whether or not a third party has notice of its terms appears only to arm transactional parties that happen to be LLCs with an extra-contractual option to repudiate commitments made by their representatives that is unavailable to businesses otherwise organized, which is likely to surprise reasonable third parties when the LLC deploys the option at a later time to avoid the legal consequences of its representative's actions.

4. POTENTIAL SOLUTIONS

Formal Statutory Reforms

Statutory drafters are aware of the problems identified in this chapter, in particular the experts charged with drafting the Revised Uniform Limited Liability Company Act (RULLCA), which was completed in 2006. RULLCA's solution is elegant and precise. It achieves clarity by jettisoning the partnership legacy of positional powers and by reattaching LLC law to common-law agency. RULLCA section 301(a)[52] provides that "[a] member is not an agent of a limited liability company solely by reason of being a member."[53] This language makes it unnecessary to clarify the relationship(s) between a partner's positional power, actual authority, and apparent authority. A reader might then wonder how an LLC might ever be bound, if the LLC lacks managers, in the absence of members' positional power; subsection (b) answers the question by providing that "[a] member's status as a member does not prevent or restrict law other than this [act] from imposing liability on a limited liability company because of the person's conduct," which acknowledges that through the application of agency law a member of an LLC may become an agent.[54] Under RULLCA an LLC is member-managed unless its operating

---

[49] La. Rev. Stat. Ann. § 12-1317(B). See also former Okla. Stat. Ann., tit. 18, § 2019C, which provided that "[p]ersons dealing with members or managers of the limited liability company shall be deemed to have knowledge of the restrictions on the authority of members or managers contained in a written operating agreement if the articles of organization of the limited liability company contain a statement that such restrictions exist."

[50] RULLCA, Prefatory Note at 4.

[51] Frost at 47.

[52] Lest a superficial reader miss the point, the title of the section is: "NO AGENCY POWER OF MEMBER AS MEMBER."

[53] RULLCA § 301(a).

[54] The language might helpfully have acknowledged that an agent's conduct may also lead to legally enforceable rights that the principal may wish to exercise as against third parties with whom the agent dealt.

agreement provides otherwise.[55] In a member-managed LLC, acts outside the ordinary course of business require the consent of all members,[56] as would be true in a general partnership. Like RUPA, RULLCA permits an LLC to file a statement of authority with the secretary of state or comparable official but it may designate positions, not just persons.[57] With stated exceptions (including filings concerning authority to transfer real property), a statement of authority "is not by itself evidence of knowledge of notice of the limitation by any person."[58] Nothing in RULLCA makes restrictions of authority contained in LLC operating agreements effective as against third parties who deal with the LLC, in particular third parties who lack notice of the restriction.

Under RULLCA, as for incorporated business entities, much work is assigned to the doctrine of apparent authority. For example, designating someone as a "manager" likely implicates the power to bind the LLC as to matters within the ordinary course of business.[59] Conferring a title such as "President" on a member or a manager implicates a large body of common-law precedent focused on the meanings ordinarily associated with formal organizational titles, as would conferring a title that designates a functional area or specialty within the LLC. To be sure, RULLCA itself does not address all questions that may surface as a consequence of jettisoning members' positional power. For example, might a newly formed LLC be "stymied" if it has not yet filed any statement of authority, and its operating agreement does not confer titles that denote authority to interact with third parties?[60] The new LLC seems to lack any agents at all, which may protect its members against liability to third parties until the members reach agreement, but may also come as a surprise to third parties who deal with the LLC through a member. Backdrop agency law seems likely to fill this lacuna for an LLC with a governance structure that is incomplete or a work-in-progress. Recall that the RULLCA default is member-management. All members in a default member-managed LLC have "equal rights in the management and conduct" of the LLC's activities,[61] and section 407(b)(3) provides that a dispute among members on a matter "within the ordinary course of the activities of the company may be decided by a majority of the members." It is likely that the new LLC members have some understanding of the point of forming it; if the member who acts takes action that the member reasonably understands to further the LLC's objective(s), the member has acted with actual authority unless on notice that other members object or would object if they but knew of the action the member intends to take.[62]

---

[55] RULLCA § 407(a).
[56] RULLCA § 407(b)(4).
[57] RULLCA § 302 (a)(2).
[58] RULLCA § 302(d). The other exceptions concern notice of an LLC's dissolution, termination, or merger or the like transaction, effective within 90 days after the relevant statement or articles have been filed; and the filing of a post-dissolution statement of authority. RULLCA §§ 103(d) and 302(d).
[59] Frost at 47. RULLCA itself provides in § 407(c)(3) that in a manager-managed LLC, "a difference arising among managers as to a matter in the ordinary course of the activities of the company may be decided by a majority of the managers." This language contemplates that a "manager" handles matters that arise in the ordinary course of an LLC's activity.
[60] Rutledge & Frost at 51.
[61] RULLCA § 407(b)(2).
[62] Rutledge & Frost at 52. The resolution for the new-LLC hypothetical, introduced in this chapter, proposes a slight variant to these authors' analysis, which is that the member in question

Alternatively, a statute might retain a partnership-derived conferral of positional power on LLC members but include provisions that mitigate its consequences. A recent (post-RULLCA) LLC statute, effective as of January 2014 in North Carolina, is an intriguing example.[63] Section 3-20(a) vests management of North Carolina LLCs in managers,[64] followed by section 3-20(d), which provides that all members are managers "by virtue of their status as members . . ." unless the operating agreement provides otherwise,[65] for example by designating less than all members as managers or designating non-members as the LLC's sole managers. Thus, member-management is the default option but the operating agreement may specify otherwise. Under section 3-20(c) "each manager may act on behalf of the LLC in the ordinary course of its business" subject to direction and control of a majority of managers. As with the Delaware LLC statute, the first question posed by these provisions is whether a member/manager's status-derived power to "act on behalf of the LLC in the ordinary course of its business" is subject to any further constraints, if the act is in the "ordinary course" of the LLC's business. Would the member/manager's power to bind encompass acts known to the third party to represent self-dealing transactions or acts effected through atypical means? Section 2-30(e) makes applicable "the laws of agency and contract" unless provided otherwise in the statute, but this section explicitly addresses only the "administration and enforcement of operating agreements."[66] If the third party has notice of terms in the operating agreement that restrict a manager's authority (including the authority of a member/manager), neither actual nor apparent authority would enable the third party to hold the LLC to the legal consequences of the manager's unauthorized act. But one wonders whether apparent-authority principles limit the status-derived power of a member to bind an LLC to a transaction that would reasonably appear to a third party not to be authorized based on the nature of the transaction or the means through which the member effects it, when the third party has no notice of any limitations imposed by the operating agreement. Perhaps such a transaction is assumed not to be in "the ordinary course" of the LLC's business, but this may require heavy lifting by "ordinary course."

In contrast with the Delaware statute, the North Carolina statute is clear about the impact of provisions in an operating agreement that restrict authority. Under section

---

"has actual authority to take actions the member reasonably believes are necessary or incidental to achieving the objectives of the LLC so long as the member is not aware of any differing belief among the members and the act is within the ordinary course of the activities of the LLC." *Id.* My proposed analysis is narrower by a smidgen: a member who anticipates that fellow members may well object would have an incentive to act before fellow members are clued in to the action the member plans to take. Perhaps the member harboring such a suspicion would not also "reasonably believe" that what the member does is necessary or incidental to the LLC's objectives, but the analytic focus within agency law in determining whether an agent acted with actual authority is consistency with the principal's known manifestations, which include "circumstances of which the agent has notice and the agent's fiduciary duty to the principal." Restatement (Third) of Agency § 2.02(2). A reasonable person in the agent's situation, with the new LLC as a principal, might be on notice of the "circumstance" of the agent's own suspicions about the principal, that is, the likely objection by fellow LLC members.

[63] For an overview of the statute from the chair of the bar committee that drafted the act, see Kean.
[64] N.C. Gen. Stats. ch. 57D, § 3-20(a).
[65] *Id.* § 3-20(d).
[66] *Id.* § 2-30(e).

2-30(b)(2), an operating agreement "does not apply" to persons "who are not parties or otherwise bound by the operating agreement."[67] A third party, neither a party to an operating agreement nor bound by it as the statute specifies,[68] would be a party to whom the operating agreement "does not apply . . . ." Admittedly, stating that an operating agreement "does not apply" to a person is not precisely the same as stating that the person is not deemed to be on notice of its contents; but notably the North Carolina statute omits any language deeming all who may deal with or otherwise encounter an LLC to have knowledge of the terms of its operating agreement. And to preserve the potential of apparent authority as a limiting constraint on unauthorized actions, it is important that the statute does not state that non-parties are not "affected by" the agreement.

Non-Statutory Solutions

By this point in the chapter, two facts may puzzle the reader. First, only a small number of cases address the problems identified in this chapter in the LLC context. Second, statutory fixes to the problems are either in their early days or limited in number. To date, seven states and the District of Columbia have adopted RULLCA; the North Carolina statute is both new and distinctive. One explanation for the evident stickiness of problematic statutory language is that other factors suppress or mitigate the occurrence of problems, including the fact that most transactions entered into on behalf of LLCs "transpire without agency issues being recognized by the parties, let alone disputed."[69] Further explanations for stickiness stem from judicial decisions and interpretations of the law by expert lawyers that can mitigate problematic statutory language.

For Delaware LLCs, opinions from Delaware courts make it clear that, in one scholarly assessment, "the law of agency remains alive and well in Delaware."[70] Indeed, it is noticeable that neither of the two cases in point applying Delaware law refers at all to the Delaware LLC statute! In *Jack J. Morris Assocs. v. Mispillion Street Partners, LLC*, an individual co-owner of the LLC that constituted one of the defendant LLC's two members was originally designated one of the defendant's general managers.[71] Two days before he executed a contract under which the plaintiff would furnish marketing services to the defendant, the defendant's operating agreement was amended to remove the individual as a general manager. The defendant paid some invoices submitted by the plaintiff but then ceased paying. The court denied the plaintiff's motion for summary judgment in its suit for breach of contract, entirely relying for analytic traction on common-law agency. The individual testified that the defendant LLC was aware that he entered into the agreement with the plaintiff, which might constitute an implied grant of actual authority to the individual, based on whether he reasonably believed the defendant authorized him

---

[67] *Id.* § 2-30(b)(2).
[68] Under section 2-31(a) & (b), non-parties bound by the operating agreement are the LLC itself and interest holders, who under section 1-03(15) are defined to include members and non-members who hold economic interests in the LLC.
[69] RULLCA, Prefatory Note at 4.
[70] Bishop & Kleinberger at ¶ 14.04[3][a] 14–116.
[71] 2008 WL 3906755 (Del. Super. Ct. May 5, 2008).

to enter into the agreement notwithstanding the earlier revocation of his position as a general manager. Separately, and requiring "factual evaluation," was whether the individual acted with apparent authority, an inquiry "which must consider whether Defendant made representations to Plaintiff indicating that [individual] was its agent, whether Plaintiff relied on them, and whether that reliance was reasonable."[72] Unremarkable as an articulation of agency doctrine, the court's opinion nonetheless is remarkable for the absence of any reference to the LLC statute. Perhaps counsel for the defendant did not think that a defense premised on the statute's "unless otherwise provided" language would be helpful.

In the second case, the Court of Chancery likewise did not refer to the LLC statute in denying motions for summary judgment; the case stemmed from an employee's use of funds embezzled from his employer to buy property on behalf of an LLC in which he and another individual were members. In *B.A.S.S. Group, LLC v. Coastal Supply Co.*, once the embezzlement came to light, the now-former employee settled with his former employer on terms that required transfer to the former employer of property purchased for the LLC with the embezzled funds.[73] After the embezzler did the transfer, the LLC's other member sued to void it, alleging that the embezzler lacked authority under the LLC agreement to make the transfer. The court found the question complicated under the LLC agreement because the embezzler, designated therein as the "Authorized Person" to execute instruments on behalf of the LLC, may not have acted in good faith, as the agreement required. Additionally debatable on the summary judgment record was whether the embezzler acted with apparent authority in transferring the property to his former employer because it was not clear whether the employer "relied upon anything" done by the LLC "in formulating its arguably reasonable belief" that the embezzler acted with authority in transferring the LLC's property.[74] Again, unremarkable applications of common-law agency doctrine, but again nowhere does the opinion refer to the Delaware LLC statute.

These opinions may furnish the backdrop for the emergence of an arguable expert consensus about the relationship between Delaware's LLC statute and the common-law doctrine of apparent authority, a consensus at odds with the reported reactions of Delaware counsel as of 2006 reported earlier in this chapter. Such a consensus could reinforce the impact of the judicial decisions to date as well as predict the likely outcome of future litigation. In 2014, the Committee on LLCs, Partnerships, and Unincorporated Entities of the ABA's Business Law section[75] prepared and published a form LLC agreement for single-individual-member LLCs organized under Delaware law.[76] Addressing management of the LLC, the form (inter alia) permits delegation by

---

[72] 2008 WL 3906755 at *4.
[73] 2009 WL 1743730 (Del. Ch. June 19, 2009).
[74] 2009 WL 1743730 at *6. Not helping the plaintiff was the strength of the former employer's counterclaim for unjust enrichment. The court held that the LLC was not a bona fide purchaser for value of the embezzled funds and denied summary judgment on the counterclaim only because the parties did not address "who should capture the upside of the Property" if any value remained net of the embezzled funds plus interest. *Id.* at *7.
[75] The same committee sponsored the meeting that generated multiple interpretations of Delaware's statute in 2006. See Frost at 11.
[76] Single-member LLCs "once suspect because novel .., are now popular both for sole proprietorships and as corporate subsidiaries." RULLCA, Prefatory Note at 1.

the member to other persons or entities, with such titles as the member may elect, of "the power and authority to act on behalf of the Company as the Member may delegate in writing to any such person or entity."[77] Recall that one literal reading of the Delaware statute is that provisions in an operating agreement (termed an LLC agreement under Delaware law) exclusively specify the power, as well as the actual authority, to bind the LLC. Inconsistent with this reading is footnote 15 to this portion of the form, which notes that "while appointed persons or entities will only have actual authority as set forth in this Agreement, they may nevertheless have apparent agency authority, including perhaps apparent authority to bind the LLC as a third party would reasonably ascribe to the titles given."[78] In light of the authors' professional and institutional stature, the form's inclusion of apparent authority as a possible basis on which an LLC may be bound by an unauthorized act may represent an informed professional consensus inclined to reject an interpretation of statutory language disconnected on this issue from the common law.

5. CONCLUSION

External agency is essential to the capacity of any business entity to engage in business dealings with other entities and with individuals. Perhaps the relatively settled nature of common-law agency makes it all the more surprising that the most basic agency question of all—the power to bind a firm—has been so muddled over the history of LLC statutes and is treated ambiguously in the Delaware LLC statute. This chapter demonstrates that the muddle is avoidable. RULLCA achieves clarity by jettisoning the partnership-derived concept of positional powers and by affirmatively embracing the common law to resolve agency questions. Separately, a statute might retain powers of position for LLC members and managers but also specify—as do partnership statutes—the circumstances under which an unauthorized act would bind the LLC, while also specifying that restrictions on authority contained in operating agreements do not affect the legal position of a third party who lacks knowledge or notice of the restrictions.

REFERENCES

American Bar Association, LLCs, Partnerships, Unincorporated Entities Committee, Business Law Section, Single-Member LLC Individual Member Form, 69 Bus. Law. 775–97 (2014).
BISHOP, CARTER G. & KLEINBERGER, DANIEL S., LIMITED LIABILITY COMPANIES: TAX AND BUSINESS LAW (2010).
BUSCH, DANNY & MACGREGOR, LAURA J., THE UNAUTHORISED AGENT (2009).
DeMott, Deborah A., The Contours and Composition of Agency Doctrine: Perspectives from History and Theory on Inherent Agency Power, 2014 U. ILL. L. REV. 1813.
Frost, Steven, Agency Law & LLCs in Delaware, Other States and under RULLCA, 10 J. Passthrough Entities 11–12, 47–48 (2007).
Gevurtz, Franklin A., Why Delaware LLCs?, 91 Or. L. Rev. 57–126 (2012).
Kean, Warren P., A Road Map for the New North Carolina Limited Liability Act, The Litigator, Nov. 2013, available at http://litigation.ncbar.org/newsletters/litigatornov2013/llclaw.

---

[77] *Id.* item 5.1 (iii).
[78] *Id.* at 780 n. 15, citing Restatement (Third) of Agency § 2.03.

Lewis, William D., The Uniform Partnership Act, 24 Yale L. J. 617–41 (1915).
McMeel, Gerard, Philosophical Foundations of the Law of Agency, 116 L. Q. Rev. 387–411 (2000).
ORTS, ERIC W., BUSINESS PERSONS (2013).
RIBSTEIN, LARRY E. et al., UNINCORPORATED BUSINESS ENTITIES (5th ed. 2013).
Rutledge, Thomas E. & Frost, Steven G., RULLCA Section 301—The Fortunate Consequences (and Continuing Questions) of Distinguishing Apparent Agency and Decisional Authority, 64 Bus. Law. 37–58 (2008).

PART 3

RELATIONSHIPS WITH THIRD PARTIES

7. Is the liability of limited liability entities really limited?*
Allan G. Donn

> If you come to grief, and creditors are craving (For nothing that is planned by mortal head Is certain in this Vale of Sorrow—saving That one's Liability is Limited)[1]

Unless there is some prohibition or other compelling reason not to, a limited liability entity ("LLE") will be used for any activity or property ownership that may give rise to a claim against the owners of the activity or the property.

Until 1988, except in the case of limited partnerships, corporate income tax treatment had been the price paid for limited liability. That year the Internal Revenue Service announced that a Wyoming limited liability company, which provided limited liability for all of its owners, would be taxed as a partnership for federal income tax purposes. Since that time, the principle of limited liability has been extended by the states to other unincorporated business organizations.

Protection against liability is the most important non-tax factor in the choice of entity. In making that choice, a number of issues must be considered. Which entities are available for particular persons and for a particular enterprise? Are there differences among the LLEs in the effectiveness and extent of liability protection within a state and from state to state? Is there a difference among the LLEs in the risk that limited liability will be undermined by courts or statutes other than those statutes under which the entity is organized?

When an LLE is used, owners assume that they will be protected from third-party claims arising out of property or activity of the entity. That liability protection is often referred to as the liability "shield" or "corporate veil." However, as will be described hereafter, there are many leaks in the limited liability shield.[2]

The liability exposure of the entity owners has three principal sources: first, explicit exceptions in the statute of the organization or judicial interpretations of the statute; second, judicial concepts, such as piercing the corporate veil and successor liability; and third, statutory override of the entity act general liability shield.

---

* This chapter will not address the policy reasons for and against limited liability, recently reviewed by Oh, Veil Piercing Unbound, 93 B.U. L. Rev. 89, 97–102 (2013). There will be references to the uniform entity acts prepared by the Uniform Laws Commission ("ULC"). The ULC has in process a project to harmonize the various acts; the draft harmonized version of those uniform acts will not be addressed in this chapter.

[1] W.S. Gilbert, Mr. Goldbury's song, Utopia Limited, Borowitz, Gilbert and Sullivan on Corporation Law, 29 Legal Stud. F. 941, 948–9 (2005).

[2] Feeley v. NHAOCG, LLC, 62 A. 3d 649 (Del. Ch. 2012).

1. GENERAL PRINCIPLES OF ENTITY LIMITED LIABILITY

Although historically a corporation was treated as a juridical entity separate and distinct from its owners, the recognition of the limited liability of its owners was a later development. "The doctrine arose in the wake of the acceptance of the entity concept but not as a necessary consequence thereof."[3] Today, the recognition of a corporation as a separate entity is viewed as the basis for the limited liability. The United States Supreme Court has said, "After all, incorporation's basic purpose is to create a distinct legal entity, with legal rights, obligations, powers, and privileges different from those of the natural individuals who created it, who own it, or whom it employs."[4]

Generally, one person is not liable for the debts or obligations of another.[5] Therefore, the owners of a legal organization that is treated as a separate entity are not liable for the debts and obligations of the entity. The relationship between being an entity and limited liability is not applicable to all business organizations. For example, although a general partnership and a limited partnership are treated as separate legal entities under the current uniform acts, the general partners of either type of partnership are personally liable for the obligations of the entity. Conversely, although what is known as a series of a Delaware Series LLC is not treated as a separate legal entity, the statutes that provide for series provide liability protection for their owners.

Corporations

Under the general rule of American law, a corporation is a separate legal entity, distinct from its owners, and the owners are not personally liable for the obligations of the corporation.[6] In most states limited liability "arises from the corporate common law . . . rather than from statutory or constitutional provisions," and the principle of limited shareholder liability is so well established that the corporate statutes of a number of states do not include an express statement of the principle.[7]

Limited Liability Companies ("LLCs")

Every state has adopted legislation authorizing LLCs. All of the LLC acts expressly provide that no member or manager of an LLC will have any personal obligation for any liabilities of an LLC, whether arising in contract, tort or otherwise, some including

---

[3] Blumberg, Corporate Groups § 3.02 (2d ed. 2005).
[4] Cedric Kushner Promotions, Ltd. v. King, 533 U.S. 158 (2001).
[5] "[T]he key point is not that the shareholder has been granted some special thing called limited liability. The real point is that *the corporation is a separate legal person*, and, thus, in the case of creditor claims against an enterprise in corporate form, *the corporation is the debtor*, not those persons who hold claim to the equity in the enterprise. . . ." (emphasis in original). Manning & Hanks, Legal Capital 16–17 (4th ed. 2013).
[6] RMBCA § 6.22(b) sets forth "the basic rule of nonliability of shareholders for corporate acts on debts that underlies modern corporation law." Official Comment. Members are not liable for the debts or obligations of a nonprofit corporation. Revised Model Nonprofit Corporation Act § 6.12.
[7] Blumberg, The Law of Corporate Groups - Substantive Law § 6.01 and n. 1 (1st ed. 1987).

the phrase "solely by reason of" being a member or acting as a manager. Some statutes include the obverse proposition, that is, the debts, obligations and liabilities of the LLC are solely those of the LLC.[8] Some statutes also provide that an LLC member is not a proper party to proceedings by or against an LLC, except where the object is to enforce the member's rights against or liability to the LLC.[9]

General Partnerships

Although a general partnership is an entity distinct from its partners,[10] in contrast to the limited liability of corporate shareholders, general partners are liable jointly and severally for the obligations of the partnership.[11]

Limited Partnerships

Under the Revised Uniform Limited Partnership Act ("RULPA"), a general partner of a limited partnership has the unlimited liability of a general partner of a general partnership.[12] However, a limited partner who is not also a general partner is not liable for the obligations of the limited partnership unless the limited partner "participates in the control of the business."[13] Even in that case, the limited partner is liable only to persons who transact business with the partnership reasonably believing, based upon the limited partner's conduct, that the limited partner is a general partner.[14] RULPA contains a "safe harbor" list of activities that a limited partner may carry on without being deemed to have participated in control.[15]

The RULPA provision defining the circumstances upon which a limited partner may be liable as a general partner has been replaced in the Uniform Limited Partnership Act (2001) ("ULPA 2001"), which provides: "A limited partner is not personally liable, directly or indirectly, by way of contribution or otherwise, for any obligation of the limited partnership solely by reason of being a limited partner, even if the limited partner participates in the management and control of the limited partnership."[16] Thus, under the new limited partnership law, a limited partner will have the general liability protection available to a corporate shareholder and an LLC member.

---

[8] Del. Code Ann. tit. 6, § 18-303(a).
[9] E.g., N.Y. LLC Law § 610.
[10] RUPA § 201(a).
[11] RUPA § 306(a). Personal liability for the firm's debts has been described as "[p]erhaps the most partneresque feature" of partners' relations to the firm. E.E.O.C. v. Sidley Austin Brown & Wood, 315 F.3d 696, 703 (7th Cir. 2002).
[12] RULPA § 403(b).
[13] RULPA § 303(a). A limited partner may also be liable for permitting his name to be used in the partnership name. RULPA § 303(d). But see, Del. Code Ann. tit. 6, § 17-303(d).
[14] The "detrimental reliance" requirement generally precludes tort creditors. IV Bromberg & Ribstein, Partnerships § 12.14[B] n.10 (2014).
[15] RULPA § 303(b).
[16] ULPA (2001) § 303.

Limited Liability Partnerships ("LLPs")

An LLP is a general partnership in which the general partners are not personally liable for the partnership's obligations solely by reason of being a partner.[17] Every state now permits LLPs. The California, New York, and Oregon LLP statutes are unusual in that they permit LLPs only for professional practices.[18] The predominant LLP form is referred to as "full shield," under which the general partners are protected against all liabilities of the partnership.[19] In full shield states, a partner of an LLP, an LLC member, and shareholder have the same liability protection.

Some states provide only a partial shield, meaning that the partners are protected against only claims arising from negligence, wrongful acts or misconduct, but not against other liabilities, such as those arising under contracts.[20] In those states, an LLC provides greater protection than an LLP.

The benefit of being a partner of an LLP is the protection against claims arising from the acts or omissions of others. However, as will be more fully described, partners remain liable for their personal misconduct. Furthermore, those partners are not entitled to require the innocent partners to share the cost of the liability.[21] In a partnership in which some partners are actively involved in the business and others are not, the managing partners who may be at risk of direct personal liability should understand that one consequence of the LLP form is that they surrender their right of contribution from the other partners, unless provided in the agreement after the vote to become an LLP.

Limited Liability Limited Partnerships ("LLLPs")

A RULPA LLLP is a limited partnership in which neither the general partners nor the limited partners, regardless of their participation in management, are personally liable for obligations the partnership incurs while the partnership is an LLLP.[22]

Under ULPA (2001), the certificate of limited partnership must state whether the limited partnership is an LLLP.[23] According to the Comment, "The requirement is intended to force the organizers of a limited partnership to decide whether the limited partnership is to be an LLLP."[24] There cannot be many circumstances in which the general partner would agree to unlimited liability.

---

[17] RUPA § 306(c).
[18] Cal. Corp. Code § 16101(b)(A); N.Y. Partnership Law § 121-1500; O.R.S. § 67.500(1)(a).
[19] E.g., RUPA § 306(c); Del. Code Ann. tit. 6, § 15-306(c); N.Y. Partnership Law § 26(b).
[20] E.g., 15 Pa. C.S.A. § 8204(a).
[21] RUPA § 306, Comment 3. The last sentence of § 306(c) provides that becoming an LLP negates any inconsistent provision in the partnership agreement, such as one for contribution, that existed before the vote to become an LLP.
[22] E.g., Del. Code Ann. tit. 6, § 17-214(c); Va. Code Ann. § 50-73.78(c). Permitted in 16 states. Prohibited by California, Oregon and New York.
[23] ULPA (2001) § 201(a)(4).
[24] ULPA (2001) Comment, subsection (a)(4) of § 201.

Professional Entities

All states permit professional practice by professional corporations. Most states permit professional practices to be conducted by LLCs and LLPs. However, California permits an LLC to render professional services only if the applicable code authorizes an LLC to hold that license, certificate, or registration.[25]

In some states, a lawyer's right to protection against vicarious liability is conditioned upon provision of certain amounts of liability insurance or alternative forms of "financial responsibility." In other states vicarious liability for malpractice claims against lawyers continues but only up to certain dollar limits or to the extent of failure to maintain required insurance.[26] No state expressly imposes unlimited vicarious liability on lawyers practicing in limited liability entities.

Business Trusts or Statutory Trusts

Generally, the beneficial owners of a business or statutory trust have the same limited liability as a shareholder.[27] In addition, the trustees are not liable to third parties.[28]

Personal or Donative Trusts

Under the common law of trusts, a trustee is personally liable for obligations of the trust, and claims by third parties are not limited to trust assets.[29] However, under the Uniform Trust Code (now adopted by 27 jurisdictions) the common law rule has been changed, and a trustee is not personally liable on a contract properly entered into in the trustee's fiduciary capacity if that capacity is disclosed in the contract, and the trustee is personally liable for tort only if the trustee is personally at fault.[30] Moreover, a trustee who holds an interest as a general partner is not personally liable on a partnership contract if the fiduciary capacity was disclosed in the contract or a filed partnership statement, and the trustee is not personally liable for torts committed by the partnership unless personally at fault.[31]

Unincorporated Nonprofit Associations

Under the common law, a nonprofit association is not a legal entity separate from its members, who are viewed as an aggregate of individuals.[32] Under the Revised Uniform

---

[25] Cal. Corp. Code § 17701.04(b).
[26] E.g., Del. S.Ct. Rule 67(h)(II); Mass. S.J.C. Rule 3.06(3).
[27] E.g., Del. Code Ann. tit. 12 § 3803(a).
[28] E.g., Del. Code Ann. tit. 12 § 3803(b). For a full discussion of business trusts, see Oh, Chapter 16.
[29] 4 Scott & Ascher on Trusts (5th ed. 2007) § 26.2 (Contractual Liability); § 26.3 (Tort Liability). Although previously it was no defense to a suit that the trust estate was insufficient to indemnify the trustee, that appears to be no longer the case. § 26.4.5.
[30] UTC § 1010(b). See also, Restatement of the Law Third Trusts §§ 105 and 106.
[31] UTC § 1011(a) and (b).
[32] Uniform Unincorporated Nonprofit Association Act (1996) § 6 Comment 1.

Unincorporated Nonprofit Association Act (2008) ("RUUNA") an unincorporated nonprofit association is a legal entity distinct from its members and managers.[33] A debt, obligation, or other liability of an unincorporated nonprofit association under RUUNA is solely that of the association and not that of a member or manager solely because of acting as a member or manager.[34]

Under the Federal Volunteer Protection Act, subject to certain exceptions and certain state conditions that are not deemed inconsistent with the statute, an uncompensated volunteer of a nonprofit organization or governmental entity is not liable for harm caused by an act or omission of the volunteer on behalf of the entity if the harm was not caused by willful or criminal misconduct, gross negligence, reckless conduct, or a conscious or flagrant indifference to the right or safety of the individual harmed, unless caused by a vehicle.[35]

Delaware Series

The Delaware limited partnership and LLC statutes contain unusual provisions. The governing instrument may create a division referred to as a series. A series under the Delaware act is not a separate legal entity.[36] However, if separate records are maintained for any series, the assets associated with any series are held and accounted for separately from the other assets of the entity or other series, and if the agreement so provides and notice of the limitation on liability is set forth in the certificate of formation, then the debts or obligations of one series may not be enforced against the balance of the entity or other series, and those of the entity and other series may not be enforced against the assets of the series.[37]

---

[33] RUUNA § 5(a). "The separate legal status of an UNA is a fundamental concept . . . that insulates the assets of the members from claims against the UNA." RUUNA § 5(a), Comment 1.

[34] RUUNA § 8(a)(2). According to Comment 3, "Solely" is intended "to make it clear that a member or manager is not vicariously liable for the liabilities of the UNA or the liabilities of another member or manager merely because of that person's status as a member or manager." However, the member or manager may have personal liability as a result of his or her own actions.

[35] 42 U.S.C.A. § 14503(a)(3).

[36] Conaway & Tsoflias, The Delaware Series LLC: Sophisticated and Flexible Business Planning, 2 Mich. J. of Private Equity & Venture Capital Law 97, 108–09 (2012). By contrast, the Illinois Series LLC statute provides that a series is treated as a separate entity to the extent set forth in the articles of organization. 805 ILCS 180/37-40(b). Similar to a Series LLC is what is known as a protected cell company. Under the applicable statute, the assets of a protected cell may not be charged with liabilities of any other protected cell or the sponsor captive insurance company generally. E.g., Del. Code Ann. tit. 18, § 6934(3). See Feetham & Jones, Protected Cell Companies (2d ed. 2010).

[37] Del. Code Ann. tit. 6, § 17-218(b); Del. Code Ann. tit. 6, § 18-215(b). Delaware also permits a statutory trust series. Del. Code Ann. tit. 12, § 3804(a).

2. EXCEPTIONS IN THE STATUTE UNDER WHICH THE ENTITY IS FORMED OR JUDICIAL INTERPRETATIONS OF THE STATUTE

Direct Liability for Own Acts or Omissions

Although a shareholder, limited partner, LLP partner and LLC member and manager generally do not have vicarious liability for the obligations of the entity, the "solely by reason" phrase is to make clear that an entity owner may have liability on other grounds. That liability results, not from status as an owner of the entity, but from the owner's personal acts or omissions that breach a duty owed to a third party.[38] However, some cases have declined to hold the person acting liable.[39] Some statutes include an express exception that a shareholder, LLC member, or LLP partner is directly liable for any negligent or wrongful act or misconduct committed by each of them,[40] but the result is generally the same under the common law in the absence of statute. That liability may include liability for negligence in selecting, training, retaining, supervising, or otherwise controlling personnel.[41] Some LLC acts expressly impose liability for negligence in supervision.[42] Some statutes go further and hold an entity owner liable for any negligent or wrongful act or misconduct committed "by any person under his direct supervision and control" while rendering professional services on behalf of the entity.[43] New York imposes the same standard of supervisory liability on professional service corporations, LLCs and LLPs.[44]

Although generally an officer is not liable for entity wrongdoing merely because of his status, the United States Supreme Court has recognized the "responsible corporate officer" doctrine, under which liability under certain federal statutes may be imposed directly on a corporate officer whose personal conduct resulted in the entity's liability.[45]

Common Law of Agency

An agent is personally liable on a contract made on behalf of a principal if the existence and identity of the principal have not been disclosed.[46] That principle has been applied to impose liability on LLC members and managers who have not given notice that they were

---

[38] E.g., Cortez v. Nacco Materials Handling Group, Inc., 337 P.3d 111 (Or. 2014); Everkrisp Vegetables Inc. v. Otto, 941 F. Supp. 2d 1132 (D.N.D. 2013); Mbahaba v. Morgan LLC, 44 A.3d 472 (N.H. 2012); Sturm v. Harb Dev., LLC, 2 A.3d 859 (Conn. 2010).
[39] E.g., Dass v. Yale, 3 N.E.3d 858 (Ill. App. Ct. 2013), appeal denied, 5 N.E. 3d 1123 (Ill. 2014) (unpublished table decision); Ogea v. Merritt, 130 So. 3d 888 (La. 2013); and 16 Jade Street, LLC v. R. Design Constr. Co., LLC, 405 S.C. 384, 747 S.E.2d 770 (2013).
[40] E.g., N.Y. B.C.L. § 1505(a); N.Y. LLC Act § 1205(b). But Del. Code Ann. tit. 6, § 15-306(d) was amended in 2001 to delete the provision as unnecessary.
[41] Restatement Third, Agency § 7.05.
[42] E.g., Md. Corp. & Ass'ns. Code section 4A-301(a)(2) (professional services).
[43] E.g., N.Y. B.C.L. § 1505(a).
[44] N.Y. LLC Act § 1205(b); N.Y. Partnership Law § 26(c).
[45] United States v. Park, 421 U.S. 658 (1975); Friedman v. Sebelius, 686 F.3d 813 (D.C. Cir. 2012).
[46] Restatement Third, Agency § 6.03(2).

acting on behalf of an LLC.[47] Furthermore, an agent may be liable to a third party to whom he owes a duty. However, "Most cases hold that an agent does not owe a duty to a third party when the agent's negligent conduct causes only pure economic loss to a third party."[48]

Voluntary Personal Liability

A member or partner will be liable for obligations undertaken by agreement, such as the guaranty of an obligation of the entity.[49] Furthermore, LLC members or LLP partners may be liable in their capacity as members or partners for all or specified debts if the document filed to form the entity so provides.[50]

Capital Contribution Deficiencies

Entity owners are liable for the difference between capital contributions made and the amount agreed to be made.[51] The rights of creditors to enforce the contribution obligation cannot be modified merely by agreement of the owners.[52] Some acts provide that conditional obligations may be enforced only if the conditions, such as a discretionary call, have been satisfied or waived.[53] Under some statutes an assignee who is admitted as a substituted member or partner is liable for the obligations of the assignor to make contributions.[54] Generally, the assignor is not released by the assignment.[55]

Interim Distributions

Many acts impose limits on distributions, providing that a distribution may be made only so long as the entity remains solvent in the equity and balance sheet sense.[56] Generally,

---

[47] E.g., Water, Waste & Land, Inc. v. Lanham, 955 P.2d 997 (Colo. 1998).
[48] Restatement Third, Agency § 7.02, Comment d. See, R. Keatinge, The Liability of Managers and Other Agents for Their Own Acts on Behalf of an LLC, Business Law Today, February 2015.
[49] E.g., Cal. Corp. Code § § 17703.04(e); Del. Code Ann. tit. 6, § 18-303(b); N.Y. LLC Law § 609(b). See Common West Office Condos. Ltd. v. Resolution Trust Corp., 5 F.3d 125 (5th Cir. 1993), holding that an individual had incurred liability in two separate and distinct capacities—as general partner under the partnership's note, and as guarantor of that note, and that the guaranty agreement under which he guaranteed only 25% of the note did not limit his 100% liability as a general partner.
[50] E.g., Del. Code Ann. tit. 6, § 18-303(b); N.Y. LLC Law § 609(b); N.Y. Partnership Act § 26(d). The waiver provision originated under the four-factor tax classification regulations when limited liability was a corporate factor, and it was desirable to negate that factor. Under the check-the-box regulations, it would be an unusual situation in which the members or partners would so elect.
[51] E.g., N.Y. LLC Law § 502(a).
[52] E.g., RMBCA § 6.22(a); Del. Code Ann. tit. 6, § 18-502(b); In re LJM2 Co. Inc., L.P., 866 A.2d 762 (Del. Ch. 2004); RULPA § 502(b).
[53] E.g., Del. Code Ann. tit. 6, § 18-502(b); ULPA (2001) § 502(c).
[54] E.g., Ohio Rev. Code § 1705.20(B); RULPA § 704(b); ULPA (2001) § 702(g).
[55] E.g., RULPA § 704(c).
[56] E.g., RMBCA § 6.40(c); Del. Code Ann. tit. 6, § 18-607(a). Most LLP statutes, including RUPA, do not impose a limitation on distributions, but among those that do are Cal. Corp. Code § 16957(a), Colo. Rev. Stat. § 7-64-1004; and Del. Code Ann. tit. 6, § 15-309.

a corporate shareholder who receives an unlawful distribution is not liable to repay it unless he knew that it was excessive.[57] By comparison, under a number of statutes an LLC member and limited partner may be liable to return distributions made in violation of the limits even if they did not know that it was excessive.[58]

Wrongful Liquidation Distributions

In addition to the statutory limitations on distributions and liability for unlawful distributions during the operation of the entity, a number of statutes address rights of creditors to assets in the winding up of the company. The company must apply its assets first to discharge or make provision to discharge obligations to creditors before distributions to members.[59] If the assets have been distributed to the members in liquidation, then, before the claim is barred by the applicable statute of limitations, a creditor may recover from the members to the extent of the lesser of the members' proportionate shares of the claim or the amounts received in liquidation.[60]

3. JUDICIALLY CREATED EXCEPTIONS TO THE LIABILITY SHIELD

Under a number of theories, courts have exercised their equitable powers to disregard the separate existence or liability shield of a legal entity to impose liability on an owner of the entity, or in effect, joint and several liability on affiliated persons.

Piercing the Veil

Notwithstanding the general liability limitation of shareholders, there is a common law concept that under certain circumstances courts will "pierce the corporate veil" to hold shareholders liable for torts and contracts of the corporation.[61] Piercing is not an independent cause of action but an equitable remedy that holds one party liable for the obligation of another.

The subject has been described as "among the most confusing in corporate law," and a

---

[57] RMBCA § 8.33(b)(2).
[58] E.g., Ribstein & Keatinge, Limited Liability Companies § 6.05; RULPA § 608. But see, Del. Code Ann. tit. 6, § 18-607(b) (knew of violation); ULPA (2001) § 509(b).
[59] RULLCA § 708(a); RULPA § 804(l); ULPA (2001) § 812(a).
[60] RMBCA § 14.07(d)(2); RULLCA § 704(d)(2).
[61] For the history of veil piercing, see Presser, Piercing the Corporate Veil § 1.03 (2014). A few states expressly provide for veil-piercing in their corporate statutes. E.g., V.T.C.A. Bus. Org. Code § 21.223(b); Nev. Rev. Stat. § 78.747.1. For recent analyses of the subject, see Macey and Mitts, Finding Order in the Morass: The Three Justifications for Piercing the Corporate Veil, 100 Cornell L. Rev. 99 (2014); Oh, Veil-Piercing Unbound, 93 B.U.L. Rev. 89 (2013); Oh, Veil-Piercing, 89 Tex. L. Rev. 81 (2010); Millon, The Still-Elusive Quest to Make Sense of Veil-Piercing, 89 Tex. L. Rev. 15 (2009); see also Boyd and Hoffman, Disputing Limited Liability, 104 Nw. U. L. Rev. 853 (2010); Matheson, Why Courts Pierce: An Empirical Study of Piercing the Corporate Veil, 7 Berkley Bus. L.J. 1 (2010).

"legal quagmire."[62] There is no definitive statement of the rule; instead there is generally said to be a two-prong test.[63] First, is separateness of the entity whose veil is sought to be pierced disregarded by the parties and is the activity giving rise to the claim controlled by the persons sought to be reached? Second, is the entity used to perpetuate a fraud, violate a public policy, or perpetuate an injustice? A number of factors are enunciated in the cases on the first prong.[64] The standards for piercing the corporate veil are not uniform from state to state, and there is a broad range of application of the concept in the reported court decisions.[65]

A few LLC statutes expressly direct that the "piercing" rule applicable to corporations and their shareholders apply to LLCs and their members.[66] There is no reason to expect that courts will not treat other LLEs in the same manner as a corporation for piercing purposes. Although some commentators have argued that piercing should not be applied to LLCs,[67] most of the courts that have addressed the issue, even without express statutory provisions, have applied or assumed the application of the piercing principle to LLCs.[68]

In addition to the piercing jurisprudence of state courts, there is also a federal common law of piercing.[69] A number of cases have held that the standard for piercing the corporate veil is often more lenient for causes of action arising under federal laws, such as pension law, maritime law, and labor law, than under state law.[70]

A special kind of federal piercing is known as "substantive consolidation." That is a judicially created remedy by which a bankruptcy court, pursuant to its general equitable

---

[62] Presser, Piercing the Corporate Veil 10 (2014 ed.).
[63] Wachovia Securities, LLC v. Banco Panamericano, Inc., 674 F.3d 743, 754 (7th Cir. 2012). Some courts employ a three prong test. In re Phillips, 139 P.3d 639 (Colo. 2006).
[64] E.g., Bank of Montreal v. SK Foods, LLC, 476 B.R. 588, 897–98 (N.D. Cal. 2012). After listing 20 factors, the court said, "This list is not exhaustive, and no one factor is determinative."
[65] Oh, Veil Piercing, 89 Tex. L. Rev. 81 (2010).
[66] E.g., Cal. Corp. Code § 17703.04(b); Ga. Code Ann. § 14-11-314; Minn. Stat. § 322B.303, subd. 2; Colorado also applies corporate veil-piercing principles to LLPs. Colo. Rev. Stat. Ann. § 7-64-1009(1).
[67] E.g., Bainbridge, Abolishing LLC Veil Piercing, 2005 Ill. L.Rev. 77 (2005).
[68] E.g., Spring Street Partners-IV, L.P. v. LAM, 730 F.3d 427, 443 (5th Cir. 2013) (Texas law); NetJets Aviation, Inc. v. LAC Commc'ns, LLC, 537 F.3d 168, 176 (2d Cir. 2008) (Delaware law). But see, Pannell v. Shannon, 425 S.W.3d 58, 75 n.15 (Ky. 2014) (acknowledging "strong arguments why LLC veil piercing should not be allowed . . . even when corporate veil piercing is viable in the jurisdiction, . . .," citing Bainbridge); In re Gigliotti, 507 B.R. 826 (Bankr. E.D. Pa. 2014) (applied corporate principles to determine whether to pierce the veil of an LLP and did not), aff'd, Black v. Gigliotti, 2014 WL 3858008 (E.D. Pa. 2014); HOK Sport, Inc. v. FC Des Moines, L.C., 495 F.3d. 927 (8th Cir. 2007) (applied veil piercing to a non-profit corporation).
[69] E.g., Williamson v. Recovery Ltd., P'ship, 542 F.3d 43, 53 (2d Cir. 2008) (federal maritime law); Unite Herte Nat'l Ret. Fund v. Kombassan Holding A.S., 629 F.3d 282 (2d Cir. 2010) (pension plan withdrawal liability); Ferrar v. Oakfield Leasing, Inc., 940 F. Supp. 2d 249, 267 (E.D.N.Y. 2012) (federal common law, not state law, controls veil piercing in ERISA actions).
[70] E.g., Blair v. Infineon Techs. AG, 720 F. Supp. 2d 462 (D. Del. 2010); NLRB v. Bolivar-Tees, Inc., 551 F.3d 722 (8th Cir. 2008). Centerpoint Energy Servs., Inc. v. Halim, 743 F.3d 503 (7th Cir. 2014) (applying Illinois law).

powers, may consolidate the assets and liabilities of a debtor and its affiliated entities so that the claims against the debtor become claims against the consolidated assets.[71]

When an entity is deemed to be acting as agent for its owner, liability of the owner is that of a principal and is governed by the general law of agency. In that case, it is not necessary to disregard the separate entity status to impose liability upon the entity owner for obligations of the agent entity.[72]

Successor Liability

Generally, the buyer of assets is not responsible for the obligations of the seller. However, the courts have created a number of exceptions to that general state law principle. Those include: (1) an express or implied assumption by the buyer of the seller's liabilities;[73] (2) fraudulent transfers, in which the obligated person attempts to transfer the assets of the selling entity to a new entity that operates the same business, with the same employees, equipment, and customers;[74] (3) de facto merger, the elements of which are continuity of ownership, cessation of the ordinary business and dissolution of the acquired entity, assumption of liabilities ordinarily necessary for uninterrupted continuation of the acquired business, and a continuity of management, personnel, physical location, assets and general business operation;[75] and (4) where the buyer is treated as a mere continuation of the seller.[76]

As the federal common law of piercing the veil is generally said to be more lenient for claims arising under federal law, the federal common law standard for successor liability "presents a lower bar to relief than most state jurisprudence. . . ."[77] Furthermore, according to a federal appellate court, ". . . . there is an interest in legal predictability that is served by applying the same [federal] standard of successor liability . . . to all federal statutes that protect employees . . . ."[78]

Additional Theories

A corporate parent of a general partner has been held to have aided and abetted the general partner's breach of fiduciary duty.[79] It may also be argued that the controlling

---

[71] E.g., In re Owens Corning, 419 F.3d 195, 205-16 (3d Cir. 2005); In re SK Foods, LP, 499 B.R. 809 (Bankr. E.D. Cal. 2013).
[72] Bates v. Bankers Life and Cas. Co., 993 F. Supp. 2d 1318, 1354 (D. Ore. 2014).
[73] E.g., Bender v. Newell Window Furnishings, Inc., 681 F.3d 253 (6th Cir. 2012); Monahan v. Emerald Performance Materials, LLC, 705 F. Supp. 2d 1206 (W.D. Wash. 2010).
[74] E.g., Baker v. Dorfman, P.L.L.C., 232 F.3d 121 (2d Cir. 2000).
[75] E.g., ePlus Group, Inc. v. SNR Denton, LLP, 976 N.Y.S.2d 20 (App. Div. 2013).
[76] E.g., Idearc Media, L.L.C. v. Palmisano & Assoc., P.C., 929 F. Supp. 2d 939 (D. Ariz. 2013).
[77] Thompson v. Real Estate Mortgage Network, 748 F.3d 143, 150 (3d Cir. 2014).
[78] Teed v. Thomas & Betz Power Solutions, L.L.C., 711 F.3d 763, 767 (7th Cir. 2013).
[79] Time Warner Entm't Co., L.P. v. Six Flags Over Georgia, LLC, 537 S.E.2d 397 (Ga. Ct. App. 2000), *cert. granted, judgment vacated*, and *case remanded* (as to punitive damage issues), 534 U.S. 801 (2001); In re Rural Metro Corp. Stockholders Litigation, 2014 WL 971718 (Del. Ch. 2014) (financial advisor held liable for aiding and abetting breach of fiduciary duty by corporate directors); Gotham Partners, L.P. v. Hallwood Realty Partners, L.P., 817 A.2d 160 (Del. 2002).

owner and the owned entity or multiple owners should be characterized as partners conducting the business giving rise to the claim.[80]

The single business enterprise doctrine is an equitable doctrine that applies partnership-type liability principles when entities combine or integrate their resources and operations for a common business purpose.[81] A court has distinguished single business enterprise liability from the "alter ego" version of the piercing principle on the basis that the "alter ego" theory generally requires proof of fraud but that no proof of fraud is required to establish single business enterprise liability.[82] Apart from fraud, many of the factors found in veil-piercing decisions are also significant in enterprise liability cases.

Single business enterprise liability is not a new theory. It developed in the railroad and taxi industry but was subordinated to veil piercing in early intragroup tort liability cases.[83] Although the two theories seem to overlap, one commentator has sought to distinguish them by describing veil piercing as a vertical form of liability, providing a mechanism for holding a shareholder personally liable for the corporation's obligations, and enterprise liability as a horizontal form of liability, providing a mechanism for holding the entire business enterprise liable.[84] Even where enterprise liability is imposed on the affiliated entities, it does not follow that the controlling shareholder will be personally liable.[85]

4. DIRECT LIABILITY IMPOSED ON OWNERS OR AFFILIATES BY OTHER STATUTES

According to recent commentary, "Perhaps the most straightforward theory that explains courts' decisions to pierce the corporate veil is furthering a regulatory or statutory scheme whose purpose would be undermined by upholding the corporate form."[86] Notwithstanding that justification for piercing by courts, direct liability is imposed upon entity owners and affiliates by a number of federal and state statutes, including by using generic terms to describe the potentially liable persons.

Employment Laws

A number of federal statutes impose obligations on an "employer" for matters relating to employment. Among those statutes are Title VII of the Civil Rights Act of 1994, the Fair

---

[80] E.g., In re Silicone Gel Prods. Liab. Litig., 887 F. Supp. 1455 (N.D. Ala. 1995) (held that Dow Corning was not a partnership of Dow Chemical and Corning).
[81] SSP Partners v. Gladstrong Inv. (USA) Corp., 275 S.W.3d 444 (Tex. 2008). A variation on the theory is liability of two or more persons for "acting in concert." Abdallah v. Bain Capital LLC, 752 F.3d 114, 122 (1st Cir. 2014), citing Restatement (Second) Torts § 876 (1979).
[82] SSP Partners v. Gladstrong Inv. (USA) Corp., 275 S.W.3d 444 (Tex. 2008).
[83] Blumberg, Corporate Groups, § 10.03[E] (2d ed. 2005).
[84] Bainbridge, Abolishing Veil Piercing, 26 J. Corp. L. 479, 526 (2005).
[85] Gartner v. Snyder, 607 F.2d 582 (2d Cir. 1979).
[86] Macey and Mitts, Finding Order in the Morass: The Three Justifications for Piercing the Corporate Veil, 100 Cornell L. Rev. 99, 115 (2014). Another commentator has said piercing the veil was developed primarily to deal with private controversies, rather than matters of statutory policy. Blumberg, Corporate Groups, § 96.01[d] (2d ed. 2005).

Labor Standards Act ("FLSA"), the Family, Medical Leave Act ("FMLA"), the Americans with Disabilities Act, and the WARN Act. In addition, to the federal statutes, a number of state statutes similarly prohibit discriminatory employment practices by "employers."[87]

The statutes do little to define "employer" other than it being a person engaged in an activity with more than a prescribed number of employees. Regulations under the federal statutes, as applied by the federal courts, make clear that "employer" is broader than the person for whom an individual nominally works directly and exclusively. For example, regulations under FMLA provide two tests to determine who is an "employer," namely, an "integrated employer" test and a "joint employment" test.[88] In order to determine an "integrated employer," a number of prescribed factors are applied to determine whether multiple entities should be considered as one all-encompassing employer for purposes of the act.[89] "Joint employment" is determined by whether "two or more businesses exercise some control over work or working conditions of the employee."[90] The analysis by the federal courts is highly fact-intensive.[91]

Federal statutes have been extended to unincorporated entities as well. In one case, the owner of an LLC was held to be an "employer" under the FLSA and, therefore, personally liable for the LLC's violating the minimum wage statute.[92]

Liability for Wage Claims of Employees

A New York statute provides that the ten largest shareholders of a non-publicly traded corporation are personally, jointly and severally, liable for "all debts, wages, salaries to and owing to any of its laborers, servants or employees other than contractors, for services performed by them for the corporation."[93] In addition, the Massachusetts Wage Act,

---

[87] E.g., Iowa Code § 216.2(7).
[88] 29 CFR § 825.104(c).
[89] 29 CFR § 825.104(c)(2).
[90] 29 CFR § 825.104(c)(1).
[91] See Knitter v. Corvias Military Living, LLC, 758 F.3d 1214 (10th Cir. 2014) (Title VII action dismissed because defendant was not her "employer"); Love v. J.P. Cullen & Sons, Inc., 779 F.3d 697, 701 (7th Cir. 2015); In re Tweeter OPCO, LLC, 453 B.R. 534 (Bankr. D. Del. 2011) (For WARN Act purposes, the court found that entity related to debtor in chain of ownership was held to be part of the single employer); Irizarry v. Catsimatidis, 722 F.3d 99 (2d Cir. 2013) (CEO of corporation was held to be an "employer" under the FLSA); Guippone v. BH S&B Holdings LLC, 737 F.3d 221 (2d. Cir. 2013) (question as to whether parent company was a single employer with its subsidiary under the WARN Act).

The scope of persons sought to be included within the concept of "employer" has been broadened to include persons other than owners and officers, such as franchisors. E.g., NLRB Office of the General Counsel determines that McDonald's, USA, LLC is a joint employer with its franchisees, NLRB Office of Public Affairs, July 29, 2014, consolidated complaint filed, NLRB Office of Public Affairs, December, 2014; Naik v. 7-Eleven, Inc., 2014 WL 3844792 (D.N.J. 2014). But see, Patterson v. Domino's Pizza, LLC, 333 P.3d 723, 60 Cal. 4th 474 (2014) (held under the facts before it, the franchisor did not stand in an employment or agency relationship with the franchisee and its employees for purposes of holding it vicariously liable for workplace injuries inflicted by an employee of a franchisee).

[92] Gray v. Powers, 673 F.3d 352 (5th Cir. 2012); Dalton v. Manor Care of West Des Moines IA, LLC, 986 F. Supp. 2d 1044 (S.D. Iowa 2013) (FMLA).
[93] N.Y.B.C.L. § 630(a).

which provides that corporate officers are deemed to be the employer of the employees of a corporation, has been interpreted to apply to a manager or other officer or agent of an LLC, LLP, or other limited liability business entity.[94]

Environmental Laws

Environmental statutes use generic terms such as "owner" or "operator" to impose liability on affiliated parties. The Comprehensive Environmental Response, Compensation, and Liability Act imposes liability on "owners" and "operators," or a person who at the time of the disposal of any hazardous substance owned or operated the facility.[95] For example, a parent corporation that actively participates in, and exercises control over, the operations of a subsidiary specifically related to pollution itself may be held directly liable as an "operator" of the facility.[96] In addition to being subject to direct liability as an owner or operator, an entity may also be subject to derivative liability for the action of another affiliate of that entity if the veil may be pierced under general corporate law principles.[97]

"Responsible Person" Tax Statutes

The Internal Revenue Code requires employers to withhold Social Security and income taxes from the wages of employees and to remit the amounts withheld to the IRS.[98] The amounts withheld constitute a special fund held in trust for the benefit of the United States, known as "trust funds."[99] If the employer fails to do so, then any person required to collect and pay over the tax who willfully fails to do so is liable for the total amount not paid over to the government.[100]

A number of states impose personal liability on a "responsible person" for a broader range of tax than trust fund taxes, including income, sales, and use taxes. A New York statute provides that every person required to collect sales or use tax will be personally liable for the tax imposed. The act defines "person required to collect tax" to include officers, directors or employees of a corporation, employees of a partnership, and employees or managers of an LLC who in that capacity are under a duty to act for the entity to comply with the law. The statute also includes "any member of a partnership or LLC" as a "person required to collect tax" but without the qualification that the person be under a duty to act for the entity in complying with the tax requirement.[101]

---

[94] Cook v. Patient EDU, LLC, 989 N.E.2d 847 (Mass. 2013).
[95] 42 U.S.C. § 9607(a)(2).
[96] United States v. Bestfoods, 524 U.S. 51 (1998). "Owner or operator" is also the standard under the Clean Air Act, 42 U.S.C. § 7413(b).
[97] Bestfoods, 524 U.S. at 63 n.9.
[98] IRC §§ 3102(a) and 3402(a).
[99] IRC § 7501.
[100] IRC § 3401(d)(1).
[101] New York Tax Law § 1133(a); In the Matter of Boissiere and Krystal, 2014 WL 482057 (N.Y. Div. Tax App. 2014). The Administrative Law Judge expressly held that the tax provision overrode the general liability shield of an LLC member or LLP partner. The New York Department of Taxation and Finance has adopted a policy to provide relief from *per se* joint personal liability for certain LLP partners and LLC members. Tech. Memo. TSB-M/11(17)S (Sept. 19, 2011).

Pension Funding

Federal law imposes joint and several liability for funding pension plans on the members of a "controlled group," that is, a group considered as a single employer under the Internal Revenue Code.[102] A "controlled group" consists of companies that are under "common control," including a parent and subsidiary.[103] On termination of a pension plan, all members of the controlled group are liable, jointly and severally, for the unfunded benefit liability to plan beneficiaries.[104]

There is a similar statute for withdrawal from a multi-employer union pension plan. Under that statute, all trades or business under common control with the withdrawn employer are treated as a single entity for purposes of withdrawal liability. Although the statute does not define "common control" or "trade or business," the Pension Benefit Guaranty Corporation issued regulations defining "common control," which is generally 80 percent or more common ownership by vote or value. The PBGC has not issued regulations defining a "trade or business," but a federal appellate court has recently held that an investment fund was a "trade or business" subject to withdrawal liability for corporations in which it had invested because of its active involvement in the management and operation of those corporations.[105]

A substantial number of additional federal statutes use generic terms to directly impose liability on the owner or affiliate of an entity. Among those statutes are the Perishable Agricultural Commodities Act,[106] the Copyright Law,[107] Patent Law,[108] Food and Drug Cosmetic Act,[109] Coal Industry Retiree Health Benefits Act,[110] and the Fair Debt Collection Practices Act.[111]

5. CONCLUSION

The answer to the question whether limited liability entities actually provide the anticipated liability protection is "Yes, generally." There is no reason to doubt that an unincorporated LLE will provide substantially the same liability protection to its owners as that

---

[102] IRC § 412(b).
[103] IRC §§ 1563(a), 414(b) and 414(c).
[104] ERISA § 4062; IRC § 412(b).
[105] Sun Capital Partners III, LP v. New England Teamsters & Trucking Indus. Pension Fund, 724 F.3d 129, 142 (1st Cir. 2013), *cert denied*, 134 S. Ct. 1492 (2014).
[106] Perfectly Fresh Farms, U.S. Dept. of Agriculture, 692 F.3d 960 (9th Cir. 2012) ("admittedly and intentionally a tough law." The court concluded that two officers of the corporation that violated the Act were "reasonably connected" with those corporations within the statutory definition of the term.)
[107] Range Road Music, Inc. v. East Coast Foods, Inc., 668 F.3d 1148 (9th Cir. 2012).
[108] Wordtech Sys., Inc. v. Integrated Networks Solutions, Inc., 609 F.3d 1308 (Fed. Cir. 2010).
[109] TMJ Implants v. U.S. Dept. of Health & Human Servs., 584 F.3d 1290, 1303 (10th Cir. 2009) (liability imposed on any "person" who violates the Act included the corporate president as well as the corporate manufacturer).
[110] "Any related person" to the operator is jointly and severally liable with the operator.
[111] Cruz v. Int'l Collection Corp., 673 F.3d 991 (9th Cir. 2012) (sole owner, officer and director of a corporation held to be a "debt collector").

available to corporate shareholders. However, as is also the case for shareholders, there are a substantial number of situations in which the anticipated liability protection may not be available. The numerous bases for imposing liability on shareholders should also be expected to apply to owners of other LLEs. Erosion of the liability shield continues not only with the application of judicial concepts, such as piercing the veil and successor liability, but by the proliferation of statutes that impose liability directly on owners and affiliates of an entity. To borrow a phrase used in a related context, the state of the principle of limited liability is less than reassuring to investors and other participants in corporate enterprises interested in knowing with certainty what the limitations are on the scope of shareholders' personal liability for corporate acts.[112]

BIBLIOGRAPHY

Amera and Kolod, Substantive Consolidation: Getting Back to Basics, 14 Am. Bankr. Inst. L. Rev. 1 (2006).
Bainbridge, Abolishing LLC Veil Piercing, 2005 Ill. L. Rev. 77 (2005).
Bishop, The New Limited Partner Liability Shield: Has the Vanquished Control Rule Unwittingly Resurrected Lingering Limited Partner Estoppel Liability as Well as Full General Partner Liability?, 37 Suffolk U. L. Rev. 667 (2004).
Blumberg, Corporate Groups (2d ed. 2005).
Blumberg, The Law of Corporate Groups—Substantive Law (1st ed. 1987).
Boyd, The Responsible Corporate Officer Doctrine, The Practical Lawyer 55 (August 2005).
Bromberg and Ribstein, Limited Liability Partnerships, The Revised Uniform Partnership Act, and the Uniform Limited Partnership Act (2001).
Bromberg and Ribstein, Partnerships (2d ed. 2014).
Construction and Application of Limited Liability Company Acts—Issues Relating to Personal Liability of Individual Members and Managers of Limited Liability Company as to Third Parties, 47 ALR 6th 1 (2009).
Erens, Friedman, and Mayerfield, Bankrupt Subsidiaries: The Challenges to the Parent of Legal Separation, 25 Emory Bankr. Dev. J. 65 (2008).
Feetham and Jones, Protected Cell Companies (2d ed. 2010).
Fry, Corporate-Participant Liability for Direct Patent Infringement: A Look to Copyright Law's Vicarious Liability Analysis, 2012 Colum. Bus. L. Rev. 284 (2012).
Gravlich, Substantive Consolidation—A Post-Modern Trend, 14 Am. Bankr. Inst. L. Rev. 527 (2006).
Herrmann, The New OIG "Responsible Corporate Officer Doctrine," 14 J. of Health Care Compliance 47 (Jan./Feb. 2011).
Hillman, Weidner, and Donn, The Revised Uniform Partnership Act (2013–14 ed.).
Jacobsen, Successor-in-Business Tax Claims: A Suggestion for Harmonization, A.B.I.J. Oct. 2013, p. 70.
Liability of Successor Corporation for Injury or Damage Caused by Product Issued by Predecessor, Based on "Product Line" Successor Liability, 18 A.L.R. 6th 629 (2006).
Liability of Successor Corporation for Injury or Damage Caused by Product Issued by Predecessor, Based on Mere Continuation or Continuity of Enterprise Exceptions to Nonliability, 13 A.L.R. 6th 355 (2006).
Liability of Successor Corporation for Injury or Damage Caused by Product Issued by Predecessor, Based on Merger or Consolidation of Transferor and Transferee, 109 ALR 5th 301 (2003).
Loewenstein, Veil Piercing to Non-Owners: A Practical and Theoretical Inquiry, 41 Seton Hall L. Rev. 839 (2011).
Lubaroff and Altman, Delaware Limited Partnerships § 6.10 (2011 Supp.).
Macey and Mitts, Finding Order in the Morass: The Three Real Justifications for Piercing the Corporate Veil. Cornell Law Review, 100 Cornell L. Rev. 99 (2014).
Mancino, The Trust Fund Recovery Penalty and Tax-Exempt Employers, 22 J. Tax. of Exempt Orgs. July/August 2010, 3, 13–14.
Matheson, Why Courts Pierce: An Empirical Study of Piercing the Corporate Veil, 7 Berkley Bus. L. J. 1 (2010).

---

[112] Macey and Mitts, Finding Order in the Morass: The Three Justifications for Piercing the Corporate Veil, 100 Cornell L. Rev. 99, 100 (2014).

McKim, Personal Liability for Unpaid Business Taxes, 69 State Tax Notes 289 (July 29, 2013).
Miller, Are There Limits on Limited Liability? Owner Protection and Piercing the Veil of Texas Business Entities, 43 Tex. J. Bus. Law 405 (2009).
Miller, Owner Liability Protection and Piercing the Veil of Texas Business Entities, University of Texas School of Law Conference on Partnerships and LLCs (July 22, 2010).
Miller, The Perils and Pitfalls of Practicing Law in a Texas Limited Liability Partnership, 43 Texas Tech L. Rev. 563 (2011).
Millon, The Still-Elusive Quest to Make Sense of Veil-Piercing, 89 Tex. L. Rev. 15 (2009).
Morrissey, Piercing All the Veils: Applying an Established Doctrine to a New Business Order, 32 J. Corp. L. 529 (2007).
Murphy, A Trap for the Unwary? Single Employer Liability for Related Entities under the WARN Act, 21 Norton J. of Bankr. L. Prac. 151 (2012).
Oh, Veil Piercing, 89 Tex. L. Rev. 81 (2010).
Oh, Veil Piercing Unbound, 93 B.U.L. Rev. 89 (2013).
Petrin, The Curious Case of Directors' and Officers' Liability for Supervision and Management: Exploring the Intersection of Corporate and Tort Law, 59 Am. U. L. Rev. 1661 (2010).
Presser, Piercing the Corporate Veil (2014 ed.).
Prestidge, Avoiding FCPA Surprises: Safe Harbor from Successor Liability in Cross-Border Mergers and Acquisitions, 55 W&M L. Rev. 3015 (2013).
Rapp, Preserving LLC Veil Piercing: A Response to Bainbridge, 31 J. Corp. L. 1063 (2006).
"Responsible Corporate Officer" Doctrine or Responsible Relationship of Corporate Officer to Corporate Violation of Law, 119 ALR 5th 205 (2004).
Ribstein, The Rise of the Uncorporation, 144 (2010).
Rutledge, Limited Liability (or Not): Reflections on the Holy Grail, 51 S.D.L. Rev. 417 (2006).
Successor Liability, Mass Tort, and Mandatory-Litigation Class Action, 118 Harv. L. Rev. 2357, 2358 (2005).
Thompson, Piercing the Corporate Veil: An Empirical Study, 76 Cornell L. Rev. 1036, 1058 (1991).

8. Mitigating the impact of a counterparty LLC's financial distress

Jennifer Ivey-Crickenberger and Michelle M. Harner

1. INTRODUCTION

Doing business by contract in an unincorporated entity form can create certainty for owners but it also can generate ambiguity and confusion for parties doing business with the entity. For example, can an LLC operating agreement alter the LLC's or its members' rights under federal bankruptcy law and in turn indirectly affect the rights of creditors in any subsequent bankruptcy case? If so, how do creditors anticipate and protect themselves against such bankruptcy clauses? This chapter summarizes certain key issues facing creditors of unincorporated entities, including: the enforceability of waivers and ipso facto (bankruptcy termination) clauses in prepetition operating and partnership agreements; the impact of the automatic stay and plan injunction provisions on creditors' rights against the members or partners of a bankrupt entity; and the effect of charging orders in the bankruptcy context. Although these issues can arise in most any bankruptcy case, the interplay of federal bankruptcy law, applicable state entity law, and the parties' contractual rights can create unique circumstances and unexpected consequences that potential creditors of an unincorporated entity should at least consider at the beginning of the business relationship.

2. GENERAL OVERVIEW

A creditor—whether a lender, supplier, or other third party—always needs to hope for the best but plan for the worst, and that planning is most effective when done at the beginning of the relationship. Admittedly, it is challenging for business people to enter into a transaction planning for its failure. Such a proactive posture, however, can be particularly valuable in the LLC context where case law is still developing, the Bankruptcy Code does not specifically reference or account for issues arguably unique to LLC entities, and state law generally does (and many argue that federal bankruptcy law should) respect parties' *ex ante* contractual bargains.

The questions that a creditor should ask concerning a potential transaction are not that different from other situations: Does the debtor have the financial wherewithal to perform? What collateral or third party guarantees are available to secure the indebtedness? What is the creditor's maximum exposure? Can the transaction be staged to mitigate the amount of exposure at any one time? What happens if the debtor fails?

Regardless of the answers to these questions, a creditor entering into a transaction with an LLC should fully understand: the LLC's ownership and operational structure; the terms of the operating agreement and the voting rights of members and any managers;

the LLC's interaction with its owners and any affiliated companies; and the state law governing the LLC. The creditor should tailor its transactional strategy based on the answers to the foregoing questions and the details of the particular transaction. In addition, the creditor should consider certain key issues discussed in this chapter.

3. KEY ISSUES

Can the LLC File for Bankruptcy?

According to the provisions and definitions provided in the Bankruptcy Code, an LLC is *eligible* to file a bankruptcy petition.[1] Whether the LLC has the *authority* to file a bankruptcy petition may depend on the law of the state in which the LLC is organized (statutory authority) and the provisions of the operating agreement (contractual authority).

In regard to statutory authority, for example, although the authority of a general partner to file bankruptcy on behalf of a general partnership is found in Bankruptcy Rule 1004(a), the authority of individuals to file on behalf of corporations is typically based on state corporate law,[2] and rests with the board of directors.[3] In an LLC, the statutory authority of managers or members to file a bankruptcy petition on behalf of the LLC is based on state law,[4] and is also less apparent; many state statutes do not directly address the ability of the LLC to file a voluntary petition, although some do.[5] Even without direct statutory authority, at least three courts have found specific indirect statutory authority,[6] and most

---

[1] In relevant part, 11 U.S.C. § 109 provides that "persons" may be a debtor under the Title; § 101(41) defines "person" as including an individual, partnership, or corporation; and § 101(9) defines the term "corporation" as including an unincorporated company or association, which includes the LLC.

[2] Price v. Gurney, 324 U.S. 100, 106–107, 65 S. Ct. 513, 516 (1945) ("The District Court in passing on petitions filed by corporations under [the Bankruptcy Code] must of course determine whether they are filed by those who have authority so to act. In absence of federal incorporation, that authority finds its source in local law."); Phillips v. First City, Texas-Tyler, N.A. (*In re* Phillips), 966 F.2d 926, 934 (5th Cir. 1992) ("[L]ook to state law to determine which people have authority to seek federal bankruptcy protection on behalf of state-created business entities.").

[3] *See, e.g., In re* Giggles Restaurant, Inc., 103 B.R. 549, 552–53 (Bankr. D. N.J. 1989) ("In the absence of a provision to the contrary, New Jersey law provides that the business and affairs of a corporation shall be managed by its board."). *See also* DEL. CODE ANN. tit. 8, § 141 (a) (West) ("The business and affairs of every corporation . . . shall be managed by or under the direction of a board of directors . . .").

[4] *See, e.g., In re* A-Z Electronics LLC, 350 B.R. 886, 889 (Bankr. D. Idaho 2006) ("State law, not bankruptcy law, is used to determine whether the party signing the entity petition had the authority to do so."); *In re* H & W Food Mart, LLC, 461 B.R. 904 (Bankr. N.D. Ga. 2011) (holding that bankruptcy petition filed on behalf of LLC was not authorized based on Georgia law and provisions in the operating agreement).

[5] MD. CODE, CORPS. & ASS'NS § 4a-403(d)(2) (providing that, unless otherwise agreed in the operating agreement, a member may not file a voluntary petition on behalf of the LLC without unanimous consent of the members).

[6] *See, e.g., In re* Avalon Hotel Partners, LLC, 302 B.R. 377, 380–81 (Bankr. D. Or. 2003) (holding the decision to file bankruptcy on behalf of the LLC should fall under the decisions requiring consent under OR. REV. STAT. ANN. § 63.130(4)(f), because "a decision to convert an LLC

others presuppose that LLCs have statutory authority to file a petition. In at least one case, the personal bankruptcy of a single-member LLC's only member removed the member's statutory authority to file a bankruptcy petition on behalf of the LLC.[7]

The contractual authority of a member or manager to file bankruptcy on behalf of an LLC may vary based on the language in the operating agreement or other organizational documents.[8] In fact, language in an operating agreement stating that "all decisions" must be made by majority consent may be enforced in the bankruptcy context.[9] Similarly, an operating agreement that was silent on the specific issue of authority to file bankruptcy but that granted broad authority to the managing member to act on behalf of the LLC was interpreted as granting authority to the managing member to file bankruptcy on behalf of the LLC.[10] Both of these circumstances support the contention that operating

---

into any other type of entity [including a debtor-in-possession] requires the consent of a majority of the members"); *In re* Delta Starr Broadcasting, LLC, No. Civ. A. 05-2783, 2006 WL 285974 (Bankr. E.D. La. Feb. 6, 2006) (referencing LA. REV. STAT. ANN. § 12:1318(B) which provides that certain extraordinary decisions require a majority vote (unless otherwise provided in the articles of organization or operating agreement) and that the decision to file bankruptcy was such an extraordinary decision, though the statute did not mention bankruptcy specifically); *In re* East End Dev., LLC, 491 B.R. 633, 638–39 (Bankr. E.D.N.Y. 2013) (holding that the affairs of an LLC are governed by state law and the LLC operating agreement, and finding indirect authority for the managing member to file a bankruptcy petition despite the fact that the operating agreement and state law default rules were silent on the specific issue).

[7] *In re* A-Z Electronics LLC, 350 B.R. 886 (Bankr. D. Idaho 2006) (U.S. Trustee successfully moved to convert or dismiss LLC's Chapter 11 petition for "cause" because the LLC's single member lacked authority to file the petition); *see also In re* B & M Land & Livestock, LLC, 498 B.R. 262 (Bankr. D. Nev. 2013) (same).

[8] *In re* Crossover Financial I, LLC, 477 B.R. 196 (Bankr. D. Colo. 2012) (discussing and enforcing the operating agreement delegation of power to the manager to make *all* decisions concerning the business affairs of the company); *In re* H & W Food Mart, LLC, 461 B.R. 904, 907–08 (Bankr. N.D. Ga. 2011) (manager of LLC who had filed personal bankruptcy not authorized to file petition on behalf of LLC); *In re* Carolina Park Assocs., LLC, 430 B.R. 744 (Bankr. D. S.C. 2010) (holding that second member's lack of consent to filing constituted a failure of the filer to satisfy a condition precedent to filing a bankruptcy petition on behalf of the LLC and dismissing bankruptcy case), *vac'd on other grounds*, No. 2:10-CV-1805-DCN, 2010 WL 3893628 (D. S.C. Sept. 30, 2010); *In re* Orchard at Hansen Park, LLC, 347 B.R. 822 (Bankr. N.D. Tex. 2006) (enforcing provisions of the operating agreement that required unanimous member consent to file a voluntary bankruptcy petition on behalf of the LLC); *In re* TAGT, L.P., 393 B.R. 143 (Bankr. S.D. Tex. 2006) (noting member of LLC had no authority to file bankruptcy on behalf of LLC where LLC's organizational documents delegated such authority to the LLC's managers), *aff'd sub nom In re* Yorkshire, LLC, 540 F.3d 328 (5th Cir. 2008); *In re* Avalon Hotel Partners, LLC, 302 B.R. 377, 380–81 (Bankr. D. Or. 2003) (discussing the "major decisions" requirements in the operating agreement, and applying those requirements to bankruptcy, though it did not specifically discuss bankruptcy). *See also In re* East End Dev., LLC, 491 B.R. 633 (Bankr. E.D.N.Y. 2013).

[9] *In re* 210 West Liberty Holdings, LLC, No. 08-677, 2009 WL 1522047 (Bankr. N.D.W. Va. May 29, 2009) (provision that "all decisions" be made by majority vote is sufficient to allow bankruptcy filing over member objection because objecting member's approval not necessary to constitute majority); *In re* Ice Oasis, LLC, No. 08-31522 TEC, 2008 WL 5753355 (Bankr. N.D. Cal. Nov. 7, 2008) (bankruptcy of two-member LLC required consent of both members because of provision that all decisions must be made by majority consent).

[10] *In re* East End Dev., LLC, 491 B.R. 633, 638–39 (Bankr. E.D.N.Y. 2013) (granting authority to file on behalf of the LLC in the managing member without consent of the other member

agreement language should be thoughtfully chosen. Additionally, if the LLC's organizational documents prescribe certain procedures for the entity to file bankruptcy, adherence to those procedures will likely be upheld in court.[11]

Can a Creditor Block or Prevent the LLC from Filing for Bankruptcy?

In some, so far unique, circumstances a creditor may be able to block or prevent an LLC from filing for bankruptcy. In one instance, a creditor who was eventually granted an equity interest in the LLC in connection with a short-term bridge loan it provided was able to prevent the LLC from filing a voluntary bankruptcy petition, due to the protections granted to it as an equity holder in the operating agreement.[12] In another instance, a creditor successfully had an LLC's bankruptcy case dismissed because the person who filed the petition lacked authority under the terms of an LLC Pledge Agreement between the LLC and the creditor, and also under the operating agreement.[13] However, in another case, a secured creditor was not able to block or prevent an LLC from filing for bankruptcy, though the creditor argued that the LLC operating agreement prohibited a bankruptcy filing and that, even if the filing had been permitted, the manager was not authorized to file the petition without the unanimous affirmative vote of all the members.[14]

In addition, although a contractual provision prohibiting the filing of a bankruptcy petition is generally unenforceable as against public policy,[15] in one case it has successfully prevented an LLC from filing bankruptcy (or more accurately, precipitated the dismissal of the case).[16]

---

even though the operating agreement was silent on the issue, noting "[t]he Operating Agreement confers broad powers upon the Managing Member to act on behalf of the Debtor . . . [i]n contrast, the actions for which the Managing Member must obtain the consent of [the other member] are narrow and specific").

[11] *See In re* Green Power Kenansville, LLC, No. 04-08384-8-JRL, 2004 WL 5413067 (Bankr. E.D. N.C. Nov. 18, 2004).

[12] *In re* Global Ship Sys., LLC, 391 B.R. 193, 203 (Bankr. S.D. Ga. 2007).

[13] *In re* Green Power Kenansville, LLC, No. 04-08384-8-JRL, 2004 WL 5413067 (Bankr. E.D. N.C. Nov. 18, 2004). The *Green Power* LLC Pledge Agreement provided that the sole member of the LLC would not allow a change of control of the LLC and upon an event of default, all of the member's voting rights would transfer to the lender. Additionally, the operating agreement provided that the Independent Manager could not be removed without the approval of all the members and all the material creditors. Despite these provisions, and after an event of default, the original member allegedly effected a change in control, which allegedly resulted in a new Independent Manager who filed the bankruptcy petition. The petition was dismissed because this new independent manager did not have the proper authority to file.

[14] *In re* Bay Club Partners-472, LLC, 59 B.C.D. 127 (Bankr. D. Ore. 2014). The secured creditor in *Bay Club* tried something clever by having the prohibition against bankruptcy language included in the LLC operating agreement along with its requests for other restrictive covenants instead of including the bankruptcy waiver provision in a loan agreement. The court noted this was "cleverly insidious" . . . and is "a distinction without a meaningful difference."

[15] *See id.* ("The Ninth Circuit has been very clear that a debtor's prepetition waiver of the right to file a bankruptcy case is unenforceable because it is a violation of public policy.").

[16] DB Capital Holdings, LLC v. Aspen HH Ventures LLC (*In re* DB Capital Holdings, LLC), 463 B.R. 142 (B.A.P. 10th 2010) (table decision) (A creditor successfully had an LLC's bankruptcy case dismissed because it was filed without authority, due to provisions in the operating agreement

Can the Creditor File an Involuntary Bankruptcy against the LLC?

Several courts have allowed involuntary petitions to be filed against LLCs under section 303 of the Bankruptcy Code.[17] The burden is on creditors that join in filing an involuntary petition to establish that they are qualified to do so,[18] and a creditor's eligibility to join an involuntary petition is determined at the time of the filing.[19]

Is the LLC's Operating Agreement an Executory Contract?

Section 365 of the Bankruptcy Code provides that, with some exceptions, a trustee "may assume or reject any executory contract or unexpired lease of the debtor."[20] The trustee's powers to act are applicable to debtors in possession as well through section 1107(a) of the Bankruptcy Code. For example, the authority to assume or reject an executory contract may be useful if the LLC seeks to shed itself of a particular member.[21]

The Bankruptcy Code does not define the term executory contract. As a result, courts generally look to the well-known Countryman definition, which provides that an executory contract is one "under which the obligation of both the bankrupt and the other party to the contract are so far unperformed that the failure of either to complete performance would constitute a material breach excusing the performance of the other."[22]

---

that: (1) expressly prohibited filing for bankruptcy, (2) required the manager to "conduct and operate its business *as presently conducted*"; and (3) provided that the Manager was to cease operating as the manager upon a bankruptcy filing of the debtor). *See also In re* NNN 123 North Wacker, LLC, 59 B.C.D. 157 (Bankr. N.D. Ill. 2014) (holding that an agreement between the LLC members limiting the power of the LLC to file bankruptcy may be valid and citing *In re DB Capital Holdings, LLC*); Green Bridge Capital S.A. v. Shapiro (*In re* FKF Madison Park Group Owner, LLC), No. 10-11857, 2011 WL 350306 (Bankr. D. Del. Jan. 31, 2011) (managing member was not authorized to convert involuntary chapter 7 case to chapter 11 due to operating agreement provision indicating unanimous written consent was required).

[17] *In re* Basil Street Partners, LLC, 477 B.R. 846, 849 (Bankr. M.D. Fla. 2012); *In re* AMC Investors, LLC, 406 B.R. 478, 483 (Bankr. D. Del. 2009); *In re* ELRS Loss Mitigation, LLC, 325 B.R. 604, 624 (Bankr. N.D. Okla. 2005).

[18] *In re* ELRS Loss Mitigation, LLC, 325 B.R. at 614; *In re* Rosenberg, 414 B.R. 826, 840 (Bankr. S.D. Fla. 2009), *aff'd*, 472 Fed. Appx. 890 (11th Cir. 2012) (unpublished). *See generally* Riverview Trenton RR Co. v. DSC, Ltd. (*In re* DSC, Ltd.), 486 F.3d 940, 944 (6th Cir. 2007).

[19] *In re* Green Hills Dev. Co., LLC, 445 B.R. 647, 654–55 (Bankr. S.D. Miss. 2011) (citing *In re* Smith, 437 B.R. 817–22 (Bankr. N.D. Tex. 2010)), *aff'd*, 741 F.3d 651 (5th Cir. 2014).

[20] 11 U.S.C. §§ 365(a), 1107(a).

[21] Dye v. Sandman Assocs., LLC (*In re* Sandman Assocs., LLC), 251 B.R. 473 (W.D. Va. 2000) (holding that LLC operating agreement in this case was not an executory contract and thus the LLC could not get rid of the dissenting member).

[22] Vern Countryman, *Executory Contracts in Bankruptcy: Part I*, 57 MINN. L. REV. 439, 460 (1973). *See, e.g.*, Gouveia v. Tazbir, 37 F.3d 295, 298–99 (7th Cir. 1994) ("[A] contract under which the bankrupt and the other party both are obligated, that such obligation remains unperformed by either party, and that failure of either to complete performance would constitute a material breach excusing the other of performance."). Northwest Airlines, Inc. v. Klinger (*In re* Knutson), 563 F.2d 916, 917 (8th Cir. 1977). *See also* Mason v. Official Comm. of Unsecured Creditors (*In re* FBI Distrib. Corp.), 330 F.3d 36, 40 n. 5 (1st Cir. 2003); ReGen Capital I, Inc. v. Halperin (*In re* Wireless Data, Inc.), 547 F.3d 484, 488 n. 1 (2d Cir. 2008); Enterprise Energy Corp. v. U.S. (*In re* Columbia Gas Sys. Inc.), 50 F.3d 233, 238 (3d Cir. 1995); Gloria Mfg. Corp. v. Int'l Ladies' Garment Workers'

Although *most* courts, when considering a partnership agreement, find that the agreement is an executory contract *per se*,[23] many courts view LLC operating agreements differently, holding that each *particular* operating agreement must be analyzed to determine if it qualifies as an executory contract under the Countryman definition; outcomes vary based on the particular circumstances.[24] For instance, in one case the non-debtor member sought to establish that the LLC operating agreement was an executory contract because the members had ongoing unperformed obligations as fiduciaries for one another and the LLC.[25] The court rejected this argument, stating that the member did not establish that applicable state law recognized fiduciary duties between members of a manager-managed LLC.[26]

Union, 734 F.2d 1020, 1021–22 (4th Cir. 1984) (citing H.R. Rep. No. 595, 95th Cong., 1st Sess. 220 (1977)).

[23] Breeden v. Catron (*In re* Catron), 158 B.R. 629, 632 (E.D. Va. 1993) (holding that a partnership agreement is an executory contract; also holding the partnership agreement constitutes a contract whereby the members agree to perform services—a non-assignable under applicable law—thus the contract may not be assumed or assigned unless the other members consent to the assumption or assignment) (citing 11 U.S.C. §§ 365(c)(1), 1107(a)), *aff'd*, 25 F.3d 1038 (4th Cir. 1994); *In re* Priestly, 93 B.R. 253, 258–59 (Bankr. D. N.M. 1988) (partnership agreement is an executory contract); Burley v. Am. Gas & Oil Investors (*In re* Heafitz), 85 B.R. 274 (Bankr. S.D. N.Y. 1988) (same); *In re* Corky Foods Corp., 85 B.R. 903, 904 (Bankr. S.D. Fla. 1988) (same); *In re* Sunset Developers, 69 B.R. 710, 712–13 (Bankr. D. Idaho 1987) (same); Skeen v. Harms (*In re* Harms), 10 B.R. 817, 821 (Bankr. D. Colo. 1981) (same). *Cf.* Samson v. Prokopf (*In re* Smith), 185 B.R. 285, 293–94 (Bankr. S.D. Ill. 1995) (holding the limited partnership agreement in question was not an executory contract).

[24] *See* Endeka Enters, LLC v. Meiburger (*In re* Tsiaouchis), No. 1:07CV436, 2007 WL 2156162 (Bankr. E.D. Va. July 19, 2007) (noting that partnership agreements are considered executory contracts *per se* "solely because partners owe fiduciary duties to each other and to the partnership"; as such, the court held that each particular operating agreement must be analyzed in order to determine if it qualifies as an executory contract); Allentown Ambassadors, Inc. v. N.E. Am. Baseball, LLC (*In re* Allentown Ambassadors, Inc.), 361 B.R. 422 (Bankr. E.D. Pa. 2007) (holding operating agreement is an executory contract because material, unperformed obligations remained on both sides); *In re* Capital Acquisitions & Mgmt. Corp., 341 B.R. 632 (Bankr. N.D. Ill. 2006) (holding operating agreement was not an executory contract utilizing similar analysis); *In re* Daugherty Const., Inc., 188 B.R. 607, 612–13 (Bankr. D. Neb. 1995) (holding operating agreement was executory contract using Countryman analysis); *In re* Garrison-Ashburn, L.C., 253 B.R. 700, 708–09 (Bankr. E.D. Va. 2000) (analyzing the specific operating agreement and holding it is not an executory contract because it "merely provides the structure for the management of the company . . . [and] imposes no additional duties or responsibilities on the members"). *See also In re* Knowles, No. 6:11-bk-11717-KSJ, 2013 WL 152434 (Bankr. M.D. Fla. Jan. 15, 2013) (holding that the operating agreement was not executory because "the Debtor's ongoing management and capital contribution duties are remote, improbable, or extremely speculative"); *In re* Strata Title, LLC, No. 12-24242, 2013 WL 1773619 (Bankr. D. Ariz. Apr. 25, 2013) (holding operating agreement was executory contract); *In re* Alameda Inv., LLC, No. 6:09-BK-10348-PC, 2013 WL 3216129 (Bankr. C.D. Ca. June 25, 2013) (holding operating agreement not an executory contract), *aff'd*, 2014 WL 868605 (B.A.P. 9th Cir. 2014); Sheehan v. Warner (*In re* Warner), 480 B.R. 641 (Bankr. N.D. W.V. 2012) (operating agreement not executory contract).

[25] *See Endeka Enters, supra* note 24.

[26] *Id.* (also noting that the debtor member had no duties as a manager or director and LLC operating agreement explicitly allowed members to engage in independent activities).

Will the Bankruptcy Court Enforce Prepetition Contractual Agreements between the Creditor and the LLC?

In general, whether the Bankruptcy Court will enforce prepetition contractual agreements between an LLC and a creditor depends on: (1) whether the contract qualifies as an executory contract and (2) whether statutory or common law precludes assignment of the contract without consent of the non-debtor.[27]

In *In re Green Power Kenansville, LLC*, the Bankruptcy Court did enforce prepetition contractual agreements between the creditor and the LLC. These agreements included a Pledge Agreement that prohibited the LLC from filing a bankruptcy petition and also provided that the membership interests (including voting rights) of the single member of the LLC would transfer to the creditor upon default.[28]

Whether a prepetition agreement regarding relief from the automatic stay will be enforceable depends on a variety of factors.[29] These factors include, for example, whether the debtor filed the bankruptcy petition in bad faith, whether there is a possibility of effective reorganization,[30] or whether the case involves a single-asset debtor.[31] Insofar as a pre-petition waiver affects the rights of third parties not bound by the agreement and

---

[27] See *In re* Footstar, Inc., 337 B.R. 785 (Bankr. S.D. N.Y. 2005); *see also In re* Dewey Ranch Hockey, LLC, 406 B.R. 30, 36 (Bankr. D. Ariz. 2009).

[28] *In re* Green Power Kenansville, LLC, No. 04-08384-8-JRL, 2004 WL 5413067 (Bankr. E.D. N.C. Nov. 18, 2004).

[29] *In re* Frye, 320 B.R. 786, 790–91 (Bankr. D. Vt. 2005) (laying out ten factors that may be considered by a court in determining whether to enforce a prepetition waiver of the automatic stay and noting "[t]he weight given to each factor will vary on a case-by-case basis and must be left to the sound discretion of the court, based upon the equities, facts and circumstances presented. Similarly, the determination of whether a hearing is necessary to make findings on some of these factors must be made on a case-by-case basis, depending upon the record available to the court") (citing *In re* Atrium High Point Ltd. P'ship, 189 B.R. 599 (Bankr. M.D.N.C. 1995)), *subsequent determination*, 323 B.R. 396 (Bankr. D. Vt.), *amended*, 2005 WL 1915845 (Bankr. D. Vt.), *denying stay*, 2005 WL 1285833 (Bankr. D. Vt. 2005).

[30] See *In re* 4848, LLC, 490 B.R. 343 (E.D. Wisc. 2013) (granting motion to lift the automatic stay where debtor's proposed plan did not have reasonable possibility of being confirmed within reasonable period of time); *In re* Jenkins Court Assocs. L.P., 181 B.R. 33 (E.D. Pa. 1995) (declining to enforce the prepetition waiver of the automatic stay without a full evidentiary hearing, and discussing the various factors deserving consideration in the decision); *In re* Club Tower, L.P., 138 B.R. 307, 310–11 (N.D. Ga. 1991) (enforcing prepetition waiver of automatic stay because petition filed in bad faith); *In re* Sky Group Int'l, Inc., 108 B.R. 86 (Bankr. W.D. Pa. 1989) (refusing to enforce a prepetition waiver of automatic stay because debtor had significant equity cushion in underlying assets).

[31] *In re* Trans World Airlines, Inc., 261 B.R. 103, 116 (Bankr. D. Del. 2001) (noting that argument in favor of enforcing a prepetition waiver of the automatic stay is strongest in single asset real estate cases); *see also* LSREF2 Baron, LLC v. Alexander SRP Apts., LLC (*In re* Alexander SRP Apts., LLC), No. 12-20272, 2012 WL 1910088 (Bankr. S.D. Ga. 2012); *In re* Jenkins Court Assocs. L.P., 181 B.R. at 37 (declining to enforce the waiver and stating that in single-asset cases, "there may be little significant distinction between enforcement of a prepetition waiver of the automatic stay . . . and enforcement of a provision prohibiting the filing of a bankruptcy case in the first place"). *See also In re* DB Capital Holdings, LLC, 454 B.R. 804, 813–14 (Bankr. D. Colo. 2011) (holding the prepetition waiver was not enforceable against the single-asset debtor, but granting creditor relief from stay because debtor could not provide adequate protection).

the prepetition agreement alters the debtor-in-possession's rights, obligations, and duties under federal bankruptcy law, the waiver will likely be held unenforceable.[32]

Members who are also creditors may be treated differently, depending on the circumstances. In *O'Donnell v. Tristar Esperanza Props.* (*In re Tristar Esperanza Props., LLC*), 488 B.R. 394 (B.A.P. 9th Cir. 2013), the Bankruptcy Court and the Bankruptcy Appellate Panel enforced both the buy-back provision and the arbitration award in favor of the departing member based on the debtor LLC's operating agreement. The courts, however, determined that the departing member's claim should be subordinated to those of the of the debtor's unsecured creditors.

In addition, the Bankruptcy Court generally will not enforce prepetition contractual agreements between a creditor and a member if it involves a pledge of the member's interest that requires prior approval of fellow members.[33]

Can a Creditor Enforce a Charging Order in Bankruptcy?

As a preliminary matter, a charging order must be perfected prior to the debtor's filing the bankruptcy petition in order for there to be any prospect of enforcement in bankruptcy.[34] In *In re Raiton*,[35] the court, applying the California Commercial Code, held that the prepetition charging order was a lien that could be enforced in bankruptcy. Moreover, the court held that the lien was superior to security interests that were perfected at a later date and that this particular "lien [was] superior to the debtor in possession's interest as a 'hypothetical lien creditor.'"[36]

A charging order that is not enforced in bankruptcy may survive postpetition if applicable state law provides that a charging order creates a lien. In *In re Keeler*, the court held that a prepetition charging order on the debtor's partnership interest was a lien and that "although any action to collect upon the lien was stayed during the bankruptcy, the lien itself 'rode through' the bankruptcy case" and the creditor was not required to file a proof of claim in order to protect the lien.[37]

Not all states, however, treat a charging order as a lien. In *Monroe v. Berger*,[38] the court discussed the creditor's efforts to collect on a charging order both during and after

---

[32] *See, e.g., In re* Trans World Airlines, Inc., 261 B.R. at 114–15 (noting the Bankruptcy Court must approve lifting the stay, and other creditors have the right to object, regardless of the prepetition agreement); *In re* Sky Group Int'l, Inc. 108 B.R. at 89 ("To grant a creditor relief from stay simply because the *debtor* elected to waive the protection afforded the debtor by the automatic stay ignores the fact that it also is designed to protect *all creditors* and to treat them *equally*. The orderly liquidation procedure contemplated by the Code would be placed in jeopardy . . .").

[33] *In re* Weiss, 376 B.R. 867 (N.D. Ill. 2007) (individual debtor and member of LLC pledged his interest in the LLC to creditors, however, the debtor had no authority to pledge the interest without the consent of the other members).

[34] *In re* Jaffe, 235 B.R. 490 (Bankr. S.D. Fla. 1999).

[35] Raiton v. G&R Props. (*In re* Raiton), 139 B.R. 931, 936 (B.A.P. 9th Cir. 1992).

[36] *Id.* (citing *In re* Stocks, 110 B.R. 65, 67 (Bankr. N.D. Fla. 1989)).

[37] Keeler v. Academy of Am. Franciscan History, Inc. (*In re* Keeler), 257 B.R. 442, 448 (Bankr. D. Md. 2001) (citing Dewsnup v. Timm, 502 U.S. 410, 416 (1992); Cen-Pen v. Hanson, 58 F.3d 89, 92–93 (4th Cir. 1995)), *aff'd*, 273 B.R. 416 (D. Md. 2002).

[38] Monroe v. Berger, 297 B.R. 97 (Bankr. S.D. Ohio 2003).

the debtor's bankruptcy; the claim was discussed and deemed virtually worthless by the Bankruptcy Court, and, though the underlying asset increased in value afterwards, the creditor could not then seek to enforce it. Because the creditor's charging order was not a lien under Ohio law, it did not "ride through" bankruptcy; it was discharged.

Can a Creditor Pursue Non-debtor Parties despite the LLC's Bankruptcy Case?

Most states' LLC legislation indicates that an LLC and its members are separate entities and recognizes that LLC property is distinct from member assets.[39] Generally, courts also recognize this distinction.[40] In addition, the automatic stay generally may not be invoked to protect non-debtors,[41] and creditors may pursue non-debtor parties such as guarantors.[42] Even so, the Bankruptcy Court may issue an injunction barring creditor pursuit of non-debtor parties, including guarantors, if "necessary or appropriate to carry out the provisions of [the Bankruptcy Code]."[43]

Does the Bankruptcy of a Member Affect the LLC (and in Turn the LLC's Creditors)?

When a member of an LLC files for bankruptcy, all of the debtor's legal or equitable interests on the date of filing become part of the debtor's bankruptcy estate.[44] There is some disagreement whether the entirety—both the economic and non-economic rights—of a debtor's membership interest in the LLC become property of the estate and remain intact.[45] This distinction may have a significant effect on the recovery of the member's creditors.

---

[39] DEL. CODE ANN. tit. 6, § 18-701 (West); MD. CODE ANN., CORPS. & ASS'NS §§ 4A-301, 4A-602, (West) (describing membership interest in LLC as personal property of the member, and stating no member is personally liable for the obligations of the LLC unless otherwise agreed); NEV. REV. STAT. ANN. §§ 86.351, 86.371 (West) (substantially similar to Maryland).

[40] See, e.g., In re HSM Kennewick, L.P., 347 B.R. 569, 571–72 (Bankr. N.D. Tex. 2006) (applying the corporate principle—that a corporation and its stockholders are separate entities and title to corporate property is vested in the corporation—to both partnerships and limited liability companies).

[41] See Saxby's Coffee Worldwide, LLC v. Larson (*In re* Saxby's Coffee Worldwide, LLC), 440 B.R. 369, 378 (Bankr. E.D. Pa. 2009) (citing McCartney v. Integra Nat'l Bank North, 106 F.3d 506, 509–10 (3d Cir. 1997)).

[42] Gander Partners LLC v. Harris Bank, N.A. (*In re* Gander Partners LLC), 432 B.R. 781, 187 (Bankr. N.D. Ill. 2010), aff'd, 442 B.R. 883 (N.D. Ill. 2011), *subsequently vac'd.*

[43] *In re* Saxby's Coffee Worldwide, LLC, 440 B.R. at 378 & n.11, 379 (Bankr. E.D. Pa. 2009) (citing and discussing 11 U.S.C. § 362, and discussing three circumstances in which entry of injunction restraining creditors from proceeding against non-debtors may be appropriate); *see also In re* Brier Creek Corp. Ctr. Assoc. Ltd., 486 B.R. 681, 684–85 (Bankr. E.D. N.C. 2013) (extending automatic stay to non-debtor guarantors under "unusual circumstances" exception).

[44] 11 U.S.C. § 541.

[45] *See In re* Garrison-Ashburn, L.C., 253 B.R. 700, 707–08 (Bankr. E.D. Va. 2000) (holding that though both the economic and non-economic rights of the bankrupt member become property of the estate, the non-economic rights terminate); Klingerman v. ExecuCorp, LLC (*In re* Klingerman), 388 B.R. 677 (Bankr. E.D. N.C. 2008) (holding that both the economic and non-economic rights become property of the estate and remain intact); LaHood & FLLZ, LLC v. Covey (*In re* LaHood), 437 B.R. 330, 336 (Bankr. C.D. Ill 2010) (same as *Klingerman*).

Many state LLC Acts specify that, as a default rule, bankruptcy of a member will be an event of dissociation,[46] and will lead to the bankrupt ceasing to be a member.[47] The dissociation may result in the member losing rights the member enjoyed prepetition; the member may not lose any rights;[48] or may lose only non-economic rights upon filing a bankruptcy petition.[49] Provisions in an operating agreement that purport to deprive a member debtor of both economic and non-economic rights in the LLC upon filing a bankruptcy petition, however, will not likely be upheld because such clauses are pre-empted by federal bankruptcy law.[50] Depending on the circumstances, creditors may be able to recover more when the non-economic rights are included in the debtor's estate.

Additionally, the bankruptcy of a member could benefit (or, theoretically harm) the member's creditors because of the law of preferences. A member's prepetition removal from an LLC or the member's prepetition assignment of his membership rights could be avoided as a preference, thus potentially adding value to the member's estate.[51] In *In re*

---

[46] *See, e.g.*, HAW. REV. STAT. ANN. § 428-601 (West); ILL. COMP. STAT. ANN. § 180/35-45 (West); N.J. STAT. ANN. § 42:2B-24 (West); VA. CODE ANN. § 13.1-1040.1 (West).

[47] *See, e.g.*, DEL. CODE ANN. tit. 6, § 18-304 (West) ("A person ceases to be a member of a limited liability company upon the happening of any of the following events: (1) Unless otherwise provided in [the operating agreement] or with consent of all the members, a member: (a) makes an assignment for the benefit of creditors; (b) files a voluntary petition in bankruptcy; (c) is adjudged a bankrupt or insolvent . . ."); MD. CODE ANN., CORPS. & ASS'NS § 4A-606 (West); N.C. GEN. STAT. ANN. § 57c-3-02 (West). *Cf.* NEV. REV. STAT. ANN. § 86.491 (West) ("Except as otherwise provided in the section, the articles of organization or the operating agreement, the . . . bankruptcy . . . [of] a member, including, without limitation, a sole member, does not: (a) terminate the status of the person as a member . . ."). *But see*, Duncan v. Dixie Mgmt. & Inv., L.P. (*In re* Dixie Mgmt. & Inv., L.P.), 474 B.R. 698, 701 (Bankr. W.D. Ark. 2011) (holding that the state's LLC Act—providing that bankruptcy of a member results in dissociation—was ineffective due to the conflict with Federal Bankruptcy Law and Supremacy Clause).

[48] *See, e.g.*, Sheehan v. Warner (*In re* Warner), 480 B.R. 641 (Bankr. N.D. W.Va. 2012) (allowing trustee of bankrupt member to step into shoes of member, with full economic and non-economic rights in the LLC as if the bankruptcy had never occurred, despite the fact that the debtor's bankruptcy caused the debtor to have no right to participate in the business of the company); Klingerman v. ExecuCorp, LLC (*In re* Klingerman), 388 B.R. 677 (Bankr. E.D. N.C. 2008) (despite a clause in the operating agreement indicating the member of the LLC would cease to be a member upon filing bankruptcy, the bankrupt member was able to commence a proceeding to compel the LLC's dissolution).

[49] *See, e.g.*, Spain v Williams (*In re* Williams), 455 B.R. 485, 501–02 (Bankr. E.D. Va. 2011) (where both of the only interest-holders in an LLC filed for bankruptcy, triggering dissociation and leaving them without non-economic rights, no one remained to wind up the business affairs of LLC; trustee was appointed to liquidate LLC); *In re* Garrison-Ashburn, L.C. 253 B.R. 700, 707–08 (Bankr. E.D. Va. 2000) (though *all* the member's LLC rights and privileges came into the bankruptcy estate, so did the duties and obligations, meaning the bankruptcy estate would only have the rights of an assignee of the membership interest under the applicable statute and, ultimately, only the economic rights); The IT Group, Inc., Co., v. The Shaw Group Inc. (*In re* IT Group, Inc., Co.), 302 B.R. 483, 487 (D. Del. 2003) (holding provision in operating agreement purporting to deprive the debtor of economic rights upon bankruptcy unenforceable).

[50] Milford Power Co, LLC v. PDC Milford Power, LLC, 866 A.2d 738 (Del. Ch. 2004).

[51] *See also* Garcia v. Garcia (*In re* Garcia), 507 B.R. 434 (Bankr. E.D.N.Y. 2014). In *Garcia*, an individual chapter 11 debtor brought an adversary proceeding to set aside a prepetition transfer of his membership interest in an LLC as a constructively fraudulent transfer or a preference, after the other members had expelled him for taking excess distributions. The Court determined that the

Lull, a member's removal from an LLC for the alleged failure to make promised contributions was deemed a preferential transfer to the remaining members of the LLC, increasing the value of the debtor member's estate.[52]

Notably, the creditors of an individual member in bankruptcy may be permitted to intervene in the LLC bankruptcy if certain conditions are met. In *In re Hyde Park P'ship*, one of the individual partners and the partnership were both in bankruptcy and the creditors' committee in the individual's bankruptcy case sought to intervene in the partnership bankruptcy case as a party in interest under 11 U.S.C. § 1109(b).[53] The court first noted that, for bankruptcy purposes, a partnership is separate and distinct from its partners and noted that the proposed intervenors had not met the burden of demonstrating inadequate representation, their interest in the outcome of the partnership's bankruptcy was contingent, and the intervention would cause undue delay and a significant unnecessary increase in costs. The creditor of an individual debtor member thus may be able to intervene in the LLC's bankruptcy case by establishing one or more of these factors.

Lastly, unscrupulous behavior by an individual LLC member in bankruptcy could benefit creditors; in an unusual case, the individual member's creditor was able to exercise rights (obtained postpetition) against the debtor's non-debtor LLC, though the creditor's original claim was against the member and not the LLC.[54]

4. ADDITIONAL CONSIDERATIONS FOR THE SERIES LLC

A number of states permit companies to operate multiple businesses under a common organizational umbrella referred to as a series LLC.[55] The series LLC typically features

---

transfer of the debtor's membership interest was not a fraudulent conveyance because he received reasonably equivalent value and the transfer was not a preference because it was not "for or on account of an antecedent debt owed by the debtor before such transfer was made."

[52] Kotoshirodo v. Dorland & Assoc., Inc. (*In re* Lull), No. 06-00898, 2008 WL 3895561 (Bankr. D. Haw. Aug. 22, 2008) (construing the definition of "transfer" in § 547(b) broadly, finding the transfer was made when the debtor was insolvent and within 90 days of the filing of the petition, finding that the effect of the transfer enabled the other member to receive more than he would have received under chapter 7 if the transfer had not occurred, and noting the parties agreed that there was an antecedent debt at issue in the case). *Cf.* Garcia v. Garcia (*In re* Garcia), 494 B.R. 799 (Bankr. E.D.N.Y. 2013) (a member's prepetition removal from an LLC was not deemed a preferential transfer to the remaining members because the transfer did not occur "'for or on account of an antecedent debt' as required by § 547(b)(2)" but occurred in accordance with the terms of the LLC's operating agreements and in response to the removed member's misconduct).

[53] 73 B.R. 194 (Bankr. N.D. Ohio 1986).

[54] Desmond v. U.S. Asset Funding, L.P. (*In re* Desmond), 316 B.R. 593 (Bankr. D. N.H. 2004). In *Desmond*, the sole and managing member of an LLC filed a bankruptcy petition in his individual capacity; the LLC did not file a petition and the individual debtor treated the LLC as a separate entity and did not inform the court of the LLC's business dealings. Postpetition, the debtor, acting as an individual and as manager of the LLC, entered into a transactional agreement with a creditor without the approval of the court. Thereafter the debtor unsuccessfully sought to enjoin the creditor from exercising its rights against the non-debtor LLC.

[55] These states are Delaware, Illinois, Iowa, Kansas, Nevada, Oklahoma, Tennessee, Texas, Utah, and Wisconsin. Both the District of Columbia and Puerto Rico have series LLC statutes as well.

a "master" or "parent" LLC with one or more separate businesses organized as limited liability companies (each a "series") under the master LLC. The relationship between the master and the series LLCs is determined by the limited liability company agreement and may be referenced in the articles of organization or certificate of formation filed with the state where the entity is organized. Distressed series LLCs face many of the same issues as other unincorporated entities, and often many more challenges because of their unique treatment under state law. For certain purposes, state law views the master LLC and the related series as one entity, yet for other purposes—primarily asset ownership and liability allocation—state law treats the master and each series as distinct entities.[56] Moreover, the series LLC is a relatively recent innovation and there is limited case law dealing with insolvent series LLCs.[57]

Because of the bifurcated treatment of series LLCs under state law—i.e., sometimes treated as the same entity, sometimes treated as separate distinct entities—several questions regarding their insolvency remain unresolved. Based on the definition of who can be a debtor, the master LLC should qualify as a debtor under the Bankruptcy Code. It is unclear, however, what would happen to the series if the master seeks bankruptcy protection or what may happen to the master or the other series if one series seeks bankruptcy protection. More basically, there may be a question of whether a single series could file independently from the master LLC.

Regardless of whether a series can file bankruptcy on an independent basis or whether it will be deemed part of the master LLC's bankruptcy case, the more important question may be what happens to the assets and liabilities of each series. Will a related series' assets be deemed available to satisfy a debtor's obligations?[58] In bankruptcy, this type of issue is often addressed under the equitable doctrine of substantive consolidation.

Substantive consolidation essentially combines the assets and liabilities of the debtor's bankruptcy estate with the assets and liabilities of another company or group of companies. The result is a larger, consolidated pool of assets to pay the obligations of all of the companies' collective creditors. Although substantive consolidation typically is used to combine the bankruptcy estates of two debtors, it also can be used to combine the assets and liabilities of a debtor with non-debtor companies.

Different courts articulate and apply the substantive consolidation doctrine in different ways. Some courts consider "two critical factors" in assessing a motion for consolidation: "(i) whether creditors dealt with the entities as a single economic unit and did not rely on their separate identity in extending credit; or (ii) whether the affairs of the debtors are so

---

[56] Michelle M. Harner et al., *Series LLCs: What Happens When One Series Fails?*, ABA BUS. L. TODAY, Feb. 2013.

[57] *See id.*; Adam Hiller, *But Series-ly Folks—The Series Laws, and How They (May) Intersect with Bankruptcy Law*, 20 AM. BANKR. INST. L. REV. 353 (2012); Shannon L. Dawson, Comment, *Series LLC and Bankruptcy: When the Series Finds Itself in Trouble, Will It Need Its Parent to Bail It Out?*, 35 DEL. J. CORP. L. 515 (2010); Michael W. McLoughlin & Bruce P. Ely, *The Series LLC Raises Serious State Tax Questions But Few Answers Are Yet Available*, J. OF MULTI-STATE TAX. & INCENTIVES 7, Jan. 2007; Nick Marsico, *Current Status of the Series LLC: Illinois Series LLC Improves Upon Delaware Series LLC but Many Open Issues Remain*, J. PASSTHROUGH ENTITIES, Nov–Dec. 2006, at 35.

[58] *Id.*

entangled that consolidation will benefit all creditors."[59] Other courts require a finding that "consolidation is necessary to avoid some harm or to realize some benefit." Still others follow an equities-of-the-case approach by "focusing on equity to creditors and refusing to 'be blinded by corporate forms.'"[60] The factors considered by courts under the substantive consolidation doctrine often resemble those considered by courts in the alter ego/veil piercing arena. Thus, substantive consolidation is a case-by-case analysis.

In the series LLC context, a substantive consolidation analysis may not only consider the applicable state statute and relevant operating agreements, but also how the master LLC and the series conduct themselves in practice. Parties doing business with a series LLC should evaluate the substantive consolidation case law in their jurisdiction and consider the doctrine in drafting their agreements and structuring any collateral package. Although there is no certainty in this analysis, it can inform the process in a meaningful way.

5. CONCLUSION

The law governing financially distressed LLCs (and other unincorporated entities) is generally well established but variations on certain, sometimes key, issues exist depending on the jurisdiction. Moreover, the treatment of distressed series LLCs is still developing. Many of the key issues highlighted in this chapter require specific consideration of the facts of each case for appropriate resolution. This need for fact-specific inquiry is attributable in large part to the structure of LLCs themselves and the contractual nature of their governance and business relationships. Although parties likely cannot avoid bankruptcy with advance planning, they can improve confidence in outcomes by thoughtfully utilizing state LLC and commercial law. As always, a creditor should hope for the best but plan for the worst, and that planning is most effective when done at the beginning of the relationship.

---

[59] First Owners Ass'n of Forty Six Hundred Condo. Inc. v. Gordon Props., LLC (*In re* Gordon Props., LLC), 478 B.R. 750, 757–58 (E.D. Va. 2012) (explaining various approaches to substantive consolidation analysis) (citations omitted).

[60] *Id.* at 758–60 (remanding for bankruptcy court to re-evaluate equities of the case from the creditors' perspective).

9. Attacking asset protection LLCs
Franklin A. Gevurtz

1. INTRODUCTION

The oft-recited justification for the explosive spread of LLC statutes throughout the United States is to enable business owners to limit their personal liability for debts of the business and at the same time obtain partnership-style tax treatment of the business' income. It is therefore a bit surprising to stumble across a law review article describing how its author uses an LLC to hold his vacation home (Callison 2011). In fact, this is illustrative of a cottage industry in which individuals have created LLCs to shield assets they personally use from their personal creditors, rather than to operate businesses.

It is now generally accepted that using legal entities to shield their owners from business debts can produce an efficient allocation of business risks. The social utility of using such entities to allow individuals to shield assets held for personal use (such as vacation homes) from their personal creditors, however, seems far more problematic. True, state laws (through homestead exemptions and the like) commonly exclude some assets (or value in the assets) from seizure by creditors. Also, creditors might voluntarily agree to limit the assets to which they can look to satisfy their loans. The use of LLCs to shield personally used assets from personal creditors, however, reflects no such carefully considered legislative policy of insulating a few critical assets from creditor claims, nor is it a highly transparent means of obtaining creditors' agreement delimiting the assets subject to their claims.

This chapter examines avenues available to protect creditors whose debtors use LLCs to shield assets held for personal, rather than business, use. My thesis, contrary to some leading scholarship in the area, is that creative judicial application of existing remedies can handle this problem, while jurisdictional competition renders a legislative solution unlikely.

2. CHARGING ORDERS AND TRANSFEREE RIGHTS

To understand asset protection LLCs, one must understand the basic remedy available to the unpaid creditor of an LLC member when seeking to levy upon the member's interest in the LLC—this being the charging order.

The Charging Order in Its Original Partnership Context

While people today focus on the advantage of corporations over ordinary partnerships in protecting the owners' personal property from the business' creditors, historically an equal if not greater advantage of corporations over partnerships was to insulate assets committed to the business from claims by creditors of the individual owners. This so-called affirmative asset partitioning protects the interests of other stakeholders (other owners, creditors, etc.) in the corporation and, at the same time, is fair to the creditors of the individual shareholder, who can look to the shareholder's stock in the corporation to satisfy their claims. If the debtor shareholder owns a majority of the stock, then the creditor or outside bidder obtaining the stock upon its sale to pay the debt can obtain control over the corporation and with this control the ability to dissolve the company or otherwise command distributions from the corporation (after payment to the corporation's creditors and along with distributions to the corporation's other shareholders). If the debtor shareholder only owns a minority interest in a publicly traded corporation, then the sale can obtain the public trading price for the benefit of the creditor. If the debtor shareholder only owns a minority interest in a closely held corporation, sale of the shares might not fetch much, but this represents the precarious value of minority interests in closely held corporations.

Ultimately, partnership law evolved to address the problem of a partner's personal creditor seizing assets used by the business. Influenced, however, by the concerns that partners normally must work closely together in managing the business and can face unlimited personal liability as a result of actions by other partners, partnership law established a different remedy from corporate law. Under both the original and Revised Uniform Partnership Act, creditors of a partner cannot seize partnership property, nor can they seize the partner's entire interest in the firm, including management rights, to satisfy the debt.[1] Instead, the creditor can obtain a charging order[2]—a garnishment-like remedy by which the court commands the partnership to give some or all of the debtor partner's share of distributions, when and if the firm makes distributions to its partners, to the creditor rather than to the debtor partner.[3] Beyond this, a creditor might be able to foreclose upon the partner's interest in the partnership; however, the party purchasing the interest would only have the rights of an assignee (more modernly called a transferee) of a partnership interest—meaning the right to receive distributions when and if made, but no management rights.[4] Obtaining management rights depends upon entry into the firm as a new partner; something that requires consent of the other partners.[5] Potentially helpfully, the assignment or a charging order, and especially the bankruptcy of a partner, might create a dissolution or dissociation event that can force the partnership to buy out the interest of the debtor partner.[6]

The Charging Order in Non-Business and Single-Owner LLCs

The very definition of a partnership—two or more persons carrying on as co-owners of a business for profit—establishes the preconditions that make the charging order remedy work. Co-owners of a business, particularly if they face unlimited personal liability for the

---

[1] See Rev. Unif. Partnership Act §§ 501–503.
[2] Id at § 504.
[3] E.g., Rev. Unif. Ltd. Liab. Co. Act § 503 Comment.
[4] Rev. Unif. Partnership Act at §504(b).
[5] Id at § 401(i).
[6] Id at §§ 601(4)(ii) (allowing other partners to expel a partner who has transferred substantially all his or her interest or is subject to a charging order), 601(6) (dissociating a bankrupt partner), 701 (providing for buy-out by the firm of a dissociated partner when the firm does not dissolve).

business' debts, normally desire to get their hands on the firm's profits. Hence, non-debtor partners will insist on receiving distributions, even if a charging order channels the debtor partner's share of partnership distributions to his or her creditor.

LLC statutes have imported the charging order remedy from partnership law,[7] but without retaining the preconditions that make the remedy work. Current LLC statutes commonly allow single-member (owner) LLCs.[8] At the same time, eliminating the threat of personal liability makes it easier to obtain nominal members for multimember LLCs. In either case, the result is to remove the pressure from non-debtor members to distribute the firm's profits. In addition, LLC statutes typically do not limit the purposes for which LLCs may be formed[9] and, accordingly, allow LLCs to exist for the purpose of owning property used solely by the company's owner.

Beyond this, LLC statutes typically do not grant any management rights to the transferee of a member's interest, but instead require consent by the members for the transferee to become a new member.[10] Hence, a buyer of the debtor member's interest through a foreclosure sale (if available under the relevant LLC act), like the beneficiary of a charging order, must wait around for those in charge of the LLC to distribute any earnings. Moreover, a charging order or a transfer of a member's interest does not necessarily dissociate a member;[11] meaning the debtor member can still have power over the LLC. LLC statutes also commonly provide that charging orders, assignments of a member's interest, and a member's bankruptcy do not trigger dissolution and liquidation of the firm or the right of those claiming through the member to demand the firm cash out the member's interest.[12] The impact of the member's bankruptcy or assignment of all interest becomes complicated, however, in a single-member LLC because of statutory provisions that might terminate a member's LLC membership in such events and might dissolve the LLC when it ceases to have any members.[13] Such provisions, however, are often subject to contrary agreement (including the "agreement" of the sole member with him- or herself).[14] Potentially better from an asset protection standpoint in light of bankruptcy case law discussed below involving single-member LLCs, parties might take advantage of state LLC law provisions allowing no-contribution and no-economic-interest members[15] to bring in trusted parties as additional members in order for an asset protection LLC to continue despite the bankruptcy of the principal member.

All told, these provisions seemingly allow an asset protection LLC to continue, and to continue to allow the debtor member to use its property, while creditors wait in vain for the firm to make any distributions subject to the charging order.

---

[7] *E.g.*, Rev. Unif. Ltd. Liab. Co. Act § 503.
[8] *See, e.g., id* at § 102(13) (implicitly recognizing single-member LLCs by defining operating agreement to include an "agreement" of the sole member of an LLC).
[9] *E.g., id* at § 104(b).
[10] *Id* at §§ 401(d)(3), 502(a)(3).
[11] *Id* at § 502(a)(2), (g).
[12] *See, e.g., id* at §§ 404(b) (no rights to compel distributions before liquidation), 701 (listing causes of dissolution).
[13] *E.g., id* at §§ 602(7), 701(a)(3).
[14] *E.g., id* at § 110(a), (c).
[15] *E.g., id* at § 401(e).

Creative Enforcement of Charging Orders

Aggressive judicial enforcement of charging orders can go far to prevent asset protection LLCs. Express or implied within the statutes creating the charging order is the court's power to undertake enforcement actions (turnover orders) against LLCs who disobey the charging order by continuing to give distributions to the debtor member instead of the creditor.[16] Of course there is a "whack-a-mole" problem if the creditor must constantly watch for surreptitious distributions to the debtor member and return to court for a turnover order every time a few dollars finds its way into the debtor's hands. Fortunately, LLC acts empower the court to appoint a receiver to ensure distributions go to the creditor and not the member.[17]

The true asset protection LLC poses a more subtle challenge to the charging order remedy. An LLC existing for the purpose of holding assets personally used by a member presumably will not be making any money to distribute either in compliance with the charging order or on the sly to the debtor member. Nevertheless, there is a failure to comply with the charging order in this situation. This is because the free use of the assets in effect constitutes an in-kind distribution to the debtor member. Income tax cases treating owner use of corporate property as a taxable in-kind dividend[18] support this characterization.

Determining the appropriate remedy for such free use gets tricky. The court might grant a turnover order requiring the LLC to pay the equivalent of back rent to the creditor. This follows what happens with monetary distributions to the debtor in violation of the charging order, where the remedy is to force the firm to pay what it should have to the creditor, rather than simply have the debtor return the money to the firm.[19] Clever debtors might anticipate the problem by paying rent to the LLC before the creditor challenges the free use of property as an in-kind distribution; albeit, this poses a practical problem for broke members. Some assets that debtors may put into an asset protection LLC (such as collections of valuable objects) might not be subject to a determinable rent and the debtor member might obtain satisfaction from a collection or other such asset simply in the knowledge of its existence. Here, the remedy under the rubric of enforcing the charging order is trickier, even though the principle that there is an in-kind distribution through the owner's enjoyment remains the same. As discussed below, avoiding such complexities, as well as the expense of a receiver, might lead a court simply to reverse pierce the asset protection LLC.

---

[16] *See, e.g.*, Rev. Unif. Ltd. Partnership Act § 703 Comment.

[17] *E.g.*, Rev. Unif. Ltd. Liab. Co. Act § 503(b)(1). This still leaves the potential for characterization disputes over whether so-called salary payments to a member who works for the LLC constitute disguised distributions—a problem that parallels the long history of similar disputes over whether corporate salary payments to principal shareholders constitute disguised and non-deductible dividends.

[18] *E.g.*, Ireland v. United States, 621 F.2d 731 (5th Cir. 1980).

[19] *See, e.g.*, Rev. Unif. Ltd. Partnership Act § 703 Comment.

Levying on the Entire Membership Interest

The assumption underlying the discussion so far is that the charging order and perhaps a foreclosure sale of the member's transferable interest in distributions are the only means for a member's creditor to levy on the member's interest in an LLC. In its controversial 2010 decision in *Olmstead v. FTC*,[20] however, the Florida Supreme Court held that Florida's LLC statute did not confine the creditor of a sole member of an LLC to these actions. Instead, the judgment creditor could use the general provision in Florida's law allowing creditors to levy on all their debtors' real and personal property (including stock in corporations) to levy on an interest encompassing all of the debtor member's rights in the LLC (including the right to dissolve the LLC and obtain its assets).

From a policy perspective, the court's decision is understandable, since the purpose for limiting members' creditors to charging orders or to selling the distribution rights of a transferee is to protect non-debtor members—who do not exist in a single-member LLC. Moreover, the facts in *Olmstead* were highly sympathetic to the creditor, which was the Federal Trade Commission seeking to recover restitution on behalf of victims defrauded by the sole member of asset protection LLCs.

The question of whether Florida's LLC act was amenable to this interpretation sparked a strong dissent. In defense of the majority opinion, the Florida legislature left the door open to the court's interpretation by not referring—in telling contrast to Florida's partnership and limited partnership acts—to the charging order as the exclusive creditor remedy in the LLC statute. LLC statutes in other states, especially after *Olmstead*, may not have this omission.[21] In any event, if the LLC act does not pre-empt the state's general levy provision, there is nothing in the LLC statute to draw the line the *Olmstead* court wished between multimember and single-member LLCs.[22] Of course, if there is no good policy reason to distinguish LLC membership interests from corporate stock in terms of creditor rights, then treating levying on LLC interests the same as levying on stock, which would be the upshot of applying the court's opinion to all LLCs, might be a good thing.

3. BANKRUPTCY LAW

Upon filing bankruptcy, the estate administered by the bankruptcy trustee generally obtains all interests in the debtor's property, and the bankruptcy trustee, with certain

---

[20] 44 So. 3d 76 (Fla. 2010).
[21] Pomeroy (2013–14) states that 34 states have exclusivity language in their LLC acts, while the acts in 16 states are silent. From the standpoint of avoiding unintended interpretations, the exclusive remedy language leaves much to be desired. *Olmstead* illustrates the hazard of putting the language in some acts and not others. On the flip side, the language fails to specify what other remedies the charging order pre-empts. For example, does it preclude the creditor seeking to set aside a property transfer to the LLC as a fraudulent conveyance or arguing that the court should reverse pierce to hold the LLC liable for the member's debt? In fact, the comment to the charging order section in the Revised Uniform Limited Liability Company Act (§ 503) states that the exclusivity language does not preclude reverse piercing.
[22] A subsequent amendment to the Florida LLC act drew this line (Pomeroy 2013–14).

exceptions, can assume any contracts to which the debtor is a party.[23] This creates several issues when the property interest or contract right in question is a membership interest in an asset protection LLC.

To begin with, contracts define the rights they create and, with one exception discussed below, the trustee cannot obtain greater rights than provided by the contract the trustee assumes. In the case of LLC membership interests, the contract consists both of the LLC agreement and the state LLC law. Since, as discussed earlier, state LLC acts typically deny transferees of membership interests and creditors any right except to wait around for distributions, members typically argue that this is the only right the trustee for a bankrupt member in an LLC obtains. The answer to this argument, however, is that the trustee is not a transferee or a creditor; rather, subject to exceptions set out in the bankruptcy code, the trustee steps into the shoes of the bankrupt member by operation of the bankruptcy code.

Still, this only gets the trustee so far, because whether stepping into the shoes of the bankrupt member turns into money for the creditors depends upon what rights the bankrupt member had. So, for example, if the bankrupt member could only transfer an interest allowing the buyer to wait around for distributions that never happen, then the trustee will not be able to get much if the trustee tries to sell the bankrupt member's interest. Similarly, if the bankrupt member could not have forced the dissolution of the LLC or a buy-out by the LLC of the member's interest, then presumably the trustee cannot either. On the other hand, if the LLC agreement granted the bankrupt member the right to use the property held by an asset protection LLC, then the trustee ought to be able to seize this right for the estate and lease the property.[24] More critically, if the bankrupt member had sufficient voting power to dissolve the LLC and distribute its assets to the member(s), or to admit into the membership a party agreeing to purchase the bankrupt member's interest, then the trustee could exercise this voting power in order to get at the LLC's assets or to sell the bankrupt member's interest including voting power. Indeed, it would not matter precisely what the LLC agreement provided as far as the power of the sole member of a single member LLC to dissolve the firm or to approve entry of a new member, since the trustee, as effectively the only party to the one-party LLC agreement, could simply agree to modify the "contract."

One problem with the analysis so far is that LLC statutes and LLC agreements commonly dissociate members upon the member's bankruptcy,[25] thereby terminating the bankrupt member's management rights and, in turn, seemingly cutting off the trustee's ability to use the bankrupt member's rights to vote for dissolution of the LLC, the admission of transferees as new members, or for anything else. Provisions terminating contract rights or preventing their assignment upon bankruptcy, however, create an externality,

---

[23] 11 U.S.C. §§ 365, 541.

[24] Things become more complicated if the LLC agreement does not grant the member the right to use the property. In this event, the trustee might at least at least attempt to kick the member out of the property; albeit a provision in the LLC agreement waiving all fiduciary and other duties could block the obvious claim that such use violates the member or manager's duty to the LLC. If the debtor claims the right to such use as the manager of the LLC, this raises the question of whether rights of a manager also go into the bankruptcy estate, which, in turn, gets into the limits on assuming executory contracts discussed below.

[25] E.g., Rev. Unif. Ltd. Liab. Co. Act § 602(7)(A).

since parties to contracts have limited incentive to protect the interests of claimants in a future bankruptcy. Accordingly, the bankruptcy code generally invalidates so-called ipso facto terms, which terminate or prevent the assignment of contract rights upon a party's bankruptcy.[26]

At first glance, the invalidation of ipso facto terms seemingly dooms provisions such as typical state LLC laws that dissociate bankrupt members from an LLC.[27] Complicating this conclusion is a critical caveat on the trustee's power to assume executory contracts. In order to protect the interest of the other party to the contract, the bankruptcy code contains various exceptions to the trustee's right to assume an executory contract. Of relevance to LLC membership interests, the code allows a party entitled under state law to accept performance only from, or to provide performance only to, the original party to the contract (a personal performance contract), to prevent the trustee's assumption of the contract.[28] The application of this provision to the typical general partnership interest, involving as it does a situation in which partners must get along and where one partner's action can create personal liability for other partners, is evident.

A number of courts have addressed whether a membership interest in an LLC, like the typical ordinary partnership interest, falls within the personal performance exception to an executory contract the trustee can assume.[29] Critically, the focus is protecting the interests of other parties to the LLC agreement against prejudice resulting from dealing with the bankruptcy trustee. Such prejudice is obviously absent if there are no parties to the LLC agreement other than the bankrupt member. Put in the language of the bankruptcy code, the personal performance exception exists if a party to the contract can object to accepting performance from or providing performance to anyone other than the debtor, which obviously cannot be the case without another party to the contract.

Based upon this analysis, the influential *Albright* decision[30] reached the correct result, even if its doctrinal explanation leaves a bit to be desired. In *Albright*, the bankruptcy court for the District of Colorado held that the trustee for the bankruptcy estate of the sole member in a Colorado asset protection LLC had the power to compel dissolution of the LLC and thereby acquire the LLC's property for the bankruptcy estate. The court's policy analysis—that the purpose for limiting creditors to the charging order is to protect other members and therefore not applicable to a one-person LLC—is largely correct and influenced the Florida Supreme Court in *Olmstead*. *Albright*'s analysis of whether Colorado's LLC law allowed the trustee to become a substituted member may be convoluted, but, in any event, was unnecessary. The bankruptcy code gave the trustee whatever rights the bankrupt member had unless the personal performance exception prevented the trustee from assuming the LLC agreement. The lack of other members meant the exception did not apply. Moreover, even if anyone had pointed to a provision in Colorado's LLC act or the LLC agreement dissociating the member upon his bankruptcy, this simply

---

[26] 11 U.S.C. §§ 365(e)(1), 541(c)(1).
[27] Because dissociation of a partner triggers liquidation or a buy-out of the partner's interest, and accordingly an immediate pay-out, trustees generally have had limited incentive to argue that dissociation upon a partner's bankruptcy constitutes an invalid ipso facto provision.
[28] 11 U.S.C. § 365(c)(1), (e)(2)(A).
[29] *E.g.*, In re Ehmann v. Fiesta Investments, 319 B.R. 200 (Bankr. D. Ariz. 2005).
[30] In re Albright, 291 B.R. 538 (D. Colo. 2003).

would have been an invalid ipso facto provision in the absence of any other members objecting to the trustee obtaining management rights.[31]

The critical limitation in the *Albright* result and in the above analysis is that it only applies to single-member LLCs. The court in *Albright* noted that other doctrines dealing with fraudulent conveyances and pre-bankruptcy transfers might void property transfers to asset protection LLCs with added "peppercorn" members, but the court did not address whether such members can block a trustee's assumption of powers under an LLC agreement by invoking the personal service exception. A creative bankruptcy court, working by analogy to the treatment of sham partners under income tax law,[32] ought to look to the reality of the situation and ignore nominal members.

4. FRAUDULENT TRANSFER LAW

Fraudulent transfer statutes[33] allow courts to set aside property transfers whose purpose is to hinder collection by creditors, as well as transfers by insolvent debtors without fair consideration (constructive fraud).[34] Because the member transferring property into an LLC typically receives an interest (or an increase in the member's interest) in the LLC in exchange for the transfer,[35] normally there would not be constructive fraud, and so the existence of a fraudulent transfer would depend upon the showing of subjective intent to hinder collection.

Showing that the transfer of property to an asset protection LLC after a debt arose was intended to hinder collection by creditors typically should not be that difficult.[36] In fact, what other purpose is there for putting assets into an asset protection LLC besides hindering creditors? This is entirely different from transfers either to or from a business conducted through an LLC. Owners transfer assets into a business normally to further the business and produce more money for the debtor (and creditors) in the future. There is also normally a perfectly legitimate explanation for owners to withdraw some assets from an LLC conducting a business—specifically the desire to enjoy through personal spending or other investments the fruits of the business. Moreover, the desire to protect assets not

---

[31] While receiving less notoriety than *Albright*, the Bankruptcy Appellate Panel for the Ninth Circuit got the doctrinal analysis, as well as the result, essentially right in *In re First Protection, Inc.* 440 B.R. 821 (Bankr. App. 9th Cir. 2010).
[32] *E.g.*, Historic Boardwalk Hall LLC v. Commissioner, 694 F.3d 425 (3d Cir. 2012).
[33] Formerly referred to as fraudulent conveyance statutes.
[34] *E.g.*, Unif. Fraudulent Transfer Act § 4.
[35] This might not be the case in some family LLCs in which the LLC agreement does not give the contributing member an increase in distribution rights based upon an increase in contributions, thereby effectively transferring some or all of the value of the contribution to other LLC members. Contributions to such family LLCs by members who are insolvent at the time of the transfer accordingly would be a fraudulent transfer without regard to intent.
[36] *E.g.*, Firmani v. Firmani, 752 A.2d 854 (N.J. Super. Ct. App. Div. 2000). In *Firmani*, the court also rejected the argument that there was no transfer of property triggering the fraudulent transfer act, but merely a change in form. Since an LLC only functions as an asset protection vehicle because it is a separate legal person from the debtor, for the debtor to claim that a transfer of property to an LLC does not constitute a transfer within the meaning of the fraudulent transfer act is frivolous.

transferred into an LLC from the LLC's creditors does not trigger the fraudulent transfer statutes regardless of this intent, since there is no transfer.

Things become less straightforward if the transfer occurred before the debt. Indeed, some scholars have asserted that the fraudulent transfer remedy will not work in situations in which parties exercise the foresight to establish asset protection LLCs to protect against possible creditors in the future (Ribstein 2005). This, however, may be taking too narrow a view. Fraudulent transfer acts expressly reach situations in which the transferor intended to hinder collection by future creditors.[37] Apologists for the asset protection industry argue that despite this language, fraudulent transfer acts do not reach transfers to asset protection vehicles intended to protect against potential future claims resulting from changes in law or, more broadly, when the debtor retains enough assets to cover some notion of reasonably expected future debts (Sullivan 1997). The cases cited in support of these propositions, however, are distinguishable. For example, cases holding that transfers by solvent parties to close relatives do not show intent to hinder collection by future creditors do not say the same about transfers to asset protection LLCs—unless persons start loving their LLCs as much as their children or parents. This said, pre-debt transfers to asset protection LLCs create one potentially significant barrier to fraudulent transfer claims: Creditors who knew that their prospective debtor did not actually own the property in question when agreeing to extend credit cannot expect much sympathy asserting a fraudulent transfer claim.[38]

5. REVERSE PIERCING

Discussion of creditor protection when dealing with entities such as corporations or LLCs inevitably brings one to the doctrine of piercing the corporate (or limited liability company) veil. In this instance, however, since personal creditors wish to go after company assets—rather than company creditors going after personal assets—we are dealing with what is referred to as reverse piercing.

Introduction to Reverse Piercing

In order to understand reverse piercing, one must first understand normal piercing in which unpaid creditors of failed corporations seek to have the court impose liability for the company's debts upon one or more of its shareholders. Both statutes and court decisions have made normal piercing applicable to LLCs.[39]

Judicial decisions on normal piercing are befuddling; often the result of courts tossing out meaningless terminology or using decisional templates made long and confusing with redundant or normatively questionable factors.[40] Such decisions typically begin with courts reciting two or three elements necessary to pierce. Under one common

---

[37] *E.g.*, Unif. Fraudulent Transfer Act § 4(a).
[38] *E.g.*, Rose v. Morrell, 259 A.2d 8, 11 (Vt. 1969).
[39] *E.g.*, In re Suhadolik, 2009 WL 2591338 (Bankr. C.D. Ill.).
[40] The discussion of normal piercing is based on Gevurtz (1997).

formulation, piercing requires: (1) control (often said to mean such complete domination that the corporation has no separate mind, will or existence of its own; ignoring the obvious fact that no corporation has a separate mind of its own); (2) use by the defendant of this control to commit fraud or wrong, to perpetrate the violation of a statutory or other positive legal duty, or dishonest and unjust act in contravention of plaintiff's legal rights; and (3) that the fraud or wrong proximately caused injury to the plaintiff (albeit many courts prefer to leave this third element implicit in the second). Instead of listing control as the first element, many courts obscure matters by referring in their first element to a unity of interest and ownership such that the separate personalities of the corporation and the individual no longer exist.

One can make sense of these two- or three-part tests by realizing that the second (and third) elements are telling the court when to pierce—when some fraud or wrongful conduct (beyond simply the failure of the corporation to pay) injures the creditor; while the first element is telling the court against whom to pierce (the shareholder who used control over the corporation to commit the fraud or wrong, rather than a shareholder who is simply an innocent investor).

One can also clarify the "fraud or wrong" element by reducing the multiple factor lists to what are essentially three possible grounds for piercing. At least since Robert Clark's classic article (Clark 1977), scholars have recognized that the owner's withdrawal of corporate assets other than in the equivalent to an arms-length exchange for the owner's work or property, and when the company is unable to pay its bills, has provided the grounds for piercing in a large proportion of the cases. Courts often speak in these cases of siphoning or commingling—albeit the later term could encompass not only informal flows of money from the company to the owner but also flows from the owner to the company, which raises entirely different justifications for piercing. Fraudulently misleading creditors into doing business with the company—for instance, by confusing the creditor as to who will be liable for the debt or what assets the debtor company has—explains as many piercing decisions as misuse of assets. The most controversy, even if impacting the least number of cases, involves inadequate capitalization. In many cases, lack of corporate assets goes to support a claim of fraud (insofar as an egregious lack of assets allows the inference that an owner who incurred additional debts on behalf of the corporation knew the corporation would be unable to repay them). Beyond this, operating a business without sufficient insurance (or self-insurance) to cover foreseeable tort liability externalizes accident costs in a way that can lead some courts to pierce.

Reverse piercing might occur when the creditor of a shareholder or of a member in an LLC seeks to hold the corporation or the LLC liable for the shareholder or member's debt, rather than the creditor of the corporation or LLC seeking to hold the shareholder or member liable for the company's debt (Crespi 1990).[41] This is far less common than normal piercing, because creditors of shareholders or of members of LLCs have another remedy, which is to levy against the debtor's stock or ownership interest in the LLC. As discussed above, the nature of corporate stock makes levying upon stock, rather than

---

[41] Reverse piercing might also occasionally occur at the behest of a shareholder, who, in a "have one's cake and eat it too" mode, seeks to gain some advantage by personally claiming rights owned by the shareholder's corporation.

seeking recovery from the corporation, generally an appropriate remedy, which normally better protects the legitimate interests of other shareholders or corporate creditors. The more limited remedy available to creditors of members in an LLC, however, makes reverse piercing an important tool to prevent abuse in the LLC context.

Asset Transfers

With normal piercing, the improper transfer of assets, which can justify piercing, involves moving assets from the company to its owner, since this is what puts the assets beyond reach of the company's creditors. By the same logic, in reverse piercing, an improper transfer of assets would involve moving the assets from the owner to the company, since this is what puts the assets beyond the direct reach of the owner's creditor. A leading case of reverse piercing with an LLC—*Litchfield Asset Management Corp. v. Howell*[42]—involved such a transfer. There, the 97 percent owner of an LLC transferred almost $150,000 (which she obtained by borrowing against the cash surrender value of her life insurance policies) to her LLC, after the plaintiff creditor had obtained a judgment against her for over $650,000.

If the remedy provided by reverse piercing in a situation like this is simply to seize the money or property transferred to the LLC, than all we have is a redundancy to the fraudulent transfer law remedy discussed earlier. Making the LLC liable for the entire debt, even it exceeded the amount transferred from the debtor to the LLC, would follow the approach of normal piercing and might be justified for deterrence or if the exact amount of the improper transfer is uncertain.

Interestingly, in deciding to reverse pierce, the court in *Litchfield* actually spent more time pointing to informal cash flows from the LLC to the 97 percent member than it spent pointing to the member's transfer of personal money to the LLC. At first glance, this appears to reflect a confused court's rote application of normal piercing analysis without recognizing the different approach demanded when dealing with reverse piercing. On further reflection, however, the court may inadvertently be on the right track. In part, informal withdrawals of funds from the LLC by the debtor member evidence that the initial transfer of funds by the member to the LLC was simply a fraudulent attempt to put money beyond the reach of the member's creditors into a piggy bank where the member could get the funds as needed, instead of a bona fide transfer.

A broader reason that member withdrawals can justify reverse piercing stems from the earlier discussion of the charging order remedy. Charging orders require distributions go from the LLC to the member's creditor, rather than to the member. Hence, the member should not be using control over the LLC to take out funds in violation of the charging order. As discussed earlier, one possible remedy for such conduct under the charging order scheme would be appointment of a receiver to oversee LLC funds and their distribution. It might be cheaper and easier, however, to reverse pierce and allow the creditor direct access to the LLC's assets. A doctrinal justification would be that the LLC cannot insist on confining members' creditors to the charging order remedy at the same time the firm disobeys the charging order. As also discussed earlier, an LLC formed to own assets

---

[42] 799 A.2d 298 (Conn. App. Ct. 2002).

personally used by its member will not typically be distributing money, even on the sly, to its member. The argument made earlier that personal use of company assets, in reality, constitutes an in-kind distribution in contravention of the charging order applies to the reverse piercing analysis as well. Indeed, the reverse piercing remedy of making the LLC liable for the member's debt may avoid the awkward questions discussed earlier regarding the appropriate action by the court (such as whether to have the LLC pay the creditor equivalent of back rent) when the violation of the charging order's command consists of such in-kind distributions through the free use of LLC property.

Fraud and Creditor Knowledge

The most likely potential claim of fraud in the case of asset protection LLCs goes to the apparent ownership of the LLC's assets. Creditors might assume that an individual residing in a luxurious home owns the place (or at least has the wherewithal to rent the place) rather than owning an LLC, which owns the home and allows its free use. Arguing that such fraud justifies reverse piercing, however, faces two serious difficulties.

The first problem is that a check of title records may have disclosed the LLC's ownership of the property in question. Should the failure to check such records preclude any claim based upon fraud? This may depend upon the nature of the creditor in question: A lending institution negotiating a large long-term personal loan may be expected to exercise a certain amount of due diligence; whereas it is not efficient to impose such a burden on a trade creditor, who gives 30 days to pay the bill.

The second problem is more analytic. With normal piercing based upon fraud, the controlling owner committed the fraud. Hence, piercing simply imposes liability upon one who would be liable for his or her fraud even without piercing. With reverse piercing based upon a misrepresentation by the controlling owner (such as appearing to own property in fact owned by the LLC), the company did not commit the fraud; the owner did. A court could impose additional liability upon the owner for his or her fraud; but presumably the owner is unable to pay judgments or else the creditor would not be seeking to reverse pierce. Whether agency principles would make the LLC liable for the owner's fraud depends upon whether the owner is acting within the scope of his or her employment, or within his or her apparent authority, as the manager or managing member of the company when committing the fraud. At first glance, creating an appearance of personally owning property in fact owned by the LLC does not seem to be conduct motivated to serve the LLC's interest or the normal activity of an LLC's manager and so beyond the situations in which fraud traditionally comes within the scope of an agent's employment or apparent authority.[43] A more creative analysis, however, might reach a different conclusion. Specifically, if the purpose of the asset protection LLC is to allow the owner to enjoy the use of property, then allowing the owner to use the property, including in such a manner as to confuse creditors, is within the scope of the owner's authority as the manager of the LLC, and so the LLC can be charged with the fraud. In any event, perhaps this is a case in which such abstractions are not as important as the underlying equities. Creditors fooled about the ownership of the LLC's property ought to be able to recover

---

[43] *See, e.g.*, Restatement (Third) Of Agency §§ 7.07, 7.08 (2006).

from the LLC without worrying too much about the fine points of whether technically the LLC, or an agent acting on its behalf, committed the fraud—at least, as discussed below, in the absence of prejudice to other significant owners or creditors of the LLC.

Suppose, however, the creditor knows about an asset protection LLC's ownership of the property at the time the creditor entered into the contract creating the member's obligation to the creditor. In this instance, there would be no basis for a claim of fraud based upon confusion about who owned the property. Perhaps the creditor might claim the member misled the creditor about whether the LLC, rather than just the member, would pay the debt, or the owner incurred personal debt at the time the owner knew he or she would never repay it—which returns us again to the question of whether to reverse pierce to make the LLC liable for the owner's misrepresentations.

The broader question is the degree to which the creditor's knowledge of property ownership by an asset protection LLC cuts off reverse piercing based upon theories other than fraud. For example, in *Braswell v Ryan Investments Ltd*,[44] an ex-wife, suing after her ex-husband breached a divorce settlement agreement, sought to reverse pierce her ex-husband's corporation, which held title to the house that had been the couple's primary residence. In refusing to reverse pierce, the court focused the bulk of its opinion on the fact that the corporation's ownership of the couple's primary residence pre-dated the agreement. The court reached the normative significance of this fact by noting that the ex-wife was aware of the corporation's ownership at the time she negotiated the settlement.

The question of whether creditor knowledge should cut off all claims to reverse pierce leads into the occasional debate over whether fraud ought to constitute the exclusive grounds for piercing generally. Here, the argument for such a conclusion would be that the creditor's knowledge of property ownership by an asset protection LLC constitutes an implied agreement to forgo collection against the property owned by the LLC. Acceptance of this argument would seem to depend upon the nature of the creditor and of the obligation, as well as the possible grounds asserted for reverse piercing. Involuntary creditors, such as tort victims, can hardly be said to have agreed to forego seeking recovery against the property held by the LLC. Even voluntary creditors have not implicitly agreed to forego claims based upon property transfers to the LLC that take place after the debt arose. Whether voluntary creditors implicitly agreed to forego claims based upon circumvention of the charging order is a more complex inquiry.

The creditor of an LLC member is entitled, barring other agreement, to seek a charging order against the LLC, which should preclude distributions, in-kind or otherwise, to the member, and which, in turn, creates the argument that circumvention of the charging order, including by free use of property, should lead to piercing. Why should a creditor need to make specific provision in its agreement in order to assert a claim based upon the creditor's legal remedies? In the end, this issue becomes a circularity: If courts decide that knowledge of use of property by an asset protection LLC waives claims based upon circumvention of the charging order, then creditors come to know they must specifically contract to look to the asset protection LLC's property; whereas if courts hold that mere knowledge does not implicitly waive the creditors' right to stand on their legal remedies, then creditors can assume they do not need to make specific provision. Given the lack of

---

[44] 989 So. 2d 38 (Fla. App. 2008).

social utility for asset protection LLCs, courts should start from the position that creditor knowledge of property ownership by an asset protection LLC does not implicitly waive creditors' piercing claims based upon circumvention of the charging order remedy, including by the member's free use of LLC property.

Inadequate Capitalization

In normal piercing, inadequate capitalization of the company might provide grounds to pierce. In reverse piercing, the relevant "capitalization" is that of the member. In both normal and reverse piercing, the primary normative grounds for piercing based upon inadequate capitalization, in itself, would be to avoid externalization of accident costs otherwise resulting when individuals, who conduct activities creating a risk of injury to others, can underinsure secure in the knowledge that property they enjoy is beyond the reach of unpaid victims. This is a concern when individuals conduct businesses through companies with few assets and little insurance, thereby justifying normal piercing. It is also a potential concern when individuals, such as professionals, use asset protection LLCs as a substitute for purchasing adequate liability insurance. Indeed, without reverse piercing, the asset protection LLC can encourage persons to conduct underinsured dangerous activities even more than does allowing parties to conduct such activities through an LLC. After all, limited liability does not relieve individuals of liability for their own torts; whereas asset protection LLCs could shield personally used property from seizure by the victims of one's own torts. Hence, courts should reverse pierce asset protection LLCs whose member(s) fail to purchase personal liability insurance sufficient to cover reasonably foreseeable damage claims. Moreover, creation of an asset protection LLC by a professional or other person engaged in risky activities is strong evidence that the individual did not view his or her insurance as adequate, which, in turn, ought to create a presumption that the insurance was not adequate.

Control and Stakeholder Equities

Just because we are dealing with reverse piercing does not mean it makes any sense to talk about the LLC controlling its member, rather than the member controlling the LLC. On the other hand, simply asking whether the member controls the LLC is not the relevant inquiry for reverse piercing. Instead, one needs to return to the normative function of requiring control as an element for normal piercing. As stated above, control serves to separate the guilty from the innocent; in other words, if some fraud or wrongdoing justifies piercing, who did it. Reverse piercing creates a similar necessity to separate the guilty and the innocent. In this instance, however, the analysis is more complex.

With normal piercing, separating the guilty and the innocent is a direct all-or-nothing proposition: One is seeking to impose liability for the entire debt upon the owner who committed the fraud or wrongful act and no liability upon the passive owners who did not commit the fraud or wrongful act. With reverse piercing, we are not talking about imposing liability upon the party who committed the fraud or wrongful act; this is the owner and that person is broke. Instead, the question is whether imposing liability upon the LLC for the owner's personal debt will unfairly harm the interests of other stakeholders in the LLC—other members, as well as creditors of the LLC itself—who did not engage in any misconduct, but who will indirectly suffer if the LLC must pay one member's personal debts.

To begin with, consider the interests of other possible members of the LLC. The presence of other members who have invested significant amounts into a business LLC counsels very strongly against reverse piercing, whereas nominal members, whose sole function is to ward off reverse piercing (or, as discussed earlier, to preclude the bankruptcy trustee's ability to exercise the management rights of the bankrupt member of a single-member LLC), should count little. In between is the common case in which the founder of an asset protection LLC establishes membership interests for family members to whom the founder wishes to pass his or her property upon his or her death. Taking a "you get what you pay for" attitude, courts might not be too sympathetic toward members receiving gratuitous, or largely gratuitous, interests in asset protection LLCs, even in circumstances of bona fide donative intent—except perhaps in situations involving modest amounts for truly dependent spouses or minor children. Moreover, the transfer is still essentially gratuitous whether an individual transfers his or her property to an LLC and then transfers interests in the LLC to other family members, or first transfers interests in the property to other family members and then has the joint owners of the property transfer the property to the LLC.

Individuals might seek to avoid piercing by having multiple members make significant money or property contributions to an asset protection LLC. The sympathy a court should show toward the non-debtor members in such a property protection LLC "co-op" may depend upon the circumstances. An asset protection LLC in which each member primarily uses the property he or she contributed may elicit little sympathy for the non-debtor members, since the cooperation simply exists in a common effort to shield assets from creditors. By contrast, an LLC in which a number of individuals pool together resources to purchase a commonly used asset (like a vacation home) can elicit a different reaction. After all, an historic purpose for corporations was to allow commonly used property—whether for business or for other activities—to remain committed to the activity without fear that claimants against any individual involved in the activity could seize some of the property (Platt 1976, discussing medieval municipal corporations). Of course, a commonly used vacation home or the like does not have the broader social utility of a business or charitable endeavor; but still the interests of the other contributors to the commonly used property are not without some equity in this situation.

Given the usual expectations, the interest of the LLC's creditors is quite strong and would normally counsel against reverse piercing absent evidence that doing so will not imperil the LLC's ability to pay its own debts.

Against these equities courts must balance the strength of the creditor's grounds for piercing. Here, in fact, is where the highly contextual, case-specific approach traditional in piercing analysis has an advantage.

Finally, notice in this analysis that, despite the label given to this discussion, "control" is largely beside the point. The fact that a controlling member in an LLC might exercise the raw power to take or use the firm's property as his or her own does not, in itself, justify further victimizing other members by also making the LLC liable for this member's debts. On the other hand, other members, who actively participate, or knowingly and voluntarily acquiesce, in the wrongful or fraudulent conduct creating grounds for reverse piercing, cannot expect much sympathy when asserting that piercing will prejudice their interests.

6. STATUTORY REFORM AND CHOICE OF LAW

Concluding that judicial remedies were inadequate, Professor Larry Ribstein argued that statutory reform was necessary (Ribstein 2005). The discussion so far suggests that Professor Ribstein was overly pessimistic regarding judicial remedies. At the same time, a statutory solution must confront the temptation of some state legislatures to raise revenues by selling asset protection LLCs to persons in other states. Previous efforts by some states to sanction asset protection grantor trusts evidence this hazard (Ribstein 2005).

This experience, in turn, makes choice of law a potentially critical concern in dealing with asset protection LLCs. State legislation that would allow LLCs only for a business purpose or that would broaden creditor remedies beyond the charging order run up against the incorporation doctrine (under which states recognize legal entities formed in other states) and the internal affairs rule (under which states apply the entity laws of the state of formation). The constitutional limit on states disregarding these rules is complex, uncertain, and beyond the scope of this chapter.

Bankruptcy, being Federal law, has an advantage here. Fraudulent transfer acts should not fall within the internal affairs rule. There is disagreement about whether piercing falls within the internal affairs rule (Gevurtz 1997), but, even if so, the equitable nature of the doctrine and the vagaries with which courts typically explain decisions to pierce gives courts in various states plenty of flexibility. The same can be said of courts' ability to creatively fashion charging orders to deal with abuse.

7. CONCLUSION

The history of liberalization of business organization law is that no good deed goes unabused. When it comes to those who exploit LLCs' laws by setting up LLCs to shelter personal assets from personal creditors, courts have the ability under existing laws to prevent abuse.

REFERENCES

Callison, J. William (2012), "Nine Bean-Rows LLC: Using the Limited Liability Company to Hold Vacation Homes and Other Personal-Use Property," *William Mitchell Law Review*, 38, 592–626

Clark, Robert C. (1977), "Duties of the Corporate Debtor to its Creditors," *Harvard Law Review*, 90, 505–562

Crespi, Gregory S. (1990), "The Reverse Pierce Doctrine: Applying Appropriate Standards," *Journal of Corporate Law*, 16, 33–69

Gevurtz, Franklin A. (1997), "Piercing Piercing: An Attempt to Lift the Veil of Confusion Surrounding the Doctrine of Piercing the Corporate Veil," *Oregon Law Review*, 76, 853–906

Platt, Colin (1976), The English Medieval Town

Pomeroy, Chad J. (2013–14), "Think Twice: Charging Orders and Creditor Property Rights," *Kentucky Law Journal*, 102, 705–738

Ribstein, Larry E. (2005), "Reverse Limited Liability and the Design of Business Associations," *Delaware Journal of Corporate Law*, 30, 199–229

Sullivan, John E. III (1997), "Future Creditors and Fraudulent Transfers: When a Claimant Doesn't Have a Claim, When a Transfer Isn't a Transfer, When Fraud Doesn't Stay Fraudulent, and Other Important Limits to Fraudulent Transfers Law for the Asset Protection Planner," *Delaware Journal of Corporate Law*, 22, 955–1049

PART 4

TAX AND ACCOUNTING

10. Tax aspects of partnerships, LLCs, and alternative forms of business organizations
Bradley T. Borden

1. INTRODUCTION

A driving force behind the growing popularity of partnerships, limited liability companies (LLCs), and other alternative forms of organizations in the United States is the preferential tax treatment such entities receive when compared to corporations.[1] As a general matter, corporations are subject to an entity-level tax,[2] and distributions from corporations to shareholders are also subject to tax.[3] Consequently, corporate income is taxed twice in the United States. In contrast, the income of partnerships, LLCs, and other alternative forms of organizations generally is not subject to an entity-level tax in the United States. Instead, all the income of such entities flows through to the owners of the entities, and the owners report their respective shares of a flow-through entity's income on their respective tax returns.[4] Additionally, partnership tax law (the tax regime most commonly associated with partnerships and LLCs) grants the members of such entities significant flexibility, which provides tax advantages that exceed mere avoidance of double taxation. The presence of corporate double tax and the tax flexibility granted to partnerships and LLCs combine to create a sophisticated flow-through partnership tax regime in the United States that is unrivaled in other countries that also have dual tax regimes for corporations and other entities. Flow-through tax also exists beyond the confines of partnership tax in several niche areas of the law. After discussing the fundamental aspects of the taxation of partnerships, LLCs, and other alternative organizations in the United States, this chapter briefly describes how the tax treatment of such entities typically differs in other countries. It concludes by describing how the different treatment of such entities in different countries creates hybrid entities that parties use in cross-border investments and transactions for tax-planning purposes.

2. OVERVIEW OF PARTNERSHIP TAXATION

Partnerships and LLCs (referred to collectively in this chapter as "partnerships" unless stated otherwise) generally are not subject to taxation in the United States.[5] Instead, they compute income and expenses, report those items on information returns filed with the

---

[1] *See* Chrisman.
[2] *See* Internal Revenue Code (I.R.C.) § 11.
[3] *See* I.R.C. § 61(a)(7).
[4] *See* I.R.C. §§ 702, 703.
[5] *See* I.R.C. § 701.

Internal Revenue Service (IRS), and allocate the items to their members.[6] The members report their respective shares of partnership income and loss on their respective tax returns and pay tax on such items as appropriate.[7] In other words, partnerships pass income through to their members, resulting in partnership taxation commonly being referred to as a form of "pass-through" or "flow-through taxation." Partnership flow-through taxation can sound simple, but its application has proven to be quite complex. Part of that complexity derives from the effort to apply both aggregate and entity concepts to partnership taxation.

Aggregate versus Entity Taxation

Partnership taxation attempts to balance aggregate and entity theories of taxation.[8] Under the entity theory, tax law treats a business or property-ownership arrangement as an entity separate from its owners. Tax law thus views the entity as owning property and earning income. The owners of the entity have interests in the entity (in many respects analogous to shareholders' interests in a corporation) that they can transfer. Under the aggregate theory, tax law would not treat a business or property-ownership arrangement as an entity separate from its owners. Instead it would treat the owners as directly owning undivided interests in the property and as directly earning income from the co-owned property. State law also has adopted both entity and aggregate theories at different times for different types of entities.[9] When the U.S. Congress enacted the current income tax Law in 1913, it treated corporations as entities separate from their owners,[10] but disregarded partnerships, treating them as aggregates of their owners.[11] The treatment reflected the then-current understanding of the non-tax distinction between corporations and partnerships. That understanding was based in part upon the historic view of the grant or concession theory of corporations, which derived from early state grant of monopolistic authority to corporations that performed government functions and were treated as legal persons.[12] From that theory evolved the entity theory and a list of entity attributes.[13] Although commentators were struggling with whether partnerships were legal persons separate from their owners at the turn of the twentieth century, the more dominant view appeared to be that they were not separate entities.[14] The theories and views of corporations, partnerships, and now LLCs have changed over time and continue

---

[6] *See* I.R.C. § 703. This chapter generally uses "member" to refer to an owner of any arrangement that is taxed as a partnership because such arrangements may be either partnerships or LLCs. It uses the term "partner" to specifically refer to a member of a state-law partnership.
[7] *See* I.R.C. § 702.
[8] *See* Borden (2009); Jackson, Johnson, Surrey, Tenen & Warren.
[9] Several commentators have discussed the theories of both corporate and partnership law. *See, e.g.*, Demsetz; EASTERBROOK & FISCHEL; Hansmann, Kraakan & Squire; Hobbs; Horwitz; Jensen & Meckling; Rosin.
[10] *See* Tariff Act of 1913, ch. 16, § II.A, 38 Stat. 114, 166.
[11] *See* Tariff Act of 1913, ch. 16, §§ II.G(a), II.D.
[12] *See e.g.*, Baldwin; Hausmann, Kraakman & Squire; Horwitz; Lobinger; Williston.
[13] *See* Kornhauser.
[14] *See* Borden (2009); Crane (1915); Horowitz; Lewis. Although the 1914 Uniform Partnership Act included entity provisions, its definition of partnership adopted an aggregate view. *See* UNIF.

to change as business and legal practices evolve and lawyers find innovative uses of entities.[15] Such changes and innovations affect the tax treatment of such entities, but current tax regimes still reflect some aspects of the early non-tax theories of the various entities.

Corporate tax remains an entity regime with an exception for qualifying small businesses. The current partnership tax regime is a mere shadow of the almost pure aggregate structure that Congress adopted in 1913.[16] Although the non-tax view of partnerships has almost universally shifted to the entity theory over the last 100 years,[17] partnership tax retains significant aggregate components. An explanation for the mixed theory of partnership taxation is that the aggregate provisions of partnership taxation accommodate the unique nature of the capital structure of traditional partnerships, which can include complex profit- and loss-sharing arrangements. The entity provisions provide the framework needed to tax partnership income, prevent the abusive use of the partnership tax rules, and facilitate tax administration.[18] The history of partnership tax reveals Congress's attempt to strike the appropriate balance between aggregate and entity provisions.[19] The development of partnership tax is one of apparent trial and error. Often Congress enacts entity provisions only to later enact other aggregate rules to take some of the edge off the earlier-enacted entity provisions. A review of some of the central rules of partnership taxation helps illustrate the interaction of the entity and aggregate rules and some of the challenges that Congress faces in maintaining those rules.

Allocating Tax Items

Partnerships, like other types of businesses or property-ownership arrangements, generate both economic items (such as rental revenue, fees for services, proceeds from the sale of property, rent expense, and payroll expenses) and tax items (such as rental income, gain or loss on the sale of property, depreciation deductions, and deductions for wages and rent).[20] Often, the most difficult challenge for partnership taxation is allocating tax items.[21] The challenge would be less onerous if all partnerships allocated economic items of profit and loss in proportion to partners' contributions, and partnerships made distributions in the same proportion.[22] With such simple arrangements, partnership tax law could simply require the partnership to allocate tax items in proportion to contributions, economic-item allocations, and distributions. Many partnerships, however, use so-called

---

P'SHIP ACT § 6, 6 U.L.A. 393 (1914). *See also* UNIF. P'SHIP ACT, Prefatory Note 1914, 6 U.L.A. 276 (2001).

[15] *See* Crane (1936); Hillman; Jensen; Kleinberger; Reyes & Vermeulen; Ribstein.
[16] *See* Borden (2006); Borden (2009).
[17] *See* Carney; Kleinberger; Rosin.
[18] *See* Borden (2009).
[19] *See* Borden (2006); Borden (2009); Jackson, Johnson, Surrey, Tenen & Warren.
[20] *See* Borden (2008); Borden (2011).
[21] *See e.g.*, Borden (2011); Hasen; Monroe (2012); Polsky.
[22] In fact, a significant difference between partnership taxation and S corporation taxation (a very simplified version of a flow-through taxation discussed below that applies to qualifying small businesses) is that S corporation taxation only applies to entities that issue a single class of stock, *see* I.R.C. § 1361(b)(1)(D), requiring the entity to allocate tax items in proportion to contributions and to make distributions in the same proportion. *See* I.R.C. § 1.1361-1(l).

"special allocations," which are not in proportion to contributions or distributions. Tax law struggles to govern the allocation of tax items to members of such arrangements.

The extent of the difficulty of allocating tax items may vary based upon the type of partnership. For example, a law firm partnership may allocate profits and losses to its members based upon a formula that considers business development and hours billed. Partnership taxation could require such a partnership, and other largely service-oriented partnerships (i.e., those with small capital investments) to allocate tax items in proportion to the allocation of profits and losses on an annual basis. Allotting tax items based upon the allocation of economic items is accurate if all of the tax items correspond with an economic item. Capital-intensive partnerships that use special allocations raise a more difficult challenge, because some of the tax items of such partnerships do not correspond with any economic items.

Capital-intensive partnerships deduct the cost of property over time in the form of depreciation. Depreciation deductions often do not correspond with any economic item.[23] For example, an office building should qualify for depreciation deductions, but generally such property increases in value over time. The increase in value is an economic item, so depreciation deductions (which decrease a partnership's tax basis in property and represent a diminution in the property's value) do not correlate with an economic item. Nonetheless, the partnership must allocate that tax item, and partnership tax law should ensure that the partnership does not allocate it in an abusive manner. For example, partnership tax should prohibit a partnership from allocating depreciation deductions to a member who can use those deductions to reduce taxable income while allocating them away from a member that has no income to offset those deductions or one that is tax exempt and would not benefit from the deductions. Such allocations would appear to be abusive because they would reduce the partners' overall tax liability but do not affect their economic rights.[24] For partnerships that do not allocate economic items in proportion to contributions and distributions, the proper allocation of tax items is difficult to determine, so the IRS may not be able to adequately prevent such abusive allocations.

To further appreciate the difficulty of governing the allocation of tax items, assume a real estate partnership allocates profits and losses using a distribution waterfall that requires the partnership to first distribute contributed capital plus some return to investors and then divide any remaining profits among investors and managers based upon a fixed percentage.[25] With such partnerships, the proper allocation of profits and losses is unknown until the partnership liquidates and computes the distribution waterfall.[26] Nonetheless, the partnership generates tax items, including depreciation deductions, throughout its life, but tax law probably should not merely require the partnership to allocate tax items in accordance with the allocation of economic items. Despite the extreme difficulty that partnership tax faces, it must attempt to govern the allocation of tax items and deter abusive allocations. The aggregate theory requires that members be taxed on their shares of partnership profits and losses as they occur. The entity theory may,

---

[23] *See* Borden (2011).
[24] *See* Monroe (2012); Polsky.
[25] *See* Borden, *Distribution Waterfalls* (2014); Carey.
[26] *See* Borden (2011); Borden (2010).

however, treat the partnership as receiving those profits and losses before the members have access to them.

Properly governing the allocation of tax items is so difficult, in fact, that partnership taxation has largely failed to adequately do so. Tax law allows partnerships to allocate tax items in accordance with partners' interests in partnerships or in such a manner that the allocations have "substantial economic effect."[27] The IRS can reallocate any tax items that do not satisfy one of these tests.[28] The first test presents a significant challenge for the IRS.[29] For example, a real estate partnership may provide for a distribution waterfall that requires the partnership to provide a 25 percent internal rate of return to the member who contributes capital to the partnership before it distributes any amount to the member who manages the partnership real estate. Early in the life of the partnership, the real estate's performance may indicate that it will never generate enough cash flow to cover the distribution to the capital partner. If the partnership agrees to allocate all of the depreciation deductions to the capital partner, the IRS would be hard pressed to present an argument based upon the partners' interests in the partnership that is strong enough to overturn such an allocation. If the partnership later generated sufficient cash flow to cover the distribution to the capital partner, the IRS may still not be able to successfully argue that the allocation does not accurately reflect the partners' interests in the partnership. In such a situation, the members may argue that their interests are based upon original contributions, not distributions. Because the capital member contributed all of the capital to the partnership, the members could argue that the capital member qualifies for 100 percent of the depreciation deduction. This one example illustrates shortcomings of the test for partners' interest in a partnership as a basis for governing the allocation of tax items. Other types of capital structures of partnerships can add further complexity.

The two-part test for substantial economic effect is no less flawed.[30] The first part of the test requires tax-item allocations to have economic effect, and the second part requires that the economic effect of the allocations be substantial.[31] For an allocation to have economic effect, the person to whom a tax item is allocated must receive the economic benefit or bear the economic burden that corresponds with the tax item.[32] Under a safe harbor, tax-item allocations have economic effect if the partnership agreement (1) requires the partnership to maintain capital accounts in accordance with prescribed rules, (2) requires the partnership to liquidate in accordance with positive capital account balances, and (3) obligates members to restore deficit capital account balances upon liquidation of their interests.[33] Members of LLCs often prefer not to include all of these requirements in their LLC agreements because the third one could make them liable for additional capital contributions. Tax-item allocations can, however, have economic effect, if the result of the allocation is the same as the one that would have occurred had the partnership satisfied

---

[27] *See* I.R.C. § 704(a), (b).
[28] *See* Treas. Reg. § 1.704-1(b)(1)(i).
[29] *See* Borden (2011).
[30] *See* Borden (2011); Monroe (2012); Polsky.
[31] *See* Treas. Reg. § 1.704-1(b)(2)(i).
[32] *See* Treas. Reg. § 1.704-1(b)(2)(ii)(*a*).
[33] *See* Treas. Reg. § 1.704-1(b)(2)(ii)(*b*).

all three safe-harbor requirements.³⁴ Ensuring that tax-item allocations have economic effect can be difficult, however, if the partnership agreement has distribution-dependent allocation provisions, such as the distribution waterfall described above.³⁵

The test for substantiality may lack any utility in many situations. The idea behind the test is that partnerships should not be able to allocate tax items in such a manner that they reduce the overall tax liability of the members without altering the economic arrangement.³⁶ Unfortunately, the wording of the rule is almost incomprehensible and incorporates terms and concepts such as "after-tax economic consequences," "present value," "strong likelihood," and "substantially diminished."³⁷ Such undefined terms and concepts in this context could render the test useless in many situations. Additionally, the test would have utility only if it could compare allocations in a partnership agreement to some baseline allocation. The rules recommend using the partners' interests in the partnership as the baseline for testing allocations,³⁸ but the tax-item allocation provisions in a partnership agreement affect the partners' interests in a partnership, if the allocations have economic effect.³⁹ As a consequence, partnerships may have no realistic baseline against which to compare allocations. Because of these shortcomings and the deficiencies in the test for economic effect, partnerships often make no attempt to ensure that tax-item allocations have substantial economic effect. Instead, they claim that their tax-item allocations are in accordance with the partners' interests in the partnership.

Despite the deficiencies in the rules governing partnership allocations of tax items, the aggregate view of partnerships requires that the rules provide enough flexibility to allow the members to allocate tax items in a manner that accurately reflects their economic arrangement. A pure entity regime would not properly account for many economic arrangements, so the law will most likely never perfectly balance entity and aggregate theories in the rules governing tax-item allocations. Thus far commentators and lawmakers have been unable to propose rules that sufficiently recognize partners' economic arrangements and prevent abusive allocations.⁴⁰ Undoubtedly future commentary will continue to propose ideas, but the goal of accurate and flexible rules may be unattainable.

Transfers of Partnership Property and Interests in Partnerships

The entity theory treats partnerships as owning property and members as owning interests in partnerships, but the aggregate theory requires the tax consequences of dispositions of partnership property to flow through to the partners. As a result, if a partnership sells

---

[34] *See* Treas. Reg. § 1.704-1(b)(2)(ii)(*i*). Allocations can also have economic effect if they do not cause members to have deficit capital account balances (or cause them to have only limited deficit capital account balances if affected members have limited deficit restoration obligations), and the partnership agreement contains a qualified income offset. *See* Treas. Reg. § 1.704-1(b)(2)(ii)(*d*).
[35] *See* Cuff, *Drafting Wonderland* (2008); Cuff, *Drafting for Idiots* (2008); Brock, Part I (2013); Brock, Part II (2013).
[36] *See* Borden (2011); Monroe (2012); Polsky.
[37] *See* Treas. Reg. § 1.704-1(b)(2)(iii)(*a*).
[38] *See id.*
[39] *See* Borden (2011).
[40] *See, e.g.*, Borden (2011); Monroe (2012).

property, it recognizes gain or loss on the sale (entity theory),[41] and it allocates that gain or loss to the members (aggregate theory).[42] If a member sells an interest in the partnership, the member recognizes gain or loss on the disposition of that interest (entity theory).[43] The interest in a partnership should be a capital interest,[44] so gain or loss that a member recognizes on the disposition of the interest generally is capital gain.[45] Nonetheless, tax law requires a selling member to recognize a portion of the gain from the sale of the partnership interest as ordinary income if the partnership holds inventory or accounts receivable (aggregate theory),[46] which generate ordinary income at the partnership level when sold or collected. Thus, the partnership includes an aggregate component in an area that is largely governed by entity concepts.

The acquirer of an interest in a partnership takes a cost basis in the acquired interest (entity theory),[47] which ensures that the acquiring member would not recognize gain or loss on the immediate disposition of such interest. Due to the application of the entity theory, however, the bases of the assets of the partnership property generally remain the same. Consequently, if the partnership were to sell any of its property immediately after the transfer of a partnership interest, the partnership could recognize gain or loss that is attributable to increases or decreases in the value of the partnership property that occurred prior to the transfer of the partnership interest. That same gain or loss should be reflected in the value of the transferred partnership interest. If tax law does not adjust the basis of partnership property to reflect that gain or loss, the acquiring member will recognize the same gain or loss when the partnership later sells its property. To prevent the double taxation of that gain or loss, partnership tax allows the partnership to elect to adjust the bases of partnership property to ensure that a person who acquires an interest in a partnership does not recognize any portion of pre-transfer built-in gain or loss (aggregate theory).[48] That ability to make such adjustments incorporates the aggregate theory into the entity-theory rules governing transfers of interests in partnerships.

Contributions and Distributions

The contribution and distribution rules of partnership taxation intricately blend aggregate and entity theories to produce somewhat complex rules. The aggregate theory would require members to be taxed on contributions to partnerships or distributions from partnerships because such transactions would represent an exchange of property with other partners. But another objective of partnership tax is to not interfere with business formation or the application of assets to their highest and best use.[49] If the law taxed the formation (i.e., contributions to partnership) of partnerships, business and property

---

[41] See I.R.C. § 703(a).
[42] See I.R.C. §§ 702, 704.
[43] See I.R.C. § 741.
[44] See I.R.C. § 1221.
[45] See I.R.C. § 741.
[46] See I.R.C. § 751(a).
[47] See I.R.C. § 1012.
[48] See I.R.C. §§ 743, 754.
[49] See Jackson, Johnson, Surrey & Warren.

owners would be less inclined to join resources. Tax-free formations and dissolutions (i.e. distributions from partnerships) of partnerships provide business and property owners a means of testing business ideas with no tax cost. For instance, if two parties wish to test whether joining resources can produce synergies, they can do so knowing that combining their resources in a partnership will not be taxed and that they can dissolve the partnership tax free, if things do not develop as planned. The ability to dissolve a partnership or distribute property tax free also allows parties to put resources to their highest and best use without concern that doing so will impose tax costs. For example, if two members wish to dissolve a partnership because one of them has lost the motivation to continue in a venture, they can do so without incurring significant tax cost. The business can continue with the remaining member as a sole proprietor or as a partnership with the remaining member and new member who is motivated to maximize the output of resources. If the dissolution were taxable, however, the partnership may remain intact with the less-motivated member failing to fully utilize partnership resources. Thus, tax-free formation and dissolution (and tax-free contributions and distributions) help ensure that resources are put to their highest and best use, and partnership tax adopts general rules allowing tax-free contributions and distributions.[50]

Even though tax-free formations and dissolutions of partnerships are appropriate goals of partnership taxation, contributions to and distributions from partnerships raise many issues that the aggregate theory requires the law to address. The tax-free contributions of property should not eliminate gain or loss inherent in contributed property.[51] Partnership tax helps ensure that such gain or loss is not eliminated on contribution by requiring the partnership to take the contributing member's tax basis in the contributed property.[52] Thus, if a person contributes appreciated property to a partnership and the partnership sells it immediately, the partnership would recognize gain on that disposition (entity theory). Because that property increased in value while held by the contributing partner, however, tax law requires the contributing member to recognize any gain that accrued prior to the contribution (aggregate theory).[53] Tax law accomplishes this by requiring the partnership to keep track of pre-contribution built-in gain or loss on contributed property and to allocate it to the contributing member when the partnership recognizes that gain or loss.[54] These contribution rules thus include components of both the aggregate and entity theories of partnership taxation

The distribution rules similarly include components of both the entity and aggregate theories. The rules provide for tax-free distribution but generally require the distributee member to take a basis in the property that the partnership had.[55] Thus, the rules preserve any pre-distribution gain or loss that the partnership had in the property. A distribution

---

[50] *See* I.R.C. §§ 721, 731(a), (b).
[51] *See* Monroe (2009).
[52] *See* I.R.C. § 723; *see also* I.R.C. § 722 (requiring the contributing member to take a basis in the partnership interest equal to the basis of the contributed property).
[53] *See* I.R.C. § 704(c).
[54] *See* Treas. Reg. § 1.704-3.
[55] *See* I.R.C. §§ 731(a), (b), 732. If the distribution liquidates the member's interest in the partnership, the member's basis in the distributed property will equal the basis of the member's interest in the partnership. *See* I.R.C. § 732(b).

could be a taxable event, however, if the distribution changes the distributee member's share of partnership inventory or unrealized receivables.[56] This aggregate aspect of the distribution rules ensures that the members do not use tax-free distributions to change their proportionate ownership of property that generates ordinary income.[57]

The rules also contain provisions that prevent members from using the contribution and distribution rules to effect tax-free disguised sales of property. Generally, transfers of property for property are taxable events.[58] Because partnership tax provides generally that contributions and distributions are not taxable events, under the general partnership tax rules two parties could each contribute property to a partnership and have the partnership distribute the respective properties to the respective partners, effecting a tax-free exchange of the properties. To prevent this type of abuse, partnership tax adopted what are commonly referred to as "anti-mixing-bowl rules" that generally tax such transactions.[59] These anti-abuse rules follow the aggregate theory by treating the contributing members as continued owners of contributed property. Thus, the partnership contribution and distribution rules generally allow for tax-free transfers of property to and from partnerships, and they include several other rules that recognize the aggregate theory or are designed to prevent abuse.

Effect of Partnership Liabilities

The rules governing the allocation of partnership liabilities to members incorporate both aggregate and entity theories. Generally, incurring a liability for business purposes outside the partnership context results in a current or deferred deduction. For instance, if an individual borrows money to pay employees, the individual generally would be able to deduct the compensation expense.[60] If the individual used the proceeds to acquire depreciable property, the individual could take depreciation deductions related to the property.[61] The entity theory of partnership tax allows members to take allocated partnership deductions only to the extent that the deductions do not exceed the bases members have in their interests in a partnership.[62] The application of the entity theory in this respect could prevent members from taking deductions that arise from partnership borrowings. To help avoid that outcome, partnership tax applies the aggregate theory to increases the basis members have in their partnership interests by the amount of the partners' respective shares of the partnership liabilities.[63] Those increases allow the members to deduct their respective shares of partnership deductions attributed to partnership liabilities.[64] The rules governing the allocation of partnership liabilities have changed significantly over the years from a

---

[56] *See* I.R.C. § 751(b); Hanna; Simmons.
[57] *See* Monroe (2014); Simmons.
[58] *See* I.R.C. § 1001(a), (c). An exception to this rule applies to certain transfers of like-kind property. *See* I.R.C. § 1031.
[59] *See* I.R.C. §§ 704(c)(1)(B); 737. An exception to this rule applies to certain contributions and distributions of like-kind property. *See* I.R.C. § 704(c)(2).
[60] *See* I.R.C. § 162(a)(1).
[61] *See* I.R.C. §§ 167, 168.
[62] *See* I.R.C. § 704(d).
[63] *See* I.R.C. §§705, 722, 752.
[64] *See* Borden, Binder, Blinder & Incatasciato.

focus on profit and loss sharing to a focus on risk of loss.[65] Now they include a complex definition of recourse liabilities and complex directions for allocating both recourse and nonrecourse liabilities.[66] As members and their advisors find ways to shift the allocations to gain maximum tax advantage,[67] the IRS must respond to help prevent such abuses.[68] The rules grow in complexity as the IRS changes them to prevent perceived abuses.

3. TAXATION OF OTHER FORMS OF FLOW-THROUGH ENTITIES

The discussion to this point has focused on partnership taxation, which is the form of flow-through taxation most often associated with partnerships and LLCs in the United States, but it is definitely not the only form in the United States. The United States also grants flow-through taxation to qualifying small business corporations (S corporations), real estate investment trusts (REITs), real estate mortgage investment conduits (REMICs), and regulated investment companies (RICs). As discussed below, such tax entities, even though not taxed as partnerships, often can be state-law partnerships, LLCs, or other forms of organizations.

S corporations qualify for a form of flow-through taxation that is much simpler than partnership taxation. The S corporation tax regime derives from the general corporate regime, so its beginning point is entity taxation. Congress took away some of the entity attributes of that regime to create the S corporation taxation. Consequently, the S corporation regime is an entity-minus regime.[69] An entity must make an election and satisfy several requirements to qualify for S corporation treatment. For example, generally only individuals can have an ownership interest in an S corporation.[70] Perhaps more importantly from a flow-through perspective, S corporations can only issue one class of stock.[71] The one-class-of-stock requirement mandates that S corporations allocate tax items and make distributions in proportion to member contributions.[72] This requirement limits the application of S corporation tax to a limited percentage of business organizations. The simplified S corporation rules also lack many of the aspects of partnership taxation. For instance, S corporation liabilities do not affect the bases that members have in their interests in the S corporation. Consequently, members of S corporations cannot deduct all of the losses that may flow through to them. Their deductions are limited to the amount of their bases in their S corporation interests, unaffected by S corporation liabilities.[73]

---

[65] See Abrams; Haden; McCarthy.
[66] See Treas. Reg. § 1.752-1, -2, -3.
[67] See King; Lipton & Golub.
[68] See Notice of Proposed Rulemaking: Section 707 Regarding Disguised Sales, Generally, REG-119305-11 (Jan. 29, 2014). Commentators were generally very critical of these proposed rules. See, e.g., Elliott; Lipton; Rubin, Whiteway & Finkelstein.
[69] See Borden (2010).
[70] See I.R.C. § 1361(b)(1)(B).
[71] See I.R.C. § 1361(b)(1)(D). Stock for this purpose includes any ownership interest, including an interest in a partnership or LLC that qualifies for S corporation treatment.
[72] See Treas. Reg. § 1.1361-1(l)(1).
[73] See I.R.C. § 1366(d).

Tax aspects 157

Also, S corporations do not have to track pre-contribution gain or loss and allocate it to contributing members. As a result, any pre-contribution gain or loss recognized by an S corporation is shared by the S corporation members in proportion to their interests in the S corporation. S corporation tax is much simpler than partnership tax, but it sacrifices accuracy and broad applicability for that simplicity.

S corporations are also subject to many of the general corporate tax rules,[74] so contributions to S corporations are more likely to be taxable to the contributing member,[75] and distributions from S corporations are subject to tax.[76] Thus, even though S corporation tax is a flow-through regime, because it is an entity-minus regime, it is different from partnership tax in many fundamental aspects. Those differences may make S corporation tax unattractive to many business and property owners, but the different regimes provide a choice of entities.

A few highly specialized flow-regimes apply to entities that hold real estate assets or other passive investments. REITs benefit from a form of flow-through taxation,[77] but REIT tax is only available to entities that meet several requirements. For example, 75 percent of a REIT's income must be from rents from real property or other sources related to real property,[78] 95 percent of its income must be from rents from real property or from other passive sources,[79] 75 percent of its assets must be real estate assets or other qualifying assets,[80] and a REIT must distribute 90 percent of its income to its members.[81] REITs also must have no fewer than 100 members.[82] REITs can be state-law corporations and still qualify for flow-through taxation, but they must elect REIT status.[83] Because REITs make distributions based upon stock ownership, REITs in effect allocate tax items to their members in proportion to their distribution rights in the REIT. Despite the restrictions that entities must satisfy to qualify for REIT flow-through taxation, REITs enjoy considerable popularity as corporations use them to divert income from the double taxation to which income from the real estate would otherwise be subject if publicly held in another form of tax entity.[84]

Another highly specialized flow-through regime is REMIC taxation. REMIC taxation only applies to securitized pools of mortgages that meet several requirements related to the quality of assets in the pool[85] and satisfy tax accounting rules for payment received on

---

[74] *See* I.R.C. § 1371(a).
[75] *See* I.R.C. § 351 (imposing strict requirements for obtaining tax-free contributions to corporations).
[76] *See* I.R.C. §§ 311(b), 331, 336.
[77] *See* I.R.C. § 857(a)(1) (allowing REITs to deduct the amounts paid in dividends); I.R.C. § 857(b)(1) (subjecting undistributed REIT income to the corporate tax regime); I.R.C. § 857(b)(3)(B) (providing that dividend income recognized by a REIT shareholder can be a capital gain dividend to reflect capital gains recognized by the REIT).
[78] *See* I.R.C. § 856(c)(3).
[79] *See* I.R.C. § 856(c)(2).
[80] *See* I.R.C. § 856(c)(4).
[81] *See* I.R.C. § 857(a).
[82] *See* I.R.C. § 856(a)(5).
[83] *See* I.R.C. § 856(c)(1). *See also* Treas. Reg. § 301.7701-3(b)(3)(v)(B) (providing that a noncorporate entity can elect to be a REIT).
[84] *See, e.g.*, Gryta & Knutson.
[85] *See* I.R.C. §§ 860D, 860G(a)(3).

mortgages and made to holders of REMIC interests.[86] The REMIC rules allow REMICs to issue multiple classes of securities (referred to as "tranches" in the REMIC industry), but they require REMICs to maintain static pools of assets.[87] REMICs are generally organized as state-law trusts, but they can be any form of entity, or simply a pool of mortgages that are so identified.[88] Although REMIC taxation tends to be the province of a very small portion of the tax bar, REMICs were an integral part of the 2008 financial crisis, and, if loan originators and promoters of mortgage-backed securities had adhered to the REMIC rules, they could have helped prevent the crisis or stemmed its severity.[89]

Tax law also grants flow-through taxation to RICs. To qualify for RIC treatment, a company must register under the Investment Company Act of 1940 as a management company or unit investment trust, elect to be treated as a business development company, and be excluded from the definitions of "investment company" and "common trust fund."[90] The company also must elect to be a RIC on its tax return and meet incoming and asset requirements.[91] At least 90 percent of the company's income must be from dividends, interest, gains from the disposition of stock or securities, or other types of income derived from investing in stock, securities, or foreign currencies.[92] The company also must maintain a diversified portfolio of securities.[93] A RIC, like a REIT, is not subject to income tax on distributed income, if it distributes at least 90 percent of its taxable income to its members.[94] The character of income recognized by RICs flows through to the RIC members as part of the dividend payments.[95] Therefore, RICs provide a specialized form of flow-through taxation for entities that hold securities. Mutual funds are the type of arrangement that qualifies for RIC taxation.

4. ELECTION OUT AND INAPPLICABILITY OF PARTNERSHIP TAXATION

Although partnerships and LLCs can qualify for partnership taxation, some such entities elect not to be taxed as partnerships. Partnership taxation provides numerous tax benefits to most types of business and property-ownership arrangements, but in some situations, corporations provide better tax benefits or non-tax factors outweigh the tax benefits that partnership tax would provide. To illustrate, S corporations are able to reduce social security tax and Medicare tax (FICA employment taxes) by designating a portion of payments made to S corporation members as compensation and treating the rest as dividends.[96] If the compensation payment is reasonable, it, but not the dividend

---

[86] *See* I.R.C. §§ 860B, 860C, 860E.
[87] *See* I.R.C. §§ 860D, 860F(a).
[88] *See* Treas. Reg. § 1.860D-1(c)(1); PEASLEE & NIRENBERG.
[89] *See* Borden & Reiss.
[90] *See* I.R.C. § 851(a).
[91] *See* I.R.C. § 851(b)(1).
[92] *See* I.R.C. § 851(b)(2).
[93] *See* I.R.C. § 851(b)(3).
[94] *See* I.R.C. § 852(a), (b).
[95] *See* I.R.C. § 852(b)(3).
[96] *See* David E. Watson, P.C. v. United States, 107 A.F.T.R.2d 311 (2010).

distributions, will be subject to the employment taxes.[97] This type of employment tax planning especially makes sense for service entities that have insignificant assets. An arrangement that holds significant assets would, however, most likely benefit from the partnership tax rules because those rules allow for tax-free contributions and distributions, which rules do not apply to S corporations. Arrangements that have both significant assets and service components may obtain the benefits of both flow-through regimes by forming an S corporation to provide the services and a partnership to own the property. Such an arrangement may require a rental or management agreement between the two entities. Even though such arrangements add complexity, the tax savings they provide can justify the additional non-tax costs.

Start-ups (entities with a goal of going public and perhaps expanding internationally) also often choose the corporate form over the partnership form for both tax and non-tax purposes. Several studies conclude that entrepreneurs and investors lose the benefit of tax losses flowing through during the early years of the start-up, which can equate to billions of dollars of lost tax savings.[98] Nonetheless, the industry resists change and continues to use corporations, but some anecdotal evidence suggests that some in the industry are working to change that general practice. With billions of dollars of tax savings at stake, surely change will come to this area as well and noncorporate entities will become more prevalent in the start-up space.

Tax law has made selecting a tax entity relatively simple with an elective regime that generally does not rely upon the state-law classification or general non-tax attributes of an arrangement.[99] Tax law subjects state-law corporations (other than those that satisfy the requirements to be an REIT, a REMIC, or a RIC) to corporate tax,[100] but partnerships and LLCs with at least two members generally can elect to be subject to partnership tax by default, or be subject to corporate tax.[101] If they otherwise satisfy the S corporation requirements, such an entity can also elect to be subject to S corporation tax, or will be deemed to have elected to be a corporation if it elects to be an S corporation.[102]

LLCs that have a single member cannot be partnerships for tax purposes because a partnership must have at least two members.[103] Tax law disregards such arrangements by default, but they can elect to be corporations.[104] If tax law disregards an LLC because it has a single member, all of the tax items of the LLC are tax items of the single member. If a corporation is the sole member of an LLC that does not elect to be a corporation, tax law treats the LLC's activities as those of a division of the corporation.[105] If an individual is the sole member of an LLC that does not elect to be a corporation, tax law treats the activities of the LLC as the individual's activities as a sole proprietor.[106]

---

[97] See id.
[98] See Bankman; Fleischer (2003); Goldberg; Morse.
[99] See Treas. Reg. § 301.7701-1(a)(1). Commentators have both praised and criticized the elective "check-the-box" classification regime. See, e.g., Borden (2010); Dean; Field; Fleisher (1996); Yin.
[100] See Treas. Reg. § 301.7701-2(b)(1).
[101] See Treas. Reg. § 301.7701-3(a)–(b).
[102] See Treas. Reg. § 301.7701-3(b)(3)(v)(C).
[103] See Treas. Reg. § 301.7701-2(c)(1), -3(f)(2).
[104] See Treas. Reg. § 301.7701-3(a), (b).
[105] See Treas. Reg. § 301.7701-2(a).
[106] See id.

A state-law partnership must have at least two members. If one member of a partnership is an individual and the other is an LLC wholly owned by the individual, state law will recognize the existence of the partnership, but tax law can treat the state-law partnership as having a single member and disregard it. For example, an individual may be the sole limited partner of a limited partnership. That individual may also be the sole member of an LLC, which is the general partner of the limited partnership. Assuming that neither the limited partnership nor the LLC elects to be a corporation, tax law will disregard the LLC and treat the individual as being both the general partner and the limited partner. Thus, tax law would treat the limited partnership as having a single member and would disregard the limited partnership.

Not all partnerships and LLCs can take advantage of the general elective classification rules. Publicly traded partnerships are not subject to the general tax entity classification rules. As a general matter, publicly traded partnerships are subject to corporate tax.[107] A publicly traded partnership will, however qualify for flow-through taxation if at least 90 percent of its income derives from passive-type income.[108] Private equity funds have devised complicated structures to take their businesses public and preserve flow-through taxation.[109] Although such arrangements have their critics,[110] the structure does not appear to present an obvious abuse.[111]

In addition to listing several entities that come within the definition of corporation, the U.S. tax entity classification system for non-U.S. entities focuses on whether partnerships, LLCs, and alternative business organizations provide limited liability for their members. Non-U.S. corporations are corporations for purposes of U.S. tax law.[112] A noncorporate non-U.S. entity that does not provide limited liability to all of its members is a partnership for U.S. tax purposes by default.[113] A noncorporate non-U.S. entity that provides limited liability for all of its members is a corporation by default for U.S. tax purposes, but such an entity can elect to be disregarded (if it has a single member) or to be a partnership (if it has multiple members).[114] The discussion below illustrates that the U.S. entity classification system and non-U.S. classification systems provide tax-planning opportunities to structure ownership using hybrid entities (those that are treated one way in one jurisdiction and another way in another jurisdiction).

5. TAX TREATMENT IN OTHER JURISDICTIONS

The use of partnerships and LLCs in the United States for conducting regular business and owning property appears to be more prevalent than in other jurisdictions. The prevalent use of such entities in the United States appears to fuel the growth and complexity

---

[107] *See* I.R.C. § 7704(a).
[108] *See* I.R.C. § 7704(c), (d).
[109] *See* Cauble.
[110] *See id.*
[111] *See* Borden, *Notable Partnership Articles* (2014).
[112] *See* Treas. Reg. § 301.7701-2(b)(8).
[113] *See* Treas. Reg. § 301.7701-3(b)(2)(i)(A).
[114] *See* Treas. Reg. § 301.7701-3(b)(2)(i)(B).

of the partnership tax rules. Partnership tax is not as developed in other jurisdictions. For example, Canada has a partnership tax system, but its use is much narrower than the U.S. system's. Canadian partnership tax only applies to partnerships.[115] Other entities, such as LLCs, are subject to corporate tax in Canada.[116] Although partnership tax in the United States has grown significantly since the IRS ruled that LLCs qualify for partnership tax treatment and every state enacted an LLC statute, the lack of similar rules in Canada does not appear to be the primary reason for the narrower use of its partnership tax system. Instead, Canadian practitioners attribute the narrower use of the rules to Canada's integrated individual and corporate taxes.[117] Canada provides a credit to shareholders to account for income tax paid by Canadian corporations, so corporate income is not subject to double tax in Canada.[118] Because taxpayers do not need to use partnership tax to avoid the corporate double tax, partnership tax is not as prevalent in Canada, and the Canadian government has been swift to act to stop partnership structures that erode the corporate tax base.[119] Nonetheless, hybrid entities are an important part of cross-border tax planning between Canada and the United States.

6. HYBRID ENTITIES

Partnerships and LLCs often can qualify as one type of entity in one jurisdiction and another type in a different jurisdiction. Cross-border planning in the United States and Canada helps illustrate the use of hybrid entities. As between the United States and Canada, hybrid entities include partnerships, U.S. LLCs, and Canadian unlimited liability companies. Partnerships are flow-through entities under Canadian tax law.[120] They can elect to be flow-through entities or corporations under U.S. tax law.[121] U.S. LLCs and Canadian unlimited liability companies are corporations under Canadian tax law.[122] They can elect to be flow-through entities (if they have more than one member), disregarded entities (if they have a single member), or corporations under U.S. tax law.[123] For instance, a U.S. corporation may form an unlimited liability company to conduct business in Canada. Canadian tax law would treat the unlimited liability company as a corporation, but the unlimited liability company could elect to be disregarded for U.S. tax purposes.[124] Income earned by the unlimited liability company would be subject to the U.S. income tax, just as it would be if the income were from a branch of the U.S. corporation. It would also be subject to Canadian corporate taxes,[125] and dividends paid to the

---

[115] *See* Canada Income Tax Act (CITA) § 96(1); Backman v. The Queen, 2001 DTC 5149 (SCC).
[116] *See* CITA §§ 2(1), 248(1).
[117] Telephone conference on November 14, 2011, with Gary Gluckman and Janice Russell in the Toronto office of Deloitte, LLP.
[118] *See* CITA §§ 82(1)(*b*); 121(a).
[119] *See* Johnson & Lille (2009).
[120] *See* CITA § 96(1).
[121] *See* Treas. Reg. § 301.7701-3.
[122] *See* JOHNSON & LILLE (2010).
[123] *See* Treas. Reg. § 301.7701-3.
[124] *See* Treas. Reg. § 301.7701-3(b)(2).
[125] *See* CITA § 2(1).

U.S. corporation would be subject to Canadian withholding rules.[126] Generally, dividends paid by Canadian corporations to U.S. shareholders qualify for favorable withholding rates under the U.S.-Canada tax treaty.[127] Hybrid entities, such as unlimited liability companies, provide the opportunity for taxpayers to reduce tax liability. As the following discussion illustrates, taxpayers use hybrid entities to stop or block certain types or character of income from flowing in particular directions or to address entity classification issues. Consequently, such entities are often referred to as "stoppers" or "blockers" when used in such a manner.[128]

U.S. taxpayers can use hybrid entities to structure "income-stripping" arrangements that reduce tax liability. Pursuant to a basic income-stripping transaction the U.S. corporation would lend money to a Canadian unlimited liability company. The unlimited liability company would be a corporation under Canadian tax law and be disregarded under U.S. tax law. The loan would be disregarded for U.S. tax purposes, so the U.S. corporation would not report payments or accruals of interest as income. The U.S. corporation would report income from the unlimited liability company, but if the U.S. corporation had offsetting losses or could otherwise exclude or defer the income, it would not pay tax on it. Canada tax law grants the unlimited liability company a deduction for interest paid on the loan from the U.S. corporation,[129] reducing the unlimited liability company's Canadian taxable income and tax liability. The U.S.-Canada tax treaty provides generally that a corporation withholds at a lower tax rate, if any, for interest paid to U.S. taxpayers.[130] Thus, the interest deduction and lower treaty withholding rate reduce the amount of tax that the unlimited liability company pays in Canada. If the U.S. corporation does not otherwise pay tax on the unlimited liability company's income, the structure reduces the U.S. corporation's tax liability.

An example illustrates an income-stripping arrangement. Assume that ULC, a Canadian unlimited liability company that is wholly owned by USCorp (a corporation resident in the United States), earns $200 before $40 of interest paid to USCorp. Canada taxes the interest paid at 25 percent or $10, so ULC pays $30 to USCorp. Canada taxes the remaining $160 at its regular rate. Assuming that rate is also 25 percent, ULC would pay $40 in Canadian income tax, so its total Canadian tax would be $50. USCorp also reports $200 of foreign-source income because it disregards ULC and the interest payment. If USCorp's effective U.S. tax rate is 35 percent, it would have $70 of U.S. tax, and the credit for Canadian taxes paid would reduce that amount to $20. Nonetheless, USCorp's total tax would be $70—the sum of $50 of Canadian and $20 of U.S. taxes. A lower withholding rate in Canada on the interest would not affect USCorp's total tax liability in this situation. For example, if the withholding rate was only 5 percent, ULC would pay $2 of tax on

---

[126] *See* CITA §§ 212(1), 215(1).
[127] *See Protocol Amending the Convention Between the United States of America and Canada*, art. X(2)(a), Sep. 21, 2007, S. TREATY DOC. No. 110-15 (2007) (limiting the withholding rate to 5 percent if the recipient holds at least 10 percent of the voting stock of the corporation paying the dividend) (hereinafter "*U.S.-Canada Treaty*").
[128] *See* Brunson; Gupta, Wach, Uffner & Cohen; Taylor.
[129] *See* CITA § 20(1)(c).
[130] *See U.S.-Canada Treaty*, art. XI(1) (providing generally that the country where interest originates does not tax the interest if beneficially owned by a member of the other country).

the interest and the same $40 of income tax for a total $42 of Canadian tax. The lower rate reduces the Canadian tax by $8. USCorp would credit the new amount of Canadian tax against its U.S. tax and pay $28 of U.S. tax. Thus, USCorp's total tax would remain $70.

The hybrid entity could, however, help the U.S. corporation reduce or defer its overall tax liability if its U.S. tax situation was such that it did not pay income tax on ULC's income. For example, if USCorp had losses to offset the income from Canada, it would pay no tax on that income in the United States. USCorp would then benefit from lower taxes in Canada. Thus, the hybrid entity could help reduce USCorp's tax liability.

One purpose of recent amendments to the U.S.-Canada tax treaty was to help reduce the use of hybrid entities to reduce the tax liability. The amendment pursues this goal by recharacterizing certain payments. In particular, the treaty now deems payments to be made to a person who is not subject to the treaty if (1) Canada tax law treats the payment as derived from an entity that is not a U.S. resident, (2) the entity is not fiscally transparent under U.S. tax law, and (3) the U.S. tax treatment would be different if derived directly from the payee and not through the hybrid entity.[131] The treaty deems payments to be made to a person who is not subject to the treaty if (1) Canadian tax law treats a person as receiving a payment from a Canadian resident, (2) the person is treated as fiscally transparent under U.S. tax law, and (3) U.S. tax law would treat the payment differently if the person was not transparent under U.S. tax law.[132] The payments in the example above comes within this latter rule because (1) Canada treats USCorp as receiving payments from ULC, (2) U.S. tax law disregards ULC, making it fiscally transparent under U.S. tax law, and (3) U.S. tax law would treat the payment as interest if ULC were a separate entity for U.S. tax purposes. Therefore, the rule applies, and Canada would treat the payments as made to a person who is not a member of a Contracting State, and the payments would lose the favorable treaty rates. The following example from the Canada Revenue Agency confirms that the treaty would prohibit the income-stripping structure described above.

Example [1]—ULC with one shareholder

> USCo is a resident of the United States and a qualifying person for purposes of the Convention. USCo holds all of the shares of an unlimited liability company ("ULC"). ULC is a resident of Canada under the Convention and carries on business in Canada. USCo has also made an interest-bearing loan to ULC. Under the taxation laws of the United States, ULC is a disregarded entity and thereby fiscally transparent.
>
> USCo is considered, for United States tax purposes, to carry on ULC's business operations and, as a result, USCo includes income from the ULC's Canadian operations in its income. In addition, USCo's shareholdings in ULC and the interest-bearing loan are disregarded for United States tax purposes. If ULC was not a disregarded entity, USCo would recognize interest income from the loan on an accrual basis and would be subject to tax under the Code on dividends received from ULC.
>
> Due to ULC's fiscal transparency under the Code, the loan interest is not recognized for United States tax purposes with the result that the interest income does not receive the same treatment (i.e., an inclusion of interest income on an accrual basis) that would be given to the interest if the ULC were not fiscally transparent. Therefore, Article IV(7)(b) [of the U.S.-Canada

---

[131] *See id.* at art. IV(7)(a).
[132] *See id.* at art. IV(7)(b).

Tax Treaty] will apply to the interest paid by the ULC to USCo such that it will be considered not to be paid to or derived by the USCo for the purposes of the Convention.[133]

Because the payment from ULC to USCo does not qualify for treaty benefits, the payment to USCo will be subject to Canada's regular 25 percent withholding rate.[134] Consequently, USCo cannot use this structure to obtain a reduced withholding rate in Canada. Nonetheless, the Canada Revenue Agency appears to read the provisions of the treaty literally, which allows for some opportunities to use hybrid entities to reduce tax liability. By merely creating another blocker entity to hold an interest in the hybrid entity, the U.S. corporation can obtain an economically equivalent result and favorable treaty rates on interest payments. The following example illustrates the type of opportunity that exists to reduce the Canadian withholding rate.

Example [2] – ULC with more than one shareholder

> Assume the facts in Example [1] except that USCo holds 90% of the shares of ULC. The other shareholder of ULC is USCo's wholly-owned subsidiary USSub, which is also a resident of the United States and a qualifying person for the purposes of the Convention. For United States tax purposes, ULC is treated as a fiscally transparent partnership. USCo and USSub are each allocated items of income and expenses from ULC on an annual basis in proportion to their shareholdings in ULC; the items of income and expense of ULC may be netted against each other before they are allocated to USCo and USSub. USCo is considered to earn interest from the loan and USCo and USSub are considered to have incurred a proportionate share of the interest expense payable by ULC on the loan from USCo. If ULC was not treated as a fiscally transparent partnership for United States tax purposes, USCo would still realize interest income from the loan to ULC, but USCo and USSub would not be considered to have incurred any portion of the interest expense on the loan.
>
> In this scenario, USSub will be considered to earn interest income from the loan to ULC regardless of ULC's status as a fiscally transparent entity for United States tax purposes. In determining whether Article IV(7)(b) [of the U.S.-Canada Treaty] applies to the loan interest, the focus is on the treatment of the interest as an item of income without reference to the allocation of other income or expense from the partnership (i.e., on the amount potentially subject to tax under Part XIII of the [Canadian Income Tax] Act). As a result, Article IV(7)(b) will not apply to the payment of interest by ULC to USCo.[135]

In this example, the interest expense allocated to USCo and USSub could offset USCo's interest income from ULC. Viewing USCo and USSub as an economic unit, the transaction is therefore similar to the transaction in Example 1. If USCo and USSub have sufficient losses to offset income allocated to them by ULC, they will not owe U.S. tax on the income of ULC. Apparently, even if USSub's interest in ULC is very small, the Canada Revenue Agency would appear to apply the treaty benefits to the interest ULC pays to USCo. The economic unit's only tax would therefore be the Canadian tax. If the interest payments qualify for treaty benefits, the entities could use ULC to reduce their Canadian tax liability. Thus, the Canada Revenue Agency appears to sanction the use of hybrid

---

[133] *See* CRA Document 2009-0318491I7, "Canada-United States Tax Treaty—Art. IV:6/IV:7 'same statement' (Nov. 13, 2009)", *cited in* JOHNSON & LILLE (2010).

[134] *See* CITA § 212(1)(b).

[135] *See* CRA Document 2009-0318491I7, "Canada-United States Tax Treaty—Art. IV:6/IV:7 'same statement' (Nov. 13, 2009)", *cited in* JOHNSON & LILLE (2010).

entities if the structure satisfies the letter of the law in the treaty. The Canada Revenue Agency's literal reading of the treaty would make other hybrid structures available for the purpose of reducing tax liability. This one example illustrates how partnerships, LLCs, and alternative business organizations facilitate cross-border tax planning, and how the motivation to reduce taxes can affect choice-of-entity decisions.

7. CONCLUSION

Partnerships, LLCs, and other forms of organizations are an important part of U.S. and international business and property ownership. Tax law in the United States provides businesses and property owners a wide array of choices when they combine resources. Those choices add complexity to choice-of-entity decisions, and the regimes are often complex, requiring additional planning and accounting efforts. Nonetheless, the freedom of choice and potential tax savings to be derived from that choice fuel that complexity. Therefore, nothing suggests that the tax treatment of partnerships, LLCs, and other noncorporate organizations will trend to greater simplicity in the near future. Instead, as parties and their advisors become more sophisticated and as they continue to pursue tax-saving strategies, they will find new ways to use the rules to reduce their taxes. Lawmakers and taxing authorities will have to respond to those actions with more rules. Such efforts add complexity to the law and further erode any effort to adopt purely aggregate or purely entity rules of flow-through taxation.

REFERENCES

Abrams, Howard E., *Long-Awaited Regulations Under Section 752 Provide Wrong Answers*, 44 TAX L. REV. 627 (1989).
Baldwin, Simeon Eben, *History of the Law of Private Corporations in the Colonies and States*, 3 SELECT ESSAYS IN ANGLO-AMERICAN LEGAL HIST. 236 (1909).
Bankman, Joseph, *The Structure of Silicon Valley Start-Ups*, 41 UCLA L. REV. 1737 (1994).
Borden, Bradley T., *The Federal Definition of Tax Partnership*, 42 HOUS. L. REV. 925 (2006).
Borden, Bradley T., *Partnership Allocations and the Internalization of Tax-Item Transactions*, 59 S.C. L. REV. 297 (2008).
Borden, Bradley T., *Aggregate-Plus Theory of Partnership Taxation*, 43 GA. L. REV. 717 (2009).
Borden, Bradley T., *Residual-Risk Model for Classifying Business Arrangements*, 37 FLA. ST. U. L. REV. 245 (2010).
Borden, Bradley T., *The Allure and Illusion of Partners' Interests in a Partnership*, 79 U. CIN. L. REV. 1077 (2011).
Borden, Bradley T., *Notable Partnership Articles from 2013*, 143 TAX NOTES 1513 (June 30, 2014).
Borden, Bradley T., *Math Behind Financial Aspects of Partnership Distribution Waterfalls*, 145 TAX NOTES 305 (Oct. 20, 2014).
Borden, Bradley T. & Reiss, David J., *REMIC Tax Enforcement as Financial-Market Regulator*, 16 U. PENN. J. BUS. L. 663 (2014).
Borden, Bradley T., Binder, Joseph, Blinder, Ethan & Incatasciato, Louis, *A Model for Measuring the Expected Value of Assuming Tax-Partnership Liability*, 7 BROOK. J. CORP., FIN. & COMM. L. 361 (2013).
Brock, Noel P., *Targeted Partnership Allocations, Part I*, 44 TAX ADV. 374 (June 2013).
Brock, Noel P., *Targeted Partnership Allocations, Part II*, 44 TAX ADV. 464 (July 2013).
Brunson, Samuel D., *Repatriating Tax-Exempt Investments: Tax Havens, Blocker Corporations, and Unrelated Debt-Financed Income*, 106 NW. U. L. REV. 225 (2012).
Carey, Stevens A., *Internal Rates of Return and Preferred Returns: What is the Difference?*, 6 Real Est. L. & Ind. Rep. 200 (Apr. 2, 2013).
Carney, William J., *Limited Liability Companies: Origins and Antecedents*, 66 U. COLO. L. REV. 855 (1995).

Cauble, Emily, *Was Blackstone's Initial Public Offering Too Good To Be True?: A Case Study in Closing Loopholes in the Partnership Tax Allocation Rules*, 14 Fla. Tax Rev. 153 (2013).

Chrisman, Rodney D., *LLCs are the new King of the Hill: An Empirical Study of the Number of New LLCs, Corporations, and LPs Formed in the United States Between 2004–2007 and how LLCs were Taxed for Tax Years 2002–2006*, 15 Fordham J. Corp. & Fin. L. 459 (2010).

Crane, Judson A., *The Uniform Partnership Act: A Criticism*, 28 Harv. L. Rev. 762 (1915).

Crane, Judson A., *Twenty Years Under the Uniform Partnership Act*, 2 U. Pitt. L. Rev. 129 (1936).

Cuff, Terrence Floyd, *Working with Target Allocations—Drafting in Wonderland*, 35 Real Est. Tax'n 162 (2008).

Cuff, Terrence Floyd, *Working with Target Allocations—Idiot-Proof or Drafting for Idiots?*, 35 Real Est. Tax'n 116 (2008).

Dean, Steven A., *Attractive Complexity: Tax Deregulation, the Check-the-Box Election, and the Future of Tax Simplification*, 34 Hofstra L. Rev. 405 (2005).

Demsetz, Harold, *The Structure of Ownership and the Theory of the Firm*, 26 J. L. & Econ. 375 (1983).

Easterbrook, Frank H. & Fischel, Daniel R., The Economic Structure of Corporate Law (1991).

Elliott, Amy S., *Practitioners Fuming After Issuance of New Bottom-Dollar Guarantee Rules*, 2014 TNT 20-1 (Jan. 30, 2014).

Field, Heather M., *Checking in on "Check-the-Box"*, 42 Loy. L.A. L. Rev. 451 (2009).

Fleischer, Victor E., Note, *"If it Looks Like a Duck": Corporate Resemblance and Check-the-Box Elective Tax Classification*, 96 Colum. L. Rev. 518 (1996).

Fleischer, Victor E., *The Rational Exuberance of Structuring Venture Capital Start-ups*, 57 Tax L. Rev. 137 (2003).

Goldberg, Daniel S., *Choice of Entity for a Venture Capital Start-Up: The Myth of Incorporation*, 55 Tax Law. 923 (2002).

Gryta, Thomas & Knutson, Ryan, *Windstream Cleared to Cut Taxes by Forming a REIT: IRS Allows Firm to Classify Its Phone Lines as Real Estate*, Wall Street Journal (July 29, 2014).

Gupta, Ash, Wach, Tim, Uffner, Jeffrey D. & Cohen, Susan R., *Tax Issues in Structuring Cross-Border Private Equity Funds*, 57 Canada Tax J. 23 (2009).

Haden, Ed R., Note, *The Final Regulations Under IRC Sections 704(b) and 752: Envisioning Economic Risk of Loss Through a Glass Darkly*, 49 Wash. & Lee L. Rev. 487 (1992).

Hanna, Christopher H., *Partnership Distributions: Whatever Happened to Nonrecognition?*, 82 Ky. L. J. 465 (1993–1994).

Hansmann, Henry, Kraakman, Reinier & Squire, Richard, *Law and the Rise of the Firm*, 119 Harv. L. Rev. 1333 (2006).

Hasen, David, *Partnership Special Allocations Revisited*, 13 Fla. Tax Rev. 349 (2012).

Hillman, Robert W., *Law, Culture, and the Lore of Partnership: Of Entrepreneurs, Accountability, and the Evolving Status of Partners*, 40 Wake Forest L. Rev. 793 (2005).

Hobbs, Patrick E., *Entity Classification: The One Hundred-Year Debate*, 44 Cath. U. L. Rev. 437 (1995).

Horwitz, Morton J., *Santa Clara Revisited: The Development of Corporate Theory*, 88 W. Va. L. Rev. 173 (1985).

Jackson, J. Paul, Johnson, Mark H., Surrey, Stanley S., Tenen, Carolyn K. & Warren, William C., *The Internal Revenue Code of 1954: Partnerships*, 54 Colum. L. Rev. 1183 (1954).

Jackson, J. Paul, Johnson, Mark H., Surrey, Stanley S., & Warren, William C., *A Proposed Revision of the Federal Income Tax Treatment of Partnerships and Partners—American Law Institute Draft*, 9 Tax L. Rev. 109 (1954).

Jensen, A. Ladru, *Is a Partnership Under the Uniform Partnership Act an Aggregate or Entity?*, 16 Vand. L. Rev. 377 (1963).

Jensen, Michael C. & Meckling, William H., *Theory of the Firm: Managerial Behavior, Agency Costs and Ownership Structure*, 3 J. Fin. Econ. 305 (1976).

Johnson, Elizabeth J. & Lille, Genevieve C., *The Taxation of Partnerships in Canada*, Bull. Int. Tax'n 381 (Aug./Sep. 2009).

Johnson, Elizabeth & Lille, Genevieve C., Understanding the Taxation of Partnerships (6th ed. 2010).

King, Tom, Note, *The Tax Court Capsizes a Leveraged Partnership in Canal Corp.*, 65 Tax Law. 713 (2012).

Kleinberger, Daniel S., *The Closely Held Business Through the Entity-Aggregate Prism*, 40 Wake Forest L. Rev. 827 (2005).

Kornhauser, Marjorie E., *Corporate Regulation and the Origins of the Corporate Income Tax*, 66 Ind. L.J. 53 (1990).

Lewis, William Draper, *The Uniform Partnership Act—A Reply to Mr. Crane's Criticism*, 29 Harv. L. Rev. 158 (1915).

Lipton, Richard M., *Proposed Regulations on Debt Allocations: Controversial, and Deservedly So*, 120 J. Tax'n 156 (Apr. 2014).

Lipton, Richard M. & Golub, Todd D., *The Tax Court Drains Canal Corporation's Leveraged Partnership Transaction*, 113 J. Tax'n 340 (2010).

Lobinger, Charles Sumner, *The Natural History of the Private Artificial Person: A Comparative Study in Corporate Origins*, 13 Tul. L. Rev. 41 (1938).

McCarthy, Edward J., *Adjustments to Partner's Basis Caused by Partnership Liabilities: Internal Revenue Code Section 752 in Action*, 10 St. Louis. U. L. J. 261 (1965).
Monroe, Andrea, *Saving Subchapter K: Substance, Shattered Ceilings and the Problem of Contributed Property*, 74 Brook. L. Rev. 1381 (2009).
Monroe, Andrea, *Too Big to Fail: The Problem of Partnership Allocations*, 30 Va. Tax. Rev. 289 (2012).
Monroe, Andrea, *Taxing Reality: Rethinking Partnership Distributions*, 47 Loy. L.A. L. Rev. 657 (2014).
Morse, Susan C., *Startup Ltd.: Tax Planning and Initial Incorporation of Location*, 14 Fla. Tax. Rev. 319 (2013).
Peaslee, James M. & Nirenberg, David Z., Federal Income Taxation of Securitization Transactions (4th ed. 2011).
Polsky, Gregg D., *Deterring Tax-Driven Partnership Allocations*, 64 Tax Law. 97 (2010).
Reyes, Francisco & Vermeulen, Erik P.M., *Company Law, Lawyers and "Legal" Innovation: Common Law versus Civil Law*, Lex Research Topics in Corp. L. & Econ. Working Paper No. 2011-3 (Aug. 10, 2011), *available at* http://papers.ssrn.com/sol3/papers.cfm?abstract_id=1907894.
Ribstein, Larry E., *The Rise of the Uncorporation*, University of Illinois Law and Economics Working Papers, no. 83, *available at* http://law.bepress.com/uiuclwps/art83 (July 2007).
Rosin, Gary S., *The Entity-Aggregate Dispute: Conceptualism and Functionalism in Partnership Law*, 42 Ark. L. Rev. 395 (1989).
Rubin, Blake D., Whiteway, Andrea M., and Finkelstien, Jon G., *A "Guaranteed" Debacle: Proposed Partnership Liability Regulations*, 143 Tax Notes 219 (Apr. 14, 2014).
Simmons, Daniel L., *The Tax Consequences of Partnership Break-Ups: A Primer on Partnership Sales and Liquidations*, 66 Tax Law. 653 (2013).
Taylor, William B., *"Blockers," "Stoppers," and the Entity Classification Rules*, 64 Tax Law. 1 (2010).
Williamson, Oliver E., *Organizational Form, Residual Claimants, and Corporate Control*, 26 J. L. & Econ. 351 (1983).
Williston, Samuel, *History of the Law of Business Corporations Before 1800*, 2 Harv. L. Rev. 105 (1888).
Yin, George K., *The Taxation of Private Enterprises: Some Policy Questions Stimulated by the "Check-the-Box" Regulations*, 51 SMU L. Rev. 125 (1997).

11. Capital accounts in LLCs and in partnerships
*Donald J. Weidner**

1. INTRODUCTION

A lawyer drafting either an operating agreement for a limited liability company or a partnership agreement will be attempting to tease out, and reduce to writing, the basic economic understanding of the co-owners. Core matters include: the contributions each owner will make; how much credit each will be given for those contributions, be they of property or of services; how the owners will share in profits; how they will share in losses; how they will share in operating distributions; the price to be paid in the event of a buyout; and the right to any liquidating distributions, including the right to require another owner to "pony up" a final amount on liquidation.[1]

Dealing with the client can be sensitive, particularly when it comes to reducing to writing exactly what happens if things do not go as well as expected. Sometimes consciously and sometimes unconsciously, the drafter also will be interacting with: (1) the organization's accountant, who may not yet be identified but who is likely to create a separate "capital account" for each owner; (2) statutory default rules that may give economic significance to those capital accounts; and (3) provisions of standard form agreements that contain impenetrable language designed to assuage federal income tax authorities who, in an audit, are likely to scrutinize the significance of capital accounts to determine the propriety of special allocations of tax benefits.

The purpose of this chapter is to provide an integrated view of capital accounts in LLCs and in partnerships. It begins with an explanation of what capital accounts are and what they are not. It emphasizes their importance as a matter of accounting practice and as a matter of state law. It also attempts to put their federal income tax significance into simple historical perspective. It assumes that the economic understanding of the parties must drive the maintenance of capital accounts and cautions that the adoption of standard form tax boilerplate may frustrate that understanding. Because of the opportunities the federal income tax law offers to these "pass-through" organizations, there are often two sets of books, one for financial accounting purposes and one for federal income tax purposes.[2] For simplicity of analysis, this chapter proceeds on the assumption that they are one and the same.

---

*   I would like to express my appreciation to Steve Johnson for his exhaustive and helpful comments and to Allan Donn, Mary McCormick and Manuel Utset, who always make things better.

[1]   Other core economic matters include: whether there is a right to make capital calls and remedies for failing to heed the call; who has the right to compel operating distributions; provisions concerning organizational continuity, such as the right or obligation to be bought out and the right to liquidate the business; and any waivers of the obligation to refrain from competing.

[2]   *See generally* Frank Lyon Co. v. U.S., 435 U.S. 561, 577 (1978): "[T]he characterization of a transaction for financial accounting purposes, on the one hand, and for tax purposes, on the

2. INTRODUCTION TO THE BALANCE SHEET

Most generally, the accounting profession will apply basic accounting principles to represent the economic understanding of firm owners. The application of these basic principles will produce at least two basic documents: an income and expense statement and a balance sheet. Even the generalist is likely to recall that the balance sheet reflects the age-old equation: Assets = Liabilities + Equity. In the case of both the LLC and the partnership, each member or partner has a specifically designated share of the equity portion of the balance sheet.[3] The owner's separate share of the organizational equity, or of the overall "owner's equity," is referred to as that owner's "capital account." This is very different from accounting for corporations, in which shareholders are not given individual equity accounts.

Consider, for example, the situation of a partnership or LLC in which owners A and B contribute $6 and $4, respectively. The double entry system of accounting will reflect where the money came from, that is, from contributions of capital, and where it went, initially into the organization's assets, that is, cash. Assume that the firm then borrows $90 in cash and uses the total $100 cash on hand to purchase a piece of real property. The balance sheet will show, on the left side, a real property asset at its $100 cost and, on the right side, $90 in the liabilities section of the balance sheet and $10 in capital accounts, with A's capital account reflecting A's $6 contribution and B's capital account reflecting B's $4 contribution.

At the most elemental level, then, each owner's capital account reflects how much the owner has a right to receive from firm equity. Thus, if the $100 asset were subsequently sold for a price equal to its acquisition cost, and the liability were repaid for $90, the asset side of the balance sheet would show $10 in assets and the capital accounts would say that, if the firm were liquidated, A would receive $6 and B would receive $4.

Restated for our present purposes, each owner has an individual capital account that reflects that owner's share of firm assets minus their share of firm liabilities. The capital account is often described, sometimes loosely and inaccurately, as the owner's "bank account" in the organization. Like a usual bank account, one's capital account may be positive (thus reflecting, at some very general level, at least the hope of a distribution) or negative (overdrawn, and thus, also at some very general level, reflecting an obligation to pay back). Unlike the usual bank account, however, the maintenance of owners' capital accounts is much more complicated and varied, even before taking into account their significance either for state law purposes or for federal income tax purposes.

---

other, need not necessarily be the same." See also Thor Power Tool Co. v. Commissioner, 439 U.S. 522, 542 (1971), referring to "the vastly different objectives that financial and tax accounting have."

[3] For the sake of simplicity, members of LLCs and partners in partnerships will both be referred to as "owners."

3. BASIC CAPITAL ACCOUNT ACCOUNTING

The Primacy of Intent

The basic rule of both LLC law and partnership law is that the owners are free to allocate each of the economic consequences of their business as they see fit (provided they do not violate the rights of third parties). As among themselves, for example, they are free to agree on how much credit they are to be given for different kinds of contributions, on how they share profits, or different kinds of profits, on how they share losses, or different kinds of losses, on when and how they receive operating, or current, distributions, and on their rights and duties when one of them is bought out or on liquidation of the business. The task of the agreement is to record these decisions. The task of the accountant is to execute the agreement on the organizational books. Sometimes, however, the written agreement may be incomplete, ambiguous or vague. Because the capital accounts reflect the sharing relationships among the owners, an accountant is likely to be filling in the gaps along the way. In filling those gaps, the accountant may be informed by a wide variety of factors, including practices of the various members, conversations with them, personal experience with them in other contexts, standard practice in the business or industry, and local statutory or decisional law. At least annually, the documents will be produced. Because of this, financial statements may be considered as evidence of the agreement of the members.

Basic Capital Account "Maintenance"

What capital accounts are and are not: equity accounts that mix apples and oranges
Because of the popularity and at least relative appropriateness of the analogy to a bank account, it is important to explain why a capital account is *not* like a normal bank account. The stereotypical bank account is a record of transactions in hard cash, increased both by dollars deposited and by interest credited and decreased by withdrawals.[4] The classic bank account does not involve any judgment calls estimating, through appraisal or otherwise, the value of assets. Although capital accounts could be similarly constructed and maintained, they rarely are. They usually reflect a mix of hard cash entries and entries that involve estimates of the value assigned to assets or, on occasion, to services. Often, and not necessarily on a regular basis, assets that are initially listed at one value are revalued, or "marked to market" (Abrams 2010). Consider some of the things usually in the mix.

Cash Hard dollar entries typically include cash contributions and loan amounts. A cash contribution of $100 will be reflected as a $100 asset, and it will be credited to the capital account of the owner who contributed it. A loan of $100 in cash will be reflected as a $100 asset and will be credited to the liability portion of the balance sheet, with no effect on the owners' capital accounts. Conversely, if $50 is transferred to an owner as a distribution, the asset account will be reduced by $50 and the recipient owner's capital account will also be reduced by $50.

---

[4] Until the recent financial crisis, there was no suggestion that bank accounts would ever be reduced by "negative interest."

Capital accounts do *not* reflect all cash transfers to and from owners. Most broadly and most importantly, capital accounts only reflect an owner's equity in the venture and transactions with regard to that owner's equity (Baker 2010). An owner's capital account does *not* reflect a transaction in which the owner is interacting with the firm as if the owner were an unrelated third party—sometimes referred to as a "third party" transaction[5] (Larson 2013). Thus, in the simple situation under discussion, if the $50 in cash were transferred to the owner as a salary rather than as a distribution of owner's equity, it will *not* reduce the recipient's capital account.

Noncash assets and transfers If $200 in firm cash is used to purchase an asset, the $200 in cash will disappear from the firm books and the new asset will be listed at its $200 cost. The liability account and the capital accounts will remain unchanged. On the other hand, if an asset that was purchased long ago outside the firm is transferred to the firm by an owner through a contribution of capital, the asset is likely to be listed on the firm's books at an estimate of its current value rather than at its historical cost[6] (Simmons 2009). If, for example, owner X contributes to firm capital an automobile that X purchased years ago for $1,000, the owners may agree it is now worth only $200 and reflect that estimate on the firm books. Thus, the automobile will be listed as a $200 asset and X will receive a credit of only $200 to capital account. The balance sheet *will* balance.

Here again, capital accounts do *not* reflect all transfers of noncash assets between the owners and the firm. Capital accounts only reflect an owner's equity and transactions with regard to that equity. Thus, if in the above example X sells the property to the firm rather than transfers it as a contribution to capital, the sale will not affect X's capital account.

Assets listed on a balance sheet are often charged with estimated depreciation. The depreciation for financial accounting purposes may be chosen as the best possible estimate of economic depreciation. Or, management may decide to overstate or understate economic depreciation on the firm books. For example, the asset could, as an economic matter, be appreciating significantly and still be "charged" with depreciation that is being claimed for financial accounting purposes, federal income tax purposes, or both.[7]

If an asset is reduced by a $100 depreciation charge, you will not be surprised to learn that the balance sheet will be made to balance. Liabilities will not be reduced by the depreciation charge and that leaves only the capital accounts, which must, in the aggregate, be reduced by a total amount equal to the depreciation charge. Someone must decide how that depreciation charge is allocated among the owners' capital accounts. For example, will a portion of it reduce the capital accounts of each of the owners or will it all be charged to reduce the capital account of the owner who contributed the asset? If

---

[5] I.R.C. § 707(a)(1) sets out the general rule that if an owner "engages in a transaction with a [firm] other than in his capacity as an [owner] of such [firm], the transaction shall, except as otherwise provided in this section, be considered as occurring between the [firm] and one who is not [an owner]."

[6] I.R.C. § 704(c) and the regulations thereunder address the appropriate tax allocations when property is contributed to a firm at a value different than its basis, that is, with a "built in" gain or loss.

[7] Federal income tax law restricts the methods taxpayers may use to compute tax depreciation. See I.R.C. §§ 167, 168 and 197.

all owners are to share in the charge, by how much will each owner's capital account be reduced? These are questions that should be answered in the agreement. If the agreement is silent, statutory default rules, to be discussed shortly, may be called upon to answer the question. As we shall see, the Internal Revenue Service (IRS) may closely examine the impact of allocations of tax depreciation on capital accounts, and on the significance given to those accounts, to determine the validity of the allocations for federal income tax purposes.

Finally, depreciation deductions aside, an asset listed at one amount can subsequently be listed at a different, or restated amount. According to popular terminology, an asset may be "marked to market." That process may entail a marking up or a marking down. For example, if a firm purchases a share of stock for $100, it is likely to be listed on the balance sheet at $100. If the stock is regularly traded and has tripled in value, it may be "marked up" on the balance sheet to its $300 market value. Because the balance sheet must balance and liabilities remain unaffected, the capital accounts of the owners must be increased to reflect the additional $200 in equity. Here again, the partnership or operating agreement should answer the question how that $200 in unrealized profit should be allocated among the owners. The same issues are presented if the asset drops in value.

Services Services contributed by an owner are not usually assigned a value for financial accounting purposes. Therefore, the value of those services will not be reflected on the balance sheets as affecting assets, liabilities or capital accounts. As we shall see, this difference in treatment from cash contributions can have unpleasant consequences for the owner who contributes services, *especially* if capital accounts are treated as bank accounts. On the other hand, the owners could conclude that an owner contributing services should indeed get a credit for the value of those services. If those services appear, for example, as a $400 asset on the firm books, perhaps described as "good will" or as "prepaid services," the balance sheet will be made to balance. The owner contributing services deemed to be worth $400 will receive a $400 credit to his, her or its capital account.

In short, an owner's capital account is the owner's share of the organization's net apples and oranges. The lawyer's job, at a minimum, is to tease out and memorialize in an agreement the intent of the owners with regard to how they will slice and dice those apples and oranges among themselves. The accounting profession will then apply the agreement to the results of operation of the business. It will produce constantly changing capital accounts that capture the cumulative impact of operations on the equity account of each owner. These individualized owner's equity accounts represent a whole additional level of accounting that does not exist on a corporate balance sheet, which does not assign shareholders their individual slices of firm equity. One way of thinking about it is by considering that standard corporate accounting reflects an entity approach whereas standard LLC and partnership accounting reflects an aggregate approach.

The maintenance rules in a nutshell
The basic rules of capital account maintenance can be stated simply. On the positive side, an owner's capital account is increased, or credited, by the cash and by the agreed net value of any property the owner contributes. It is also increased by the owner's share of any firm profits. On the negative side, an owner's capital account is decreased, or debited, by the amount of cash and by the net value of any property the owner receives as a distribution.

It is also decreased by any depreciation charged to the owner and by the owner's share of any other losses.

The owners may not think about their capital accounts until one or more of them leaves or until the firm is liquidated. At either one of those points, the intent of the owners, ideally reflected in their agreement, is of course the ultimate driver. The intent of the owners may be to carve up the equity pie in specific ways completely independent of capital accounts. On the other hand, the owners' agreement may specifically provide that capital accounts determine, for example, the amount of a buyout price or the allocation of liquidating distributions. The most difficult situations to deal with are those in which the owners' agreement is ambiguous, vague, silent on the point or completely nonexistent. In those situations, the capital accounts may be deemed to be the best evidence of their agreement.

There are two fundamental ways in which capital accounts may be given significance, either expressly, by statutory default rule or inferentially. First, the owner's positive capital accounts may direct the distribution of the net assets that remain in the firm. Second, an owner's negative capital account may be deemed to reflect a debt to the firm that must be repaid to the firm, either to be paid to firm creditors or to be distributed to the other owners. Not all owners may have intended giving either or both of these kinds of significance to capital accounts.

Misunderstandings and unintended consequences
There are two basic aspects of normal capital account maintenance that often either cause or reflect unintended consequences. The first is that a negative capital account may be regarded as reflecting a debt to the firm, which can come as a particular shock to an owner who contributes services. The second is that there will be a need to mark assets to market before capital accounts can be given their "normal" significance upon either a liquidation or a buyout.

Negative account shock to service partner   Consider again the often oversimplified statement that a capital account can be analogized to a bank account. The statement persists because there is some truth to it. Viewed as a bank account, a negative capital account is like an overdrawn bank account—there is an obligation to repay the firm. The question is whether that obligation is nonrecourse or recourse.

Consider the situation of a complete liquidation of the business. Capital accounts can have one of the two basic functions alluded to earlier. First, they can direct the distribution of any net equity that remains in the firm after the business has been wound down and outsider creditors have been satisfied. Second, they can reflect that an owner with a negative capital account has an obligation to contribute additional assets to the firm so that those fresh assets can be distributed to unsatisfied firm creditors or to other owners.

Consider the example of an extremely simple liquidation of a two-person firm. Assume that all the firm's assets have been sold and reduced to cash. Assume that cash has then been used to satisfy all the firm's outside creditors. Although there are no remaining assets inside the firm, and no remaining liabilities to third parties, the two owners of the firm are left with "opposite-signed" capital accounts. That is to say, one owner has a positive capital account and the other has a negative capital account. Because the balance sheet must balance, if there are no remaining assets or third-party liabilities, one capital account will be negative in the same amount as the other capital account will be positive.

Putting some meat on the bones of this example, assume that, after all assets have been liquidated and the proceeds paid to satisfy creditors, the firm is an empty shell that reports owner *A* with a positive capital account of $100 and owner *B* with a negative capital account of $100. The normal application of capital accounts analysis provides that *B* must contribute $100 to the firm to bring *B*'s capital account up from minus $100 to zero. The balance sheet must still balance, and the new cash asset of $100 would be attributed to *A*'s $100 positive capital account. As a result, *A* would receive a liquidating distribution of that $100. After that distribution, the balance sheet would continue to balance, with zero assets, zero liabilities and two zero capital accounts. As we shall see, this is the result of the default capital account reconciliation rules in the Revised Uniform Partnership Act. In short, these rules give the capital accounts both kinds of significance. They guide the distribution of what is in the firm at liquidation. They also require that a negative capital account be treated as reflecting a recourse obligation to pay more money into the firm.[8]

The classic and most controversial situation in which opposite-signed capital accounts can have unexpected consequences involves a mixture of owners who contribute services and owners who contribute capital. Consider a hypothetical two-person firm made up of one owner, Property, who contributes property and another owner, Services, who contributes services. If Property pays $100 for property and contributes it to the firm, the balance sheet will balance. The contribution of the $100 piece of property is reflected on the firm books both as a $100 property asset and as a $100 credit to Property's capital account. Unless otherwise agreed, Services will not be treated as contributing an asset and hence will not receive any credit to Services' capital account. Assume that nothing else happens except that the property is subsequently sold for only $20, that is, at an $80 loss. The question is how that loss will be shared. If Property and Services have agreed to share all losses equally, the $80 loss will be charged 50/50 to their respective capital accounts. The result is that there will be $20 cash left in the firm. The equal sharing of the $80 loss will reduce Property's capital account from $100 to $60 and Services' capital account from zero to negative $40, or ($40).

Make no mistake about it. Two things are clear. First, the analogy to bank accounts and the default rules in the case of partnerships both say that Services must contribute $40, thus bringing Services' capital account from ($40) up to zero and the total firm cash up from $20 to $60. The $60 is then distributed to liquidate the equity interest of Property, taking Property's capital account from $60 to zero. After the distribution, the balance sheet balances. Zero assets equal the sum of zero liabilities and zero capital accounts.

The second thing that is clear is that this may come as a complete surprise to Services. Services may not have understood that the general agreement to share losses equally applied to losses from the sale of property contributed by Property. The fundamental problem, if there is one, is not with capital accounts or their analysis. The fundamental problem is that the owners never reached a common understanding of the meaning of the agreement that all losses will be shared equally.

Confusion regarding impact on current versus liquidating distributions and on buyouts
There is a second, more general way in which capital accounts maintenance, and the

---

[8] Except in the case of a negative capital account of a limited liability partner.

analogy to a bank account, can lead to misunderstanding. We have seen that a failure to understand that capital accounts represent a mix of apples and oranges can lead to the inaccurate assumption that an owner's capital account represents a reasonably accurate snapshot of the value of the owner's equity. This basic misunderstanding can lead to the further mistaken assumption that capital accounts have equal predictive value, if not mandatory force, in the case of a current distribution, in the case of a liquidating distribution and in the case of a buyout.

Capital accounts generally have different consequences in each of these three situations. Capital accounts do not address when current distributions should be made. Nor do they address when additional contributions must currently be made. In the case of a liquidation or a buyout, unlike the situation of a bank account, a firm's assets will generally either have to be sold or marked up to market or down to market before capital accounts give a clearer picture of the value of an equity interest. Capital accounts address the liquidation most directly and the buyout derivatively.

CURRENT DISTRIBUTIONS   It is important to emphasize that capital accounts say very little about the right to a current distribution. Even if a capital account accurately reflects the value of an owner's equity to the penny, it does not say anything about the right to receive a current distribution. Indeed, even if the firm's only asset is cash, the capital accounts do not even suggest that the holder of a positive capital account has any right to a current distribution. Such a right, if it exists, must be found in the agreement of the owners, which may be in writing or may be established in parol. As we are about to see, statutory default rules, both for partnerships and for LLCs, are notably silent on the basic issue of when an owner has a right to a current distribution. Much to the chagrin of the creditors of owners, capital accounts, standing alone, do not fill the void. An owner's creditors cannot levy upon a right the owner does not have.

LIQUIDATIONS AND BUYOUTS   Capital accounts, subject always to the agreement of the owners, have more to say when an owner exits the firm. Owner exit can be effected in one of two ways. First, the owner can be "cashed out" as part of a liquidation of the firm. Most simply, liquidation can be accomplished either by sale of the entire business as a going concern or by selling the firm's assets and satisfying its liabilities. Second, the owner could be simply "bought out" of a firm that will continue. As always, in both these situations, the partnership or operating agreement controls the rights among the owners and between the owners and the firm. However, unlike the situation involving a current distribution, the statutory default rules may give the capital accounts great economic significance, and it is to these rules that we now turn.

4. STATUTORY DEFAULT RULES ON CAPITAL ACCOUNTS

Partnerships

Partnership law is more detailed regarding the maintenance and significance of capital accounts than is the law of LLCs in most states. Most states have adopted the Revised

176 *Partnerships, LLCs and alternative forms of business organizations*

Uniform Partnership Act of 1994 ("RUPA")[9] and many of the subsequent amendments to it. RUPA introduced extensive default rules on the relations among partners and between partnerships and partners that were unprecedented in scope (Donn, Hillman & Weidner 2014). In particular, RUPA introduced default rules that "deem" capital accounts to be maintained for each partner and give those capital accounts important economic significance when a partnership is being liquidated and when a departing partner is being bought out.

RUPA's capital account maintenance rules
RUPA makes clear that its capital account rules are all default rules, rather than mandatory rules. That is, as among themselves, the partners' agreement controls.[10] The partners are free to agree to give capital accounts any significance they like, or none at all.

If the partnership agreement is silent on the point, RUPA deems that capital accounts are maintained in a certain way.

Each partner is deemed to have an account that is:

(1) credited with an amount equal to the money plus the value of any other property, net of the amount of any liabilities, the partner contributes to the partnership and the partner's share of the partnership profits; and
(2) charged with an amount equal to the money plus the value of any other property, net of the amount of any liabilities, distributed by the partnership to the partner and the partner's share of the partnership losses.[11]

These rules do not provide for crediting a capital account for a contribution of services. Accompanying default rules provide how much of the firm's profits or losses are to be credited or charged to each partner. Profits are to be shared and credited equally and losses are to be shared and charged "in proportion to the partner's share of the profits."[12] The Official Comments to these unprecedented provisions are brief but make four basic points.

First, the Official Comments explain that RUPA's capital account maintenance rules reflect the basic accounting practice described earlier in this chapter. This is an important point to be made in response to those who believe that RUPA's new provisions on capital accounts are inappropriate. RUPA's rules on capital accounts reflect what is taking place in the world of business, particularly small business. More precisely, even if the partners in their agreement do not specifically agree to construct and maintain a capital account for each partner, the accounting profession is likely to do it as a matter of course. The partners, or their attorneys, may not be aware of that. Furthermore, they may not be aware that proper capital account creation and maintenance may be critical if the IRS challenges the validity of special allocations of tax benefits among the partners.

---

[9] In 1996, RUPA was modified to include limited liability partnership provisions. Uniform Partnership Act (1997), 6 UNIF. LAWS ANN. Part I. The Uniform Law Commission, which promulgated the RUPA in 1994 and its 1997 revision, has recently proposed "harmonized" provisions that would eliminate the capital account provisions that most states have adopted.
[10] R.U.P.A. § 103(a).
[11] R.U.P.A. § 401(a).
[12] R.U.P.A. § 401(b).

Second, the Official Comments underscore that RUPA's capital account rules are default rules rather than mandatory rules.[13] As is almost always the case with RUPA's rules regulating the rights among partners and between partnership and partners, RUPA's capital account rules can be set aside by the agreement of the partners. In statutory language, RUPA's capital account rules apply only "[i]n the absence of another system of partnership accounts" chosen by the partners.[14] Sophisticated parties can craft economic agreements among themselves as they see fit, provided the rights of third parties are not violated.

Third, the Official Comments acknowledge that RUPA's capital account rules are "rudimentary."[15] Why enact statutory default rules that simply scratch the surface of sophisticated business practice? As the Reporter on the project, I can write with confidence that the Drafting Committee concluded that some guidance was better than none at all. The fundamental reason for including "rudimentary" rules on the construction and maintenance of capital accounts is to give an analytical starting point to small business people, to their lawyers and other advisors, and to the judges or mediators who might be resolving their disputes. The core function of RUPA is, after all, to provide a "residual" set of rules to govern unincorporated businesses. That is, RUPA controls co-owners of a business for profit who have not formed any other business organization. It is a package of clear and predictable rules for the participants, and for the resolvers of their disputes, to turn to when they have no provable agreement. In particular, RUPA's capital account rules tell all involved how to begin to analyze who gets what in the event of commercial divorce.

Finally, reflecting the importance of capital accounts in the event of commercial divorce, the Official Comments direct the reader to the provisions on partnership liquidations, in which the capital accounts are given their most direct and explicit significance.[16] As we shall see, these capital accounts-driven liquidation rules are in turn the starting point for the default rule on the price that must be paid to buy a partner out (Golub 2009).

Impact on liquidating distributions: the capital account reconciliation requirement

RUPA gives the most direct significance to capital accounts in the case of a liquidation of the partnership. The key provision is Section 807, which is entitled "Settlement of Accounts and Contributions Among Partners." It provides that the firm assets "must be applied to discharge its obligations to creditors" and that "[a]ny surplus must be applied to pay in cash the net amount distributable to partners in accordance with their right to distributions" under RUPA's capital account reconciliation rule. This "in cash rule" means that, in the case of a liquidation of the business, a "mark to market" approach is not sufficient. Unless the partners have agreed to the contrary, any partner has the right to insist that the assets be sold and the proceeds used to satisfy creditors. No partner may either insist upon or be forced to accept a liquidating distribution in any form other than cash.[17]

---

[13] R.U.P.A. § 103.
[14] R.U.P.A. § 401, Official Comment 2.
[15] Indeed, they are so rudimentary they include no reference to a charge for depreciation.
[16] "The rules regarding the settlement of the partners' accounts upon the dissolution and winding up of the partnership business are found in Section 807." Id.
[17] RUPA § 402 provides: "A partner has no right to receive, and may not be required to accept, a distribution in kind."

What happens after the assets are sold? Section 807's capital account reconciliation rule first provides that the profits and losses "from the liquidation of the partnership assets must be credited and charged to the partners' accounts."[18] It then gives the capital accounts both kinds of significance discussed earlier. First, the capital accounts guide the liquidating distribution of any cash that remains after creditors are satisfied: "The partnership shall make a distribution to a partner in an amount equal to any excess of the credits over the charges in the partner's account." Second, a negative capital account must be treated as reflecting a debt to the partnership. In the statutory language: each partner "shall contribute to the partnership an amount equal to any excess of the charges over the credits in the partner's account."[19] All of this makes sense under standard accounting practice. Because the balance sheet will always be in balance, one partner's negative capital account means that there is an "opposite signed" amount somewhere else. The negative capital account of Partner *A* means either that one of the other partners has a positive capital account or that there is an outstanding liability to a creditor. Thus, the additional money contributed by the partner with the negative capital account will either be paid out to an unsatisfied creditor or be distributed to another partner with a positive capital account balance.

Significance on buyout

RUPA also contains default provisions of unprecedented detail defining what happens when a partner is to be bought out of a partnership that will continue. Among other things, and most importantly for our purposes, it defines the price that must be paid to the partner being bought out. In the case of a buyout, the basic price that must be paid is the amount the partner being bought out would have received if the partnership were being liquidated.[20] Stated differently, the buyout price is theoretically determined by a hypothetical liquidation of the business. Hence, Section 807's capital account reconciliation rule must be applied, although in a modified way. Because the partnership assets are not being sold as they would be in the case of a "true" liquidation, they must be valued—they must be "marked to market." As in the case of a liquidating distribution, when the reconciliation rule requires gain or loss on the sale of partnership assets to be credited or charged to capital accounts, gain or loss on the hypothetical sale of those same assets must also be reflected in capital accounts. Liabilities must then be hypothetically satisfied. The result is a hypothetical balance in the capital account of the partner being bought out.

Significance on current distribution

RUPA's capital account maintenance and reconciliation rules were not intended to have any effect either on the right to receive a current distribution or on any current obligation to make an additional contribution.

---

[18] R.U.P.A. § 807(b).
[19] R.U.P.A. § 807(b). The deficit makeup calculation does not include "charges attributable to an obligation for which the partner is not personally liable under" the limited liability partnership shield of R.U.P.A. § 306(c). Id.
[20] R.U.P.A. § 701(b). For further discussion of this provision, see R. Hillman, D. Weidner and A. Donn, The Revised Uniform Partnership Act S 701, Authors' Comment 4 (2014).

Limited Liability Companies

The LLC acts in the various states were typically crafted by drafting committees made up of corporate lawyers more comfortable with the corporate form and real estate, probate and trust lawyers, who were more comfortable with the partnership form. The resulting LLC acts draw both from partnership law and from corporate law. The state statutes vary greatly and in particular diverge based on how much, and what, they draw from each of the two pre-existing bodies of law. One thing is clear: most do *not* borrow heavily from RUPA's capital account maintenance and reconciliation rules.

The Revised Uniform Limited Liability Company Act

The Uniform Law Commission, which promulgated RUPA, subsequently promulgated the Revised Uniform Limited Liability Company Act ("RULLCA").[21] RULLCA has not been adopted nearly as widely as RUPA. However, it is instructive for the purpose of our focus on capital accounts. Although RULLCA borrows liberally from RUPA in other respects, it rejects RUPA's treatment of capital accounts.[22] It does so in a provision that addresses something that RUPA does not: the right to share in a current distribution. RUPA did not contain a separate provision on the right to current, or non-liquidating, distributions. Indeed, RUPA had no provision at all on current distributions. It is interesting that, to address something that RUPA did not, the RULLCA drafters felt it necessary to scrap all of RUPA's capital accounts rules affecting liquidating distributions and buyouts.

The RULLCA rule on current distributions is a free-standing provision, Section 404, entitled "Sharing of and Right to Distributions before Dissolution." It provides that a member has a right to a distribution before dissolution "only if the company decides to make an interim distribution."[23] However, if a distribution is made, it "must be in equal shares among members."[24] In the process, RULLCA completely discards RUPA's capital account reconciliation rules. The Official Comment to the current distribution rule explains the reason for eliminating "the default structure for maintaining capital accounts" as follows:

> Capital accounts are maintained for one purpose, to determine how distributions will be made.... If the statute has a simple default rule for how distributions will be made to the members, providing an additional set of default profit and loss allocation provisions and capital account rules will be, at best, duplicative and, at worse, inconsistent with the distribution rules.[25]

---

[21] Uniform Limited Liability Company Act (2006), last amended 2011.

[22] Indeed, a recent "harmonized" version of RUPA proposes to abandon the capital accounts rules. It remains to be seen whether this change will be widely adopted. Even if all statutory capital account default rules were to be eliminated, partnerships and LLCs would continue to generate capital accounts, absent a shift to a corporate approach that has no separate equity account for each owner.

[23] RULLCA § 404(b).

[24] The full provision is RULLCA § 404(a): "Any distribution made by a limited liability company before its dissolution and winding up must be in equal shares among members and persons dissociated as members, except to the extent necessary to comply with a transfer effective under Section 502 or charging order in effect under Section 503."

[25] RULLCA § 404, Official Comment 1.

The Delaware Limited Liability Company Act

The Delaware LLC Act is probably the most influential statute governing LLCs. Here, as in many other cases, Delaware sets the standard for business law. Like RULLCA, the Delaware LLC Act declines to address the maintenance or significance of capital accounts.[26]

5. FEDERAL INCOME TAX SIGNIFICANCE OF CAPITAL ACCOUNTS

As mentioned earlier, capital accounts can exist and be maintained entirely apart from federal income tax purposes. Here, as in other areas, two sets of books are often maintained, one for financial accounting purposes and the other for federal income tax purposes. The two sets of books can be quite different. For tax purposes, capital accounts must also include items of taxable income, gain, loss, deduction or credit allocated to the owners.

Origin of Tax Rules on Capital Accounts that Bind Both Partnerships and LLCs

Even though partnerships and LLCs are not bound by common state statutory default rules regulating the maintenance and significance of capital accounts, they continue to be linked both by a common accounting practice and by the treatment they share for federal income tax purposes. For federal income tax purposes, most multi-member LLCs are "pass through" entities, just like partnerships.[27] Indeed, they are governed by the partnership tax rules of Subchapter K, the magic 700's as I like to think of them, which enable an aggregate approach to taxation.[28] The LLC, being the newcomer on the block, simply got swept up into Subchapter K. Under these rules, there is no tax at the entity level. Rather, firm taxable income or loss, or items thereof, are "passed though" to the individual firm owners. As a general rule, Subchapter K has long given the owners great freedom to allocate items of income, gain, loss, deduction or credit among themselves as they see fit. If their so-called "special" allocations are "disregarded" by the IRS, the IRS will reallocate them in a manner it deems more appropriate.

There have long been rules on special allocations, also known as the "704(b)" rules because of the Internal Revenue Code section under which they were promulgated (Monroe 2010). In 1985, those rules were made much more complicated, and it may be useful to explain how they got that way. For many years prior to 1986, passive investors were being allocated hundreds of millions in tax losses from pass-through investments in which they took no active part and in amounts far beyond any amounts they had at risk.

---

[26] By contrast, Delaware's partnership law includes RUPA's capital account maintenance rule and RUPA's capital account reconciliation rule. Del. Code Ann. tit. 6, §§ 15-401(g) and 15-807(b).

[27] A multi-member LLC may "check the box" and be treated as a corporation. I.R.C. § 7701 and Treas. Reg. §§ 301.7701-2 and -3.

[28] The entity approach continues for many purposes under Subchapter K. Most basically, the firm is a reporting entity.

If investors made cash contributions, they were minor compared to the total amount of "basis" they were allowed to claim in their partnership interests. "Basis" is tax-speak for a taxpayer's unrecovered investment in the eyes of the tax law. In the heyday of real estate and other tax shelters, limited partners were claiming and using deductions up to the full amount of a basis that included not only the cash they contributed, and hence had at risk, but also their share of nonrecourse liabilities, with respect to which they took no risk. They were being "specially allocated" items of deduction and credit in a way that the Treasury saw as significantly damaging the effectiveness of the personal income tax. "Investors" were sheltering from tax their income from other sources.

The Tax Reform Act of 1976 introduced "at risk" rules to limit deductions from certain investments to amounts taxpayers had at risk.[29] Amounts at risk included cash and recourse liabilities, but not nonrecourse liabilities. Nevertheless, these rules let a great deal through, and real estate tax shelters in particular continued to spread and grow. Ultimately, the 1986 "passive loss" rules denied limited partners and other nonprofessional passive investors the ability to offset either their portfolio income or their personal service income with these partnership deductions.[30] Theoretically, they "get" their allocations of deduction or loss, they just can't use them. The passive loss rules went to the heart of the tax shelters and were a crowning victory for opponents of the limited partnership tax shelters that had spread from the top 1 percent deep into the middle class.

In 1983, three years before the passive loss rules were enacted, the IRS proposed dramatic amendments to the 704(b) regulations, which were designed primarily to tighten down on tax shelters. Section 704(b) had itself been amended by the Tax Reform Act of 1976, which replaced 704(b)'s "principal purpose of . . . the avoidance or evasion of any tax" limitation with the current requirement that allocations have "substantial economic effect." The substantial economic effect language had previously appeared in the legislative history of the 1954 Code and in the regulations. (Weidner 1981). The 1983 proposals officially announced a shift to heavy reliance on capital accounts to probe, among other things, substantial economic effect. They also included extensive provisions on nonrecourse financing (McKee, Nelson & Whitmire 2014). One wonders whether these 704(b) regulations, which were ultimately adopted and subsequently modified, would have been quite so complex had they been drafted subsequent to the passage of the passive loss rules. Although special allocations continue to pose important issues, most of the war against pass-through tax shelters was won with the passive loss rules.

Section 704(b) and the Three Ways to Defend Tax Allocations Among Owners

Section 704(a) provides the general rule that owners are free to agree among themselves how they will share income gain, loss, deduction or credit. The limitation in Section 704(b) is that an allocation they agree upon will be disregarded if it "does not have substantial economic effect."[31] The item subject to the disregarded allocation will be reallocated "in

---

[29] I.R.C. § 465. These rules were strengthened in 1986.
[30] I.R.C. § 469.
[31] I.R.C. § 704(b)(2). As indicated above, the substantial economic effect language was added to the statute by the Tax Reform Act of 1976.

accordance with the [owner's] interest in the [firm] (determined by taking into account all facts and circumstances)."[32] An owner's "interest in the [firm]" is also the default rule for guiding the allocations of tax items that the members never agreed upon.[33] The terribly complex 704(b) regulations promulgated under these simple statutory rules place considerable emphasis on an analysis of the owners' capital accounts.

The 704(b) regulations tell owners that an allocation they agree to may be justified, or respected, in one of three ways.[34] First, if the allocation has substantial economic effect, as that term is defined in the regulations. Second, if the allocation *is* in accordance with the owner's interest in the firm, as that term is defined in the regulations. Third, if the allocation is *deemed* to be in accordance with an owner's interest in the firm pursuant to one of the special rules contained in the regulations.[35]

Substantial economic effect: strict capital account observance
In order for a firm's allocation to have substantial economic effect, the regulations emphasize, there must be an economic effect and it must be substantial. The "fundamental principle" is that, in order for an allocation to have economic effect, it must be consistent with the economic arrangement of the owners. The basic policy judgment is clear: "[I]n the event there is an economic benefit or economic burden that corresponds to an allocation, the [owner] to whom the allocation is made must receive such economic benefit or bear such economic burden."[36] The regulations then set out a "safe harbor" that is based on satisfying three prongs of capital accounts analysis.

Capital accounts must be properly maintained Capital accounts must be maintained throughout the life of the firm in accordance with the capital account maintenance rules in the regulations. Those rules essentially require a basic capital account maintenance that also reflects tax allocations. That is, capital accounts must be maintained as described earlier in this chapter and also must reflect tax allocations of income, gain, loss, deduction or credit.[37]

Liquidating distributions must be made in accordance with positive capital account balances Upon liquidation of the firm, or of an owner's interest in the firm, liquidating distributions must "in all cases . . . be made in accordance with the positive capital account balances" of the owners.[38]

Negative capital accounts must be treated as debts to the firm If liquidation of an owner's interest results in a "deficit balance" (negative) capital account, the owner must

---

[32] I.R.C. § 704(b) (flush language). The "interest in the [firm]" language was also added in 1976.
[33] I.R.C. § 704(b)(1).
[34] Technically, the 704(b) regulations only describe whether an allocation will be respected *as a matter of Section 704(b)*. They are explicit that overarching tax avoidance principles, or other specific provisions, may cause an allocation to be disregarded even if it is respected as a matter of 704(b). Treas. Reg. § 1.704-1(b)(i)(iii).
[35] Treas. Reg. § 1.704-1(b)(1)(i).
[36] Treas. Reg. § 1.704-1(b)(2)(ii)(a).
[37] Treas. Reg. § 1.704-1(b)(2)(iv)(b).
[38] Treas. Reg. § 1.704-1(b)(2)(ii)(b)(2).

be "unconditionally obligated to restore the amount of such deficit balance" to the firm, "which amount shall, upon liquidation of the [firm], be paid to creditors of the [firm] or distributed to other [owners] in accordance with their positive capital account balances."[39] As explained earlier, this is the same as RUPA's capital account reconciliation rule.

The regulations contain an alternative test for economic effect. The alternate test also engages basic capital accounts analysis. Under this test, as under the basic substantial economic effect test, capital accounts must be properly maintained and liquidation proceeds must be distributed in accordance with positive capital accounts balances. However, in lieu of requiring an owner to restore any capital account deficit, the firm may provide for a "qualified income offset." The basic idea is that an owner who unexpectedly receives certain allocations that drive the owner's capital account negative must be allocated offsetting allocations that drive the owner's capital account positive "in an amount and manner sufficient to eliminate such deficit balance as quickly as possible."[40]

Accordance with owner's interest in the firm

The regulations essentially provide that a tax allocation *is* in accordance with the owner's interest in the firm if the allocation also reflects the economic benefits or burdens, if any, behind it.[41] Thus, for example, an owner who bears all the expenses with respect to a particular asset may be allocated all the corresponding deductions. In general, the broad factors to be considered include the owners' relative contributions, their interests in economic profits and losses, their interests in cash flow and current distributions, and their interests in liquidating distributions.[42] Although capital accounts can feature in the inquiry, this approach does not require the same strict observance as the substantial economic effect test.

***Deemed* in accordance with owner's interest in the firm**

The core operation of this third way to justify allocations of tax benefits treats situations in which the economic risk that theoretically justified a deduction falls outside the firm rather than upon any owner. As the regulations explain: "Allocations of losses, deductions ... attributable to [firm] nonrecourse liabilities ... cannot have economic effect because the creditor alone bears any economic burden that corresponds to those allocations."[43] In short, an allocation will be *deemed* in accordance with an owner's interest in a firm if it provides that the recipient of the tax benefit will also receive any ultimate related tax burden. For example, assume that three of four owners are allocated all the depreciation deductions attributable to a building that was purchased for $100 with 100 percent nonrecourse financing. The allocation will not be deemed to be in accordance with the owners' interest in the firm unless the three owners who were allocated the deduction are also allocated the tax burden attributable to the basis reduction caused by the allocation. There must be, in the words of the regulations, a "minimum gain chargeback."[44]

---

[39] Treas. Reg. § 1.704-1(b)(2)(ii)(b)(3).
[40] Treas. Reg. § 1.704-1(b)(2)(ii)(d).
[41] Treas. Reg. § 1.704-1(b)(3)(i).
[42] Treas. Reg. § 1.704-1(b)(3)(ii).
[43] Treas. Reg. § 1.704-2(b)(1).
[44] Treas. Reg. § 1.704-2(f).

Thus, if the property is depreciated down to an adjusted basis of $20 and no principal has been paid on the mortgage, there will be a minimum gain of $80 when the property is sold or foreclosed upon because the "relief" from the nonrecourse mortgage will be taxed, usually as "amount realized."[45] Absorbing that tax burden is the price to be paid for the depreciation deductions that reduced basis. The tax burden must go to the recipient of the tax benefit.

Varying Drafting Challenges and Strategies: Layer Cake and Target Allocations

The more complex a firm's economic arrangements, the more difficult it is to reduce them to writing. The difficulty is compounded by the need to include provisions to assure with some measure of confidence that any special tax allocations of tax benefits or burdens will be respected under the 704(b) rules. A significant body of literature has developed discussing various drafting strategies to allocate economic and tax consequences (Garcia, Hallmark, Kuller, McKee, Nelson, & Whitmire 2014) and a detailed discussion of these strategies is beyond the scope of this chapter. These strategies have their own vocabulary and can differ in significant ways, both in their approach and in their vulnerability. For example, under the "layer cake" approach, allocations of income or loss are reflected in capital accounts that ultimately will affect how cash is distributed in the event of a liquidating distribution (Gerson, Lohnes & Schmalz 2006). In more recent years, "target" (Golub 2009) or "forced" allocation provisions have become popular (Cuff 2013a; Cuff 2013b). These provisions do not require that liquidating distributions be made in accordance with whatever capital account balances have resulted from previous allocations. They direct how liquidating distributions will be made, and they provide for allocations of income, gain, loss, deduction or credit that will help achieve "target" capital account balances consistent with the desired distributions in the event of hypothetical liquidation. In some cases, the allocations of each year's tax consequences are not made until after all the results for a year are clear. "In its purest form, this technique results in an agreement that contains no precise allocations" (Garcia, Hallmark, Kuller, McKee, Nelson & Whitmire 2014). For present purposes, suffice it to say that, under either approach, capital accounts maintenance is central.

Frequent Lack of Clarity in Agreements

Attempts to assure compliance with the byzantine 704(b) regulations have resulted in operating and partnership agreements that are unclear in one of two ways. First, they can be unclear because they include complex capital account provisions, including perhaps provisions dealing with nonrecourse deductions and minimum gain chargebacks. I have seen these complex provisions even in the agreements of smaller law firms that do not involve a complex financial structure, nonrecourse financing or special tax allocations. The provisions seem to have migrated from much more complex firms on the assumption that they are tried and true. The complex provisions can also make the agreements quite lengthy. As mentioned above, proper drafting is a matter of professional judgment

---

[45] Commissioner v. Tufts, 461 U.S. 300 (1983).

(O'Connor & Schneider 2009). A case can certainly be made that it is good to anticipate and address in an agreement almost any financing arrangement or special allocation that might arise. However, it strikes me as overkill in many cases. It surely is unfortunate and ironic when lawyers and other owners of small businesses cannot possibly comprehend their written agreements. To the extent portions of an agreement are impenetrable and make it too lengthy, the agreement as a whole is a less effective guide or counseling document for the owners.

The second type of tax provision basically says that the owners agree to do whatever it takes to achieve tax compliance in the event of a challenge by the IRS. This approach has the advantage of allowing the agreement to be shorter and more confined to a clearer vision of the owners' economic arrangement. The disadvantage with this second approach is the risk caused by its vagueness. Perhaps that risk is reduced if it is clear that, wherever possible, the trade-off for tax benefits will be with tax burdens rather than with hard cash. The risk is surely reduced by maximum clarity with respect to the economic arrangement.

6. CONCLUSION

In the financial crisis that started to unfold in 2007, it became widely known that investment bankers, and their lawyers and accountants, had drafted documents for financial instruments so complex as to be beyond comprehension. However impenetrable, language and structures migrated and became widely accepted once they passed muster. Former Federal Reserve Chairman Allan Greenspan quipped that, even with more than 100 economists at his disposal, he could not untangle the agreements or structures behind billions of dollars of collateralized debt obligations (Sorkin 2009). Unfortunately, something similar, although perhaps not quite as extreme, has happened within the more modest arena of LLCs and partnerships. Despite the fact that these are two premier vehicles for small businesses with two or more owners,[46] they are often governed by agreements that are very difficult to understand. Operating and partnership agreements are often drafted by generalists who incorporate standard form language that attempts to validate special allocations of tax benefits that might be made, even if implausible. Although the relevant federal income tax regulations focus heavily on capital accounts, those capital accounts can have significant and unintended economic consequences.

My thesis is twofold. First, even apart from federal income tax law, attorneys must have at least a rudimentary understanding of what capital accounts are and are not, as well as any state default rules regulating them. The accounting profession typically *is* generating individual capital accounts for each owner, even if those accounts are not required either by the owners' agreement or by law.[47] In the world of small business, often characterized by incomplete or vague agreements and by poor record-keeping, those accounts provide at least some standardized measure of an owner's net equity in the firm. Second, capital

---

[46] Subchapter S corporations are also quite popular.
[47] There is nothing preventing owners or their agents or representatives from dispensing with capital accounts, that is, from moving to more of a corporate approach that dispenses with an equity account for each owner.

account analysis is a useful analytical device. Walking the standard range of anticipated transactions through a capital accounts analysis can raise with great clarity and precision basic economic decisions that might otherwise be overlooked, particularly decisions regarding the sharing of different kinds of losses among the owners.

REFERENCES

Abrams, Howard E. (2010), "Partnership Book-Ups," *Public Law & Legal Theory Research Paper Series*, available at *http://papers.ssrn.com/sol3/papers.cfm?abstract_id=1652569* (last accessed August 2014).

Baker, Donald H. (2010), "What Does that Operating Agreement Mean? A Primer on LLC Capital Accounting for the Non-Specialist," *Michigan Business Law Journal*, Summer 2010, 13–19.

Cuff, Terence F. (2013a), "Some Conjecture on Target Allocation Provisions," *Real Estate Taxation*, 40(3), 127.

Cuff, Terence F. (2013b), "Some Further Conjectures on Target Allocation Provisions," *Real Estate Taxation*, 40(4), 156.

Donn, Allan, Robert W. Hillman & Donald J. Weidner (2014), *The Revised Uniform Partnership Act*, New York: Thomson West.

Garcia, Joe, Jr., Sandra W. Hallmark, Mark A. Kuller, William S. McKee, William F. Nelson & Robert L. Whitmire (2014), *Structuring and Drafting Partnership Agreements: Including LLC Agreements* (3d ed.), New York: Warren, Gorham & Lamont.

Gerson, Craig, Karen T. Lohnes & John Schmalz (2006), "Value Equals Basis and Partners' Distributive Share: Stuffing, Fill-Ups, and Waterfalls," *Journal of Taxation*, 105, 109–119.

Golub, Todd D. (2009), "How to Hit Your Mark Using Target Allocations in a Real Estate Partnership," *Tax Management Memorandum*, 50, 403.

Larson, Joni (2013), *Partnership Taxation: An Application Approach* (2nd ed.), Durham, NC: Carolina Academic Press.

McKee, William S., William F. Nelson & Robert L. Whitmire (2014), *Federal Taxation of Partnership and Partners*, New York: Warren, Gorham & Lamont.

Monroe, Andrea (2010), "Too Big to Fail: The Problem of Partnership Allocations," *Virginia Tax Review*, 30, 465–522.

O'Connor, Brian J. & Steven R. Schneider (2009), "Partnership and LLC Agreements: Learning to Read and Write Again," *Tax Notes*, 1323–1340, December 21.

Simmons, Daniel L. (2009), "Built-in Gain and Built-in Loss Property on Formation of a Partnership: An Exploration of the Grand Elegance of Partnership Capital Accounts," *Florida Tax Review*, 9(6), 599–696.

Sorkin, Andrew Ross (2009), *Too Big to Fail*, New York: Penguin Group.

Weidner, Donald J. (1981), "Partnership Allocations and Capital Accounts Analysis," *Ohio State Law Journal*, 467, 468.

PART 5

DISSOLUTION AND FUNDAMENTAL CHANGES

12. Fundamental changes in the LLC: a study in path-divergence and convergence
Joan MacLeod Heminway

1. INTRODUCTION

As most commentators note, architects of the law governing the limited liability company business form (LLC) in the United States (a relatively late entrant in the U.S. business entity race) could, and did, look to the law of partnerships, limited partnerships, and corporations in formulating LLC law. The Revised Uniform Partnership Act (RUPA) was, rather transparently, the original basis for many of the statutory rules in the Uniform Limited Liability Company Act (ULLCA). The RUPA codified partnership norms that focus on the co-equal consent of partners for the entity's formation, maintenance, wind-up, and termination. As a result, the ULLCA's RUPA foundation gave the LLC form, in a simple, direct way, the attributes needed to secure pass-through treatment for the entity under federal income tax law while providing limited liability to owners under state entity law, a major driving force behind the LLC. Specifically, under the pre-existing federal income tax regulations, an unincorporated business entity enjoyed pass-through tax treatment if it lacked at least two of four core characteristics of corporations: (1) continuity of life, (2) centralization of management, (3) limited liability, and (4) free transferability of interests.[1] However, because aspects of the LLC deviated from general partnership law, limited partnership and corporate law policy also have played a role in the creation of LLC rules, and limited partnership and corporate doctrine was grafted onto the RUPA base to some extent in creating the Revised Uniform Limited Liability Company Act (RULLCA). As a result, courts have used both partnership and corporate law principles in deciding LLC controversies that require statutory interpretation or gap-filling. Moreover, the doctrinal rules relating to LLCs have changed over the years, including in response to developing decisional law and federal income tax law changes in 1997 that allowed for more liberal pass-through treatment for unincorporated business entities. Accordingly, the ULLCA had—and each successor uniform act has continued to have—a palpable, albeit tentative and shifting, hybrid quality about it.

Many aspects of this crossbred existence have generated significant scholarly attention. In particular, issues relating to limited liability (including veil piercing), taxation, management and control (including fiduciary duties), and the overall flexibility of internal governance rules have been well analyzed in the literature—and rightly so. These are important doctrinal concerns, and they are considerations central to the formation and day-to-day operation of a business organized as an LLC.

---

[1] *See* Treas. Reg. § 301.7701-2(a) (1980); *see also Morrissey v. Comm'r of Internal Revenue*, 296 U.S. 344 (1935).

Issues relating to fundamental changes in LLCs, however—matters such as amendments to organizational documents, mergers, conversions, domestications, and dissolutions—have received measurably less consideration. While they are regular occurrences in the lifecycle of a firm, they are not in front of an LLC's management or legal counsel every day. Having said that, they are critically important aspects of the law governing LLCs, especially in transformative times.

Accordingly, this chapter reviews the current state of fundamental change doctrine in the LLC form in the United States, collects and describes key observations on the current (and continually evolving) U.S. laws governing these important transactions, and draws related summary conclusions.

2. A BRIEF DOCTRINAL OVERVIEW

By the end of the 20th century, every state in the union had introduced an LLC statute of one form or another. The first uniform LLC act in the United States, the ULLCA, was formalized in 1996, four years after the drafting of the Prototype Limited Liability Company Act (PLLCA) by a working group of the American Bar Association's Committee on LLCs, Partnerships and Unincorporated Entities. LLC law continued to develop rapidly through state legislatures in its wake. As a result, The National Conference of Commissioners on Uniform State Laws adopted a new version of the uniform act, the RULLCA, in 2006. Innovations continued. In 2011, in response to significant changes in LLC law introduced in Delaware, the Revised Prototype Limited Liability Company Act Editorial Board of the LLCs, Partnerships and Unincorporated Entities Committee of the American Bar Association introduced a Revised Prototype Limited Liability Company Act (RPLLCA). State LLC laws are at varied stages of development and include assorted provisions from these uniform and prototype acts, as well as rules individually crafted to meet specific state policy needs.

The introduction of the series LLC has been an important, complex innovation of state LLC law. In states adopting Delaware-style series LLC provisions, LLC series are treated for most purposes as separate entities within a single LLC entity. Delaware's law serves as the model for this type of LLC, and its statement of this general rule reads as follows:

> A series . . . may carry on any lawful business, purpose or activity, whether or not for profit, with the exception of the business of banking . . . . Unless otherwise provided in a limited liability company agreement, a series . . . shall have the power and capacity to, in its own name, contract, hold title to assets (including real, personal and intangible property), grant liens and security interests, and sue and be sued.[2]

Other states have implemented their own series provisions in their statutes. Some deviate from the Delaware model, and most rely on written terms (statutorily authorized provisions in, for example, an LLC operating agreement or limited liability company agreement), at least to some extent, to formalize the specific rights inuring to those holding interests in the series. Accordingly, it is difficult to generalize governance rules

---

[2] DEL. CODE ANN. tit. 6, § 18-215 (West 2014).

in this area across multiple jurisdictions and firms. The series LLC is a relatively new statutory addition and has not yet been widely tested practically or judicially, including in the area of fundamental change transactions. It remains, however, an area to watch.

Notwithstanding series LLC doctrine and other examples of recognized individuality in state approaches to LLC law, there are certain generalizable standards and trends in LLC law concerning fundamental organizational changes. These standards and trends are summarized in the sections below. They highlight a number of important themes and reveal undeniable patterns of interest to businesses and their legal counsel.

The summary offered below focuses on certain key aspects of the law relating to fundamental change transactions. Fundamental change doctrine in LLC law, as in corporate law, comprises legal rules that focus on the nature of transactional authority. Specifically, fundamental change transactions are those that are so basic to the firm that non-manager owners are given an element of control—a right to vote or consent. The summary of fundamental change doctrine in the LLC context that follows therefore focuses on the approval rights of LLC members over basic structural transactions.

Amendments to Organizational Documents

LLC organizational documents typically consist of a chartering document—the document that, when filed with the office of the secretary of state of a state, constitutes the LLC as a legal entity—and an agreement among the members (owners) of the LLC as to the governance rules by which the LLC will operate. The labels for LLC organizational documents have evolved over the years. For example, the ULLCA and PLLCA both use the term "articles of organization" to describe the LLC charter and "operating agreement" to describe the governance agreement among members. However, the RULLCA uses "certificate of organization," and the RPLLCA uses "certificate of formation," to refer to the LLC charter. In addition, while the RULLCA continues to refer to the governance agreement among members as an operating agreement, the RPLLCA refers to that governance agreement as a "limited liability company agreement." State statutes predictably employ a similarly varied set of terms to refer to LLC organizational documents, most of them using the terms provided in the prototype or uniform acts.

Amendments to these LLC organizational documents enjoy a special legal status. As a general matter, the consent of all members is required to amend LLC organizational documents, at least by default. Section 404(c) of the ULLCA, Sections 407(b)(4) and (c)(4) & (5) of the RULLCA, and Section 406(c)(1) of the RPLLCA, for example, all provide for unanimous consent for amendments to the articles (or certificate) and operating (or limited liability company) agreement. In some cases, these statutes rely on language providing for approval by all members of any matter outside the ordinary course of business of the LLC. Unanimity by default is the rule in some state LLC statutes.[3]

---

[3] See, e.g., COLO. REV. STAT. ANN. § 7-80-209 (West 2014) ("An amendment to the articles of organization is invalid unless approved by all of the members or in such other manner as may be provided in the operating agreement"); MICH. COMP. LAWS ANN. § 450.4603 (West 2014) (requiring in a certificate of amendment "[a] statement that the amendment or amendments were approved by the unanimous vote of all of the members entitled to vote or by a majority in interest if an operating agreement authorizes amendment of the articles of organization by majority vote.");

However, other variations also are common and seem to be proliferating. Some state LLC statutes allow the required consent of members to be varied only by provision in the chartering document. Other state LLC statutes specify the required vote (typically majority, but sometimes supermajority) of members unless the charter or governance agreement provides for a different—sometimes only a greater—vote.[4] Some state LLC statutes provide for different votes based on the subject matter of the amendment, with more fundamental, core changes requiring a unanimous vote and other changes requiring a majority vote.[5] Some states allow managers in manager-managed LLCs (LLCs in which the management function is performed by one or more persons, who need not be members, named or designated in the manner set forth in the statute) to adopt limited, clerical charter amendments (rather than requiring that members consent to those amendments).[6] Some states—most notably Delaware—treat amendments of the operating, LLC, or other governing agreement as a matter of contract by default.[7]

Mergers, Conversions, and Domestications

Doctrinal rules relating to LLC mergers, conversions, and domestications also vary and have evolved significantly over the years. The trend has been toward more types of transactions between and among more and more forms of domestic and foreign business entity. This liberalization generally tracks and follows on developments in corporate doctrine and is illustrated well by the progression of the prototype and uniforms acts.

Section 904 of the ULLCA provides for mergers of a limited liability company with or into a domestic or a foreign limited liability company or companies, or one or more domestic or foreign corporations, partnerships, limited partnerships, or other entities. For

---

OR. REV. STAT. ANN. § 63.444 (West 2014) ("Except as otherwise provided in ORS 63.441 [regarding amendments that can be approved by a manager or managers of a manager-managed LLC] or in the articles of organization or any operating agreement, all amendments to the articles of organization or any operating agreement must be approved unanimously by the members.").

[4] *See, e.g.*, LA. REV. STAT. ANN. § 12:1318 (West 2014) (providing for a majority vote of the members to approve all amendments to the articles or operating agreement, unless otherwise provided in the articles or a written operating agreement); N.Y. LTD. LIAB. CO. LAW § 213 (McKinney 2014) ("Except as provided in the operating agreement, an amendment of the articles of organization shall be authorized by at least a majority in interest of the members entitled to vote thereon.").

[5] *See, e.g.*, OKLA. STAT. ANN. tit. 18, § 2020 (West 2014) (providing for a majority vote of the members for approval of an amendment to the articles of organization or operating agreement, subject to certain exceptions where a unanimous vote is required, unless in either case a different vote is provided in the LLC's articles or operating agreement—a written operating agreement being required to vary the unanimity requirement); TENN. CODE ANN. § 48-249-204(c) (West 2014) (requiring approval for an amendment of the LLC's articles by all members, except for an amendment changing the LLC's name or making other specified ministerial changes).

[6] *See, e.g.*, 805 ILL. COMP. STAT. § 180/5-15 (West 2014); OR. REV. STAT. ANN. § 63.441.

[7] *See, e.g.*, DEL. CODE ANN. tit. 6, § 18-302(e) ("If a limited liability company agreement provides for the manner in which it may be amended, including by requiring the approval of a person who is not a party to the limited liability company agreement or the satisfaction of conditions, it may be amended only in that manner or as otherwise permitted by law . . . ."); TENN. CODE ANN. § 48-249-204(c) ("Any amendment to an LLC's operating agreement shall be approved by the method provided in its LLC documents. If the LLC documents do not provide for the method by which an operating agreement may be amended, all of the members shall approve any amendment to the operating agreement.").

a domestic LLC that is a party to the merger, the plan of merger must be approved by all of the LLC's members or by the number or percentage of members required in the operating agreement. Conversions, however, were only covered in the ULLCA in a limited way. The relevant provision, Section 902 of the ULLCA, only permits conversions of domestic partnerships and domestic limited partnerships into LLCs. The conversion requires the unanimous approval of the partners or approval in accordance with the terms of the partnership agreement. Domestications are not covered at all in the ULLCA.

What a difference ten years makes. The adoption of the RULLCA reflected significant changes in the doctrine relating to organic transactions—mergers, conversions, and domestications—that constitute fundamental change transactions. Article 10 of the RULLCA provides broadly for LLC mergers, conversions, and domestications. Under Sections 1003(a), 1007(a), and 1011(a) of the RULLCA, respectively: all members of an LLC that is party to a merger must consent to the plan of merger; all members of a converting LLC must consent to the plan of conversion; and all members of a domesticating LLC must consent to a plan of domestication. Sections 1002(a) and 1006(a) of the RPLLCA carry forward the same unanimous approval rules set forth in the RULLCA, but Article 10 of the RPLLCA classifies a domestication transaction as a type of conversion. Accordingly, the RPLLCA only references mergers and conversions.

Individual states have adopted many different versions of these rules, customized to reflect unique provisions and policy attributes. A number of states do not have domestication provisions in their LLC law; some of these jurisdictions have plans to add domestications to their statutes. In addition, state legislatures have continued to innovate from the evolving rules represented in the uniform and prototype LLC acts. Florida, for example, recently added an "interest exchange" transaction to the list of organic transactions permitted to be entered into by LLCs.[8] Under the new Florida LLC law, interest exchange transactions are the LLC equivalent of the corporate statutory share exchange transaction (an alternative form of business combination provided for in Section 11.03 of the Model Business Corporation Act). Also, Wyoming, in the 2010 revisions to its LLC Act, continued to provide for both continuances (which operate like RULLCA domestications) and domestications (in which a foreign LLC is not required to abandon its foreign domicile but is also permitted to validly exist under Wyoming law).[9] Among states that provide for domestications, some provide a narrow meaning to the term "domestication," defining it as only applying to applications of non-U.S. entities for continued existence under domestic LLC law.[10] Other states construe domestication transactions more broadly as repatriations to the state of any U.S. or non-U.S. firm organized under the laws of another jurisdiction.[11] Tennessee, which is unique in recognizing a director-managed form of LLC in addition to the more standard manager-managed and member-managed forms, requires the majority approval of directors or managers, as applicable, and members for "[t]he sale, lease, transfer or other disposition by an LLC of all, or substantially all, of its property and assets not in the usual and regular course of business."[12]

---

[8] See FLA. STAT. ANN. §§ 605.1031–1036 (West 2014).
[9] See WYO. STAT. ANN. §§ 17-29-1010 & 17-29-1012 (West 2014).
[10] See, e.g., DEL. CODE ANN. tit. 6, § 18-212.
[11] See, e.g., WYO. STAT. ANN. § 17-29-1012 (West 2014).
[12] TENN. CODE ANN. § 48-249-705.

Most strikingly, however, state statutes, unlike the prototype and uniform LLC acts, have begun to eschew unanimous member consent requirements in favor of majority approval requirements, especially for mergers.[13] Delaware law provides for approval of a merger plan "by members who own more than 50 percent of the then current percentage or other interest in the profits of the domestic limited liability company owned by all of the members."[14] Conversions and non-U.S. domestications are subject to approval "in the manner provided for by the document, instrument, agreement or other writing, as the case may be, governing the internal affairs" of the converting or domesticating entity "and the conduct of its business" or, as appropriate, by applicable law.[15] This shift has brought with it the addition of dissenters' (appraisal) rights under certain state LLC laws.[16] Delaware's LLC law authorizes contractual appraisal rights.[17] Other states have followed.[18] These provisions are relatively new and their value has not yet been fully demonstrated.

The overall trajectory of modifications to state LLC merger, conversion, and domestication statutes has been toward enhanced flexibility as to both the form of the transaction and the organizational form of the transaction's participants. This trend has principally been executed through the tailored grafting of nomenclature and processes from corporate laws onto LLC statutory frameworks. States that are moving away from requiring unanimous member consent for organic transactions like mergers, conversions, and domestications also are largely following corporate models.

Yet, the corporatization of fundamental change rules does not portend the corporatization of LLC law as a whole. A 2013 Delaware Chancery Court case reviewing a post-conversion claim for advancement and indemnification from an LLC illustrates this point. The LLC was the successor of a corporation in a conversion. The claimant was a director and chairman of the predecessor corporation and a member of the governing board and chairman of the successor LLC. The claim for indemnification related to actions taken by the claimant during the time that he was working for the predecessor

---

[13] See, e.g., FLA. STAT. ANN. §§ 605.1023(1)(a) & 605.1043(1)(a) (requiring approval for mergers and conversions by a majority-in-interest of all members with voting rights); NEV. REV. STAT. ANN. § 92A.150 (West 2014) ("A plan of merger, conversion or exchange involving a domestic limited-liability company must be approved by members who own a majority of the interests in the current profits of the company then owned by all of the members"); N.H. REV. STAT. ANN. § 304-C:156 (2014) ("Unless the operating agreement provides otherwise, a limited liability company that is a party to a proposed merger shall approve the merger agreement by majority vote of the members"); id. § 304-C:150 ("If the limited liability company agreement of the limited liability company referred to in paragraph II does not specify the manner of authorizing a statutory conversion of the limited liability company or a merger that involves the limited liability company as a constituent party and does not prohibit a statutory conversion of the limited liability company, the statutory conversion shall be authorized by majority vote of the members of the limited liability company"); TENN. CODE ANN. § 48-249-702 & 704 (providing for a majority vote of managers or directors, as applicable, and a majority vote of members to approve a merger or the conversion of a domestic LLC to another entity).
[14] DEL. CODE ANN. tit. 6, § 18-209(b).
[15] Id. §§ 18-212(c)(6) & 18-214(h).
[16] See, e.g., FLA. STAT. ANN. §§ 605.1061–605.1072; NEV. REV. STAT. ANN. §§ 92a.300–92a.500; N.H. REV. STAT. ANN. §§ 304-C:160–C:172.
[17] See DEL. CODE ANN. tit. 6, § 18-210.
[18] See, e.g., TENN. CODE ANN. § 48-249-706.

corporation. The Chancery Court denied the plaintiff's claim for advancement and indemnification because the successor LLC's operating agreement did not authorize the advancement and indemnification.

> The change of the entity from Ashbridge Corporation to Ashbridge LLC was a fundamental change in identity. The advancement and indemnification scheme of Ashbridge Corporation's bylaws was re-written into contractual terms in Ashbridge LLC's operating agreement in a manner that substantially altered the rights and obligations of the parties.... The Court will therefore not impose retroactive obligations on a limited liability company when the plain language of its operating agreement would not permit predecessor or affiliate liability and when the indemnification schemes of the predecessor corporation and successor limited liability company differ.[19]

Thus, as this opinion illustrates, there may be significant potential traps for the unwary that emanate from the relative merger, conversion, and domestication freedom permitted in the LLC context.

Dissolutions

Dissolution rules in LLC statutes were originally derived from a partnership model in order to assure pass-through treatment for LLCs under then applicable federal income tax law. Specifically, partnership norms that provided for dissolution in the event of the dissociation of a partner from the firm were incorporated into the LLC form to avoid the continuity of existence attribute of the corporate form, since pass-through income tax status under pre-existing federal law was linked in part to limited (as opposed to perpetual) entity existence. Once pass-through tax status was de-linked from continuity of interest and other core corporate attributes in the late 1990s, LLCs were free to innovate toward individualized contractual dissolution events that allow for perpetual existence.

Section 801 of the ULLCA, introduced almost coincident with these federal tax law changes, edged toward that objective. Under the ULLCA, while the separation (dissociation) of an LLC member from the LLC has the potential to dissolve the LLC, dissolution is not an automatic effect of LLC member dissociation. Although members can apply to a court for dissolution under specified circumstances set forth in the ULLCA (frustration of the LLC's economic purpose, the conduct of another member making continuation of the business with that member reasonably impracticable, the reasonable impracticability of conducting the company's business in conformity with the articles of organization and the operating agreement, and illegal, oppressive, fraudulent, or unfairly prejudicial managerial action), for the most part, dissolution events can be set forth in or varied in the LLC operating agreement.

The RULLCA and the RPLLCA retain this relative freedom of contract and push further toward corporate dissolution rules, including in the case of the RULLCA those applied by legislatures and courts for principal use in the close corporation context. For example, Section 701 of the RULLCA adds both the consent of all of the members as a

---

[19] *Grace v. Ashbridge LLC*, CIV.A. 8348-VCN, 2013 WL 6869936 (Del. Ch. Dec. 31, 2013) (footnotes omitted) (citing to *Bernstein v. TractManager, Inc.*, 953 A.2d 1003 (Del. Ch. 2007) for support).

default dissolution event and also an express provision for an alternative (non-dissolution) remedy for illegal, fraudulent, or oppressive managerial conduct. The latter allows for buyouts of member interests on a showing of managerial oppression without triggering dissolution of the firm in a manner akin to that provided for in Section 14.34 of the Model Business Corporation Act. The RPLLCA provides for only five simple, straightforward dissolution triggers: (1) an event or circumstance set forth in the limited liability company agreement, (2) the consent of all the members, (3) with the requisite consent, LLC delinquency that is not cured over a three-year period, (4) 90 days after dissociation of the last remaining member, and (5) on application by a member, a court order because it is not reasonably practicable to carry on the LLC's activities in accordance with the LLC agreement.

Like the RULLCA, some state laws combine partnership dissolution and dissolution-related provisions from the RUPA (including, for example, dissolution events that include member dissociation and buyouts) with corporate law dissolution concepts (including, for example, authority to dissolve an LLC or authorize a member buyout based on managerial oppression, detailed provisions on other forms of judicial dissolution, and rules providing for administrative dissolution).[20] Some of these state LLC laws provide that dissolutions require the approval of a majority, rather than all, of the members of the LLC.[21] Delaware law provides for five dissolution events: (1) the time specified in the limited liability company agreement (acknowledging expressly that the LLC otherwise has a perpetual existence by default), (2) the happening of events specified in the limited liability company agreement, (3) "unless otherwise provided in a limited liability company agreement, upon the affirmative vote or written consent of the members of the limited liability company ... by members who own more than 2/3 of the then-current percentage or other interest in the profits of the limited liability company owned by all of the members," (4) with certain exceptions, when there are no remaining members, and (5) by judicial decree on application "whenever it is not reasonably practicable to carry on the business in conformity with a limited liability company agreement."[22]

3. RESULTING OBSERVATIONS

The history and current state of fundamental change doctrine in the LLC form of business association give rise to a number of important observations. Several of these merit a

---

[20] See, e.g., COLO. REV. STAT. ANN. §§ 7-80-801–80-813 (West 2014); FLA. STAT. ANN. §§ 605.0701–.0717; N.H. REV. STAT. ANN. §§ 304-C:98–C:105-A & §§ 304-C:127–C:146; N.M. STAT. ANN. §§ 53-19-38–53-19-46; TENN. CODE ANN. §§ 48-249-601–622; WYO. STAT. ANN. §§ 17-29-601–701(a)(v)(B).

[21] See, e.g., N.H. REV. STAT. ANN. § 304-C:129 ("Unless the operating agreement provides otherwise, a limited liability company shall be dissolved by majority vote of the members."); N.M. STAT. ANN. § 53-19-39 (West) ("A limited liability company is dissolved ... except as otherwise provided in the articles of organization or an operating agreement, upon the written consent of members having a majority share of the voting power of all members."); TENN. CODE ANN. § 48-249-603(b)(2) ("If the proposed dissolution of the LLC is approved at a meeting of the members by a majority vote, or such other vote as may be provided for in the LLC documents, the LLC shall be dissolved.").

[22] DEL. CODE ANN. tit. 6, §§ 18-801 & 18-802.

brief commentary. These observations are set forth below grouped under three principal subject matter headings: the influence and interplay of corporate law and freedom of contract, vested rights and fundamental changes, and legislative drafting choices.

Influence and Interplay of Corporate Law and Freedom of Contract

No accurate summary of fundamental change doctrine in LLC law could fail to highlight two key drivers of the development of that doctrine: corporate law rules (noted at the outset in this chapter) and principles of freedom of contract. These two influences on fundamental changes under LLC law are both predictable and potentially contradictory. As a result, policy considerations played out in the courts and the legislature have been and continue to be important to LLC fundamental change doctrine.

Corporate law is both familiar and well developed. Those who formerly organized corporations and are familiar with corporate norms now often choose the LLC form for their businesses because of its inherent flexibility. Repeat players in the entity formation game—business lawyers included—are accustomed to corporate norms and understand the ways in which those norms solve recurrent, common problems in business entity formation and maintenance. Fundamental changes in LLCs resemble and raise questions similar to those raised by fundamental changes in the corporate context. It is unsurprising, and perhaps even rote and efficient, that the judiciary and legislators solve these problems, including those involving LLC fundamental changes, using the time-tested (albeit sometimes imperfect) solutions offered by corporate law. Tennessee LLC law has gone so far as to provide expressly for a director-managed form of LLC that incorporates corporate law structures and norms into LLC law in their entirety.[23]

The trend away from unanimous consent, especially as an immutable rule, illustrates the influence of corporate law. In an entity of any size, unanimous consent may be difficult to obtain. A business entity's inability (1) to amend its chartering document or governance rules, (2) to obtain approval of a business combination or a change in entity form or domicile, or (3) to dissolve, liquidate, and terminate its existence distracts management and imposes weighty costs on operations that decrease the value of the business unnecessarily. Corporate law had already traveled this path by providing for majority and supermajority votes in these circumstances, balanced by other governance rules that protect or compensate shareholders (notably, in specific cases, fiduciary duties of the majority to the minority, entire fairness review for cash-out mergers, and appraisal rights for dissenting shareholders). LLC law has looked to and incorporated many of these same rules.[24]

Dissolution provides another good example of the effects of corporate law on LLC doctrine. The description of legislative changes provided in the preceding part of the

---

[23] *See, e.g.*, TENN. CODE ANN. § 48-249-401(c) & (d), 402(c) & (d), and 403(i).

[24] *See, e.g.*, sources cited *supra* notes 16–18 (regarding statutory institution and facilitation of LLC appraisal rights); *Allen v. Devon Energy Holdings, L.L.C.*, 2012 Tex. App. LEXIS 2110, at *87 (Tex. App. Houston 1st Dist. Mar. 9, 2012) (recognizing a fiduciary duty of the majority to the minority under Texas LLC law); *Anderson v. Wilder*, 2003 Tenn. App. LEXIS 819, at *9 (Tenn. Ct. App. Nov. 21, 2003) (recognizing a fiduciary duty of the majority to the minority under Tennessee LLC law); *Brazil v. Rickerson*, 268 F. Supp. 2d 1091, 1097, 1099 (W.D. Mo. 2003) (recognizing a fiduciary duty of the majority to the minority under Missouri LLC law).

chapter belies an interest in using corporate law as a foundation to evolving LLC dissolution doctrine. But courts also have contributed to this corporatization.

Specifically, some courts applying and construing the original RUPA partnership-based dissolution schemes compellingly analogized closely held corporations to closely held LLCs—entities, in each case, operated and controlled by a small number of members, often comprising friends and family. These courts interpreted and filled gaps in LLC statutes in a manner consistent with corporate doctrine, including by ordering dissolution when it had not been requested as a remedy or fashioning alternative remedies when dissolution had been requested as a remedy. The opinions in these cases note circumstances substantially similar to those underlying court determinations made under corporate law and apply corporate law rules.[25]

An accompanying trend in LLC law toward freedom of contract is sometimes at odds with the movement toward incorporating corporate law principles into LLC law. Partnership law under the RUPA places heavy emphasis on the contractual relations of the partners. Under the RUPA, with minor exceptions, the partnership agreement controls the relations between and among partners and between partners and the partnership. Corporate doctrine is a very detailed, rich body of law that includes comprehensive substantive and procedural rules. Most of these rules are default rules rather than immutable rules, but corporate law tends to employ majoritarian default rules rather than more tailored, bespoke principles. LLC law's origins in partnership law norms responded in part to a perceived need for more flexibility and customization than typically is provided in corporate law. The preservation and enhancement of freedom of contract principles in LLC law tends to create some tension with the increasing influence of corporate law on LLC law.

Delaware is the leading and classic example of a state that has more frequently chosen to evolve its law toward increased freedom of contract, although other jurisdictions have adopted some of Delaware's specific pro-contract rules. Delaware LLC law serves as a primary model for the RPLLCA, which has a decidedly contractarian tilt. The statutory law in Delaware expressly incorporates a freedom of contract objective by articulating a policy "to give the maximum effect to the principle of freedom of contract and to the enforceability of limited liability company agreements."[26] Other states also have adopted this express statutory norm.[27]

The legislature has spoken, and the Delaware courts understand their marching orders. The Delaware case on post-conversion advancement and indemnification described earlier in the chapter relies heavily on notions of freedom of contract, for example.[28] In another case, the Delaware Chancery Court denied an LLC member's request for judicial dissolution based on the court's interpretation of the LLC's governance agreement.

---

[25] See, e.g., Dickson v. Rehmke, 78 Cal. Rptr. 3d 874 (3d Dist. 2008); Kirksey v. Grohmann, 754 N.W.2d 825 (S.D. 2008).

[26] DEL. CODE ANN. tit. 6, § 18-1101(b).

[27] See, e.g., KAN. STAT. ANN. § 17-7662 (West 2014) ("The policy of the Kansas Revised Limited Liability Company Act . . . is to give the maximum effect to the principle of freedom of contract and to the enforceability of operating agreements."); KY. REV. STAT. ANN. § 275.003(1) (West 2014) ("It shall be the policy of the General Assembly through this chapter to give maximum effect to the principles of freedom of contract and the enforceability of operating agreements.").

[28] See supra note 19 and accompanying text.

> I have found that Section 2.2 of the LLC Agreement applies generally to exclude all rights associated with membership not required by law or expressly granted in the LLC Agreement. Because a right to judicial dissolution is not required by law or expressly granted in the LLC Agreement, and because reading the Agreement as a whole it is clear that the parties meant to exclude any right to judicial dissolution, I find that the Plaintiff does not have a right to seek a dissolution . . . .[29]

That trial court judgment, affirmed by the Delaware Supreme Court, illustrates the triumph of contract law over corporate principles applicable to closely held entities that have been applied, as earlier noted, by courts in other states.

In all jurisdictions, courts must determine the extent to which statutory provisions, including those imported from corporate law, foreclose the exercise of freedom of contract by LLC members. Often, the job is made more difficult by a lack of clear policy directives from the legislature. In those circumstances, general common law norms tend to form the basis of the courts' judgments. One scholar in the area describes this environment in a compelling way. Her words in this regard are worth repeating here.

> The developing strains of business entity governance hold the promise of promoting the interest in contractual freedom while, at the same time, balancing the important need for minimum standards to protect legitimate expectations of fair and equitable conduct on the part of one's business partners. The contractarian model should acknowledge the need for and importance of such mandatory minimum standards to govern business relationships.
>
> Regardless of how courts articulate their judicial tests, reverence for the written contract must be tempered with the recognition that judicial review is a good and essential thing, as is a mandatory core of acceptable manager and/or member conduct. It has been said that the "defining tension" in corporate governance today is the tension between deference to directors' decisions and the scope of judicial review. In this debate, I have suggested that the uncertainty of the law, and the corresponding specter of judicial intervention, are not unfortunate consequences to be avoided by the creation of a perfect statutory phrase or judicial test. Rather, judicial review is the healthy price and the all-important force that deters overreaching and enables the application of behavioral constraints within the context of our contractual scheme of self-governance.[30]

This quoted passage identifies statutory and common law elements of business entity governance, which include especially the existence and application of fiduciary duties in the LLC context, as central, foundational standards that courts use in mediating the tension between standardized entity law norms and contractual freedom. The quoted passage suggests that this judicial oversight is both constant and beneficial as a check on opportunistic behavior in business entities.

However, there is some sentiment favoring and movement toward making fiduciary duties in the LLC context purely contractual or fully waivable. Delaware LLC law, for example, allows for the full customization of fiduciary duties in the limited liability company agreement but also provides that the implied contractual covenant of good

---

[29] *Huatuco v. Satellite Healthcare*, CV 8465-VCG, 2013 WL 6460898 (Del. Ch. Dec. 9, 2013), aff'd, 93 A.3d 654 (Del. 2014); see also, e.g., *R & R Capital, LLC v. Buck & Doe Run Valley Farms, LLC*, CIV.A. 3803-CC, 2008 WL 3846318 (Del. Ch. Aug. 19, 2008).

[30] Sandra K. Miller, *The Role of the Court in Balancing Contractual Freedom with the Need for Mandatory Constraints on Opportunistic and Abusive Conduct in the LLC*, 152 U. Pa. L. Rev. 1609, 1654 (2004) (footnotes omitted).

faith and fair dealing may not be eliminated.[31] New York law also permits the waiver of fiduciary duty in LLCs.[32] The implementation of rules of this kind will change the role that judicial enforcement of fiduciary duties has played in adjusting the equities among business venturers participating in LLCs.

Vested Rights and Fundamental Changes

Ownership interests—member interests—in LLCs are personal property. Initial LLC rules requiring unanimous member consent for fundamental changes derived from the belief that an LLC member, as a business owner, has a vested property right in his, her, or its ownership interest in the LLC. The recognition of the vested rights doctrine vis-à-vis fundamental change transactions, however, imbued minority ownership interests with hold-up value that had the capacity to foster inefficiencies and stagnate the firm. The summary of fundamental change law in the LLC context provided earlier in the chapter demonstrates that few fundamental changes currently require unanimous consent. LLC law has moved away from the recognition of vested rights that require the unanimous consent of members for the approval of fundamental change transactions.

Some state legislatures have made this choice quite explicitly by including a renunciation of vested rights in their LLC statutes. For example, Utah law generally provides that "[e]xcept as may otherwise be expressly provided in the articles of organization or operating agreement, a member has no vested property right resulting from any provision in the articles of organization, including any provision relating to management, control, capital structure, purpose, duration of the company, or entitlement to distributions."[33]

Some states make more specific express provision on the lack of vested rights of LLC members. Tennessee law offers an example of this approach in the form of an immutable rule that disclaims vested rights under both chartering (articles) and governance (operating agreement) documents. Tennessee's original LLC law (which continues to exist in parallel with its revised LLC Act) provides that an LLC member "does not have a vested property right resulting from any provision in the articles or operating agreement, including provisions relating to management, control, capital structure, distribution entitlement or purpose or duration of the LLC."[34] Virginia law includes a similar provision referencing the articles only.[35]

In a rudimentary sense, the developments in LLC law relating to the vested rights doctrine exemplify the overall evolution of LLC law. Specifically, the decline of unanimous

---

[31] DEL. CODE ANN. tit. 6, § 18-1101(c) & (e). In 2013, the Delaware legislature clarified that default fiduciary duties do, in fact, exist under Delaware LLC law, a matter that, together with fiduciary duty waivers, had been a litigable issue. *See* DEL. CODE ANN. tit. 6, § 18-1104; *Gatz Props., LLC v. Auriga Capital Corp.*, 59 A.3d 1206 (Del. 2012); *Feeley v. NHAOCG, LLC*, 62 A.3d 649 (2012) (Del. Ch. 2012).

[32] *See Pappas v. Tzolis*, 20 N.Y.3d 228 (2012).

[33] UTAH CODE ANN. § 48-2c-407(2) (West 2014); *see also* KY. REV. STAT. ANN. § 275.003(6) ("No member or other person shall have a vested property right resulting from any provision of the operating agreement which may not be modified by its amendment or as otherwise permitted by law.").

[34] TENN. CODE ANN. § 48-209-101(b).

[35] VA. CODE ANN. § 13.1-1014.E. ("A member of a limited liability company does not have a vested property right resulting from any provision of the articles of organization.").

consent provisions—especially mandatory ones—and the abandonment of the vested rights doctrine in LLC fundamental changes manifest both the comparable evolution in corporate law and notions of freedom of contract. Business owners that choose to organize their firm as an LLC understand that the state can alter LLC law and that, consistent with that law as in effect from time to time, they have the ability to agree around a variety of statutory default rules, including many of those relating to fundamental changes. Although other aspects of LLC law (notably, fiduciary duties, the obligation of good faith and fair dealing, and oppression relief in the dissolution setting) continue to protect minority interests in the fundamental change environment, vested property rights no longer provide that protection under most state LLC acts.

Legislative Drafting Choices

The history and current state of LLC fundamental change doctrine offer legislatures the motive and opportunity to create more streamlined, coherent, user-friendly statutes governing LLCs and business entities more generally. In particular, similarities in filing processes, the liberalization of organic transactions to allow for mergers, conversions, and domestications in and among all statutory business forms, and the adoption of significant corporate law norms in LLC law fairly beg for rationalization. Commentators have been suggesting consonant changes to entity law since the 1990s.

The bar undertook to create legislative change momentum. The American Bar Association established a Business Law Ad Hoc Committee on Entity Rationalization in 2001. In 2002, the committee released the Model Inter-Entity Transactions Act (MITA), which focused on simplifying statutory entity rules relating to fundamental changes. The MITA was later combined with a similar initiative undertaken by the National Conference of Commissioners on Uniform State Laws (the Uniform Entity Transactions Act), resulting in the publication of and subsequent revisions to the Model Entity Transactions Act (META). The advent and transformation of LLC law—and especially the fundamental change provisions—were strong motivations for these projects.

A few state legislatures have begun to undertake the task of revising, consolidating, and generally simplifying their business entity statutes. The development of fundamental change doctrine and, more particularly, the evolution of the law governing organic transactions, have been catalysts for those legislative initiatives. Some state initiatives focus only on reorganizing the law applicable to organic transactions. Other states have incorporated broader changes in corporate governance rules in their reform efforts. Although the details of the amendments (like the rules being amended) vary from state to state, several different general ways of approaching the relevant legislative drafting have emerged.

Traditionally, all of the fundamental change rules for each form of business entity were located in the statute for that particular business entity. In other words, the rules for amendments to organizational documents, mergers, conversions, domestications, and dissolutions for LLCs in any individual state were located solely in the state's LLC Act. That remains true in most states.

However, a few states have adopted "junction box" statutes. In these states, the common substantive and procedural rules for organic transactions are collected in a separate act among the business entity statutes of the state. Alabama, Colorado, Connecticut, and Nevada are four states that have adopted a "junction box" approach. The META also represents a version of this approach. In each case, the fundamental change provisions in individual entity statutes within the adopting state are preserved to some extent despite the adoption of a separate statute governing these transactions. This aspect of junction box statutes limits the value of those statutes as simplification measures in that practitioners may need to look at two or more separate laws—the junction box statute and the statutes governing the individual entities subject to the action.

Texas has taken a related but distinct approach that addresses this inefficiency to some extent. The Texas law expressly articulates its purpose: "to make the law encompassed by this code more accessible and understandable by: (1) rearranging the statutes into a more logical order; (2) employing a format and numbering system designed to facilitate citation of the law and to accommodate future expansion of the law; (3) eliminating repealed, duplicative, expired, executed, and other ineffective provisions; and (4) restating the law in modern American English to the greatest extent possible."[36] To achieve these aims, Texas organizes all of its business entity laws under a comprehensive business organizations code. The code begins with a title that incorporates consolidated fundamental change rules and other provisions generally applicable to all forms of business entity. The individual entity laws are separate titles within the Texas Business Organizations Code, the code having replaced in their entireties all of the predecessor standalone state entity laws. These separate entity law titles state the required vote for actions by LLCs (including the required vote for fundamental changes), but otherwise do not address fundamental changes. Accordingly, to a great extent, the Texas model keeps all fundamental change provisions in one place, in one title, regardless of the form of entity.

Other states have reformed their LLC laws, including especially their fundamental change provisions within those laws, to make them more internally consistent and more consistent with analogous provisions across forms of entity while keeping all fundamental change rules within each distinct entity law statute. Florida undertook this kind of legislative overhaul. The revisions were effective on January 1, 2014 and, effective January 1, 2015, all Florida LLCs were required to comply with the revised LLC Act.

> The structure of the new act for organic transactions is a big improvement over existing law, with the provisions for each organic transaction modeled in the same manner (there are six sections for each of the four types of transactions, each set in the same order and having the same descriptive captions, with the subsections of each section in the same order). Generally, these provisions correspond to article 10 of the uniform act, except that the definitions (other than those dealing with appraisal rights) have been relocated to the general definition section of the new act and the appraisal rights provisions in the existing law have been placed at the end (the uniform act does not contain appraisal rights).[37]

Changes of this nature are common as bar association groups and legislatures struggle with how to best accomplish improvements in the evolving law of fundamental changes for LLCs and other forms of entity without undertaking large, time-consuming revision projects.

---

[36] TEX. BUS. ORGS. CODE ANN. § 1.001 (West 2014).
[37] Louis T. M. Conti & Gregory M. Marks, *Florida's New Revised LLC Act, Part IV*, FLA. B.J., March 2014, at 27, 28 (footnotes omitted).

4. CONCLUSION

The law applicable to fundamental changes in LLCs has been developing both rapidly and continuously since the introduction of the LLC form. These changes have not been entirely consistent from state to state. Nevertheless, they do have certain commonalities.

Both corporate law and freedom of contract principles have influenced developments in the legal doctrine of LLC fundamental changes. For example, approval requirements for fundamental changes have largely moved away from unanimity, and dissenters' rights and a dissolution remedy for member oppression have been grafted into LLC law from corporate law. Yet LLC statutes also have increasingly comprised default rules that allow LLC constituents to order the affairs of the LLC for themselves.

The corporatization of and contractarian bent to LLC law sometimes come into conflict. Fiduciary duty law, historically a mediating factor in that conflict, threatens to evolve toward freedom of contract norms. If taken to an extreme, this trend would compromise fiduciary duty's historical role as interstitial doctrine that preserves equitable conduct in business enterprises.

Dominant corporate law rules coexist peacefully with freedom of contract norms in the LLC response to vested rights, however. Contemporary LLC law has rejected the original emphasis on the vested personal property rights of business entity equity holders (owners), earlier eschewed under corporate law. Unanimous consent requirements for fundamental changes have all but disappeared. In some cases, appraisal rights have arisen, as they did under corporate law, on a mandatory or default or contractual basis. In other cases, freedom of contract in the LLC form has completely supplanted any vested rights previously recognized in the LLC law governing fundamental changes.

These developments put pressure on the drafting of LLC law by state legislatures. There is wide acknowledgement of redundancies in the laws governing fundamental changes within LLCs and as among different forms of entity and a perceived overall need for simplification of LLC law generally and fundamental change doctrine specifically. Model statutes and legislative initiatives offer varied approaches to LLC law reform, and modifications to the laws governing organic transactions and other fundamental changes have been the foundation of many of these projects.

While LLC fundamental change law has been understudied, it is important to the development of LLC law and the overall law of business entities. Although LLC law originally was patterned after partnership law, LLCs often operate more like corporations in fundamental change contexts. Doctrine has developed to respond to that fact. Having said that, the LLC law applying to fundamental changes also retains (and in some cases has returned to or built on) the contractarian roots of LLC law, incorporating freedom of contract principles that distinguish LLC law meaningfully from corporate law. In this environment, state legislatures struggle with the complexity of and arising from changes in LLC fundamental change doctrine. Some have begun to respond to these challenges with creative approaches to structuring LLC law. More innovation in this respect can be expected and should be welcomed.

BIBLIOGRAPHY

ABA Ad Hoc Committee on Entity Rationalization, *Proposed Model Inter-Entity Transactions Act*, 57 BUS. LAW. 1569 (2002)

ABA COMM. ON LLCS, P'SHIPS AND UNINCORP. ENTITIES, PROTOTYPE LIMITED LIABILITY COMPANY ACT (1992)

ABA Comm. on LLCs, P'ships and Unincorp. Entities, *Revised Prototype Limited Liability Company Act*, 67 BUS. LAW. 117 (2011)

ABA CORPORATE LAWS COMM, MODEL BUSINESS CORPORATION ACT (2010)

Art, Robert C., *Conversion and Merger of Disparate Business Entities*, 76 WASH. L. REV. 349 (2001)

Blackwell, Thomas F., *The Revolution Is Here: The Promise of a Unified Business Organization Law*, 24 J. CORP. L. 333 (1999)

Bratton, William W. & Joseph A. McCahery, *An Inquiry into the Efficiency of the Limited Liability Company: Of Theory of the Firm and Regulatory Competition*, 54 WASH. & LEE L. REV. 629 (1997)

Callison, J. William & Maureen A. Sullivan, LIMITED LIABILITY COMPANIES: A STATE-BY-STATE GUIDE TO LAW AND PRACTICE (2014)

Campbell, Jr., Rutheford B., *Bumping Along the Bottom: Abandoned Principles and Failed Fiduciary Standards in Uniform Partnership and LLC Statutes*, 96 KY. L.J. 163 (2007–2008)

Clark, Jr., William H., *What the Business World is Looking for in an Organizational Form: The Pennsylvania Experience*, 32 WAKE FOREST L. REV. 149 (1997)

Conti, Louis T. M. & Gregory M. Marks, *Florida's New Revised LLC Act, Part IV*, FLA. B.J., March 2014, at 27

Cottam, Dale W. et al., *The 2010 Wyoming Limited Liability Company Act: A Uniform Recipe with Wyoming "Home Cooking"*, 11 WYO. L. REV. 49 (2011)

Geu, Thomas & Robert Keatinge, *The Proposed Model Inter-Entity Transactions Act: A Proposal to Rationalize Changes in Forms of Business Organizations*, 37 REAL PROP. PROB. & TR. J. 385 (2002)

Hillman, Robert W., *Limited Liability and Externalization of Risk: A Comment on the Death of Partnership*, 70 WASH. U. L.Q. 477 (1992)

Hillman, Robert W., *Limited Liability In Historical Perspective*, 54 WASH. & LEE L. REV. 615 (1997)

Johnson, Lyman P. Q., *Delaware's Non-Waivable Duties*, 91 B.U. L. REV. 701 (2011)

Keatinge, Robert R., *Corporations, Unincorporated Organizations, and Unincorporations: Check the Box and the Balkanization of Business Organizations*, 1 J. SMALL & EMERGING BUS. L. 201 (1997)

Keatinge, Robert R., *Universal Business Organization Legislation: Will It Happen? Why and When*, 23 DEL. J. CORP. L. 29 (1998)

Kleinberger, Daniel S., *The Closely Held Business Through the Entity-Aggregate Prism*, 40 WAKE FOREST L. REV. 827 (2005)

Kleinberger, Daniel S., *Two Decades of "Alternative Entities": From Tax Rationalization Through Alphabet Soup to Contract as Deity*, 14 FORDHAM J. CORP. & FIN. L. 445 (2009)

Kleinberger, Daniel S. & Carter R. Bishop, *The Next Generation: The Revised Uniform Limited Liability Company Act*, 62 BUS. LAW. 515 (2007)

Lion, III, Paul "Chip" L., *Cross Entity Merger and Conversion Statutes*, ALI-ABA LIMITED LIABILITY ENTITIES IN TIMES OF CHANGE (March 12, 2002)

Loewenstein, Mark J., *A New Direction For State Corporate Codes*, 68 U. COLO. L. REV. 453 (1997)

Matheson, John H. & Brent A. Olsen, *A Call for a Unified Business Organization Law*, 65 GEO. WASH. L. REV. 1 (1996)

Miller, Sandra K., *The Role of the Court in Balancing Contractual Freedom with the Need for Mandatory Constraints on Opportunistic and Abusive Conduct in the LLC*, 152 U. PA. L. REV. 1609 (2004)

Miller, Sandra K., *Discounts and Buyouts in Minority Investor LLC Valuation Disputes Involving Oppression or Divorce*, 13 U. PA. J. BUS. L. 607 (2011)

Moll, Douglas K., *Minority Oppression and the Limited Liability Company: Learning (or Not) from Close Corporation History*, 40 WAKE FOREST L. REV. 883 (2005)

NATIONAL CONFERENCE OF COMMISSIONERS ON UNIFORM STATE LAWS, MODEL ENTITY TRANSACTIONS ACT (2007), available at http://www.uniformlaws.org/shared/docs/entity_transactions/meta_final_07.pdf

Oesterle, Dale A. & Wayne M. Gazur, *What's in a Name?: An Argument for a Small Business "Limited Liability Entity" Statute (with Three Subsets of Default Rules)*, 32 WAKE FOREST L. REV. 101 (1997)

REVISED UNIFORM LIMITED LIABILITY COMPANY ACT (2006)

Ribstein, Larry E., *The Deregulation of Limited Liability and the Death of Partnership*, 70 WASH. U. L.Q. 417 (1992)

Ribstein, Larry E., *A Critique of the Uniform Limited Liability Company Act*, 25 STETSON L. REV. 311 (1995)

Ribstein, Larry E. & Robert R. Keatinge, RIBSTEIN AND KEATINGE ON LIMITED LIABILITY COMPANIES (2014)

Ribstein, Larry E. & Bruce H. Kobayashi, *Uniform Laws, Model Laws and Limited Liability Companies*, 66 U. COLO. L. REV. 947 (1995)
Rutledge, Thomas E., *Waiving Fiduciary Obligations*, J. PASSTHROUGH ENTITIES, Mar.–Apr. 2009, at 43
Rutledge, Thomas E., *The 2010 Amendments to Kentucky's Business Entity Laws*, 38 N. KY. L. REV. 383 (2011)
UNIFORM LIMITED LIABILITY COMPANY ACT (1996)

13. Care and loyalty after the dissociation from or dissolution of an unincorporated entity
Thomas E. Rutledge

> How come we don't always recognize the moment love begins, but we always know the moment it ends?
> *LA Story*

The discharge of fiduciary obligations at the time of dissolution and during the winding-up phase is a troubling issue. Questions include to whom the duties are owed and the aim of those duties. Participants in the now dissolved venture may misapprehend continuing obligations, especially when, rightly or wrongly, there is the belief that one or more of the other participants in the venture have engaged in inappropriate or dishonest conduct in its operation, thereby giving rise to the belief that those other participants are owed nothing. Unfortunately neither the statutes nor case law provides comprehensive guidance, leaving each situation to resolution by what may be expensive private ordering and even more expensive resolution before a tribunal. While we may know the moment love ends, seldom do we know when fiduciary obligations end.

Adding further complexity to the matter are the facts that (a) different unincorporated forms provide greater and lesser degrees of detail as to the survival of fiduciary duties after dissolution and (b) individual ventures have great flexibility in providing different rules by private ordering. It is therefore not possible to say that "in the realm of unincorporated business entities, after dissolution the rule is _____." Rather, at best we can say "in a venture organized under the ____ act, assuming no private ordering to the contrary, the rule is ____." Even that statement cannot be made with respect to a venture organized under an act that does not specify the effect of dissolution upon fiduciary duties.

To foreshadow a point to be addressed in greater detail below, the best practice is to by private ordering address a priori in the partnership or operating agreement the fiduciary duties that will continue to bind the venture's former participants. This guidance should address both the obligations of a person who leaves a venture during its duration and as well the obligations of the participants after the dissolution of the firm and during the winding-up phase. By doing so the participants have guidance as to what is and is not expected of them and avoid another basis for conflict among the participants in a venture that may have failed or been driven to dissolution by a breakdown from inter-personal relationship.

We begin with the presumption that our actor owes a fiduciary duty to either the venture or to the venture and its owners. From that starting point there is the question of the nature and ultimate effect of the separation of the actor from the venture. Under traditional partnership law a partner's departure from the venture, whether voluntary or involuntary (identified as a "dissociation"),[1] typically effected a "dissolution" of

---

[1] *See, e.g.*, UNIF. PART. ACT ("LIPA") § 29, 6 (pt. II) U.L.A. 349 (2001).

the partnership. While the remaining partners could reconstitute the partnership, that reconstituted partnership is deemed to be a new legal entity.[2] The more modern Revised Uniform Partnership Act does not dictate this result and does not provide that the legal existence of the partnership is interrupted simply because of a partner's withdrawal from the venture.[3] While certain early LLC Acts provided for the entity's dissolution upon a member's dissociation, nearly all if not all of the Acts now provide that an LLC will have continuity of life notwithstanding the loss of a member.

Typically herein the "dissolution" of the venture will refer to its termination as an ongoing venture as contrasted with the technical termination which was a consequence of a dissociation under the Uniform Partnership Act and similar partnership laws. Consideration is given, but to a lesser degree, to the situation of an individual participant separating from an ongoing venture and that former participant's ongoing obligations to the venture.

It is important to appreciate that dissolution is not so much an event in time as it is an alteration in purpose. While typically an unincorporated entity may engage in any legal business activity,[4] upon dissolution the purpose of the venture is altered to the winding up and liquidation of its activities, the satisfaction of creditor claims, and either the final distribution of net assets among the participants or, in the case of a general partnership, the collection of additional contributions from the partners for the purpose of satisfying creditor claims. As such, upon dissolution the venture is not concluded, but rather it enters a phase during which it will be concluded. During this phase of dissolution the venture's assets need to be collected and disposed of in a manner most advantageous to creditors and the venture's participants.[5] It is to be expected that fiduciary obligations will continue to police the activities undertaken as part of the winding up and liquidation. At the same time, as the activities of the venture are restricted after dissolution to those necessary to wind up and liquidate, we would not expect that fiduciary obligations will attach to conduct not necessary in connection with the winding up and liquidation. The difficulty arises in drawing that distinction.[6]

---

[2] *See, e.g., Fairway Dev. Corp. v. Title Insurance Co. of Minn.*, 621 F.Supp. 120 (N.D. Ohio 1985).

[3] *See* REV. UNIF. PART. ACT ("RUPA") § 603, 6 (pt. I) U.L.A. 172 (2001).

[4] *See, e.g.*, REVISED UNIFORM LIMITED LIABILITY COMPANY ACT ("RULLCA") § 104(b), 6B U.L.A. 437 (2008) ("A limited liability company may have any lawful purpose, regardless of whether for profit."); DEL CODE ANN. tit. 6, § 18-106(a); N.H. REV. STAT. ANN. § 304-C:21; *see also* 1 RIBSTEIN AND KEATINGE, appx. 4–9.

[5] The ability of the venture's creditors to enforce the fiduciary obligations owed by the venture's participants is a question outside the scope of this chapter. For a trio of Delaware decisions addressing these issues, see *Production Resource Group, L.L.C. v. NCT Group, Inc.*, 863 A.2d 772 (Del. Ch. 2004); *North American Catholic Educational Programming Found., Inc. v. Gheewalla*, 930 A.2d 92 (Del. 2007); *Trenwick America Litigation Trust v. Ernst & Young, L.L.P.*, 906 A.2d 168 (Del. Ch. 2006).

[6] The fiduciary duties upon and after either dissociation or dissolution has received little systematic attention. An exception is Hart (1954).

THE SOURCE—*MEINHARD v. SALMON*

Meinhard v. Salmon,[7] the archetypical case on partner fiduciary obligations, by at least one reading, arose in connection with a partnership's dissolution. Meinhard and Salmon were the two partners in a venture organized in 1902 to hold and exploit a 20-year lease. Salmon had made the contacts for the original lease and had then brought Meinhard into the deal in order to provide necessary financing.[8] By all indications the venture was successful during that intended term. As the leasehold was coming to an end, Salmon negotiated a new lease for the same and additional adjacent property, a lease which among other things obligated Salmon to demolish an existing structure and erect a new building three times larger. What was different, and the genesis of this famous suit, was that Meinhard was not included in the new venture. It was over that exclusion that Meinhard brought suit, alleging, *inter alia*, that Salmon was required to include him in the exploitation of the new lease on the same terms as the prior lease. Notwithstanding a spirited dissent that appears more grounded in the law than does the majority opinion, Justice Cardozo wrote some of the more (perhaps the most) cited prose in business entity law, stating:

> Joint adventurers, like copartners, owe to one another, while the enterprise continues, the duty of the finest loyalty. Many forms of conduct permissible in a workaday world for those acting at arm's length, are forbidden to those bound by fiduciary ties. A trustee is held to something stricter than the morals of the marketplace. Not honesty alone, but the punctilio of an honor the most sensitive, is then the standard of behavior. As to this there has developed a tradition that is unbending and inveterate. Uncompromising rigidity has been the attitude of courts of equity when petitioned to undermine the rule of undivided loyalty by the "disintegrating erosion" of particular expectations . . . . Only thus has the level of conduct for fiduciaries been kept at a level higher than that trodden by the crowd. It will not consciously be lowered by any judgment of this court.

Whether this is a correct statement of the law is open to debate. For example, did Meinhard have a reasonable expectation that he would be included in the exploitation of a lease subsequent to that which he and Salmon agreed to jointly exploit? The dissent found that he did not. Still, the majority required that Meinhard be admitted as a partner in the new and substantially larger venture. Meinhard's victory was in part pyrrhic; in the subsequent downturn of the New York real estate market after the 1929 stock market crash and the ensuing Great Depression, Meinhard was required to make significant capital contributions to the partnership. As a matter of law, the Uniform Partnership Act, not adopted in New York until 1919, sets forth a significantly more restricted formulary as to a partner's fiduciary obligations.

Still, regardless of whether *Meinhard v. Salmon* accurately reflects the laws as they stand today,[9] its language permeates the understanding of what is expected of participants in

---

[7] 249 N.Y. 458, 164 N.E. 545 (1928).
[8] *See generally* Miller, *Meinhard v. Salmon*.
[9] *See, e.g.*, Hillman (1987), which observed:

> Although colorful, the judicial rhetoric inevitably overstates the standard of conduct the law actually imposes on partners. If partners truly are fiduciaries, they are a unique species

unincorporated entities,[10] suggesting at least that the participants in a venture concluded as to its object continue to owe obligations to protect the interests of co-venturers in related future activities. It is against this background that this chapter is written and that questions of post-dissolution fiduciary obligations must be made.

THE STATUTORY GUIDANCE

Assuming the particular venture has not by private ordering modified the default fiduciary obligations, in which case the first inquiry must be of the particular standards therein set forth, it is important to ascertain what the controlling statute says about the fiduciary obligations among the participants in the venture and the degree to which the statute has addressed their application either after the venture's dissolution or the separation of a participant therefrom.

UPA

The Uniform Partnership Act (1914) ("UPA") Section 21(1) mandates that:

> Every partner must account to the partnership for any benefit, and hold as trustee for it any profits derived by him without the consent of the other partners from any transaction connected with the formation, conduct, or liquidation of the partnership or from any use by him of its property.

Note that the obligation continues through the "liquidation of the partnership." Still, the obligation is tied to status as a "partner." A partnership is not terminated by reason of dissolution (UPA § 30), and the remaining partners have an obligation to complete performance on the partnership's executory contracts for the benefit of the partnership.[11] The UPA is silent as to any modification of fiduciary obligations upon dissolution.

RUPA

The Revised Uniform Partnership Act (1997) ("RUPA"), at § 404, defines an exclusive listing of partner's fiduciary duties as being loyalty and care under the following formulae:

---

of this group and cannot be subjected to traditional standards applicable to other types of fiduciaries . . . . Partners . . . are always joint owners . . . . Partners are not disinterested trustees, and the likelihood that most partners operate under a "punctilio of an honor the most sensitive" standard is remote.

[10] For example, in *Mason v. Underhill*, No. 2006-CA-002144-MR, 2008 WL 1917179 (Ky. App. May 2, 2008), notwithstanding that Kentucky had adopted both the Uniform Partnership Act (1914) and the Revised Uniform Limited Partnership Act (1985), neither of which was actually mentioned, the court quoted *Meinhard v. Salmon* at length in describing what are the fiduciary duties of the general partner of a limited partnership.

[11] See, e.g., *Platt v. Henderson*, 361 P.2d 73 (Or. 1961). But see *In re Thelen*, 24 N.Y.3d 16 (existing hourly matters of defunct law firm would transfer to new firm of attorney without a right in the prior firm to a claim on fees earned after transfer of file).

- A partner's duty of loyalty is:
    (1) to account to the partnership and hold as trustee for it any property, profit, or benefit derived by the partner in the conduct and winding up of the partnership business or derived from a use by the partner of partnership property, including the appropriation of a partnership opportunity;
    (2) to refrain from dealing with the partnership in the conduct or winding up of the partnership business as or on behalf of a party having an interest adverse to the partnership; and
    (3) to refrain from competing with the partnership in the conduct of the partnership business before the dissolution of the partnership.[12]
- A partner's duty of care is as follows:
    (c) A partner's duty of care to the partnership and the other partners in the conduct and winding up of the partnership business is limited to refraining from engaging in grossly negligent or reckless conduct, intentional misconduct, or a knowing violation of law.[13]

From there, RUPA § 603 provides that upon a partner's dissociation from the partnership:

(2) the partner's duty of loyalty under Section 404(b)(3) terminates; and
(3) the partner's duty of loyalty under Section 404(b)(1) and (2) and duty of care under Section 404(c) continue only with regard to matters arising and events occurring before the partner's dissociation, unless the partner participates in winding up the partnership's business pursuant to Section 803.

RULLCA

The Revised Uniform Limited Liability Company Act ("RULLCA") § 409(b) provides that if the LLC is "member-managed," then each member is subject to a duty of loyalty which includes the obligations:

(1) to account to the company and to hold as trustee for it any property, profit, or benefit derived by the member:
    (A) in the conduct or winding up of the company's activities;
    (B) from a use by the member of the company's property; or
    (C) from the appropriation of a limited liability company opportunity;
(2) to refrain from dealing with the company in the conduct or winding up of the company's activities as or on behalf of a person having an interest adverse to the company; and
(3) to refrain from competing with the company in the conduct of the company's activities before the dissolution of the company.

Section 409(c) of RULLCA defines, in a member-managed LLC, each member's duty of care as follows:

Subject to the business judgment rule, the duty of care of a member of a member-managed limited liability company in the conduct and winding up of the company's activities is to act with

---

[12] RUPA § 404(b), 6 (pt. I) U.L.A. 143 (2001).
[13] RUPA § 404(c), 6 (pt. I) U.L.A. 143 (2001).

the care that a person in a like position would reasonably exercise under similar circumstances and in a manner the member reasonably believes to be in the best interests of the company. In discharging this duty, a member may rely in good faith upon opinions, reports, statements, or other information provided by another person that the member reasonably believes is a competent and reliable source for the information.

RULLCA § 603(2) provides that upon a member's dissociation from the LLC "if the company is member-managed, the person's fiduciary duties as a member end with regard to matters arising and events occurring after the person's dissociation." Curiously this provision is far less specific than is the predecessor RUPA as to how the various aspects of the duty of loyalty are modified upon dissociation from the venture. The RULLCA is silent as to the impact of dissolution upon the obligations owed by the members.

RPLLCA

The Revised Prototype Limited Liability Company Act ("RPLLCA") is silent as to the fiduciary obligations of a member, entirely leaving that question to the private ordering of the participants in the venture.[14] In consequence the Act is silent as to the impact upon fiduciary obligations consequent to either dissociation or dissolution. While there is great benefit to leaving the nature and application of fiduciary duties to private ordering, it creates as well the burden to account for the effect of dissociation and dissolution upon those obligations; else the agreement is incomplete and must be completed through ex ante dispute resolution.

The Statutory Lacunae

Tellingly for our purposes, none of the Uniform Acts nor the RPLLCA address the degree and manner in which the duties owed by the participants in the venture are modified, if at all, by the venture's dissolution (note that a venture's dissolution is not of itself an event of dissociation of the participants therefrom). This is curious in that the winding up and liquidation of a venture may take a significant period of time during which those participants may seek to affiliate themselves with a new venture and engage in activities that are subject to characterization as conflicting with the original venture or which utilize to a greater or lesser degree what may be characterized as its property including good will. Those activities may have the effect of reducing the value of the prior venture and limit its ability to liquidate on other than fire sale terms. A former participant may argue that there can be no competition vis-à-vis a venture that is restricted to winding up and liquidation and that absent direct use of firm assets for the purpose of generating gain for another firm there can be no breach of duty. The Uniform and the Revised Prototype may each be faulted for not addressing these issues.[15]

---

[14] See 67 BUS. LAW. at 120. In contrast, the original Prototype Limited Liability Company Act (1992) sets forth a statutory duty of loyalty and as well a standard of care set forth in the terms of a standard of culpability. See PROTOTYPE § 402.

[15] This critique is offered even as the author has been involved in the drafting of a number of these statutes.

There is an additional lacuna in the differential treatment of one who has withdrawn from a venture versus, for example, what is a company "opportunity"[16] when the LLC is being wound up and liquidated? Is any new prospect not an opportunity because the purpose of the business in now limited to activities appropriate for winding up? Conversely, is an opportunity which affords the ability to dispose of venture assets on advantageous terms something which must be afforded the dissolving venture? Imagine a retail flooring company that is being dissolved consequent to disagreements between the two owners. Should one of them, during winding up, learn of the opportunity to make a full-price retail sale of certain inventory, we would expect there to be an obligation to offer that opportunity to the dissolving firm. However, if the dissolution of the firm is consequent to that participant's withdrawal from the firm, at least RULLCA and RUPA would indicate that there is no duty to share this opportunity with the original firm.

For these reasons, and again in the absence of clear private ordering, it is necessary to assess the common law that has arisen, primarily under UPA, as to the obligations that continue to exist after the venture's dissolution. Unfortunately, that guidance is often confusing.

CASE LAW

The initial problem with relying upon the existing case law is its paucity except with respect to decisions under UPA. The relative novelty of the LLC form and the various LLC statutes have not yet afforded the opportunity to develop a deep body of decisions. In certain instances, it will be possible to use decisions based upon UPA in assessing conduct in LLCs consequent to the LLC Act in question using an UPA formula for fiduciary obligations.[17] Often this will not be possible as the statutory formula differs from that employed in UPA, a fact which may preclude the application of case law decided under UPA to disputes arising under RUPA or one of the LLC Acts.[18]

Continuing Fiduciary Duties of the Resigning and Remaining Partners After a Partner's Withdrawal

When a partnership is continued by the remaining partners after a partner's dissociation, the dissociated partner and remaining partners retain fiduciary duties to one another and to the business in multiple regards. One of the most basic involves any and all business opportunities that originated with the partnership. The fiduciary duty of loyalty restricts a dissociated partner from taking personal advantage of any information or opportunities which came to his or her attention prior to withdrawal and which were not abandoned or otherwise refused by the partnership. This principle is illustrated by *Fouchek v. Janicek*,[19]

---

[16] *See, e.g.*, RULLCA § 409(b)(1)(C), 6B U.L.A. 488 (2008).
[17] *See, e.g.*, Rutledge and Geu (2010).
[18] *See, e.g.*, *TM2008 Investment, LLC v. ProCon Capital Corp.*, 323 P.3d 704 (Ariz. App. 2014) (trial verdict reversed where instructions spoke of generic obligation of LLC members to one another and did not reflect obligations undertaken in operating agreement).
[19] *Fouchek v. Janicek*, 225 P.2d 783 (Or. 1950).

wherein the Supreme Court of Oregon held a partner responsible for breach of his fiduciary duties when he withdrew from the partnership in order to personally pursue an opportunity originally belonging to the partnership. The partnership, a wholesaling business, had been approached by a group of investors seeking to enter into a joint venture with the partnership.[20] Around 30 days after that offer was made, and before negotiations commenced between the partnership's members and the investors, one of the partners, Janicek, suddenly withdrew from the partnership, solicited the investors on his own, and ultimately obtained the opportunity for himself.[21]

The remaining partners brought suit against Janicek for breach of fiduciary duty in usurping the business opportunity, but the suit was dismissed by the trial court. On appeal by the remaining partners, Janicek defended his actions by arguing that in order for a disassociated partner to be held liable for breach of fiduciary duty, "[t]he partnership must have owned and held [a] *tangible asset or property* and the withdrawing partner must have taken that valuable asset or property to the detriment of the preceding partnership."[22] The court disagreed with that characterization of the facts, and instead called the business opportunity at issue "a species of preemptive privilege or, better, a preemptive opportunity that was an incident of the [partnership] enterprise."[23] The court further stated that "[i]nformation belongs to a partnership in the sense of property in which it has a valuable right, if it is of the character which might be employed to the partnership's advantage. Such information cannot be used by one partner for his private gain."[24]

The court ultimately held that even though the partner had voluntarily dissociated from the partnership before obtaining for his own account the business opportunity offered to his former firm, his fiduciary obligations to the firm continued into his future dealings since the opportunity had arisen out of his former partnership. The court declared that "[w]hen a partner wrongfully snatches a seed of opportunity from the granary of his firm, he cannot, thereafter, excuse himself from sharing with his copartners the fruits of its planting, even though the harvest occurs after they have terminated their association."[25] Partners, therefore, cannot simply eliminate their fiduciary duties to the partnership entity by dissociating from the partnership.

Fouchek and similar decisions caution against a participant in a venture seeking to exploit for themselves what could be exploited by the firm.

It has been held that when a partner dissociates from the partnership in contravention of the partnership agreement, the remaining partners may not be held to the same fiduciary standards as they would have otherwise been in relation to that dissociating partner. In *Bluestein v. Davis*,[26] the court held that when a partner dissociated from a partnership in violation of the controlling agreement, the fiduciary relationship between the partners ended to the extent it protected the interests of the now dissociated partner, such that

---

[20] *Id.* at 787.
[21] *Id.* at 788.
[22] *Id.* at 790 (emphasis in original).
[23] *Id.*
[24] *Id.* at 791.
[25] *Id.* at 793.
[26] *Bluestein v. Davis*, 230 N.E.2d 61 (Ill. App. 1967).

the remaining partners could conduct business without accounting to that withdrawing partner.

Generally, fiduciary duties must continue despite strained relations between the partners, even after a partner has informed co-partners that he or she will not be continuing in the partnership after the termination date.[27] Even if the partners are no longer working together amicably, the relationship of trust that initially gave rise to the fiduciary duties among the partners still exists.[28] In a buy-sell situation, the partners' principal fiduciary duty is primarily one of full disclosure, but also can include a fiduciary duty to pay a fair price to the withdrawing partner or the estate of a deceased partner.[29] These concepts are exemplified by *Lund v. Albrecht*,[30] wherein the Ninth Circuit was asked to review the fiduciary duties of two feuding former partners. After 13 years of partnership in real estate acquisitions, development, and sales, two partners began to discuss the possibility of dissolution effected through Albrecht's purchase of Lund's interest in the business and its assets.[31] They negotiated for several months over the purchase price, during which time Albrecht secretly solicited and received four offers to sell Lund's portion of the property at a price much higher than that which Albrecht was offering to Lund in their negotiations.[32] Lund was never aware of these offers, and presumably did not know the true value of the property he was selling to his partner Albrecht. After selling the property and interests to Albrecht, Lund discovered the earlier offers when he was made aware of Albrecht's substantial profit from selling the properties to a third party.[33] Lund brought suit against Albrecht for breach of his fiduciary duty in failing to disclose material information about the purchase of Lund's shares of the business.[34]

The court's decision on liability hinged on the effective date of the partnership termination, as it was undisputed that Albrecht's non-disclosure of the third party offers to purchase partnership property would have been a breach of fiduciary duty if the partnership was still in existence at that time.[35] Under California law, the court explained, "consummation occurs, and a partner's fiduciary duty ends, when the parties have formed and signed a contract to purchase the partnership interest."[36] The court reviewed negotiation documents and determined that the purchasing contract had not yet been completed at the time that Albrecht began soliciting and concealing offers and, as such, the trial court had properly found him liable for breach of his fiduciary duty to Lund when he failed to disclose material information about the sale.[37]

The Second Circuit addressed the issue of a departing partner and the continuing duties

---

[27] BROMBERG AND RIBSTEIN ON PARTNERSHIP 6:130.
[28] *Id.*
[29] *Id.* at 6:149 (2011–3 Supplement).
[30] *Lund v. Albrecht*, 936 F.2d 459 (9th Cir. 1991).
[31] *Id.* at 461.
[32] *Id.* at 462.
[33] *Id.*
[34] *Id.*
[35] *Id.* at 463.
[36] *Id.*
[37] *Id.* at 464. *Accord Harris v. Archer*, 134 S.W.3d 411 (Tx. Ct. App. 2004).

of the remaining partners in *Newburger, Loeb & Co. v. Gross*,[38] where a managing partner withdrew from an investment advisor partnership amidst disagreements over the handling of business records. In the case, the managing partner, Gross, gave a four-week notice of his departure from the firm and demanded the return of certain capital investments.[39] However, the partnership agreement provided that at least 85 percent of the partnership interest of a withdrawn general partner must remain in the firm, at the risk of the business, for 12 months after that partner's withdrawal.[40]

Several months later, the remaining partners attempted to transfer the assets of the partnership to reorganize into a corporation, a move that would have jeopardized Gross's financial investment still locked in with the firm.[41] The remaining partners tried several coercive tactics, including threats of legal action, to convince Gross to consent to the transfer, but eventually executed the reorganization without Gross's permission.[42] When the remaining partners later sued Gross for fraud related to his earlier handling of certain business affairs, Gross countersued, claiming breach of fiduciary duty by those partners for their improper coercive activities and other misconduct. Gross argued that their breach of fiduciary duty entitled him to a return of his capital investment in the partnership, an argument accepted by the Second Circuit Court of Appeals.[43]

Looking to the partnership fiduciary duties of utmost good faith, fairness, and loyalty put forth by Chief Judge Cardozo in *Meinhard v. Salmon*, the *Newburger* court found that although Gross withdrew from the partnership, the fiduciary obligations of his co-partners to him had not terminated.[44] The court explained that:

> as a withdrawn general partner Gross no longer had any voice in management, although his capital remained in the firm at the risk of the business and Gross continued to share in an allocated portion of the firm's profits and losses. Thus, we conclude that at least up to and perhaps after the transfer, the Partnership and its members owed to Gross the duties of good faith, fairness and loyalty in their dealings with him regarding the Partnership business.[45]

Decisions such as *Newburger* caution against the view that a dissociated participant from the firm is "fair game," a caution especially applicable when the dissociated participant remains at risk for the venture success.

In sum, when a partner withdraws from a partnership but the partnership business continues, ongoing fiduciary duties restrict the withdrawn partner from taking personal advantage of any business opportunities arising from his or her connection with the

---

[38] *Newburger, Loeb & Co. v. Gross*, 563 F.2d 1057 (2d Cir. 1977), *cert. denied*, 434 U.S. 1035 (1978).
[39] *Id.* at 1062.
[40] *Id.*
[41] *Id.* at 1063.
[42] *Id.*
[43] *Id.* at 1078.
[44] *Id.*
[45] *Id. See also Johnson v. Peckham*, 120 S.W.2d 786 (1938) (stating that if a fiduciary were allowed to void his or her duties simply by withdrawal from the partnership, there would be a risk of abusive bargaining); *Ong. Intl. (U.S.A.) v. 11th Ave. Corp.*, 850 P.2d 447 (Utah 1993) (finding that a fiduciary relationship existed at the time of redemption of a partnership interest despite adversarial dealings).

former partnership. The remaining partners must continue in their fiduciary duties of loyalty, good faith, and full disclosure to the withdrawing partner between the time of the withdrawal announcement and that partner's official departure, despite any ill will that may arise between them. Where the partner properly dissociates, the remaining partners must honor their fiduciary arrangement until the completion of partner withdrawal, but where a partner dissociates in contravention of the partnership agreement, the remaining partners may relax their fiduciary duties as to their interaction with that withdrawn partner.

Continuing Fiduciary Duties of Partners During and After Dissolution and Winding Up of the Partnership

The dissolution of a partnership triggers many responsibilities for the partners participating in the dissolution and winding-up process for the business. They include powers and duties to the partnership and to each other to do all acts necessary to complete the partnership business and engage in the winding up of the partnership affairs,[46] and continue to have certain fiduciary duties to the partnership and to their co-partners during that period and beyond.[47]

Initially, the fiduciary duties extend to include the duty to complete all outstanding contracts of the partnership as of the dissolution date.[48] As explained in *Frates v. Nichols*,[49] a partner in dissolution owes a duty to his former partnership to wind up the pending business, since every member is personally obligated to fulfill partnership contracts. In *Frates*, one member of a dissolved law firm secretly obtained retainer agreements from multiple clients of his former firm to continue with their negligence cases through his new firm, an act which occurred between the dissolution date and the final wind-up date of the former firm.[50] That partner kept all fees from those cases for himself. His former co-partners objected, insisting that as part of his ongoing fiduciary duty to not compete for partnership business or wrongly usurp partnership opportunities, he should take nothing from the client business that originated with the former firm.[51]

The court adopted and followed the rule that "the retention of a law firm obligates every member thereof to fulfilling that contract, and that upon a dissolution any of the partners is obligated to complete that obligation without *extra* compensation."[52] It found that the dissolution date of the partnership did not put an immediate end to the partnership, but that it continued for the purposes of winding up its affairs, which included the completion of outstanding contracts such as those the partner solicited for his own benefit.[53] Thus, the independent retainer agreements signed post-dissolution were deemed void, since the partner's ongoing duty to wind up partnership affairs eclipsed his apparent

---

[46] See CALLISON & SULLIVAN at 426.
[47] *Id.* at 429.
[48] *Id.*
[49] *Frates v. Nichols*, 167 So. 2d 77 (Fla. App. 1964).
[50] *Id.* at 79.
[51] *Id.*
[52] *Id.* at 81 (emphasis in original).
[53] *Id.* at 80.

transfer of firm-wide contracts to himself.[54] As a result, the fees accrued by that partner for the work performed on the contracts were assets of the former firm, and should have been split between them as part of the winding up of business affairs.[55]

The Supreme Court of Colorado illustrated the continuation of fiduciary duties during the wind-up period in *Hooper v. Yoder*,[56] a case that tracked a partnership through its later incorporation and interpreted the effect of incorporation on the rights and duties of the former partners with respect to each other. The partnership business was a manufacturing and sales operation for frozen yogurt bars, which Hooper and Yoder organized without a formal written partnership agreement.[57] A year later, the partners incorporated the business and expanded their production and distribution operations, but elected to defer the issuance of stock in the newly formed corporation.[58]

As new members were added to the corporation's board of directors, the relationship between Hooper and Yoder began to deteriorate, ultimately leading to Yoder's termination from the business he had founded with Hooper.[59] Yoder later learned that Hooper had been issued corporate stock without Yoder's consent, in addition to earning a salary from the business while Yoder received no compensation whatsoever.[60] Yoder then brought suit against Hooper and the corporation for compensation.

The Supreme Court of Colorado reviewed the facts of the interaction and concluded that the partnership between Hooper and Yoder was dissolved upon the formation of the corporation, but that the partnership did not terminate at that time, continuing to exist for the purposes of winding up.[61] It also found that Hooper breached his fiduciary duty to Yoder during the course of the winding-up process by excluding Yoder from participating equally in the issuance of corporate stock and by secretly withdrawing salary from the business.[62] In doing so, the court acknowledged the general rule that "when partners organize a corporation to operate the business of the partnership and transfer the assets to the corporation, the partnership is dissolved."[63] However, the court explained that the winding up of the partnership includes the transfer of the partnership assets to the corporation in exchange for corporate stock, extending the winding-up period in this instance through Hooper's self-issuance of stock and denial of that same benefit to Yoder.[64]

Thus, the partnership continued to exist, and so did the fiduciary duties that Hooper owed to Yoder, including "the right to demand and expect from the other a full, fair, open and honest disclosure of everything affecting the relationship" and the same duty of loyalty and fair dealing as before dissolution and winding up occurred.[65] The court found that Hooper's actions during the winding-up process were in violation of Hooper's

---

[54] *Id.*
[55] *Id.* at 82.
[56] *Hooper v. Yoder*, 737 P.2d 852 (Colo. 1983).
[57] *Id.* at 854.
[58] *Id.* at 854–855.
[59] *Id.* at 856.
[60] *Id.*
[61] *Id.* at 857.
[62] *Id.*
[63] *Id.*
[64] *Id.* at 858.
[65] *Id.*

fiduciary duties of good faith and fair dealing, and affirmed the lower court's award to Yoder of one-half of the shares of stock and salary improperly taken by Hooper.[66]

At least as much as in any other area of the law, there are the decisions as to post-dissolution fiduciary obligations that are simply hard to understand, but which remain viable and therefore cautionary. One such decision is *Monin v. Monin*,[67] which addressed the dissolution of a partnership between two brothers. Sonny advised his brother Charles that he was no longer willing to continue their existing partnership, it being in the milk hauling industry. Anticipating the partnership's dissolution, Sonny advised the dairy cooperative that the agreement for hauling would not be renewed as of the next renewal date. Sonny as well advised Charles that he would be for his own account seeking to enter into the hauling contract with the cooperative. Ultimately Sonny and Charles entered into a "Partnership Sales Agreement" pursuant to which Charles bought out Sonny, with the contract being contingent upon Charles being awarded the hauling contract with the cooperative going forward. The agreement also contained a non-compete agreement binding upon Sonny.

The cooperative declined to award the hauling contract to Charles and instead awarded it to Sonny. Charles then brought suit. While the trial court found no violation of duty by Sonny,[68] the Court of Appeals held that Sonny violated a fiduciary duty to Charles by continuing to pursue for his own account the hauling contract. "We conclude the trial court's reasoning is flawed in that it ignores Sonny's duties to the partnership with respect to the most valuable asset of that entity, the milk hauling contract."[69] The court ignored, however, the fact that the partnership was dissolved by virtue of Sonny's express notice of withdrawal and that the dairy cooperative decided unilaterally whether the contract, what the court described as the partnership's "most valuable asset," would be awarded to Charles, to Sonny, or to anyone else. Still, "Sonny's continuing duty was especially applicable here as he agreed to sell his interest to Charles so Charles could continue the partnership business," even though the purchase contract apparently contained a price adjustment should Charles not be awarded the new hauling contract.

Again, it is difficult to reconcile the ultimate ruling with the underlying facts and law. That does not mean, however, that confused decisions will not continue to plague this area of law.

The Particular Problem of Term and Undertaking Partnerships

As previously noted, *Meinhard v. Salmon* may be read as a decision on the obligation of a partner in what is today described as a partnership for a particular term or for a particular undertaking and a determination that each partner is obligated to invite other

---

[66] *Id.* at 861.
[67] 785 S.W.2d 499 (Ky. App. 1989).
[68] *Id.* at 500 (as to the cooperative's refusal of the contract to Charles, "the affairs of the Monin Brothers partnership were finally settled on September 27, 1984. As a result of the actions of that date, the assets of the partnership were finally valued at $22,000.00. When Charles was rejected as the D.I.'s milk hauler on that date, the partnership had no interest in the milk routes and neither partner had any claim to same as part of their partnership interests.").
[69] *Id.*

partners into the continued venture. That is necessarily a disturbing holding in that it cuts against the purpose of a term or undertaking partnership, namely to limit the scope of the partnership relationship and provide for its termination.[70] Fortunately that reading of *Meinhard v. Salmon* does not to this day continue as the rule of law, and partners have been afforded greater flexibility to structure their post-term or post-undertaking activities.

For example, in *Cass JV, LLC v. Host International, Inc.*,[71] Cass and Host jointly bid on and were awarded the right to operate concessions at an airport for a franchise period of ten years. During that period the relationship between Cass and Host deteriorated. Prior to the time that solicitations were made for the concession franchise for the next ten-year period, Host advised Cass that it would not be bidding with Cass for the next period. Host, with a new partner, was awarded the franchise for the next period, and Cass brought suit alleging breach of fiduciary duty. The court found there to be no breach of duty. Initially, the purpose of the partnership was defined as exploitation of the concession franchise, that being defined as that for a specific ten-year period. Second, Host had advised Cass that they would not be together bidding to receive the franchise for the next period. On that basis there was no concealment of intentions.

Approaching the Dispute

While the resolution of a dispute involving an allegation that fiduciary obligations have been violated depends upon a unique set of facts, there are certain principles that guide the analysis. First, careful attention must be paid to the particular agreement of venture. The assumption that in unincorporated ventures of a particular form (partnership, limited partnership, LLC, etc.), the fiduciary duties are standard is simply wrong. Rather, by private ordering the participants may modify the statutory default rules and impose different standards.[72] Furthermore, various of the LLC Acts, and to a lesser degree partnership and limited partnership acts, allow the entire waiver of some or all otherwise applicable fiduciary obligation.[73] To state the obvious, asserting that there has been a breach of fiduciary obligations when said obligation has been waived in the controlling organic document is a pointless effort unless it can be demonstrated that the underlying Act allows the waiver or limitation of that duty.[74]

If and to the extent that the venture's organic documents do not address the applicable

---

[70] Whether a particular partnership is for a particular term or a particular undertaking is beyond the scope of this chapter. As to that question, *see, e.g.*, *Fischer v. Fischer*, 197 S.W.3d 98 (Ky. 2006). Certain LLCs are by statute either for a term or a particular undertaking (*see, e.g.*, ULLCA § 203(a)(5), 6B U.L.A. 574 (2008)), and by private ordering the purpose of any LLC could be limited to a term or undertaking.

[71] No. 312-CV-00359-CRS-DW, 2014 WL 3955366 (W.D. Ky. Aug 13, 2014).

[72] *See, e.g.*, KY. REV. STAT. ANN. § 275.170 ("Unless otherwise provided a written operating agreement"); SARGENT & SCHWIDETZKY, app. KY-9 (setting forth an operating agreement in which the manager's duty of loyalty is based upon the formula employed in the Kentucky Revised UPA).

[73] *See, e.g.*, *Hite Hedge LP v. El Paso Corp.*, Civ. Act. No. 7117-VCG, 2012 WL 4788658 (Oct. 9, 2012); *Xcell Energy and Coal Company, LLC v. Energy Investment Group, LLC*, C.A. No. 8652-VCN, 2014 WL 2964076 (Del. Ch. Feb. 18, 2014).

[74] *See, e.g.*, RULLCA § 110(d), 6B U.L.A. 442 (2008).

standards, it is necessary to ascertain what the particular statute defines as the applicable default.[75] Again, it is crucial to focus upon the laws governing that particular form of entity in its jurisdiction of organization. For example, LLCs formed in different jurisdictions may have different default formulae of fiduciary duties,[76] just as may partnerships.[77] Consequent to the increased specificity of business entity statutes, including as to the default formulae of fiduciary obligations and their modification upon either dissociation or dissolution, the room for common law is reduced, and "courts *should* exercise great care when analyzing or generalizing from one statute to another where the different statutory schemes vary in manner of expression, detail of regulatory method, and scope of application."[78]

It is not enough to know that there is a duty of care; the focus needs to be upon which duty of care. A Kentucky-organized LLC requires that conduct of a member or manager subject thereto not be "wanton or reckless."[79] In contrast, common law agents and auctioneers are bound to a duty of reasonable care (*i.e.*, simple negligence).[80] Under the Uniform Condominium Association Act, the officers and executive board of a condominium association are held to a standard of simple negligence.[81]

For that reason it is important to focus on that particular formula and as necessary distinguish law developed under other organizational forms or on other states when the standards are dissimilar. Having identified the default fiduciary obligation, it is then necessary to determine whether and how the statute addresses the impact of either dissociation or dissolution upon those duties.

There is as well the possibility that by statute the actor in question does not owe fiduciary obligations by virtue of his or her position.[82]

---

[75] In those states which do not impose a statute of frauds requiring that departures from the default be in writing (*see, e.g.*, Del. Code Ann. tit. 6, § 18-101(7)), there will be questions as to whether the duties have been modified by course of conduct or oral agreement.

[76] Compare DEL. CODE ANN. tit. 6, § 18-1104 ("In any case not provided for in this chapter, the rules of law and equity, including the rules of laws and equity relating to fiduciary duties and the law merchant, shall govern.") with KY. REV. STAT. ANN. § 275.170(1) (statutory standard of care set forth as a standard of culpability); *id.* § 275.170(2) (statutory standard of loyalty).

[77] Compare RUPA § 404(c) *with* KY. REV. STAT. ANN. § 362.1-404(3).

[78] Rutledge & Geu, *supra* note 17 at 502. *See also Pannell v. Shannon*, 425 S.W.3d 58, 68 (Ky. 2014) ("In fact, 'limited liability companies are creatures of statute,' controlled by Kentucky Revised Statutes (KRS) Chapter 275, not primarily by the common law. To the extent that common law doctrines could arguably govern limited liability companies, the Kentucky Limited Liability Company Act 'is in derogation of common law,' and the traditional rule of statutory construction that 'require[s] strict construction of statutes that are in derogation of common law shall not apply to its provision.' Thus, to the extent the statutes conflict with common law, the common law is displaced.") (citations omitted).

[79] KY. REV. STAT. ANN. § 275.170(2).

[80] *See* RESTATEMENT (THIRD) OF AGENCY § 8.08 (2006); 201 KY. ADMIN. REGS. 11:121(1)(4)(e) (2010).

[81] *See* UNIF. CONDO. ACT § 3-103(a), 7 (pt.II) U.L.A. 503 (2009).

[82] *See, e.g.*, ULPA (2001) § 305(a), 6A U.L.A. 424 (2008) (limited partner as such does not owe fiduciary obligations); KY. REV. STAT. ANN. § 275.170(4) (member in LLC that has elected to be manager-managed does not as a member owe fiduciary obligations).

It is only from a careful determination of the applicable standard, whether set by private agreement or by statute, of the fiduciary obligations undertaken that the facts alleging a breach may be assessed.

THE NECESSITY OF CAREFUL DRAFTING

As previously indicated, the best practice is to, a priori, define what obligations, including the fiduciary obligations, continue to bind one who dissociates from what is otherwise an ongoing venture and as well the obligations of the venture's participants upon its final dissolution. Prior agreement, entered into at a time when the interests of the participants are not antagonistic as to expectations and limitations, will provide a degree of certainty that is not available when the parties must rely upon an often incomplete statutory background and inconsistent case law.

Initially, careful consideration of the purpose of the venture is crucial. A venture with the purpose of "engaging in any activity that may be validly undertaken by a partnership/limited partnership/LLC" provides no guidance as to the nature of the participant's intended activities and the scope of their obligations to one another. The purpose clause modifies and informs a number of issues including fiduciary duties and judicial dissolution. Assume a manager is offered the opportunity to participate in the development of the property at 234 Chestnut Street; the LLC's business to date has been to develop the property at 123 Main Street. If the purpose of the LLC is to engage in real estate development or any other lawful activity, the development of 234 Chestnut Street falls within its permitted purpose. If the manager does not disclose the opportunity to the LLC he may be charged with having diverted a company opportunity to his personal gain in breach of his fiduciary duties to the LLC. If, in contrast, the purpose of the LLC had been defined as the development of the property at 123 Main Street, the development of 234 Chestnut Street is outside the LLC's purpose, and there is no claim for the improper diversion of an opportunity and a breach of duty. Therefore, in the LLC's dissolution, there can be no claim that the exploitation of 234 Chestnut Street is a venture asset whose proceeds must be shared among all of the participants.[83]

Second, the operating provisions as to fiduciary obligations need to address both dissociation and dissolution and the impact thereon of the duties owed. These provisions require equally as much attention as the provisions addressing the fiduciary duties as originally owed. Initially they should create separate paths for separation from an ongoing venture as distinct from the venture's dissolution. In the former instance it is necessary to protect the venture's ongoing activities while affording the separating participant the opportunity to continue in business.

Upon separation from an ongoing venture there is a desire to capture for the firm's benefit the gain realized upon the exploitation of venture assets. Defining what are those assets is often difficult. While a participant's generalized business knowledge is something they may not be deprived of, they may be deprived of the ability to exploit trade secrets, business opportunities of which they became aware prior to separation, and other

---

[83] See also *Cass JV, LLC*, supra note 71; *Whalen v. Connelly*, 545 N.W.2d 284 (Iowa 1986).

confidential information such as client contacts. For these and similar reasons it may be appropriate to incorporate in the partnership/operating agreement confidentiality, non-competition and non-solicitation limitations that are binding subsequent to separation from the venture. A simple but easily overlooked requirement is to provide that these limitations will be and remain binding notwithstanding dissociation from the firm and termination of status as a party to the operating/partnership agreement. Another drafting point is to address whether the obligations are fixed as of the time of dissociation, thereafter being static as to now dissociated participant, or whether they remain dynamic. For example, if the obligation is to not solicit business from existing clients of the venture, is that universe of clients to be determined as of the date of dissociation or does it rather include clients of the venture who become so after dissociation? As another example, does an obligation to not solicit venture employees to abandon employment apply only to the employees in place as of dissociation or rather to all employees of the firm during the non-solicitation period?

The objective is to ascertain the obligations that bind a member and to assess how those obligations should be affected by each of (i) dissociation and (ii) dissolution, thereby appreciating that dissociation and dissolution may have different impacts upon a particular obligation. Again employing the non-solicitation obligation, while it may continue as to a dissociated member or partner for the duration of the venture, it could be lifted a reasonable period of time after dissolution.[84] Whether and how these obligations survive will be dependent upon the venture; the participants in a firm of software engineers and the participants in a legal or accounting firm have different needs and pressures that need to be accommodated.

The other side of the coin must be considered as well, namely obligations of the venture and its continuing participants to dissociated participants. Decisions such as *Newburger* caution against a view that those who remain at risk of the venture's continued vitality may not be owed fiduciary obligations.

CONCLUSION

Various of the existing statutory schemes are either silent as to or minimally address the continuing application of fiduciary obligations post-dissociation or post-dissolution. These periods are obviously a fertile time for disputes as to what duties are owed and whether they have been violated. Setting aside those circumstances in which ambiguity may be advantageous, it is crucial that the drafter address these issues in the partnership or operating agreement.

---

[84] Care should be taken in the drafting of eliminating or modifying fiduciary duties upon dissolution to exclude inadvertent administrative dissolution for failure to make ministerial filings with the Secretary of State or similar state or other regulatory bodies. *See, e.g.*, KY. REV. STAT. ANN. § 14A.7-010.

REFERENCES

CALLISON, J. WILLIAM & MAUREEN SULLIVAN, PARTNERSHIP LAW AND PRACTICE.
HART, CHRISTINE ET AL., BROMBERG AND RIBSTEIN ON PARTNERSHIP (2014).
Hart, Janet, *Termination of the Fiduciary Duty of Business Associates Not to Compete for the Firm's Customers and Supplies*, 4 DUKE BAR J. 16 (1954).
Hillman, Robert W., *Private Ordering Within Partnerships*, 41 U. MIAMI L. REV. 425, 458 (1987).
Miller, Geoffrey P., "*Meinhard v. Salmon*", *New York University Law and Economics Working Papers*. Paper 105 (2007); http://lsr.nellco.org/nyu_lewp/105.
PROTOTYPE LIMITED LIABILITY COMPANY ACT, reproduced in 3 LARRY E. RIBSTEIN AND ROBERT R. KEATINGE, RIBSTEIN AND KEATINGE ON LIMITED LIABILITY COMPANIES, App'x C (2nd ed. December 2014).
REVISED PROTOTYPE LIMITED LIABILITY COMPANY ACT ("RPLLCA"), 67 BUS. LAW. 117 (Nov. 2011).
REVISED UNIFORM LIMITED LIABILITY COMPANY ACT ("RULLCA"), 6B U.L.A. 407 (2008).
REVISED UNIFORM PARTNERSHIP ACT ("RUPA") (1997), 6B U.L.A. 1 (2001).
RIBSTEIN, LARRY E. AND ROBERT R. KEATINGE, RIBSTEIN AND KEATINGE ON LIMITED LIABILITY COMPANIES (2nd ed., December 2014).
Rutledge, Thomas E. and Thomas Earl Geu, *The Analytic Protocol for the Duty of Loyalty Under the Prototype LLC Act*, 63 ARK. L. REV. 473, 475–77 (2010).
SARGENT, MARK A. AND WALTER D. SCHWIDETZKY, LIMITED LIABILITY COMPANY HANDBOOK (2013–14 ed.).
UNIFORM LIMITED LIABILITY COMPANY ACT ("ULLCA"), 6B U.L.A. 545 (2008).
UNIFORM PARTNERSHIP ACT (1914) ("UPA"), 6 (pt. I) U.L.A. 275 (2001).

PART 6

SPECIALIZED ENTITIES

14. Nonprofit and charitable uses of LLCs
Cassady V. "Cass" Brewer

1. INTRODUCTION

The overwhelming first choice in new, for-profit business entity formations is the limited liability company ("LLC").[1] Less well known, however, is the increasing use of LLCs for nonprofit and charitable endeavors. Accordingly, this chapter explores in four sections the emerging use of LLCs for nonprofit and charitable purposes, including the use of LLCs in hybrid for-profit/nonprofit arrangements. Section 2 provides necessary background information on the nonprofit and charitable sector. Section 3 surveys the relatively common use of LLCs as nonprofit subsidiaries or affiliates. Section 4 examines how LLCs are used to facilitate certain charitable or quasi-charitable activities, including program-related investments and social enterprise. Section 5 concludes with some very recent, innovative uses of LLCs by donors to charities.

2. AN OVERVIEW OF THE NONPROFIT AND CHARITABLE SECTOR

Two Bodies of Law Govern

The nonprofit and charitable sector consists of an incredibly diverse group of organizations formed and operated primarily to serve purposes other than pure profit-making. The sector sometimes is referred to as the "voluntary sector" or "community sector." A recent Congressional Research Service report defined the nonprofit and charitable sector as follows: "The term 'nonprofit sector' is generally intended to include all organizations with federal tax-exempt status. The term 'charitable sector' is used to refer to one type of tax-exempt organization, specifically those organizations with 501(c)(3) public charity status."[2] This chapter essentially adopts the Congressional Research Service definition of the nonprofit and charitable sector, but it also elaborates.

In particular, although federal income tax law controls whether an organization is tax-exempt, state law governs the legal form that the organization may take. Organizations exempt from federal income taxation thus may choose from different legal forms: unincorporated associations, trusts, nonprofit corporations, and as this chapter explains, even LLCs. Therefore, to appreciate the existing and potential roles that LLCs have in

---

[1] See JOINT COMMITTEE ON TAXATION, SELECTED ISSUES RELATING TO CHOICE OF BUSINESS ENTITY at 8–9 (Aug. 1, 2012).
[2] Molly F. Sherlock & Jane G. Gravelle, "An Overview of the Nonprofit and Charitable Sector," Congressional Research Service Report #40919 at 2 (Nov. 17, 2009).

the nonprofit and charitable sector, one must understand the codependent relationship between federal and state law governing the sector.

Federal Income Tax Law

The Internal Revenue Code ("IRC") lists the various types of organizations that normally are exempt from federal income taxation: instrumentalities of government; title-holding corporations; charities; unions; trade associations; social clubs; fraternities and sororities; and a number of other, specified organizations.[3] Within this diverse list, however, certain types of so-called "charitable" organizations receive extraordinarily favorable treatment under the IRC and have come to dominate the nonprofit sector. Specifically, entities that are organized and operated exclusively for religious, charitable, scientific, educational, or other eleemosynary purposes specified in IRC §§ 170(c)(2) and 501(c)(3) not only are exempt from federal income tax, but contributors to such organizations generally are permitted a special tax deduction.[4] These favored, tax-exempt organizations are often referred to as "(c)(3)s" or sometimes as "charities."

Within the dominate category of (c)(3) organizations, the IRC further divides charities into two subcategories: private foundations and organizations that are not private foundations, commonly known as "public charities." Generally, public charities consist of churches, nonprofit hospitals, private schools and universities, and organizations that ordinarily depend upon broad-based contributions and grants for their financial support. Charitable private foundations, on the other hand, typically depend upon a founding individual or family for their financial support and usually remain controlled by the founder and his or her family.[5]

Furthermore, within the subcategory of private foundations, most are classified as "nonoperating foundations," meaning that they do not conduct charitable activities directly, but that they provide financial support in the form of contributions and grants to public charities and other charitable causes. A prominent example of a nonoperating (or as it is sometimes called, "grantmaking") private foundation is the Bill & Melinda Gates Foundation. Distinct from grantmaking foundations, *operating* foundations directly conduct charitable activities rather than simply make grants; yet, they remain controlled and financially supported by relatively few individuals. For example, the J. Paul Getty Trust, which owns and operates the J. Paul Getty Museum, is classified as a private operating foundation.

In general, public charities and private operating foundations are subject to much less IRS regulation and scrutiny (because they presumably are accountable to the public), while nonoperating private foundations are subject to substantial constraints and IRS oversight.

Finally, although the IRC exempts many types of nonprofit and charitable organizations from federal income taxes, these organizations are not immune from all taxation. Nonprofit and charitable organizations pay employment taxes in the same manner as

---

[3] *See* I.R.C. § 501(c)(1)–(29).
[4] *See* I.R.C. § 170(c)(2).
[5] *See* SHERLOCK & GRAVELLE, at 2.

for-profit organizations.⁶ Nonprofit and charitable organizations (especially private foundations) are subject to a complex array of federal excise taxes designed to encourage or discourage certain behavior.⁷ Further, nonprofit or charitable organizations regularly engaged in trades or businesses that are substantially unrelated to their eleemosynary purpose, or in certain debt-financed activities, can be subject to the unrelated business income tax ("UBIT").⁸ Lastly, as discussed below, certain state and local taxes can apply to nonprofit and charitable organizations.

State Law and the Prevalence of Nonprofit Corporations

As noted above, the state law entities that traditionally are used to qualify for tax-exempt status consist of unincorporated associations, charitable trusts, and nonprofit corporations. Unincorporated associations generally are used only by very small, informal organizations. Charitable trusts, even though they are the oldest form, tend to be limited to fairly narrow exempt purposes. For instance, trusts are sometimes used to hold title to property used for charitable purposes or to serve as the legal form for pure grantmaking foundations. More often than not the chosen form is the nonprofit corporation.⁹ Nonprofit corporations typically are chosen because they offer limited liability; a well-understood governance structure; flexibility in operation; adaptability to unforeseen circumstances; better protections and indemnification for fiduciaries; and perpetual existence.

In general, nonprofit corporations come in two varieties: public benefit and mutual benefit. Public benefit corporations are designed to serve public and charitable purposes. Public benefit corporations may or may not have "members" who control the organization. Public benefit corporations *without* members ordinarily are governed by a self-perpetuating board of directors. Public benefit corporations *with* members also are governed by a board of directors, but the members vote on the board of directors and on certain other matters involving the corporation similar to shareholders in a for-profit corporation. Unlike shareholders of a for-profit corporation, however, members of a public benefit corporation have no economic rights to the assets of the corporation upon dissolution. Thus, regardless of whether it has members, the assets of a public benefit corporation are held strictly for public or charitable purposes.

Mutual benefit corporations, on the other hand, generally serve the needs of a specified set of individuals or entities. Individuals or entities served by a mutual benefit corporation typically are designated as "members" of the corporation. Unlike members of a public benefit corporation, members of a mutual benefit corporation may have an economic interest in the corporation in addition to voting rights. Nevertheless, the members' economic rights are limited. Members do not participate in a mutual benefit corporation's earnings while it is operating, but the members may receive distributions when the corporation dissolves.

---

⁶ *See* I.R.C. § 3121. *But see* I.R.C. § 3127 (granting a narrow exception for members of certain religious faiths).
⁷ *See* I.R.C. §§ 4911–4948.
⁸ *See* I.R.C. §§ 511–514.
⁹ For purposes of this chapter references to "nonprofit corporations" includes non-stock corporations. *See, e.g.*, Del. Code Ann. tit. 8, § 114.

In general, regardless of whether it is a public benefit corporation or a mutual benefit corporation, the Attorney General of the state of incorporation is responsible for monitoring nonprofit corporations and taking action if necessary to protect the state's interest with respect to the corporation.

Merely organizing and operating as a nonprofit corporation, though, does not automatically entitle an organization to federal tax-exempt status or to receive tax-deductible charitable contributions. Rather, to qualify as tax-exempt under federal law, a nonprofit corporation must satisfy the particular requirements of one of the listed types of exempt organizations set forth in the IRC. Moreover, to qualify as both exempt and eligible to receive tax-deductible charitable contributions (i.e., a (c)(3) organization), a nonprofit corporation ordinarily must apply to the IRS for recognition of its charitable status.[10] And, to be so recognized by the IRS, the nonprofit corporation must include in its governing documents certain restrictive language, especially language that satisfies the so-called "nondistribution constraint." In essence, the "nondistribution constraint" imposes limitations on the disposition of the corporation's assets so that its property and earnings forever will benefit the charitable sector.[11]

Assuming that a nonprofit corporation is granted (c)(3) status, the IRS provides the organization with a determination letter confirming its exemption. Thereafter, the organization typically provides copies of its (c)(3) determination letter to state authorities, contributors, and other interested parties in order to prove its exempt status.

Primarily because they cater to a public or charitable purpose and sometimes have a built-in "nondistribution constraint," most nonprofit corporations that seek to qualify as (c)(3)s are organized as public benefit corporations without members.[12] Some (c)(3) organizations, though, are formed as public benefit corporations with members in order to vest ultimate control in persons other than a self-perpetuating board of directors. In the author's experience, for instance, churches occasionally are organized as public benefit corporations with members. Moreover, public benefit corporations with members can be used to serve as controlled "subsidiaries" of other (c)(3)s. The parent charity is the sole member of the public benefit corporation and thereby in control, but the "subsidiary" corporation applies for and obtains tax-exempt status as a (c)(3) independent of the parent charity. Affiliated health care systems, for example, often use structures whereby a parent charity serves as the controlling member of a number of distinct public benefit corporations that operate separate hospitals. Mutual benefit corporations are not used for (c)(3) status—because they serve members, not the public—but they are used for trade associations, homeowners' associations, and

---

[10] *See* I.R.C. § 508. Churches and charities with $5,000 or less in gross receipts, however, are not required to apply. Organizations covered by a group exemption letter ruling also do not have to apply. *See* Reg. 1.508-1(a)(3). If an organization is not seeking (c)(3) status, then it is not *required* to apply to the IRS for recognition of its exemption, but many non-(c)(3) organizations nevertheless do apply using IRS Form 1024 to secure an IRS determination letter.

[11] The IRS has ruled that nonprofit corporation statutes in a few states per se meet the requirements of the nondistribution constraint. Rev. Proc. 82-2, 1982-1 C.B. 367.

[12] To clarify, for public relations purposes many nonprofit organizations call their donors and patrons "members" even though those individuals have no legal right to participate in the governance of the organization.

similar exempt organizations that are intended to serve a specified group of individuals or entities.

3. CHARITABLE SUBSIDIARY AND AFFILIATED LLCs

LLCs increasingly are being used in the nonprofit and charitable sector as wholly owned subsidiaries or as partially owned affiliates for many of the same reasons LLCs are popular among for-profit businesses:

- Freedom of contract: Many LLC statutes embrace the principle of freedom of contract and grant broad latitude to an LLC's members in determining their respective economic, voting, transferability, and other legal rights concerning the LLC. Corporate statutes, on the other hand, tend to be more rigid with respect to the legal rights of shareholders.
- No limitations on members: There are no limitations as to who may be members of an LLC. Thus, an LLC can bring together on a flow-through tax basis an assortment of different types of parties, such as private foundations, for-profit entities, public charities, individuals, and government.
- Liability protection: Despite their contract-like nature, LLCs nevertheless offer absolute liability protection like a corporation.
- Malleable tax treatment: LLCs are the shape-shifters of the federal income tax system. By default, wholly owned, single-member LLCs are disregarded for federal income tax purposes, but they may elect corporate tax treatment if desired. Multiple-member LLCs default to partnership tax status (as long as the entity is intended to share profits among co-owners), but multi-member LLCs also may elect corporate tax treatment if desired.[13]
- Any lawful purpose: Under the laws of most states, LLCs are like nonprofit corporations in that they may have "any lawful purpose," including a charitable purpose. Going even further, four states expressly allow the formation of nonprofit LLCs.[14]

Disregarded Single-Member Limited Liability Companies

The use of wholly owned, single-member LLCs ("SMLLCs") as subsidiaries of nonprofit and charitable organizations is well accepted and IRS approved.[15] To wit, the IRS announced in 1999 that the activities of 100 percent-owned disregarded federal income tax entities (such as SMLLCs) must be reported by charities on their annual IRS Form

---

[13] *See* Reg. § 301.7701-3.
[14] The four states are Kentucky, Minnesota, North Dakota, and Tennessee. *See* KY. REV. STAT. ANN. § 275.520-540 (2014); MINN. STAT. § 322B.975 (2014); N.D. CENT. CODE § 10-36-01 TO -09 (2014); TENN. CODE ANN. § 48-101-809 (2014).
[15] The IRS has a website devoted to "Limited Liability Companies Associated with Tax-Exempt Organizations." *See* http://www.irs.gov/Charities-&-Non-Profits/Limited-Liability-Companies-Associated-with-Tax-Exempt-Organizations (last visited Aug. 15, 2014).

990 information return.[16] Moreover, SMLLC disregarded subsidiaries of charities are not required to include any "nondistribution constraint" or similar charitable purpose language in their governing documents, presumably because the assets may benefit only the charitable parent.[17] Additionally, the IRS ruled in 2012 that disregarded SMLLCs of (c)(3)s are eligible to receive tax-deductible contributions as if the contributions had been made directly to the parent charity itself.[18]

Even prior to 2012, the IRS had ruled privately on the use of disregarded SMLLCs by charitable organizations in several circumstances:

- Liability protection and segregating operations: A (c)(3) educational organization formed a disregarded SMLLC to provide fee-based investment administration services to school districts and local governments within the state,[19] while another used a number of distinct SMLLCs to meet unique regional needs within the state it served.[20]
- Developing adjacent land as rental property: A (c)(3) continuing care retirement community used a disregarded SMLLC to develop a specialized medical office building on adjacent land. The building eventually would be leased to a regional hospital that would sublease some of the space to physicians.[21]
- Similar: A private foundation planned to own and manage its real estate investment portfolio through one or more disregarded SMLLCs,[22] and an exempt community development organization envisioned using SMLLCs to provide student housing.[23]
- Accepting private foundation grants: A private foundation grant to a disregarded SMLLC of a public charity was treated for tax purposes as a "qualifying distribution" to the charity itself.[24]

The growing use of disregarded SMLLCs in the nonprofit and charitable sector is not merely an outgrowth of the general popularity of LLCs. Rather, there are at least three situations where a disregarded SMLLC has distinct advantages over other types of subsidiaries historically used in the nonprofit and charitable sector.

First, prior to the existence of disregarded SMLLCs, charitable organizations or their donors primarily used supporting organizations or title-holding corporations to function as exempt subsidiaries.[25] Generally speaking, such exempt subsidiaries are used for

---

[16] Announcement 99-102, 1999-43 I.R.B. 545.
[17] See IRS website, *supra* note 15.
[18] Notice 2012-52, 2012-35 I.R.B. 317.
[19] Priv. Ltr. Rul. 200606047 (Feb. 10, 2006).
[20] Priv. Ltr. Rul. 200551023 (Dec. 23, 2005).
[21] Priv. Ltr. Rul. 200538027 (Sept. 23, 2005).
[22] Priv. Ltr. Rul. 200637041 (Sept. 15, 2006).
[23] Priv. Ltr. Rul. 200304036 (Jan. 24, 2003).
[24] Info. Ltr. 2010-0052 (June 25, 2010). Nonoperating private foundations generally are required to make annual "qualifying distributions" of at least 5% of the value of the foundation's investment assets. *See* I.R.C. § 4942.
[25] To clarify, the reference here to "exempt subsidiaries" is meant to distinguish supporting organizations and title-holding corporations from regular corporate subsidiaries. If a nonprofit

the same reasons as for-profit subsidiaries: to segregate assets or activities and to provide liability protection for the parent entity. By virtue of their dedication to one or more public charities, supporting organizations avoid private foundation status even if the organization is controlled by relatively few individuals; however, supporting organizations must apply to the IRS for recognition of their exempt status and are highly regulated.[26] Title-holding corporations are, as the name suggests, exempt organizations formed for the purpose of holding title to real property.[27] Although not required to separately apply for exempt status, title-holding corporations are subject to strict limitations on their activities. With the advent of disregarded SMLLCs, nonprofit and charitable organizations may accomplish the dual objectives of segregating assets or activities and providing liability protection without the constraints imposed upon supporting organizations and title-holding corporations. Moreover, as noted above, contributions to such disregarded SMLLCs are tax-deductible.

Second, nonprofit and charitable organizations that regularly engage in trade or business activity substantially unrelated to their eleemosynary activities can be subject to the federal unrelated business income tax ("UBIT"). For instance, if a (c)(3) routinely allows third parties to use its facilities for weddings, receptions, and other private events, and if services (e.g., food and beverage, entertainment, security, etc.) are provided in connection therewith, the fees paid to the charity for hosting such events give rise to UBIT.[28] If unrelated business income becomes predominant, then a (c)(3) theoretically can lose its exempt status because it no longer operates primarily for exempt purposes.[29] Using a disregarded SMLLC to conduct such UBIT-generating activities has at least three advantages over other types of exempt subsidiaries:

- If such UBIT-generating activity is conducted through an exempt subsidiary, and if the exempt subsidiary has no other activities, then it will lose its exempt status. The activities of the parent charity apparently are not attributed to the exempt subsidiary for purposes of meeting the operated "primarily" test for (c)(3) status.[30] The activities of the exempt parent are attributed, however, to the activities of a disregarded SMLLC.[31]
- If the UBIT activities produce net losses instead of net income, then as long as the SMLLC is disregarded for income tax purposes those UBIT losses can be used by

---

or charitable organization uses a for-profit corporation as a subsidiary, such a subsidiary is fully taxable and not eligible for tax-deductible contributions.

[26] *See* I.R.C. §§ 508; 509.

[27] See I.R.C. §§ 501(c)(2) and (c)(25).

[28] Reg. § 1.512(b)-1(c)(5). *See also* Rev. Rul. 80-297, 1980-2 C.B. 196 (summer tennis camp paying private school for use of tennis facilities); Tech. Adv. Mem. 9702003 (Jan. 10, 1997) (exempt art gallery providing space for corporate and other special events).

[29] *See Associated Master Barbers and Beauticians v. Commissioner*, 69 T.C. 53 (1977) (30%); *Orange County Agricultural Society, Inc. v. Commissioner*, 893 F.2d 529 (2nd Cir. 1990) (30%); *Bethel Conservative Mennonite Church v. Commissioner*, 746 F.2d 388 (7th Cir. 1984) (22%).

[30] *See, e.g., Redlands Surgical Services v. Commissioner*, 113 T.C. 47 (1999) aff'd by 242 F.3d 904 (9th Cir. 2001) (affiliate with no other assets or activities was denied exempt status for entering into a joint venture with physicians even after arguing that the exempt hospital group's activities should be attributed to the affiliate).

[31] Announcement 99-102, 1999-43 I.R.B. 545.

the parent charity to offset unrelated business income from other sources.[32] The losses would not be available to the parent charity if the unrelated business activity is conducted through an exempt subsidiary such as a supporting organization or title-holding corporation.
- If the UBIT-generating activities of a disregarded SMLLC subsidiary become so substantial that they threaten the parent charity's exempt status, then there is a simple solution. The parent charity can elect under the check-the-box regulations to treat the SMLLC as a corporation for tax purposes, thereby "blocking" the subsidiary's activities and income from adversely affecting the parent charity's exemption.[33] Of course, once such an election is made, the taxable SMLLC will be treated as a taxable subsidiary for income tax purposes, and all of its income will be subject to federal income tax. In addition, payments to the parent charity that are deductible by the taxable subsidiary (e.g., interest, rent, royalties, etc.) will constitute unrelated business income to the parent even if such payments might otherwise qualify for an exception from UBIT.[34]

Third, due to ease of formation and automatic treatment as an exempt subsidiary, a disregarded SMLLC can be the perfect vehicle for a (c)(3) to receive a charitable contribution of an asset subject to contingent liabilities.[35] Alternatively, a disregarded SMLLC can be set up quickly by a (c)(3) to acquire sensitive or risky charitable assets.[36] Another example: A (c)(3) interested in sponsoring a summer camp to be conducted by a group of teachers might form a disregarded SMLLC to receive the required funds and to enter into the necessary contracts. Disregarded SMLLCs also may be used by charities in certain circumstances to solicit donations or conduct activities overseas.

Despite the advantages associated with the use of disregarded SMLLCs by nonprofit and charitable organizations, some caveats are in order. For instance, SMLLCs are not disregarded for employment tax purposes.[37] Therefore, if a nonprofit or charitable organization's disregarded SMLLC has employees, it ordinarily will be subject to employment tax filings and payments distinct from the parent organization.[38] Although most states follow the default federal income tax classification of SMLLCs as disregarded entities,

---

[32] *See* I.R.C. § 512(b)(6).

[33] *See, e.g.*, Priv. Ltr. Rul. 200602039 (Jan. 13, 2006) (where an exempt hospital formed a taxable subsidiary to license intellectual property to third parties without jeopardizing the hospital's exemption).

[34] *See* I.R.C. § 512(b)(13).

[35] *See, e.g.*, Priv. Ltr. Rul. 200150027 (Dec. 14, 2001) (disregarded SMLLC established by (c)(3) to receive contribution of real property subject to potential environmental liabilities).

[36] *See, e.g.*, Shalia Dewan, *The Deal That Let Atlanta Retain Dr. King's Papers*, New York Times (June 27, 2006) *available at* http://www.nytimes.com/2006/06/27/us/27king.html?_r=0 (last visited Sept. 1, 2014) and 2007 Consolidated Financial Statements, The Community Foundation for Greater Atlanta, Inc. at 13 (footnote 9) *available at* http://cfgreateratlanta.org/Repository/Files/2007AFS1.pdf (last visited Sept. 1, 2014).

[37] Reg. § 301.7701-2(c)(2)(iv)-(v) *rev'g* Notice 99-6, 1999-1 C.B. 321.

[38] *See* Reg. §§ 31.3121(b)(3)-1T; 31.3127-1T; 31.3306(c)(5)-1T; 301.7701-2T (generally treating SMLLC as separate entity for employment tax purposes but also permitting SMLLC to be disregarded for certain religious exceptions).

not all states do so. Moreover, non-income based state taxes—such as franchise, sales, use, and property taxes—can apply to nonprofit and charitable SMLLCs unless a specific exception applies.

Another potential disadvantage of SMLLCs relates to so-called "veil piercing" arguments made by claimants against parent organizations. Because for federal income tax purposes a disregarded SMLLC is treated as mere division and thereby included in a parent nonprofit or charitable organization's tax return, there is a tendency in practice to ignore the separate legal existence of the LLC. Repeated failure to respect the separate legal existence of a SMLLC opens the door to claims that the liability shield should be ignored as well.[39] In general, though, if the disregarded SMLLC is regularly treated by the parent nonprofit or charitable organization as a separate legal entity and transactions between the parent and the SMLLC are conducted on arm's length, fair-market-value terms, the liability shield will be upheld. In a similar vein, it currently is unclear whether federal or state laws protecting volunteers to nonprofit organizations from personal liability apply equally to volunteers to disregarded SMLLCs of nonprofit organizations.

Lastly, in a decision with potentially far-reaching implications, the Tax Court recently determined in *RERI Holdings I, LLC* that a disregarded SMLLC interest should *not* be ignored for purposes of determining whether a taxpayer is entitled to a charitable contribution deduction.[40] The taxpayer in *RERI Holdings I, LLC* contributed an interest in a disregarded SMLLC holding real property to the University of Michigan. The taxpayer claimed a charitable deduction of approximately $33 million in connection with the donation of the SMLLC interest. As required for tax purposes, the taxpayer obtained an appraisal substantiating the amount of its claimed deduction; however, the taxpayer's appraisal was of the underlying real property held by the disregarded SMLLC, not the membership interest in the SMLLC itself. Because the interest in the SMLLC, not the underlying real property, was donated to the University of Michigan, the IRS argued in a motion for summary judgment that the taxpayer's charitable deduction should be disallowed. In particular, the IRS argued that the deduction must be disallowed because the appraisal was of the wrong property and therefore failed the "qualified appraisal" requirements for charitable contributions of property.[41]

Without much fanfare, Judge Halpern accepted the argument of the IRS that a charitable contribution of an interest in a disregarded SMLLC should be viewed differently than a charitable contribution of the underlying asset. Judge Halpern so held notwithstanding the fact that the SMLLC otherwise is ignored for federal income tax purposes.[42] Judge Halpern's opinion relies heavily on the Tax Court's earlier decision in *Pierre*[43] that, for *gift tax valuation purposes*, a taxpayer's gifts of membership interests in the taxpayer's SMLLC are distinct from gifts of partial interests in the underlying property. *Pierre* arguably is distinguishable, though, from *RERI Holdings I, LLC*, because (i) *Pierre* is

---

[39] See, e.g., *Soroof Trading Development Co., Ltd. v. GE Fuel Cell Systems, LLC*, 842 F. Supp. 2d 502, 522 (S.D.N.Y. 2012) (all activities of SMLLC were conducted by employees of sole member).
[40] *RERI Holdings I, LLC v. Commissioner*, 143 T.C. No. 3 (2014).
[41] *Id.* at 7.
[42] *Id.* at 8.
[43] *Pierre v. Comm'r*, 133 T.C. 24 (2009), *supplemented by* 99 T.C.M. (CCH) 1436 (2010).

a gift (not income) tax case and (ii) the gifts in *Pierre* transformed the SMLLC into a multi-member LLC held by four trusts. This latter point of distinction, though, may not be significant as it appears the trusts were grantor trusts such that the taxpayer in *Pierre* remained the income tax owner of the SMLLC.

Despite the fact, however, that Judge Halpern agreed with the IRS's view that an interest in a disregarded SMLLC should be respected for charitable contribution deduction purposes, all was not lost for the taxpayer in *RERI Holdings I, LLC*. Rather, perhaps to avoid so easily granting summary judgment against the taxpayer and in favor of the IRS, Judge Halpern reasoned that there was an unresolved issue of material fact whether a valuation of the property held by the SMLLC rather than a valuation of the SMLLC interest itself nevertheless could "stand proxy"[44] for the otherwise required qualified appraisal. The ultimate outcome of the case, therefore, remains to be seen.

Given the uncertainty created by the Tax Court's decisions in *RERI Holdings I, LLC* and *Pierre* regarding the tax *valuation* treatment of membership interests in disregarded SMLLCs, donors to charitable organizations should transfer the underlying property itself to charity rather than transferring an interest in an SMLLC holding the property. If the property must be wrapped inside a disregarded LLC for liability protection or other reasons, then the donee charity should form the disregarded SMLLC to receive the contribution rather than receiving an interest in the property-holding SMLLC formed by the donor. Otherwise, due to the quirky way in which SMLLC membership interests apparently are valued for federal tax purposes, the donor inadvertently may be reducing the amount of his or her expected charitable contribution deduction. On the other hand, for estate and gift tax purposes, a donor presumably would rather transfer a membership interest in a disregarded SMLLC to a non-charitable donee in order to minimize the value of the transfer and thereby reduce potential estate and gift taxes.

Regarded But Nonetheless Tax-Exempt LLCs

The foregoing section focuses upon the use of *disregarded* SMLLCs as subsidiaries and affiliates of tax-exempt nonprofit and charitable organizations. This section briefly examines the evolving use of a *regarded* LLC as a substitute for the most popular legal form of exempt organization, the nonprofit corporation.

Since at least 2001 the IRS has recognized that an LLC may qualify as a (c)(3) organization.[45] In order to so qualify, however, an LLC must apply for (c)(3) status just as most nonprofit corporations must apply.[46] Further, claiming to be tax-exempt (including for this purpose submission of an application for (c)(3) status) constitutes an election by the LLC to be classified as a corporation for federal income tax purposes.[47] Most importantly, to be successful in securing (c)(3) status, it is the IRS's position that the LLC must

---

[44] See *RERI Holdings I, LLC v. Commissioner, supra* note 40, at 10.
[45] See Richard A. McCray and Ward L. Thomas, I.R.S., US Dep't of Treasury, *Limited Liability Companies as Exempt Organizations—Update* 29-32 (2001) *available at* http://www.irs.gov/pub/irs-tege/eotopicb01.pdf (last visited Sept. 3, 2014).
[46] See I.R.C. § 508; text accompanying *supra* notes 31–34.
[47] Reg. § 301.7701-3(c)(1)(v)(A).

meet 12 specific requirements set forth in prior IRS continuing professional education materials.[48]

The IRS continuing professional education materials reflect the IRS's position that an LLC cannot function as a (c)(3) organization unless all of its members are (c)(3) organizations, governmental units, or instrumentalities thereof; however, this is only the IRS's position. It is not settled law. A public benefit corporation may have non-exempt, non-governmental members and nevertheless qualify as a (c)(3) organization provided the "nondistribution constraint" is met and other necessary provisions are set forth in the organization's governing documents. The IRS's guidance regarding exempt LLCs does not explain why it believes the (c)(3) standards for an LLC should be any more stringent than for a public benefit corporation. If the IRS's position is litigated, it is conceivable that a properly organized and operated LLC could qualify as a (c)(3) organization even if it has non-exempt, non-governmental members. This especially should be the case if the LLC is formed in one of the four states that statutorily authorize nonprofit LLCs.[49] Those four states impose the "nondistribution constraint" (as well as other requirements) on nonprofit LLCs similar to the restrictions imposed upon public benefit corporations. It is unlikely, though, that a taxpayer would be willing to challenge the IRS's position when a duly formed public benefit corporation can easily obtain IRS approval for (c)(3) status.[50]

Even if a court were to agree with the IRS's position that an LLC seeking exempt status as a (c)(3) organization must have (c)(3) or governmental members only, that would leave open the issue of whether an LLC could qualify for some other tax-exempt status such as a trade association, social club, fraternity or sorority, or homeowners' association.[51] These types of exempt organizations are not eligible to receive deductible charitable contributions and typically take the legal form of a mutual benefit corporation, but they nevertheless can be tax-exempt if they meet certain strict requirements. Theoretically, it should be possible for an LLC to qualify as an exempt trade association, social club, fraternity or sorority, or homeowners' association since these exempt organizations are meant to provide limited benefits to individual and business members. As far as the author is aware, however, this theory has not been tested and may never be as long as a duly formed nonprofit corporation is a viable alternative.[52]

---

[48] I.R.S., U.S. Dep't of Treasury, *Limited Liability Company Reference Guide Sheet* (2011) *available at* http://www.irs.gov/pub/irs-tege/llc_guide_sheet.pdf (last visited Sept. 3, 2014).

[49] *See* KY. REV. STAT. ANN. § 275.520–540 (2014); MINN. STAT. § 322B.975 (2014); N.D. CENT. CODE § 10-36-01 TO -09 (2014); TENN. CODE ANN. § 48-101-809 (2014).

[50] On August 15, 2014, the author emailed 673 subscribers to an ABA listserv for nonprofit organizations—tax-nonprofit@mail.americanbar.org—asking whether anyone on the listserv had ever encountered a (c)(3) LLC with non-(c)(3) members. No one responded affirmatively.

[51] *See* I.R.C. § 501(c)(6)-(8); 528.

[52] On August 29, 2014, the author emailed the same ABA listserv subscribers as described in footnote 50 asking whether anyone had ever encountered an LLC that was tax-exempt as a member-based organization like a trade association, social club, fraternity or sorority, or homeowners' association. No one responded affirmatively. One respondent indicated that, after initially applying for (c)(4) [social welfare organization] status as an LLC with a (c)(4) and (c)(6) [trade association] members and getting IRS resistance, the client changed course and used a nonprofit corporation instead with IRS approval.

Nonprofit/For-Profit Joint Ventures and Ancillary Joint Ventures

LLCs also are used for joint ventures and so-called ancillary joint ventures between nonprofit organizations and for-profit organizations or investors. Joint ventures and ancillary joint ventures essentially are formal, legal arrangements where a nonprofit participates in a business partnership with individuals or for-profit enterprises. With respect to joint ventures and ancillary joint ventures between (c)(3) organizations and for-profit enterprises (whether taking the legal form of an LLC or another entity), the courts and the IRS have developed a complex set of guidelines that charities must follow. Otherwise, charities participating in joint ventures risk losing their exempt status. A thorough discussion of the IRS's joint venture guidelines is beyond the scope of this chapter; however, a summary is set forth below.

If a "substantial"[53] part of a public charity's[54] activities and assets are held as a member of an LLC with for-profit members, then the LLC must further the (c)(3) member's exempt purpose *and* the (c)(3) member must retain management control over the LLC.[55] Otherwise, the (c)(3) member jeopardizes its tax-exempt status. In fact, for "substantial" activities and assets held through an LLC, the (c)(3) member must possess control even if the assets it contributes to the LLC are proportionately less than assets contributed by for-profit members.[56] Moreover, since the activities of the LLC must further a charitable purpose, income produced by the LLC does not generate UBIT for the (c)(3) member.[57]

On the other hand, if an "insubstantial" part of a public charity's activities and assets are held as a member of an LLC, then the (c)(3) member generally can maintain its tax-exempt status without retaining control over the LLC;[58] however, a secondary analysis then applies. If the "insubstantial" activity conducted through the LLC is substantially related to the (c)(3) member's exempt purpose, then the income generated by the LLC typically will not give rise to UBIT.[59] If the "insubstantial" activity conducted through the LLC is unrelated to the (c)(3) member's exempt purpose, then the income may give rise to UBIT depending upon the nature of the income and the application of numerous other technical rules.[60]

---

[53] See Rev. Rul. 2004-51, 2004-1 C.B. 975, 975–76 (attributing "insubstantial" activities of an ancillary LLC joint venture to an exempt member); Rev. Rul. 98-15, 1998-1 C.B. 718, 719–20 (attributing "substantial" activities of a whole hospital LLC joint venture to an exempt a member).

[54] Exempt private foundations are subject to separate rules—the excess business holdings rules—that severely limit a private foundation's ability to invest in an arrangement that even remotely resembles a "joint venture" or "ancillary joint venture." See I.R.C. § 4943. With respect to non-(c)(3) exempt organizations, there is very little authority about applying the joint venture and ancillary joint venture rules, but it appears the IRS's approach to the analysis is the same. See Priv. Ltr. Rul. 200528029 (July 15, 2005) (62.5% interest in an LLC held by for-profit corporation while 37.5% interest held by IRC § 501(c)(6) trade association did not adversely affect trade association's tax-exempt status).

[55] See Rev. Rul. 98-15, *supra* note 53.
[56] Id. at 721.
[57] See Treas. Reg. § 1.501(c)(3)-1(b)(1)(iii).
[58] See Rev. Rul. 2004-51, *supra* note 53.
[59] See Treas. Reg. § 1.501(c)(3)-1(b)(1)(iii).
[60] Id. § 1.501(c)(3)-1(e).

Furthermore, even in connection with an "insubstantial" activity conducted through an LLC, if the value of the assets contributed to the LLC by the (c)(3) member is proportionately greater than the value of the assets contributed by for-profit members, the (c)(3) member would be well advised to maintain control over the LLC. If the (c)(3) member contributes proportionately greater value than for-profit members but does not retain control of the LLC, the IRS may challenge the arrangement as constituting impermissible private benefit even if the LLC's activity is "insubstantial" with respect to the (c)(3) member.[61]

The key to the joint venture/ancillary joint venture analysis, therefore, is determining whether a public charity's membership interest in an LLC is considered a "substantial" or "insubstantial" part of its activities and assets. Frustratingly, however, there is no clear guidance in this regard. If the question is litigated, the "substantial" versus "insubstantial" dividing line apparently is open to interpretation and hindsight by the IRS and the courts.[62] Thus, the uncertainty both as to whether a (c)(3) member of an LLC must have control and whether its activities and assets held through an LLC are "substantial" or "insubstantial" makes tax-exempt joint ventures and ancillary joint ventures extremely delicate undertakings.

Finally, as if it were necessary to complicate matters further, it is well established that, as part of its regular endowment, an exempt nonprofit or charitable organization may hold passive investments in an LLC similar to passively holding corporate stock. Such passive investments, certainly if they are only a small fraction of a (c)(3) organization's assets, apparently are not considered by the IRS to be subject to the joint venture or ancillary joint venture rules. Presumably such passive investment in an LLC is not a "joint venture" in the eyes of the IRS even though the LLC generally would be treated as a partnership for tax purposes.[63] Put differently, as far as the author is aware, there is no clear rule as to when an ostensibly "passive" investment in an LLC either is so large or borders so closely on being "active" that the joint venture rules are implicated.

Further IRS guidance concerning the application of the joint venture and ancillary joint venture rules would be welcome, but given that the IRS's last significant public

---

[61] See *St. David's Health Care Sys. v. United States*, 349 F.3d 232, 239 (5th Cir. 2003) ("[W hen a non-profit organization forms a partnership with a for-profit entity, the non-profit should lose its tax-exempt status if it cedes control to the for-profit entity."); *Redlands Surgical Servs. v. Comm'r*, 113 T.C. 47, 92–93 (1999) (holding a non-profit organization under I.R.C. § 501(c)(3) did not operate "exclusively for exempt purposes . . . by ceding effective control over its operations to for-profit parties" because it "impermissibly serve[d] private interests").

[62] Practitioners sometimes advise that "insubstantial" means 15% or less of an exempt organization's activities, but this is by no means a bright-line test binding on taxpayers, the IRS, or the courts. See *Best Lock Corporation v. Commissioner*, 31 TC 1217 (1959) (holding that a loan comprising 15% of a charitable foundation's expenditures was a "substantial" non-exempt activity).

[63] Specifically, the IRS's instructions provide that joint venture disclosure and reporting is not required if the arrangement meets two conditions: (1) 95% or more of the venture's or arrangement's income is passive income (e.g., rents, dividends, etc.) as described in § 512(b)(1)-(5); *and* (2) the "primary purpose of the organization's contribution to, or investment or participation in, the venture or arrangement is the production of income or appreciation of property." IRS Instructions (2013) to Form 990 at page 24.

pronouncement in this area was in 2004,[64] such guidance may not be forthcoming anytime soon.

4. STRICTLY FOR-PROFIT BUT NEVERTHELESS CHARITABLY USED LLCs

Outside of the joint venture and ancillary joint venture realm, for-profit LLCs also are used in collaboration with nonprofit and charitable organizations to further exempt purposes. These collaborative arrangements are slightly different from joint ventures and ancillary joint ventures. They are different because the participating nonprofit or charitable organization economically has a very finite role vis-à-vis the LLC engaged in the activity. The two primary examples of this type of collaboration via a for-profit LLC are (i) low-income housing and new-markets tax credit structures and (ii) program-related investments.

Low-Income Housing and New Markets Tax Credit LLCs

Both the low-income housing tax credit[65] and the new markets tax credit[66] are designed to spur investment in affordable housing and in community development. Affordable housing and community development have long been recognized as permissible purposes for (c)(3) organizations.[67] Because tax credits normally cannot be used by tax-exempt organizations, it seems commonsensical that charities should be able to partner—for instance, via an LLC—with for-profit businesses to further tax-exempt purposes and take advantage of federally sanctioned tax incentives. In this instance, however, common sense is misleading.

In particular, the ability of tax-exempt organizations to become members in affordable housing or community development LLCs alongside for-profit members has become a highly specialized area subject to extraordinarily technical and complex rules. It is beyond the scope of this chapter to delve into the nuances of such tax-credit LLCs. Moreover, numerous other commentators already have done so. The point of the brief discussion here is to highlight that, in most cases, charitable organizations participating in such tax-credit LLCs have insignificant membership interests: often 1 percent or less.[68] These (c)(3) organizations generally do have, though, an active role in managing the LLC and in most cases the (c)(3) organizations serve as managing-members of the LLC that owns the

---

[64] See Rev. Rul. 2004-51, *supra* note 53.
[65] I.R.C. § 42.
[66] I.R.C. § 45D. The new markets tax credit expired at the end of 2014. See I.R.C. § 45D(f)(1)(G). If, however, past history is any indication, Congress likely will extend the credit with retroactive effect at the end of 2015.
[67] See Rev. Rul. 70-585, 1970-2 C.B. 115 (affordable housing); Rev. Rul. 74-587, 1974-2 C.B. 162 (community development).
[68] See, e.g., Rev. Rul. 2003-20, 2003-1 C.B. 465 (new markets tax credit); Priv. Ltr. Rul. 9736039 (June 9, 1997) (exempt general partner of low-income housing limited partnership had .15% interest).

project. It is in this role as manager that (c)(3) organizations must carefully comply with the applicable rules to safeguard their tax-exempt status. To safeguard their tax-exempt status, the (c)(3)s must be able to demonstrate that their activities as manager align closely with their exempt purpose.

Program-Related Investments and LLCs

Statutorily authorized since 1969, program-related investments ("PRIs") are special types of investments made by private foundations. PRIs are special because they simultaneously can be both charitable and profitable.[69] PRIs are an exception to the jeopardizing investment excise taxes imposed on abusive or imprudent investments made by private foundations and their managers.[70] As stated by the Joint Committee Bluebook to the Tax Reform Act of 1969:

> The Act makes it clear that a program-related investment—such as low-interest or interest-free loans to needy students, high risk investments in low-income housing, and loans to small businesses where commercial sources of funds are unavailable—is not to be considered as an investment which might jeopardize the foundation's carrying out of its exempt purposes (since such an investment is classified as a charitable expenditure). To qualify as program related, the investment must be primarily for charitable purposes and not have as one of its significant purposes that of deriving a profit for the foundation.[71]

Treasury regulations specify that although a PRI primarily must be motivated by charitable desires, "the fact that [a PRI] subsequently produces significant income or capital appreciation" is not, absent other factors, conclusive evidence that profit-making was the primary motive behind the investment.[72] Recently-proposed regulations[73] illustrate the charitable versus profit-making balancing act with an example of a PRI made to protect the environment. The private foundation in the example purchased common stock in a new recycling company on the same high-risk/high-reward terms as other investors. Even though there was a potential for significant profit, the investment qualified as a valid PRI because other sources of capital were scarce and the investment aligned with the private foundation's environmental mission.[74] If a PRI is financially successful, then to avoid certain excise taxes an amount equal to the profit as well as the recovered capital ordinarily must be redeployed (in the form of another PRI or a grant) by a private foundation within one year of receipt.[75]

---

[69] See I.R.C. § 4944(c); Reg. § 53.4944-3.
[70] I.R.C. 4944(a) & (b).
[71] See STAFF OF JOINT COMMITTEE ON TAX'N, GENERAL EXPLANATION OF THE TAX REFORM ACT OF 1969 (H.R. 13270), 91ST CONGRESS, PUB. LAW 91-172 AT 46 (DEC. 3, 1970) available at https://www.jct.gov/publications.html?func=startdown&id=2406 (last visited Sept. 7, 2014).
[72] Reg. §53.4944-3(a)(2)(iii).
[73] Prop. Treas. Reg. § 53.4944-3(b) exs. 11–19, 77 Fed. Reg. 23,430, 23,430–32 (Apr. 19, 2012).
[74] Prop. Treas. Reg. § 53.4944-3(b) Ex. 12.
[75] See I.R.C. § 4942(f)(2)(C)(i) (stating that "amounts received or accrued as repayments of amounts which were taken into account [previously] as a qualifying distribution . . . for any taxable year" must be added to the required annual distribution amount for the current taxable year under I.R.C. § 4942.

The regulations also mandate that private foundations comply with the so-called "expenditure responsibility" rules with respect to PRIs.[76] Generally, the expenditure responsibility rules require the investing foundation to undertake all reasonable efforts and establish adequate procedures to (i) see that the PRI is spent only for the purpose for which it is made; (ii) obtain full and complete reports from the recipient organization on how the funds are spent; and (iii) make full and detailed reports on the PRI to the IRS.[77] Finally, the regulations provide that PRIs may not be used to support lobbying or political campaign activities.[78]

Although they do entail additional compliance burdens, PRIs arguably are superior to private foundation grants in many respects. For instance, PRIs (including administrative costs incurred in making them) count toward a private foundation's annual 5 percent minimum distribution requirement.[79] As distinguished from grants, however, PRIs hold the very real promise of being repaid and perhaps even earning a profit. PRIs also qualify as an exception to the excess business holdings rule, which generally prohibits private foundations from owning more than 20 percent (but less than 100 percent) of a for-profit business.[80] Furthermore, because they generally require repayment of some kind, PRIs may encourage greater accountability than grants, which ordinarily are not required to be repaid by the recipient organization.

Nevertheless, despite their potential advantages, PRIs are rarely used. It is estimated that less than 1 percent of the amount expended each year by private foundations takes the form of PRIs.[81] The relatively rare use of PRIs is attributable to several causes. One, except for the fairly sophisticated, most private foundations lack awareness of PRIs and assume that outright grants to public charities are the only means to satisfy their annual distribution requirement. Two, private foundation managers (except among sophisticated private foundations) generally are uncomfortable conducting the business, financial, and tax underwriting required for PRIs. Three, program officers at most private foundations have a deeply held (albeit largely unsubstantiated) bias against charitable expenditures that require repayment. Their view is that any required return reduces the benefit of the expenditure; therefore, program officers believe that grants inherently are better than PRIs at maximizing the private foundation's charitable efforts.

Furthermore, the limited technical guidance available regarding PRIs focuses almost exclusively upon investments in corporate stock or in low-interest or no-interest loans.[82]

---

[76] I.R.C. § 4945; Reg. § 53.4945-5(a)(1).
[77] Id. § 53.4945-5(b)(1)(i–iii).
[78] Reg. § 53.4944-3(a)(1)(iii) provides that "[n]o purpose of the [PRI may be] to accomplish one or more of the purposes described in § 170(c)(2)(D)." I.R.C. § 170(c)(2)(D) restricts activities that involve influencing legislation and participating in political campaigns.
[79] See I.R.C. § 4942.
[80] See I.R.C. § 4943.
[81] See Steven Lawrence, *Doing Good with Foundation Assets: An Updated Look at Program-Related Investments*, THE PRI DIRECTORY: PROGRAM RELATED INVESTMENTS AND LOANS BY FOUNDATIONS (Jeffrey A. Falkenstein & David G. Jacobs Eds., 3d ed. 2010).
[82] None of the examples set forth in the PRI regulations address an equity investment in an LLC or partnership. See Reg. § 53.4944-3(b) exs. 1-10; Prop. Treas. Reg. § 53.4944-3(b) exs. 11–19, 77 Fed. Reg. 23,430, 23,430–32 (Apr. 19, 2012).

There is virtually no guidance concerning equity-based PRIs in LLCs, apparently because of the number of very subtle, technical issues that arise in connection therewith.[83] The complexity and corresponding lack of guidance no doubt impedes the use of equity-based PRIs in LLCs. The relevant issues include:

- Joint Venture Rules: An equity-based PRI in an LLC implicates the joint venture and ancillary joint venture rules.[84] These rules are notoriously ambiguous, and a misstep has potentially disastrous consequences: loss of tax-exempt status. At least in the IRS's view, the joint venture rules simply are not implicated by an investment in corporate stock or in true debt.
- Co-Investment and Self-Dealing Rules: If a private foundation is interested in making a PRI into an LLC, then it is probable that the private foundation's founders or managers likewise will be interested. If, however, private foundation founders or managers co-invest along with the private foundation, self-dealing and possibly other excise taxes can apply.
- UBIT Rules: The application of the UBIT rules to PRIs in LLCs is not clear.

The Rise of Impact Investing and For-Profit Social Enterprise

Although historically underutilized, especially in the context of LLCs, more recent developments perhaps foreshadow a different future for PRIs and LLCs. In particular, the concept of "impact investing" is gaining popularity among high-net-worth individuals and their family offices.[85] Impact investing is a catchphrase used to describe investments intended to generate positive social or environmental impact in addition to financial returns, similar to PRIs. A related concept, "social enterprise"—a business that emphasizes social or environmental goals alongside profits—is becoming widely recognized both in the business world[86] and in the law.[87]

Very recently, states have begun modifying their business laws to authorize hybrid forms

---

[83] See Letter to Hon. Douglas Shulman, IRS Commissioner, from ABA Section of Taxation, *Comments on New Examples of Program-Related Investments in Proposed Regulations Section 53.4944-3(b)* (Aug. 8, 2012) ("We understand that a decision was made not to include an equity investment in a limited liability company [in the proposed regulations] because of the complexity of the issues around investments in pass through entities.").

[84] PRIs in LLCs apparently are not excluded from the joint venture rules in the IRS's view because they (1) typically generate active (not passive) income and (2) expressly may not be made for the primary purpose of producing income or realizing appreciation in property. *See* IRS Instructions (2013) to Form 990 at page 24.

[85] *See, e.g.*, Margaret Collins, *Steve Case Backs Brain Device as Wealthy Push Do-Good Investing*, Bloomberg News (Sept. 5, 2014) *available at* http://www.bloomberg.com/news/2014-09-05/case-backs-brain-device-as-wealthy-push-do-good-investing.html (last visited Sept. 8, 2014).

[86] *See* Inc. Staff, *How a Business Can Change the World*, INC. Magazine (May 2011) *available at* http://www.inc.com/magazine/20110501/how-a-business-can-change-the-world.html (last visited Sept. 8, 2014).

[87] See Cassady V. Brewer, Elizabeth Carrott Minnigh & Robert A. Wexler, *Social Enterprise by Non-Profits and Hybrid Organizations* (2014) 489 TAX. MGMT., at A-42 to -45.

of for-profit enterprises that cater to social enterprise.[88] These new legal forms (which are best understood simply as variants of existing forms) include benefit corporations, flexible purpose corporations, social purpose corporations, benefit limited liability companies, and low-profit limited liability companies.[89] Other chapters of this book examine the corporate forms for social enterprise. Therefore, in the section below, this chapter provides an overview of the low-profit limited liability company. Immediately thereafter, benefit limited liability companies are explained.

L3Cs

The first low profit limited liability company ("L3C") statute was passed by Vermont in 2008.[90] Seven other states, Illinois, Louisiana, Maine, Michigan, Rhode Island, Utah, Wyoming,[91] and two Native American tribes, Oglala Sioux Tribe and the Crow Indian Nation of Montana,[92] have followed Vermont by adopting their own versions of L3C legislation. North Carolina is another state that initially followed Vermont in authorizing L3Cs, but effective January 1, 2014, North Carolina repealed its L3C statute.[93]

The L3C is best understood as a variant form of a regular LLC. Therefore, the L3C retains all of the basic characteristics (e.g., flexibility, limited liability, malleable tax treatment, etc.) of a regular LLC. In addition, the L3C statutes mandate that the federal income tax rules for PRIs be part of an L3C's governing documents. Specifically, all of the state L3C statutes provide that (1) the L3C must further the accomplishment of a charitable purpose, (2) the L3C would not have been formed but for its relationship to the accomplishment of a charitable purpose, (3) the L3C has no significant purpose of the production of income or the appreciation of property, and (4) the L3C has no political or legislative purpose. This cumbersome language is designed to dovetail with and satisfy the PRI requirements set forth in the IRC and in corresponding regulations.

Essentially, the L3C is intended to tip the balance in favor of finding a valid PRI for equity-based investments in LLCs by private foundations. The balance ostensibly is tipped in favor of finding a valid PRI because the L3C itself must be organized and operated in accordance with the above-noted basic requirements applicable to PRIs. Theoretically, then, a private foundation should be more comfortable making a PRI into an L3C than into a regular LLC. Moreover, due to its unique name, an L3C arguably is easier to identify, thereby better enabling the IRS and other interested parties to monitor PRI-related ventures. Furthermore, the statutorily-imposed charitable or educational purpose

---

[88] Id. at A-33. See also Cassady V. Brewer, *Social Enterprise Entity Comparison Chart* (Aug. 1, 2014) available at http://papers.ssrn.com/sol3/papers.cfm?abstract_id=2304892 (last visited Sept. 8, 2014).

[89] Id.

[90] VT. STAT. ANN. TIT. 11, § 3001(27).

[91] 805 ILL. COMP. STAT. 180/1-26; LA. REV. STAT. ANN. § 12:1302.C; ME. REV. STAT. TIT. 31, § 1611; MICH. COMP. LAWS § 450.4204; R.I. GEN. LAWS § 7-16-76; UTAH CODE ANN. § 48-2c-412; WYO. STAT. ANN. § 17-29-102(A)(IX).

[92] OGLALA SIOUX TRIBAL COUNCIL ORDINANCE 09-23; CROW LAW AND ORDER CODE §§18-5-102, 18-5-108, 18-5-705.

[93] SEE N.C. GEN. STAT. § 57C-2-01 (REPEALED EFF. JAN. 1, 2014). SEE S.B. 439, 2013–2014 NC GENERAL ASSEMBLY.

and mission of the L3C arguably ameliorates the fiduciary-duty constraints that purely for-profit entities and their managers must consider when making business decisions that favor mission over profit. Thus, deciding upon a course of action that *heavily favors* mission over profit-making theoretically is permissible for the managers of an L3C.

Critics justifiably point out that because the IRS has not preapproved L3Cs for PRIs, unless and until such preapproval is possible, the L3C has no real advantage over a traditional LLC. Critics further argue that every PRI is unique and requires a comprehensive analysis of all the facts and circumstances surrounding the investment. Thus, each L3C and private foundation investment in an L3C must be evaluated on its own merits because federal law, not state law, determines whether an investment qualifies as a PRI. Therefore, the critics argue, the L3C provides no blanket PRI protection and is misleading because a well-advised private foundation must perform the same level of due diligence when investing in an L3C. Some critics also have argued that the L3C statutes technically are flawed because they require the *entire* L3C entity to be charitable or educational, whereas the test for a PRI only requires that the investment itself, not the entire entity, further a charitable or educational purpose. Clearly, there are some valid concerns among commentators and lawmakers as most-recently evidenced by North Carolina's repeal of its L3C statute effective January 1, 2014.

A final note: Although the L3C originally was envisioned as a vehicle for PRIs, there is no statutory requirement that an L3C be funded by a PRI or that an L3C have even one tax-exempt member. In fact, some L3Cs are being formed with no intention of ever receiving a PRI. These non-PRI L3Cs presumably are being formed because the L3C provides nonprofit or charitable "branding" for the organization and potential fiduciary liability protection for its managers. Alternatively, these non-PRI L3Cs perhaps are being organized as the legal form for social enterprises. Similarly, among exempt organizations, the eleemosynary nature of the L3C may be appealing as a substitute for using a regular SMLLC as a subsidiary or affiliate, Using L3Cs as affiliated entities also may be advantageous. For example, L3Cs may be particularly well suited for joint ventures with tax-exempt hospitals or similar operating charities. The mixed charitable and profitable nature of such ventures aligns well with the L3C format without regard to whether any investment in the venture is designed to qualify as a PRI.

Benefit LLCs

The benefit LLC is a variant of the benefit corporation, discussed elsewhere in this volume. Two states, Maryland[94] and Oregon,[95] have authorized benefit LLCs. The Maryland and Oregon benefit LLC statutes essentially mirror the respective authorizing statutes for a Maryland or Oregon benefit corporation.

A Maryland benefit LLC must have the purpose of creating a "general public benefit."[96] General public benefit is defined for this purpose as "a material, positive impact on society and the environment, as measured by a third-party standard, through activities that

---

[94] MD. CODE ANN., CORPS. & ASS'NS §§ 4A-1201 TO -1208.
[95] OR. REV. STAT. §§ 60.750 TO -.770.
[96] MD. CODE ANN., CORPS. & ASS'NS § 4A-1206(A).

promote a combination of specific public benefits."[97] Specific public benefits include the following: (1) providing individuals or communities with beneficial products or services; (2) promoting economic opportunity for individuals or communities beyond the creation of jobs in the normal course of business; (3) preserving the environment; (4) improving human health; (5) promoting the arts, sciences, or advancement of knowledge; (6) increasing the flow of capital to entities with a public benefit purpose; or (7) the accomplishment of any other particular benefit for society or the environment.[98] Maryland benefit LLCs also are required to produce an annual benefit report that includes an assessment against a third-party standard of the benefit LLC's performance in accomplishing its general and specific benefits.[99] As noted above, this language mirrors the statutory language authorizing Maryland benefit corporations.[100]

Unique, however, among most states with benefit corporation law, Maryland requires a benefit LLC to use the term "Benefit" in its name.[101] Maryland apparently uses this unique naming requirement to track the number of benefit entities formed under its law. This unique name requirement conceivably is the principal motivation behind the Maryland benefit LLC statute because a regular Maryland LLC may engage in any lawful activity, "whether or not for-profit."[102] Thus, a regular Maryland LLC could be formed and organized for social enterprise purposes. Requiring a distinct name, however, presumably allows Maryland to track those LLCs that affirmatively have chosen to organize as a "benefit" LLC, as opposed to organizing as a regular LLC.

Similar to the directors and officers of a Maryland benefit corporation, the person or persons managing the business and affairs of a Maryland benefit LLC (i.e., either managing-members or designated managers) are required to consider not only the interests of the members but also the interests of nonmember stakeholders (e.g., customers, employees, community, etc.) of the LLC.[103] With respect to the duty of the managers or managing-members to consider these diverse interests, however, the Maryland benefit LLC statute takes a curious turn. On one hand, the law provides that a person managing a Maryland benefit LLC "shall consider" the effects of any action or decision not to act on members and stakeholders.[104] Yet, on the other hand, the statute provides that a person managing a Maryland benefit LLC "does not have any duty" to either the members or the stakeholders of the LLC.[105] Accordingly, a manager of a benefit LLC seems to be accountable to no one unless otherwise provided in the articles of organization or written operating agreement.

Beyond the foregoing, the Maryland benefit LLC statute, like all LLC statutes, leaves the details of the economics, management duties, transaction approvals, voting, indemnification, and other matters of the LLC to the articles of organization and the operating

---

[97] Id. at § 4a-1201(c).
[98] Id. at § 4a-1201(d).
[99] Id. at § 4a-1208.
[100] Id. at §§ 5-6C-01 to -08.
[101] Id. at § 1-502.
[102] Id. at § 4a-201.
[103] Id. at § 4a-1207.
[104] Id. at § 4a-1207(a).
[105] Id. at § 4a-1207(b).

agreement. In essence then, aside from the specific statutory provisions summarized above, Maryland benefit LLCs should be treated just like any other Maryland LLC.

Oregon took a slightly different approach when enacting its benefit LLC statute. Like Maryland, Oregon adopted both the benefit corporation and the benefit LLC forms; however, unlike Maryland, which separately modified its business corporation law and its LLC law, Oregon's statute creates a "benefit company," which can be either a corporation or an LLC.[106] It appears Oregon may have taken this approach because both an Oregon business corporation and a regular Oregon LLC are required to have a "lawful business"[107] purpose. In theory, a lawful business purpose does not include an eleemosynary purpose. Moreover, unlike Maryland, an Oregon benefit LLC is not required to have a special name. To be formed as an Oregon benefit LLC, the company so provides in its articles of organization.[108]

If an Oregon LLC chooses to be a benefit company, then the LLC must pursue a "general public benefit" and may adopt a "specific public benefit" as well.[109] An Oregon benefit LLC also may (but is not required to) appoint one or more "benefit governors" who are individuals (not entities) and who are members in a member-managed LLC or managers in a manager-managed LLC.[110] Any benefit governor is not personally liable for an action or omission taken (or not taken) in his or her capacity as such unless the action or omission constitutes self-dealing, willful misconduct or a knowing violation of law. With respect to all governors (i.e., managing-members or managers) of an Oregon benefit LLC, in determining the best interests of the benefit company, consideration should be given to how any action or inaction will affect the members of the LLC, its employees, its subsidiaries and suppliers, customers, the community, the environment, and other stakeholders of the benefit LLC.[111] In exchange for considering the interest of stakeholders, a governor of a benefit LLC is not personally liable for monetary damages for the benefit company's failure to provide a general or specific public benefit.[112] An Oregon benefit company also is required to produce an annual benefit report.[113]

5. DONOR USES OF LLCs

LLCs also are being used by donors to charities. Sophisticated donors to charity are using LLCs to preserve anonymity and to provide flexibility beyond traditional charitable-giving vehicles.

Subject to certain exceptions, donors contributing $5,000 or more in cash or property to a (c)(3) organization are disclosed on Schedule B to the charity's annual Form 990.[114]

---

[106] OR. REV. STAT. TIT. 7 §§ 60.750 TO -.770.
[107] *Id.* at § 60.074.
[108] *Id.* at § 60.754(1)(b).
[109] *Id.* at § 60.758.
[110] *Id.* at § 60.762.
[111] *Id.* at § 60.760(1).
[112] *Id.* at § 60.760(5)(b).
[113] *Id.* at § 60.768.
[114] IRS Instructions (2013) to Form 990 at page 75.

Although the names listed on Schedule B are not required to be made public like much of the rest of Form 990, inadvertent disclosures happen[115] and, regardless, the IRS obviously will learn of the donor. This motivates some donors to take extraordinary measures to remain anonymous. One of those measures involves forming a disregarded SMLLC through which the charitable contribution is made. Because the SMLLC is disregarded for federal income tax purposes, the donor takes the charitable deduction on his or her tax return. The required disclosure on Schedule B, however, reveals only that "Anonymous, LLC" made the contribution, with a post office box listed as the address.

Very sophisticated and wealthy individuals have found ways to use an LLC to support both philanthropy and entrepreneurship. And, if they so desire, they can do so while remaining anonymous. For instance, Emerson Collective, LLC, founded by Laurene Powell Jobs, Steve Jobs's widow, reportedly has given away millions without having to report donations and grants as otherwise would be required if a private foundation had been used.[116] Emerson Collective's website indicates that the organization focuses upon justice, students, and innovation and "invest[s] ... time, energy and resources in people who blend optimism with pragmatism, people who have the audacity to dream up new ways to improve the world and the determination to make them a reality."[117]

Although one can only speculate, Emerson Collective, LLC presumably takes the position that it is either a disregarded SMLLC held by Ms. Jobs or, assuming it has multiple members, an agent acting on behalf of the members of the LLC. It would seem unlikely that Emerson Collective, LLC would take the position for federal income tax purposes that it is a partnership because it appears to lack a profit motive.[118] In addition, electing corporate status for federal income tax purposes would seem unnecessary as well. Thus, as either a disregarded SMLLC or an agent for its members, Emerson Collective, LLC likely does not file a federal income tax return. The funds contributed to Emerson Collective, LLC, to the extent those funds are donated to (c)(3) organizations, would be deductible only if and when the funds actually were contributed. Moreover, the Schedule B of the Form 990 of a (c)(3) receiving funds from Emerson Collective would not disclose the identity of Ms. Jobs or other members (if any) of Emerson Collective. Therefore, at the price of deferring the charitable deduction until a contribution is actually made to a (c)(3) organization, Ms. Jobs or other members (if any) of Emerson Collective retain anonymity and are freed from all the constraints imposed upon most nonprofit or charitable organizations.

---

[115] For example, see Barnaby Zall, Donor Q&A, Philanthropy Roundtable (May/June 2002) available at http://www.philanthropyroundtable.org/topic/excellence_in_philanthropy/donor_q_a5 (last visited Sept. 10, 2014).
[116] Claire Cain Miller, *Laurene Powell Jobs and Anonymous Giving in Silicon Valley*, New York Times (May 24, 2013) available at http://bits.blogs.nytimes.com/2013/05/24/laurene-powell-jobs-and-anonymous-giving-in-silicon-valley/?_php=true&_type=blogs&_r=0 (last visited Sept. 10, 2014).
[117] *See* http://www.emersoncollective.com/about/.
[118] See, e.g., *McElroy v. Commissioner*, T.C. Memo 2014-163 (2014) (state law general partnerships formed to make charitable contributions are not federal income tax partnerships because they lack a profit motive).

6. CONCLUSION

This chapter provides a broad overview of the use of LLCs in the nonprofit and charitable sector. There is little doubt that uses of LLCs not touched upon in this chapter will evolve. That is a testament to the incredible utility of the LLC for both business and eleemosynary endeavors. Sort of like duct tape,[119] LLCs can be used for just about anything.

BIBLIOGRAPHY

Alexander, Robert G. & Dallas E. Klemmera (2010), "Creative Wealth Planning with Grantor Trusts, Family Limited Partnerships, and Family Limited Liability Companies," Estate Planning & Community Property Law Journal, 2, 307, 359–361.
Arnsberger, Paul, Melissa Ludlum, Margaret Riley & Mark Stanton (2008), "A History of the Tax-Exempt Sector: An SOI Perspective," IRS Statistics of Income Bulletin 27, 105.
Bayona, Dennise & Ken Milani (2011), "The L3C Low-Profit Limited Liability Company: Investment Option for Societal Impact," Practical Tax Strategies, 86, 66.
Bishop, Carter G. (2010), "The Low-Profit LLC (L3C): Program Related Investment by Proxy or Perversion?," Arkansas Law Review, 63, 243.
Bishop, Carter G. & Daniel S. Kleinberger (2009), LIMITED LIABILITY COMPANIES: TAX AND BUSINESS LAW, ¶¶ 3.01–3.12.
Brewer, Cassady V. (2012), "A Novel Approach to Using LLCs for Quasi-Charitable Endeavors (a/k/a 'Social Enterprise')," William Mitchell Law Review, 38, 678.
Brewer, Cassady V. (2013), "Seven Ways to Strengthen and Improve the L3C," Regent University Law Review, 25, 329.
Brewer, Cassady V., Elizabeth Carrott Minnigh & Robert A. Wexler (2014), "Social Enterprise by Non-Profits and Hybrid Organizations," Bloomberg BNA Tax Management Portfolio 489, A-42 to -45.
Brewer, Cassady V. & Sean J. Reynolds (Jul./Aug. 2007), "Business and Tax Planning with Controlled Organizations," Taxation of Exempts, 19, 3.
Brewer, Cassady V. & Michael J. Rhim (2009), "Using the 'L3C' for Program-Related Investments," Taxation of Exempts, 21, 11.
Brody, Evelyn (2010), "All Charities Are Property-Tax Exempt, But Some Charities Are More Exempt Than Others," New England Law Review, 44, 621.
Callison. J. William & Allan W. Vestal (2010), "The L3C Illusion: Why Low-Profit Limited Liability Companies Will Not Stimulate Socially Optimal Private Foundation Investment in Entrepreneurial Ventures," Vermont Law Review, 35, 273.
Chiodini, Steven & Gregory L. Colvin (2011), "The Use of LLCs in Fiscal Sponsorship—A New Model," Taxation of Exempts 22, 7.
Collins, Margaret (Sept. 5, 2014), "Steve Case Backs Brain Device as Wealthy Push Do-Good Investing," Bloomberg News, available at http://www.bloomberg.com/news/2014-09-05/case-backs-brain-device-as-wealthy-push-do-good-investing.html (last visited Sept. 8, 2014).
Coverdale, John F. (2013), "Of Red Bags and Family Limited Partnerships: Reforming the Estate and Gift Tax Valuation Rules to Achieve Horizontal Equity," University of Louisville Law Review, 51, 239.
Dagher Jr., Peter G. (2013), "Social Impact Bonds and The Private Benefit Doctrine: Will Participation Jeopardize a Nonprofit's Tax-Exempt Status?," Fordham Law Review, 81, 3479, 3519.
Daher, Dominic & Barry Brents (Nov./Dec. 2006), "Achieving Enhanced Liability Protection Through SMLLCs," Taxation of Exempts, 18, 137.
Dana, Andrew F. (2010), "Structuring Separate and Subsidiary Entities for Private Operating Foundations," Taxation of Exempts, 22, 33.

---

[119] According to the Science & Technology Channel, duct tape has been used for everything from saving lives to removing warts. See Science & Technology Channel, Top 10 Uses for Duct Tape available at http://www.sciencechannel.com/science-technology/10-uses-for-duct-tape.htm (last visited Sept. 10, 2014).

Ely, Bruce P., William T. Thistle, II & J. Sims Rhyne III (2014), "State Tax Treatment of LLCs and LLPs: Update for 2014," Journal of Multistate Taxation, 24, 12.

Fishman, James F. & Stephen Schwarz (4th ed. 2010), "Nonprofit Organizations: Cases and Materials," 48–53.

Fritz, Robert W. (2001), "The Evolving Use of Limited Liability Companies by Tax-Exempt Organizations," Taxation of Exempts 13, 112.

Hill, Frances R. & Douglas M. Mancino (2010), TAXATION OF EXEMPT ORGANIZATIONS, ¶¶ 2.01 to 2.05.

Inbar, Tomer J. (May 11, 2012), "Joint Ventures: The Legal Basics," ABA Section of Taxation, Exempt Organizations Section Meeting.

Inc. Staff (May 2011), "How a Business Can Change the World," INC. Magazine, available at http://www.inc.com/magazine/20110501/how-a-business-can-change-the-world.html (last visited Sept. 8, 2014).

Internal Revenue Service (2010), "Statistics of Income OneSheet: Charities and Other Tax-Exempt Organizations," available at http://www.irs.gov/pub/irs-soi/2010ExemptOrganizationsOneSheet.pdf (last visited Aug. 14, 2014).

Internal Revenue Service (2011), "U.S. Dep't of Treasury, Limited Liability Company Reference Guide Sheet," available at http://www.irs.gov/pub/irs-tege/llc_guide_sheet.pdf (last visited Sept. 3, 2014).

Joint Committee on Taxation (Aug. 1, 2012), "Selected Issues Relating to Choice of Business Entity," 8–9.

Joseph, James P. & Andras Kosaras (2008), "New Strategies for Leveraging Foundation Assets," Taxation of Exempts, 20, 22.

Keatinge, Robert R. (2009), "LLCs and Nonprofit Organizations—For-Profits, Nonprofits, and Hybrids," Suffolk University Law Review, 42, 553.

Kelley, Thomas (2009), "Law and Choice of Entity on the Social Enterprise Frontier," Tulane Law Review, 84, 337.

Kleinberger, Daniel S. (2010), "A Myth Deconstructed: The 'Emperor's New Clothes' on the Low-Profit Limited Liability Company," Delaware Journal of Corporate Law, 35, 879.

Lang, Robert & Elizabeth Carrott Minnigh (2010), "The L3C, History, Basic Construct, and Legal Framework," Vermont Law Review, 35, 15.

Lawrence, Steven (2010), "Doing Good with Foundation Assets: An Updated Look at Program-Related Investments, in THE PRI DIRECTORY: PROGRAM RELATED INVESTMENTS AND LOANS BY FOUNDATIONS xiii, xiii," (Jeffrey A. Falkenstein & David G. Jacobs eds., 3d ed.).

Lion, Ofer and Douglas M. Mancino (2012), "PRIs—New Proposed Regulations and the New Venture Capital," Taxation of Exempts 24, 2.

Mancino, Douglas M. (Jan. 25, 2013), "Use of Single Member Limited Liability Companies by Tax Exempt Organizations," 2013 Midyear Meeting, ABA Section of Taxation.

Mayer, Lloyd Hitoshi & Joseph R. Ganahl (2014), "Taxing Social Enterprise," Stanford Law Review, 66, 387.

McCray, Richard A. & Ward L. Thomas (2001), "I.R.S., US Dep't of Treasury, Limited Liability Companies as Exempt Organizations—Update 29–32" available at http://www.irs.gov/pub/irs-tege/eotopicb01.pdf (last visited Sept. 3, 2014).

McDowell, Suzanne Ross & David Shevlin (Nov. 14–15, 2013), "Tax Exempt Organizations: An Advanced Course, Creative and Practical Uses of Single Member LLCs," American Law Institute Continuing Legal Education.

Murray, J. Haskell & Edward Hwang (2011), "Purpose with Profit: Governance, Enforcement, Capital-Raising and Capital-Locking in Low-Profit Limited Liability Companies," University of Miami Law Review, 66, 1.

O'Donohoe, Nick, Christina Leijonhufvud & Yasemin Saltuk (Nov. 29, 2010), "Impact Investments: An Emerging Asset Class," J.P. Morgan Global Research available at http://www.jpmorgan.com/cm/cs?pagename=JPM/DirectDoc&urlname=impact_investments_nov2010.pdf (last visited Sept. 9, 2014).

Outenreath, Alyson (2013), "'Uncharitable' Policy for Charities: Use of Disregarded LLCs by I.R.C. § 501(c)(3) Organizations is a Trap for the Unwary in Certain States," South Texas Law Review, 54, 685.

Pacific Community Ventures, "The Social Enterprise Census," available at http://socialenterprisecensus.org/about-us/ (last visited Sept. 8, 2014).

Purcell, Elizabeth A. (1987), "Using For-Profit Subsidiaries to Preserve Exempt Status," Journal of Taxation, 67, 180.

Ragin, Jr., Luther M. (2010), "Program-Related Investments in Practice," Vermont Law Review, 35, 53.

Sanders, Michael I. (4th ed. 2013), JOINT VENTURES INVOLVING TAX-EXEMPT ORGANIZATIONS.

Sanders, Michael I. (2005), "Can the Commercial Model of 'Unorthodox' Joint Ventures Meet The Service's Control Objectives?" Taxation of Exempts 17, 99, 108.

Schmidt, Elizabeth (2010), "Vermont's Social Hybrid Pioneers: Early Observations and Questions to Ponder," Vermont Law Review, 35, 163.

Sherlock, Molly F. & Jane G. Gravelle (Nov. 17, 2009), "An Overview of the Nonprofit and Charitable Sector," Congressional Research Service Report #40919, 1.

Staff of Joint Committee on Taxation, "General Explanation of the Tax Reform Act of 1969 (H.R. 13270), 91st Congress, Pub. Law 91-172," 46 (Dec. 3, 1970) available at https://www.jct.gov/publications.html?func=startdown&id=2406 (last visited Sept. 7, 2014).

Tyler, John (2010), "Negating the Problem of Having 'Two Masters': A Framework for L3C Fiduciary Duties and Accountability," Vermont Law Review, 35, 117.

Upton, Richard R. & Carl Merino (2012), "IRS Allows Charitable Contributions to Disregarded Entities," Tax Notes 137, 1327.

Vishnepolskaya, Marina (2014), "International Charitable Giving Using Single-Member LLCs Under Notice 2012–52," Journal of International Taxation 25, 43.

Walker, David S. (2012), "A Consideration of an LLC for a 501(c)(3) Nonprofit Organization," 38 William Mitchell Law Review, 38, 628.

Wilson, Brendan M. (2010), "Using Subsidiaries to Hold and Manage Real Property," Real Estate Taxation, 38, 28.

Wilson, Brendan M. (2012), "Planning For Co-Investments Between a Private Foundation and a Disqualified Person," Journal of Taxation, 116, 45.

15. State laboratories and social enterprise law
J. Haskell Murray

1. INTRODUCTION

In her iconic book *The Genius of American Corporate Law*, Professor Roberta Romano claims "federalism spurs innovation in public policy because of the incremental experimentation afforded by fifty laboratories of states competing for citizens and firms." The legal academy has given much attention to jurisdictional competition for traditional business associations such as corporations and limited liability companies ("LLCs"). Delaware has long been recognized as the clear winner in the competition among the states for traditional corporations and LLCs, with some academics arguing that the competition has been a "race to the bottom" and others contending that the competition has been a "race to the top." To date, however, the behavior surrounding emerging social enterprise forms, such as low-profit LLCs and benefit corporations, has not been thoroughly discussed or analyzed. Also, unlike the situation with the more traditional business associations, Delaware does not seem to have dominated the social enterprise law market yet.

Section 2 of this chapter provides an overview of the social enterprise forms in the United States and the early academic literature regarding these forms. Section 3 describes many of the innovations in the social enterprise law area and the various iterations of the laws. Section 4 asks why states are passing these social enterprise laws, while Section 5 suggests that jurisdictional positioning and interest group theory may hold some answers. The chapter concludes by drawing on the Delaware experience to predict the characteristics of the winning state in any future jurisdictional competition that may arise over social enterprises.

2. OVERVIEW OF U.S. SOCIAL ENTERPRISE LAW AND LITERATURE

Low-Profit Limited Liability Companies (L3Cs)

The 2008 Vermont Low-Profit Limited Liability ("L3C") statute was both the first L3C statute and the first social enterprise statute in the United States. Since 2008, eight additional states and two Indian tribes have passed L3C statutes. Effective January 1, 2014, North Carolina became the first of the nine states to repeal its L3C statute, though it allowed previously formed L3Cs to continue to exist in the state. The L3C concept was championed by Robert "Bob" Lang, the Chief Executive Officer of the Mary Elizabeth & Gordon B. Mannweiler Foundation. Mr. Lang worked with attorneys on the L3C concept, but is not a lawyer himself.

L3C statutes were drafted, primarily, to target Program Related Investments ("PRI") from foundations and thereby address the funding issues facing social enterprises (Lang & Minnigh 2010). The statutes mirror, in many respects, the PRI regulations and replace "investment" in the regulations with "company" in the L3C statutes. The L3C statutes require that the company "(i) significantly furthers the accomplishment of one or more charitable or educational purposes . . .; and (ii) would not have been formed but for the company's relationship to the accomplishment of charitable or educational purposes."[1] The L3C statutes also require that "[n]o significant purpose of the company is the production of income or the appreciation of property" but the statutes also make clear that the production of significant income or appreciation of property is not conclusive evidence of a statutory violation.[2] The L3C proponents believed that if the L3C statutes required of companies the same thing that the PRI regulations require of investments, an L3C would become a safe place for foundations to make PRIs without as much need for an expensive and time-consuming written opinion from counsel or advanced ruling by the Internal Revenue Service ("IRS"). To date, however, the IRS has not expressly endorsed the L3C as a safe harbor for PRIs (Hopkins 2014). Despite the lack of a clear safe harbor, Lang has promoted a tranched investment structure for L3Cs where foundations provide high-risk and low-return capital, allowing more traditional investors to obtain a market return.

The L3C has been touted by Lang and his supporters as: (1) aiding private foundations in the PRI process; (2) a "for-profit with a nonprofit soul" that serves both profit and social purpose; (3) a branding vehicle; and (4) a way, through his proposed tranched investment structure, to provide each set of investors their desired social and financial returns (Lang & Minnigh 2010, Wood 2010). Professors and practitioners quickly launched criticism against the L3C, stating, *inter alia*, that: (1) the statutes did not significantly protect or aid private foundations in the PRI process; (2) LLCs could serve the same purpose as L3Cs under the current tax law; (3) the statutes were over-hyped and bordered on fraudulent in their claims; (4) the skeletal L3C statute was insufficient to deal with the complexities stemming from the conflicts between the "two masters" of profit and purpose; and (5) the proposed tranched investments were impractical and could lead to private inurement that may jeopardize the investing foundations' tax exemptions (Bishop 2010, Callison & Vestal 2010, Chernoff 2010, Kleinberger 2010). A few professors, while largely agreeing with the criticisms, suggested reforms for the L3C law, including: (1) amend the proposed tranched model by replacing traditional investors with social investors; (2) require at least one tax-exempt investor; (3) add reporting and registration requirements for certain L3Cs; (4) require at least a partial asset lock for L3Cs engaged in mergers and acquisitions activity; and (5) provide free transferability and withdrawal by any tax-exempt member of an L3C (Murray & Hwang 2011, Brewer 2012).

Possibly in response to the academic and practitioner criticism, the passing of the L3C statutes has been at a relative standstill, with the last L3C statute passed in 2012. From 2012 to present, over a dozen state social enterprise statutes, of types other than the L3C, were passed. The number of L3C statutes has actually decreased since 2012; as mentioned above, effective January 1, 2014, North Carolina repealed its L3C statute (Brewer 2014).

---

[1] Vt. Stat. Ann. tit. 11, § 3001 (27A). Other state L3C statutes largely follow Vermont's lead.
[2] *Id.* at § 3001 (27B).

Currently, there are reported to be approximately 1,100 L3Cs and most are small, closely held entities (interSector 2014).

Benefit Corporations and Benefit LLCs

In 2010, Maryland passed the first benefit corporation statute. Currently, over two dozen states have passed benefit corporation statutes, a few of which are public benefit corporation statutes, discussed below in a separate section. Nonprofit organization B Lab, which has been privately certifying companies as "certified B corporations" since June of 2007, has been a major force behind the passing of benefit corporation statutes. According to a Benefit Corporation White Paper drafted by the proponents of the legislation ("Proponent White Paper"), the benefit corporation law is intended to expressly expand the concept of corporate purpose to include a mandatory focus on society and the environment, while adding accountability and transparency to combat "greenwashing" (Clark & Vranka 2013). Critics of the benefit corporation statutes note the lack of enforcement mechanisms in the law and that benefit corporation legislation is propped up by marketing from well-funded B Lab (Callison 2012, Groshoff 2013).

The authors of the Proponent White Paper claim that the market (including consumers, investors, and social entrepreneurs) is demanding a society-focused, for-profit entity form like the benefit corporation. The Proponent White Paper's authors also argue that existing case law hinders socially focused for-profit entities, citing *Dodge v. Ford, Unocal, Revlon*, and *eBay v. Newmark*. The centerpiece of the benefit corporation statutes is its purpose clause, which states that each benefit corporation must have a "general public benefit purpose," defined as "[a] material positive impact on society and the environment, taken as a whole, assessed against a third-party standard, from the business and operations of a benefit corporation."[3] The benefit corporation movement has been spurred, in part, by statements by the current Chief Justice of the Delaware Supreme Court, Leo Strine, including: "as a matter of corporate law, the object of the corporation is to produce profits for the stockholders . . . the social beliefs of the managers, no more than their own financial interests, cannot be their end in managing the corporation" (Strine 2012) and by statements by former Delaware Chancellor William Chandler in the *eBay v. Newmark* case, including, "[h]aving chosen a for-profit corporate form, the Craigslist directors are bound by the fiduciary duties and standards that accompany that form. Those standards include acting to promote the value of the corporation for the benefit of its stockholders."[4]

Proponents of the benefit corporation form claim that the benefit corporation law provides a higher level of accountability and transparency than traditional corporate law. Accountability is increased, they claim, by mandatory language requiring consideration of various corporate stakeholders by directors, and by the provision of benefit enforcement proceedings for resolution of complaints related to failure to pursue the benefit

---

[3] MODEL BENEFIT CORP. LEGIS. § 201.
[4] eBay Domestic Holdings, Inc. v. Newmark, 16 A.3d 1, 34 (Del. Ch. 2010). Professor Lyman Johnson has questioned the *eBay* decision and noted the lack of citation to authority for the court's statement about the mandated focus on shareholder profits. Johnson (2013) at 274–75.

corporation's purpose. Transparency is increased, they argue, by the benefit corporation statutes requiring an annual benefit report and by requiring the measurement of general public benefit against a "comprehensive, credible, independent and transparent" third-party standard (Clark & Vranka 2013, Clark & Babson 2012).

Both academics and practitioners have contested the claims made in the Proponent White Paper. Only approximately 1,000 benefit corporations have been formed in the first four years of the legislation, suggesting the market demand may be less than was claimed.[5] For comparison, Delaware is home to over one million entities, and in 2007 an average of 430 LLCs were formed each weekday in Delaware (Manesh 2011). Additionally, some commentators contend that existing law already provides sufficient solutions for social entrepreneurs, including: (1) the flexible, contract-based LLC form, (2) the constituency statutes in over 30 states, and (3) the express allowance of social or environmental purpose in states such as Oregon (Murray 2012). Certain academics have also argued that social entrepreneurs could avoid the cases cited in the Proponent White Paper by incorporating in more stakeholder-friendly states, and even in the states of the cited cases, the business judgment rule provides significant protection for social entrepreneurs. Some professors have countered that even if benefit corporations are not technically needed, they might serve as a useful signaling device (Murray 2012, Yockey 2015). Moreover, commentators have claimed that the "general public benefit purpose" is too vague and provides insufficient guidance to directors when they face zero-sum games; these critics have suggested amending benefit corporation statutes to require the prioritization of the interests, or at least the identification of the benefit corporation's primary interest (Murray 2012). Others have suggested that the "general public benefit purpose" mandate is too broad and statutes should be made flexible enough to allow social entrepreneurs to focus on one or more specific social or environmental issues without being forced to consider all stakeholders (Callison 2012, Loewenstein 2013).

Various academic authors have called into question the strength of the accountability measures of the benefit corporation law, noting that among all of the stakeholders that directors are required to consider, the benefit corporation statutes only provide shareholders with standing to bring a benefit enforcement proceeding (Brakman Reiser 2011, Murray 2012). Some articles have suggested statutory amendments to provide more serious accountability, including imposing a charitable giving floor, adding a partial asset lock, instituting stakeholder standing, and regulating the third-party standard providers that currently vary wildly in quality (Murray 2012, 2013, 2014). At least one author has noted that benefit enforcement proceedings may be used by shareholders to "greenmail" benefit corporations into buying off those particular shareholders, possibly to the detriment of the corporation, its mission, and the other stakeholders (Callison 2012).

On the transparency front, authors have noted that the statutes' benefit reporting requirements are extremely vague, susceptible to white- and green-washing, and lack an express enforcement mechanism for punishing benefit corporations that do not provide

---

[5] The number of benefit corporations has continued to grow during the publication process, estimated to exceed 1,500 in April 2015. Relatedly, as of April 2015, there are approximately 1,200 "certified B corporations" in existence, but benefit corporations are not required to be certified, and the certified B corporations, oddly, include partnerships, LLCs, and traditional corporations, in addition to benefit corporations.

the reports at all (Callison 2012, Murray 2012). Delaware Supreme Court Chief Justice Leo Strine criticized benefit corporations, writing that "[benefit corporations exist in] a fictional land where you can take other people's money, use it as you wish, and ignore the best interests of those with the only right to vote" (Strine 2012). At least one academic article has suggested that financial tools may be more effective than the statutes in preventing mission drift by social enterprises like benefit corporations (Brakman Reiser & Dean 2013).

Currently, Maryland and Oregon provide for formation of benefit LLCs. The benefit LLC statutes are nearly identical to the benefit corporation statutes, but the benefit LLC law relies on the state LLC statute, instead of the state corporate statute, to fill in the gaps left by the benefit LLC law. Most proponents of the benefit corporation statutes, including B Lab, claim that they are not encouraging the passage of benefit LLC legislation at this time because they believe the traditional LLC law to be flexible enough to address the needs of social entrepreneurs who are not interested in the corporate form (Murray 2012).

Flexible Purpose Corporations and Social Purpose Corporations

In response to some of the mandatory provisions of the benefit corporation statutes, such as the required "general public benefit purpose," and the expressed desire to give companies more freedom, two states have passed more flexible social enterprise statutes. California passed a flexible purpose corporation ("FPC") statute, in addition to its benefit corporation statute, and Washington state passed a "social purpose statute," ("SPC"), which is similar to the FPC statute (Brakman Reiser 2012, Plerhoples 2012, ABA White Paper 2013).[6]

Unlike the Model-based benefit corporation statutes, the FPC and SPC statutes require adoption of one or more specific purposes. The Model-based benefit corporation statutes require pursuit of a "general public purpose" and require benefit corporation directors to consider all stakeholders, not just a sub-set of stakeholders as is allowed by the FPC and SPC laws. The FPC and SPC statutes expressly provide for dissenters' rights, for shareholders who object to conversion to that entity type. Dissenters' rights have been included in a few benefit corporation statutes, including California's, but are not included in the statutes that follow the Model Benefit Corporation Legislation. Bill Clark, the primary drafter of the benefit corporation legislation, has argued that dissenters' rights might harm cash-poor corporations that wish to convert, but do not have the resources to pay the shareholders who do not want to make the change to a social enterprise form (Clark & Vranka 2013).

Supporters of the benefit corporation statutes have stated that the FPC and SPC statutes are too weak to support the dual mission of social entrepreneurs. Benefit corporation proponents worry about FPCs and SPCs that might harm society by focusing on only one group of stakeholders, for example, caring for the environment, while treating their employees poorly. Critics of the benefit corporation framework respond that the benefit corporation legislation has overpromised, will suffocate companies with its mandatory provisions, and has not provided the means to live up to its bold claims of achieving both profit and broad purpose (Loewenstein 2013).

---

[6] California amended its FPC statute, effective in January 2015, to switch its name to SPC.

Public Benefit Corporations

In 2013, Delaware, the leader in U.S. corporate law, entered the social enterprise law scene with its own statutory innovation: the public benefit corporation ("PBC"). B Lab places Delaware's PBC statute under the benefit corporation umbrella, but the Delaware statute differs from the Model in a number of ways. Colorado and Minnesota have already adopted large parts of Delaware's statute, and other states are considering using portions of or all of Delaware's framework. The Colorado statute largely followed the Delaware PBC law, but Colorado has reporting requirements that more closely follow the Model (Lidstone 2014). The Minnesota law allows the formation of two types of entities under its PBC law: general benefit corporations and specific benefit corporations (Walker 2014).

The Delaware statute is more permissive than the benefit corporation statute in most areas, but has more mandatory provisions in the corporate purpose area than either the FPC or SPC statute. According to the Delaware PBC statute, the PBC "is a for-profit corporation . . . intended to produce a public benefit or public benefits and to operate in a responsible and sustainable manner."[7] The statute also requires PBCs to choose a specific purpose and to "manage or direct the business and affairs of the public benefit corporation in a manner that *balances* [1] the pecuniary interests of the stockholders, [2] the best interests of those materially affected by the corporation's conduct, and [3] the specific public benefit or public benefits identified in its certificate of incorporation."[8] The Delaware law only requires a benefit report every two years, instead of the annual requirement under the Model benefit corporation law, and the Delaware PBC law does not require the report to be publicly posted. Further, the Delaware law allows, but does not require, appointment of a Benefit Director or use of a third-party standard. In short, Delaware's PBC law mostly moves the Model's benefit corporation framework toward increased private ordering, enabling entrepreneurs to make a wider range of choices for their businesses.

The PBC law is recent, so relatively little legal scholarship has been published on this specific entity type as of the publication of this chapter. The articles that have been written, some of which are only in draft form, have largely praised the PBC form as an improvement on most of the existing social enterprise laws (Callison 2013, Murray 2014). The same articles, however, have noted various issues with the PBC law, including continued lack of clarity for directors and the seeming lack of effective enforcement mechanisms.

3. ITERATIONS AND INNOVATIONS IN SOCIAL ENTERPRISE LAW

As Section 2 demonstrates, states have passed a variety of social enterprise statutes and social enterprise law has drawn a number of critiques in the literature. Social enterprise law has evolved over time, sometimes due to the passage of a statute that creates a new

---

[7] DEL. CODE ANN tit. 8, § 362(a).
[8] *Id.* at § 365(a) (emphasis added).

entity type and sometimes due to changes within statutes providing for the same entity type. The L3C statutes are very thin and have few requirements, but the L3C statutes do clearly state that the common good must be the primary purpose. The benefit corporation statutes, along with the FPC, SPC, and PBC statutes, are less clear on the priorities of the entities than the L3C, but add significant additional detail in other areas through the statutory requirements described below.

Defining entity purpose has been at the heart of many of the social enterprise statutes. For L3C statutes, the law is clear that the "charitable or education purposes" must dominate the "production of income." Subsequent statutes have defined entity purpose, but most have not clearly explained priorities and how the interests of shareholders and other stakeholders should be prioritized. For example, the Model Benefit Corporation Legislation and most states that follow the Model require pursuit of a "general public benefit purpose."[9] Shareholders are included among the stakeholders that directors of benefit corporations must consider, but no prioritization among stakeholders is provided in the Model. The FPC and SPC statutes address what Bill Callison calls the illiberalism problem, created by the broad, mandatory "general public benefit purpose," by the FPC's and SPC's provision of more flexibility in the definition of entity purpose (Callison 2013). The FPC and SPC statutes allow the entity's focus to be on one or more specific stakeholders. The PBC stakes out middle ground by requiring both a specific public benefit purpose and a more general public purpose. The FPC, SPC, and PBC statutes, however, do not clearly addresses the issue of prioritization among shareholders and other stakeholders.

L3C statutes do not require use of a third-party standard in measuring the social impact of an entity. Benefit corporation statutes, mostly passed after the L3C statutes, do require use of a third-party standard, while Delaware's PBC statute expressly allows, but does not require, use of a third-party standard. Colorado's PBC statute follows the Model in requiring a third-party standard, while the FPC and SPC statutes do not require entities to use a third-party standard to measure social impact.

The L3C statutes do not expressly require any social reporting. The Model and most state benefit corporation statutes require annual benefit reports that must be posted on a public portion of the firm's website. A few of the benefit corporation statutes, namely Massachusetts, Nevada and New Jersey, create express penalties for failing to provide benefit reports. For example, in New Jersey, if an annual benefit report is not filed for two years, that benefit corporation will lose its benefit corporation status. Most of the state benefit corporation statutes, however, have no express enforcement mechanism related to social reporting. The FPC statute requires both annual and special reports. The Delaware PBC statute requires only biennial reports and the report only has to be shared with shareholders and not the general public, unless the PBC decides to require public disclosure. A few states, including Arkansas, Massachusetts, New Jersey, Pennsylvania, and South Carolina, require filing the annual benefit corporation report with the state.

Neither the L3C statutes nor the Model Benefit Corporation Legislation address dissenters' rights for shareholders opposing the transition to or from social enterprise status. California's benefit corporation and FPC statutes were the first to expressly

---

[9] MODEL BENEFIT CORP. LEGIS. § 102.

address and require dissenters' rights. Colorado, Delaware, Massachusetts, Nevada, and South Carolina addressed dissenters' rights in their later adopted social enterprise statutes, but those statutes only expressly provide dissenters' rights when adopting benefit corporation status, not when terminating benefit corporation status. Virginia addresses the issue of potentially unwanted entity conversion by requiring 100 percent shareholder approval for a traditional for-profit corporation to adopt benefit corporation status, instead of the typical two-thirds shareholder vote; Delaware currently requires 90 percent.

The Model and most benefit corporation state statutes require acknowledgment that the firm is a benefit corporation in the articles of incorporation. L3C statutes require that the firm name include the abbreviation L3C. California (FPC), Colorado (PBC), Delaware (PBC), Louisiana (BC), and Washington (SPC) also require the entity type in the firm name. Most benefit corporation statutes do not require inclusion of the entity type in the firm name, due to a fear that requiring a name change will be a barrier for conversion to the benefit corporation form.

As the reader can see, the state laboratories have been at work. With the assistance of proponents like B Lab, the states have created various iterations of the social enterprise statutes and entirely new social enterprise entity types. This evolution is likely to continue with over a dozen states actively considering social enterprise statutes. This experimentation by the states, allowed by federalism, is part of what Professor Roberta Romano calls "the genius of American corporate law" (Romano 1993). The evolution of social enterprise laws may be the most significant business law product of the state laboratories in the past decade. Professors Erin O'Hara and Larry Ribstein remind us in their book *The Law Market* that firms are free to shop for these new laws (2009).

Sections 2 and 3 have described "what" has come into being and what has changed in social enterprise law. Sections 4 and 5 will attempt to describe "why" the evolution of social enterprise law occurred and "how" states may proceed in the future.

4. JURISDICTIONAL COMPETITION?

Jurisdictional competition for corporation charters has been heavily analyzed and hotly debated in the literature. In 1974, William Cary, then a law professor at Columbia University, wrote a seminal article in the *Yale Law Journal* where he argued that Delaware corporate law was leading a "race to the bottom." In basic terms, the race to the bottom theory posits states competing for charters have enacted management-friendly enabling statutes and "have watered the rights of shareholders vis-à-vis management down to a thin gruel" (Cary 1974). Professor Cary's seminal article has been cited over 1,000 times and a popular legal academic blog even bears the title "The Race to the Bottom."

Others, including Judge Ralph Winter of the Second Circuit and Professor Roberta Romano of Yale Law School, have argued that Delaware has led a "race to the top" (Winter 1977, 1982, 1989, Romano 1987, 1993). Proponents of the "race to the top" theory argue that investors will prefer firms that do not excessively favor management and that competition for charters creates incentives to construct the optimal corporate code. Over time, the choice regarding where to incorporate has essentially boiled down to two potential states: Delaware and the home state of the firm (Daines 2002). As explained by Professor Daines, "[f]ederalism has thus resulted in a series of local markets with one national producer, rather than a nationwide "race to the top/bottom" (*id.*). Professor Romano mentioned Delaware's "reputation for responsiveness to corporate concerns . . . . comprehensive body of case law, judicial expertise in corporation law, and administrative expertise" as reasons for Delaware's preeminence (Romano 1993).

Professor Ehud Kamar has argued that the indeterminacy of Delaware's corporate law prevents other states from benefiting from Delaware's learning and network externalities and increases Delaware's market power (Kamar 1998). Professor Kamar and Professor Marcel Kahan have stated that Delaware uses its significant market power to increase its profits through price discrimination (Kahan & Kamar 2001). Professor Moshen Manesh has claimed that Delaware does not have the same market power with LLCs because of, *inter alia*, the contractibility and reduction of legal indeterminacy in LLC law (Manesh 2011). Professors Bruce Kobayashi and Larry Ribstein concluded that Delaware has won the competition for LLCs for many of the same reasons Delaware has won the competition for corporate charters, and that most other states seem more interested in retaining local LLCs than fighting for LLCs from outside their state (Kobayashi & Ribstein 2011).

Benefit corporation statutes provide even more room for judicial intervention as they currently mandate a plethora of interests that directors of benefit corporations must consider. As mentioned above, the benefit corporation must serve a general public benefit purpose, defined as: "[a] material positive impact on society and the environment, taken as a whole, assessed against a third-party standard, from the business and operations of a benefit corporation."[10] Almost each word in this key definition could use judicial interpretation. Further, benefit corporation statutes do not allow contracting around or out of the "general public benefit purpose" which takes the issue out of the hands of private parties and leaves significant questions for the courts to answer (Callison 2012, Murray 2012).

The indeterminacy of benefit corporations allows for at least the possibility of significant price discrimination, if benefit corporations become a more popular vehicle in the future and if at least one state can differentiate its product sufficiently. The best data to date suggests that there is currently very little at stake for states in the social enterprise area with only approximately 1,100 L3Cs and 1,000 benefit corporations having been formed as of late 2014 (Cooney et. al. 2014). This number is insignificant in the face of almost six million corporations and over three million partnerships currently in existence.[11] The interest in social enterprises would have to increase exponentially for any state to make considerable revenue off of social enterprise franchise fees. States like Louisiana, New Jersey, and South Carolina have been stuck at single-digit benefit corporations for well over 12 months. Washington D.C.'s first and only benefit corporation was formed with the assistance of the Georgetown Law Center Social Enterprise and Nonprofit Clinic. Professor Eric Talley of UC Berkeley School of Law found that only 60 benefit corporations and 15 FPCs were formed in the first eight months of the California laws being enacted (Talley 2012). Only 5 percent of the entities formed were headquartered outside of California, suggesting that virtually no revenue was brought in from companies

---

[10] MODEL BENEFIT CORP. LEGIS. § 102.
[11] U.S. CENSUS DEPARTMENT, 2012 STATISTICAL ABSTRACT 491 (2012) (based on 2008 federal tax filings).

outside of the state (*id.*). Currently, there does not appear to be vigorous competition for out-of-state social enterprises because so few exist, making the potential financial rewards for states negligible.

5. JURISDICTIONAL POSITIONING AND INTEREST GROUPS

If the financial rewards related to social enterprises are currently so small, why are states passing social enterprise laws? The two most logical explanations are jurisdictional positioning and the interplay of the interest groups involved.

Jurisdictional Positioning

Some of the states passing social enterprise laws may be positioning themselves so that they have the legal framework in place if social enterprise, and the related phenomenon of "impact investing," become more popular. Impact investing and Socially Responsible Investing (SRI) are both terms that are being used with increasing frequency in the investment community. Between the two terms, SRI is usually the more inclusive term and can even mean merely avoiding certain "sin stocks" in an investment fund. Other SRI measures include investing in companies with above-average environmental, social, and corporate governance ("ESG") practices or investing in companies that focus on certain issues (such as human rights issues or climate change). SRI in equity investments in the United States has reportedly grown from less than $1 trillion in 1995 to nearly $4 trillion in 2012.[12] "Impact investing" is generally treated as a more narrow term, and "recognizes that investments can pursue financial returns while also intentionally addressing social and environmental challenges" (Bugg-Levine and Emerson 2011). The Global Impact Investor Network (GIIN) states that "[i]mpact investments are investments made into companies, organizations, and funds with the intention to generate measurable social and financial return" (Saltuk 2013). While there is not agreement on the amount of capital designated for "impact investments," an admittedly incomplete J.P. Morgan survey identified $8 billion in dedicated funds in 2012 (*id.*).

As previously mentioned, Delaware has long dominated the corporate law market. However, it has not always been the leader in corporate law. New Jersey was the leading state for incorporations as early as 1881, and passed what many consider the first modern, liberal corporate law statute in 1896; a number of states, including Delaware, followed New Jersey's lead. In 1913, New Jersey passed the so-called seven sisters law that resulted in a tightening of its corporate law. Delaware did not amend its corporate law, had been chipping away at New Jersey's lead through price competition, and took the lead from New Jersey in the early 1900s (Yablon 2007).

Currently, Delaware enjoys the ability to price discriminate and charge large firms a premium for incorporation, a fee of up to $180,000 per year. As mentioned above, some modern scholars attribute this ability to engage in price discrimination, *inter*

---

[12] US SIF—The Forum for Sustainable and Responsible Investment, *Growth of Sustainable and Responsible Investing* 1995 to 2012 http://www.ussif.org/photogallery/SRI1995to2012.jpg.

alia, to the indeterminacy of Delaware's law. Looking forward, states may be anxious to capture the potentially significant revenue from social enterprise formation. For the social enterprises built on a corporate base (BC, SPC, PBC, FPC), the law is likely to be indeterminate and the judicial interpretation questions may be even more complex because of all the stakeholders that must be considered or balanced under social enterprise law. The social enterprises built on the LLC base (L3C and BLLC) lean toward increased contractibility where Professor Manesh believes the market power will not be as strong. In those areas, price may be more important. That said, initially in the competition for corporate charters, Delaware competed with New Jersey on price, and Delaware was later, after it was more established as the corporate leader, able to engage in price discrimination. After the passage of time, a state may solidify its leadership in the social enterprise area and be able to price discriminate successfully, as Delaware has in the traditional corporate arena. While there might not be much competition currently, states may wish to position themselves to win the race because being an early mover in jurisdictional competition can be important due to migration costs associated with firms switching their state of incorporation and the time generally required for the emergence of significant network and learning effects (Romano 1985, Macey & Miller 1987).

Interest Group Theory

Nearly 30 years ago, Professors Jonathan Macey and Geoffrey Miller applied an interest group theory borrowed from economists George Stigler and Sam Peltzman to describe corporate law development. Macey and Miller discussed the interests of and the rent-seeking provisions extracted by corporate lawyers, corporate managers and government officials. This interest group theory also works well to explain the widespread adoption and development of social enterprise law. The various interest groups involved in the passage of social enterprise laws have much to gain and little to lose in the passing of these laws.

For the state politicians, the reasons to support the social enterprise laws are readily apparent. Social business is popular; Wall Street and traditional for-profit corporations are not. Social enterprise laws can even appeal to the pro-market, pro-Wall Street politicians, because these laws purport to embrace freedom, do not force anyone to incorporate under the laws, and expressly deny altering the existing corporate laws. The social enterprise laws allow the market to operate. The statutes appear to appeal to both the social justice advocates on the left and to the free market proponents on the right (Westaway 2012). Research has shown that a "larger 'green' workforce exerts a mildly positive influence on Benefit Corporation legislation passage," suggesting that environmentally friendly states are especially interested in social enterprise law (Rawhouser, et. al. 2014). Additionally, social enterprise laws have been promoted as no cost or low cost to states. Currently, there are no state-level tax breaks for social enterprises, and the adoption of social enterprise laws do not even require much in the way of necessary changes at the secretary of state's office, as the social enterprises are often simply included in the LLC or corporation framework. Given the low cost of social enterprise laws, the benefits do not have to be large to justify passage of these laws from a politician's perspective. States may attract some businesses to the state and may gain some revenue, with negligible costs, or so the social enterprise pitch goes.

Another interest group, corporate managers, have been able to limit their liability in the benefit corporation and PBC statutes. Those laws limit standing of those who can bring a claim and make building a successful claim extremely difficult. External stakeholders are not given standing to sue even though the statutes require consideration of their interests. The Model Benefit Corporation Legislation, upon which most state benefit corporation statutes are based, provides that directors are not personally liable for monetary damages "for failure of the benefit corporation to pursue or create general public benefit or specific public benefit."[13] Delaware's PBC statute makes clear that directors will not be liable for any decision that "is both informed and disinterested and not such than no person of ordinary, sound judgment would approve."[14] In addition to the liability protection, many corporate managers see the social enterprise entity types as a way to brand their business and increase goodwill.

For lawyers and business people looking for a new way to pitch their products and services, or a new area in which to become expert, social enterprise is appealing. B Lab appears to have exerted significant effort to recruit supportive professionals. Most of the professionals hope to gain some financial rewards from their newfound expertise in the social enterprise law. Many of the professionals are already marketing their expertise and are hoping to benefit from the marketing.

Academics and some sophisticated lawyers have been largely critical of the social enterprise law. Politicians, however, seem to be catering to much broader constituencies than academics and a subset of lawyers. While state bar associations and academics have been consulted prior to the passage of some social enterprise laws, they have been largely ineffective in stopping the benefit corporation statutes from being passed. Critics have, however, contributed to the evolution of the social enterprise laws. Also, academics such as Daniel Kleinberger and Carter Bishop, along with practitioner Bill Callison, played a large role in the current stalling and decline of the L3C form. B Lab has done a better job than the L3C leaders in making an effort to include academics and high-level legal practitioners in the conversations around the legislation, though B Lab has been criticized as well for being unwilling to modify certain controversial provisions (Callison 2013). As Macey and Miller recognize, lawyers often act as the gatekeepers of corporate law, but frequently, in the social enterprise context, bar association committees are being overruled or pressured into approving the laws by other interest groups.

Potential Future Jurisdictional Competition for Social Enterprises

States interested in competing for social enterprises can learn from the vast legal academic literature on state competition for traditional corporate charters. Academics have floated various theories for Delaware's success in attracting corporate charters. Some attribute Delaware's success to its indeterminate case law and expert judiciary (Kamar 1998). Others credit, at least in part, Delaware's appropriately responsive legislature, its admired

---

[13] MODEL BENEFIT CORP. LEGIS. §§ 102, 201(a)–(b) (2014).
[14] *Id.* § 365(b); Delaware Public Benefit Corporations: FAQs (on file with author).

Chancery Court, and its administrative expertise (Romano 1993). Commentators point to Delaware's credible commitment to maintaining its focus on meeting the legal needs of corporations incorporated in the state due to Delaware's relative reliance on franchise taxes and Delaware's past, significant investment in its legal infrastructure (Romano 1993, Simmons 2008). Still others point to Delaware's small size, limited alternative economic options, and prime location, situated between the financial capital (New York City) and the political capital (Washington D.C.) of the United States (Bruner 2013). Delaware was not, and often is not, the first mover in the corporate law area, but Delaware generally does act early and gain some early-mover advantages. Other commentators mention the networking and learning effects that have accumulated over time. As mentioned earlier, some have argued that jurisdictional competition has been a race to the bottom, others a race to the top, but history seems to suggest that Delaware provides the appropriate balance between meeting shareholder needs and the needs of management. Focusing on only shareholder rights (North Dakota) or only management's desires (West Virginia, South Dakota, and Nevada) has not allowed states to overtake Delaware (Yablon 2007, Barzuza 2012).

Delaware's success is likely a combination of the factors mentioned above, and to the extent the above are replicable, states could take cues from Delaware in attempting to carve out a niche in social enterprise law. States could learn from the Delaware experience with traditional business forms and may attract social enterprises through: (1) being an early mover (perhaps, leading to learning and network effects); (2) passing balanced statutes; (3) appointing judges with subject matter expertise; (4) providing a responsive legislature; (5) making a credible commitment to continue the state's concern for the firms by investing in legal and social enterprise infrastructure; (6) touting any geographic proximity to major business centers; and (7) engaging with the corporate bar and legal academy. Smaller states may have more incentive to pursue social enterprise, due to the proportional returns, but states like Delaware, New York, California, Nevada, and Maryland, which already have significant infrastructure built for related entity forms, may have a sizeable lead on other states. In fact, early data on the benefit corporation formation, shows those five states with significant infrastructure as leading in the number of benefit corporations formed, though it is still much too early to declare a clear winner. In any event, the state laboratories, prompted by social enterprise proponents like Bob Lang and B Lab, have produced a variety of social enterprise laws, and the evolution of these forms will be interesting to watch over coming years.

CONCLUSION

Since 2008 we have seen a proliferation of social enterprise forms in the United States. This chapter has described some of the variations in forms and within forms. Given the indeterminacy of benefit corporation law, this chapter has posited that if social enterprises become more popular, a dominant state could eventually engage in significant price discrimination and collect significant revenue. Currently, only a relatively small number of social enterprises have been formed and thus the financial stakes are quite low. This chapter has suggested that jurisdictional positioning and interest group theory, rather than current jurisdictional competition, explain why states are passing social enterprise statutes. If social enterprise forms become more widely used in future years, states may choose to compete more vigorously in the social enterprise area. This chapter has suggested that interested states could learn from the Delaware experience with traditional corporations in any attempt by those states to attract social enterprises.

ACKNOWLEDGMENT

With permission of the publisher and editors, this chapter will be published, with significant additions and modifications, in the *Maryland Law Review* under the title *Social Enterprise Law Market*.

REFERENCES

ABA Business Law Section, Corporate Laws Committee, *Benefit Corporation White Paper*, 68 BUS. LAW. 1083 (2013).

Barzuza, Michal, *Market Segmentation: The Rise of Nevada as a Liability-Free Jurisdiction*, 98 VA. L. REV. 935 (2012).

Bishop, Carter G., *The Low-Profit LLC (L3C): Program Related Investment by Proxy or Perversion?*, 63 ARK. L. REV. 243 (2010).

Brakman Reiser, Dana, *Benefit Corporations—A Sustainable Form of Organization?*, 46 WAKE FOREST L. REV. 591 (2011).

Brakman Reiser, Dana, *The Next Big Thing: Flexible Purpose Corporations*, 2 AM. U. BUS. L. REV. 55 (2012).

Brakman Reiser, Dana and Steven A. Dean, *Hunting Stag with FLY Paper: A Hybrid Financial Instrument for Social Enterprise*, 54 B.C. L. REV. 1495 (2013).

Brewer, Cassady V., *Seven Ways to Strengthen and Improve the L3C*, 25 REGENT U. L. REV. 329 (2012).

Brewer, Cassady V., *Hybrid Business Entities in 2014*, SOCENTLAW.COM, January 6, 2014, http://socentlaw.com/2014/01/hybrid-business-entities-in-2014/.

Bruner, Christopher M., *Market-Dominant Small Jurisdictions in a Globalizing Financial World*, Washington & Lee Legal Studies Paper No. 2013-19, October 21, 2013, http://papers.ssrn.com/sol3/papers.cfm?abstract_id=2343111.

Bugg-Levine, Antony & Jed Emerson, Impact Investing: Transforming How We Make Money While Making a Difference (2011).

Callison, J. William, *Putting New Sheets on a Procrustean Bed: How Benefit Corporations Address Fiduciary Duties, the Dangers Created, and Suggestions for Change*, 2 AM. U. BUS. L. REV. 85 (2012).

Callison, J. William, *Benefit Corporations, Innovation, and Statutory Design*, 26 REGENT U. L. REV 143 (2013).

Callison, J. William & Allan W. Vestal, *The L3C Illusion: Why Low-Profit Limited Liability Companies Will Not Stimulate Socially Optimal Private Foundation Investment in Entrepreneurial Ventures*, 35 VT. L. REV. 273 (2010).

Cary, William L., *Federalism and Corporate Law: Reflections upon Delaware*, 83 YALE L. J. 663 (1974).

Chernoff, David S., *L3Cs: Less There than Meets the Eye*, TAX'N EXEMPTS, May–June 2010.

Clark, Jr., William H. & Elizabeth K. Babson, *How Benefit Corporations Are Redefining the Purpose of Business Corporations*, 38 WM. MITCHELL L. REV. 817 (2012).

Clark, Jr., William H. & Larry Vranka, *The Need and Rationale for the Benefit Corporation: Why It Is the Legal Form that Best Addresses the Needs of Social Entrepreneurs, Investors, and, Ultimately, the Public*, January 18, 2013, http://benefitcorp.net/storage/documents/Benecit_Corporation_White_Paper_1_18_2013.pdf.

Clarke, Christen, *California's Flexible Purpose Corporation: A Step Forward, A Step Back, or No Step at All*, 5 BUS., ENTREPRENEURSHIP, & L. 301 (2012).

Cooney, Kate, Justin Koushyar, Matthew Lee & Haskell Murray, *Benefit Corporation and L3C Adoption, A Survey*, STANFORD SOCIAL INNOVATION REVIEW, December 5, 2014, http://www.ssireview.org/blog/entry/benefit_corporation_and_l3c_adoption_a_survey.

Daines, Robert, *The Incorporation Choices of IPO Firms*, 77 N.Y.U. L. REV. 1559 (2002).

Groshoff, David, *Contrepreneurship? Examining Social Enterprise Legislation's Feel-Good Governance Giveaways*, 16 U. PA. J. BUS. L. 233 (2013).

Hopkins, Jamie, *Low-Profit Limited Liability Companies: High-Risk Tax Fad or Legitimate Social Investment Planning Opportunity?*, 2014 CARDOZO L. REV. DE NOVO 35 (2014).

interSector Partners, *Here's the Latest L3C Tally*, L3C, March 3, 2014, http://www.intersectorl3c.com/l3c_tally.html.

Johnson, Lyman, *Pluralism in Corporate Form: Corporate Law and Benefit Corps.*, 25 REGENT U. L. REV. 269 (2013).

Kahan, Marcel & Ehud Kamar, *Price Discrimination in the Market for Corporate Law*, 86 CORNELL L. REV. 1205 (2001).

Kamar, Ehud, *A Regulatory Competition Theory of Indeterminacy in Corporate Law*, 98 COLUM. L. REV. 1908 (1998).

Kleinberger, Daniel S., *A Myth Deconstructed: The "Emperor's New Clothes" on the Low-Profit Limited Liability Company*, 35 DEL. J. CORP. L. 879 (2010).

Kobayashi, Bruce H. & Larry E. Ribstein, *Delaware for Small Fry: Jurisdictional Competition for Limited Liability Companies*, 2011 U. ILL. L. REV. 91.

Lang, Robert & Elizabeth Carrott Minnigh, *The L3C, History, Basic Construct, and Legal Framework*, 35 VT. L. REV. 15 (2010).

Lidstone, Herrick K., *The Long and Winding Road to Public Benefit Corporations in Colorado*, 43 COLO. LAW. 39 (2014), http://papers.ssrn.com/sol3/papers.cfm?abstract_id=2266654.

Loewenstein, Mark J., *Benefit Corporations: A Challenge in Corporate Governance*, 68 BUS. LAW. 1007 (2013).

Macey, Jonathan R. & Geoffrey P. Miller, *Toward an Interest-Group Theory of Delaware Corporate Law*, 65 TEX. L. REV. 469 (1987).

Manesh, Mohsen, *Delaware and the Market for LLC Law: A Theory of Contractibility and Legal Indeterminacy*, 52 B.C. L. Rev. 189 (2011).

Murray, J. Haskell, *Choose Your Own Master: Social Enterprise, Certifications and Benefit Corporation Statutes*, 2 AM. U. BUS. L. REV. 1 (2012).

Murray, J. Haskell, *Defending Patagonia: Mergers & Acquisitions with Benefit Corporations*, 9 HASTINGS BUS. L. J. 485 (2013).

Murray, J. Haskell, *Social Enterprise Innovation: Delaware's Public Benefit Corporation Law*, 4 HARV. BUS. L. REV. 345 (2014).

Murray, J. Haskell & Edward I. Hwang, *Purpose with Profit: Governance, Enforcement, Capital-Raising and Capital-Locking*, 66 U. MIAMI L. REV. 1 (2011).

O'Hara, Erin A. & Larry E. Ribstein, The Law Market (2009).

Peltzman, Sam, *Towards a More General Theory of Regulation*, 19 J. LAW & ECON. 211 (1976).

Plerhoples, Alicia E., *Can an Old Dog Learn New Tricks?: Applying Traditional Corporate Law Principles to New Social Enterprise Legislation*, 13 TRANSACTIONS: TENN. J. BUS. L. 221 (2012).

Rawhouser, Hans, Michael Cummings, and Andrew Crane, *The Diffusion of New Legal Forms for Social Hybrids*, March 31, 2014 (unpublished manuscript, on file with author).

Rodrigues, Usha, *Entity and Identity*, 60 EMORY L.J. 1257 (2011).

Romano, Roberta, *Law as a Product: Some Pieces of the Incorporation Puzzle*, 1 J.L. ECON. & ORG. 225 (1985).

Romano, Roberta, *The State Competition Debate in Corporate Law*, 8 CARDOZO L. REV. 709 (1987).

Romano, Roberta, The Genius of American Corporate Law (1993).

Saltuk, Yasemin, *Perspectives on Progress: The Impact Investor Survey*, J.P. MORGAN SOCIAL FINANCE RESEARCH LIBRARY, http://www.jpmorganchase.com/corporate/socialfinance/document/207350_JPM_Perspectives_on_Progress_2013-01-07_1018749_ada.pdf (2013).

Simmons, Omari Scott, *Branding the Small Wonder: Delaware's Dominance and the Market for Corporate Law*, 42 U. RICH. L. REV. 1129 (2008).

Stigler, George J., *The Theory of Economic Regulation*, 2 BELL J. ECON. & MGMT. SCI. 3 (1971).

Strine, Jr., Leo E., *Our Continuing Struggle with the Idea That For-Profit Corporations Seek Profit*, 47 WAKE FOREST L. REV. 135 (2012).

Talley, Eric L., *Corporate Form and Social Entrepreneurship: A Status Report from California (and Beyond)*, September 10, 2012, http://papers.ssrn.com/sol3/papers.cfm?abstract_id=2144567.

Walker, Deborah J., *Please Welcome the Minnesota Public Benefit Corporation*, http://papers.ssrn.com/sol3/papers.cfm?abstract_id=2408241 (2014).

Westaway, Kyle, *Something Republicans and Democrats Can Agree On: Social Entrepreneurship*, STANFORD SOCIAL INNOVATION REVIEW, April 17, 2012.

Winter, Jr., Ralph K., *State Law, Shareholder Protection, and the Theory of the Corporation*, 6 J. LEGAL STUD. 251 (1977).

Winter, Jr., Ralph K., *Private Goals and Competition Among State Legal Systems*, 6 HARV. J. L. & PUB. POL'Y 127 (1982).
Winter, Jr., Ralph K., *The "Race for the Top" Revisited: A Comment on Eisenberg*, 89 COLUM. L. REV. 1526 (1989).
Wood, Arthur, *New Legal Structures to Address the Social Capital Famine*, 35 VT. L. REV. 45 (2010).
Yablon, Charles M., *The Historical Race Competition for Corporate Charters and the Rise and Decline of New Jersey: 1880–1910*, 32 J. CORP. L. 323 (2007).
Yockey, Joseph W., *Does Social Enterprise Law Matter?*, 66 ALA L. REV. 767 (2015).

16. Business trusts
Peter B. Oh

1. INTRODUCTION

Virtually ignored by academics, the business trust arguably is the most prominent organizational form used today. This claim is disputable essentially only insofar that no one knows the actual composition, scale, and volume of trusts used for commercial purposes.[1] Yet no one doubts that trusts are the dominant form for massive employee pensions and mutual funds, as well as for a myriad of asset securitization and structured finance transactions.[2]

The multi-trillion dollar question is why.[3] To arrive at an answer, one first must delve into the historical origin and growth of the business trust. Grasping this in turn enables one to comprehend and evaluate the diverse modern permutations of this organizational form, which has been described as a "mystery" with a "secret life."[4] Demystifying the business trust is difficult, because it has the ability to assume many different forms, bear many labels, and perform many functions. This versatility resists the conventional approach of using a template of features (e.g., formation, limited liability, management structure, transferability) to compare the business trust to other types of organizational forms. Instead, the common functions of the business trust are delineated to evince some of its objective merits and, incidentally, its comparative advantages over other forms.

---

[1] *See, e.g.*, Robert Flannigan, *Business Applications of the Express Trust*, 36 ALTA. L. REV. 630, 630 (1998) ("The extent to which the trust is employed to serve commercial purposes is unknown and probably unknowable."). Part of the problem is a lack of reliable data, as there is no registration requirement for trusts. *See, e.g.*, John H. Langbein, *The Secret Life of the Trust: The Trust as an Instrument of Commerce*, 107 YALE L.J. 165, 178 (1997) ("The data available on the asset values of the various forms of trust has many shortcomings, but the drift is unmistakable. . . . [T]he data leave[ ] me on solid ground asserting . . . that well above 90% of the wealth in trust in the United States is held in commercial as opposed to personal trusts."). This problem is compounded by the "considerable conceptual difficulty in distinguishing between commercial and non-commercial activities," Flannigan, *supra*, at 631, as well as between business and commercial activities, Steven L. Schwarcz, *Commercial Trusts as Business Organizations: Unraveling the Mystery*, 58 BUS. LAW. 559, 562 n.18 (2003).

[2] *See, e.g.*, Robert H. Sitkoff, *Trust as "Uncorporation": A Research Agenda*, 2005 U. ILL. L. REV. 31, 38.

[3] *See, e.g.*, Langbein, *supra* note 1, at 168–78 (estimating conservatively $11.6 trillion in commercial trusts almost two decades ago).

[4] *See supra* note 1.

2. THE NASCENT BUSINESS TRUST

From Britain to Massachusetts

The business trust arose as a subversive alternate to the British company. In response to numerous speculative commercial ventures gone awry, Parliament enacted the Bubble Act of 1720, requiring all corporate forms with transferable stock to obtain formal permission to do business "either by act of Parliament, or by a charter from the Crown,"[5] which thereby "drastically limited the development of business corporations in Britain."[6] But these corporations were not the target of the Bubble Act; rather, the legislation's aim was to eliminate the slew of voluntary associations that had emerged as a way to circumvent the charter requirement. And after Parliament repealed the Bubble Act in 1825, these voluntary associations re-flourished. By the 1860s British investors began to flock to what became known as the investment trust, "the earliest of [which] were unincorporated, of a voluntary nature, and of a fiduciary character, and hence were called trusts in accordance with the custom of that time."[7] Although registration later was required by the Companies Acts, these voluntary associations were permitted to retain their form as a trust.[8]

Across the Atlantic business trusts already had begun to germinate in a concurrent, similar manner. Decades before the Companies Acts, various American state legislatures had enacted their own general incorporation statutes; and all of these statutes prohibited use of the corporate form for real estate, an apparent hold-over from medieval English mortmain statutes.[9] To circumvent this prohibition, real property owners formed business trusts, which also were not subject to any of the capital limits or regulatory disclosure requirements applicable to corporations.[10]

The incubator for these alternate corporate forms was Massachusetts. Although it was the first state to enact a general incorporation statute in 1809, Massachusetts was one of the last to permit incorporation without legislative sanction.[11] And, like other states, Massachusetts prohibited corporations from dealing in real estate,[12] which in turn spawned the use of business trusts. But what set Massachusetts apart was a series of early court decisions ruling that real estate business ventures would be treated as trusts, and not as corporations or partnerships, in matters of tax[13] and limited

---

[5] 6 Geo. I c. 18 (1720).
[6] Ronald E. Seavoy, *The Public Service Origins of the American Business Corporation*, 52 BUS. HIST. REV. 30, 32 (1978).
[7] THEODORE J. GRAYSON, INVESTMENT TRUSTS, THEIR ORIGIN, DEVELOPMENT AND OPERATION 1–2 (1928).
[8] *See* The Companies Acts, 25 & 26 Vict. ch. 89, § 180 (1862).
[9] *See* Sheldon A. Jones et al., *The Massachusetts Business Trust and Registered Investment Companies*, 13 DEL. J. CORP. L. 421, 426 (1988) (citing *Report of the Massachusetts Tax Commissioner on Voluntary Associations*, Mass. House Rep. No. 1646, at 2 (1912)).
[10] *Cf.* Mass. Pub. Stat. tit. XV, ch. 106, § 14 (1882).
[11] *See, e.g.*, E. Merrick Dodd, Jr., *Statutory Developments in Business Corporation Law*, 50 HARV. L. REV. 27, 31 (1936).
[12] *Id.*
[13] *See, e.g.*, Williams v. Inhabitants of Milton, 102 N.E. 355 (Mass. 1913); *see also* Wheeler A. Rosenbalm, Comment, *The Massachusetts Trust*, 31 TENN. L. REV. 471, 472–76 (1964).

liability.[14] By recognizing these ventures as a distinct commercial entity, Massachusetts courts "provide[d] a hospitable environment for the business trust"[15] whose jurisdictional superiority was so manifest that these entities became known as "Massachusetts Trusts."[16]

Numerous advantages set this commercial form apart from its rivals. As with other jurisdictions, business trusts in Massachusetts were not subject to any minimum or maximum capital limits, nor were they subject to the annual financial disclosure requirements that applied to corporations.[17] But equally important, investors held only a beneficial interest within, and a not a share of, a Massachusetts Trust, and thus had "no right to manage it by themselves nor to instruct the trustees how to manage it for them";[18] to obtain, much less exercise, any control over the trustees would result in the entity being treated as a general partnership, and not a Massachusetts Trust.[19] On the other hand, though, Massachusetts business trustees were not afforded limited liability or indemnification protection that corporate directors enjoy;[20] absent an exculpatory clause, Massachusetts business trustees were allowed only an equitable right to reimburse themselves for "obligations incurred for the benefit of the trust."[21]

From Common Law to Statutory Trusts

Until the early 1900s the business trust thrived in the common law.[22] On the one hand, the business trust thus represented an attractive alternative to the myriad of statutory limitations and regulations applicable to early corporations and later also general partnerships.[23] On the other hand, a consequence of being grounded in the law of trusts was that business trusts were not a legal entity, and thus only could sue (or be sued) and transact in the name of the trustee. All of this was compounded by judicial confusion and inconsistency across jurisdictions about how to treat business trusts.[24] And in some

---

[14] *See, e.g.*, Dolben v. Gleason, 198 N.E. 762 (Mass. 1935).
[15] Jones *et al.*, *supra* note 9, at 429.
[16] *See, e.g.*, EDWARD H. WARREN, CORPORATE ADVANTAGES WITHOUT INCORPORATION 328 (1929) ("A business trust is often called a Massachusetts Trust, because such trusts have probably been used in Massachusetts more than in any other one state.").
[17] *See supra* notes 13–14.
[18] Williams, 102 N.E. at 357.
[19] *See, e.g.*, Frost v. Thompson, 106 N.E. 1009 (Mass. 1914). The right to elect trustees initially was among the disqualifying types of control, but later was held not to result in treatment as a partnership. *See* Commissioner of Corporations and Taxation v. City of Springfield, 71 N.E.2d 593 (Mass. 1947).
[20] *See, e.g.*, Dolben v. Gleason, 198 N.E. 762, 763 (Mass. 1935) ("[I]n the absence of a stipulation to the contrary a trustee is personally liable in an action on a contract made by him for the benefit of the trust estate.").
[21] Town of Hull v. Tong, 442 N.E.2d 427, 429 (Mass. 1982).
[22] *See, e.g.*, Sitkoff, *supra* note 2, at 32 ("In the late 1800s and early 1900s, before the corporate form had matured, the common-law business trust . . . was a strong competitor to corporation as a mode of business organization.").
[23] *See* UNIFORM PARTNERSHIP ACT (1914). *See also* WILLIAM C. DUNN, TRUSTS FOR BUSINESS PURPOSES 230–68 (1922).
[24] *See, e.g.*, Tamar Frankel, *The Delaware Business Trust Act Failure as the New Corporate Law*, 23 CARDOZO L. REV. 325, 326 n.4 (2001) (citing Herbert B. Chermside, Jr.,

jurisdictions the business trust even was denounced altogether as an "impermissible evasion of local corporate law."[25]

These developments did not escape the attention of the federal government. In 1939 the Securities and Exchange Commission (SEC) undertook a massive study of business trusts, specifically those used in connection with securities investments, and released a multi-volume report.[26] Although that report did examine trusts with individual investors, as well as Massachusetts Trusts,[27] the SEC was far more interested in the use of structures such as "a pyramided system of investment companies, based upon one company holding a controlling block of stock of other investment companies and noninvestment companies."[28] In direct response to the increasing use of trusts for mutual funds and investment companies Congress implemented the Investment Company Act of 1940.[29]

Waves of state trust statutes then followed during the 1960s and 1980s, including Delaware's contribution in 1988.[30] The reason for this surge in trust regulation is not entirely clear, but one distinct possibility is an apparent consensus among jurisdictions by the late 1950s that "employment of trust in the carrying on of trade or business" was "per se imprudent unless expressly authorized by the trust instrument."[31] Accordingly, state legislatures perhaps decided to take matters into their own hands to eschew any confusion or uncertainty within the common law about whether trusts could be used for business or commercial purposes. Delaware, for instance, reportedly adopted its Act for the "principal purpose of . . . recogniz[ing] the statutory trust as an alternate form of business organization."[32]

Not surprisingly, Delaware crafted a pivotal business trust statute. Interestingly, Delaware's Statutory Trust Act appears in Title 12, "Decedents' Estates and Fiduciary Relations," and not within Title 6, "Commerce and Trade," where all other business

---

Annotation, *Modern Status of the Massachusetts or Business Trust*, 88 A.L.R.3d 704 (1978 & Supp. 2001)).

[25] Sitkoff, *supra* note 2, at 36 (citing Leland S. Duxbury, *Business Trusts and Blue Sky Laws*, 8 MINN. L. REV. 465 (1924)).

[26] *See* I SECURITIES AND EXCHANGE COMMISSION, INVESTMENT TRUSTS AND INVESTMENT COMPANIES, REPORT OF THE SECURITIES AND EXCHANGE COMMISSION PURSUANT TO SECTION 30 OF THE PUBLIC UTILITY HOLDING COMPANY ACT OF 1935 (1939) (hereinafter SEC, INVESTMENT TRUSTS).

[27] *See, e.g., id.* at 29–34.

[28] *Id.* at 100.

[29] *See, e.g.*, IV SEC, INVESTMENT TRUSTS, *supra* note 26, at 383 (describing the 1940 Act as being designed "to eliminate and prevent deficiencies and abuses in these organizations"). For a more detailed examination of the 1940 Act's impact on trusts, see, for example, Thomas S. Harman, *Emerging Alternatives to Mutual Funds: Unit Investment Trusts and Other Fixed Portfolio Investment Vehicles*, 1987 DUKE L.J. 1045; Jay B. Gould & Gerald T. Lins, *Unit Investment Trusts: Structure and Regulation Under the Federal Securities Laws*, 43 BUS. LAW. 1177 (1988).

[30] According to one prominent commentator, there are "perhaps as many as four generations of business trust legislation," with the first being colonial acts such as the Massachusetts statute, followed by those in the 1960s, then "legislation passed in the 1980s but before the Delaware Act," and finally post 1988 enactments. Sitkoff, *supra* note 2, at 36.

[31] *Id.* at 37 (quoting RESTATEMENT (SECOND) OF TRUSTS § 227 cmt. f (1959)).

[32] Wendell Fenton & Eric A. Mazie, *Delaware Statutory Trusts*, in THE DELAWARE LAW OF CORPORATIONS & BUSINESS ORGANIZATIONS § 19.2 (9th ed. 2004 Supp.).

organizations are located; nevertheless, the statute defines a "statutory trust" as "an unincorporated association" that:

> (1) Is created by a governing instrument under which property is or will be held, managed, administered, controlled, invested, reinvested and/or operated, or business or professional activities for profit are carried on or will be carried on, by a trustee or trustees . . . including but not limited to a trust of the type known at common law as a "business trust," or "Massachusetts trust," or a [Real Estate Investment Trust].[33]

And, consistent with its approach to all business organizations, Delaware treats a statutory business trust as a "separate legal entity,"[34] subject to "maximum effect to the principle of freedom of contract."[35] Accordingly, while "the laws of [Delaware] pertaining to trusts are hereby made applicable to statutory trusts,"[36] they still benefit from the same contractarian framework that contributes to the state's durable dominance as the jurisdiction of choice for all other business entities.

Delaware's statute also implemented two significant refinements. First, the statute resolved a persistent common law ambiguity about the partitioning of the business trust's assets from the personal assets of beneficiaries and owners; as the statute now makes clear, beneficial owners are "entitled to the same limitation of personal liability extended to stockholders of private corporations for profit," and no personal liability can be imposed on a trustee unless provided by contract.[37] Second, as is the case for its limited liability companies, Delaware adopted a *laissez faire* conception of trustees' fiduciary duties, in that they "may be expanded or restricted or eliminated by provisions in the governing instrument" beyond the "implied contractual covenant of good faith and fair dealing";[38] accordingly, unlike other jurisdictions, Delaware features a complete opt-out regime as to whether any kind of trust-based duties of care or loyalty exist.[39] In these regards, then, Delaware's statutory business trusts offer some of the same fundamental benefits that the state's most popular business organization forms do, leading some to conclude that, "[i]n theory, any entity that can be formed as a business corporation, an LLC, an LLP, or an LLLP could be formed instead as a statutory business trust."[40]

Currently at least 18 states have some type of business trust statute. And at least 29

---

[33] DEL. CODE ANN. tit. 12 § 3801(g)(1) (2012).
[34] *Id.* at § 3801(g)(2); *see also* I.R.S. Rev. Rul. 2004-86 (ruling that Delaware statutory trusts are a separate entity that "will be classified as a trust for federal tax purposes").
[35] DEL. CODE ANN. tit. 12 § 3825(b) (2012). *See also* Frankel, *supra* note 24, at 326–27 ("[T]his marvelous contract-like organizational form, [with] its liberal contractarian approach and the freedom to . . . take on such characteristics of traditional *inter vivos* trusts, business trusts, corporations, or partnerships . . . may be the greatest advantage of the business trust over alternative forms of business organizations."); Professor Frankel, however, offers some persuasive criticisms that the Delaware act actually fails to deliver fully on these promises. *See generally id.*
[36] DEL. CODE ANN. tit. 12, § 3809 (2012).
[37] *Id.* at § 3803; *see also id.* at § 3817 (providing for trustee indemnification). However, beneficial owners do have a right to bring a derivative action against a trustee, *id.* at § 3816.
[38] *Id.* at § 3806(c).
[39] *See, e.g.*, Sitkoff, *supra* note 2, at 38 ("[T]rust law's more rigorous duties of loyalty and care . . . appear to be incorporated by reference by the modern business trust statutes.").
[40] Henry Hansmann *et al.*, *The New Entities in Historical Perspective*, 2005 U. ILL. L. REV. 5, 14; *see also infra* notes 68–78 and accompanying text.

states have legislation permitting the trust for business or commercial uses,[41] while 47 states have provisions that at least recognize the existence of a statutory trust.[42] The most recent, significant contribution is the Uniform Statutory Trust Entity Act, which was introduced in 2009 and has been adopted by two jurisdictions.[43] Slowly, but surely, the statutory business trust is becoming an established part of the business organizations landscape.

3. THE MODERN BUSINESS TRUST

The business trust is a mercurial entity that resists precise definition. The most "current" definition from the Supreme Court was formulated in 1924,[44] well before states proceeded to enact multiple generations of business trust statutes. But most of these recent statutes do not displace common law trusts; on the contrary, these statutes typically "provide that the common law of trusts applies unless otherwise displaced by a specific statutory provision or the terms of the trust instrument."[45] Moreover, jurisdictions such as Delaware subscribe to an overt contractarian approach, conferring parties with tremendous flexibility in constructing and operating a business trust. All of this suggests that trying to define the business trust may not be necessary to understand it—all we have to do is see it at work.[46]

---

[41] *Cf. id.* at 35–36 ("The existing literature . . . puts the count of states with general business trust legislation anywhere from seventeen to thirty-four. Based on fresh electronic searches, I put the current count at twenty-nine.") (citing sources).

[42] My electronic searches revealed that only the state codes of Indiana, New Mexico, and Vermont lack any reference to the term "statutory trust."

[43] *See* Uniform Law Commission, *Statutory Trust Entity Act*, http://uniformlaws.org/Act.aspx?title=Statutory%20Trust%20Entity%20Act (last visited August 23, 2014) (listing the District of Columbia and Kentucky as having adopted the model act).

[44] In a case concerning the applicability of the Revenue Act of 1916 to three Massachusetts trustees, the court stated:

> The "Massachusetts Trust" is a form of business organization . . . consisting essentially of an arrangement whereby property is conveyed to trustees, in accordance with the terms of an instrument of trust, to be held and managed of such persons as may from time to time be the holders of transferable certificates issued by the trustees showing the shares into which the beneficial interest in the property is divided. These certificates . . . entitle the holders to share ratably in the income of the property, and, upon termination of the trust, in the proceeds. (Hecht v. Malley, 265 U.S. 144, 146 (1924) (Sanford, J.))

This evidently remains the operative definition used by the court. *See* Navarro Sav. Ass'n v. Lee, 446 U.S. 458, 467–68 (1980) ("In *Hecht v. Malley* . . . this Court described the Massachusetts business trust in terms that have come to be accepted as the classic definition") (Blackmun, J., dissenting) (citing 16A R. Eickhoff, Fletcher Cyclopedia of the Law of Private Corporations §8228 (1979))

[45] Sitkoff, *supra* note 2, at 38.

[46] *Cf.* Jacobellis v. State of Ohio, 378 U.S. 184, 197 ("I shall not today attempt further to define the kinds of material I understand to be embraced within that shorthand description; and perhaps I could never succeed intelligibly in doing so. But I know it when I see it") (Stewart, J., concurring); The Departed (2006) ("I know what you are, and what you aren't.") (Mark Wahlberg aka Det. Sgt. Dignam).

One useful approach is to view business trusts through a taxonomy. According to one prominent commentator,

> [c]ommercial trusts can be categorized in two ways: by the "type" of trust, where labels have been given to commercial trusts, and by the business use to which the trust has been placed. Both ways are needed because there is sometimes an imprecise correlation between labels and functions: certain entities called trusts are not trusts, and other entities may be trusts even though they do not go by that name.[47]

While not without merit, cataloging the entire universe of business trusts by label or name is a difficult, and perhaps futile, exercise. Past attempts have been helpful in identifying a broad range of business trust-like entities, but many of them can be denominated or described in multiple ways;[48] moreover, this population is potentially too numerous to yield a wieldy list.[49]

The superior approach is thus to focus just on different functions. Business trusts have at least five discrete, categorical functions: (1) property holding, (2) asset securitization, (3) risk management, (4) pooled asset management, and (5) tax advantages. Each of these applied features of the business trust is described concisely here, with reference to more detailed treatment in academic literature.

Property Holding

Trusts are a useful commercial vehicle for simply holding property. This is because trusts serve as an intermediary entity through which developers or owners can transact via a trustee, without having to reveal their own identity.[50] Trusts also can facilitate transactions involving multiple parties by having property centralized within the custody and control of a trustee.[51] Typically, the trustee performs the function of "nothing more than a nominee or 'bare' trustee . . . [who] holds the legal title, but has no power to deal independently with the property."[52] In both scenarios the operative rationale is a mitigation of collective action problems; shielding identities can avoid potential hold-out problems by third-parties, while representation by a fiduciary can reduce the number of creditors or litigants who are directly involved in decision-making.

This rationale is clearly illustrated by transactions under the Trust Indenture Act of 1939. When, for example, a corporate entity issues debt securities, a trustee is appointed to represent the interests of all securityholders. Effective representation is possible because while the indenture is by and between the issuer and trustee, the latter has no control, custody, or right of the property unless a default occurs, and instead bears fiduciary duties that inure to the benefit of securityholders.[53] By occupying this peculiar intermediary role

---

[47] Schwarcz, *supra* note 1, at 563–64.
[48] *Compare, e.g., id.* at 566–73, *with* Langbein, *supra* note 1, at 168–77.
[49] *See, e.g., id.* (listing at least 12 distinct types of business trusts).
[50] *See, e.g.*, Flannigan, *supra* note 1, at 631.
[51] *Id.* at 631 and 633.
[52] *Id.* at 632.
[53] *See, e.g., id.* ("The trust is associated with a notorious set of default fiduciary rules and principles that . . . is a considerable convenience to settlors . . .").

between the issuer and the securityholders, the trustee serves to "overcome[ ] the coordination problem that inheres in widespread public ownership of debt securities."[54]

Asset Securitization

Business trusts also serve an integral role in structured finance deals. Although data on the size of the structured finance market are elusive, $21.7 billion in asset-backed securities were traded in 2013,[55] a large fraction of which "is financed—or somewhat more accurately, refinanced—through asset securitization trusts."[56] Undoubtedly, even after the recent global financial crisis, structured finance continues to thrive, and it does so primarily in the form of the business trust.

In this arena the trust typically serves as a special purpose entity (SPE). Although the range of potential transactions is diverse, in essence an operating company can transfer assets (e.g., receivables) or even liabilities (e.g., mortgages) to a trust, which in turn issues securities to third-party investors, whose cash largely will flow back to the company.[57] The trust thus performs a crucial function as an intermediating shield; while the company enjoys a lack of privity with investors, the SPE trust's "bankruptcy remote" status protects investors should the company become insolvent.[58]

Risk Management

Related to its role in securitization, business trusts diversify risk. Traditionally, lenders would guard against overextended liabilities by selling undivided interests to other banks;[59] under this approach, however, selling each interest to a separate bank quickly accrued substantial transaction costs to achieve a level of sufficient diversification.[60]

Instead, businesses use a variety of different types of trusts. Rather than the traditional method, a simple statutory business trust can diversify risk easily by the issuance of trust certificates, with a so-called residual class that is retained by the lender for the purposes of recouping any remaining value after all senior investors have been paid as well as providing an incentive for the lender to monitor the originating debtor's financial situation.[61] Another common diversification vehicle is a master trust, which enables a party to create multiple classes of trust certificates for a specific set of financial assets; as with

---

[54] Langbein, *supra* note 1, at 174.
[55] *See* Securities Industry and Financial Markets Association, *US SF Trading Volume*, www.sifma.org/research/statistics.aspx (last visited August 29, 2014).
[56] Langbein, *supra* note 1, at 172 (reporting "'[p]atchy Federal Reserve data show[ing] nearly $1.9 trillion in mortgage pools," albeit in 1996).
[57] For an excellent diagram of this structured transaction, see, for example, Paul Halpern & Oyvind Norli, *Canadian Business Trusts: A New Organizational Structure*, 18 J. APP. CORP. FIN. 66, 67 fig.1 (2006) ("Business Trust Structure"). And for excellent information and insight into the benefits of asset securitization, see Steven L. Schwarcz, *What Is Securitization? And for What Purpose?* 85 S. CAL. L. REV. 1283 (2012).
[58] *See, e.g.*, Schwarcz, *supra* note 1, at 564; Langbein, *supra* note 1, at 173.
[59] *See, e.g.*, Schwarcz, *supra* note 1, at 565.
[60] *See, e.g., id.* at 565–66.
[61] *See, e.g., id.*

corporations, different classes can have entirely different terms, which can appeal to a broader population of potential investors and thus increase the amount of investments.[62]

Pooled Asset Management

The majority of pension and mutual funds are organized as trusts.[63] Pension funds assume this form because the Employee Retirement Income Security Act of 1974 (ERISA) "codifies the central principles of trust fiduciary law, and ERISA's legislative history makes clear that Congress meant to track the common law of trusts."[64] In contrast mutual funds have a choice to form either as an investment company or investment trust, but the majority reportedly favor the latter option.[65]

Trusts are preferred pooled investment vehicles for multiple reasons. Beyond ERISA's mandatory regulatory framework,[66] pension funds resort to the trust for its structural relationship with beneficiaries, since undistributed funds may be transferred to a pension plan owner's survivors; in this way, "the pension trust exhibits a hybrid trait: Although it is a commercial trust, it commonly gives rise to a gratuitous transfer."[67]

The trust rationale for mutual funds, however, is far more complex. As one prominent commentator has observed, "[t]here are not . . . clear answers to the fundamental question of whether trusts are a better form of business organization than corporations . . . ."[68] According to the commentator, one possibility is that the corporate form may be better suited for more unilaterally aggressive mutual funds, because the presence of strong limited liability and the Business Judgment Rule may shield managers from litigation risks, versus "where all of the fund's beneficiaries want the manager to take these risks, there would be no real conflicting interests, and the trust form is sufficient."[69] This seems somewhat dubious, given that the Investment Company Act of 1940 provides identical fiduciary standards to managers of investment companies and investment trusts.[70]

A more plausible reason is governance. The choice of entity for mutual fund managers largely is not between a trust and a generic corporation, but rather what is known as the

---

[62] *See, e.g., id.* at 567.

[63] *See, e.g.*, Langbein, *supra* note 1, at 168–71 and 178; Flannigan, *supra* note 1, at 633 ("Most mutual funds in Canada are in fact trusts.").

[64] Langbein, *supra* note 1, at 169 (citing sources).

[65] *Id.* at 171.

[66] Cf. *id.* at 169 ("Actually, the federal policy of promoting the trust form for pension funds is older than ERISA.").

[67] *Id.* at 170; *see also* Paul B. Miller, *The Future for Business Trusts: A Comparative Analysis of Canadian and American Uniform Legislation*, 36 QUEEN's L.J. 443, 449 (2011) ("The popularity of the trust for managing funds is understandable given similarities between the management of pooled assets of multiple investors and the management of trust property for multiple beneficiaries of an ordinary private donative trust.").

[68] Schwarcz, *supra* note 1, at 560 (noting also the vagaries of the trust's superiority over partnerships); *see also* Langbein, *supra* note 1, at 188 ("[W]e should in principle be able to specify why one or the other prevails in a particular setting. I am not yet able to do this.").

[69] Schwarcz, *supra* note 1, at 571.

[70] *See* 15 U.S.C. § 77b, 80a-1 to 80a-64, 80b-1 to 80b-21 (1994). *See also* Miller, *supra* note 67, at 450 ("As in corporations, [trust] management is subject to fiduciary strictures to guard against careless and disloyalty.").

Maryland corporation. According to a survey, "half of all newly organized mutual funds took the form of [Massachusetts business] trusts, but . . . a further 28% were organized as Maryland corporations."[71] During the late 1980s Maryland's legislature revamped its corporation statute "to ape the flexibility of the commercial trust in governance."[72] Specifically, Maryland investment company boards are not required to hold annual meetings merely for informational purposes,[73] thereby avoiding "attendant proxy costs, one of the distinctive advantages of trust-type mutual funds,"[74] and may modify unilaterally the aggregate number of shares.[75]

The business trust, however, features a unique structural advantage. In essence the trustee can be understood as "two distinct legal persons: a natural person contracting on behalf of himself, and an artificial person acting on behalf of the beneficiaries."[76] The distinction turns on asset partitioning, whereby the trustee represents an agent whose personal assets are shielded from any of the trust's creditors while the trust is managed by a "de facto office of the trustee" that "serves as the organizing hub for the various relations that aggregate into the trust."[77] Put differently, individual trustees can come and go, but the office of the trustee is a stable entity that actually performs the function of handling all of the trust's creditors and facing their claims. And, most crucially, "[t]his creation of two distinct persons c[an] not feasibly be reproduced with explicit contracting" due to excessive transaction costs.[78] No exact structural counterpart exists within any other kind of business organization, including the Maryland corporation.

Tax Advantages

Tax considerations also cannot be discounted from the business trust. Pursuant to the Check-the-Box regulations, American business trusts are not treated the same as so-called "ordinary," or donative, trusts, but rather as a business entity;[79] nevertheless, under this regime, business trusts can elect to be taxed on a "pass-through" basis, thereby avoiding the entity-level tax applied to all corporations.[80] And for those business trusts beyond the reach of the Check-the-Box regulations, the same effect can be obtained by utilizing internal debt to offset any profits, with cash distributed in the more favorably taxed form

---

[71] Langbein, *supra* note 1, at 187 (citing Jones *et al.*, *supra* note 9, at 422).
[72] *Id.*
[73] *See* MD. ANN. CODE § 2-501 (requiring an annual meeting only when there is an election of directors, approval of the investment advisory agreement, ratification of selection of independent accountants, or approval of a distribution agreement). *See also* Jones *et al.*, *supra* note 9, at 422 n.5 (describing some interpretative ambiguities within this statutory provision).
[74] Langbein, *supra* note 1, at 187.
[75] *See* MD. ANN. CODE § 2-105.
[76] Henry Hansmann & Reinier Kraakman, *The Essential Role of Organizational Law*, 110 YALE L.J. 387, 416 (2000).
[77] Robert H. Sitkoff, *An Agency Costs Theory of Trust Law*, 89 CORNELL L. REV. 621, 641 (2004).
[78] *Id.* at 632 (citing Henry Hansmann & Ugo Mattei, *The Functions of Trust Law: A Comparative Legal and Economic Analysis*, 73 N.Y.U. L. REV. 434, 466 (1998)).
[79] *See* 26 C.F.R. § 301.7701-4(a)–(c) (2014).
[80] *See id.* at § 301.7701-2.

of interest, rather than as capital gains or dividends.[81] Moreover, unlike partnerships, business trusts functioning as pension funds or other types of retirement accounts have their tax deferred to a later period, thereby yielding further gains.[82]

Summary

Business trusts can bear many names and assume an even greater number of forms. More importantly, business trusts can perform multiple functions in a wide variety of settings, only some of which have been described here. At the risk of stating the obvious, these functions are neither mutually exclusive nor singularly dispositive in explaining why business trusts are preferred in certain industries or transactions. On the contrary the diverse array of functions and context in which business trusts thrive bespeaks to a versatility that few other organizational forms can exhibit; this advantage is only reinforced when one considers the contractual flexibility permitted in business trust instruments, particularly in *laissez faire* jurisdictions such as Delaware. Accordingly, the pertinent question is not really why business trusts exist, but rather why they are not used to an even greater extent than what the available data already suggest.[83]

4. CONCLUSIONS

Despite its venerable history, the business trust continues to be a dynamic organizational form. Over the past two centuries the business trust has evolved from an almost purely common law creature into a contractarian entity governed by modern statutory defaults that incorporate traditional trust principles. Recent academic and legislative attention only promise to further refine the business trust and unlock its true potential.

For this to occur, however, a great deal of work remains to be done. Among the most significant and pressing deficiencies with regard to the business trust is a virtual dearth of empirical evidence. Official and private regulatory bodies here and abroad currently do not compile reliable, much less textured, data on the frequency, scale, and types of business trusts in use, despite clear indications of their ubiquity. Moreover, we lack even any anecdotal evidence from users of business trusts about why they have chosen that form over any other alternatives. Finally, there are thousands of published legal decisions concerning business trusts, which would benefit from systematic treatment of the issues that tend to arise with these entities. Obtaining all of these sorts of information would go a long way to establishing a clear positive portrait about the business trust and how it enhances value in various settings and transactions.

There is also a fundamental conceptual issue that merits serious attention. The modern

---

[81] *See, e.g.*, Halpern & Norli, *supra* note 57, at 70.
[82] *See, e.g., id.*; Miller, *supra* note 67, at 451 ("Income trust conversions in Canada were largely driven by preferred tax status.").
[83] A plausible explanation may lie in network effects and status quo bias, whereby entrepreneurs favor more established and familiar types of organizations rather than the business trust. *See, e.g.*, Sitkoff, *supra* note 2, at 46. Or perhaps the reason is simple ignorance. Regardless, the answer requires some empirical evidence.

business trust is viewed conventionally from the robust contractarian approach, which fruitfully frames and guides our understanding of unincorporated and corporate entities; indeed, Delaware's statute explicitly embraces contract as the natural legal foundation for business trust.[84] But, at the same time, the trust is grounded in property law; this the basis for the materially distinct set of fiduciary relationships within trusts,[85] as well as the structurally peculiar relationships between the trustee, the underlying *res*, and beneficiaries.[86] The relationship between contract and property is not mutually exclusive,[87] and so perhaps the most apt characterization of the trust is as a "hybrid of contract and property, [where] . . . contractarian elements do[ ] not require disregard property components whose convenience abides."[88] But that nevertheless renders the business trust a meaningfully different kind of form than the partnership, corporation, and limited liability company.[89] To be sure, all of these forms conform to various cost-structure or feature-based analysis.[90] The challenge, however, is not confined simply to finding some kind of golden thread that runs through the entire universe of business organizations; rather, the trust's quirky nature presents a rich array of provocative questions about what is and potentially what should be the proper paradigmatic way to view business law in general.

---

[84] *See supra* note 35 and accompanying text.
[85] *See, e.g.*, Gregory S. Alexander, *A Cognitive Theory of Fiduciary Relationships*, 85 CORNELL L. REV. 767, 768 (2000).
[86] *See, e.g.*, Hansmann & Mattei, *supra* note 78, at 147.
[87] *See, e.g.*, Thomas W. Merrill & Henry E. Smith, *The Property/Contract Interface*, 101 COLUM. L. REV. 773 (2001).
[88] Langbein, *supra* note 1, at 669; *see also generally* John H. Langbein, *The Contractarian Basis of the Law of Trusts*, 105 YALE L.J. 625 (1995).
[89] *Cf.* Navarro Sav. Ass'n v. Lee, 446 U.S. 458, 476–77 (1980) (questioning "the Court's distinction between business trusts and . . . other enterprises . . . on the locus of title to the trust assets") (Blackmun, J., dissenting).
[90] *See generally* Sitkoff, *supra* note 2; Hansmann & Kraakman, *supra* note 76. One also could apply an information or transaction cost analysis or focus on differences within the conventional matrix of attributes derived from the Kintner Regulations.

17. The law firm as an industry model for entity choice and management
Allison Martin Rhodes and Robyn Axberg

1. INTRODUCTION

The selection and management of a business entity is driven by the particular business at hand. Every business is shaped by the history of its industry, the culture of its owners, the needs of its customers and regulatory and legal pressures. The law firm is a particularly instructive example of how these forces shape entity selection and management. The law firm as a business is driven by service to clients, by regulation, by historically rigid ownership notions, by imminent threats of litigation, and by culture. These forces have resulted in an entity unlike any other.

The legal profession once enjoyed a reputation as an almost untouchable learned profession, driven by the pursuit of intellectual and professional artistry. Notions of entity selection, everyday managerial considerations, and liabilities were beneath it. To whatever extent that was ever the case, it is no longer. The law firm is a high-risk, business-driven enterprise tied to its history and its regulatory restraints. Although lawyers prefer a more precious reputation, the law firm is just a service company and its revenue is generated by a fee structure (typically, the billable hour) charitably described as arcane. It is also one of the most regulated professions that modern industry has ever sustained—boasting advertising regulations that at one time prohibited so much as a sign on one's door for fear of appearing untoward and unworthy of the profession. Finally, it bears signs to this day of a culture of the most traditional and loyal to the true partnership—men in business together for profit, sharing risk, reward and liability as brothers. Of course, with better than 60 percent of law school graduates as women and women leading law firm growth (albeit with still improperly proportioned partnership ranks), the culture of the brotherhood has withered just as the general partnership has given way to reality. The model of the law firm as entity is new in as many ways as it is the same.

Due to the strong influences of clients, regulation, history, and liability the law firm is a case study in how the nature of a profession drives the selection and operation of its entities. Put plainly, a nail salon is not an auto parts store any more than a venture capital partnership is a law firm or The Coca Cola Company is a soda counter in a drug store. By breaking down those influences that truly drive the entity selection and its operation we begin to understand how the bones of the business should be the first step in any entity selection decision and, ultimately, its management structure. This chapter will analyze the forces that shape intelligent law firm formation and management and suggest ways in which changes in the industry might shape the future law firm entity.

2. THE REGULATORY BACKDROP

There are a variety of regulatory requirements that influence how a law firm chooses to organize. Lawyers are not simply business organizers and owners—they are regulated professionals who face personal consequences far beyond those considered by a typical business owner: A lawyer who fails to abide by ethics rules is at risk of losing his or her license to practice law. Similarly, law firms that fail to abide by jurisdictionally specific regulations are at risk of prosecution under criminal unauthorized practice of law statutes. Finally, because lawyers and law firms operate in a highly litigious environment, they face the constant threat of lawsuits for malpractice and professional negligence and, with that, the possibility of vicarious liability for the acts of others.

To understand how and why law firms are best organized, the best place to begin is with an understanding of the overlapping regulations that drive the profession.

The Ethics Rules

The legal profession has long been the subject of regulation. Lawyer and law firm regulation is best understood based on the American Bar Association Model Rules of Professional Conduct. Every U.S. state, with the exception of California, has adopted a variation on the Model Rules. The California rules, although articulated differently, are in accord with Model Rule concepts. Ethics rules relating to management considerations, lawyer exclusivity, the paramount rights of clients, and an unusual micromanagement of the purchase and sale of law firms should all be taken into consideration during the process of forming a law firm.

Management considerations

There are two Model Rules that govern how a law firm must structure its management and, by extension, its entity. Law firms are unique business forms to the extent that management and supervision are not just a good idea, but are regulatory requirements. Model Rule 5.1 pertains to the responsibilities of partners, managers, and supervisory lawyers. Model Rule 5.1 requires partners or those with comparable managerial authority to ensure that the law firm has in place measures to assure compliance with the ethics rules across the firm and further requires a lawyer with supervisory responsibility over another lawyer to take steps to assure that the subordinate lawyer conforms to the rules. The rule further imposes disciplinary liability on lawyers who direct, supervise, or fail to intervene on the ethics violations of other lawyers in the same firm.

Model Rule 5.2, in turn, sets out the responsibilities of a subordinate (or non-managing) lawyer and provides that a subordinate lawyer may only avoid personal responsibility for ethics violations when the lawyer acts at the direction of a supervising lawyer who is providing direction on a reasonable resolution of an arguable question of professional duty.

The above managerial obligations and responsibilities are frequently reflected in the law firm's organizational framework or policy statement. Because of the nature of firm regulation, we should expect to see far more management and collaboration details in a law firm partnership agreement than we would see in an agreement for a widget business. For instance, partnership and operating agreements may include management structures consistent with the rules obligating new matter review protocol as well as supervision of associates. The ethical obligation to supervise may also mean that a law firm should have expulsion as an option to manage lawyer partners who put the law firm, and therefore, the law firm's other partners, at risk. What is plainly improper in the law firm context (but is totally proper and typical in many manager-managed entities) is completely centralized authority absent personal professional obligation. Lawyers must be responsible for lawyering in the same way that doctors must be responsible for deciding which treatments suit a patient. This autonomy, together with its supervisory counterparts, are often reflected in entity structuring through the management provisions of partnership agreements.

Lawyer exclusivity in ownership
Because lawyers are highly regulated, there is a companion ethical obligation to insulate lawyers from the influence of unregulated non-lawyers. In essence, personal and ethical regulatory obligations will sometimes cause a lawyer to make a decision that is not in the best business interest of the enterprise. The exclusivity rules are intended to promote the ethical, rather than the profitable, decision tree. The concept of preserving a lawyer's professional independence is in tension with law firm ownership and economics. Law firms, like any other business, seek to organize with an eye toward stability in ownership and client relations. The following rules substantially curtail, but do not eliminate, such efforts.

Model Rule 5.4 addresses the relationships between lawyers and non-lawyers. The rule prevents non-lawyer ownership of law firms and, some say, interferes with many creative business relationships between non-lawyer professionals and their lawyer counterparts. Traditional investment strategies are not possible in light of the restriction against dividing legal fees with non-lawyers. Model Rule 5.4 both prohibits the sharing of legal fees with non-lawyers and prevents lawyers from entering into a partnership with a non-lawyer if any of the activities of the partnership consist of the practice of law. The rule sets out in further detail a variety of prohibitions aimed at preventing any non-lawyer having influence over the practice of law.

Lawyer exclusivity is not limited to entity ownership, but extends to any business relationship based on earned legal fees. Organizational choices may also be driven by the regulation of legal fees. Just as the rules disfavor non-lawyer influence over lawyer decision making, the rules require that clients be informed of the economics of the lawyer's relationship with other lawyers. The division of legal fees between lawyers, whether by referral fee or other support, must be disclosed, and in some states the specifics of the division (i.e. percentage splits) also must be disclosed.[1] These disclosure requirements are not required in the typical commercial partnership context, where the customer receives one bill and has no right to know how the partners might later divide the profits. The operative organizational question becomes whether a like-minded group of lawyers must form a full-fledged partnership or whether a looser affiliation will allow them to enjoy the nuanced benefits of their relationship without the migraine headache of a law firm partnership. The California Supreme Court elaborated on those structural considerations in 2002 when it held that a joint venture was not a law firm partnership for purposes of the

---

[1] *See* Model Rule 1.5(e) (division of fees between lawyers of different firms "may be made only if the division is in proportion to the services provided by each lawyer" and "the client agrees to the arrangement, including the share each lawyer will receive, and the agreement is in writing").

fee-splitting rule in *Chambers v. Kay*.² Under *Chambers*, joint ventures and other similarly loose associations must comply with disclosure and consent obligations involving information about the economics of law firm management that are not otherwise necessary in a business context.

The micromanagement of law firm ownership and control arises again in Model Rule 1.17, which addresses the sale of law practices. This rule states that a law practice may only be sold when the selling lawyer will cease the practice (as defined by either geography or area of law) and only when the entire practice will be sold to a single lawyer or law firm. The rule further dictates the treatment of firm clients during that process, affording advance notice of a proposed sale and the client an opportunity to leave the firm before the sale.

A far more influential ethics rule, however, relates to the movement of lawyers across competitors in the industry. Non-competition clauses in partnership agreements, and provisions that resemble such clauses, are prohibited as a matter of legal ethics, an extension of the client's rights to choose her lawyer over any trivial business consideration of the lawyer. Model Rule 5.6 places the following restrictions on a lawyer's right to practice:

> A lawyer shall not participate in offering or making:
>
> (a) a partnership, shareholders, operating, employment, or other similar type of agreement that restricts the right of a lawyer to practice after termination of the relationship, except an agreement concerning benefits upon retirement; or
> (b) an agreement in which a restriction on the lawyer's right to practice is part of the settlement of a client controversy.

As a result of Model Rule 5.6, there is tremendous volatility in law firm ownership, a trend not common in other business models.

Model Rule 5.6 has been interpreted broadly, including as support for the proposition that a term of a partnership agreement that *indirectly* restricts a lawyer's mobility between firms can constitute a violation of the rule and thus is unenforceable. That analysis is routinely applied to prevent enforcement of non-competition provisions and restrictive covenants, as well as more subtle provisions that functionally handcuff the lawyer to his or her firm (Hillman 2014).

The leading case on restricting a lawyer's practice is *Cohen v. Lord, Day & Lord*.³ The court reasoned:

> [W]hile the provision in question does not expressly or completely prohibit a withdrawing partner from engaging in the practice of law, the significant monetary penalty it exacts, if the withdrawing partner practices competitively with the former firm, constitutes an impermissible restriction on the practice of law. The forfeiture-for-competition provision would functionally and realistically discourage and foreclose a withdrawing partner from serving clients who might wish to continue to be represented by the withdrawing lawyer and would thus interfere with the client's choice of counsel.⁴

The Comments to Model Rule 5.6 agree with the *Cohen* analysis and provide:

---

² 56 P.3d 645 (Cal. 2002).
³ 550 N.E.2d 410 (1989).
⁴ *Id.* at 411.

An agreement restricting the right of lawyers to practice after leaving a firm not only limits their professional autonomy but also limits the freedom of clients to choose a lawyer. Paragraph (a) prohibits such agreements except for restrictions incident to provisions concerning retirement benefits for service with the firm.

At the other end of the spectrum is *Howard v. Babcock*,[5] which indicates that the economic interests of law firms should merit protection. In *Howard*, the court held that '[a]n agreement that assesses a reasonable cost against a partner who chooses to compete with his or her former partners does not restrict the practice of law. Rather, it attaches an economic consequence to a departing partner's unrestricted choice to pursue a particular kind of practice.'[6] Although *Howard* is not widely followed, similar reasoning has appeared in decisions in Illinois,[7] and Arizona[8] (Hillman 1994). Those authorities address provisions that are clearly tied to competition and acknowledge that the free movement of lawyers and their clients is not the only fair consideration in interpreting a rule based on Model Rule 5.6. It is also important for law firms to be permitted to have reasonable business policies.

Lease obligations are a frequent problem facing law firms, and associated off-sets are a common partnership agreement provision. In *Shuttleworth, Ruloff & Giordano v. Nutter*,[9] the court enforced an employment contract that required departing lawyers to make lease payments unless termination was for death, disability, or judicial appointment. The court found that the provision was not intended to restrict the lawyer's mobility and was not triggered by competition per se; rather, it was designed to insure that the firm had the means to make its lease payments. Similar results can be achieved with thoughtfully designed compensation systems, including those that time or stagger the timing of bonus schedules.

State Regulation

In addition to the ethics rules, another source of external regulation that influences the manner of a law firm's organization is state business law. Although state law is not uniform, entities generally must register with the secretary of state in the state of organization and as a foreign entity in those other states where it does business. Moreover, many states impose an additional layer of regulation specific to law firms. State regulations can significantly impact entity selection for law firms. Prime among those regulatory impacts is the almost universal requirement that law firms maintain some form of professional malpractice insurance for liability-limiting entities. Even within one state, however, different associational forms may require different amounts of coverage, and the steps involved in assuring compliance may also be different.

Those sorts of inconsistent regulatory requirement present a myriad of difficulties for growing and expanding law firms. For instance, notwithstanding findings showing some

---

[5] 863 P.2d 150 (Cal. 1993).
[6] *Id.* at 156.
[7] *See Hoffman v. Levstick*, 860 N.E.2d 551 (Ill. App. Ct. 2006).
[8] *See Fearnow v. Ridenour, Swenson, Cleere & Evans, P.C.*, 138 P.3d 723 (Ariz. 2006).
[9] 493 S.E. 2d 364 (Va. 1997).

limited liability company (LLC) law firms within the state of California, that state does not permit the LLC law firm form.[10] Because of that prohibition, a law firm organized as an LLC may expand into California either as affiliated entity or by conversion.[11] Another California inconsistency is the requirement that all shareholders in a professional corporation sign a personal guarantee as a form of securing malpractice obligations; the state does not, however, extend that same requirement to partners in a limited liability partnership (LLP).[12] Similarly, some states require materially different compliance obligations for each entity, making expansion into new states expensive and administratively burdensome (Martin Rhodes, Hillman & Tran 2014).

Liability

Finally, the environment of legal malpractice claims against lawyers and law firms plays an important role in defining the law firm form. As with, for example, the medical profession, every act of the lawyer/partner is an opportunity to create substantial liability of and monetary damages against the entity, and, therefore, its individual owners. Organization of the entity, adequate insurance, shielding personal liability, and attention to corporate formalities become of paramount importance. There was a time when law firms existed as truly shared risk and reward professional associations, but that was also a time when legal malpractice suits against lawyers were rare. The entity choice of a law firm will govern the degree to which the personal assets of partners may be reached by a professional negligence claim and, therefore, the extent to which individual partners might expect to be named in a lawsuit involving partners (Mallen & Martin Rhodes 2015). Concerns regarding limitations of liability are shared by non-lawyer partners in other entities, but in law firms (and other professional entities), the practical consequences are far more serious because substantial liability may arise from the personal legal services provided by a partner directly to a client.

3. OPERATION CONSIDERATIONS FOR THE LAW FIRM ENTITY

Management

Management and control represent critical elements of entity selection analysis for the law firm. As noted above, the ethics rules impose certain requirements, but historical and cultural influences play an even larger role. In traditional partnerships, all member partners participate in management of the business. That makes good sense in many businesses, just as it did in the traditional law firms of the 19th and early 20th centuries. However, modern law firms, where the label "partner" is not a sign of traditional ownership but

---

[10] *See* Cal. Corp. Code § 17375 (West 2013). *See also* New Mexico Formal Ethics Opinion 2009–1, which discusses whether law firm LLCs are permitted in New Mexico. Arguably, law firm LLCs are not permitted in New Mexico.
[11] *See* Cal. Corp. Code § 17540.8 (West 2013).
[12] *Compare* Cal. Bar Rule 3.158 *with* Cal. Corp. Code § 16956 (West 2013).

instead is merely an indication of status within the firm, are notoriously top heavy. As a consequence, inviting the complete participation in management of hundreds of partners in a large law firm (or even 10 partners in a small law firm) is tantamount to allowing the inmates to run the asylum. A law firm is not a normal partnership—it is a business in which the partners are providing direct services to the clients and are partners, some say, in name only.

In larger law firms, regardless of the entity utilized, some form of centralized management in an executive or management committee is common, with wider partnership participation limited to the most significant decisions. Centralization may be an especially important consideration for growing law firms in which, at first, a model of management where every partner is involved makes the most sense, but as the firm expands, a more defined management team makes more sense. A well-crafted partnership agreement offers the opportunity to thoughtfully control the management and the growth of the organization.

Corporate formality is another concern and argues heavily against relying on the corporate form for law firms. While operational requirements on LLCs and LLPs are generally relatively minimal, corporations tend to face much more defined rules and requirements. Annual meetings, the recording of minutes, and the proceedings that take place at these meetings are all usually defined in corporate statutes, whereas most LLC and LLP statutes are silent on these areas. Legal professionals further are notoriously poor at maintaining these corporate formalities, which can put the critical personal liability protections at risk.

Compensation

Certainly, differences among entity types affect the manner in which management and control may be influenced within the particular organization. A technical difference between LLPs and general partnerships on the one hand and LLCs and corporations on the other is how profits are presumed to be shared. Partners all are presumed to equally share profits, whereas members and shareholders in LLCs and corporations are entitled to proportional shares of profits based on their capital investments. Once a law firm expands beyond a handful of owners, pro rata profit sharing quickly presents problems. Wide variations in skill, business development talents, management responsibility and personal profitability make it difficult to attract and sustain productive partners when all partners share equally in the fruits of the firm's labors. Resentment grows fast and the most profitable partners leave the firm. Compensation ultimately must yield to these realities.

Flexibility in compensation should also drive the entity form choice. Shareholders in a corporation generally enjoy dividends paid on profits based on the number of shares owned, and partners similarly often enjoy distribution of profits based on their partnership share. Neither of those concepts account for the fact that law firm partners are also revenue-generating workers who sustain the organization and are responsible for growing the business and serving existing clients. Traditional compensation and profit distributions based entirely on firm profits without regard to individual partner performance create a rigid system that most law firms have found disadvantages business development in a service industry. Devising a compensation system for law firm owners is acknowledged as the most difficult management and structure-related task of a law firm. Strategies are generally comprised of three elements: First, remuneration for the individual's personal contribution to revenue; second, return on capital investment; and third, profit allocation among owners (Cotterman 2010). In light of the interplay among those factors, they must be addressed in some fashion in the organizational elements of the entity.

All of the entity forms discussed in this section will allow for management flexibility and compensation systems based on performance metrics proven to support law firm stability. In a corporation, compensation is inextricably tied to share value. Although it is certainly possible to create a merit-based compensation system in a corporate agreement, it is cumbersome at best.

The LLC operating agreement and the partnership agreement provide the blank canvas on which to craft a compensation system. Agreements often include complicated compensation systems conferring substantial discretion on compensation committees or managers. Such agreements offer an opportunity for the partner to agree to cede this important function to a system that promotes the business goals of the law firm and all of its partners over the formulaic-based profit participation of more traditional business models.

Emergence of the "Non-Equity Partner"

In an effort to maximize partnership profits (both actual profits and the often-cited profits-per-partner metric) and to add flexibility to attorneys' career trajectories, the legal industry has shifted to a two-tier partnership structure. Most law firms, particularly larger firms, now distinguish between the equity partner and the non-equity partner. The non-equity partner, sometimes called an income partner (or more pejoratively, a fake partner), provides an interim step or even an alternative to traditional equity partnership.

A partner or shareholder is, by definition, an equity owner of some share of the business. Over time, law firms have created the legal fiction of non-equity partner (Richmond 2010). The mere term "non-equity partner" is itself an "oxymoron" since partnership is defined by "co-ownership and shared personal responsibility," neither of which exists with the non-equity partner (Hillman 2005). In other words, one cannot be a non-owner owner. The terminology has nevertheless survived and become an industry norm.

Instead of connoting ownership, a modern interpretation of "partner" in a law firm is a status suggesting a level of experience and peer respect that comes with advancement within the firm. To the average client or prospective client the term partner brings stature and, as such, carries business development gravitas.

The non-equity partner title is used regardless of entity structure, including in professional corporations (where the term might more properly but even more confusingly be non-equity shareholder) as well as in LLPs and LLCs.

Although the term reflects a tier of partnership, in reality there is no tier. A non-equity partner is generally nothing more than an employee who enjoys none of the risks or benefits of partnership. She will not make capital contributions and will not participate in profits or receive a liquidation distribution upon dissolution. To whatever extent the law firm chooses to give non-equity partners participation in partnership-like activities, such as meetings, committee appointments, or even the partnership compensation process, such participation stems from contractual rights and obligations rather than from co-ownership or shared responsibility.[13]

But that conclusion regarding the clear distinction between equity and non-equity partners is not free from doubt. Modern law firms have revised the conception of equity partners such that they often look more like employees or their non-equity partner cousins (Hillman 2005). As law firms have become larger, the actual management of law firms is frequently concentrated in management or executive committees. Gone are the days of full partnership control or votes on business direction, other than the election of the managing committees and perhaps certain big-ticket items, such as votes for dissolutions or mergers.

In addition, one of the underpinnings of the emergence of the non-equity partner stems from the industry recognition that not all partners are created equal. Only a small number—an often coveted upper echelon of partners—are the seasoned rainmakers of the firms. As discussed above, law firms often vary compensation even among equity partners on the basis of factors other than ownership percentage, such as productivity measured in new clients, collections on hours worked, or similar performance metrics. Equity and non-equity partners alike may receive bonuses that are based in part on individual performance metrics and on overall firm profitability.

Further, modern trends in liability-limiting entity options cast doubt on traditional notions that "partners" share risk for the endeavor. Often, non-equity partners are held out to the public as "partners" with no outwardly visible distinctions made between the different tiers. Equity and non-equity partners alike may sign fee agreements with clients on behalf of the firm, be listed as partners on firm stationery, and otherwise engender traditional notions of apparent authority. Moreover, those trends among equity partners erode the concepts that once were hallmarks of true partnership in the traditional sense and which distinguished true partners from non-equity partners (Richmond 2010).

Notwithstanding the fiction of the title, the IRS permits law firms to include non-equity partners in the ranks of k-1 partners for purposes of pass-through taxation. In reality, many non-equity partners receive k-1 forms that traditionally are reserved for the true owners who share in the profits of the firm. Using that technique, firms shift the burden for certain self-employment taxes to the non-equity partners. The k-1 phenomenon further blurs the lines between equity and non-equity partners and may cast doubt on the non-equity partner as an employee under employment law tests. The result insulates firms from liability for workplace discrimination claims, for example, which apply only to employees and not to owners.

4. HISTORICAL ENTITY FORMS

Today, law firms are free to choose among a variety of associational forms, including a sole proprietorship, a general partnership, an LLP, an LLC, or a professional corporation. Of course, as discussed above, the availability of different entity forms and the regulations

---

[13] *See, e.g., D'Esposito v. Gusrae, Kaplan & Bruno PLLC*, 844 N.Y.S.2d 214, 215 (N.Y. App. Div. 2007).

pertaining to each form depends on state law. Historically, however, the forms available to lawyers in forming their firms were significantly more limited. At common law, lawyers could choose between sole proprietorships and general partnerships. Beginning in the 20th century, new entity forms were invented. But with each new entity form came form-specific nuances tied to state-specific concerns that emerged as states adopted laws to make the formation of the new entities possible.

The first significant uniform codification for business entities occurred in 1914 when the Commission on Uniform State Laws approved the Uniform Partnership Act (UPA). Before the creation of the UPA, general partnerships were subject to common law and civil law, applied through state statute. There was great variation between state laws as a result. In 1915, the American Bar Association (ABA) approved the UPA, and within a short period of time, nearly every state had adopted the UPA, standardizing the laws, rules, and regulations pertaining to general partnerships. More recently, the Revised Uniform Partnership Act (RUPA) has been promulgated and is in effect in a majority of the states.

A general partnership is defined by the UPA and RUPA as an association of two or more persons to carry on as co-owners a business for profit.[14] As with a sole proprietorship, the pure general partnership as a business entity does not provide any protection to its partners' personal assets—the liabilities of the partnership extend to all of the assets of the partners. Thus, if one partner commits malpractice, other potentially innocent partners could lose their homes, savings, or any other assets as a result. Although commercial businesses long had the ability to protect the personal assets of owners from the businesses' liability by incorporating, lawyers and others did not have this option. Deciding to partner with another professional amounted to risking one's assets for the benefit of that partnership. The unavailability of the corporate form to professionals was rooted in the idea that limited liability was incompatible with the professional relationship (Johnson 1995). It was not until the development of the professional corporation in the 1960s that the concept of limited liability was extended to professional service firms.

In 1961, the ABA Committee on Ethics and Professional Responsibility issued an opinion concluding for the first time that attorneys could practice through corporations if a series of safeguards were met. Specifically, those safeguards were: (1) the lawyer remains personally responsible to the client for the services rendered; (2) restrictions on liability of other lawyers in the firm must be made apparent to the client; (3) none of the stockholders may be non-lawyers; (4) there must be no sharing of profits with employees who are not lawyers; and (5) only lawyers may participate in the management of the firm (Hillman 2014).[15] One of the primary impetuses for the creation of professional corporations was the desire to give professionals access to certain tax benefits, such as higher pension plan contributions (Martin Rhodes, Hillman & Tran 2014). As the first alternative to the standard general partnership form, the professional corporation paved the way for other limited liability entity forms that become available to law firms over the next few decades, such as the LLP and the LLC. With the concept of limited liability extended to the legal profession, entity selection became a true decision, rather than a de facto selection.

---

[14] *See* Revised Uniform Partnership Act §101(6) (1996); Uniform Partnership Act §6(1) (1914).
[15] Citing ABA Committee on Professional Ethics, Formal Opinion 303 (1961).

5. MODERN SURVEY OF ENTITY FORMS AVAILABLE TO LAW FIRMS

The most basic of business entity forms is not an entity at all—it is the sole proprietorship. A sole proprietorship consists of an individual operating a business for his/her own profit. The sole proprietor is personally liable for all of the debts of the business. As a self-employed person, the sole proprietor pays taxes as an individual on all income, including income derived from the legal practice. A sole proprietorship offers no shield to protect the lawyer's personal assets because no distinction exists between personal and business assets. Thus, due to the lack of liability protection, a sole proprietorship is a risky and disfavored entity form.

Only slightly more complex than the basic sole proprietorship is the general partnership. The general partnership is nothing more than two or more individuals engaged in a profit-seeking endeavor. Hallmarks of the general partnership are common ownership and shared personal responsibility. Each partner in a general partnership is jointly and severally liable for the obligations of the partnership, just as a sole proprietor would be for the sole proprietorship.

Although it is declining in popularity, the professional corporation, or PC, remains one of the most prevalent entity forms employed by law firms (Martin Rhodes, Hillman & Tran 2014). Professional corporations are a distinct entity form despite the fact that historical tax benefits that set corporations apart from sole proprietorships and partnerships have now been extended to those entity forms (Martin Rhodes, Hillman & Tran 2014). Professional corporations, like all corporations, are owned by shareholders. In most instances, the shareholders elect directors who serve as the management body of the professional corporation. The directors, in turn, appoint officers who perform the daily business of the entity. Significantly for the legal profession, directors and officers may also be shareholders of the corporation. Typically, the shareholders in a corporation are protected from personal liability for the actions of the professional corporation. Similarly, in the case of a law firm, the lawyers (as shareholders) may be shielded from personal liability for the business obligations and from the negligence of other shareholders. That shield, however, may be limited by state law.

Under Federal tax law, professional corporations can be designated either C-corporations or S-corporations. The extent to which these designations have meaning under state law varies by the state. With respect to Federal taxation, the C-corporation's income is taxed at the corporate rate. When that income is subsequently disbursed to the shareholders, the shareholders are taxed for their individual income. In contrast, the S-corporation is treated as a "pass-through" entity for Federal tax purposes. Corporate income is allocated to shareholders, who are then taxed at their individual rate for the gains and losses of the corporation. For S-corporations, therefore, there is only one round of taxation where C-corporations face two. Because of this more advantageous tax treatment, S-corporations must meet certain criteria, such as having no more than 100 shareholders, having only one class of stock, and being a domestic corporation with domestic shareholders.

The registered limited liability partnership is a relatively new sub-form of the general partnership. In 1991, Texas became the first state to recognize the LLP form. Today, every state has enacted comparable legislation, making the LLP a universally available entity form for law firms. The most attractive aspect of most LLP legislation is that the LLP presents the option of functioning as a general partnership, while allowing for some insulation of the general partners from risks of personal liability (Goforth 1996). An LLP thus marries the benefits of partnership taxation with the limited liability more characteristic of a corporation.

Traditionally, the extent of LLP limited liability protection varied from state to state, with some states choosing to be "partial shield" states and some choosing to bestow "full shield" protection to LLPs. Under a "partial shield" scheme, partners in an LLP may be protected from others' negligent acts and omissions but may, for example, be held personally liable for the contractual obligations of the LLP. Under a "full shield" rule, partners enjoy limited liability protection equal to that of the owners of an LLC or a corporation. Currently, only nine states retain partial shield statutes, while the balance of states and the District of Columbia have full shield statutes (Martin Rhodes, Hillman & Tran 2014).

Along with the development of the LLP came the creation of a wholly new entity known as the limited liability company. LLCs are like LLPs in blending elements of partnerships and corporations. The owners of an LLC are referred to as members, and they benefit from the same limited liability as a shareholder in a corporation. Like corporations, LLCs may be run by member or non-member managers (the equivalent of a corporation's directors). With respect to taxation, however, LLCs function more like a partnership than a corporation. The LLC itself is not taxed. Instead, the income that is deemed passed on to the members is taxed at the individual member level. Further, although a partnership may be dissolved when one partner leaves, an LLC can survive such an event.

6. TRENDS IMPACTING ENTITY SELECTION

Law firms were late to the limited liability structures. While other businesses enjoyed choice of corporate or partnership forms, professionals (such as lawyers and physicians) were prohibited from incorporating until the 1960s and, in some states, as late as the 1980s. The only entity available to professionals was the general partnership, which offered no protection from vicarious liability.

The 1960s development of the professional corporation as a means of extending tax advantages to professional service firms offered law firms the first alternative to the general partnership associational form. By the turn of the century, lawyers in various jurisdictions had the option of the professional corporation, the LLC and the LLP. This slow evolution of the law tracks the even slower evolution of law firm entity choices.

A survey conducted in 2002 offered the first comprehensive look at what firms actually were doing in the new era of enhanced associational choices (Hillman 2003). The survey revealed that firms were accepting new organizational options, but they were doing so at a somewhat slower pace than might be expected. Excluding sole proprietorships, professional corporations were the dominant form (53%), with general partnerships a distant second (29%). LLCs (8%) and LLPs (10%) significantly trailed more traditional organizational forms. When, however, the survey was limited to large law firms, the LLP was the organizational form of choice.

The data were partially updated in 2011, and little appears to have changed. Although the professional corporation obviously remains the dominant form (51%), LLCs have surged in popularity (22%), presumably at the expense of general partnerships (down to 16%). Interestingly, LLPs are the least popular associational form and have shown little increase in popularity over the last decade (Martin Rhodes, Hillman & Tran 2014).

7. THE LAW FIRM AS AN EVOLVING BUSINESS MODEL

As should be clear, the regulation of the law firm has strong historical roots that are not always consistent with modern law practice, partnership law, or the future needs of the industry. External forces continue to put pressure on the industry, which is slow to evolve. Evolution, however, is inevitable. This section discusses three areas in which we believe evolution is necessary for the future of the law firm entity as a thriving business—non-lawyer ownership, multijurisdictional growth of firms, and the globalization of the practice of law.

The Future of Model Rule 5.4

As discussed above, Model Rule 5.4 prohibits law firm entities from having any non-lawyer owners, including corporate partners that are not themselves authorized to practice law. This historical prohibition has shaped not only law firms, but the entire delivery of legal services to consumers. Modern business may have reached the point where its counter pressure will prevail. Perhaps sadly, the legal profession is viewed by the public more as a commodity service and less as a "profession." A survey of editorials and even lawyer jokes demonstrates the public's distrust of lawyers and the prevailing perception of lawyers as greedy.

As just another commodity business, consumers of legal services may look for short-cuts in terms of price or bundling of legal services with other types of services, such as consulting services, professional relations services and even accounting or tax services. Model Rule 5.4 functionally prohibits such bundling or comingling and perpetuates the traditional conception of legal practice as a profession.

In practice, however, many professionals blur that distinction. Consulting firms often hire attorneys to help structure tax arbitrage plans, but the attorneys claim that they are practicing tax accounting or tax consulting rather than practicing law (Fisher 2000). Similarly, corporations hire in-house counsel for certain legal needs, such as contract drafting and review. Other creative minds have created entities that hold themselves out as "law firms" but function more like temporary agencies (such as Axiom). Entities that are not law firms in the traditional sense are providing competition to law firms, such as LegalZoom for incorporation services. These alternatives are a modern curiosity and it remains to be seen whether the substantial regulatory pressures on the pure law firm entity form will ultimately catch up and shape these business models.

Various committees of the ABA and many states have formed commissions or task forces to study potential liberalization of Model Rule 5.4 to permit multidisciplinary practice (Adams 2013). International trends lend credence to arguments in favor of liberalizing Model Rule 5.4 to permit multidisciplinary practices. Australia and the United Kingdom, for example, permit law firm ownership by corporations and without regard to whether ownership consists of lawyers or non-lawyers (Adams 2013).

The ABA formally created its commission on multidisciplinary practice in 1998, although other studies of the ABA date back to 1977 (Adams 2013). The ABA and several states' bar associations have examined whether revising the rules to focus on lawyer conduct rather than on law firm structure might be beneficial to the profession. Certainly, access to capital and more efficient business structures would benefit a liberal corporate structure that includes non-lawyers. Efficient business structures may enhance the competitiveness of U.S. firms in the global setting and enable firms to offer legal services at more affordable prices to consumers.

Several concerns counterbalance arguments that attempt to liberalize the rules. For example, some question whether non-lawyers who may have influence or power in such entities may adhere to the conflict rules or confidentiality rules or other rules of professional conduct that remain important cornerstones of the legal profession.

The District of Columbia in 1991 adopted a form of Model Rule 5.4 that permits lawyers and non-lawyers to share ownership and control in the provision of legal services. The D.C. formulation requires such entities to have, as their sole purpose, the provision of legal services. That limitation has prevented many D.C. firms from taking advantage of the rule.

The Future of Multijurisdictional Practice

Like Model Rule 5.4's prohibition of non-lawyer ownership, the jurisdictionally centric licensing of lawyers has a dramatic impact on how a law firm is organized. As a general rule, a lawyer may not maintain a systematic presence in a state unless the lawyer is licensed by that state. By extension, a law firm may not expand or open offices across state borders unless it employs lawyers licensed in those states. As discussed above, each state in turn imposes regulation on the entity itself. Simply put, growth is difficult. Issues surrounding the prohibition on the unauthorized practice of law, although not necessarily of direct concern during entity selection, are likely to come into play as law firms, large and small, continue to strive for solid footing in an increasingly national and even global legal market.

State by state licensing is the most persuasive explanation for the prevalence of the small regional law firm. At both the organizational and individual lawyer level, the regulations impose geographic boundaries that may or may not protect clients but certainly protect local lawyers from out-of-state competition.

Changes in the national and international legal market are driving a lively discussion about the need to allow lawyers and law firms more flexibility to engage in multijurisdictional practice without requiring admission to each and every jurisdiction in which the lawyer practices (Greenbaum 2010; Gillers 2012). Technological developments that allow lawyers to practice anywhere with an internet connection, along with the increasing accessibility and uniformity of the law as a general matter, mean that it is quite possible for a lawyer admitted in a single jurisdiction to competently practice in any state. However, the growth of multijurisdictional practice is suppressed by regulations that seem to allow for virtual practice based in the state of licensure but prohibiting physical presence as the unauthorized practice.

Model Rule 5.5(a) prohibits lawyers from "practic[ing] law in a jurisdiction in violation of the regulation of the legal profession in that jurisdiction, or assist[ing] another in doing so." Lawyers who are not admitted to practice in a jurisdiction may not "establish an office or other systematic and continuous presence in [the] jurisdiction for the practice of law" or represent that they are admitted to practice in the jurisdiction.[16] The policy underlying Model Rule 5.5 addresses states' interest in protecting residents and their justice system from incompetent or unscrupulous lawyers (Gillers 2002). Most states have adopted some form of temporary presence rule, but those rules vary dramatically and managing their overlapping and inconsistent requirements further pushes law firms back to their home state. Even *pro hac vice* rules vary greatly by jurisdiction and are not a solution to the dilemma of avoiding the unauthorized practice of law while maintaining a multijurisdictional practice.[17] Law firms that seek to practice in jurisdictions in which they do not maintain an office will have difficulty competing for business against local firms or the larger law firms that have a presence, however small, in that jurisdiction.

The Future of the Global Law Firm

The complexity of law firms operating across U.S. jurisdictions is multiplied in the international context. The inconsistent state regulation pales in comparison to the inconsistent international regulation. Lawyers with exceptional training may not be eligible for licensing in other countries if for no other reason than a single regulatory framework cannot account for the vast array of licensing requirements and stylings of global neighbors. Similarly, a law firm that organizes as a particular type of entity in one nation may be ineligible to perform professional services in that entity form in another nation. For example, the personal liability protections afforded a shareholder under U.S. law are strictly forbidden for professionals under Japanese law. How then does a global law firm offer the same personal liability protections to its partners in the U.S. and Japan? Global law firms have sought solutions as they expand. For many it is the realization that with each country a different entity form is appropriate, yet the firm wishes to feel like a single entity and most certainly wishes to market itself as a global powerhouse.

One popular solution for law firms seeking to have a global presence is the Swiss *Verein*, which is an association that permits existing organizations in various jurisdictions to partner together in a common enterprise. The *Verein* structure provides flexibility among disparate entity types and has become a favorite method to combine firms together internationally (Simpson 2014). Other law firms turn to complex affiliated entity structures, essentially cobbling the law firm together. Ultimately, globalization must present a solution that allows the law firm to exist as an international entity with some sense of singular ownership. That day, however, seems distant.

---

[16] Model Rule 5.5(a).
[17] *See* ABA Center for Professional Responsibility CPR Policy Implementation Committee, *Comparison of ABA Model Rule for Pro Hac Vice Admission with State Versions and Amendments since August 2002* (2012) (in 36 jurisdictions, the number of appearances is purely at the court's discretion, whereas in Montana, a lawyer may have a total of two appearances ever, and in other jurisdictions, the number of appearances is limited over a one- or two-year period).

8. CONCLUSION

The law firm is a business like any other. Its most influential feature may not be the regulatory, historical, and commercial influences discussed in this chapter, but stems instead from the entities' "parents." Like the cobblers' children who have no shoes, law firms are organized by lawyers. They are not usually the same lawyers, however, that form the various other entities discussed in this text. Rather, the law firm is organized by the very lawyers who are its owners, whether they know what they are doing or not. The extent that this consideration has influenced popular law firm forms over centuries cannot be measured. Lawyers also write the regulations that govern the firms. They write the legislation and tax codes that drive the corporate and partnership structures, and they own and manage their business often with little or no assistance from business executives. Query whether the resulting unique entity model is the tail or the dog.

REFERENCES

Adams, Edward S. (2013), "Rethinking the Law Firm Organizational Form and Capitalization Structure," *Missouri Law Review*, 78, 799, 800–805, 807–808.
Cotterman, James ed. (2010), *Compensation Plan for Law Firms*, 15.
Fisher, Susan Smith (2000), "Multidisciplinary Practice: Mission Impossible, Brave New World, Or Something More Elegant?," *Ethics and Professional Responsibility in the New Millennium* (West), 5.
Gillers, Stephen (2012), "A Profession, If You Can Keep It," *Hastings Law Journal*, 63, 958–959.
Gillers, Stephen (2002), "Lessons from the Multijurisdictional Practice Commission: The Art of Making Change," *Arizona Law Review*, 44, 686.
Goforth, Carol R. (1996), "Limiting the Liability of General Partners in LLPs: An Analysis of Statutory Alternatives," *Oregon Law Review*, 75, 1143.
Greenbaum Arthur F. (2010), "Multijurisdictional Practice and the Influence of Model Rule of Professional Conduct 5.5—An Interim Assessment," *Akron Law Review*, 43, 956–958.
Hillman, Robert W. (2014), *Hillman on Lawyer Mobility: the Law and Ethics of Partner Withdrawals and Law Firm Breakups*, § 2.3.3–2.3.4, Supplement 6:2 n 3.
Hillman, Robert W. (2005), "Law, Culture, and the Lore of Partnership: Of Entrepreneurs, Accountability, and the Evolving Status of Partners," *Wake Forest Law Review*, 40, 820.
Hillman, Robert W. (2003), "Organizational Choices of Professional Services Firms: An Empirical Study," *The Business Lawyer*, 58, 1387.
Hillman, Robert W. (1994), "The Law Firm as Jurassic Park: Comments on Howard v Babcock," *U.C. Davis Law Review*, 27, 533.
Johnson, Jennifer J. (1995), "Limited Liability for Lawyers: General Partners Need Not Apply," *The Business Lawyer*, 51, 92–102.
Mallen, Ronald E. & Martin Rhodes, Allison (2015), *Legal Malpractice* § 5:2 et seq.
Martin Rhodes, Allison, Hillman, Robert W. & Tran, Peter (2014), "Law Firms' Entity Choices Reflect Appeal of Newer Business Forms," *Business Entities*, 16 No. 4, 16–20.
Richmond, Douglas R. (2010), "The Partnership Paradigm and Law Firm Non-equity Partners," *Kansas Law Review*, 58, 508, 551.
Simpson, Jake (2014), "Verein Tie-Ups Gain Allure as Firms Eye Global Expansion," available at www.law360.com/articles/563434/verein-tie-ups-gain-allure-as-firms-eye-global-expansion (last accessed September 2014).

PART 7

JUDICIAL AND LEGISLATIVE RESPONSES

18. Harmonization, rationalization, and uniformity
Robert R. Keatinge

1. INTRODUCTION AND OVERVIEW

A juridical form of business or nonprofit organization ("Form of organization" or simply "Form") such as a business corporation, limited liability company ("LLC"), or partnership is generally organized or recognized under a state statute (an "Organic statute"). An organization formed in accordance with an Organic statute is generally regarded as a coherent and distinct legal entity.[1] The organization may be thought of as an aggregation of component characteristics ("Characteristics") which provide for the nature of the organization and its property and liabilities and the rights and duties of the organization, its owners, its managers, those who deal with it, and the governmental authorities that recognize and regulate it.[2] These Characteristics range from the mundane (such as the name and designator that the organization may use in registering with the state) to the sublime (such as the default or mandatory rights and duties among the owners, managers, and the organization and the ability to order these rights and duties by agreement). Some Characteristics are common to many or all Forms of organization while others are unique to a single Form, but in any case, the aggregate combination of Characteristics comprising a Form of organization defines that Form in contrast to others.

The increase in the pace of change in existing Forms and the addition of new Forms have been significant since the middle of the 1980s. With each change or addition, there has been the creation of new Characteristics, a change in the aggregation of Characteristics comprising a Form, or both. In response to these changes and, in particular, to address transactions common to all or most Forms of organization, such as

---

[1] Until the Uniform Partnership Act of 1994 (which subsequently became the Uniform Partnership Act (1997) ("UPA (1997)"), partnership statutes had not expressly stated that partnerships were legal entities. Because both the original Uniform Partnership Act ("UPA (1914)") and UPA (1997) have Characteristics that are more aggregate in nature (such as limitations on the ability of partner to transfer governance rights) and others that are more entity-like (such as the ability of the partnership to hold property and sue in its own name), the "entity" nomenclature may be more illusion than reality. In other words, a UPA (1914) partnership was an aggregate except when it was an entity, while a UPA (1997) partnership is an entity except when it is an aggregate. To avoid the question of "entityness," as a concession to the brevity of life, this chapter refers to each firm as an "organization" rather than an "entity."

[2] While the total number of Characteristics is probably unknowable, compare Robert R. Keatinge, Corporations, Unincorporated Organizations, and Unincorporations: Check the Box and the Balkanization of Business Organizations, 1 J. Small & Emerging Bus. L. 201, 233–34 (1997) (listing a handful of Characteristics) with Ribstein and Keatinge on Limited Liability Companies attempts to compare various Characteristics of different state limited liability company statutes in Appendices appearing at the end of some chapters. In the June 2015 edition of these appendices there were 76 charts each of which compared the state, uniform and prototype statutes with respect to a distinct issue, often with two or more discrete or complementary Characteristics.

filing of documents and use of names, and transactions involving more than one Form of organization such as the merger, conversion, interest exchange, domestication, or division involving different Forms of organizations (Inter-Form transactions), the drafters of Organic statutes have used the processes which this chapter describes as Harmonization and Rationalization. In addition, the pursuit of Uniformity, which pre-existed the recent increase in Forms, has also played a role in responding to these changes. Each of Harmonization, Rationalization, and pursuit of Uniformity is distinct in goals, benefits, and risks, and the processes are often confused with each other.

This chapter discusses each of the processes, its respective benefits and drawbacks, and the problems created when the processes are combined or confused with one another.

As a result of the confusion and conflation of the processes of Harmonization, Rationalization, and pursuit of Uniformity, it is important to understand how these terms and the term "Characteristic" are used in this chapter.

Characteristics

Until the early 1990s there were three principal Forms of organization in the United States: business corporations, general partnerships, and limited partnerships. Since the mid-1980s all of the Organic statutes have been changed or replaced.[3] In addition, a new business Form—the LLC—has evolved as have a variety of other legal Forms (such as statutory trusts). In addition, new sub-Forms (such as the limited liability partnership ("LLP") and the limited liability limited partnership ("LLLP")) have come into being.

As noted above, each of these Forms of organization may be considered as an aggregation of Characteristics that, taken together, comprise the identity of an organization as being a particular Form. Generally, the relationship between the organization, its owners, decision-makers, and agents on the one hand, and those dealing with the organization, on the other ("External Characteristics"), will largely be determined by the statutory and regulatory law of the jurisdictions to which the organization is subject[4] and case law interpreting the statutes. External Characteristics include such matters as the vicarious liability to third parties of the organization and its owners, decision-makers, and agents for the debts of the organization, the organization's competence to deal in commerce and law, and the manner in which the organization conducts such dealings. These include the organization's ability to hold property in its own name, to sue and be sued, and how the organization may act and become bound.

---

[3] See the Model Business Corporation Act (1984), the Uniform Partnership Act (1997), the Uniform Limited Partnership Act (1976, 1981, and 2001).

[4] As this chapter is limited to consideration of United States organizations, it would be tempting to think of these jurisdictions as states, but it is important to remember that organizations are subject to regulation by the Federal and, at times, local jurisdictions as well, as, for example, where federal or local law imposes restrictions on the Forms of organization that may conduct certain activities or treats different forms of organization differently for tax purposes. Other laws and regulations may have an impact on the Characteristics. For example, rules of professional conduct applicable to attorneys or others such as Model Rules of Professional Conduct Rules 1.8 and 5.4 may require special liability Characteristics and exchange rules adopted by the New York Stock Exchange or NASDAQ may require certain governance Characteristics, both of which are beyond the scope of this chapter.

Those Characteristics that are related to the relationship among the organization's owners, decision-makers and other Constituents with each other and the organization ("Internal Characteristics") are determined by three sources: the statutory and regulatory law of the jurisdictions to which the organization and its members and managers are subject (including, and generally principally, the Organic statute), the case law interpreting those statutes and the relationships in general, and the agreement of the owners.[5]

Obviously, these sources are not discrete, but are highly interactive. With respect to Internal Characteristics, the statutory rules may be mandatory or "default" (i.e., subject to modification by the agreement of those organizing or operating the organization (the "Constituents")) and where incomplete or unclear may be subject to interpretation or augmentation by the case law. The case law may: (i) be modified by the agreement; (ii) may make any modification by agreement ineffective, or (iii) may be overridden by subsequent statutory provisions. The agreement may be subject to, or supersede, the statutory and case law and, where incomplete or unclear, may be interpreted or supplemented by case law—often with helpful judicial comments on the competence of the drafting. This rock-paper-scissors process makes it difficult to make determinations of what the Internal Characteristics of a particular Form of organization are in a particular jurisdiction. Thus, in order to consider questions of Harmonization and Rationalization of Internal Characteristics, one must start with certain aspects of state statutory law, particularly the ability of the Constituents to order the Internal Characteristics.

With respect to External Characteristics, the agreement of the owners occupies a more modest role than it does with respect to Internal Characteristics. The agreement has a more limited impact on third parties whose interests are affected by External Characteristics and who do not participate in the bargaining for the provisions in the agreement and often do not have notice of such provisions.[6]

---

[5] Of course, like the distinction between Harmonization and Rationalization discussed below, the distinction between Internal and External Characteristics is not as sharp as the discussion in this chapter suggests it is. Almost every Characteristic affects both the rights and duties of the organization vis-à-vis third parties and property and the internal affairs of the organization. Some, like the name and identity of the organization, the organization's ability to conduct certain types of activities, and the manner in which the organization or a Constituent becomes obligated to a third party are predominantly External, even though they may be of great interest to the Constituents, and will thus be considered External Characteristics. Similarly, the relationship, rules, rights, and duties of the organization and its owners and agents, while predominantly of interest to the organization and its Constituents and thought of as Internal Characteristics, even though third parties may have some interest in these rights, as in the case of lenders to organizations and other third parties who do not wish to find themselves in a position of, for example, aiding and abetting a breach of fiduciary duty. In the discussion below, it may be helpful to think of Characteristics as being predominantly External or Internal, and in any case, in each case to think about the External or Internal effect of the Characteristic.

[6] See, e.g., UPA (1997) § 103(b)(10) ("The partnership agreement may not ... restrict rights of third parties under this [Act].") and Keatinge, Closely-Held Business Symposium: The Uniform Limited Partnership Act, The Partnership Agreement and Third Parties: ReRULPA § 110(B)(13) v. RUPA § 103(B)(10), 37 Suffolk U. L. Rev. 873 (2004). An interesting and perhaps troubling exception to this rule is the ability to establish series of assets the access to which by creditors may be limited or precluded and which need only be generally referred to in the public document. See, e.g., 6 Del. C. § 18-215. Whether a particular asset is subject to the protection of the series and the

Harmonization

For purposes of this chapter, "Harmonization" is defined as the process by which the drafter of Organic statutes attempts to identify those Characteristics with respect to which there are inadvertent inconsistencies, i.e., those reflecting unintentional differences among Forms of organization.[7] The National Conference of Commissioners on Uniform State Laws ("NCCUSL") has a project entitled "Harmonization of Business Entity Acts" ("NCCUSL Harmonization Project")[8] the product of which will be a code of acts comprising uniform statutes for general and limited partnerships, LLCs, unincorporated nonprofit associations, statutory trusts, and cooperative associations as well as the Model Entity Transactions Act ("META")[9] and the Model Registered Agents Act ("MRAA").[10] The NCCUSL Harmonization Project defined Harmonization as an attempt "to make similar provisions in all unincorporated business entity acts the same, while also recognizing the differences between unincorporated business forms and maintaining those distinct differences."[11]

The Characteristics that are the best candidates for Harmonization are those related to Inter-Form transactions and those that may be thought of as "plumbing." As noted below in the discussion of the development of Harmonization, Inter-Form transactions such as mergers and conversions put a premium on being able to describe Characteristics of the surviving organization in a manner consistent with that used for the Characteristics of the merging or converting organizations. Plumbing Characteristics are almost always Characteristics that are not heavily policy driven such as available names, contents of filed documents, rules applicable to registered agents and therefore the argument for Harmonization is quite strong. Names are a particularly easy example: a jurisdiction that establishes rules for when a name is either "deceptively

---

extent to which any creditor may reach such asset are determined by the nonpublic limited liability company agreement and the internal accounting for such asset.

[7] The distinction between Harmonization and Rationalization that this chapter employs is a distinction not always observed in discussions of Harmonization, Rationalization or both. Much of the discussion uses the terms interchangeably, although, as discussed herein, the difference between the two concepts can be significant.

[8] The Harmonization of Business Entity Acts Project, although not formally completed was, according to the NCCUSL website, approved by NCCUSL in 2011 and amended in 2013, and has been adopted in the District of Columbia and introduced in Idaho. Nonetheless, as of November 7, 2014, according to the NCCUSL website, the final act was "unavailable." See www.uniformlaws.org/Act.aspx?title=Harmonization of Business Entity Acts. References to language from the Harmonization of Business Entity Acts Project are to the most recent public documents available on the NCCUSL website.

[9] META is an act dealing with certain Inter-Form transactions such as mergers, conversions, interest exchanges, domestications, and divisions of organizations.

[10] As the name suggests, MRAA deals with the procedures for registering, including contents of a registration application, changing a prior filing, or resigning as a registered agent. Like META, MRAA is a "model act" which indicates that the language is more precatory than that of "uniform" acts, which are intended not as a flexible model but as a rigorously orthodox statement of both the policies and syntax of the statute to be adopted without modification.

[11] Memorandum from Chairman Harry J. Haynsworth to Drafting Comm. On Harmonization of Unincorporated Entity Acts 1 (Sept. 29, 2009) cited in Dylla, A Case for The Adoption of the Revised Uniform Limited Liability Company Act in South Dakota, 56 S.D. L. Rev. 285 (2011).

similar" to, or not "distinguishable on the records" from, another name already on the records (and therefore not available for use by a new organization) should not vary depending on the Form of organization being formed.[12] Characteristics which are good candidates for Harmonization—particularly plumbing Characteristics—are generally External Characteristics. This is the case because third parties are generally not in a position to affect the Internal Characteristics and ordinarily will not be affected by them. While in a broad sense, those establishing an organization may affect the rights of third parties in their selection of Form of organization, once that selection is made, the rights and expectations of the third parties will generally be those for which the Organic statute provides and not subject to the internal agreement of the Constituents of the organization.

Rationalization

"Rationalization" is an approach to changing Organic statutes that compares provisions of different Organic statutes dealing with the same Characteristic to determine which statutory construction is superior and to conform the Characteristic deemed by the statutory drafter to be an inferior rule to the one the drafter considers superior.

Joan Heminway described "rationalization" as "a consideration of parallel rules from the different forms of entity in light of underlying policy and applicable theory."[13] As Heminway indicates, this Rationalization goes beyond the Harmonization, the attempt to coordinate inconsistently worded—but otherwise policy-indistinguishable—pronouncements in the statutes, by allowing those drafting statutes to remove Characteristics of Organic statutes with which they disagree and replace them with Characteristics they find more attractive. Unlike Harmonization, Rationalization does not concern itself with inadvertent inconsistencies, but rather with the "improvement" of all Organic statutes by engrafting Characteristics from one Form onto the Organic statute of another. As such, Rationalization tends to reduce distinctions among Organic statutes that may have been developed intentionally, or if developed inadvertently, may have come to be accepted and expected by those using the statutes.

The effect of Rationalization is to negate the choice of Characteristic within a particular jurisdiction though choice of Form of organization. This is accomplished by reducing the extent to which Characteristics under any Organic statute vary from the Characteristic deemed by whomever is doing the Rationalizing to be the optimal Characteristic for all Forms.

---

[12] Robert R. Keatinge, Plumbing and Other Transitional Issues, 58 Bus. L. 1051 (May 2003) (discussing the importance of Characteristics of this sort and noting that such Characteristics are important and do not get the attention and respect they deserve. The title comes from the John Gardner quote "The society which scorns excellence in plumbing because plumbing is a humble activity, and tolerates shoddiness in philosophy because philosophy is an exalted activity, will have neither good plumbing nor good philosophy. Neither its pipes nor its theories will hold water.").

[13] Joan MacLeod Heminway, Rationalizing Entity Law: Corporate Law And Alternative Entities (Part II) 2013-DEC Bus. L. Today (December 2013) available at www.americanbar.org/content/dam/aba/publications/blt/2013/12/full-issue-201312.authcheckdam.pdf.

Pursuit of Uniformity

"Uniformity" refers to the conforming of the Organic statutes of different jurisdictions relating to the same Form of organization. There are two principal bodies promulgating recommended national business organization legislation. NCCUSL principally pursues Uniformity by drafting "uniform" legislation, which is intended to be adopted *verbatim* or as close thereto as possible, and, in some instances "model" legislation where NCCUSL determines that Uniformity is impractical either as result of the failure of a NCCUSL project to attain Uniformity or because the statute being considered will be subject to particularized state rules or interstate compacts.[14] In contrast to Harmonization and Rationalization, which is the vertical coordination of Characteristics of the organic statutes within a particular jurisdiction to eliminate non-policy-driven distinctions, the pursuit of "Uniformity" represents an attempt to make statutes in different jurisdictions consistent.

In the area of new or changing Forms of organization, there is a natural tendency of each jurisdiction, often through state bar associations (or what the Delaware courts refer to as the "organs of the bar"[15]) to look at the Organic statutes of other states and imitate those provisions that the adopting jurisdiction finds agreeable. This was the manner in which LLCs were developed. Occasionally a special interest group will make a national effort for the adoption of a statute in every state. A successful example of this process was one conducted by the American Association of Certified Public Accounts together with major accounting firms for the adoption of LLP legislation.[16]

---

[14] NCCUSL has as its mission "to promote uniformity of law among the states, and to support and protect the federal system of government by seeking an appropriate balance between federal and state law." Its principal purpose is the adoption of uniform legislation, i.e., a statute that does not vary from the orthodox NCCUSL-promulgated statute. Reluctantly, NCCUSL will propose a "model act" which "a) provides, on a matter of interstate interest, a comprehensive well-worked-out model whose provisions can be lifted in whole or in part by a state, or b) provides uniformity of underlying principle on a point of importance; but in the absence of interstate implications acts of this sort are definitely discouraged; or c) provides a model for handling an emergent need to keep emergent legislation sane and harmonious." Nat'l Conference of Comm'rs on Unif. State Laws and Proceedings of the 55th Annual Meeting 57 (1946) cited in Robert A. Stein, Forming A More Perfect Union, A History of the Uniform Law Commission, available at www.uniformlaws.org/Shared/Publications/ULC%20History%20Book/Forming%20a%20More%20Perfect%20Union.pdf at page 70. In its Statement of Policy Establishing Criteria and Procedures for Designation and Consideration of Acts (July 13, 2010) 143–144, NCCUSL expressed this policy by distinguishing between "uniform acts" as those with respect to which "uniformity of the provisions of the proposed enactment among the states is a principal objective" and "model acts," which are those with respect to which "(A) uniformity is a desirable objective, though not a principal objective; (B) the act may promote uniformity and minimize diversity, even though a significant number of states do not enact the act in its entirety; or (C) the purposes of the act can be substantially achieved even though it is not adopted in its entirety by every state."

[15] See, e.g., Auriga Capital Corp. v. Gatz Properties, 40 A.3d 839, 856 (Del. Ch. 2012) judgment entered sub nom. Auriga Capital Corp. v. Gatz Properties, LLC, 4390-CS, 2012 WL 598121 (Del. Ch. Feb. 23, 2012) aff'd, 59 A.3d 1206 (Del. 2012); Feeley v. NHAOCG, LLC, 62 A.3d 649, 662 (Del. Ch. 2012); Gatz Properties, LLC v. Auriga Capital Corp., 59 A.3d 1206, 1219 (Del. 2012).

[16] Robert R. Keatinge et. al., Limited Liability Partnerships: The Next Step in the Evolution of the Unincorporated Business Organization, 51 Bus. Law. 147, 159 (1995); Robert A. Prentice,

A less successful example of this process is that conducted by B Lab to have states adopt "benefit corporation" statutes.[17] In other cases, groups of professionals from various states have combined through national bar associations in order to consider business organization legislation with the intention of offering their drafting to assist state drafting committees in developing their statutes. The Model Business Corporation Act ("MBCA") and Prototype LLC Act and their revisions are such statutes. Unlike NCCUSL and the sponsors of special interest legislation and like all state Organic statutes, the MBCA and Prototype statutes are offered in the marketplace of ideas to be drawn upon if felt appropriate but without proselytizing zeal.[18] In this chapter, "Uniformity" refers to the sort of orthodoxy that NCCUSL espouses, as opposed to the more precatory approach pursued by the statutes developed by American Bar Association committees.

2. ALTERNATIVE APPROACHES TO HARMONIZATION

Harmonization, in its earliest forms, was done in response to the need to facilitate the mergers or conversions involving more than one Form of organization. Alternatives for Harmonized statutes had been discussed as early as 1967.[19] Colorado adopted a separate

---

Anatomy of a Fraud: Inside the Finances of the PTL Ministries. Gary L. Tidwell. John Wiley & Sons, Inc., 1993. Pp. 357, 31 Am. Bus. L.J. 519, 534 (1993) citing Accountants Coalition, The Liability Crisis in the United States: Impact on the Accounting Profession — A Statement of Position (1992) and Ed Roberts, Big Six Firms Branch Out to Create Lobby, Making Liability Reform Top 1993 Priority, Thomson's Int'l Bank Accountant, May 10, 1993, at 5 (describing the Accountants Coalition as group comprising what were at that time the Big Six major accounting firms).

[17] See Benefit Corp Information Center at benefitcorp.net. B Lab, like NCCUSL, wants to mandate the language of benefit corporation statutes to benefit its activities of evaluating the benefits conferred by the organizations and, like NCCUSL, has not been successful in maintaining orthodoxy in those states it has been successful in convincing to adopt its special interest product. Mark J. Loewenstein, Benefit Corporations: A Challenge in Corporate Governance, 68 Bus. Law. 1007, 1010 (2013).

[18] On its website, www.uniformlaws.org/, NCCUSL makes it clear at the outset with its slogan "Diversity of Thought, Uniformity of Law" suggesting, one supposes, the interesting concept that although there may be different ideas about the policy or particulars of a statute, those inconsistent ideas may only be expressed in one orthodox statutory formulation. NCCUSL's passion for Uniformity is interesting as it perceives itself as a defender of Federalism, but were it to attain its goal of universal state acceptance of a single Organic statute, the result would be difficult to distinguish from a Federal Organic statute.

[19] Robert A. Kessler, With Limited Liability For All: Why Not a Partnership Corporation?, 36 Fordham L. Rev. 235 (1967) and Harry J. Haynsworth, The Need for a Unified Small Business Legal Structure, 33 Bus. Law. 849 (1978); On August 7, 1995, George Coleman of Texas and the author in connection with the American Bar Association's Business Law Section Committee on Taxation and Partnerships and Unincorporated Business Organizations, presented a draft argument for and proposed the Azle Society, UNIversal [Contractual] ORgaNization Act (or Unicorn), which, for a time was available at www.stcl.edu/lnet-llc/commllo.html but, like its eponym, the Unicorn has vanished from the world and lives on only in literature as described in Haynsworth. See also, Dale A. Oesterle & Wayne M. Gazur, What's In A Name?: An Argument for a Small Business "Limited Liability Entity" Statute (With Three Subsets of Default Rules), 32 Wake Forest

Inter-Form transaction statute in 1997,[20] which was followed six years later when Texas adopted the Texas Business Organization Code with a deferred effective date.[21]

Ad hoc Harmonization (Delaware)

Delaware is an example of one form of Harmonization wherein, rather than having a single "hub" or "junction box" statute, the organs of the bar that create preliminary drafts of business organization statutes attempt to assure that the statutes each contain the same language.[22] This conformity of language in Delaware statutes has been done traditionally over many years and reflects the approach to Harmonization historically followed by most states before the advent of statutes like those described below.

This approach is probably most effective in avoiding inadvertent undermining of the policy underlying each Organic statute as the Harmonized language is included in the Organic statute itself. In this way, the Harmonization is done using the language and structure of each Organic statute without the problems and risks attendant to coordinating differences in definitions and structures among different Organic statutes.

"Junction Box" Harmonization (Colorado and META)

The initial impetus for the Harmonization of Organic statutes was the desire to facilitate the transformation of existing organizations—especially general and limited partnerships—into LLCs as efficiently as corporations combine under merger and consolidation statutes. The ability to transform an organization from one Form to another or to combine organizations of two different Forms into a surviving organization through a process that does not involve more than a single filing with the state filing officer was particularly important once the LLC became widely accepted and the tax and state law questions had been resolved. Inter-Form transactions required changes to the organizational statutes to ensure that the transactions could be accomplished smoothly and easily.

In response to this need, state Organic statutes were modified, first to permit partnerships to convert into LLCs and then to permit an organization of one Form to convert into, or merge with, an organization of any other Form. These statutes tended to be based on the merger provisions of corporate statutes, but, because different Forms of organization have different Characteristics, the new Organic statutes had to provide for these differences. The Organic statutes did this by considering the transformation of one Form of organization to another through merger or conversion as having three issues to be resolved: (1) How is the transaction approved by the organization? (2) How

---

L. Rev. 101 (1997) and Mark J. Loewenstein, A New Direction for State Corporation Codes, 68 U. Colo. L. Rev. 453 (1997).

[20] Colorado Session Laws 1997 Chapter 260 (approved June 3, 1997).

[21] The Texas Business Organization Code Acts 2003, 78th Leg., ch. 182, Sec. 1, eff. Jan. 1, 2006.

[22] Thus, for example, the 2014 amendments to the Delaware alternative entity statutes, H.B. 327, 147th Gen. Ass. (dealing *inter alia* with the request for information from a limited liability company) corresponds with the language of H.B. 328, 147th Gen. Ass. (dealing with limited partnerships) and 326 (dealing with general partnerships).

is the transaction effected by the organization? and (3) what is the effect of the transaction (on the owners, the property of the organization, the creditors of the organization, and those dealing with the organization)? Statutory drafters were required to identify the Characteristics that were implicated by each of the issues. As the earliest of these Inter-Form transactions were between partnerships and LLCs, the issues were not particularly hard because, as contractually based unincorporated organizations, they have many Characteristics in common.[23] It was determined that, in the case of a merging or converting limited partnership, the approval of the transaction and the liability of partners for obligations incurred before the transaction would continue to be governed by the Characteristics of the limited partnership statute,[24] the manner of effecting the merger or conversion would be governed by the Organic statute authorizing the merger or conversion (in this case, the LLC statute), and that, except to the extent that former Characteristics would be carried over as described above, the surviving organization's Characteristics would be governed by the surviving organization's Organic statute. This mixing and matching of Characteristics from two Organic statutes militated in favor of some coordination of the language between the two statutes, although an effort was made not to allow this coordination to upset the basic traditional structure of the two statutes. Thus, after a conversion, the general partner would be a member of the surviving LLC but would continue to have vicarious liability for pre-conversion debts assumed by the LLC in the conversion to the same extent as had been the case before the conversion.

As increasing flexibility was sought—such as statutory simplification for conversions of LLCs to or from business and nonprofit corporations—the issues of coordination of the Organic statutes became complicated, so a movement began to remove these Inter-Form reorganization provisions from the Organic statutes of the Forms of organization and into a statute through which an organization could enter as one Form and emerge as another—thus the term "junction box" statutes. Colorado adopted its first Inter-Form transaction statute in 1997 (the "Colorado Corporations and Associations Act" or "Colo. CCA").[25] The Colo. CCA was initially limited to Inter-Form transactions (now available for all Forms of organization including corporations and foreign organizations) but has since been expanded to deal with filing documents,[26] powers of the secretary of state,[27] annual reports,[28] entity names,[29] registered agents,[30] foreign entities,[31] delinquency and

---

[23] See Colorado Session Laws 1994 Chapter 139 § 34 (approved April 19, 1994) (adding provisions allowing a partnership or limited partnership to convert into, or merge with, an LLC).

[24] See, e.g., C.R.S. § 7-80-1001(1994) (providing, for example, in the case of the conversion of a limited partnership to an LLC, that the approval of a conversion is governed by the limited partnership agreement and that after the completion of the conversion, the general and limited partners would continue to have the same liability with respect to liabilities incurred before the conversion as they had had before the conversion).

[25] C.R.S § 7-90-101 *et seq.* (1997) adopted as Colorado Session Laws 1997 Chapter 260 (approved June 3, 1997).

[26] C.R.S § 7-90-301, *et seq.*

[27] C.R.S § 7-90-401, *et seq.*

[28] C.R.S § 7-90-501, *et seq.*

[29] C.R.S § 7-90-601, *et seq.*

[30] C.R.S § 7-90-701, *et seq.*

[31] C.R.S § 7-90-801, *et seq.*

dissolution of entities,[32] and reinstatement of dissolved entities.[33] In each case, the junction box statute balanced deferral to Characteristics of the Form of organization to the greatest extent possible.

Complex Hub-and-Spoke and Unified Statutes (Texas Business Organization Code –"TBOC")

Some statutes, seeking to address all aspects of business organizations in a single statute with a complex hub-and-spoke system, have been adopted in Texas[34] and Alabama.[35] These statutes attempt to Harmonize the statutes applicable to all business Forms within a separate code containing some "hubs" addressing particular business Forms (such as LLCs and corporations) and some addressing particular characteristics (such as merger, purpose, powers, filing or formation, names, indemnification, and foreign entities). This is the approach taken by the NCCUSL Harmonization Project.

3. EVALUATION OF HARMONIZATION EFFORTS

Evaluating Harmonization requires separation of Harmonization efforts from those related to Rationalization and the Pursuit of Uniformity. Of course it is impossible to completely separate the processes. The sort of close examination of the Organic statutes necessary to effectively Harmonize them will, perforce, cause the statutory drafter to note more substantial issues that, while not related to Harmonization, may be changed through Rationalization. Once the statutory drafter has embarked on improving the Organic statute, there will be a temptation to fall prey to the ease of Rationalization rather than thinking through issues related to one Form of organization with an eye toward preserving the unique aspects of the Form. In other words, it is easy enough to ask, "if this provision works for corporations, why shouldn't we include it in the partnership act?" The danger of such facile analysis is that because it often overlooks the distinctions among the essences of the various Forms, it permits the drafter to do violence to the Forms with which the drafter is less familiar or comfortable.

The Benefits and Drawbacks of Harmonization

As noted above, Harmonization was initially inspired by the need to bring some order to the new (and new combinations of) Characteristics resulting from the proliferation of Forms of organization.[36] Reducing the number of inconsequential

---

[32] C.R.S § 7-90-901, *et seq.*
[33] C.R.S § 7-90-1001, *et seq.*
[34] The Texas Business Organization Code Acts 2003, 78th Leg., ch. 182, Sec. 1, eff. Jan. 1, 2006.
[35] The Alabama Business and Nonprofit Entities Code (Act 2009-513, p. 967).
[36] See, e.g., the discussion of the Colorado experience at the text accompanying footnote 23 above. Inter-Form transactions are those in which the one Form of organization is transmogrified into another either as a result of a merger of two different Forms of organization or the conversion

differences between (and occasionally even within) Organic statutes facilitates the work of those working with both the new Forms of organization and the developments in older Forms in several ways. Harmonized Characteristics make it easier for filing officers to develop processes for organizing and maintaining organizations that are simpler and more intuitive, than might be the case if, for example, the filed documents of different Forms of organizations had to provide different types of information. In similar fashion, the judicial and regulatory interpretations of Harmonized Characteristics will apply to all of the Forms of organization sharing those common Characteristics. By eliminating idiosyncratic differences in Characteristics in filing and interpretation, Harmonization allows those organizing, operating, and winding up to focus on Characteristics that are significantly distinct. In addition, Harmonization, particularly in the hub-and-spoke statutes in which the Harmonized Rule is stated once for many or all Forms of organization rather than separately in each Organic statute, makes the modification of Characteristics in future amendments of the statute more efficient and effective than it would be if the same change had to be made in each Organic statute.

As the number of Forms of organization has increased, the common law available for the understanding of particular Characteristics has become diluted by an increase in both the number of discrete Characteristics a court may need to consider and the percentage of disputes resolved through alternative dispute resolution methods that do not provide a body of public opinions upon which business people and their advisors may draw.[37] Common Harmonized Characteristics across Forms allow guidance provided to one Form to be applicable to other Forms.

Appropriately done, Harmonization would appear to provide some benefit in both of these areas. A reduction in the number of distinct Characteristics eliminates some of the translation issues that arise when one Form of organization becomes another through an Inter-Form transaction and enables business people and their advisors to apply judicial and regulatory interpretations of the Characteristic of one Form of organization to the corresponding Characteristic of another. This benefit may be less available under the ad hoc Harmonization described above because in that case the Harmonization has a greater tendency to maintain differences in terminology and structure of corresponding statutory Characteristics.

Several states have undertaken to Harmonize their statutes in whole or in part in a variety of ways. Those efforts are touched upon in Section 2 above. In light of the definition of Harmonization set forth above, the appropriate test of the success of Harmonization would be to determine whether the changes had eliminated non-policy-driven distinctions within the statutes while preserving the Characteristics of each Form of organization that make it unique. This can probably be done through a before-and-after

---

of an organization of a particular From to another Form as when a limited partnership is merged with and into a corporation or an LLC coverts to a limited partnership.

[37] Robert R. Keatinge, Plumbing and Other Transitional Issues, 58 Bus. Law. 1051, 1059 (May, 2003) (citing Hope Viner Samborn, The Vanishing Trial, A.B.A. J., Oct. 2002, at 26 noting the decline in the number of public trials and quoting U.S. District Court Judge Sarah S. Vance of the Eastern District of Louisiana to the effect that the decline in trials has reduced the amount of "publicly made law," causing a decline in the amount of precedent).

comparison to determine whether the integrity of the statute has been violated or whether the Harmonization has made changes to a Characteristic.

That Harmonization has benefits is clear. Harmonization may serve to eliminate distinctions without intended differences that arise from the capricious way in which legislation is adopted. For example, where a time period for taking a certain action is 30 days in the statute for one Form of organization, and one month for the corresponding provision of the statute for another Form, the difference makes it difficult to standardize procedures and may result in capricious and surprising results.

In proper cases, Harmonization may assist in counteracting the arrest of common law. As noted above, many important Characteristics have not had the benefit of much, or in some cases any, published judicial interpretation or construction. Where the Characteristic is common to more than one Form of organization an interpretation of the Characteristic in the context of one Form will be helpful to those attempting to construe a similar Characteristic in another, thereby reducing the costs of uncertainty to those attempting to work with evolving Forms of organization. As discussed below, this virtue, imprecisely employed by the statutory drafter, may become a vice. The insertion of an inappropriate Characteristic into the statute governing one Form simply to conform it to another Form of organization may have the deleterious result of blurring important distinctions between the two Forms.

Harmonization provides additional efficiency and clarity of decision-making in connection with the selection of a Form of organization by eliminating idiosyncratic differences that otherwise would need to be considered. For example, to the extent that the rules applicable to plumbing or other common issues are handled in the same manner in all Forms of organization—or, commonly, in all Forms of unincorporated organizations—such items can be disregarded in selecting a Form of organization. This allows the selection of a Form to be better and more exclusively focused on those Characteristics that are truly distinct. Similarly, in operation and interpretation in the event of dispute, it reduces the number of extraneous differences that need be considered.

Finally, Harmonization, particularly in a hub-and-spoke regime, facilitates the coherent management of statutory change. Often, unintended statutory inconsistencies between corresponding Characteristics of different Forms of organization arise from imperfect or inconsistent statutory modifications, i.e., circumstances in which the amendment of corresponding provisions of the Organic statutes for different Forms of organization is done inconsistently or overlooked. The possibility of such problems is reduced by having the Characteristic in a hub in which a single amendment revises the Characteristic in each of the Organic statutes served by the hub. Of course this benefit comes with a concomitant risk. Statutory drafters need to consider the effect of an amendment of a hub on all the Forms of organization affected by that hub. Even in a Harmonized world, it is never easy.

Harmonization, again particularly when accomplished through a hub or unified statute, may cause some experienced practitioners some confusion in finding the appropriate statutory rules. This should not be a major issue, as over the past three decades all business organization lawyers have been forced to relearn and adjust to a volume of new and reorganized law heretofore known only to lawyers practicing federal tax law. This problem should not be minimized but should be remedied through clear commentary and education programs.

A much greater problem arises when the harmonizer, like the Sorcerer's Apprentice, does not know when to stop. If Harmonization is allowed to morph into Rationalization and is not undertaken thoughtfully and with restraint, it will do far more damage than good. As stated by Mark Loewenstein:

> Corporate law and the law of alternative entities need not be harmonized solely for the sake of harmonization. I have tried to show some instances in which harmonization has already occurred, others where it makes sense for it to occur, and still others where harmonization makes little sense. While the end of the 20th century saw a significant increase in the number of entities available to the entrepreneur, the challenge of the 21st century will be to consider whether the legal differences among those entities makes sense and, if not, how the law should be harmonized.[38]

A risk related to those set forth above is that in the course of Harmonization words will be given new meanings that are inconsistent with the meanings that have been assigned them by statutes and common law in the past. For example, concepts such as "entity," "formation," and "interest" (as in "partnership interest," "LLC interest" and the like) may have nuanced meanings that are based on the particular Characteristics of the Form of organization. These nuances may be lost if the Harmonization is not done thoughtfully. A particularly clear example of this appears in the NCCUSL Harmonization Project, which, attempting to Harmonize language, substituted "consent or vote" for consent in the Uniform Partnership Act.[39]

The Benefits and Drawbacks of Rationalization

Like Harmonization, Rationalization has the beneficial effect of coordinating Characteristics, thereby facilitating Inter-Form transactions and making the limited case law more useful. Unlike Harmonization, Rationalization attains this benefit through the conscious changing of Characteristics of the Organic statute governing one Form of organization to correspond with the different Characteristics of the Organic statute governing another Form. Forms of organization have proliferated because the market seeks Forms with different Characteristics for a large variety of reasons. In evaluating Rationalization and Uniformity, it is important to start by deciding whether there is value in being able select from a menu of alternative Forms of organization.[40] Rather than eliminating inadvertent differences, Rationalization dictates that with respect to a particular Characteristic, the only correct answer for all Forms is the Characteristic already inherent in one of the Forms. Examples of such Rationalization would be to say that the charging

---

[38] Mark J. Loewenstein, Rationalizing Entity Law: Corporate Law and Alternative Entities (Part I) 2013-DEC Bus. L. Today (December 2013) available at www.americanbar.org/content/dam/aba/publications/blt/2013/12/full-issue-201312.authcheckdam.pdf.

[39] See the text accompanying footnote 44 below.

[40] This chapter assumes that, because newer organizations such as LLCs and LLPs have grown as rapidly as they have, there is a market for such variations, which should be allowed to grow. For charts comparing Characteristics of various Forms of organization, see, Thomas E. Rutledge, Let's Stop Describing LLCs as "Hybrids," Jour. of Passthrough Entities 33, 35 (September–October 2014) and Robert R. Keatinge, Ann Conaway, and Bruce Ely, Keatinge and Conaway on Choice of Business Entity (2015) Appendix A. For statistics on the growth of various Forms of organization see Keatinge and Conaway on Choice of Business Entity, Appendix D.

order as an exclusive remedy for creditors of a partner or member of an LLC is such a salutary Characteristic that it should be made a Characteristic of corporate law or that a corporate concept of democratic governance, even in the case of the most fundamental of decisions, by the holders of a majority of the outstanding stock should replace the contract-based partnership Characteristic that all extraordinary decisions, the amendment of an inter-partner contract, require the consent of all the partners.

Although Harmonization adds efficiency and facilitates consistent evolution of the statutes, if not applied thoughtfully Harmonization may become Rationalization without the different level of thoughtfulness that Rationalization requires. The eugenic Rationalization process may be one approach to the improvement to the Organic statutes, but differs significantly from Harmonization in both benefits and dangers. The benefits of consistent thoughtful review and improvement of Organic statutes are manifold, including providing certainty in planning and behavior in light of highly contextual and sometimes confusing case law; eliminating ambiguity without the cost and disruption of judicial proceedings; and addressing new questions raised by changes in business (some of which arise in response to previous "improvements" to Organic statutes). Unlike the elimination of unintentional discontinuities that comprise Harmonization, Rationalization—like all statutory improvements—has the effect of changing significant rules upon which some may have relied in selecting an Organic statute under which to organize. And statutory improvement should always involve a thoughtful approach based on principles related to the Characteristic being considered, not the mere elimination of unprincipled differences that is the stuff of Harmonization. As such, Rationalization is quite different from Harmonization.

As a Form statutory improvement, Rationalization presents subtle risks that Characteristics that have evolved under the regime applicable to one Form may be efficiently engrafted on another Form having a different evolution. As such, attempting to Rationalize Organic statutes at the same time as they are being Harmonized runs the risk that neither Harmonization nor Rationalization will be done well. As part of an attempt to Harmonize a statute it is easy to lose perspective on those aspects of the Organic statute that support the unique Characteristics of a particular Form of organization. Harmonization should not be an excuse to eliminate the Characteristics that distinguish one Form of organization from another.[41]

Rationalization may sometimes play a role in developing External Characteristics as such Characteristics affect third parties. Such External Characteristics as vicarious liability of owners and agents for the debts and obligations of the organization and the power of agents to bind the organization may benefit from some coordination among Forms. Many of the state Inter-Form transaction statutes and hub-and-spoke arrangements have accomplished this by creating new language that accommodates the language of the respective Organic statutes governing the various Forms of organization involved in the transaction. This respectful coordination facilitates transactions involving different Forms of organization while preserving the integrity of the respective Forms and their Organic statutes.

---

[41] See "The Danger of Over-Harmonization—The Rise (and One Hopes Fall) of Frankencluster" below.

A very different dynamic is involved when it comes to Internal Characteristics. These Characteristics will affect the rights and duties of the owners and other Constituents who have voluntarily subjected themselves to the rules of the Organic statute, either (in the case of corporate organizations) by acquiring stock with the constructive notice provided by the articles or certificate of incorporation, or (in the case of unincorporated organizations) by entering into the agreement which forms the basic governing document of the organization. In the case of Internal Characteristics there is little benefit to Rationalization, and Rationalization of Internal Characteristics may result in an Organic statute which is, at best, a confused and unhappy amalgam of inconsistent Characteristics, and, at worst, one which undercuts the basic nature of the Form of organization into which the Rationalized Internal Characteristics are engrafted.[42]

For example, the corporate process of formation entails a filing by an incorporator who is not, or not yet, a shareholder, followed by an organizational meeting at which either the incorporator or directors designated by the incorporator, adopt the internal rules and sell shares of stock to the shareholders. After this two-step filing/organization process, the corporation is formed, capable of doing business and the shareholders are the owners of the corporation. In contrast, a partnership is formed by the association of the partners, without the intercession of a non-owner such as an incorporator or the necessity of a post-formation issuance of partnership interests—essentially the agreement of the partners forms the partnership. The same principle—basing the formation of the organization on the association of the owners—applies to other contract-based organizations, such as limited partnerships and LLCs. Attempting to conform the partnership formation Characteristics to those applicable to the corporation would create the confusion of whether the fundamental concept of an "association" or agreement of partners or members is either necessary or sufficient for the creation of a competent organization.

The Benefits and Drawbacks of the Pursuit of Uniformity

The pursuit of Uniformity, like Harmonization, seeks to conform unintentional differences in Organic statutes by providing standard language for the sorts of Characteristics that are common to all statutes and may provide a statutory organizational framework making it easier to compare the Characteristics in one jurisdiction with those in another. Like Rationalization, it looks, *inter alia*, at the way in which different Organic statutes seek to deal with the same Characteristic, either in search of the superior or the most popular, as a model for a "uniform" statute that should be adopted by all. Uniformity has some benefits when it seeks to truly Harmonize statutes, as it will facilitate interstate

---

[42] Bruce H. Kobayashi & Larry E. Ribstein, Delaware for Small Fry: Jurisdictional Competition for Limited Liability Companies, 2011 U. Ill. L. Rev. 91, 100 (2011). ("Terms affecting third parties present the strongest case for uniformity because the smaller transaction amounts associated with infrequent third-party dealings are unlikely to motivate firms to engage in customized drafting or to search for different statutory terms. Firms, therefore, may economize on transaction costs by adopting uniform statutory provisions as to terms that mainly affect third parties. By contrast, provisions affecting the members involve frequent and repeated interaction where the net benefits from variation and innovation are likely to be high and the net benefits of uniform rules are likely to be the lowest.")

transactions by using common terminology for common Characteristics and facilitate coordination of the ministerial functions of filing officers. When Uniformity acts to improve statutes, it creates the same risks that Rationalization does and, if effective, would arrest the benefits recognized through individual jurisdictional competition.

While Harmonization, dealing with unintentional or insignificant differences, will leave the Forms largely intact, Rationalization and the pursuit of Uniformity have had the effect of eliminating substantive distinctions from the Forms of organization.

Like Rationalization, Uniformity seeks to determine the "right" rule for all organizations of a particular Form. Just as Rationalization would prevent a person from selecting a particular Characteristic by choosing to organize as a different Form of organization, Uniformity would deny owners the ability to select to organize under the Organic statute of another jurisdiction. When Rationalization is combined with the pursuit of Uniformity, as is the case with the NCCUSL Harmonization Project, the result is doubly pernicious. Were this legislation to be widely adopted, it could arrest business creators' ability to order their relationship either through the choice of Form of organization or choice of jurisdiction of formation. Fortunately, based on lack of success that NCCUSL has had with the statutes it has promulgated over the last 20 years (i.e., since the adoption of the 1994 version of the Uniform Partnership Act), one may hope that the NCCUSL Harmonization Project will enjoy the same lack of acceptance as have its other statutes and, in spite of itself, will be relegated to being but one entry in the marketplace of statutory ideas.

While statutes promulgated under the banner of Uniformity are designed to limit state experimentation and diversity, model statutes, although drafted in the context of fully integrated statutes, are intended to provide ideas which may be drawn upon in whole or in part or not at all by state stator drafting groups.

The Danger of Over-Harmonization—The Rise (and One Hopes Fall) of Frankencluster

There are unquestionable benefits of Harmonization, and each of Rationalization and Uniformity, if approached carefully and thoughtfully, can improve Organic statutes. Nonetheless, when Rationalization and pursuit of Uniformity are done for their own sake and without careful consideration of the fundamental natures of the discrete Forms of organization, Rosalind must be answered in the affirmative,[43] it is possible to have too much of a good thing. This is particularly true when the processes address Internal Characteristics and even more so when the Rationalization of those Internal Characteristics is done through mandatory rather than default internal matters. The result of such over-Harmonization is, at best, the mismatch of Characteristics that do not necessarily play well together, and, at worst, the doing of such violence to the structure of a Form of organization as to fundamentally alter or eliminate its utility.

The NCCUSL Harmonization Project provides clear examples of the overdoing of Harmonization, Rationalization, and pursuit of Uniformity. An example of the most pernicious consequences of Rationalization and Uniformity is the violence done to evolving unincorporated organization law that would result from wide acceptance of the

---

[43] As You Like It, Act IV scene 1.

NCCUSL Harmonization Project, either *in toto* or through the adoption of any of the Organic statutes it comprises. The project began as an effort to do simple Harmonization, but its leadership saw it as an opportunity to use Rationalization and Uniformity for conforming unincorporated organization law more closely to corporate law. The conflicts and confusion in motivation have led to something of a "Frankencluster"—a statute that attempts at once to combine, convert, and coordinate Characteristics of different Forms—in which none of the underlying purposes of the endeavor have been accomplished. The result is a confused combination of inconsistent Characteristics in which Harmonization is frustrated by the other changes the drafters are seeking to accomplish, the desired Rationalization is hopelessly distorted by the pretense of Harmonization, and uniform adoption is unlikely, at least in states in which the drafting process is subject to any thoughtful review. The NCCUSL Harmonization Project is an example of such a Frankencluster.

A sample of the confusion that can occur from excessive Rationalization is the changing of references to a partner's right to consent to a right to "vote or consent" in the Uniform Partnership Act (2011) (last amended 2013)[44] issued as part of the NCCUSL Harmonization Project. While the purpose of the changes is not yet available from NCCUSL, the addition either reflects an intent to engraft a corporate concept of voting (presumably including such concepts as record date, voting groups, and proxies) which heretofore have not been traditional elements of partnership jurisprudence except where partners intentionally use such concepts as a method of "consenting" to transactions under their agreement, or, in the alternative, it may intend no change at all in which case the added language will serve to confuse partners, opinion givers, litigants, and courts without providing any other benefits. This confusion will result, in part, from the introduction of a portion of Characteristic from corporate law into an unincorporated organizational setting. The Model Business Corporation Code devotes two entire subchapters to explaining the rules applicable to voting and voting trusts.[45] It is not clear how much of this statutory gloss is intended to be imported into the partnership act by these changes, but it may reasonably be expected that the issue will be raised at some point in the future when some clever litigant argues that the legislature would not have added the concept of "voting" to the partnership act unless it wished to make a change to the statute and that the change is intended to incorporate some or all of the recondite requirements of the corporate statute.

Fundamental changes in the policy underlying a Form of organizations should not be made as an afterthought or byproduct of Harmonization—such important policy

---

[44] See UPA (2011 last amended 2013) §§ 105(c)(13), 401(k), and 404(c)(1). As noted above, the final integrated example of this statute has not been published by NCCUSL, but it has been subject to legislative consideration in at least two states. As the final versions of the "Harmonized" acts have not been published, it is unclear how they will be designated, and to date drafts have been designated in different ways. For example the Uniform Limited Liability Company Act that was adopted in 2006 was known as the Revised Uniform Limited Liability Company Act. Its designation was changed to the Uniform Limited Liability Company Act (2006) and, the first iteration of the "Harmonized" act was referred to as: the Harmonized Revised Uniform Limited Liability Company Act (2006) (Last Amended 2011) and, most recently, as the Uniform Limited Liability Company Act (2013 Amendments to 2011 Revisions).

[45] Model Business Corporation Code §§ 7.20 through 7.32.

decisions should be based upon focused and careful study and debate. The NCCUSL Harmonization Project demonstrates the deleterious effects that occur when attempts to Harmonize Organic statutes morph into a program of Rationalization and Uniformity with the purpose of making a fundamental change in the policy underlying a Form. Trying to mask Rationalization and Uniformity as Harmonization is like trying to teach a pig to sing: it sounds terrible and irritates the pig. In this case, the efforts to Harmonize the statute will be undermined by the efforts to conceal fundamental Rationalization and Uniformity within that Harmonization, thereby distorting and misleading in an effort that should result in greater clarity and simplicity. The Rationalization and pursuit of Uniformity will also be diminished as a result of the attempt to conceal the attempt to vitiate or eliminate Forms in changes that can be presented as simple Harmonization—often leaving statutes that are more confused and inconsistent than those they replace. For example, the NCCUSL Harmonization Project, as an attempt to eliminate flexibility and contractually based rules, would be more effective were it to be honest about its goals and not attempt to bury its intentions in language purporting to Harmonize or in commentary.[46]

Unincorporated entities like partnerships, limited partnerships, LLCs and the various alternative Forms of partnership such as LLPs and LLLPs, are fundamentally based on the "association" or agreement of their members.[47] As such, the Organic statute provides that the partnership agreement, as the contract among the partners, has primacy in determining the Internal Characteristics of partnerships and other unincorporated organizations. This contractual freedom has been memorialized in many Organic statutes.[48]

Recent NCCUSL statutes culminating in the NCCUSL Harmonization Project have evinced strong hostility to contractual freedom to modify the fiduciary duties and, in particular, to the language respecting freedom of contract. The comment to Uniform Limited Liability Company Act ("ULLCA") (2006) § 110(d) explains why that statute does not contain a reference to freedom of contract:

> Delaware recently amended its LLC statute to permit an operating agreement to fully "eliminate" fiduciary duty within an LLC. This Act rejects the ultra-contractarian notion that fiduciary duty within a business organization is merely a set of default rule [sic] and seeks instead to balance the virtues of "freedom of contract" against the dangers that inescapably exist when some have power over the interests of others.

Fortunately, this attempt to use Rationalization and Uniformity to undermine the fundamental nature of the unincorporated Form of organization has not met with much success. The ULLCA has been adopted by 12 states since its promulgation in 2006.[49]

---

[46] As of November 7, 2014, the final commentary for the changes made in 2011 and 2013 have not yet been posted on the NCCUSL website, so whether the final commentary will express the intention of the drafters still remains to be seen.

[47] See, e.g., UPA (1914) § 6(1) ("A partnership is an association of two or more persons to carry on as co-owners a business for profit.").

[48] See, e.g., 6 Del. Code § 18-1101(b) ("It is the policy of this chapter to give the maximum effect to the principle of freedom of contract and to the enforceability of limited liability company agreements."). Language identical or similar to this appears in the LLC statutes of approximately half of the United States. See Ribstein and Keatinge at Appendix 9–8.

[49] Alabama (although the Alabama Limited Liability Company Law of 2015 more closely resembles the Revised Prototype LLC Act than the most current iteration of ULLCA), California,

Of those 12, five have included an explicit statement to the effect that it is the policy of the state with respect to limited liability companies to give maximum effect to the principle of freedom of contract and to the enforceability of operating agreements.[50] In this respect, the careful consideration of revised legislation may, to some extent, offset NCCUSL's passion for Rationalization to the corporate model and its pursuit of Uniformity.

The NCCUSL Harmonization Project exemplifies another drawback with respect to Rationalization and Uniformity. As statutes that attempt to limit contractual freedom, ULLCA (2006) and the Harmonized ULLCA do not permit many of the Internal Characteristics that were allowable under previous acts. This regressive approach to freedom of contract not only makes it more difficult for owners to order their relationship by agreement, but it has the pernicious effect of potentially invalidating agreements drafted under previous Organic statutes. The effect of this regression on existing agreements creates additional inefficiency and uncertainty—just the thing that Harmonization is supposed to reduce.

An example of the uncertainty created by regressive legislation occurred in California when it adopted a revision to its LLC act based on ULLCA (2006). The Beverly-Killea Limited Liability Company Act, as in effect before 2014, provided a list of permissible remedies which the operating agreement could provide if a member failed to make a contribution, including the dilution, reduction, subordination, forced sale, or elimination of the member's interest.[51] This explicit list was not included in the corresponding provision of the California Revised Uniform Limited Liability Company Act which went into effect on January 1, 2014.[52] It is unclear whether this change was intended to eliminate the availability of the remedies the former statute permitted (and which, presumably, many operating agreements provide), but the better analysis is that the fact that such remedies were provided for by statute indicated that they are not per se violative of public policy, and allowing such contractual remedies would be consistent with the enunciated policy favoring freedom of contract.[53] Regardless of whether the intention was to eliminate the ability to use forfeiture as a remedy, the ambiguity created by this change makes the California statute less usable. Regardless of whether a court ultimately upholds such a

---

District of Columbia, Florida, Idaho, Iowa, Minnesota, Nebraska, New Jersey, South Dakota, Utah, Wyoming.

[50] Alabama (Ala. Code 1975 § 10A-5A-1.06(a)); California (Cal.Corp.Code § 17701.07(a)); Florida Statutes § 605.0111(1); New Jersey (New Jersey Stat. Ann. §42:2C-11(i)); South Dakota (South Dak. Cod. Laws§ 47-34A-114). Three other states, Hawaii, Illinois, and Montana, which adopted a previous version of ULLCA, do not have such a provision. One state, Utah, eliminated this language in adopting the most recent version of ULLCA and another, Alabama, added it. Altogether 25 states and the Prototype LLC Act have such as provision. See Ribstein and Keatinge on Limited Liability Companies (2015) Appendix 9–8.

[51] Cal. Corp. Code § 17201(a)(3) (providing that remedies for failure to make a required contribution could include reduction or eliminating of a defaulting member's interest for failure to make a contribution).

[52] Cal. Corp. Code §17704.03.

[53] Cal. Corp. Code § 17701.07 subd. (a) ("It is the policy of this title and this state to give maximum effect to the principles of freedom of contract and to the enforceability of operating agreements.").

provision, both parties will have incurred significant legal costs and delay as a result of the ambiguity created by the negligence of the statutory drafters.

That this result is uncertain reflects the problem with trying to modify the NCCUSL products promulgated over the last 20 years. The Uniform Limited Partnership, and LLC statutes and those comprising the NCCUSL Harmonization Project are all much more recondite than their forbears. This statutory complexity makes modifying one of the statutes like trying to defuse a very intricate bomb: if not done properly the results could be almost as bad as if no attempt to remedy the situation had been made.

Nonetheless, a fundamental change in policy with respect to a Form of organization should not be undertaken without full consideration of the consequences of the changes, and such changes should not be buried in a Bill that purports to Harmonize the Organic statutes.

4. CONCLUSION

Each of Harmonization, Rationalization, and the pursuit of Uniformity entails much thought and is attended by complexity and nuances (for example, Rationalization between Characteristics of corporate and unincorporated Forms is more treacherous than among unincorporated Forms, but even unincorporated Forms have important distinctions), and each has its own objectives and benefits. Combining the processes makes a difficult undertaking much more difficult and dangerous. Each process should be accomplished discretely so that the ultimate users of the Organic statutes, the business people who organize firms thereunder and the courts and lawyers who attempt to understand them in operation, can obtain the benefit of each process. To combine Harmonization, Rationalization, and the pursuit of Uniformity in a single process that seeks to universally limit contractual freedom with respect to Internal Characteristics, as does the NCCUSL Harmonization of Business Entity Acts Project, runs the risk of resulting in Organic statutes that are not harmonious, rational or uniform. One may hope, based on the continuing independent thought at state and national bar associations and elsewhere, that this project will be ignored or significantly modified at the state level and that the progress toward Harmonization will go forward.

19. Casual convergence in unincorporated entity law
Nadelle Grossman

1. INTRODUCTION

On the surface, the ocean looks like a big expanse of uniform blue, with a rhythmic roll of majestic tides. Yet one look below the surface reveals an underwater world much richer and more diverse than the unvarying surface suggests.

Similarly, on the surface, the laws governing unincorporated entities such as partnerships and limited liability companies (LLCs) often superficially look the same from state to state. That is because many state partnership and LLC acts are drafted from the same uniform acts put forth by the National Conference of Commissioners on Uniform State Laws (NCCUSL). In fact, there is much momentum behind making these laws uniform. According to proponents, uniformity not only facilitates the convergence toward beneficial laws, but also brings about administrative savings (Goforth 2007; Bishop & Kleinberger 2007).

Yet one look below the surface reveals that state unincorporated entity laws are quite divergent. In particular, in a qualitative study of state LLC acts, I found extensive divergences, even though those statutes were all based on the same uniform act—NCCUSL's Revised Uniform Limited Liability Company Act (RULLCA). Those divergences are especially strong in provisions governing internal affairs as well as those governing the relationship of the LLC with the state. I also found, from interviews of members of LLC act committees charged with effecting new LLC acts, that the tide pulling toward uniformity is quite weak in most states. As that qualitative research reveals, the appearance of uniformity has more to do with the practicalities of drafting a new LLC act than with achieving the goal of uniformity.

This chapter offers a framework for LLC law that comports with the divergent nature of LLC law, as well as with the weak uniformity goals of the LLC act committees at the heart of the LLC lawmaking process. Specifically, my findings support a framework referred to as "casual convergence." The term *casual* is used for two reasons. First, it captures the reality that while convergent in some respects, state LLC laws diverge in significant ways. The word *casual* thus refers to this loose level of convergence. Second, the term *casual* refers to the fact that most LLC act committee members do not chiefly seek to achieve interstate convergence. In fact, other factors such as a desire to achieve uniformity among a state's unincorporated entity statutes, the need to draft from a model, and the need to obtain legislative passage, indirectly lead to convergence. Thus, *casual* also refers to the fact that convergence is happening more coincidentally than intentionally.

2. ORGANIZATION OF THE CHAPTER

This chapter begins by explaining the dominant framework that is currently used to characterize unincorporated entity law—uniformity. As the discussion explains, unincorporated entity law is characterized as uniform because of the trend toward state adoptions of NCCUSL's uniform unincorporated entity acts. That discussion also reviews the primary critique of uniformity as a policy objective in the area of unincorporated entity law.

The chapter next explains why uniformity fails to capture the actual state of unincorporated entity law. Specifically, the chapter reports my findings from a qualitative study conducted of state LLC acts adopted since 2006, the year NCCUSL published RULLCA, its latest uniform act in the area of unincorporated entities.

As the chapter reports, there is a clear trend toward state adoptions of RULLCA. Yet, as the discussion also reports, states depart regularly, at times significantly, from RULLCA. In addition to reporting the results of the study, the chapter also discusses some of the reasons why states adhered to, and departed from, uniformity. That part of the discussion is largely based on interviews with practicing lawyers who were on LLC act committees, as well as my experience on such an LLC act committee where passage of a new LLC act is in process.

The study and interviews depict a different framework for unincorporated entity law from the traditional uniformity framework. Specifically, the next part of this chapter explains why a casual convergence framework best describes state LLC law.

The conclusion of this chapter highlights the importance of identifying the proper framework that applies to LLC law.

3. A UNIFORMITY FRAMEWORK IN UNINCORPORATED ENTITY LAW

Reasons for Uniformity

Unincorporated entities such as partnerships and LLCs are governed by state law (Bishop & Kleinberger 2014). That means each state enacts its own laws to regulate each type of legal entity. Despite varying state regulations, independent organizations such as NCCUSL advocate for unincorporated entity law uniformity. Specifically, NCCUSL is a nonprofit organization that drafts and promotes enactment of uniform laws across states.[1] NCCUSL is an especially strong advocate for interstate uniformity, including in the area of unincorporated entities laws.

In the area of unincorporated entity law, NCCUSL has promulgated a model

---

[1] THE NATIONAL CONFERENCE OF COMMISSIONERS ON UNIFORM STATE LAWS, www.uniformlaws.org/Act.aspx?title=Limited%20Liability%20Company%20%28Revised%29 (last visited Aug. 19, 2014).

partnership act,[2] a model limited partnership act,[3] and a model LLC act.[4] On its website, NCCUSL tracks the number of adoptions of each of these model acts.[5]

According to NCCUSL, uniformity "brings clarity and stability to critical areas of state statutory law."[6] Moreover, NCCUSL declares that uniformity "reduce[s] the need for individuals and businesses to deal with different laws as they move and do business in different states."[7] In the area of unincorporated entity law in particular, NCCUSL concludes that uniformity "reduce[s] compliance costs, streamline[s] administration (which reduces costs to states) and [provides] decisive consistency across jurisdictions."[8]

Some commentators applaud efforts at uniformity in the area of unincorporated entity law. For example, according to Professor Carol Goforth, uniformity in state business law is increasingly important as interstate business transactions become more prevalent (Goforth 2007). Interstate uniformity decreases the costs associated with becoming informed of other states' laws when advising multi-jurisdictional clients on their business needs. Goforth also lauds RULLCA for employing "terminology and concepts that appear in other modern business and commercial statutes" (Goforth 2007). Employing familiar terminology and concepts is beneficial because it, too, simplifies the task of becoming informed under a state's statute modeled on RULLCA. Employing the same terminology and concepts from other statutes might also help lawyers, litigants, and courts resolve disputes by allowing them to expand the body of case law to which they might look for guidance.

In addition to achieving desirable uniformity, NCCUSL boasts the quality of its uniform lawmaking process. Specifically, the extent of individual state participation in the drafting of its uniform statutes allows its statutes to reflect diverse state experiences.[9] According to NCCUSL, its "deliberative and uniquely open drafting process draws on the expertise of commissioners" as well as "legal experts, and advisors and observers

---

[2] *See Uniform Partnership Act (1997), replacing Uniform Partnership Act (1914)*, THE NATIONAL CONFERENCE OF COMMISSIONERS ON UNIFORM STATE LAWS, www.uniformlaws.org/Act.aspx?title=Partnership%20Act (last visited Aug. 19, 2014).

[3] *See Uniform Limited Partnership Act*, THE NATIONAL CONFERENCE OF COMMISSIONERS ON UNIFORM STATE LAWS, www.uniformlaws.org/Act.aspx?title=Limited%20Partnership%20Act (last visited Aug. 19, 2014).

[4] THE NATIONAL CONFERENCE OF COMMISSIONERS ON UNIFORM STATE LAWS, www.uniformlaws.org/Act.aspx?title=Limited%20Liability%20Company%20%28Revised%29 (last visited Aug. 19, 2014).

[5] *See, e.g., Limited Liability Company Act (Revised)*, THE NATIONAL CONFERENCE OF COMMISSIONERS ON UNIFORM STATE LAWS, www.uniformlaws.org/Act.aspx?title=Limited%20Liability%20Company%20%28Revised%29 (last visited Aug. 19, 2014) (showing 12 state adoptions of RULLCA).

[6] *Uniform Law Commission*, THE NATIONAL CONFERENCE OF COMMISSIONERS ON UNIFORM STATE LAWS, www.uniformlaws.org/Narrative.aspx?title=About%20the%20ULC (last visited Aug. 19, 2014).

[7] *Id.*

[8] *Why States Should Adopt RULLCA*, THE NATIONAL CONFERENCE OF COMMISSIONERS ON UNIFORM STATE LAWS, www.uniformlaws.org/Narrative.aspx?title=Why%20States%20Should%20Adopt%20RULLCA (last visited Aug. 19, 2014).

[9] *See Uniform Law Commission*, THE NATIONAL CONFERENCE OF COMMISSIONERS ON UNIFORM STATE LAWS, www.uniformlaws.org/Narrative.aspx?title=About%20the%20ULC (last visited Aug. 19, 2014).

representing the views of other legal organizations."[10] In short, NCCUSL provides quality drafting services to states that could not afford these services on their own.[11]

Much of the academic commentary in support of NCCUSL's efforts praises these statutory drafting benefits, as well as the virtues of the model acts that result from these efforts, rather than the benefits of uniformity *per se*. For example, in the same article mentioned above, one of the key advantages Goforth identified with RULLCA is that it was drafted with recent developments in mind (Goforth 2007). Moreover, Goforth delved into RULLCA's many substantive virtues. Similarly, Professors Carter Bishop and Daniel Kleinberger, the two co-reporters for the NCCUSL committee that drafted RULLCA, boast the quality of RULLCA's drafting process as well as its substantive legal innovations (Bishop & Kleinberger 2007).

Arguments against Uniformity

Notwithstanding the many benefits of uniformity, critics, chief among them the late Professor Larry Ribstein and Professor Bruce Kobayashi, oppose uniformity as a policy goal in the area of unincorporated entity law.

As Ribstein and Kobayashi have argued, "the collective wisdom over time of fifty-one legislatures and bar drafting committees must be far greater than that of one uniform or model law drafting organization" (Ribstein & Kobayashi 1995a). Uniformity, in contrast, prevents states from experimenting with improvements to existing organizational law. That is true both at the time of the statute's initial adoption as well as at the time of ongoing changes.

Ribstein and Kobayashi are especially concerned that NCCUSL is undermining states' realization of uniformity in those areas where uniformity is efficient. Examples identified in the context of unincorporated entity law include provisions that deal with third parties who have only casual dealings with the entity.[12] In those transactions, "parties need standardized provisions" because it is "uneconomical for them to engage in customized drafting or investigate legislative alternatives" (Ribstein & Kobayashi 2009). Ribstein and Kobayashi believe this kind of efficient uniformity can occur spontaneously, where the legal system fosters efficient rules (Ribstein & Kobayashi 1996). Further, they believe this efficiency is achieved without regard to the "incentives, motivation, or foresight of ... lawmakers." In their view, NCCUSL undermines this efficient uniformity, causing some states to adopt NCCUSL's idiosyncratic approach rather than the efficient approach.

Ribstein and Kobayashi attribute NCCUSL's idiosyncratic, inefficient provisions to the process through which NCCUSL creates its model acts (Ribstein & Kobayashi 1995b). In particular, the commissioners who are on the uniform act drafting committee are generalists who may not be sensitive to the nuances of the applicable law. Moreover, those commissioners are prone to influence by expert advisors, who have opportunities to advance their special interests.

---

[10] *Id.*
[11] *Id.*
[12] While Ribstein and Kobayashi concede the potential for benefits of uniformity to outweigh its costs in this context, they do not endorse uniformity around RULLCA (Ribstein & Kobayashi 1995a).

Even if NCCUSL facilitated efficient uniformity, Ribstein and Kobayashi remain opposed to NCCUSL's uniform unincorporated entity acts. That is because "states might select the entire NCCUSL proposals, including inefficient provisions, rather than only the sections for which uniformity is efficient" (Ribstein & Kobayashi 1995a).

4. STUDY OF STATE LLC LAW

Professors Goforth, Kleinberger, and Bishop persuasively argue why NCCUSL's uniformity objective is beneficial in the area of unincorporated entity law. On the other hand, Ribstein and Kobayashi make a compelling case that uniformity in the area of unincorporated entity law is inefficient and thus inadvisable. However, as I show in this section of the chapter, these debates about uniformity are misguided. That is because the concept of uniformity fails to capture the fragmented nature of uniformity of state LLC law. Moreover, these debates fail to reflect that uniformity is not a policy objective sought by most LLC act committees who lead states' efforts at adopting new LLC legislation. Rather, as this part of the chapter explains, a framework of casual convergence better captures the state of LLC law.

This chapter focuses on LLC law because LLCs are the leading unincorporated entity form.[13] In addition, because the LLC is a relatively recent organizational form, studying trends in LLC law provides useful insights into the evolution of unincorporated entity law without having to reckon with much historical baggage. Moreover, the LLC is the subject of NCCUSL's latest efforts at achieving uniformity in the area of unincorporated entities.

This section of the chapter first reviews the results of a qualitative study I conducted of state LLC law. The study is intended to provide a picture of the extent of uniformity, and frequent lack of uniformity, in LLC law. Next, this discussion describes the nature of the qualitative research I conducted in the form of interviews of members of LLC act committees. I conducted those interviews to better understand the considerations affecting LLC act committees' adherence to, and departure from, uniformity under RULLCA. In contrast to Ribstein and Kobayashi's belief that a properly functioning legal system will lead to efficient laws without reference to specific individuals in that process, the premise of this chapter is that one cannot truly understand the legal landscape, at least in the area of LLC law, without understanding the reasons for the choices made by the individuals driving the lawmaking process. To ensure the proposed LLC act passes the legislature, these committees take into account the interests of parties with voices in the political process who have interests to be protected; that is necessary to ensure the proposed LLC act passes the legislature. I have found, however, that it is usually the members of the LLC act committee who play the leading role in determining which model or uniform act to start from, and whether and how to depart from that model or uniform act.

The discussion then explains why a uniformity framework fails to capture the actual state of LLC law. To summarize, not only does describing LLC law as uniform

---

[13] In a study, Jens Dammann and Matthias Schündeln found that in many states, the number of newly formed LLCs greatly exceeds the number of newly formed corporations and other legal entities (Dammann & Schündeln 2012).

mischaracterize the reasons why state LLC laws have converged, but it also fails to capture the extent of their divergence. As this discussion demonstrates, therefore, a framework of casual convergence more accurately reflects the current state of LLC law as well as the fact that convergence is usually attributable more to circumstantial factors than to the strength of uniformity as a policy goal.

Study of State LLC Law

To better conceptualize the existing framework for LLC law, I conducted a qualitative study of state LLC laws. In particular, I compared the texts of LLC acts of all states that revised their LLC act since 2006, when NCCUSL adopted RULLCA, through 2013.[14]

Table 19.1 presents a sampling of the study results for different types of provisions, separated by category. The first category, labeled "Internal Affairs," refers to provisions affecting relationships between and among members, managers, and the LLC. The five provisions shown on the table cover quintessential internal affairs: the scope, function, and limitations of the operating agreement; the sharing and right to distributions (before dissolution); management; standards of conduct for members and managers; and rights of members and managers to information. While other provisions of RULLCA clearly fall under the rubric of internal affairs, these provisions undoubtedly give a sense for the extent of convergence in provisions on internal affairs.

The second category, labeled "Third Parties," refers to provisions relating to the relationship between the LLC, a member, or a manager, on the one hand, and non-governmental third parties on the other. The five provisions shown on the table cover some of the more significant provisions affecting third parties: agency power of members; liability of members and managers to third parties; liability of members for contributions (including third parties' ability to enforce that); limitations on distributions to protect third parties; and charging orders as a remedy for a creditor seeking to satisfy a debt from a member's LLC interest. The sampling provides insight into the extent of convergence in provisions affecting third parties generally.

The third category, labeled "Governmental/Admin," refers to provisions that relate primarily to the relationship of the LLC or a member or manager to the state. Given the numerous statutory provisions that fall under the heading "Governmental/Admin," it was challenging selecting only five provisions. The ones the chapter covers are provisions on entity name; appointment of an agent and designation of office in the state; signing of records to be delivered to the state for filing; delivery and filing of records and effective date and time of those filings; and annual reports. This sampling should provide some insight into the extent of convergence in provisions affecting the state generally.

Each section of the table denotes with an "X" a state-specific variation from RULLCA. Where a state either followed RULLCA exactly, or made only technical, stylistic, or

---

[14] While the District of Columbia updated its LLC act in this time range, I excluded it from my study on the basis that the process for legislative adoption in D.C., and the role of lawyers in the D.C. Bar, are so different from the states, it would be difficult to compare my findings from D.C. with the results from the states.

Table 19.1 Study results for state LLC acts: convergence with RULLCA

Internal Affairs

RULLCA	California	Idaho	Iowa	Nebraska	New Jersey	Utah	Wyoming
§110. Operating Agreement: Scope, function, and limitations	X	No change	No change	X	No change	X	X
§404. Sharing of and Right to Distributions Before Dissolution	X	No change	No change	No change	No change	No change	X
§407. Management of Limited Liability Company	X	No change	X	No change	No change	X	X
§409. Standards of Conduct for Members and Managers	X	No change	X	No change	X	X	X
§410. Right of Members, Managers, and Dissociated Members to Information	X	No change	No change	X	No change	X	X

Third Parties

RULLCA	California	Idaho	Iowa	Nebraska	New Jersey	Utah	Wyoming
§301. No Agency Power of Member as Member	X	No change	No change	No change	No change	No change	No change
§304. Liability of Members and Managers	X	No change	No change	X	No change	No change	No change
§403. Liability for Contributions	X	No change	X	No change	No change	X	X
§405. Limitations on Distributions	No change	No change	No change	No change	No change	X	X
§503. Charging Order	X	X	X	X	X	X	X

Governmental/Admin

RULLCA	California	Idaho	Iowa	Nebraska	New Jersey	Utah	Wyoming
§108. Name	X	X	X	X	X	X	X
§113. Reservation of Name	X	X	X	No change	X	X	X
§203. Signing of Records to be Delivered for Filing	X	X	No change	No change	X	X	No change
§205. Delivery to and Filing of Records; Effective Time and Date	X	X	X	No change	X	X	X
§209. Annual Report	X	X	X	X	X	X	X

conforming change based on changes made elsewhere in the statute, this is denoted by the words "No change."

As Table 19.1 shows, there is much convergence among state LLC act provisions. The table also depicts many state-specific divergences.

In terms of convergence, most obviously, all of the above statutes were drafted from RULLCA. Moreover, each of these states' acts generally follows RULLCA's organizational structure. It was the similarities in organizational structure, such as consistency in section numbering, ordering, and headings, that allowed me to create the table and identify where the statutes diverged from RULLCA.

In provisions relating to third parties, there is especially strong convergence. Specifically, 22 out of a total of 35 provisions (seven states multiplied by five provisions studied) were not changed from RULLCA.[15] In fact, three states (Idaho, Iowa, and New Jersey) either made no changes to these provisions, or made only one change.[16] Nebraska changed only two of these provisions, and arguably its change to Section 503 on charging orders, permitting a member to extinguish a charging order only before *completion* of a foreclosure sale, is either a clarification or not material.

These findings are largely consistent with a study conducted by Professors Ribstein and Kobayashi on uniformity in LLC law pre-RULLCA (Ribstein & Kobayashi 2009). In that study, Ribstein and Kobayashi found the highest level of uniformity in LLC law around third-party provisions.[17] According to Ribstein and Kobayashi, this is so because standardized terms are efficient for the smaller, episodic transactions engaged in with third parties.

On the other hand, in my study, two of the five third-party provisions were changed by more than half of the states. Section 403 on liability for contributions is one of those provisions. Four states altered that provision, with changes ranging from requiring consent from all members to compromise a member's contribution obligation (California and Utah) to eliminating a creditor's ability to enforce a member's contribution obligation (Wyoming). Four states also altered Section 503 on charging orders. Here, two states eliminated a court's power to foreclose on a member or transferee's LLC interest where a judgment remains unsatisfied (New Jersey and Wyoming). New Jersey rejected RULLCA's language entirely in drafting this provision.

This finding, too, reinforces what Ribstein and Kobayashi found when studying LLC law pre-RULLCA. Specifically, they found that after NCCUSL enacted the Uniform Limited Liability Company Act (ULLCA), the predecessor to RULLCA, there was less uniformity (Ribstein & Kobayashi 2009). They largely attribute this finding to the fact that NCCUSL's model act was driving states away from spontaneous uniformity and

---

[15] This does not count as a "change" a clarification that every state I studied made to RULLCA Section 503 to reflect that the charging order covers only the unsatisfied amount of a judgment. Because the change was made by all states, there remains uniformity.

[16] On the other hand, New Jersey's change to its provision on charging orders is substantial, and the provision does not resemble the RULLCA provision. That discrepancy is discussed further below.

[17] Ribstein and Kobayashi found that NCCUSL's adoption of the uniform limited liability company act (ULLCA), the predecessor to RULLCA, actually reduced uniformity (Ribstein & Kobayashi 2009).

toward adoption of a non-leading form. Here, the extent of divergence I found in third-party provisions suggests some non-uniformity in this area despite RULLCA's attempt at achieving uniformity and the benefits Ribstein and Kobayashi have identified with uniformity in these types of third-party provisions.

In provisions relating to LLC internal affairs, there is some convergence, albeit less than with third-party provisions. Of the total of 35 provisions, just under half—16 provisions—were unchanged from RULLCA. Idaho actually made no changes to the five studied provisions from RULLCA, and New Jersey changed only one of the five provisions. Moreover, New Jersey's changes are consistent with changes made by many other states. Iowa and Nebraska made no changes to three of the five provisions. While they made changes to the other two provisions, those changes tailored RULLCA's language rather than introducing entirely separate language.

California, Utah, and Wyoming made the most changes to these provisions. In fact, California and Wyoming changed every single one of the studied provisions, and Utah changed all but one. Moreover, many of those changes are significant, including a removal of RULLCA's limit on contracting around fiduciary duties in an operating agreement (Utah and Wyoming) and a change from RULLCA's default of sharing distributions equally to sharing distributions based on relative value of contributions (California).

I found the least amount of convergence in the governmental/administrative provisions. Of the 35 provisions, only five were not changed from RULLCA. The rest—30—were modified by the states. Of the five provisions not changed from RULLCA, the majority were in one section: Section 203 on signing of records to be delivered for filing.

In contrast, every state modified RULLCA Section 108 on name. Nearly all states tailored the requirements to what name an LLC could use and extended the requirement that an LLC's name be distinguishable from foreign LLCs. In addition, two states (California and Nebraska) created a different standard for testing whether a name was too similar to an existing business entity's name to be eligible for use. Section 209 on annual report was also modified by every state. In fact, three states replaced the RULLCA provision with their own provisions (California, New Jersey, and Wyoming). Section 205 on delivery to and filing of records; effective time and date was also modified by all but one state. Those modifications ranged from eliminating the concept of a future effective time for a filing (California, Idaho, and New Jersey) to replacing the entire provision with an entirely different provision (Utah and Wyoming with respect to effective date and time).

One final observation is that states vary widely in the extent to which they depart from RULLCA's governmental/administrative provisions. For example, Nebraska made no substantive changes to the governmental/administrative provisions other than to Section 108 on name. California, New Jersey, Idaho, and Utah, on the other hand, made changes to all of these provisions. Still, with some limited exceptions, states drafted their LLC act's governmental/administrative provisions from RULLCA and tailored RULLCA to their needs rather than replacing the language entirely.

It is in part because of all of these departures from RULLCA, especially in the provisions on internal affairs and governmental/administrative, but even in the provisions relating to third parties, that I characterize state LLC law as casually convergent. While those laws are clearly convergent around RULLCA, the term *casual* captures the intermittent nature of that convergence. However, this does not explain *why* state LLC laws converge in some respects and diverge in others. The next section of this chapter is intended to explore the reasoning behind this casual convergence.

Interviews of LLC Act Committee Members

To better understand the results of my study, in addition to researching commentary, I interviewed one practitioner[18] from each state LLC act committee.[19] I conducted these interviews to better understand the reasons for state adoptions of RULLCA as well as state variations from RULLCA.

In these interviews, I focused on three broad questions: (1) why did the LLC act committee draft the state's LLC act from RULLCA (versus alternative acts, such as the American Bar Association (ABA) Revised Prototype LLC Act), (2) to what extent did the LLC act committee, by adopting a RULLCA-based statute, seek to achieve interstate uniformity in LLC law and why, and (3) what are the primary reasons why the LLC act committee departed from RULLCA.

The first question was designed to elicit information about the intent of the LLC act committee in using RULLCA; that is, whether the committee used RULLCA to achieve intrastate uniformity, to achieve interstate consistency among unincorporated entity statutes, because it wanted to follow the trend seen through other states' adoptions of RULLCA, because it was not aware of other model LLC acts, or for other reasons. If the interviewee did not comment on the relative importance of achieving interstate uniformity in proposing a new LLC act, the second question would elicit this information.

The second question was intended to gather information about the extent to which the LLC act committee sought to achieve interstate uniformity in LLC law by adopting a RULLCA-based statute. To the extent the LLC act committee member did report an objective of interstate uniformity, this question also sought to discover why the committee sought that uniformity.

The third question was designed to discover why each LLC act committee departed from RULLCA. This question was intended to reveal other committee objectives in addition to uniformity. It was also designed to gauge the relative importance of an interstate uniformity objective (if one was reported) as compared to other LLC act committee objectives.

Based on the answers given to each question, I sometimes posed follow-up questions. For example, when one LLC act committee member informed me that the member's committee departed from RULLCA to maximize the chances of legislative passage, I asked what changes were made to that state's LLC act toward that end.

---

[18] I either interviewed the chair or a co-chair of an LLC act committee, if someone was publicly identified as having acted in this capacity. If no chair or co-chair was publicly identified, I interviewed one of the practitioners on the committee. I did not interview any non-practitioners, as I sought to discover the relative importance of uniformity to practitioners.

[19] In the case of one state, there was no formal LLC act committee; rather, a new LLC act was proposed by a state legislator, and members of the state bar got involved to ensure certain changes were made to the act that was adopted. For purposes of this discussion, references to LLC act committees includes the informal association of those members of the state bar who sought to influence the LLC act legislation in their state.

I did not specifically ask about how an LLC act committee decided that the benefits of varying from uniformity outweighed the costs. As mentioned above, Ribstein and Kobayashi have argued that apart from NCCUSL's misguided uniform acts, states achieve uniformity on their own where that is efficient because of legal processes supporting that. I did not specifically pose this question because I did not want to put committee members on the defensive if the committee did not use any tools to weigh costs and benefits, as I suspected they did not. On the other hand, I did ask questions designed to get a sense of the relative priorities of committee objectives.

I also asked interviewees two background questions. First, I asked them about the composition of their committees. That question, while not focused on uniformity, sought to determine the extent to which practitioners, academics, state representatives, and others were involved in the process of LLC act adoption. This question also elicited information about the extent to which an NCCUSL Commissioner was involved in the state's adoption of a RULLCA-based statute. Second, I asked LLC act committee members how long it took their states to pass a new LLC act. I thought this information would be relevant in determining which model acts were available at the time each committee began its work. Incidentally, this question also generated information about the political process and the extent to which interests not represented on the LLC act committee influenced the content of the LLC act.

I informed the LLC act committee members I spoke with that I would not report any state-specific information—rather, I would only report my findings either anonymously or in aggregate. I thought this was appropriate to ensure speakers were as candid as possible.[20]

Reasons for Convergence

I found that there are numerous reasons for the interstate convergence in LLC law described above.

First, convergence results from a process through which states keep their organizational laws current. As numerous interviewees noted, states try to keep their organizational laws current to deal with emerging legal issues. They also keep their organizational laws current to demonstrate that they are business friendly. As one commentator noted, a new LLC act is a great, and relatively inexpensive, way to signal that the state is business friendly. Updating is especially needful where other states are updating their organizational codes, as a state does not want to appear as if it is lagging behind its peers.

As I found from my interviews and own experience on an LLC act committee, the process of updating an unincorporated organizational code is typically undertaken by practitioners, along with one or two legal academics.[21] Some committees also included, either as a committee member or as an advisor, a member of state government. Most of

---

[20] I should note that all practitioners I contacted for this qualitative research responded to my request and generously gave of their time to provide the information I sought.
[21] One exception was a state in which a legislator initiated a revision to the state's LLC act based on RULLCA. In another state, a legislative committee tasked a committee of the state bar to advise the legislative committee on revisions to that state's corporation code. Once that work was completed, the state bar committee undertook to also update that state's LLC act.

these committees were also advised by a member of NCCUSL, though two of those committees actually included NCCUSL Commissioners as committee members. All of these individuals volunteered their time and efforts to the process. For this reason, interviewees identified the need to start drafting from a model act, to avoid having to draft a statute from scratch. Moreover, many of the lawyers on these drafting committees were transactional lawyers accustomed to drafting from models.

In the area of LLC law, there are two potential models. One is RULLCA, though as mentioned above, RULLCA is actually a uniform act rather than a model act. That is because rather than serving solely as a model for drafting, it reflects NCCUSL's effort to achieve uniformity across state LLC laws. However, it can serve as a useful model for states even where they do not strive for uniformity.

The other model LLC act, prepared by a working group of the ABA's committee on LLCs, Partnerships and Unincorporated Entities, is the Revised Prototype LLC Act. Before my study, the Revised Prototype LLC Act was last updated in May 2011. The Revised Prototype LLC Act is intended by the ABA working group to serve as a drafting resource in addition to RULLCA and other state LLC acts.[22] Thus, in contrast to RULLCA, it is not designed to achieve uniformity.

As discussed above, all of the states I studied based their new LLC acts on RULLCA rather than the ABA's Revised Prototype LLC Act. As two interviewed committee members stated, their committees used RULLCA as a "starting point."

In my interviews, I found a number of reasons why LLC act committees drafted from RULLCA. For one, many did so because they thought it was well drafted and thoughtful. They also thought it clarified some ambiguous aspects of LLC law, and it reflected recent developments in LLC law. Moreover, most of these committees started their statutory revision work before the ABA working group finalized the Revised Prototype LLC Act. While the ABA released the initial Prototype LLC Act in 1992, by 2006 that act had become stale, not reflecting innovations and changes in LLC law in the intervening years. Thus, another reason why states drafted their LLC acts using RULLCA rather than an ABA prototype act during the period of my study was because there simply was no updated prototype act available at the time.

While no interviewee directly mentioned this, it is possible that states in my study used RULLCA as a starting point even after the ABA released the Revised Prototype LLC Act because those states did not want to be different from other states, which had already drafted their statutes based on RULLCA. This may in part be due to the perception, if not the reality, that a state will be left behind if it does not keep up with the legal innovations of other states.[23] Moreover, as at least one of my interviewees did mention, it is surely easier to persuade one's state legislators to adopt an act where that state is adopting an act already in effect in other states.

On the other hand, two of my interviewees said that adopting a RULLCA-based statute impaired their states' abilities to distinguish themselves from other states. As one interviewee noted, the LLC act committee avoided mentioning uniformity as a benefit to

---

[22] REVISED PROTOTYPE LIMITED LIABILITY COMPANY ACT (May 1, 2011).
[23] As Professor Roberto Romano has found, states amend their corporate codes in response to other states' innovations (Romano 1985).

RULLCA when reporting on the new act to the state legislature, worrying that the legislature might not support an effort to genericize the state's LLC law.

Another reason LLC act committees reported using RULLCA as a starting point was to create consistency with their states' other unincorporated entity statutes. Specifically, two interviewees' states adopted RULLCA so that their LLC acts were consistent with their laws applicable to partnerships, which were governed by NCCUSL's model partnership act.[24] Thus, state LLC laws might be converging around RULLCA as an effect of already convergent partnership law.

Almost all of my interviewees said that their states adopted a RULLCA-based statute so that lawyers, litigants, and courts in their states could consult the case law of other states for guidance, both in planning and in litigating, where those other states have adopted similar statutory provisions. That is especially useful in states with courts that only see a handful of lawsuits relating to the governance of unincorporated entities. A similar benefit two interviewees noted is that by adopting RULLCA, state courts and practitioners could benefit from commentary written about RULLCA generally, or about other state's RULLCA-based statutes.

However, convergence for this purpose could be risky where it leads a court to borrow "bad" case law from another state. A court can create bad case law, for example, where the judge does not have experience working with business organizational law and either misunderstands or misapplies the law. This is especially concerning in the area of business organizations because, as Professor Eric A. Posner has observed, "courts have trouble understanding the simplest of business relationships" (Posner 2000).

Two LLC act committee members identified the cost savings created by interstate LLC act convergence as a reason to adopt a RULLCA-based statute. States achieve cost savings because with convergence, attorneys can more easily become informed of other state's laws as they advise multi-jurisdictional clients. Even if different states' statutes vary in substance, convergence in the states' statutory structures and terminology facilitates the lawyer's task of becoming informed of the other state's laws. It is likely this quality that Professor Goforth and other supporters of uniformity refer to when they describe the cost-savings benefits of uniformity.

Still, no interviewee described this factor as a primary reason to draft an LLC statute based on RULLCA. Moreover, as one interviewee acknowledged, this benefit might not be all that significant because a client will have to retain a lawyer in another state where the client needs legal advice on a matter specific to the laws of that other state. This is especially so where the client needs a legal opinion under the laws of the other state. On the other hand, it is not uncommon for a client to ask its counsel for preliminary advice on the organizational laws of another state, such as advice as to whether the client should even consider forming an entity in that other state or whether it should invest in an entity formed in that other state. There, again, interviewees thought it was useful to at least be familiar with the other state's LLC act's organizational structure and terminology.

---

[24] *Partnership Act*, THE NATIONAL CONFERENCE OF COMMISSIONERS ON UNIFORM STATE LAWS, www.uniformlaws.org/Act.aspx?title=Partnership%20Act (last visited Aug. 19, 2014) (showing that most jurisdictions have adopted one of NCCUSL's model partnership acts).

Oddly, this cost-savings benefit of interstate convergence was mentioned by only two interviewees. And those interviewees did not mention it as one of the primary reasons to adopt a RULLCA-based statute. The low priority that the committee members who identified it gave to interstate statutory uniformity to achieve cost savings contradicts the importance NCCUSL and supporters give to this benefit. Moreover, to the extent what is useful is convergence as to statutory structure and terminology, that benefit does not necessarily justify uniformity as to substantive statutory terms.

Finally, two interviewees described a process of statutory revision in which the LLC act committee had very little say in which act was used to draft the state's LLC act. In those states, the choice of starting points was essentially a foregone conclusion because members of the state legislature were NCCUSL Commissioners,[25] though one of these interviewees noted that most members of the LLC act committee independently supported adopting a RULLCA-based statute. Moreover, one other LLC act committee included an NCCUSL Commissioner, and one other state's LLC act committee was regularly advised by a Commissioner. These findings reveal that uniformity might not always derive from a conscious desire by lawyers on an LLC act committee to achieve that goal, but from NCCUSL's influence, including through the political process. Hence, contrary to Ribstein and Kobayashi's hope, the political process might not always be the most effective method to filter out what they view as inefficient provisions of uniform law.

Reasons for Divergence

As discussed above, my study found many state-specific departures from RULLCA as well. There are several reasons for these departures.

First, most interviewees noted that their committees made some changes to their state's LLC act from RULLCA to reflect the common-sense and practical experiences of the members of the LLC act committee. For example, New Jersey eliminated the requirement that there be a member at the time of LLC formation based on the practical experiences of the lawyers on the LLC act committee that this was "hyper-technical and unnecessary" (Marcus 2010). Perhaps for similar reasons, the other states in my study also eliminated RULLCA's requirement that an LLC's certificate of formation state if there will be no members at the time of formation, presumably for similar reasons.[26]

Similarly, several interviewees noted that their committees retained desirable provisions of existing LLC law. Thus, states departed from RULLCA to maintain consistency with existing LLC law.

Moreover, several LLC act committees departed from RULLCA where necessary to ensure passage of the act. However, only one interviewee identified more than modest changes to the statute to address the interests of non-governmental third parties not on

---

[25] In addition, one of those state's LLC act committees included an NCCUSL Commissioner.

[26] Idaho requires that the certificate of formation include the name of either a member or manager. *See* IDAHO UNIFORM LIMITED LIABILITY COMPANY ACT § 205 (2008). Because the certificate need not include the name of a member, I included it here.

the LLC act committee.[27] When asked what changes were made to RULLCA to ensure its passage, the committee member in that state noted that changes were largely made to maintain key protections for investors and creditors available under existing LLC law. In the states where only modest changes were made to reflect the interests of non-governmental third parties, not surprisingly, those changes were also to provisions affecting third-party rights.

These comments might explain some of the departures from RULLCA's provisions, especially those affecting third parties. In the area of charging orders in particular, no state adopted RULLCA's provision entirely. Ignoring the three states that made minor clarifications made by all states, two states removed a creditor's power to foreclose on an LLC interest and one state provides that, following the foreclosure sale of an LLC interest in a single-member LLC, the member is dissociated and the purchaser becomes a member. Based on my interviews it was clear some of these changes were made to address concerns of parties who could, if they opposed the new LLC act, affect the prospects of legislative passage.

These changes to third-party provisions lend support to Ribstein and Kobayashi's theory that the political process filters out instances where the costs of uniformity outweigh the benefits. It also provides further evidence that RULLCA is driving states further apart in the area where Ribstein and Kobayashi believe uniformity is most beneficial—provisions affecting third parties. This support comes not merely through empirical evidence, but through qualitative accounts from individuals central to the legislative process.

On the other hand, with the exception of the one interviewee mentioned above, interviewees did not identify many changes that were necessitated to accommodate outside interests. This revelation raises some doubt as to the ability of the political process to check LLC act legislation, including to ensure only efficient rules are adopted.[28]

Similarly, most LLC act committee members reported departing from RULLCA to maintain state powers, processes, and forms under existing LLC law. Several interviewees specifically noted that this was necessary to ensure state support for the new act. One interviewee noted that the committee had to be especially careful not to change any of the state revenue-generating provisions. This likely explains many of the divergences in the governmental/administrative provisions.

Another reason several interviewees mentioned for departing from RULLCA was to eliminate vague standards and discretions given to courts under RULLCA, and to replace those with standards courts were already familiar with. As three interviewees noted, these changes were made to simplify the task for courts in resolving disputes under LLC law in those states. This was important given that the courts in many of the states included in my survey did not have much experience resolving disputes under LLC law.

Moreover, several committee members noted that their states departed from RULLCA to ensure their states' LLC acts were consistent with other state organization statutes. For example, New Jersey tailored Section 108 to permit alternate names, similar to its

---

[27] This statement does not apply to the lawyers in the state where a new RULLCA-based LLC act was proposed by a state legislator. In that state, the lawyers had to agitate for numerous changes to RULLCA.

[28] In addition, as discussed above, the presence of an NCCUSL Commissioner in the legislature in two states essentially made those states' adoptions of RULLCA a foregone conclusion.

corporate statute. Similarly, Utah and Wyoming simply referred to their corporation codes for provisions on appointment of agents in the state.

All of these divergences from RULLCA contradict the notion that LLC law is becoming uniform for the sake of uniformity. Admittedly, in two states, there was a legislative directive to follow RULLCA because of the presence of members of NCCUSL in the state legislature. Moreover, there was universal acknowledgment that one desirable effect of uniformity was to increase the relevant body of case law. On the other hand, as the above discussion shows, convergence in LLC law is occurring in most states not because of the strength of uniformity as a policy goal, but as a practical consequence of the state lawmaking processes. Thus, the concept of *casual* convergence also captures the fact that convergence in LLC law is happening incidentally rather than intentionally.

5. CONCLUSIONS

My study has revealed three primary conclusions. First, most state LLC acts depart, often in significant ways, from RULLCA. I found the most departures from RULLCA in provisions affecting internal affairs as well as in the governmental/administrative provisions regulating the relationship of the LLC and its members and managers to the state. I also found some divergence among state LLC acts in their third-party provisions, despite more convergence in those provisions.

Second, not only are most states failing to achieve uniformity in their LLC laws, but interstate uniformity is not even a primary objective of the majority of individuals leading the effort to adopt new LLC acts. In other words, the uniformity framework fails to capture the actual state of LLC law as well as the policy goals of most LLC act committees. My qualitative research suggests that most LLC act committees converged around RULLCA not out of a desire to achieve uniformity, but because RULLCA was a modern, well-drafted "model" that saved the committee the time and energy that would be needed to draft a new LLC act from scratch. All interviewees acknowledged that their committees discussed benefits to uniformity, especially the expansion of case law from which judges and lawyers in that jurisdiction might draw. However, uniformity was simply not a primary goal of most committees. The low priority these LLC act committees gave to uniformity explains why these committees disregarded that goal, and varied RULLCA's terms, so often and so pervasively to achieve other goals.

Third, a framework of casual convergence more accurately characterizes unincorporated entity law, or at least LLC law, given the extent of divergences among LLC acts and the absence of a common uniformity objective in lawmaking. This shift in thinking can help drive a shift in the nature of the dialogue about this area of the law. For example, my interviewees confirmed that it is helpful to lawyers representing multi-jurisdictional clients to have other states adopt statutes with similar organizational frameworks, statutory terminology, and legal concepts. Yet this type of convergence is all but ignored where commentators debate the merits and drawbacks of statutory uniformity. Thus, rather than debating whether uniformity is being achieved or is desirable, academic and political discussions should instead focus on whether it is good policy for state LLC laws to be loosely convergent and if so, in what ways this effort can be facilitated or improved.

Importantly, those debates could also ask whether casual convergence achieves a desirable balance between state experimentation and uniformity.

Admittedly, my results found that NCCUSL Commissioners did influence state adherence to uniformity, especially in the two states with NCCUSL Commissioners in the legislature on state LLC act committees. Because of this, the debate about the merits of uniformity in different statutory contexts will likely persist. But as the present state of LLC law reveals, despite NCCUSL efforts at uniformity as to LLC law, only casual convergence exists. Thus, it is time to refocus the discussion in this area of law away from uniformity and toward casual convergence.

REFERENCES

Bishop, Carter G. & Daniel S. Kleinberger (2007), "The Next Generation: The Revised Uniform Limited Liability Company Act," 62 *Business Lawyer* 515, 520–44.

BISHOP, CARTER G. & DANIEL S. KLEINBERGER (2014), LIMITED LIABILITY COMPANIES: TAX AND BUSINESS LAW ¶ 1.01.

Dammann, Jens & Matthias Schündeln (2012), "Where are Limited Liability Companies Formed? An Empirical Analysis," 55 *Journal of Law & Economics* 741, 774.

Goforth, Carol A. (2007), "Why Arkansas Should Adopt the Revised Uniform Limited Liability Company Act," 30 *University of Arkansas Law Review* 31, 51, 80.

Marcus, Ira B. (2010), "Why New Jersey Should Adopt RULLCA," NEW JERSEY STATE BAR ASSOCIATION, Business Law Section, Jan. 2010, available at www.saiber.com/news/publications/Why%20New%20Jersey%20Should%20Adopt%20RULLCA_3.PDF.

Posner, Eric A. (2000), "A Theory of Contract Law under Conditions of Radical Judicial Error," 94 *Northwestern University Law Review* 749, 758.

Ribstein, Larry E. & Bruce H. Kobayashi (1995a), "Uniform Laws, Model Laws and Limited Liability Companies," 66 *Colorado Law Review* 947, 951–53.

Ribstein, Larry E. & Bruce H. Kobayashi (1995b), "An Economic Analysis of Uniform State Laws," 25 *Journal of Legal Studies* 131, 182–83.

Ribstein, Larry E. & Bruce H. Kobayashi (1996), "Evolution and Spontaneous Uniformity: Evidence From the Evolution of the Limited Liability Company," 34 *Economic Inquiry* 464–83, ¶¶13, 34.

Ribstein, Larry E. & Bruce H. Kobayashi (2009), "The Non-Uniformity of Uniform Laws," 35 *Journal of Corporation Law* 327, 339–41.

Romano, Roberta (1985), "Law as a Product: Some Pieces of the Incorporation Puzzle," 1 *Journal of Law, Economics, and Organization*, 225, 235

20. Dictum in alternative entity jurisprudence and the expansion of judicial power in Delaware
Mohsen Manesh

1. INTRODUCTION

In the common law tradition, under the doctrine of *stare decisis*, a judicial decision is binding precedent for future cases involving similar issues and circumstances. Yet, only that portion of a court's opinion that is the holding—namely the ultimate result of the case as well as those portions of the decision necessary to obtain that result—is considered binding precedent. *Obiter dictum*, or more simply *dictum*, is that part of a court's opinion that is unnecessary to the ultimate result of the decision. Unlike the holding, dictum has no precedential value. It is not binding on future cases.

Despite this fact, curiously, Delaware courts regularly indulge in dictum. Indeed, the judicial practice is a celebrated facet of the state's rich corporate law tradition. Academics, practitioners and jurists alike have praised the state courts' liberal use of dictum as a distinguishing and invaluable feature of Delaware corporate law and its law-making process. Less noticed, however, is dictum's importance in Delaware's burgeoning unincorporated alternative entity jurisprudence. As this chapter shows, when one probes Delaware's limited partnership ("LP") and limited liability company ("LLC") decisions, one sees the same judicial hallmarks of dictum familiar to the state's corporate law precedents.

This chapter begins by first highlighting the Delaware courts' liberal use of dictum in the corporate context and describing the valuable guidance, regulatory, and responsiveness functions served by the judicial practice. This chapter then examines Delaware's alternative entity jurisprudence to demonstrate the courts have similarly employed dictum to serve like functions in the law governing LPs and LLCs. Finally, this chapter describes how the use of dictum, in both the corporate and alternative entity contexts, is only one element of a larger legal system that has evolved in Delaware to empower the state bench to act as the chief regulator of Delaware businesses.

2. DICTUM'S RECOGNIZED ROLE IN DELAWARE CORPORATE JURISPRUDENCE[1]

As anyone familiar with Delaware law knows well, dictum is a staple of Delaware corporate jurisprudence. As shown below, both the Delaware Supreme Court and the lower Court of Chancery have long employed dictum in their written opinions to resolve

---

[1] This Section 2 draws significantly from Manesh (2013a).

uncertainty, instill "best practices," and incrementally update the law to ensure it is current and responsive.

Dictum in Delaware Corporate Law

Perhaps the most notable example of Delaware Supreme Court dictum is *Weinberger v. UOP*, the case most famous for the high court's articulation of the entire fairness standard in the context of a controlling shareholder squeeze-out merger.[2] Counterfactually, the supreme court famously observed in a footnote that "the result [of the case] could have been entirely different if [the defendant] had appointed an independent negotiating committee of its outside directors to deal with [its controlling shareholder] at arm's length."[3] Unsurprisingly, the use of independent committees has become standard practice since this footnoted observation.

Of course, *Weinberger* is not an isolated instance of the supreme court's deliberate use of dictum. Consider, the *Disney* decision, in which the high court provided a lengthy— and what it recognized was unnecessary—elaboration on the fiduciary duty of good faith because the duty "is not a well-developed area of our corporate fiduciary law" and, therefore, "some conceptual guidance to the corporate community may be helpful."[4] Likewise, even as it rejected the plaintiffs' claims against the defendant-directors, the *Disney* court found it "helpful" to outline "best practices" with respect to board oversight of executive compensation.[5] Like *Weinberger*, this portion of the *Disney* decision has since transformed from dictum into standard corporate practice.

Such examples of dictum abound in the Delaware Supreme Court's corporate law decisions.[6] But dictum is also a staple of Delaware Court of Chancery jurisprudence. At the chancery, *In re Caremark* is possibly the most famous example.[7] In reviewing the fairness of a proposed settlement to which no party objected, Chancellor Allen took the opportunity to reformulate the oversight responsibilities of corporate directors to reflect the growing severity of corporate sanctions imposed under new federal regulations. In doing so, the chancellor implicitly overturned an antiquated supreme court precedent.[8] *Caremark* became, literally, the textbook articulation of directors' oversight obligation and was eventually adopted by the Delaware Supreme Court as binding precedent some 20 years later.[9]

While *Caremark* is perhaps the most famous example of chancery court dictum, it also typifies the lower court's practice in corporate law cases. Consider a string of chancery

---

[2] *See* Weinberger v. UOP, Inc., 457 A.2d 701 (Del. 1983).
[3] *Id.* at 709 n.7.
[4] *In re* Walt Disney Co. Deriv. Litig. 906 A.2d 27, 63–64 (Del. 2006).
[5] *Id.* at 56.
[6] *See, e.g.*, Sagarra Inversiones v. Cementos Portland Valderrivas, 34 A.3d 1074, 1080–81 n.13 (Del. 2011) (using dictum to reject three facets of a chancery court opinion in a separate, unrelated case); Ark. Teacher Ret. Sys. v. Caiafa, 996 A.2d 321, 322 (Del. 2010) (using dictum to consider whether plaintiffs' derivative claim could have been fashioned as a direct claim instead).
[7] *In re* Caremark Int'l Inc. Derivative Litig., 698 A.2d 959 (Del. Ch. 1996) (Allen, Ch.).
[8] *Caremark*, 698 A.2d at 969–70 (questioning the continued validity of Graham v. Allis-Chalmers Mfg. Co., 188 A.2d 125 (Del. 1963)).
[9] *See* Stone v. Ritter, 911 A.2d 362, 365 (Del. 2006).

court decisions incrementally clarifying the applicability of the *Revlon* doctrine in mixed consideration transactions.[10] Although Delaware Supreme Court precedent supports the proposition that all-cash consideration triggers so-called *Revlon* duties for the directors of a target corporation, while all-stock consideration does not (unless it is a change-of-control transaction), the high court has not squarely addressed the applicability of *Revlon* to transactions in which the target shareholders receive a mix of cash and stock in the acquirer as consideration for their shares in the target (Manesh 2014). Filling this gap, the chancery court has over the course of four decisions addressed the applicability of *Revlon* to transactions involving varying mixes of cash versus stock consideration. The court has done so despite the fact that in each case the court acknowledged the *Revlon* question was ultimately unnecessary to the resolution of the motion before it (Manesh 2014). By addressing the applicability of *Revlon*, however, these mixed consideration decisions have provided important guidance to transactional attorneys and clients about the scope of the ill-defined doctrine.

More recently, consider the role of chancery court dictum in reshaping long-standing supreme court precedent. In *Kahn v. Lynch Communications*, the high court ruled that *Weinberger*'s exacting entire fairness standard applies to all squeeze-out mergers, regardless of the procedural safeguards adopted by the controlling shareholder in negotiating the transaction.[11] In subsequent opinions addressing the *Lynch* decision, then Vice Chancellor Strine indulged in lengthy dicta to decry it, echoing the frustrations of many directors, practitioners, and scholars with the supreme court precedent.[12] By requiring entire fairness, irrespective of procedural safeguards adopted by the controlling shareholder, the vice chancellor explained, *Lynch* encouraged plaintiffs' attorneys to bring meritless suits while undercutting any incentive for controlling shareholders to embrace robust procedural safeguards that would meaningfully protect minority shareholders in such transactions. Responding to these frustrations, in *Kahn v. M&F Worldwide*, the high court eventually curtailed the application of *Lynch*, essentially adopting the vice chancellor's position.[13]

As these examples suggest, Delaware courts are not shy to indulge in dictum in their corporate law decisions. Indeed, the judicial practice has been widely praised as a distinguishing and invaluable feature of the state's legal system. By employing dictum, the Delaware bench serves three important, overlapping functions key to the development of the state's law and regulation of all Delaware corporations.

---

[10] In re Synthes, Inc. S'holder Litig, 50 A.3d 1022 (Del. Ch. 2012) (Strine, Ch.); In re Smurfit-Stone Container Corp. S'holder Litig., 2011 WL 2028076 (Del. Ch. May 20, 2011) (V.C. Parsons); In re NYMEX S'holders Litig., 2009 WL 3206051 (Del. Ch. Sept. 30, 2009) (Noble, V.C.); In re Lukens Inc. S'holders Litig., 757 A.2d 720 (Del. Ch. 1999) (Lamb, V.C.).

[11] Kahn v. Lynch Commc'n Sys., Inc., 638 A.2d 1110, 1117 (Del. 1994). The use of a special negotiating committee comprised of independent directors, as suggested by *Weinberger*, would only shift the burden to the plaintiffs, the *Lynch* court decided.

[12] In re Pure Resources, Inc. S'holders Litig., 808 A.2d 421, 444 (Del Ch. 2002); In re Cysive, Inc. S'holders Litig., 836 A.2d 531, 547–551 (Del. Ch. 2003); In re Cox Commc'ns, Inc. S'holders Litig., 879 A.2d 604, 605–07, 642–48 (Del. Ch. 2005); see also In re CNX Gas Corp. S'holders Litig., 4 A.3d 397 (Del. Ch. 2010) (Laster, V.C.) (endorsing the proposed modification of the *Lynch* doctrine).

[13] See Kahn v. M&F Worldwide Corp., 88 A.3d 635, 642–47 (Del. 2014).

The Guidance Function of Dictum

Perhaps most visibly, Delaware courts have used dictum to serve a valuable guidance function by addressing areas where existing law is ambiguous or otherwise uncertain. (Steele & Verret 2007; Manesh 2013a; Cleveland 2008; Fisch 2000). For example, in the mergers and acquisitions context, where the fiduciary duties of directors can be notoriously indeterminate (Manesh 2011; Kahan & Kamar 2001), Delaware courts have often used dictum to provide crucial direction to corporate boards and the attorneys advising them (Fisch 2000; Cleveland 2008; Rock 1997; Gilson 1997; Branson 1990). *Weinberger*'s dictum exemplifies this guidance function. The supreme court's famous footnote provided a blueprint for future squeeze-out mergers to meet the fiduciary standard of entire fairness.

The judicial guidance afforded by such dictum enhances the clarity and certainty of Delaware law in situations where an applicable legal standard is vague or indeterminate. But it has also proven useful where the law is simply silent. For example, the chancery court's dicta applying *Revlon* to various mixed consideration transactions (Manesh 2014), like the supreme court's *Disney* dictum elucidating the fiduciary good faith obligation, provided clarity by filling gaps in existing judicial precedents.

The guidance function of dictum extends beyond simply clarifying ambiguous or otherwise uncertain law. By criticizing existing precedents, Delaware courts have also used dictum to portend future doctrinal changes (Savitt 2012; Cleveland 2008). Consider, for instance, the chancery court dicta decrying the *Lynch* doctrine and presaging the high court's *M&F Worldwide* decision. By using dictum to revisit existing doctrines or to address unresolved legal questions, Delaware courts give relevant stakeholders advance notice of where the law is heading before it gets there. In this way, dictum's guidance function also enhances the predictability of Delaware law, even as it is constantly updated.

The Regulatory Function of Dictum

Beyond mere guidance, Delaware courts have also used dictum to regulate prospectively in order to shape the future behavior of corporate actors. (Manesh 2013a). The courts often employ this regulatory function of dictum by simply emphasizing where a particular litigant's conduct fell short of ideal standards (Rock 1997; Gilson 1997). *Disney*'s judicially blessed "best practices," for instance, provided unsubtle notice of the conduct that will be expected of corporate directors in future lawsuits (Steele & Verret 2007).

Such use of dictum to announce new rules or make doctrinal changes enables the Delaware bench to shape future behavior without imposing unfair results on the hapless parties who brought the litigation generating a newly announced standard (Savitt 2012; Cleveland 2008). Thus, in *Caremark*, Chancellor Allen introduced the enhanced oversight obligation for corporate directors in a case where, given the procedural posture, the newly announced rule had no effect on the litigants before him.

In addition to its procedural advantages, dictum also enables the Delaware courts to reach beyond the narrow issues presented in cases brought before them. The courts are instead able to prospectively address and decide salient issues that affect all Delaware corporations. The regulatory function of dictum thus empowers the Delaware courts to be more effective regulators, with the reach and flexibility to craft new rules and make subsequent changes like a rule-making agency or legislature (Fisch 2000; Savitt 2012).

The Responsiveness Function of Dictum

Related to its regulatory function, Delaware courts have used dictum to ensure the law is responsive, always adaptive to changes in the market and regulatory climate. (Manesh 2013a; Fisch 2000; Savitt 2012; Cleveland 2008). Through dictum, Delaware judges have often updated the law to tackle the emergent concerns of managers, investors, and even federal regulators. For example, *Caremark*'s enhanced oversight obligation for corporate directors was, in part, aimed at growing concerns over corporate criminal malfeasance among federal regulators and, therefore, investors. Likewise, *Disney*'s "best practices" regarding executive compensation addressed populist outrage over the seemingly excessive pay packages awarded to corporate executives. Such use of dictum to continuously modernize and refine existing doctrines ensures that Delaware law is agile and current, without the need to wait for legislative action or the right case to squarely raise a particular question (Fisch 2000). Moreover, the frequency with which Delaware courts face corporate litigation means that this updating process is both rapid and constant (Savitt 2012; Parsons & Tyler 2013).

Beyond updating the law to tackle emergent concerns, dictum's responsiveness function also has a more subtle facet. Without even changing the law, dictum allows Delaware courts to acknowledge and, thereby, legitimize the frustrations of various stakeholders with existing doctrines. Thus, the chancery court dicta presaging *M&F Worldwide* gave voice to mounting unhappiness among investors, directors, and many lawyers over the scourge of meritless lawsuits and nuisance-value settlements made possible by *Lynch*'s plaintiff-friendly entire fairness standard. While such dicta may not change existing law, by giving judicial voice to stakeholder frustrations, such dicta signals that future doctrinal changes may be warranted.

Recognition of Dictum's Valuable Functions

The Delaware courts' use of dictum in the service of these guidance, regulatory, and responsiveness functions has been widely praised by corporate law scholars, practitioners, and judges as an important facet of Delaware's lawmaking process—a distinctive judicial practice vital to the state's success in attracting corporate charters (Manesh 2013a; Cleveland 2008). For example, Professor Jill Fisch has argued that the liberal use of dictum, in part, makes the Delaware courts peculiarly important to the state's success in attracting corporate charters (Fisch 2000). As Fisch explained, the Delaware courts have, by employing dictum, created a lawmaking process "characterized by a high degree of flexibility and responsiveness," one that is "ideally suited to respond to developments in the business world." Likewise, noted attorney William Savitt has written in "praise of dictum," describing it as the "genius" of the Delaware legal system (Savitt 2012). And the former Chief Justice of Delaware, Myron Steele, has described the use of "dicta to give valuable guidance to deal lawyers on unanswered questions" as "an important element of Delaware's unique advantage as a forum for the resolution of the disputes of business entities" (Steele & Verret 2007).

Despite such praise, there is, naturally, a danger presented by dictum—namely, that it can be the product of unconsidered judgment. In the absence of concrete facts, an actual dispute, and real world litigants, the court may lack a clear understanding of how a new rule announced in dictum may affect parties in the broader gamut of cases. Despite the best judicial intentions, the rule may have pernicious, unintended consequences. Thus, courts have cautioned that "dicta, like the proverbial chickens of destiny, [can] come home to roost sooner or later in a very uncomfortable way [becoming] a great source of embarrassment in future cases."[14] In Delaware, however, concerns of judicial carelessness are less problematic, given the state judiciary's expertise in business law, its intensive engagement with the corporate bar and scholars, and the frequency with which it faces business-related litigation (Savitt 2012; Fisch 2000; Cleveland 2008). In this regard, Delaware's apolitical and engaged judges are likely more capable rulemakers than politically minded, often part-time state legislators who may be inexpert in business law matters.

3. DICTUM'S EMERGENT ROLE IN DELAWARE ALTERNATIVE ENTITY JURISPRUDENCE

In contrast to the corporate context, where Delaware has long been the dominant jurisdiction, the rise and popularity of alternative entities is relatively recent. As a consequence, scholars and practitioners have focused comparatively little attention on the state's LLC and LP precedents—and even less on the role of dictum in shaping that jurisprudence. A brief survey of alternative entity decisions, however, reveals the Delaware bench has comfortably embraced the practice pioneered in corporate law cases.

The Guidance Function of Dictum

In the corporate context, Delaware offers a highly refined, intricate statute and an expansive body of case law interpreting practically every facet of that statute applied to a variety of factual circumstances. By contrast, Delaware's alternative entity statutes and case law are relatively spartan. Consider that until very recently, even seemingly fundamental legal questions, like the default rules to amend an LLC operating agreement, or the default fiduciary duties owed by a manager to an LLC's members, were left unanswered by the state's statute and judicial precedents (Rutledge 2013). Unsurprisingly then, given the frequent absence of express statutory guidance or binding judicial precedent, Delaware courts have regularly employed dictum to provide attorneys and their clients with guidance on unresolved legal questions.

Consider *Olson v. Halvorsen*, in which the Delaware Supreme Court addressed whether the statute of frauds applies to oral LLC agreements.[15] At the time of the *Olson* decision, Delaware's statute did not specifically address the matter, and leading treatises on LLC law had taken opposing views on the question. Although the high court recognized that the issue did not affect the outcome of the *Olson* litigation, the court nonetheless tackled the question because it "could considerably impact the drafting and enforcement of LLC agreements."[16]

---

[14] *E.g.*, Darr v. Burford, 339 U.S. 200, 214 n.38 (1950); Opinion of the Justices, 198 A.2d 687, 689 (Del. 1964).
[15] *See* Olson v. Halvorsen, 986 A.2d 1150, 1159–61 (Del. 2009).
[16] *Id.* at 1159.

Consider also *Gotham Partners v. Hallwood Realty*, in which the supreme court addressed whether an LP could contractually eliminate the fiduciary duties of its general partner through the terms of its partnership agreement.[17] At the time, Delaware's LLC and LP statutes simply provided that fiduciary duties "may be expanded or restricted" by contractual agreement. Nowhere did the statutes mention whether such duties may be waived altogether. The only guidance on the question was a pair of chancery court decisions, which stated in passing dicta that the statutory "expanded or restricted" language permitted fiduciary duties to be wholly eliminated.[18] Although the *Gotham Partners* case did not squarely present the Delaware Supreme Court with the fiduciary waiver question, the court felt it necessary to confront what it viewed as the chancery court's "dubious dictum," lest it be "misinterpreted in future cases as a correct rule of law."[19] Thus, the high court engaged in its own dictum "in the interest of avoiding the perpetuation of a questionable statutory interpretation that could be relied upon adversely by courts, commentators and practitioners in the future."[20]

While the courts in both *Olson* and *Gotham Partners* attempted to use dictum to provide definitive guidance on then-unanswered legal questions, a notable facet of both decisions is that the dictum in each was swiftly reversed by legislative action. *Olson* opined that the statute of frauds applies to oral LLC agreements. The same year, the Delaware General Assembly amended the LLC statute to overrule *Olson*.[21] And *Gotham Partners* declared that fiduciary duties cannot be waived altogether. Shortly thereafter, the state legislature amended the LP and LLC statutes clarifying that fiduciary duties "may be expanded, restricted *or eliminated*" by the terms of a governing agreement.[22]

But even in cases where the judicial guidance is statutorily overturned, the use of dictum has helped clarify uncertainty by hastening its ultimate resolution. By employing dictum to pre-emptively stake out a judicial position, the Delaware courts force the state legislature to either take action or otherwise, through inaction, acquiesce to a pronouncement made in dictum. This symbiotic lawmaking link between the bench and legislature, facilitated by dictum, is most recently demonstrated by the Delaware Supreme Court's 2012 *Gatz v. Auriga Properties* decision.[23]

---

[17] *See* Gotham Partners, L.P. v. Hallwood Realty Partners, L.P., 817 A.2d 160, 167–70 (Del. 2002).

[18] Sonet v. Timber Co., L.P., 722 A.2d 319, 323 (Del. Ch. 1998) (Chandler, Ch.) ("Considering § 17-1101(d) of the Delaware Revised Uniform Limited Partnership Act's apparently broad license to enhance, reform, or even *eliminate* fiduciary duty protections . . . ") (emphasis added); Gotham Partners, L.P. v. Hallwood Realty Partners, L.P., 2000 WL 1476663, at *10 (Del. Ch. Sept. 27, 2000) (Strine, V.C.) ("§ 17-1101(d)(2) of DRULPA expressly authorizes the *elimination*, modification, or enhancement of these fiduciary duties in the written agreement governing the limited partnership.") (emphasis added).

[19] *Gotham Partners*, 817 A.2d at 167.

[20] *Id.*

[21] *See* DEL. CODE ANN. tit. 6, § 18-101(7) (effective Aug. 2, 2010) ("A limited liability company agreement is not subject to any statute of frauds . . . ").

[22] *See* DEL. CODE ANN. tit. 6, § 17-1101(d) (2013) (emphasis added) (governing LPs); *id.* § 18-1101(c) (emphasis added) (governing LLCs).

[23] Gatz Props. LLC v. Auriga Capital Corp., 59 A.3d 1206 (Del. 2012).

In *Gatz*, the supreme court addressed the uncertainty surrounding default duties in the alternative entity context (Manesh 2013a). At the time of *Gatz*, Delaware's LLC and LP statutes did not specify that fiduciary duties are the default duties owed by managers and general partners. Although after *Gotham Partners*, the statutes clearly allowed for fiduciary duties to be contractually eliminated, the statutes never confirmed that fiduciary duties are owed in the absence of a contractual waiver. Instead, the statutes simply stated that "*to the extent [one] has duties* (including fiduciary duties) ... [such] duties ... may be expanded, restricted or eliminated" by the terms of an LLC or LP agreement. In *Gatz*, the chancery court, per then Chancellor Strine, confirmed what was the widely held assumption that fiduciary duties are indeed the default duties, ruling that the defendant LLC manager had breached both his contractual obligations under the relevant LLC agreement as well as his default fiduciary duty owed to the LLC and its members.[24]

On appeal, the high court in *Gatz* resolved the parties' claims relying solely on the express terms of the LLC agreement and, therefore, dismissed the chancery court's ruling on the default duties question as "unnecessary" dictum. Nonetheless, the high court "pause[d] to comment"—that is, indulged in its own dictum—to renounce the chancery court's ruling lest it should be "misinterpreted as a correct rule of law" in future cases.[25] The supreme court observed that Delaware's statutes are "ambiguous" and that "reasonable minds could differ"[26] on the default duties question—making it altogether clear that contract drafters and alternative entity participants should not presume fiduciary duties are the default standard.

As with *Olson* and *Gotham Partners* before it, within weeks of *Gatz*, the Delaware legislature responded to clarify the matter, passing an amendment to the state's LP and LLC statutes confirming that fiduciary duties are the default duties owed in the absence of a contractual waiver.[27] Thus, even while *Gatz* was reversed by legislative action, the impact of its dictum expedited definitive resolution of the unresolved question by prompting the legislature.

While the examples above—*Olson*, *Gotham Partners* and *Gatz*—demonstrate the role of dictum to resolve legal uncertainty in the alternative entity context, recall that dictum's guidance function extends beyond simply addressing novel or otherwise unanswered legal questions. As in the corporate context, Delaware courts have also in alternative entity cases used dictum to reconsider existing precedents and signal the possibility of future doctrinal revisions.

This use of dictum to foreshadow future developments may be seen in a series of chancery court decisions questioning the 1991 *USACafes* decision.[28] In *USACafes*, Chancellor Allen held that where the general partner of an LP is itself an entity (for example, a corporation), the individuals who control the general partner entity owe fiduciary duties to the LP's limited partners. Although the chancery court has consistently followed

---

[24] Auriga Capital Corp. v. Gatz Props., LLC, 40 A.3d 839, 849–60 (Del. Ch. 2012), *aff'd on other grounds sub nom.* 59 A.3d 1206 (Del. 2012).
[25] *Gatz*, 59 A3d at 1218.
[26] *See Id.* at 1218–19.
[27] *See* H.R. 126, 147th Gen. Assemb., Reg. Sess. (Del. 2013).
[28] *In re* USACafes, L.P. Litig., 600 A.2d 43 (Del. Ch.1991).

USACafes—and even extended it to the analogous LLC context[29]— the court has also on multiple occasions used dictum to criticize the precedent.[30] While such dictum does not clarify any ambiguity in the existing doctrine, it nonetheless serves a guidance function by providing advance notice that changes may be afoot in the future.

The Regulatory Function of Dictum

Given the freedom of contract afforded under Delaware LLC and LP law, the rules of internal governance for alternative entities vary from one another substantially more than in the corporate context, where certain mandatory rules, like the fiduciary duties of directors and the right of shareholders to elect the board, apply to all corporations (Manesh 2011; Manesh 2009). As a consequence, opportunities to utilize dictum's regulatory function, to craft new rules to shape future behavior, have been infrequent in the alternative entity decisions.

Where appropriate, however, Delaware courts have been able to profitably exploit dictum's regulatory function. The most notable example has been the supreme court's application of the implied contractual covenant of good faith and fair dealing. Under Delaware's LP and LLC statutes, the implied covenant is unwaivable,[31] making it one of the only mandatory rules applicable to all alternative entities. In light of its mandatory status, consider the Delaware courts' use of the implied covenant in dictum to police so-called "special approval" provisions.

"Special approval" provisions are a standard feature of governing agreements for publicly traded alternative entities (Horton 2013; Manesh 2012). In essence, a "special approval" provision allows an LLC manager or LP general partner to engage in a self-dealing transaction with the alternative entity business, provided the transaction has been approved by individuals deemed "independent," as that term is defined under the relevant governing agreement. By providing a contractual procedure to approve conflict-of-interest transactions, "special approval" provisions effectively replace a key facet of the fiduciary duty of loyalty with a contractual standard that purports to wholly eliminate any judicial scrutiny of the underlying transaction. As such, "special approval" provisions are widely viewed as favoring managers, general partners, and

---

[29] *E.g.*, Bay Ctr. Apartments Owners, LLC v. Emery Bay PKI, LLC, 2009 WL 1124451, at *8 (Del. Ch. Apr. 20, 2009) (Strine, V.C.).

[30] *E.g.* Feeley v. NHAOCG, LLC, 62 A.3d 649, 667–72 (Del. Ch. 2012) (Laster, V.C.) (noting the tension between *USACafes* and the principle of corporate separateness); Paige Capital Mgt., LLC v. Lerner Master Fund, LLC, 2011 WL 3505355, at *30 (Del. Ch. Aug. 8, 2011) (Strine, Ch.) (describing *USACafes* as an "oddment" in alternative entity law decided "without much analysis"); *Bay Ctr.*, 2009 WL 1124451, at *9 n.44 (Strine, V.C.) (observing that *USACafes* "raises some difficult policy issues and disregards corporate formalities"); Gelfman v. Weeden Investors, L.P., 792 A.2d 977, 992 n.24 (Del. Ch. 2001) (Strine, V.C.) (noting the "awkward position occupied by directors of corporate General Partners" under *USACafes*); Gotham Partners, L.P. v. Hallwood Realty Partners, L.P., 2000 WL 1476663, at *19–21 (Del. Ch. Sept. 27, 2000) (Strine, V.C.) (noting the tension between *USACafes*, contractual principles, and the "potentially conflicting and irreconcilable fiduciary duties" owed by directors of a corporate general partner).

[31] *See* Del. Code Ann. tit. 6, § 17-1101(d) (2011) (governing LPs); Del. Code Ann. tit. 6, § 18-1101(c) (2011) (governing LLCs).

their affiliates (Horton 2013) and have been, in practice, frequently used to orchestrate self-dealing squeeze-out transactions that allegedly under-compensate public investors.[32]

Given the state's statutory policy to "give the maximum effect to the principle of freedom of contract" in alternative entities,[33] Delaware courts have been loath to ignore the considerable barriers against judicial intervention erected by an unambiguous "special approval" provision. Even so, Delaware courts have, in dictum, deftly employed the unwaivable implied covenant to limit abuse of the contractual safe harbor.

First, in *Brinkerhoff v. TEPPCO*, in considering the fairness of a settlement agreement to which no party objected, Vice Chancellor Laster signaled that a "special approval" provision does not give *carte blanche* to managers and general partners to engage in self-dealing conflict-of-interest transactions.[34] "While I agree that those provisions establish a weighty defense, the syllogism of 'if [special approval], then judgment for the defendants' does not automatically follow ... At a minimum, the approval must have been given in compliance with the implied covenant of good faith and fair dealing, which a partnership agreement may not eliminate."[35]

Although the vice chancellor did not elaborate on this point, three years later, the supreme court did in *Gerber v. Enterprise Products*.[36] In interpreting the scope of the "special approval" provision at issue in *Gerber*, the high court enumerated three "hypothetical example[s]" where a party's overreaching conduct would taint the "special approval" process, rendering reliance on the contractual safe harbor a potential breach of the implied covenant. Although the *Gerber* defendants were not accused of engaging in the conduct described in the high court's "hypothetical example[s]," the court effectively signaled to all managers and general partners that such conduct would be impermissible in future cases, notwithstanding technical compliance with a "special approval" process. This dictum in *Gerber* complemented the court's holding in the decision, which found that the defendants' alleged *actual* conduct (in contrast to "hypothetical example[s]") would, if proven, also breach the implied covenant.

Beyond prospectively creating new rules, Delaware courts have also used dictum to nudge contract drafters to draft clearer, more comprehensible LLC and LP agreements. For example, in interpreting alternative entity agreements, the chancery court has at various times offhandedly belittled poorly-written provisions as "convoluted,"[37]

---

[32] *See, e.g., In re* Encore Energy Partners LP Unitholder Litig., 2012 WL 3792997 (Del. Ch. Aug. 31, 2012) (Parsons, V.C.); Gerber v. Enterprise Prods. Holdings, LLC, 2012 WL 34442 (Del. Ch. Jan. 6, 2012) (Noble, V.C.); Lonergan v. EPE Holdings LLC, 5 A.3d 1008 (Del. Ch. 2010) (Laster, V.C); *In re* Atlas Energy Res., LLC, 2010 WL 4273122 (Del. Ch. Oct. 28, 2010) (Noble, V.C.).
[33] *See* Del. Code Ann. tit. 6, § 17-1101(b) (2011) (governing LPs); Del. Code Ann. tit. 6, § 18-1101(b) (2011) (governing LLCs).
[34] Brinkerhoff v. Texas Eastern Prods. Pipeline, Co., 986 A.2d 370, 390 (Del. Ch. 2010).
[35] *Id.*
[36] Gerber v. Enterprise Prods. Holdings, LLC, 67 A.3d 400, 420–21 (Del. 2013).
[37] Forsythe v. ESC Fund Mgmt. Co. (U.S.), Inc., 2010 WL 3168407, at *6 (Del. Ch. Aug. 11, 2010) (Laster, V.C.).

"inelegant,"[38] "contradictory and confusing,"[39] "linguistically challenging,"[40] and downright "head-spinning."[41] The supreme court has been similarly critical, decrying the "Gordian knot of interrelated standards" presented by one LP agreement and citing the principle of *contra preferentum*, although the court conceded the interpretive canon was inapplicable to its decision.[42] Such candid critiques and oblique observations re-emphasize to contract drafters the imperative to avoid sloppily written or needlessly complex agreements, lest the freedom of contract afforded in alternative entities should backfire with adverse consequences for their clients.

The Responsiveness Function of Dictum

Dictum's responsiveness function in alternative entity jurisprudence has been less conspicuous than in the corporate context. The vast majority of alternative entity businesses are private, rather than publicly traded. And the few that are publicly traded—often referred to as "master limited partnerships"—operate mostly in arcane industries, such as midstream energy transportation (Manesh 2012). As a result, Delaware's alternative entity law has not faced the same degree of scrutiny from academics, federal regulators, the investing public, or the press. Of the few that have focused on publicly traded alternative entities, however, the attention has largely centered around the limited legal protections afforded public investors as compared to corporations (Manesh 2012; Horton 2013; Morgenson 2011).

As illustrated by the above example of "special approval" provisions, the governing agreements of publicly traded alternative entities tend to modify or displace the traditional fiduciary protections that are mandatory under corporate law and replace them with contractual duties that are less protective of public investors. Thus, even where an investor brings a claim alleging inequitable conduct or self-dealing by a manager or general partner, courts have been compelled to dismiss such actions based on the unambiguous express terms of the governing LLC or LP agreement.[43]

At the same time, however, recognizing the vulnerabilities of public investors in alternative entities as compared to corporations, Delaware courts have used dictum to express concerns about the limited rights afforded in the alternative entity context. In *Encore Energy*, for instance, after finding the "near absence under the [LP agreement] of any duties whatsoever [owed] to the public equity holders," Vice Chancellor Parsons observed in dictum that "[i]nvestors apprehensive about the risks inherent in waiving the fiduciary duties of those with whom they entrust their investments may be well advised to avoid master limited partnerships."[44] And on appeal, the supreme court likewise gratuitously

---

[38] Stockman v. Heartland Indus. Partners, L.P., 2009 WL 2096213, at *9 (Del. Ch. July 14, 2009) (Strine, V.C.).
[39] Ishimaru v. Fung, No. 929, 2005 WL 2899680, at *12 (Del. Ch. Oct. 26, 2005) (Strine, V.C.).
[40] Gelfman v. Weeden Investors, L.P., 859 A.2d 89, 112 (Del. Ch. 2004) (Strine, V.C.).
[41] Gelfman v. Weeden Investors, L.P., 792 A.2d 977, 986 (Del. Ch. 2001) (Strine, V.C.).
[42] Norton v. K-Sea Transp. Partners L.P., 67 A.3d 354, 360–61 (Del. 2013).
[43] Representative cases are cited *supra* note 32.
[44] *In re* Encore Energy Partners LP Unitholder Litig., 2012 WL 3792997, *13 (Del. Ch. Aug. 31, 2012) (Parsons, V.C.).

cautioned that if a public investor "seeks the protections the common law duties of loyalty and care provide, he would be well-advised to invest in a Delaware corporation."[45]

In addition to steering public investors away from alternative entities and toward traditional corporations with their more robust fiduciary protections, Delaware courts have also used dictum to caution against overreach by the drafters of publicly traded alternative entity governing agreements. Thus, in *Gerber v. Enterprise Products*, Vice Chancellor Noble remarked subtly in footnoted dictum that if the protections afforded public investors are "scant, then ... *another governmental entity* might step in and provide more protection,"[46] implicitly warning publicly traded alternative entity sponsors that abuse of the freedom of contract afforded under Delaware law could provoke intervention by federal regulators. While such dictum does nothing to change existing Delaware law, it does signal the courts' unease with an emerging dynamic in which alternative entity sponsors have exploited the freedom of contract at the expense of the investing public.

Beyond simply acknowledging the frustrations of public investors or brushing back overreach in alternative entity governing agreements, Delaware courts have also used dictum to discreetly refine existing doctrine to address the vulnerabilities of public investors. Consider the Delaware Supreme Court's recent rehabilitation of the implied contractual covenant of good faith and fair dealing in the already-discussed *Gerber v. Enterprise Products* to deal with the proliferation of "conclusive presumption" provisions.[47]

Before *Gerber*, the last time the high court had addressed the implied covenant was in 2010 in *Nemec v. Shrader*,[48] a case decided outside of the alternative entity context. In *Nemec*, a divided 3-2 court majority held the implied covenant is a mere contractual "gap filler," judicially invoked to imply terms only when it is necessary to address matters not otherwise addressed by the express terms of an agreement. This "gap-filler" conception of the implied covenant marked a departure from prior Delaware case law, which had described the implied covenant as a broader obligation, beyond those defined by the express terms of a contract, requiring each party to the contract to refrain from arbitrary or unreasonable conduct that would frustrate the other party's reasonable expectations (Manesh 2013b). Under the narrower "gap-filler" conception, the implied covenant is subject to and limited by the express terms of an agreement; if the express terms of a contract address a particular matter, the implied covenant could not override those terms.

Applied to the LLC and LP context, the narrow "gap-filler" conception endorsed by *Nemec* presented two potential problems. First, as a practical matter, it invited the sponsors of publicly traded alternative entities to contrive contractual language that would purport to fill any possible gap in the LLC or LP agreement, thus precluding any public investor lawsuit based on the implied covenant. Second, as a doctrinal matter, the notion that the implied covenant is a mere "gap filler" when combined with a contract term purporting to fill any gaps in an agreement conflicted with Delaware's statutory mandate that the implied covenant cannot be eliminated.

---

[45] Allen v. Encore Energy Partners, LP, 72 A.3d 93, 109 (Del. 2013).
[46] Gerber v. Enterprise Prods. Holdings, LLC, 2012 WL 34442, *10 n.42 (Del. Ch. Jan. 6, 2012) (Noble, V.C.).
[47] Gerber v. Enterprise Prods. Holdings, LLC, 67 A.3d 400 (Del. 2013).
[48] Nemec v. Shrader, 991 A.2d 1120, 1128 (Del. 2010).

These problems quickly came to bear, as the chancery court began facing LLC and LP governing agreements that included express terms purporting to create a "conclusive presumption" that those acting on behalf of the alternative entity acted in good faith.[49] The aim of these "conclusive presumption" provisions was to fill any gap in the governing agreement through which a public investor might challenge an LLC manager or general partner's actions as a breach of the implied covenant. More problematic, these "conclusive presumption" provisions were often invoked in connection with a "special approval" to facilitate self-dealing transactions benefitting the manager or general partner.[50] Because the "special approval" provisions expressly permitted these types of self-dealing transactions, the public investors challenging the manager or general partner's actions were forced to rely solely on the implied covenant.

Dutifully applying the supreme court's *Nemec* precedent, in 2012 three successive chancery court decisions held that a "conclusive presumption" provision fills any gap in which the implied covenant might operate.[51] As a consequence, the chancery court dismissed the public investors' claims despite allegations that the manager or general partner had engaged in an unfair self-dealing transaction.

Faced with the palpably inequitable results of these chancery court decisions, the high court in *Gerber* sought to temper the narrow "gap-filler" conception of the implied covenant endorsed by its earlier *Nemec* decision. But it did so in dictum. In *Gerber*, the court held that the "conclusive presumption" provision at issue addressed a contractual "good faith" standard set forth in the relevant LP agreement, rather than the "good faith" required by the implied covenant.[52] Having thus dealt with the "conclusive presumption" provision, the court nonetheless continued in dictum to quash the suggestion that a "conclusive presumption" provision, in the abstract, could "be used to fill every gap" in an agreement.[53] To explain this assertion, the high court, in again footnoted dictum, sought to recast its earlier *Nemec* decision: "Although our Opinion in *Nemec* characterized the implied covenant as a 'gap filler,' that description . . . was not intended to be, nor should it be read as, an open-ended invitation to scriveners of partnership agreements to 'fill [every] gap' by employing 'express' contractual provisions."[54]

By uncabining the implied covenant from its narrow gap-filler function, the high court reanimated the doctrine to police against seemingly inequitable behavior. Indeed, as noted above, the court in *Gerber* went on to hold that the defendants' alleged conduct orchestrating the self-dealing transaction breached the implied covenant, notwithstanding the

---

[49] *E.g.* Lonergan v. EPE Holdings LLC, 5 A.3d 1008, 1022 (Del. Ch. 2010) (Laster, V.C); Brinckerhoff v. Enbridge Energy Co., Inc., 2011 WL 4599654, at *9 (Del. Ch. Sept. 30, 2011).
[50] *E.g. In re* Encore Energy Partners LP Unitholder Litig., 2012 WL 3792997, at *14–15 (Del. Ch. Aug. 31, 2012) (Parsons, V.C.); *In re* K–Sea Transp. Partners L.P. Unitholders Litig., 2012 WL 1142351, at *9–10 (Del. Ch. Apr. 4, 2012) (Parsons, V.C.); Gerber v. Enterprise Prods. Holdings, LLC, 2012 WL 34442, at *11–13 (Del. Ch. Jan. 6, 2012) (Noble, V.C.).
[51] *See supra* note 50.
[52] *See Gerber*, 67 A.3d at 419 ("[The] conclusive presumption must be read together with Section 7.9(b) [of the LP agreement, which] imposes a contractual fiduciary duty to act in 'good faith' . . . . Nothing in [the conclusive presumption provision] pertains to or addresses the implied covenant.").
[53] *Id.* at 420.
[54] *Id.* at 419–20, n.48.

"special approval" and "conclusive presumption" provisions in the governing agreement. *Gerber*, thus, is a textbook example of the Delaware courts' use of dictum to subtly refine its law to adapt to new challenges. With this doctrinal tweak, the high court revitalized the implied covenant, creating a judicial means to intervene on behalf of public investors and, perhaps, pre-empting federal intervention that would displace Delaware law to mandate greater investor protections.

4. DICTUM AS AN ELEMENT OF JUDICIAL EMPOWERMENT IN DELAWARE

As shown above, the liberal use of dictum, a judicial habit that evolved first in the corporate law context, has been readily transplanted by the Delaware courts to alternative entity cases. Rather than simply applying statutes and established doctrine in their written opinions, Delaware judges have deftly employed dictum to clarify uncertainty, regulate prospectively, and respond nimbly to emergent challenges. Thus, the effect of any given Delaware judicial opinion goes beyond the resolution of the specific dispute presented or even the precedential value of the holding on future cases involving similar issues and circumstances. Quite often through dictum, an opinion may have import that reaches all Delaware businesses.

This strategic manipulation of dictum has enabled the Delaware courts to play an active role in the development of Delaware law and, therefore, the regulation of the many corporations and alternative entities that are subject to it. Yet, when viewed in a broader context, the use of dictum is just one aspect of a larger legal system that has evolved in Delaware to expand the regulatory reach and lawmaking power of the state's judges over Delaware businesses.

Alongside dictum, the Delaware bench has long employed other means to shape the law beyond the holdings of written opinions. For example, Delaware's judges have an admirable tradition of engagement with business law practitioners and scholars. In their extra-judicial capacity, through participation in national bar groups and law reform projects, public speeches and scholarly articles addressing contemporary business law matters, the Delaware judges have sought to clarify and signal changes in existing law, provide guidance on novel legal questions, and communicate aspirational "best practices" in a variety of transactional contexts to shape the conduct of private business actors (Steele & Verret 2007).

More recently, the Delaware chancery court judges have leveraged so-called "transcript opinions" as yet another platform from which to develop the law to address emergent and unresolved legal questions. The availability of these bench rulings—recorded in court transcripts of oral arguments—has proliferated in recent years on practitioner-oriented websites, making them a source of growing interest among those mining for judicial direction on cutting-edge legal questions (McNally 2012). Although transcript opinions are considered to be limited to the specific facts of a case and, thus like dictum, not binding precedent,[55] Delaware courts have used these bench rulings tactically, like

---

[55] *See In re* NYSE Euronext S'holder Litig., C.A. No. 8136-CS (Del. Ch. May 10, 2013) (Strine, Ch.) (transcript opinion) (explaining that transcript opinions are "provisional," "case-specific" and therefore not binding precedent).

dictum, to respond nimbly to market dynamics and signal the law's future direction. Consider the novel legal questions raised by "don't ask, don't waive" provisions in standstill agreements,[56] which the chancery court first approached in successive bench rulings, before staking out a more definitive position in the dictum of a written opinion.[57] Thus, remarkably, without a single holding addressing "don't ask, don't waive" provisions, the court was able to respond quickly and provide timely regulatory guidance on this contractual innovation.

Transcript opinions, like dictum and the bench's professional and scholarly engagement, have provided Delaware's judges with alternative means by which to mold and refine the law, beyond the holdings of their written opinions. Leveraging these non-traditional lawmaking methods has enabled Delaware judges—rather than the state's legislature—to play the lead role in regulating the internal governance of Delaware businesses (Fisch 2000; Savitt 2012). The state legislature has largely supported this expansion of regulatory power by the state bench, instead of resisting it. Indeed, the Delaware General Assembly has sought to further concentrate regulatory authority in the state's judges by empowering the state courts to hear and decide Delaware law disputes that would be otherwise dealt with elsewhere.

Most prominently Delaware General Assembly has passed successive amendments to the state constitution, first enabling and then expanding the state supreme court's authority to accept certified questions from other jurisdictions (Ridgely 2010). Under Delaware's unusually expansive certified question procedure, any federal appellate and trial court, any supreme court of another state, and even the U.S. Securities and Exchange Commission, may request the Delaware Supreme Court to resolve questions involving Delaware law on which there is no definitive existing precedent.[58] While the authority to accept certified questions does not ensure the Delaware high court will have final say in matters involving Delaware law being litigated in another jurisdiction, it does facilitate and implicitly encourage non-Delaware tribunals to refer such matters to the Delaware justices (Winship 2014). Indeed, Delaware's certified question procedure has, in recent years, produced some of the state supreme court's most significant precedents.[59]

---

[56] In the context of a corporate auction, where a target corporation seeks to sell itself to the highest bidder, the target may require potential bidders to enter into a standstill agreement, pursuant to which a potential bidder is precluded from purchasing or making a bid for shares of the target outside of the target-controlled auction process. A "don't ask, don't waive" provision further strengthens the target's control over the auction process by prohibiting a potential bidder from even requesting that the target's board consider waiving the standstill restriction.

[57] See In re Complete Genomics, Inc. S'holder Litig., C.A. No. 7888-VCL (Del. Ch. Nov. 27, 2012) (Laster, V.C.) (transcript opinion) (questioning the enforceability of a "don't ask, don't waive" provision under applicable fiduciary standards); In re Ancestry.com Inc. S'holder Litig., C.A. No. 7988-CS (Del. Ch. Dec. 17, 2012) (Strine, C.) (transcript opinion) (asserting that "don't ask, don't waive" provisions are not categorically unenforceable and may be appropriate under some circumstances); Koehler v. Netspend Holdings Inc., 2013 WL 2181518, at *10 (Del. Ch. May 21, 2013) (Glasscock, V.C.) (finding the use of a "don't ask, don't waive" provision to be inconsistent with the defendant-directors' fiduciary duties, even though the facts presented did not merit injunctive relief).

[58] Del. Const. art. IV, § 11(8) (amended as of July 2013).

[59] See, e.g., ATP Tour, Inc. v. Deutscher Tennis Bund, 91 A.3d 554 (Del. 2014) (certified question from U.S. District Court); Ark. Teacher Ret. Sys. v. Countrywide Fin. Corp., 75 A.3d 888,

The legislative effort to channel Delaware law questions to Delaware's judges is also reflected in various of the state's statutes. Consider the Delaware LLC and LP acts, which, while professing fidelity to the freedom of contract, nonetheless prohibit alternative entity agreements from waiving the jurisdiction of the Delaware courts.[60] More recently, consider the state legislature's now stalled effort to enable Delaware chancery court judges to conduct confidential arbitrations. Although the initial iteration of the arbitration statute was ruled invalid in 2013 under the U.S. Constitution,[61] the statute's central aim was to empower the Delaware bench to adjudicate Delaware law disputes that would otherwise be decided by private arbitrators (Quinn 2013).

Regardless of the ultimate fate of the chancery court's arbitration procedure, the court may still conduct confidential mediations. Under a unique statute passed in 2003 by the state legislature, any Delaware business may elect to privately mediate a dispute before a chancery court judge as an alternative to litigation.[62] Like the arbitration statute, this mediation procedure thus represents yet another legislatively created forum in which Delaware judges may settle Delaware law disputes that may otherwise be resolved elsewhere.

The Delaware bench has joined the legislative efforts to expand the state courts' control over the law governing Delaware businesses. Through its recent *Boilermakers v. Chevron* decision, the chancery court upheld the validity of an "exclusive forum" bylaw requiring shareholders of a Delaware corporation to litigate any intra-corporate dispute in the state courts of Delaware.[63] Appropriately enough, the imprimatur for such a provision came from judicial dictum, namely Vice Chancellor Laster's unsubtle observation in an earlier decision that "if boards of directors and stockholders believe that *a particular forum* would provide an efficient and value-promoting locus for dispute resolution, then corporations are free to respond with charter provisions selecting an exclusive forum for intra-entity disputes."[64] Following the vice chancellor's dictum, exclusive forum bylaws proliferated among public Delaware corporations. More importantly, since *Boilermakers*, non-Delaware courts have followed the decision when presented with an exclusive forum bylaw, refusing to hear intra-corporate disputes of a Delaware corporation (Cleary Gottlieb Steen & Hamilton LLP 2014).

Thus, viewed in this broader context, the liberal use of dictum, in both corporate and alternative entity jurisprudence, is merely one element of a larger legal ecosystem that has sought to empower Delaware's judges to control the law governing Delaware businesses. The evolution of this regulatory system likely reflects the growing recognition that the Delaware courts—and in particular, its expert and engaged judges—are key to the state's

---

890 (Del. 2013) (certified question from U.S. Court of Appeals); CA, Inc. v. AFSCME Employees Pension Plan, 953 A.2d 227, 229 (Del. 2008) (certified question from the Securities and Exchange Commission).

[60] *See* DEL. CODE ANN. tit. 6, § 17-109(d) (governing LPs); DEL. CODE ANN. tit. 6, § 18-109(d) (governing LLCs).

[61] Del. Coal. for Open Gov't, Inc. v. Strine, 733 F.3d 510, 521 (3d Cir. 2013) *cert. denied*, 134 S. Ct. 1551, 188 L. Ed. 2d 581 (U.S. 2014).

[62] *See* DEL. CODE ANN. tit. 10, §§346–47.

[63] *See* Boilermakers Local 154 Ret. Fund v. Chevron Corp., 73 A.3d 934 (Del.Ch. 2013) (Strine, Ch.).

[64] *In re* Revlon, Inc. S'holders Litig., 990 A.2d 940, 960 & n.8 (Del. Ch. 2010).

success in the jurisdictional competition for corporate, LLC and LP charters. This view, long held in corporate law literature (Fisch 2000; Savitt 2012), has also found support in the alternative entity context (Kobayashi & Ribstein 2011; Gevurtz 2012).

By empowering its judges to shape the law, and ensuring that intra-firm disputes are ultimately resolved by those same judges, Delaware has evolved an unusual legal system that uniquely leverages the state's bench. As a result, what Delaware can offer businesses is the comfort that the rules of internal governance will be defined and applied by an apolitical cadre of informed, agile, and pragmatic regulators. And it is this comfort that is, perhaps, Delaware's principal attraction.

5. CONCLUSION

Given dictum's capacity to develop the law and to guide private actors, it is unsurprising that Delaware judges so frequently indulge in the practice in their written opinions. Nor is it surprising that the Delaware bench has taken this practice developed in the corporate context and applied it readily in alternative entity jurisprudence. Reaching beyond the holdings of their written opinions, Delaware judges have through dictum continuously shaped and reshaped the rules governing the internal affairs of Delaware LLCs, LPs, and corporations. But whether it is dictum or transcript opinions, exclusive forum bylaws, or private arbitrations, all are elements of an unusual legal system that uniquely entrusts the Delaware bench with the primary responsibility to regulate the many corporations and alternative entities organized under the laws of the state.

REFERENCES

Branson, Douglas M. (1990), "Indeterminacy: The Final Ingredient in an Interest Group Analysis of Corporate Law," 43 *Vanderbilt Law Review*, 85.
Cleary Gottlieb Steen & Hamilton LLP (2014), "Alert Memorandum: Forum Selection Clauses in the Foreign Court."
Cleveland, Steven J. (2008), "Process Innovation in the Production of Corporate Law," 41 *U.C. Davis Law Review*, 1829.
Fisch, Jill E. (2000), "The Peculiar Role of Delaware Courts in the Competition for Corporate Charters," 68 *University of Cincinnati Law Review*, 1061.
Gevurtz, Franklin A. (2012), "Why Delaware LLCs?" 91 *Oregon Law Review*, 57.
Gilson, Ronald J. (1997), "The Fine Art of Judging: William T. Allen," 22 *Delaware Journal of Corporate Law*, 914.
Horton, Brent J. (2013), "The Going-Private Freeze-Out: A Unique Danger for Investors in Delaware Non-Corporate Business Associations," 38 *Delaware Journal of Corporate Law*, 53.
Kahan, Marcel & Ehud Kamar (2001), "Price Discrimination in the Market for Corporate Law," 86 *Cornell Law Review*, 1205.
Kobayashi, Bruce H. & Larry E. Ribstein (2011), "Delaware for Small Fry: Jurisdictional Competition for Limited Liability Companies," 2011 *University of Illinois Law Review*, 91.
Manesh, Mohsen (2009), "Legal Asymmetry and the End of Corporate Law," 34 *Delaware Journal of Corporate Law*, 465.
Manesh, Mohsen (2011), "Delaware and the Market for LLC Law: A Theory of Contractibility and Legal Indeterminacy," 52 *Boston College Law Review*, 189.
Manesh, Mohsen (2012), "Contractual Freedom and Delaware Alternative Entity Law: Evidence from Publicly Traded LPs and LLCs," 37 *Journal of Corporation Law*, 555.
Manesh, Mohsen (2013a), "Damning Dictum: The Default Duty Debate in Delaware," 39 *Journal of Corporation Law*, 35.

Manesh, Mohsen (2013b), "Express Contract Terms and Implied Contractual Covenant of Delaware Law," 38 *Delaware Journal of Corporate Law*, 1.

Manesh, Mohsen (2014), "Defined by Dictum: The Geography of Revlon-Land in Cash and Mixed Consideration Transactions," 59 *Villanova Law Review*, 1.

McNally, Edward M. (2012), "The Court of Chancery Speaks by Transcript," Delaware Business Court Insider.

Morgenson, Gretchen (2011), "When Two-Thirds Isn't Enough," *New York Times* June 11.

Parsons, Jr., Donald F. & James S. Tyler (2013), "Docket Dividends: Growth in Shareholder Litigation Leads to Refinements in Chancery Court Procedures," 70 *Washington and Lee Law Review*, 473.

Quinn, Brian J.M. (2013), "Arbitration and the Future of Delaware's Corporate Law Franchise," 14 *Cardozo Journal of Conflict Resolution*, 829.

Ridgely, Henry duPont (2010), "Avoiding the Thickets of Guesswork: The Delaware Supreme Court and Certified Questions of Corporation Law," 63 *SMU Law Review*, 1127.

Rock, Edward B. (1997), "Saints and Sinners: How Does Delaware Corporate Law Work?," 44 *UCLA Law Review*, 1009.

Rutledge, Thomas E. (2013), "Going to Delaware (?)" *Journal of Passthrough Entities*, 59.

Savitt, William (2012), "The Genius of the Modern Chancery System," 2012 *Columbia Business Law Review*, 570.

Steele, Myron T. & J.W. Verret (2007), "Delaware's Guidance: Ensuring Equity for the Modern Witenagemot," 2 *Virginia Law & Business Review*, 189.

Winship, Verity (2014), "Delaware Invites Certified Questions from Bankruptcy Courts," 39 *Delaware Journal of Corporate Law*, 427.

PART 8

INTERNATIONAL PERSPECTIVES ON ALTERNATIVE FORMS

21. Partnership options in the UK: good things come in threes
Elspeth Berry

1. INTRODUCTION

The UK offers a range of business organizations including three types of partnership and five types of company, but competition to be the vehicle for a professional or trading business exists primarily among the three partnerships and the private company limited by shares, the other forms of company[1] having much more specialized uses. There is also the possibility of carrying on business as a sole trader, but this option is not underpinned by specialist business organization laws.

The three types of partnership are the general partnership, the limited partnership and the limited liability partnership (LLP) although, as will be seen, the latter is in fact a corporate body and in some ways more akin to a private limited company. These partnerships are significant both numerically and financially; it is estimated that they make up 10 percent of UK businesses with combined turnover of £150 million (Office of Tax Simplification 2014). Partnerships generally are intended to provide flexible and informal business vehicles (Law Commissions 2003: 3.3–3.6) and have traditionally offered autonomy and collegiality to professionals (Empson 2007).

This chapter will provide a brief initial outline of each type of partnership and then evaluate their key attributes. These include integration of management and ownership, lack of a model agreement, tax transparency, and the application of company insolvency legislation, all of which are common to all three partnerships. They also include ease and certainty (or otherwise) of formation; the availability (or unavailability) of flexibility, privacy, legal personality, continuity, limited liability, and automatic dissolution; and the ability (or inability) to grant floating charges. In addition, areas of uncertainty will be discussed; whether partnerships themselves can be partners/LLP members, the activities which a limited partner may undertake without incurring unlimited liability, mutual duties and their enforcement, particularly within an LLP, and whether LLP members can also be employees.

General Partnerships

The general partnership is the longest established business organization, and the second most numerous with 456,000 firms (BIS[2] 2014), after the private limited company with 2.5 million (Companies House 2014).

---

[1] These are public companies limited by shares, private companies limited by guarantee, and private unlimited companies with or without shares.
[2] UK Department for Business, Innovation & Skills.

It is governed by the Partnership Act 1890, which has been described as "one of the most ideal pieces of legislation" (Cousins 2000) for its brevity (50 sections) and simplicity. Section 1 defines a partnership as "the relation which subsists between persons carrying on a business in common with a view of profit;" it is not registered with the Registrar of Companies and comes into existence as soon as this definition is fulfilled. Its basis is the "relation" between partners; the partnership itself does not have separate legal personality, partners are personally liable for its debts, and they owe each other an overriding duty of good faith. There is no legal separation of roles, and partners are normally, although not necessarily, both managers and owners.

Limited Partnerships

The limited partnership was established only shortly after the general partnership, but by then the limited company had also been given a statutory basis and the limited partnership struggled to compete. However, although they number only 27,000 (Companies House 2014), this number has been increasing steadily in recent years and they have a significant economic impact, in particular as private equity vehicles (BERR[3] 2008: ch 3), and family (Law Commissions 2003: 1.2) and agricultural businesses (Law Commissions 2001: 1.3).

Limited partnerships are governed by the Partnership Act as modified by the even shorter Limited Partnerships Act 1907, a combination which causes some lack of clarity and also omissions. The definition in the Partnership Act (see above) applies, but the partnership must also be registered (s 5 of the Limited Partnerships Act) and there must also be at least one general and one limited partner, the latter having liability limited to his capital contribution unless he engages in management.

Limited Liability Partnerships (LLPs)

The limited liability partnership, commonly referred to as an LLP, is a much more recent creation but there are already 59,000 and increasing (Companies House 2014). It was introduced by the Limited Liability Partnerships Act 2000 (the LLP Act) in response to pressure from the accountancy profession and, to a lesser extent, the legal profession, after the combination of unlimited personal liability and "deep pockets" as compared to other potential defendants led to a number of significant claims against professional partnerships, and the introduction of LLPs in Jersey, to which a number of firms threatened to decamp if their demands were not met by the UK government (Deards 2000: 74; Freedman and Finch 1997: 399).

The LLP derives most of its features from either existing partnership or company law. From partnership law comes part of its definition in s 2(1)(a) of the LLP Act ("two or more persons associated for carrying on a lawful business with a view to profit"), the combined management and ownership roles of its members, and a number of default provisions on the operation of the firm.

From company law come the other two key elements of its definition—it is "a body corporate (with legal personality separate from that of its members)"—as well as its

---

[3] UK Department for Business, Enterprise and Regulatory Reform.

continuity, members' limited liability, the requirement to register,[4] and the disclosure of accounts in return for limited liability.[5] It also, regrettably, derives from company law the complexity of its governing legislation (Freedman 2004: 298–299), which consists primarily—although not exhaustively—of the LLP Act, the Limited Liability Partnership Regulations 2001[6] (LLP Regulations 2001) which supplement the LLP Act, including default rules modeled on the Partnership Act, and apply with modifications the Insolvency Act 1986 (IA 1986), and the Limited Liability Partnerships (Application of Companies Act) Regulations 2009[7] (LLP Regulations 2009) and Limited Liability Partnerships (Accounts and Audit) (Application of Companies Act 2006) Regulations 2008[8] (LLP Accounts Regulations) which each apply with modifications provisions of the Companies Act 2006 (CA 2006), the primary UK legislation governing companies.

The LLP is unique chiefly in its particular combination of aspects of both partnership and company law. However, it also possesses a number of unique features of its own, including the requirement to have at least two designated members who have additional responsibilities for statutory compliance,[9] and the insolvency "clawback" (discussed further below).

2. FORMATION

The definition of all three forms of partnership (see above) is similar, in that two or more persons must carry on business together and intend to make a profit.

One area of uncertainty is whether these "persons" can include general or limited partnerships, which in England and Wales (but not Scotland) are neither natural nor legal persons (discussed further below). There is no statutory or case law directly on this point and s 5 and Sch 1 of the Interpretation Act 1978 merely provide that a "person" includes a body corporate or unincorporate unless the contrary intention appears.[10] The Law Commissions (2003: 4.15) assumed that a partnership could be a partner, as does s 168(5A) of the Insolvency Act 1986, which refers to "any person (including an insolvent partnership . . .) [who] is a member of an insolvent partnership." However, leading commentators take the opposite view, either expressly (Blackett-Ord & Haren 2011[11]) or impliedly (Banks 2010[12]).

Another area of uncertainty is the extent to which business must have commenced in order for it to be "carried on" and thus a partnership formed. This difficulty has been

---

[4] Section 3 of the LLP Act.
[5] Sections 441 et seq of the Companies Act 2006 as modified by Regs 17 et seq of the LLP Accounts Regulations and ss 854–855 and 859A–Q of the Companies Act as modified by Regs 30–32 of the LLP Regulations 2009.
[6] SI 2001/1090.
[7] SI 2009/1804.
[8] SI 2008/1911.
[9] Section 8 of the LLP Act.
[10] See further Berry 2014 at 590–591.
[11] At 3.17, citing *Jai Dayal Madan Gopal* (1932) ILR 54 All 846 (India).
[12] At 11.02, note 5, arguing that an LLP can be a partner (only) because it is a corporate body—which, of course, a general or limited partnership is not.

resolved for limited partnerships and LLPs by making registration conclusive proof that the limited partnership has come into existence[13] or the LLP has been incorporated.[14] For general partnerships, the leading case is *Khan v Miah*[15] in which the restaurant that the parties had agreed to operate did not open until after the alleged partnership had been dissolved. The court held that actual trading need not have commenced, but the parties must have done enough to commence the joint enterprise on which they had agreed to engage. This was satisfied on the facts because they had acquired assets, incurred liabilities, and laid out expenditure in the course of the joint enterprise and with the authority of all parties.

The absence of any registration requirements means that general partnerships are in principle simpler, quicker, and cheaper to form. However, if a comprehensive agreement is put in place at the start (advisable for the reasons discussed below) this will increase cost and delay, while the initial registration requirements for limited partnerships and LLPs are in fact minimal.[16] Furthermore, the informality of general partnership formation has the disadvantage that such a partnership can come into existence without the parties intending it, and many disputes turn on whether a partnership exists at all, and thus whether the rights and obligations imposed on partners apply to the parties (for example, *Coward v Phaistos Ltd*[17] and *Ilott v Williams*[18]).

3. PARTNER/MEMBER AGREEMENTS

The partnership relationship is based both on equity, in the form of mutual trust (discussed below), and contract, in the form of the partnership/LLP agreement, to which the ordinary principles of contract law generally apply although there are exceptions such as the doctrine of repudiation (discussed below). However, all three types of partnership benefit from the inherent flexibility of not having to have a comprehensive or written agreement, and from the privacy of any agreement not being registrable. Unfortunately, this makes it more likely that a firm has no agreement, or none which can be proved, as to such key issues as management roles, profit and capital sharing, property ownership, retirement, and dissolution, although in limited partnerships and LLPs prior agreement has to be reached at least on the minimum details required for registration. Disputes as to what has been agreed are thus frequent, particularly in general partnerships (for example, *Castledine v RSM Bentley Jennison (a firm)*[19] and *Drake v Harvey*[20]).

The considerable benefit of this "private ordering" (Vestal 2010) or "contractability" (Ribstein 2004) would remain, however, and the risk of there being no substantial agreement (or none which can be evidenced) minimized, were a model partnership agreement

---

[13] Section 8C(4) of the Limited Partnerships Act.
[14] Section 3(4) of the LLP Act.
[15] [2000] 1 WLR 1232.
[16] Section 8A of the Limited Partnerships Act and s 2 of the LLP Act.
[17] [2013] EWHC 1292 (Ch) unreported, judgment of 21 July 2013.
[18] [2013] EWCA Civ 645 unreported, judgment of 7 June 2013.
[19] [2011] EWHC 2363 (Ch) [2012] Bus LR D77.
[20] [2011] EWCA Civ 838 [2012] Bus LR D44.

to be made readily available, in the same way as model company articles are[21] but without the requirement that they be registered.[22] A model agreement could be based in part on the existing statutory default provisions which already apply in the absence of contrary agreement.[23] These include neutral provisions such as equal sharing of capital and profits, and majority decisions on ordinary matters, as well as provisions which could easily be made more appropriate for most firms, such as departure on notice as currently but with a specified minimum notice period. Omissions in the existing default provisions could be supplemented, for example by including provisions on time devoted to business, on holiday/parental/illness leave, on arbitration and mediation, on the valuation of an outgoing partner's share, and on restrictive covenants. Improvements could also be made, for example to prevent—or mitigate the effects of—the dissolution of general or limited partnerships (discussed below).

Several versions of the model agreement would be required (as is currently the case for different types of company) to reflect the differences in the law applying to the three forms of partnership. For example, a limited partnership agreement must reflect the fact that limited partners cannot engage in management (or, at least, not without losing their limited liability) or bind the firm,[24] and that their departure, bankruptcy, or death does not dissolve the firm;[25] while an LLP agreement must reflect the fact that members are agents of the LLP rather than other members,[26] may also be designated members with associated additional statutory compliance duties, do not share losses, and may wish to exclude s 994 CA 2006 (discussed below).

4. SEPARATE PERSONALITY AND CONTINUITY

Two of the most significant potential disadvantages of general and limited partnerships in England and Wales are their lack of separate legal personality and associated lack of continuity when partners leave or new partners join (Palmer 1892: 7). Scottish partnerships do have separate personality[27] but there is some doubt as to whether this survives a change of membership (Law Commissions 2000: 2.34–2.35). The Partnership Act provides that a partnership is dissolved automatically, subject to contrary agreement, if a (general) partner leaves (ss 26 and 32), dies, or becomes bankrupt (s 33). This can, of course, be highly inconvenient to the business and although it is possible to continue with a changed membership instead of winding up, contracts with the old partnership still come to an end and partners are still entitled to leave and withdraw their respective shares. The Partnership Act provides that contracts with third parties may be novated, but this is subject to agreement by the third party. It provides no mechanism for the valuation of

---

[21] Companies (Model Articles) Regulations 2008 SI 2008/3229.
[22] Cf s 20 CA 2006.
[23] Sections 19, 24, 25, 28, 29, and 30 of the Partnership Act/Regs 7 and 8 of the LLP Regulations 2001 (the latter substantially reproducing the former).
[24] Section 6(1) of the Limited Partnerships Act.
[25] Section 6(5)(e) of the Limited Partnerships Act.
[26] Section 6(1) of the LLP Act.
[27] Section 4(2) of the Partnership Act.

partners' shares or for the imposition of restrictive covenants, although the partnership agreement may do so and the courts have provided guidelines for valuations.[28]

The lack of separate legal personality has a number of other potential disadvantages (Palmer 1892: 11–15), but these can be overcome; the partners can collectively enter into contracts and own property other than land, or set up a service company (in which partners are shareholders) to do so; land can be owned by two to four partners on trust for all the partners;[29] and the Civil Procedure Rules 1998[30] (CPR) enable a partnership to sue or be sued in the firm name.

LLPs do have separate personality, but this has its own disadvantages. First, if a wrong is done to the LLP, it is the LLP that must bring any claim (known as the proper plaintiff principle or the rule in *Foss v Harbottle*[31]) and, if it does not, it is very difficult for a minority of members to bring a claim on its behalf. The position is further complicated by the fact that ss 260–264 CA 2006, which now largely regulate derivative claims in relation to companies, are not among the provisions of CA 2006 applied to LLPs.[32] Although CPR r 19.9C provides that the procedural provisions in ss 261, 262, and 264 do apply to LLPs, and so an LLP member must apply for the court's permission to continue a derivative claim, the substantive grounds in s 263 on which permission may be granted do not, and therefore a member must satisfy the requirements previously established by the courts by way of exception to *Foss v Harbottle*. These are that the wrongdoing members are in control (*Burland v Earle*[33]) and have received personal benefits at the expense of the LLP (*Daniels v Daniels*[34]) (neither of which is now required under s 263, with the result that it is now more difficult for an LLP member to bring a claim than a shareholder), and it must be an act which could not be authorized or ratified by a simple majority of the independent members (*Smith v Croft (No 1)*.[35] Alternatively, an LLP member may petition for an order under s 994 CA 2006 (discussed below) authorizing civil proceedings on behalf of the LLP.[36]

A second disadvantage of separate personality is that, unlike a partner, an LLP member cannot unilaterally terminate the business to release his share. However, they may be able to petition the court under s 994 CA 2006[37] for an order providing for the purchase of their rights and interests by the other members or by the LLP itself.[38] The grounds for a s 994 petition are that the LLP's affairs are being or have been conducted in a manner which is unfairly prejudicial to the interests of the members generally or some part of the members, including at least the petitioner, or that an actual or proposed omission of the LLP is or would be so prejudicial. For example, in *Eaton v Caulfield*[39] the court

---

[28] *O'Neill v Phillips* [1999] BCC 600.
[29] Section 34 of the Law of Property Act 1925.
[30] SI 1998/3132 at r 5A.3.
[31] (1843) 2 Hare 461.
[32] By the LLP Regulations 2009.
[33] [1902] AC 83.
[34] [1978] Ch 406.
[35] [1986] 1 WLR 580 at 591.
[36] Section 996(2)(c) CA 2006 as modified by Reg 48 of the LLP Regulations 2009.
[37] As modified by Reg 48 of the LLP Regulations 2009.
[38] Section 996(2)(e) CA 2006 as modified by Reg 48 of the LLP Regulations 2009.
[39] [2011] EWHC 173 (Ch) [2011] BCC 386.

held that Eaton had been wrongly expelled by the other LLP members, since Reg 8 of the LLP Regulations 2001 provides that members cannot expel another member unless a power to do so has been expressly agreed, and the parties had not so agreed. The resulting exclusion from management was "one of the clearest examples of conduct which equity regards as unfair prejudice,"[40] because it prevented Eaton from participating in the LLP and from contributing to business which could lead to profits in which he was entitled to share. Moreover, as the House of Lords (now the Supreme Court) had stated in *O'Neill v Phillips*, "the unfairness does not lie in the exclusion alone but in exclusion without a reasonable offer."[41] The other members' failure to make a reasonable offer to purchase Eaton's interest thus also caused him unfair prejudice.

The court in *Eaton* also held that, by way of secondary relief, Eaton was entitled to have the LLP wound up under s 122(1)(e) IA 1986,[42] which would enable him to recover his share of its assets, because there had been a complete breakdown in the relationship between the members and it was therefore just and equitable to do so under the principles laid down in *Ebrahimi v Westbourne Galleries*.[43] In *Ebrahimi* the House of Lords suggested that winding up would be just and equitable where a member had been excluded from management if it were found that one, or probably more, of the following were satisfied: the business was formed or continued on the basis of a personal relationship involving mutual confidence, there had been an understanding that all or some of the members would participate in its conduct, and the transfer of the members' interests was restricted. The first two of these are almost inevitably satisfied where the business operates as an LLP (see below) and, in default of contrary agreement, Reg 7(5) of the LLP Regulations 2001 provides for the third.

The possibility of winding up by the court under this or the other grounds in s 122(1) IA 1986 may be of greater significance for LLP members than company members because the modified version of s 994 CA 2006 applicable to LLP members provides that they (unlike company members) may unanimously agree to exclude the right to petition. Admittedly, it has been argued that a member will be released from an LLP agreement excluding s 994 if another member commits a repudiatory breach of the agreement which he accepts, and that the entire agreement will then fall away because it is no longer unanimous (Whittaker & Machell 2009: 9.34). However, the courts have declined to apply the doctrine of repudiatory breach to the relationship between general partners (*Mullins v Laughton*[44] and *Hurst v Bryk*[45]), and while those judgments were based on aspects of general partnership law, particularly dissolution and remedies, which do not apply to LLPs, and some leading commentators argue that the doctrine does apply to LLP agreements (Whittaker and Machell 2009: 9.34), the courts have not yet confirmed that this is the case.

---

[40] *Ibid* per Proudman J at [66].
[41] Per Lord Hoffmann [1999] BCC 600 at 164.
[42] As modified by Sch 3 of the LLP Regulations 2001.
[43] [1973] AC 360.
[44] (2003) Ch 250.
[45] (2002) 1 AC 185.

5. EMPLOYMENT STATUS

It is common in professional firms to have true partners/members, employees, and an intermediate category who may be described by the firm as salaried or employed partners/members but who do not have the power or profit shares of true partners/members. It is not always easy to distinguish between partners/members, and employees, but it can be important for a number of reasons.

First, recent tax reforms mean that an LLP member will be taxed as an employee rather than a self-employed member if he receives payment of which 80 percent is "disguised salary" (an amount which is fixed, or variable but without reference to profits, or is not in practice affected by the amount of the profits), is not given a significant influence over the LLP, and has contributed capital of less than 25 percent of his disguised salary.[46] There is no equivalent provision for partnerships.

Second, a true partner cannot also be an employee of the partnership because it is not possible for an individual to be an employee of himself and his co-partners (*Ellis v Joseph Ellis & Co*[47] and *Cowell v Quilter Goodison Co Ltd*[48]). Although this view was challenged by counsel in *Clyde & Co LLP v Bates van Winkelhof*[49] and Lady Hale, giving the leading judgment, described it as "a serious challenge," she explicitly left the point undecided and Lord Carnwath, citing also the Law Commissions (2003) and Banks (2010) at 5.55, was "unpersuaded." The position for partners is directly relevant to LLP members because s 4(4) of the LLP Act provides that an LLP member may be regarded as employed by the LLP if, had he and the other members been partners in a partnership, he would have been regarded as employed by that partnership. The difficulty with s 4(4) is that, as the court noted in *Tiffin v Lester Aldridge LLP*, if it were to be applied literally, no LLP member could ever be an employee since he could not have been an employee when a partner but "[u]nfortunately, the authors of section 4(4) were apparently unaware of this."[50] In *Clyde* the Supreme Court stated that s 4(4) meant that a member would be a member or an employee in the same circumstances that a partner would be a partner or an employee. However, that case involved a dispute as to whether a member was a worker for the purpose of the protection given to "whistleblowers" under the Employment Relations Act 1996; the court held that s 4(4) did not apply to the status of worker and thus an LLP member could qualify as a worker in circumstances where a partner would not (although whether LLP members are also workers for the purposes of other statutes remains to be seen (Greenwood & Hitchens 2014)). The Supreme Court's comments on employment status may therefore not be strictly binding, but in *Reinhard v Ondra LLP and others*[51] the court expressly declined to decide this point and noted that the application of the similar (but more complicated) interpretation of s4(4) in *Tiffin* – requiring an examination of whether the member would have been a partner had the firm been a partnership and only if

---

[46] Sch 17 Pt 1 of the Finance Act 2014.
[47] [1905] 1 KB 324.
[48] [1989] IRLR 392.
[49] [2014] UKSC 21 [2014] 1 WLR 2047.
[50] [2012] EWCA Civ 35 [2012] 1 WLR 1887 at [31].
[51] [2015] EWHC 26 (Ch), [2015] All ER (D) 69 (Jan.) at [44]–[45].

this was not the case an examination of whether he was an employee – produced the same result on the facts.

6. GOVERNANCE

The social values and structures which emerge through the medium of a business organization can have far-reaching effects on its members and on those who interact with the business, including suppliers, customers, and competitors (Child 1969: 1). In UK partnerships, two features are particularly evident: the integration of management and ownership, and the principle of equality.

The sharing of net profits is prima facie evidence of partnership[52] and, in default of contrary agreement, partners/members share equally in capital (to which limited partners are obliged to contribute[53]) and profits,[54] and thus their financial reward is linked directly to the financial success of the business (Martin 2014).

Subject to contrary agreement, all partners/members have the right to manage,[55] although limited partners may not take part in management without losing their limited liability.[56] Significant decisions are taken unanimously[57] and ordinary decisions by simple majority.[58] The right to manage, equal voting, and unanimity for the most important decisions make the minority in a partnership less vulnerable than in a company (Griffiths 1999: 25, 29–30).

This integrated structure allows the most important part of the business, its human capital, to be rewarded with involvement in both management and profit sharing (Ribstein 2004: 211), producing job satisfaction and reducing the likelihood of alienation (Child 1969). Integrated management and ownership is ideal for professional practices because the professional desire for autonomy can conflict with a more bureaucratic control structure (Child 1969: 68–69). In contrast, companies risk focusing on the interests of investors at the expense of those of the workers, including the managers, whereas partnerships inherently focus on both. For a professional services firm, such equality can also promote the firm's professional identity over its business identity (Albert & Adams 2002), and for all firms the integration of roles streamlines decision making and integrates functions in pursuit of a common goal rather than creating a company-style coalition of conflicting interests or, worse still, an exploitative controlling elite (Child 1969: 12). Although company managers and investors have a common interest in the success of the business, there is a potential conflict between those whose only interest is financial and those who work in the business (Child 1969: 37, 40). Furthermore, "the managers rather of other people's money than of their own . . . cannot well be expected . . . [to] watch over

---

[52] Section 2(3) of the Partnership Act.
[53] Section 4(2) of the Limited Partnerships Act.
[54] Section 24(1) of the Partnership Act/Reg 7(1) of the LLP Regulations 2001.
[55] Section 24(5) of the Partnership Act; Reg 7(3) of the LLP Regulations 2001.
[56] Section 6(1) and (5) of the Limited Partnerships Act.
[57] Admission of a new partner/member (s 24(7) of the Partnership Act/Reg 7(5) of the LLP Regulations 2001) and change of business (s 24(8)/Reg 7(6)).
[58] Section 24(8) of the Partnership Act/Reg 7(6) of the LLP Regulations 2001.

it with the same anxious vigilance with which the partners . . . frequently watch over their own" (Smith 1776: 330); partnerships will "be more productive and skillfully managed by those whose *all* is responsible for their proceedings [than] by those whose responsibility is limited to some part . . . of their fortune, and to whom, consequently, their success or failure is a matter of comparative indifference" (McCulloch 1856: 5). Integration of roles also ensures that both management and capital are likely to be in place long term, whereas the enforced division of management and investment in a company means that each has less personal commitment to the business.

While larger firms may create their own hierarchical structure, which can diminish integration, egalitarianism (Hillman 2005: 180–181, 193), and commonality of purpose, the risks of unlimited liability reduce the likelihood that general partners will delegate their management powers entirely. Admittedly this incentive does not apply to LLP members or limited partners, but the latter at least have little power to delegate. The government recently proposed a statutory list of activities falling short of management and thus permissible for limited partners (BERR 2008) but this has, fortunately, not been adopted. It was stated to be exhaustive, which would have removed any flexibility as to activities not listed, and included activities which would otherwise properly be regarded as management, such as investments by the partnership and the disposal or acquisition of a business (Law Commissions 2003: 17.17; BERR 2008; Berry 2013).

7. DUTIES

The courts have established that partners owe each other a general duty of good faith[59] and, since LLP members are agents of the LLP,[60] they owe it fiduciary duties (such as good faith) when acting as such.[61] Three examples of the duty are included in the Partnership Act/LLP Regulations 2001: to provide true accounts and full information, to account for private profits from a transaction involving the firm or its name or connection, and to account for profits of a competing business.[62]

Partners also owe a duty of care to each other[63] and while it has not yet been established that LLP members owe such a duty to the LLP, it is likely that they do, based either on their fiduciary duties or on ordinary principles of tort law. The exact standard of the duty is not entirely clear. In *Tann v Herrington*[64] the court held that a partner must perform his duties with all reasonable skill and care, judged objectively as in *Winsor v Schroeder*, in which the court stated that a partner must carry out his work according to "the standards of a reasonable businessman in the situation" but that this duty would not be breached where he made innocent mistakes in good faith.[65] In the Scottish case of *Ross Harper*

---

[59] *Const v Harris* (1824) Turn & R 496 (general partners) and *BBGP Managing General Partner Limited v Babcock & Brown Global Partners* [2010] EWHC 2176 (Ch), [2011] Ch 296 (limited partners).
[60] Section 6(1) of the LLP Act.
[61] *White v Jones* [1995] 2 AC 207.
[62] Sections 28–30 of the Partnership Act/Regs 7(8)–(10) of the LLP Regulations 2001.
[63] See, for example, *Tann v Herrington* [2009] EWHC 445 (Ch), [2009] Bus LR 1051.
[64] Ibid.
[65] (1979) 129 NLJ 1266 per Woolf J at 1266.

& *Murphy and others v Banks* the court held that a partner must exercise "reasonable care in all the relevant circumstances,"[66] which included recognition that the partnership relationship may involve "some mutual tolerance of error," the nature of the particular business, and any practices adopted by that partnership. The standard for LLP members may be that applicable to partners, or equivalent to that owed by a director under s 174 CA 2006 (the care exercised by a reasonably diligent person having the knowledge, skill, and experience which he actually has and that which may reasonably be expected of a person carrying out his functions), although the fact that s 174 is not one of the provisions of CA 2006 applied to LLPs[67] militates against the latter. If the firm is insolvent, the standard for both partners and LLP members under the Insolvency Act 1986 is similar to s 174.[68]

However, LLP members are not agents of each other and so their mutual duties are uncertain. No duty of care applies as between directors,[69] and in *F&C Alternative Investments (Holdings) Ltd v Barthelemy (No 2)*[70] the court noted that the inclusion of a duty of good faith between members in the LLP Act had been considered and rejected. It concluded that "it is difficult to make generalizations about the circumstances in which a duty of good faith or other fiduciary duties as between the members in a limited liability partnership may arise."[71]

Statutory duties are imposed on LLP members and general partners in a limited partnership to register changes to the registered details (s 9 of the LLP Act and s 9 of the Limited Partnerships Act) and on LLP members, and in particular designated members, to draw up, distribute, and file accounts under CA 2006 as modified by the LLP Accounts Regulations.[72]

8. FINANCES

As discussed above, profits and capital are shared equally in all three forms of partnership (s 24(1) of the Partnership Act/Reg 7(1) of the LLP Act), and thus many of the comments on collegiality and shared purpose made above in relation to governance apply equally to financial equality. However, this equality is subject to contrary agreement, and indeed sharing profits at all is not an essential element of partner/LLP member status (*M. Young Legal Associates v Zahid*[73]).

In raising capital, LLPs have the advantage that, unlike the other forms of partnership, they can grant floating charges to secure loans because they are exempted from the requirements of the Bills of Sale Act 1878 and the Bills of Sale Act (1878) Amendment

---

[66] [2000] PNLR 631 per Lord Hamilton at [36].
[67] By the LLP Regulations 2009.
[68] Section 214(4) 1986 as applied to partnerships by s 221(5) as modified by the Insolvent Partnerships Order 1994 (SI 1994/2421) Schs 3, 4, 5 and 6 and to LLPs by Art 5 of the LLP Regulations 2001.
[69] *Kohn v Meehan*, unreported, judgment of 31 January 2003.
[70] [2011] EWHC 1731 (Ch), [2012] Ch 613.
[71] *Ibid* at [211].
[72] See further supra n. 5.
[73] [2006] EWCA Civ 613, [2006] 1 WLR 2562.

Act 1882[74] by s 17 of the 1882 Act. A consultation on whether general and limited partnerships should also be exempted "revealed wide-ranging support" (Law Commissions 2003: 13.32) but no legislation has been proposed, in part because of the difficulty of registering charges when general partnerships are not themselves able to register. Limited liability may also give LLPs an advantage in raising capital internally (Djelic 2013) because members are not, simply by virtue of investing, risking their other personal assets (discussed below).

9. LIABILITY

A general or limited partnership is liable for partners' acts within their actual or apparent authority,[75] for the acts of those who appear to be partners,[76] and for partners' torts and other wrongful acts committed by them in the course of business.[77] General partners are jointly and severally liable without limit for the partnership's liabilities,[78] as are limited partners if they engage in management[79] although, if they do not, their liability is limited to their capital contribution.[80] In contrast, as an LLP is a separate legal person, its members have personal liability for its debts only in exceptional circumstances.

The position of general partners is thus consonant with natural justice, which implies individual responsibility with unlimited liability for one's own acts (Djelic 2013; McCulloch 1865), and it can be argued in particular that "the professional nature of law and accounting practice and its obligations to the public interest require that each professional partner be civilly responsible for his [or her] professional acts" (Alexander 2002: 26). Unlimited liability also tempers individualistic impulses and incentivizes collective behavior and collegiality (Empson 2007).

The position of LLP members is consistent with natural justice only in the narrow range of circumstances in which they can incur personal liability for their actions: if they personally guarantee the LLP's debts, are made subject to a costs order in proceedings brought by another member against them and the LLP,[81] agree to make a contribution on winding up,[82] carry on business as a sole member for more than six months,[83] commit a wrongful

---

[74] The Acts impose complex requirements on charges over "personal chattels," in default of which the charge is void and, since most goods fall within the definition of "personal chattels," a partnership cannot in practice grant floating charges. By way of exception, a farmer (who can be an individual or partnership, but not an LLP or company) is permitted by the Agricultural Credits Act 1928 to grant a floating agricultural charge over agricultural assets.
[75] Sections 5 and 6 of the Partnership Act.
[76] Sections 14 and 36 of the Partnership Act.
[77] Sections 10 and 11 of the Partnership Act.
[78] Sections 9 and 12 of the Partnership Act and s 3 of the Civil Liability (Contributions) Act 1978.
[79] Section 6 of the Limited Partnerships Act.
[80] Section 4(2) of the Limited Partnerships Act.
[81] *Eaton v Caulfield* [2013] EWHC 2214(Ch), judgment of 3 July 2013, unreported.
[82] Section 74 IA 1986 as modified by Sch 3 of the LLP Regulations 2001.
[83] Section 4A of the LLP Act.

act or omission in the course of the LLP's business or with its authority[84] or are guilty of other wrongdoing such that a court is prepared to pierce the corporate veil (for example because the entity is a sham (*Gilford Motor Co Ltd v Horne*[85]), or if sanctions under the insolvency legislation apply (see below). LLP members are thus largely protected from liability for contractual debts and obligations incurred by other members and from vicarious liability for their negligence or misconduct. Furthermore, while natural justice also implies collective responsibility for collective acts, even when LLP members incur personal responsibility they do so only for their own personal acts, despite having benefited from the collective enterprise (Alexander 2002). Limited partners, of course, effectively cannot act.

The provision of limited liability has long been argued to promote economic progress by encouraging investment in business, thereby benefiting both investor and enterprise (Select Committee on Investments for the Savings of the Middle and Working Classes 1850: vi), and encouraging investors to invest widely (Easterbrook & Fischel 1996). However, diversified investments have not been evident in the LLP context, with LLP members tending to invest only in their own LLP, although the recent introduction of alternative business structures (ABS), in which outside investment in law firms is permitted, may encourage some diversification (Varley 2012).

Furthermore, although limited liability can reduce the costs to investors of monitoring managers and other investors (Easterbrook & Fischel 1996: 41–42; Hansmann & Kraakman 2004: 54), it transfers these costs to creditors. Risks are externalized because they are shifted from members to outsiders, despite the fact that members are in a much better position to ensure that quality monitoring systems are in place and risks minimized (Alexander 2002).

In contrast, the risk of unlimited liability clearly provides a strong incentive to work both diligently and prudently (Becerra 2009), and limited liability can be harmful to the business and to investors (Labouchere 1850; Select Committee on the Law of Partnership 1851: xvi) because it enables managers to reduce their exposure to risk without taking risk mitigation measures in the provision of services (Alexander 2002: 2), such as training, supervision, and appropriate contractual terms. Even commentators who argue that there is no need to protect third parties because they are capable of protecting themselves admit that where members have limited liability the business offers "somewhat less security" to third parties (Mill 1871: 511–512). While more sophisticated or powerful clients or creditors may be able to negotiate personal guarantees of performance or liability, the problem remains for "unsophisticated, smaller enterprises or clients" (Alexander 2002: 27). Limited liability may also encourage members to divert the firm's assets in order to protect them from creditors (Griffiths 1999: 23).

The risk of fraudulent behavior sheltering behind limited liability could be reduced if members had to contribute capital which they could not withdraw for a minimum period and which must be publicized (Select Committee on the Law of Partnership 1851). However, LLP members are not required to contribute capital; and although limited partners are, must register the amount, and remain liable for any sums withdrawn,[86] no minimum is specified and so only a nominal amount need be contributed as capital, with

---

[84] Section 6(4) of the LLP Act.
[85] [1933] Ch 935.
[86] Section 4(2) and (3) of the Limited Partnerships Act.

370 *Partnerships, LLCs and alternative forms of business organizations*

any additional investment by way of loan. In fact the government proposed removing this obligation and ending liability for any withdrawn capital after 12 months (BERR 2008), although no legislation has yet been enacted.

None of the three types of partnership themselves benefit from limited liability, but LLPs benefit from much stronger entity shielding, as members' creditors have no direct claim against the LLP, while partnership creditors have first claim on partnership assets and only if there is a surplus will partners' private creditors receive anything.[87]

10. DISCLOSURE AND FILING

The absence of registration and filing requirements means that general partnerships enjoy a considerable degree of privacy and flexibility compared to the other forms of partnership. There are only two disclosure requirements, and one of these applies to very few partnerships. First, if the names of all partners do not appear in the partnership name, they must be disclosed on all business documents and at the partnership premises.[88] Second, if all general partners are limited companies, or Scottish partnerships, or unlimited companies all of whose members are limited companies, the partnership accounts must be prepared as if it was a company; and either partners which are limited companies must disclose them in their company accounts or, if no partners are limited companies, the partners must make them available at the principal place of business.[89]

Limited partnerships are also relatively private and flexible because the information that they are required to register is (as explained above) minimal.

In contrast, as well as registering on formation, LLPs must keep a register of members available for inspection[90] and have considerable filing obligations, including an annual return (confirming the address of the registered office, details of members, and the address at which any register of debenture holders is available for inspection)[91] and audited accounts which must include the aggregate of members' profit shares and, if the total profit exceeds £200,000, the highest profit share paid to a member.[92] Compulsory disclosure of profit shares reflects the interests of creditors in ensuring that members' drawings are proportionate to the finances of the business, and disclosure generally enables outsiders to assess the financial risks of transacting with a business whose members have limited liability.

---

[87] Sections 175A(5) and 328(1)–(3) and (6) IA 1986 as modified by the Insolvent Partnerships Order 1994 (SI 1994/2421) Sch 4 Pt II para 23, and s 328A(5) IA 1986 as modified by Insolvent Partnerships Order Sch 7 para 21.
[88] Sections 1200–1204 CA 2006.
[89] Partnerships (Accounts) Regulations 2008 SI 2008/560.
[90] Sections 162–165 CA 2006 as modified by Reg 18 of the LLP Regulations 2009.
[91] Section 854 CA 2006 as modified by Reg 30 of the LLP Regulations 2009. The annual return is to be replaced by an annual confirmation statement confirming the accuracy of the registered information (s 853A CA 2006) but the legislation effecting the amendment (s 92 of the Small Business, Enterprise and Employment Act 2015) is not yet in force (provisionally due to come into force April 2016) and the consequential amendments to the LLP Regulations 2009 have not yet been drafted.
[92] Section 441 CA as modified by Reg 17 of the LLP Accounts Regulations.

11. TAX

One area of general satisfaction is the tax-transparent treatment of all three forms of partnership, which means that only the partners/members pay tax, and not the partnership/LLP.[93] However, recent changes to the taxation of LLP members perceived by the authorities to be employees rather than true members (discussed above) has provoked criticism (Cross 2014), as have changes aimed at ensuring that profits are not allocated between individual and corporate partners (in "mixed partnerships") so as to avoid tax and that assets are not disposed of by or through a partnership to secure a tax advantage.[94]

12. INSOLVENCY

The complexity of the provisions of the Insolvency Act 1986 (IA 1986) is exacerbated by their partial modification and application to partnerships (by the Insolvent Partnerships Order 1994[95] (IPO)) and LLPs (by Sch 3 of the LLP Regulations 2001). The opacity of the IPO, in particular, is typified by its invention of four different types of winding up petition against a partnership, with IA 1986 provisions applied, excluded, or modified, differently for each (Deards 1995).

The application of IA 1986 also means that partners and LLP members are subject to the same statutory sanctions for insolvency-related malfeasance that apply to companies and individuals.[96] However, LLP members are additionally liable to a unique sanction known as the "clawback." If a member withdrew LLP property within two years prior to its winding up, and knew or had reasonable grounds for believing that it was at that time unable to pay its debts or would become so as a result of the withdrawal, and knew or ought to have concluded that there was no reasonable prospect of it avoiding insolvent liquidation, then the court may order the member to contribute to the LLP's assets.[97]

Where a partnership/LLP is wound up under IA 1986, partners/members are liable to disqualification from acting as company directors or LLP members (but not as partners) under the Company Directors Disqualification Act 1986 (CDDA) if the court considers that their conduct makes them unfit to be concerned in the management of a company or LLP. However, the application of the CDDA to partners is inappropriate given that its purpose is to protect against abuse of limited liability. Furthermore, if general partners are not deterred by the prospect of unlimited personal liability, it is unlikely that they will be deterred by disqualification from a status that they have not previously sought, while limited partners are unlikely to engage in any conduct that would indicate their unfitness to manage.

---

[93] Sections 848, 852, and 863 of the Income Tax (Trading and Other Income) Act 2005.
[94] Finance Act 2014, Sch 17.
[95] SI 1994/2421.
[96] For example, ss 213, 214, 238, and 239 IA 1986.
[97] Section 214A IA 1986 as inserted by Sch 3 of the LLP Regulations 2001.

13. CONCLUSION

All three forms of partnership offer the benefits of integrated management and ownership, collegiality, streamlined and long-term decision making, and long-term investment, features which compare favorably with companies. All three share the relatively minor disadvantage of lack of a model agreement.

General and limited partnerships additionally offer the benefits of simplicity, accessibility, privacy, and flexibility. Although they were originally subject to a 20-partner limit and the legislation was thus designed for small firms, the fact that partnerships today come in all sizes (Law Commissions 2003: 1.4) and number almost half a million indicates that the original legislation remains broadly fit for purpose. However, disadvantages include lack of separate personality, lack of continuity, the IPO and, in the view of some, lack of limited liability.

In contrast, LLPs offer the benefits of separate personality, continuity, and (at least in principle) limited liability. However, they also possess a number of disadvantages, including the requirement to disclose accounts and other statutory filing obligations and, for the time being, uncertainty over a number of issues not clarified in the legislation and not yet dealt with by the courts, for example as to whether members owe duties to other members.

REFERENCES

Albert, Stuart & Edward Adams (2002), "The Hybrid Identity of Law Firms," in *Corporate and Organizational Identities* (Bertrand Moingeon & Guillaume Soenen eds.), 35–50.
Alexander, Kern (2002), "Lessons from the Rise of the US Limited Liability Partnership: Regulating Risk-taking in the Large Professional Firm" (ESRC Centre for Business Research, University of Cambridge Working Paper WP 255, Dec 2002).
Banks, Roderick l'Anson (ed.) (2010), *Lindley & Banks on Partnership* (19th edn), 5.5, 11.02.
Becerra, Manuel (2009), *Theory of the Firm for Strategic Management*, 40.
BERR (2008), "Legislative Reform Order to Repeal and Replace the Limited Partnerships Act 1907: A Consultative Document," available at www.berr.gov.uk/files/file47577.pdf (last accessed July 2014).
Berry, Elspeth (2013), "Limited Partnership Law in the United States and the United Kingdom: Teaching an Old Dog New Tricks?," 2 *Journal of Business Law* 160–185.
Berry, Elspeth (2014), "The Criminal Liability of Partnerships and Partners: Increasing the Divergence between English and Scottish Partnership Law?" 7 *Journal of Business Law* 587–591.
BIS (2014), "Business Population Estimates for the UK and Regions 2014: detailed tables," available at www.gov.uk/government/statistics/business-population-estimates-2014 (last accessed December 2014).
Blackett-Ord, Mark & Sarah Haren (2011), *Partnership Law* (4th edn), 3.17.
Child, John (1969), *The Business Enterprise in Modern Industrial Society*, 1, 12, 30, 37, 40, 60–63, 68–69.
Companies House, "Statistical Release: Companies Register Activities 2013–2014," available at www.companieshouse.gov.uk/about/busRegArchive/CompaniesRegisterActivities2013-2014.pdf (last accessed July 2014).
Cousins, Jim (2000), HC Deb 28 June 2000 cols 887–1024.
Cross, Michael (2014), "Lords Call for Delay to LLP Tax Changes," *Law Society Gazette*, available at www.lawgazette.co.uk/practice/lords-call-for-delay-to-llp-tax-changes/5040324.article (last accessed July 2014).
Deards, Elspeth (1995), "When the View is No Longer of Profit," 4(2) *Nottingham Law Journal* 165–197.
Deards, Elspeth (2000), "Partnerships and the Problem of Unlimited Liability," *Commercial Liability Law Review* 73–91.
Djelic, Marie-Laure (2013), "When Limited Liability was (Still) an Issue: Mobilization and Politics of Signification in 19th-Century England," 34 *Organization Studies* 595–621.
Easterbrook, Frank H. & Daniel R. Fischel (1996), *The Economic Structure Of Corporate Law*, 41–42, 47.
Empson, Laura (2007), "Surviving and Thriving in a Changing World: The Special Nature of Partnership," in *Managing the Modern Law Firm* (Laura Empson ed.), 10–36.

Freedman, Judith (2004), "Limited Liability Partnerships in the United Kingdom: Do They Have a Role for Small Firms?" in *The Governance of Close Corporations and Partnerships: US and European Perspectives* (Joseph A. McCahery, Theo Raaijmakers, & Erik P.M. Vermeulen eds.), 293–316.

Freedman, Judith & Vanessa Finch (1997), "Limited Liability Partnerships: Have Accountants Sewn Up the 'Deep Pockets' Debate?" Sep., *Journal of Business Law* 387–423.

Greenwood, Clive & Christopher Hitchens (2014), "Pensions: Enrolment and Partnerships," *Law Society Gazette*, available at www.lawgazette.co.uk/law/legal-updates/pensions-enrolment-and-partnerships/5042023. article (last accessed July 2014).

Griffiths, Andrew (1999), "The Future of the Partnership: Does the Unincorporated Firm with Unlimited Liability have a Role to Play in the New Millennium?" in *Regulating Enterprise: Law and Business Organisations in the UK* (David Milman ed.), 18–40.

Hansmann, Henry & Reinier Kraakman (2004), "The Essential Role of Organizational Law," in *The Governance of Close Corporations and Partnerships: US and European Perspectives* (supra), 23–71.

Harris, Ron (2013), "The Private Origins of the Private Company: Britain 1862–1907," 33(2) *Oxford Journal of Legal Studies* 339–378.

Hillman, Robert W. (2005), "The Bargain in the Firm: Partnership Law, Corporate Law, and Private Ordering Within Closely-Held Business Associations," *University of Illinois Law Review* 171–194.

Labouchere, Henry (1850), HC Deb 16 April 1850 cols 420–426.

Law Commission & Scottish Law Commission (2000), "Partnership Law: A Joint Consultation Paper," 2.34–2.35, available at http://lawcommission.justice.gov.uk/docs/cp159_Partnership_Law_Consultation.pdf (last accessed July 2014).

Law Commission & Scottish Law Commission (2001), "Limited Partnerships Act: A Joint Consultation Paper," 1.3, available at http://lawcommission.justice.gov.uk/docs/cp161_Limited_Partnerships_Act.pdf (last accessed July 2014).

Law Commission & Scottish Law Commission (2003), "Report on Partnership Law," 1.2-1.4, 4.15, 13.31, 17.17, available at http://lawcommission.justice.gov.uk/docs/lc283_Partnership_Law.pdf (last accessed July 2014).

Martin, Charles (2014), "Partnership: An Idea on the Brink?" 28(21) *The Lawyer* 10.

McCulloch, J.R. (1856), *Considerations on Partnerships with Limited Liability*, 5.

Mill, John Stewart (1871), *Principles Of Political Economy Vol. II*, 511–512.

Office of Tax Simplification (2014), "Review of Partnerships: Interim Report," Jan. 2014, available at www.gov.uk/government/uploads/system/uploads/attachment_data/file/274278/PU1619_OTS_Partnerships_Interim_report.pdf (last accessed July 2014).

Palmer, Francis Beaufort (1892), *Private Companies and Syndicates, Their Formation and Advantages* (10th edn) (MOML Legal Treatises, 1800–1926), 7, 11–15.

Ribstein, Larry E. (2004), "Why Corporations?," 1(2) *Berkeley Business Law Journal* 183–232.

Select Committee on Investments for the Savings of the Middle and Working Classes (1850), Report.

Select Committee on the Law of Partnership (1851), Report.

Smith, Adam (1776), *The Wealth Of Nations: Books IV–V* (Andrew Skinner ed., Penguin Books 1999), 330.

Varley, Martin (2012), "Is External Investment the Future for Law Firms?," *Solicitors Journal*, available at www.solicitorsjournal.com/management/business-development/external-investment-future-law-firms (last accessed July 2014).

Vestal, Allan W. (2010), "The Social-Welfare Based Limits on Private Ordering in Business Association Law," in *Private Company Law Reform: International and European Perspectives* (Joseph A. McCahery, Levinus Timmermans & Erik P.M. Vermeulen eds.), 311–319.

Whittaker, John & John Machell (2009), *The Law of Limited Liability Partnerships* (3rd edn), 9.23, 9.34, 11.1–11.24.

22. Legislative policy of alternative forms of business organization: the case of Japanese LLCs
*Zenichi Shishido**

1. INTRODUCTION

This chapter will raise two questions based on a comparison between the Stock Company (*kabushiki kaisha*, equivalent to the stock corporation in the United States) form and the LLC (*godo kaisha*) form in Japan. First, how do the players choose between one of these two legal forms of closely held business organizations? Second, what is the optimal legislative policy for providing a set of legal forms of closely held business organizations?

To answer these questions, this chapter will focus on the different degrees of freedom of contract—i.e., the different sets of mandatory laws and enabling laws—made available by the Stock Company form and the LLC form. In particular, the chapter takes up three issues relating to freedom of contract that distinguish the two legal forms and are important for the incentive bargaining among the players.[1] These three issues are (i) order-made membership rights, (ii) exit options, and (iii) fiduciary duties.

The bargaining situation, which describes the circumstances in which players try to give incentives to each other to provide capital to the joint project (Shishido 2014c), differs depending on the type of closely held business organization. Drawing on the perspective of players in the bargaining situation, this chapter will categorize closely held business organizations into three types: (i) family firms, (ii) partnership-type firms, and (iii) VC (venture capital)-backed firms.

This chapter focuses on the choice between the Stock Company form and the LLC form for the following three reasons. First, the LLC form can be used only for closely held firms in Japan, while, in the United States, the LLC form is available for both closely held *and* publicly held firms (Manesh 2012). Second, the Stock Company is the only legal form available for publicly held firms in Japan. And third, the Stock Company form and the LLC form are the only two practically meaningful choices for closely held business organizations now in Japan, as I will explain in the next section.

Section 2 provides a brief overview of Japanese corporate law and a general comparison between the Stock Company form and the LLC form. Section 3 will categorize closely held business organizations into the three types mentioned above: (i) family firms, (ii) partnership-type firms, and (iii) VC-backed firms, analyzed from the "bargaining

---

* The author wishes to acknowledge the helpful comments of Bruce Aronson, Robert Bartlett, Richard Buxbaum, Munetaka Fukuda, Mark Gergen, Robert Hillman, Robert Keatinge, Kenichi Osugi, Roberta Romano, and Masato Umetani. Alexander Coley and Lexi Rubow provided skillful research assistance.

[1] "Players" refers to the shareholders in a Stock Company and members in an LLC. Hereinafter, "members" is used to describe both.

situation" point of view. Sections 4, 5, and 6 will analyze the varying demands for freedom of contract in each type of closely held business organization, along with a comparison between the Stock Company form and the LLC form with respect to three major issues of freedom of contract: (i) order-made membership rights (Section 4), (ii) exit options (Section 5), and (iii) fiduciary duties (Section 6). Section 7 will propose a hypothesis that there is a complementarity between exit options and fiduciary duties, and suggest a legislative policy for providing closely held business organizations with certain sets of legal forms. Section 8 will conclude.

2. THE STOCK COMPANY FORM AND THE LLC FORM IN JAPAN

Overview of Legal Forms of Business Organizations in Japan

The principal legal form for closely held business organizations in Japan is still the Stock Company (*kabushiki kaisha*), which is the equivalent of the stock corporation in the United States.[2] Although the GmbH form (*yugen kaisha*) was introduced from Germany in 1938, it never achieved the popularity of the Stock Company. Finally, in 2005, the GmbH was replaced by the "Stock Company without a Board" (*torishimariyakukai hisechi kaisha*).[3]

Non-large companies with stock transfer restrictions can elect to be a Stock Company without a Board, which requires only a single director in addition to holding shareholders' meetings.[4] Although most newly founded closely held corporations, especially of the family firm type, are likely to choose the Stock Company without a Board, partnership-type firms (particularly joint ventures) and VC-backed firms will choose the Stock Company with a Board from the beginning.

Although alternative forms such as the Limited Liability Company (hereinafter LLC) (*godo kaisha*) and Limited Liability Partnership (hereinafter LLP) (*yugen-sekinin jigyo kumiai*) were established in 2005,[5] neither has been widely adopted so far. As of 2013, 95.1 percent of Japanese corporations take the form of Stock Companies, and LLCs make up only 1.1 percent.[6] The prevalence of the Stock Company form is overwhelming. That being said, the number of LLCs has been gradually increasing (Egashira, et al., 2011).

---

[2] The principal piece of legislation governing close and public corporations, including LLCs, is the Companies Act of 2005. The most recent reform of the Companies Act in 2014 does not include any particular reform for close corporations.

[3] Even after this change, GmbHs that were already in existence have been allowed to keep their trade name and maintain the legal characteristics of the GmbH, but the incorporation of new GmbHs is not permitted.

[4] In a Stock Company without a Board, a board of directors is not required and only a single director is necessary to meet the formalities (art. 326 para.1). In Stock Companies without a Board, the shareholders' meeting is empowered to decide everything (art. 295 para.1).

[5] The LLC law came into effect as of 2006 and the LLP law came into effect as of 2005.

[6] www.nta.go.jp/kohyo/tokei/kokuzeicho/kaishahyohon2013/pdf/11.pdf.

The LLP is a pass-through entity for tax purposes, while the LLC is not.[7] This could be a major reason why the number of Japanese LLCs has not grown as rapidly as the U.S. counterpart. On the other hand, even though the LLP is a pass-through entity, it has not gained popularity because it has no corporate personality and has a strong partnership nature.[8] That is, all partners must be managing partners who can be held personally liable against creditors under Japanese law.[9]

It is not too much of an exaggeration to say that under the current circumstances in Japan, there are only two practically reasonable choices of legal forms for closely held business organizations: the Stock Company and the LLC.[10] Therefore, this chapter will focus on the comparison between the two legal forms.

Comparison Between the Stock Company and the LLC

Distinct legislative policies underlying the Stock Company and the LLC forms give rise to varying degrees of freedom of contract and different default rules, both of which may affect the incentive bargaining among the players.

The legislative policy underlying the LLC is to let the parties freely plan their relationship so as to optimize their interests without focusing on the protection of minority shareholders (Aizawa & Koriya 2005). Such a legislative policy is totally different from that of the Stock Company, which still preserves several limitations on freedom of contract from the point of view of minority protection, despite significant deregulation in the Companies Act of 2005.[11]

Another important difference in the legislative policies of the two legal forms is between the default rule of separation of ownership and management in the Stock Company and the default rule of non-separation of ownership and management in the LLC. In Stock

---

[7] Originally, METI (Ministry of Economy, Trade and Industry) planned to introduce the LLC as a pass-through entity just like the U.S. LLC. MOF (Ministry of Finance), however, refused to admit a legal form having corporate personality as a pass-through entity. Therefore, METI hastily introduced the LLP as the first pass-through entity with limited liability for all members in Japan.

[8] Such a strong partnership nature is required to prevent the LLP form from being used for tax avoidance purposes.

[9] A principle of Japanese business organization laws is that in a firm in which all members enjoy limited liability, individual managers must still be personally liable to third parties, either creditors or shareholders, in cases of gross negligence in managing the firm. See Companies Act Article 429.

[10] The Companies Act divides companies into two categories: the Stock Company (*kabushiki kaisha*) and the Membership Company (*mochibun kaisha*). The LLC (*godo kaisha*) was implemented as a Membership Company, in addition to the two traditional legal forms: the General Partnership Company (*gomei kaisha*) and the Limited Partnership Company (*goshi kaisha*). The General Partnership Company and the Limited Partnership Company share the same governance structure and the same freedom of contracts as the LLC. The only difference is whether or not there is at least one member who owes unlimited liability. Therefore, it is not realistic for newly founded business organizations to choose either the General Partnership Company or the Limited Liability Company.

[11] Although the Companies Act requires that certain items be recorded in a company's charter (art. 27), which must be certified by a notary before incorporating the Stock Company (art. 30), notary certification is not necessary in LLCs. In practice, this difference gives LLCs much broader freedom of contract than Stock Companies.

Companies, managerial decisions must be made by directors. Even in a Stock Company without a Board, a director must be appointed. On the other hand, in LLCs, owners (members) are supposed to manage themselves. Decisions are basically made by consensus among the members. Neither directors' nor shareholders' meetings are necessary, although members are free to create equivalents of both by charter. As a corollary, the default rule in LLCs gives every member a veto, while the stock majority default rule in Stock Companies does not.

In sections 4, 5, and 6, I will discuss three major legislative policy issues relating to freedom of contract in which significant variance is observed between the two legal forms: (i) order-made membership rights, (ii) exit options, and (iii) fiduciary duties.

3. VARYING BARGAINING SITUATIONS OF THE THREE TYPES OF CLOSE CORPORATIONS

The "bargaining situation" describes the circumstance in which players (i.e., members) try to give each other incentives to provide capital (either monetary capital or human capital) to their joint business. Bargaining situations exist as long as all players need to incentivize each other, but emerge in different ways, depending upon the relative bargaining power of the players and the characteristics of their joint projects.

In this section, I will categorize closely held business organizations into three types based on different bargaining situations that arise: (i) family firms, (ii) partnership-type firms, and (iii) VC-backed firms.

Family Firms

In typical family firms, there is no bargaining situation, either because there is only one shareholder (in a Stock Company) or member (in an LLC), or because the controlling member does not need to incentivize minority members. Instead, the controlling member has the incentive to squeeze out minority members.

Founders disfavor easy exit options because exit options make the enterprise fragile. Founders generally wish their company to continue long after succession.

Partnership-Type Firms

Bargaining situations do exist in partnership-type firms. By definition, partnership-type firms are organized by members who are expected to provide both monetary capital and human capital to their joint projects. Therefore, monetary capital providers and human capital providers are not separated. This creates a bargaining situation in which it becomes necessary to adjust the imbalance between human capital and monetary capital (Shishido et al. 2013). Otherwise, the incentives of the player who provides more important human capital will be distorted. Note this is not a typical principal-agent situation, but rather a double moral hazard situation (Bhattacharyya & Lafontaine, 1995).

There are three types of conflicts of interest in the partnership-type company: (i) self-dealing, (ii) corporate opportunity, and (iii) disclosure (Shishido, 1987).

Directors (and members in the United States) bear the legal risk of breaching their fiduciary duties.[12] Therefore, partners have incentives to contract around fiduciary duties.

Exit options will make partners more willing to provide their own monetary capital to the joint project, but also make it more difficult to persuade other partners to provide human capital because each partner cannot make a binding commitment to the joint project.

Venture Capital-Backed Firms

Bargaining situations exist in VC-backed firms, too, but manifest differently from those in partnership-type firms. Human capital providers (entrepreneurs) and monetary capital providers (venture capitalists—VCs) are separated. Therefore, there is no necessity of adjusting the imbalance between monetary capital and human capital. The bargaining situation in VC-backed firms is basically the same as the dynamic seen in publicly held business organizations: human capital providers need autonomy and monetary capital providers need monitoring power (Shishido 2014c). This describes a typical principal-agent situation.

In addition, VCs attempt to give entrepreneurs hyper incentives through the scheme of sweat equity (Halloran et al. 2000), which allocates entrepreneurs more cash-flow rights than their share of monetary capital contribution. VCs, in turn, require stronger control than that enjoyed by shareholders in publicly held firms.

There is a risk of conflicts of interest in the cases of fund raising and exit. VC directors face the legal risk of breaching fiduciary duties.[13] Thus, VCs have an incentive to contract around fiduciary duties, while entrepreneurs prefer to preserve them. Conversely, VCs will prefer to keep the exit option as a threat to entrepreneurs, while restricting entrepreneurs' ability to exit.[14]

4. ORDER-MADE MEMBERSHIP RIGHTS

As explained below, the bargaining situation of each of the three types of closely held business organization requires some degree of separation between control rights and cash-flow rights.

Stock Companies vs. LLCs

The basic idea of the Stock Company form is that control rights and cash-flow rights should not be separated in order to give shareholders adequate incentive to exercise control (through voting rights, in particular) for the maximization of firm value. Traditionally, Japanese corporate law was very loyal to this idea and reluctant to deviate from the "one share one vote" principle. The Companies Act of 2005 changed this policy and deregulated the use of different classes of stock.

---

[12] *See, e.g.*, Meinhard v. Salmon, 164 N.E. 545 (N.Y. 1928).
[13] *See, e.g.*, In re Trados Inc. Shareholder Litigation, 73 A.3d 17 (Del. Ch. Ct. 2013).
[14] The model agreement in Halloran, et.al. (2000) stipulates no restrictions on the transfer of preferred stock, only common stock.

The LLC form, which was introduced by the Companies Act of 2005, is even more flexible in allowing a separation between control rights and cash-flow rights. Members can create, by charter, order-made membership rights for individuals based on unanimous agreement.

One of the major restrictions on freedom of contract in the Japanese LLC form is the prohibition on providing human capital in exchange for membership rights (this kind of prohibition is a matter of course for the Japanese Stock Company form). The Companies Act limits capital contributions to cash or its equivalents, for so long as the member enjoys limited liability. This reflects a different legislative policy from the LLC laws in the United States.[15]

Such a restriction, however, does not necessarily mean that the scheme of sweat equity, which is indispensable in VC-backed firms, cannot be implemented in Japan. Although it is not possible under Japanese law to evaluate promises to perform services in the future on a monetary basis and give such human capital providers the same membership rights as a member contributing an equivalent amount of cash, there is, in any event, little practical necessity for such a scheme. The practice of sweat equity, which is well established in Silicon Valley, is to give human capital providers, in addition to dividend rights, a right to participate in the liquidation value of the firm only when it exceeds the liquidation preference of monetary capital providers. At the corporate law level, such a scheme can be used either in Stock Companies or LLCs in Japan.[16]

As discussed next, demands for separation between control and cash-flow rights also differ depending on the type of closely held business organization.

Family Firms

In family firms, when the founder considers a future succession event, his goal is to let his successor heir dominate voting rights and let his other heirs have cash-flow rights, on a perpetual basis. To realize these objectives, it is easier for the founder to use the Stock Company form than the LLC form. Issuing common stock to a successor and issuing non-voting dividend preferred stock to the other heirs is simpler than contracting around the "one member one vote" default of the LLC form.

Partnership-Type Firms

In partnership-type firms, each partner would like to keep certain veto rights (the choice of which is a matter of bargaining), thereby decreasing risk through sharing control, as well as giving fellow partners a cash-flow incentive to provide their human capital. In joint venture (JV) corporations in particular, it is important to fix the incentive distortion of a partner who provides relatively valuable human capital compared to his contribution of monetary capital (Shishido, et al 2013).

---

[15] *See* Uniform Limited Liability Company Act (2006) §402; 6 Del. Code §18-501; 301(d). *See also* Ribstein & Keatinge (2013) §5:4.

[16] One possible barrier to the sweat equity scheme, however, is tax law. The Japanese National Tax Agency considers the sweat equity practice a virtual gift and thus, recipients are required to pay gift tax at a prohibitively high rate (Shishido 2014b).

To accomplish this purpose, JV corporations use shareholder agreements, substantial parts of which cannot be written in the corporate charter. In LLCs, however, most parts of these shareholder agreements can be provided in the charter, improving the enforceability of the agreements. The unanimity default requirement of the LLC form is also suitable for most JVs or partnership-type firms for preserving every member's veto rights (Shishido et al. 2013).

Venture Capital-Backed Firms

In VC-backed firms, VCs want to obtain control on a contingent basis (conditioned on, e.g., contract performance or reaching certain milestones) until the IPO, and to let entrepreneurs share cash flow disproportionate to their monetary capital contribution (sweat equity). In Silicon Valley, this is achieved using different classes of stock. But the same arrangements are already made, in practice, using the LLC form.[17]

To summarize: the choice between the Stock Company form and the LLC form makes little difference in terms of freedom of contract with respect to order-made membership rights, and particularly the separation between control rights and cash-flow rights. However, there are material differences associated with each type of closely held business organization.

5. EXIT OPTIONS

Stock Companies vs. LLCs

Both in Japan and the United States, freedom of contract with respect to exit options is one of the major policy issues raised by the LLC form, and is a feature that distinguishes LLCs from Stock Companies.

State LLC laws in the United States can be categorized into three types based on the various legislative choices made regarding exit options. The first type of legislation gives members mandatory withdrawal rights, which cannot be abandoned (e.g., California[18]). The second type of legislation gives members default withdrawal rights, which can be modified by charter (e.g., Uniform Limited Liability Company Act[19]). The third type of legislation does not stipulate anything about withdrawal rights, although it does allow members to create withdrawal right in their charters (e.g., Delaware[20]).

Japan's LLC law resembles the first type. The Companies Act has a provision on withdrawal right of members in a Membership Company (which includes LLCs as well as General Partnership Companies and Limited Partnership Companies), which reads:

---

[17] *See, e.g.*, Zimmerman v. Crothall, 62 A.3d 676 (Del. Ch. Ct. 2013).
[18] California Corporations Code §17706.01(a).
[19] Uniform Limited Liability Company Act (2006) §§601, 602(1), 110.
[20] 6 Del. Code §18-603.

Article 606
(1) In cases where the duration of a Membership Company is not provided by the articles of incorporation, or in cases where the articles of incorporation provide that the Membership Company shall continue to exist for the life of a particular partner, each partner may withdraw at the end of the business year. In such cases, each partner must give advance notice of withdrawal to the Membership Company more than six months in advance.
(2) The provisions of the preceding paragraph do not preclude the Membership Company from provision to the contrary in the articles of incorporation.
(3) Notwithstanding the provisions of the preceding two paragraphs, if there are any unavoidable grounds, any partner may withdraw at any time.

Article 606 clearly stipulates that members of Japanese LLCs can withdraw "at any time" if there are "any unavoidable grounds." This is one of the few mandatory provisions for a Membership Company, and therefore cannot be eliminated.[21] Members of Japanese LLCs, who enjoy limited liability, can withdraw even where the equity interest refund exceeds the surplus as of the day on which such refund takes place by providing a scheme of creditor protection.[22] This is an important distinction from the Stock Company, in which shareholders who have redemption rights cannot withdraw if there is not enough surplus.

Another exit option for LLC members is to transfer membership rights. The default rules require unanimous agreement of members to transfer membership rights of managing members[23] and unanimous agreement of managing members to transfer membership rights of non-managing members.[24] The rules are interpreted to allow both relaxation of the default requirement as well as stricter restrictions on transfer of membership rights, including prohibition on transfer, because of the existence of withdrawal rights as an alternative scheme for exit (Shishido 2013). That is, LLC law permits complete freedom of contract with respect to the transferability of membership rights.

In Stock Companies, the exit option for members (shareholders) is basically limited to the transfer of stock. Stock transferability can be restricted by charter and the process for restriction is stated in the Companies Act. If a shareholder wants to sell her stock to a third party, she needs the agreement of the shareholders meeting (or board of directors, if the company has a board). If the company does not ratify the transfer, it must either purchase the stock by itself (contingent on the existence of surplus for the purchase) or nominate a designated purchaser. If the seller and the buyer cannot agree on the purchase price, either party can ask the court to decide a fair price. Although the Companies Act does show an interest in guaranteeing the possibility of exit, shareholders need to find a potential purchaser of their stock in order to realize their exit option.

Such a stock transfer restriction scheme in Stock Companies was once considered not modifiable by charter. Even after the Companies Act of 2005 relaxed this rigid policy and allowed most parts of the scheme to be modified by charter, it is still not possible to fix the purchase price or a specific valuation method of stock by charter. Here, the complete freedom of contract regarding membership transferability in the LLC form provides an important practical advantage over the Stock Company by allowing specific valuation

---

[21] One issue is how far the "unavoidable grounds" can be limited by charter (Shishido 2013).
[22] Companies Act Article 635.
[23] Companies Act Article 585 I IV.
[24] Companies Act Article 585 II III IV.

methods to be fixed in the charter. This is particularly important when using rights of first refusal, which are widely seen in practice (Shishido 2013).

In Japan, differences in legal form become salient in the case of exit options: hard exit in the Stock Company and easy exit in the LLC. This distinction will significantly affect the choice of legal form.

Family Firms

In family firms, hard exit is preferable, at least for the founder and his successors, to ensure continuation of the business. Easy exit—particularly, the withdrawal right of members—threatens to disperse the assets of the firm. On the other hand, hard exit will increase the minority members' risk of being squeezed out in family firms, in which there is no bargaining situation.

From the point of view of the persons who actually make the choice of legal form for their business (founders, in most cases), it is unlikely that the LLC form will be chosen for family firms, even though the LLC form does provide more protections for the minority than the Stock Company form.

Partnership-Type Firms

In partnership-type firms, choosing easy exit or hard exit is a trade-off for each partner. Each partner wants easy exit rights for herself and hard exit for her partner. Easy exit will decrease the risk of participating in a joint project, particularly for a partner who will provide relation-specific assets, such as a factory or intellectual property.[25] On the other hand, a situation where a fellow partner can exit at any time by taking back assets indispensable for the joint project creates a risk of opportunistic behavior. Under the easy exit setup, partners cannot commit to the joint project and each partner's incentive to provide its own capital (particularly human capital) is therefore distorted.

Thus, although the easy exit option in Japanese LLCs is attractive to potential partners of partnership-type firms, it is necessary to modify by charter the default "exit at will" rule into an "exit with reasonable conditions" clause in order to use the LLC form for continuous business organizations.[26]

Venture Capital-Backed Firms

Generally speaking, in VC-backed firms, VCs want an easy exit for themselves, to use as a threat when bargaining with entrepreneurs, while simultaneously seeking to restrict the exit of entrepreneurs (Halloran, et al. 2000). However, the Japanese LLC form is inadequate to create such a discriminatory arrangement because of its mandatory withdrawal right. Therefore, it is easier to use the Stock Company form to issue different classes of

---

[25] The withdrawal right could include the right to take specific assets back if members agree. This is impossible in the case of Stock Companies (Shishido 2013).

[26] As an interpretation of Article 606, an LLC should be allowed to limit "unavoidable grounds" to situations of either deadlock or squeeze-out. Otherwise, the LLC form will not be used for partnership-type firms (Shishido 2013).

stock: (i) stock with redemption rights and without transfer restrictions to VCs, and (ii) stock with transfer restrictions to entrepreneurs.

Easy exit is, however, not so harmful either to VCs or to entrepreneurs. VCs will, in any event, pose a threat of exit, either through staged financing or by redemption rights (Halloran et al. 2000). Even if entrepreneurs have withdrawal rights, they do not provide substantial monetary capital that they can withdraw. Although VCs may want to keep entrepreneurs' human capital, VCs cannot in any case restrict the exit of human capital. Instead, VCs give entrepreneurs incentives to stay on as management through the scheme of vesting (Halloran et al. 2000).

In sum, the mandatory withdrawal right of the Japanese LLC form may affect the choice of form depending on the type of closely held business organization. It is unlikely to be chosen by family firms. On the other hand, even though the mandatory withdrawal right is foreign to current Silicon Valley-style practice, it poses little harm to VC-backed firms. For partnership-type firms, choice of the LLC form is a possibility, assuming modification of the default exit option by charter. Ultimately, the range of freedom of contract with respect to exit will be a key issue for the LLC form in practice.

6. FIDUCIARY DUTIES

Stock Companies vs. LLCs

Another major legislative issue distinguishing the LLC and Stock Company forms is fiduciary duties. The degree of room to contract around fiduciary duties is importantly different in LLCs and Stock Companies. A simple illustration on this point is the mandatory nature of fiduciary duties in the Stock Company form and the possible fiduciary exculpation in the LLC form.

Before analyzing the issue of freedom of contract in the fiduciary duty context, it is necessary to explain the three major differences in fiduciary duty law in the United States and Japan. First, in the United States, fiduciary duties are categorized into the duty of care and the duty of loyalty, which are treated as distinct, and each permits differing degrees of freedom of contract. In Japan, traditional case law has not distinguished the duty of care and the duty of loyalty and treats the fiduciary duty as encompassing both. Second, in the United States, not only directors and officers, but also majority shareholders owe fiduciary duties. In Japan, by contrast, only directors and officers owe a fiduciary duty, whereas majority shareholders do not. Third, it is not entirely clear whether directors of Japanese companies owe fiduciary duties directly to shareholders.

With respect to freedom of contract, the duty of care can be contracted around in stock corporations in the United States, but the duty of loyalty cannot.[27] In Delaware LLCs, both the duty of care and the duty of loyalty can be contracted around, and can

---

[27] In 2000, the Delaware General Corporation Law (DGCL) was amended and now allows stock corporations to renounce any interest of the corporation in any business opportunities that are presented to the corporation's officers or directors (8 Del. C. §122(17)).

even be totally eliminated by charter (Steele 2009).[28] In Japan, the fiduciary duty (without distinction between the duty of care and the duty of loyalty) cannot be contracted around in either Stock Companies or LLCs. In LLCs, however, exculpation is possible by amendment of the charter (Shishido 2013). In Stock Companies, non-executive directors can limit, by charter, ex ante damages from breach of their fiduciary duties to two years of compensation. Officers and executive directors can only limit such possible damages ex post, either by shareholder resolution or resolution of the board of directors, to four to six years of compensation (depending on rank).

As discussed below, demand for freedom of contract with respect to fiduciary duties differs depending on the type of closely held business organization.

Family Firms

In a family firm, at the company's inception the founder does not care about fiduciary duties because he is the sole owner and sole manager. If, however, he anticipates future scenarios involving other managers or directors, he will realize that fiduciary duties are necessary. Further, in anticipating future scenarios following a succession event, he will want his successor to treat his other heirs—possibly non-voting members—fairly, which will also lead him to conclude that fiduciary duties are necessary. Therefore, demand for contracting around fiduciary duties is not strong in most cases of family firms.

Partnership-Type Firms

In partnership-type firms, while demand for contracting around fiduciary duties is strong, drafters of charters must confront the trade-off between the risk of being sued for breach of fiduciary duties and the risk of opportunistic behavior by fellow partners.

Typically, there are three types of conflicts of interest in partnership-type firms: (i) self-dealing, (ii) corporate opportunity, and (iii) disclosure (Shishido 1987). In particular, self-dealing conflicts of interest are built into most partnership-type firms because adjustment of the imbalance between human capital and monetary capital is ordinarily made by self-dealing transactions. Partners (members) and directors in partnership-type firms regularly confront conflicts of interest and bear the risk of being sued for breach of fiduciary duties. Therefore, demand for contracting around fiduciary duties is strong.

In Japanese Stock Companies, self-dealing transactions generally need ratification by the board of directors.[29] Ratification by the board is not necessary if all shareholders agree,[30] but if the company suffers damage from the transaction, directors will be personally liable.[31] On the other hand, in Japanese LLCs, self-dealing transactions require agreement by a majority of non-interested members (head count) as a default. This means that as long as a member (partner) secures agreement of the other members (partners), no liability issue will arise even if the company suffers damage from the transaction.

---

[28] Del. Code Ann. Tit. 6, §§17-1101(d) & 18-1101(c).
[29] Companies Act Article 356 I (2) (3).
[30] Sup. Ct., Sept. 26, 1974, 28-6 Minshu 1306.
[31] Companies Act Article 423 III.

On the other hand, there is always the risk of opportunistic behavior by a fellow partner in partnership-type firms. For example: a partner may obtain intellectual property, which is the result of the joint project, free or very cheaply; a partner may run a competing business, which is in the same line of business as the partnership-type firm; a partner may transact with the partnership-type firm and manipulate the transfer price; or a partner may transact with the partnership-type firm without notifying the other partners.[32] It is therefore risky to eliminate fiduciary duties entirely.

In sum, demand to contract around fiduciary duties in partnership-type firms lies in a middle ground.

Venture Capital-Backed Firms

In VC-backed firms, potential conflicts of interest for VCs are expected, e.g., in the valuation of new financing or timing of M&A activity, particularly when the interest of common stockholders and the interest of preferred stockholders are adverse. This type of conflict of interest faced by VC-backed directors is different from cases of either self-dealing conflicts of interest or corporate opportunity conflicts of interest, and is difficult to mitigate by agreeing on procedural schemes. VC-backed directors have a high risk of being sued for breach of fiduciary duties. The demand for contracting around fiduciary duties is therefore strong.

The risk of opportunistic behavior by entrepreneurs can be decreased by aligning their incentives with the firm's value, and through VC monitoring achieved by obtaining corporate control, staged financing, or contractual measures. Further, in most cases, VCs have greater bargaining power. Therefore, it is likely that fiduciary duties in VC-backed firms will be eliminated, if possible.

When an entrepreneur has stronger bargaining power than VCs and VCs cannot obtain sufficient monitoring measures, the risk of opportunistic behavior by the entrepreneur to pursue his private benefit will increase.[33] In that case, VCs prefer to preserve fiduciary duties. The entrepreneur will also like to preserve fiduciary duties to prevent the VC from making an untimely exit. Therefore, in this scenario, there is no demand to contract around fiduciary duties.

7. COMPLEMENTARITIES BETWEEN POSSIBLE SETS OF LEGAL FORMS

This section will propose a hypothesis that there is a complementarity between exit options and fiduciary duties, and suggest that lawmakers enact regulations regarding fiduciary duties and exit options that allow the players of closely held business organizations to choose an optimal environment for their incentive bargain.

In other words, if there is a bargaining situation, since each party needs to incentivize

---

[32] On the other hand, simple inaction by a partner, e.g., opportunistic non-disclosure of know-how or rejection of additional capital investment, cannot be prevented by fiduciary duties.

[33] Such cases are not rare in Japan (Shishido 2014b).

the others, it will be both efficient and fair to let the parties bargain and enforce their agreements as they are. The court should try to realize what the parties would have wanted (Ayres & Gertner 1989). The problem is that contracts for organizing firms are long term and inevitably incomplete. Corporate law fiduciary duties should therefore play a gap-filling role.

Traditionally, fiduciary duties have been considered mandatory rules. In Delaware, the duty of loyalty cannot be contracted around in the stock corporation, but can be eliminated in the LLC.[34] In Japan, fiduciary duties cannot be contracted around either in the Stock Company or LLC forms, although exculpation is possible in LLCs.

Parties bargaining over the organization of a firm will face trade-offs on risks. In a relationship with fiduciary duties, each party wants to decrease the risk of being sued, while at the same time decreasing the risk of opportunistic behavior of other parties. The costs and benefits of contracting around fiduciary duties are different case by case. There are certain cases where the benefit of eliminating fiduciary duties, including the duty of loyalty, overwhelms its cost—that is, the risk of opportunistic behavior of other parties. In such cases, parties will eliminate fiduciary duties. There are also certain cases where the benefits and costs of eliminating fiduciary duties are almost the same. In these cases, parties will not entirely eliminate fiduciary duties, but will try to modify default rules in order to avoid the risk of being sued so far as possible. In both cases, if courts intervene to reverse the parties' contract, it will distort the ex ante incentives of anyone who may participate in such contracts.

When there is no bargaining situation, such as in typical family firms,[35] the risk of squeeze-out is heightened and eliminating fiduciary duties becomes problematic. Even in VC-backed and partnership-type firms, initially complete bargaining situations may turn into incomplete bargaining situations where there is a high risk of squeeze-out. In these cases, a problem of fairness arises.

Although exit options cannot entirely eliminate the risk of opportunistic behavior, they may decrease the risk of squeeze-out, which is one of the worst scenarios of opportunistic behavior. Easy exit with fair value[36] becomes a threat and creates bargaining situations. Therefore, exit options can be complements of fiduciary duties.

The practice of closely held business organizations also demands a complementary set of exit options and fiduciary duties.

In family firms, members tend to be divided into controlling members and non-controlling members. The person responsible for the initial choice of legal form of any business—the founder in most cases—will not choose a form with easy exit, such as a Japanese LLC that gives each member withdrawal rights as mandatory law, because easy exit will cause a dispersion of the company's assets and create difficulties for

---

[34] The subject of freedom of contract with respect to fiduciary duties in Delaware LLCs is a live debate (Steele 2009; Strine and Laster, Chapter 1).

[35] American investment funds organized as listed LLCs have incomplete bargaining situations, where general managers draft charters eliminating their fiduciary duties and make take-it-or-leave-it deals with investors (Strine and Laster, Chapter 1).

[36] Although it is an important issue what fair value is, both from a business planning point of view and from a judicial interpretation point of view, I will not discuss the point in this chapter. For a discussion of fair value, see Shishido (1993); Shishido (2014a).

continuing the business. On the other hand, there is usually no bargaining situation in family firms and controlling members have an incentive to squeeze out non-controlling members. The high risk of squeeze-out therefore requires mandatory fiduciary duties, not only as a matter of fairness but also from the perspective of what the parties would have wanted.

In VC-backed firms (typically Silicon Valley types), VC-backed directors face a high risk of being sued for violation of fiduciary duties, and the demand for contracting around fiduciary duties—and for eliminating the duty of loyalty in particular—is strong. If a duty of loyalty to common stockholders is imposed, the Coasian bargaining will be disturbed and firm value may fail to be maximized (Bartlett 2015). Total freedom of contract on fiduciary duties, however, raises issues of fairness (Strine & Laster, Chapter 1). Easy exit may coordinate such a trade-off. If each member has an easy exit right, particularly a right of withdrawal, he can protect himself and decrease the risk of squeeze-out. Easy exit does not necessarily require strict fiduciary duties. Further, in VC-backed firms, easy exit does not pose much harm either to VCs or to entrepreneurs.

In partnership-type firms there is a trade-off. First of all, easy exit—particularly withdrawal at will, which is the default in Japanese LLCs—does not fit well in partnership-type firms. Easy exit will make the firm too fragile for each partner to provide his own human capital. Therefore, if the default rule is easy exit, it is necessary for partners to modify the default into a more moderate exit option, which preserves the possibility of exit in the worst scenarios, such as deadlock and squeeze-out, but prevents partners from exiting in ordinary scenarios (Shishido 2013). Secondly, although partners will try to decrease the risk of being sued for breaching fiduciary duties by agreeing on procedures anticipating conflict of interest scenarios, they will not eliminate fiduciary duties entirely because the risk of opportunistic behavior is high. Therefore, a middle ground exit option and middle ground arrangement for fiduciary duties should be allowed.

In most cases, the desirability of total freedom of contract, particularly the combination of *no* fiduciary duties and *no* exit options, is the subject of controversy.[37] However, complementary sets of fiduciary duties and exit options appear workable. Legislatures and courts should therefore let the parties bargain on their trade-off situations and choose a suitable complementary set of fiduciary duties and exit options. This is ideal both from a fairness point of view and the point of view of what the parties would have wanted.

The two choices of legal forms for closely held business organizations in Japan, the Stock Company and the LLC, offer reasonable alternative sets of exit options and fiduciary duties: (i) hard exit and strict fiduciary duties in Stock Companies, and (ii) easy exit and relaxed fiduciary duties in LLCs. "In-between" options should also be made available to allow parties to realize their incentive bargain. For that purpose, LLC law should be interpreted flexibly enough to allow modification of its default rules.

---

[37] Delaware LLC law is a typical example of a regime allowing total freedom of contract, including the set of total elimination of fiduciary duties and exit options. Two judges in the Delaware courts have expressed a skeptical view toward such complete freedom of contract (Strine and Laster, Chapter 1).

8. CONCLUSION

In this comparison of the Stock Company form and the LLC form in Japan, the following three points were recognized. First, regarding the freedom of contract with respect to order-made membership rights, there are few differences between the Stock Company form and the LLC form. Second, exit options differ significantly between the Stock Company form and the LLC form and are the key consideration in choice of legal form. And third, the range of freedom of contract with respect to fiduciary duties is wider in the LLC form than in the Stock Company form.

By categorizing closely held business organizations into three types, it was found that for each type, preferences for exit options and fiduciary duties typically come in the following pairs: (i) in family firms, the combination of hard exit and strict fiduciary duties, (ii) in VC-backed firms, the combination of easy exit and relaxed fiduciary duties, and (iii) in partnership-type firms, a combination of "in-betweens."

The trade-off between the demand for freedom of contract and the gap-filling role of fiduciary duties is hard to solve. A possible solution is to recognize the complementary relationship between exit options and fiduciary duties. It is optimal from both the efficiency and fairness points of view to let the parties bargain and choose a complementary pair of exit options and fiduciary duties for themselves.

Finally, from the perspective of legislative policy, the two choices of legal forms for closely held business organizations in Japan offer reasonable sets of exit options and fiduciary duties for all three types of business, so long as the LLC laws are interpreted flexibly enough.

REFERENCES

Aizawa, Tetsu, & Daisuke Koriya (2005), "Mochibungaisha [Limited Liability Companies]," *Shojihomu*, 1748, 11.
Ayres, Ian, & Robert Gertner (1989), "Filling Gaps in Incomplete Contracts: An Economic Theory of Default Rules," *Yale Law Journal*, 99, 87.
Bartlett, III, Robert P. (2015), "Shareholder Wealth Maximization as Means to an End," *Seattle University Law Review*, 38, 255.
Bhattacharyya, Sugato, & Francine Lafontaine (1995), "Double-sided Moral Hazard and the Nature of Share Contracts," *Rand Journal of Economics*, 26, 761.
Egashira, Kenjiro et al. (2011), "Godogaisha to no Jittai to Kadai [Current Practice and Problems of LLCs]," *Shojihomu*, 1944, 6.
Halloran, Michael J. et al., (2000), *Venture Capital and Public Offering Negotiation* (3rd edn).
Manesh, Mohsen (2012), "Contractual Freedom Under Delaware Alternative Entity Law: Evidence from Publicly Traded LPs and LLCs," *Journal of Corporate Law*, 37, 555.
Ribstein, Larry E., & Robert R. Keatinge (2013), *Ribstein and Keatinge on Limited Liability Companies*, vol. 1. (2nd edn.).
Shishido, Zenichi (1987), "Conflicts of Interest and Fiduciary Duties in the Operation of a Joint Venture," *Hastings Law Journal*, 39, 63.
Shishido, Zenichi (1993), "The Fair Value of Minority Stock in Closely Held Corporations," *Fordham Law Review*, 62, 65.
Shishido, Zenichi (2013), "Goben Godo Kaisha [Joint Venture LLCs]," in *Kigyoho, Kinyuho no Shin Choryu [New Trends of Law of Enterprise and Finance]* (Atsushi Koide et al. eds.).
Shishido, Zenichi (2014a), "Godo Kaisha no Taishain no Mochibun Hyoka [Valuation of Membership Right of Withdrawing Members of LLCs]," in *Kigyoho no Genzai [Contemporary Laws of Enterprise]* (Masayoshi Deguchi et al. eds.).

Shishido, Zenichi (2014b), "Does Law Matter to Financial Capitalism: The Case of Japanese Entrepreneurs," *Fordham International Law Journal*, 37, 1087.

Shishido, Zenichi (2014c), "Incentive Bargain of the Firm and Enterprise Law: A Nexus of Contracts, Markets, and Laws," in *Enterprise Law: Contracts, Markets, and Laws in the US and Japan* (Zenichi Shishido ed.) 1.

Shishido, Zenichi, Munetaka Fukuda, & Masato Umetani (2013), *Jointo Bencha Senryaku Taizen* [*Joint Venture Strategy: Design, Bargaining, Law*].

Steele, Myron T. (2009), "Freedom of Contract and Default Contractual Duties in Delaware Limited Partnership and Limited Liability Companies," *American Business Law Journal*, 46, 221–242.

Strine, Jr., Leo E., & J. Travis Laster (2015), "The Siren Song of Unlimited Contractual Freedom," in *Research Handbook on Partnerships, LLCs and Alternative Forms of Business Organizations* (Robert W. Hillman and Mark J. Loewenstein eds.) (supra Chapter 1).

23. Return of the prodigal form? Partnerships and partnership law in the People's Republic of China
*Nicholas Calcina Howson**

1. INTRODUCTION

This chapter addresses the partnership form in the People's Republic of China (PRC, or China), and the national government-promulgated legal and regulatory norms which govern such partnership establishments. This writing does not address:

- other non-corporate law-authorized, or non-corporate, Chinese business organization forms with a basis in national law or regulation, or
- other non-corporate business organizations in the PRC: (i) without any formal legal basis, or (ii) authorized solely in local level regulation, even those which gain formal registration at the PRC State Administration of Industry and Commerce (SAIC).

Accordingly, this chapter will not describe or analyze, among many possible examples, the following decidedly partnership-type[1] forms in contemporary China: (i) collectively owned enterprises (*jiti qiye*) existing in China since the start of de-Collectivization in the mid-1950s; (ii) legal person or non-legal person Chinese-foreign cooperative joint ventures (*zhongwai hezuo jingying qiye*) (CJVs) with a legal basis since 1988; (iii) the great PRC reform-era organic precursor to formal partnerships, joint enterprises (*lianying qiye*) between legal persons, addressed in national law in 1986 but still omnipresent throughout

---

* The author would like to thank Dr. Shen Zhaohui, PhD, Peking University Law School and Tsinghua University Law School post-doctoral fellow, Wang Yang, Michigan Law School JD, 2008, and Simpson, Thacher & Bartlett LLP associate, and Alex Zhang Xiaomeng, Michigan Law School Library, for their aid and insights in assembling this chapter.

[1] A definitional note: For China, this chapter alludes to historical and contemporary self-declared "partnerships," but also what I perceive to be "partnership-type" establishments. The latter category comprehends business organizations which, first, are defined in the negative, or which do not have strong "corporate" characteristics: real separation of ownership and management, equity shares that are readily transferrable, fiduciary duties that run from traditional fiduciaries to the legal person firm or its shareholders, more shareholders who might not have other ties ex ante, default limited liability for shareholders, etc.; and second, those which have some of the characteristics of organic partnerships, including: less or no separation of ownership and management, ownership interests (whether partnership interests, illiquid "equity" interests, or what the PRC calls interests in the "registered capital" of a legal person entity) that are less readily transferrable, fiduciary duties that run between firm owners as well as between some firm owners and the common investee entity, a lesser number of investors and who have stronger ex ante ties (whether familial, geographical, sectoral or political), the absence or partial application of limited liability for investors, etc. As will be described below, the taxation of the firm and its investors cannot be dispositive for these characterizations, given the early confusion evidenced by Chinese tax authorities in the modern era of partnership and partnership-type entity establishments.

China in regulation and in fact; (iv) so-called shareholding cooperative enterprises (*gufen hezuozhi qiye*)² first subject to regulation in 1987 in the Zhejiang Province city of Wenzhou and equally omnipresent in local regulation and fact; (v) the entirely precocious "limited liability partnership" form purportedly authorized by Beijing Municipal-level legislature regulations for the (Beijing) Zhongguancun Science and Technology Park in 2000;³ (vi) the agricultural economy's rural village credit cooperative societies (*nongcun xinyong hezuoshe*) established within the parameters of national regulation and model (mandatory) articles of association; or (vii) the multiple hybrid forms spawned over many decades (e.g., the "stock cooperative economic cooperation society" (*gufen jingji hezuoshe*)).

The apparent slighting of these forms, and the many other non-corporate forms of business organization which dominate the contemporary Chinese landscape in law and in fact, is not meant to imply that such forms are subordinate, rare, or do not engage with China's formal legal institutions. Quite the opposite in fact, as a great deal of investment and business in China has been, and continues to be, undertaken pursuant to these non-corporate, non-(formal) partnership, establishments—many the legacy of the nation's rapid political, economic and legal system transitions over the past three decades⁴—in the same way formal adjudication in China features them in abundance.⁵ Indeed, and as is described below, it is these other alternative forms of business in China which are consistently the subject of ex post judicial intervention making them partnerships after the fact, or to which partnership law principles are applied by the same judicial institutions.

Notwithstanding the above, it is instructive in a volume of this kind to explain contemporary China's formal, national-level, establishment of the partnership form in law, if only because these norms and related practices will increasingly dominate capital formation and business in the non-corporate sector, for purely domestic investors and foreign capital alike. One only needs to consider the rise of venture capital and private equity activity in

---

² Formed on the back of either a pre-existing factory under a state-owned enterprise (SOE) or a collective, whereby the workers at the factory/members of the collective "purchase" (or are allocated) divided interests in the pre-existing enterprise's hard assets, whereupon the former workers/members are transformed into equity holders/investors of a newly established shareholding cooperative enterprise with enhanced governance rights.

³ For a nuanced consideration of what these locally authorized business forms mean for the Chinese legal system generally, see Clarke (2005: 57–61)

⁴ For example, the World Bank estimated that for 1983 fully 10% of China's net industrial output, and 25% of industrial employment, was related to large urban collectively owned enterprises. In 1984 the PRC State Council estimated that rural collective businesses accounted for Renminbi yuan (RMB) 55 billion of total national industrial output of over RMB 700 billion. See Chao and Yang (1985: 1215). Many of China's contemporary global champions have their roots in the collectively owned enterprise, such as Lenovo (computer hardware), Hai'er (white goods), and Huawei (telecoms).

⁵ See, for example, the case opinions and final judgments reported and analyzed in one 2013 collection published by two PRC lawyers, Zhang and Tang (2013): 25–8, 104–7, 122–26 (2005–2010 judgments concerning collectives), 343–86 (multiple judgments between 2006 and 2011 concerning joint operation contracts/enterprises), 19–24, 53–56, 107–9, 122–26 and 135–69 (judgments from 2001 to 2011 regarding shareholding cooperative enterprises or shareholding economic cooperation societies adjudicated under Beijing, Chongqing, Hangzhou and Shanghai Municipal-level regulations still in effect), and 60–65 (2009 judgment regarding a rural village cooperative society). The same is evidenced in the more than 1,000 PRC partnership-related case opinions the author is reviewing in the separate project referred to below.

or regarding the PRC in the last decade (some driven by foreign private equity specialists under the Qualified Foreign Limited Partnership (QFLP) pilot initiative started in February 2011, but also by Chinese investment institutions), and hoped-for subsequent exits into the more legal form-demanding capital markets sourced in such activity, to understand the strength of this assumption. To that end, in this chapter I will:

- summarize the historical antecedents of the PRC's partnership form and contemporary partnership legal norms,
- explain the most important aspects of China's current partnership statute and the partnership forms on offer;
- address critical issues arising in connection with the contemporary partnership form in China; and
- show the ways in which China's judicial institutions appear to be engaging with the partnership form and related legal norms, and with respect to all formally declared partnerships, non-authorized partnership-like entities, and even declared corporate entities.

2. FROM IMPERIAL CHINA TO THE 2006 PARTNERSHIP ENTERPRISE LAW

The partnership form, broadly speaking, has an extremely rich history in the Chinese world. Indeed, organic partnership-type establishments and/or parent-subsidiary partnership clusters were the default norm for Chinese business activity for several thousands of years until just before the demise of imperial rule in 1911. That changed with the first attempt to legalize both corporate and partnership establishments in the Qing Dynasty's 1904 Company Law—which provided for the first time in law what I translate as "partnerships" (*hezi gongsi*) and "limited partnerships" (*hezi youxian gongsi*)[6]—and then subsequent enactments by the Republican and Guomindang successors to China's last imperial dynasty in 1914, 1929, and 1946.[7] Partnership-type establishments before 1904 and thus pre-legalization took innumerable forms, and were based (or not) in contract or kinship, guild or shared locality/origin ties, sometimes focused on a project-specific production

---

[6] Which tracked pre-existing imperial-era customary, non-legal person, partnership forms—the shared management (*hehuo*) partnership, and the sleeping partnership with dormant partners (*yinming hehuo*), respectively. As with the limited partnership (*hezi youxian gongsi*) introduced in the 1904 Qing Company Law, in the sleeping partnership managing partners and dormant partners were distinguished, with the former acting to manage the business and suffering unlimited liability, and the dormant partners (or limited partners in the post-1904 form) only contributing capital and having some measure of limited liability.

[7] See Fang (1989), Kirby (1995), Lin (2013), Ruskola (2000), and Zelin (2009). The 1914 Beiyang Government ordinance allowed for what I translate as "unlimited liability partnerships" (*wuxian gongsi*) and "joint partnerships" (*lianhe gongsi*), and "joint share partnerships," the first two being nearly identical to the 1904 Qing statute's partnerships and limited partnerships (but with the additional attribute of legal personality), and the third merely an elaborated version of a partnership involving both unlimited liability (managing) partners and those having limited liability.

activity, were supported by cross-guarantees to give some measure of enhanced access to capital or limited liability, and obtained (or did not) some aspect of legal personality and/ or limited liability for some partners.

Perhaps most interesting in the post-1904 period, thus after the legalization of company and partnership forms alike, was the persistence of extra-legal partnership norms, and indeed resistance against or even cannibalization of newly introduced corporate law norms by pre-existing partnership expectations and practices. Sherm Cochran relates the example of the founding family behind the Nanyang Brothers tobacco business in early 20th-century China, and that family's internal struggle over proposed conversion of their firm into a joint stock company. In that case, the family patriarch articulated strong resistance to any such conversion because it would attract family authority-undermining, "disloyal," short term-interested, non-family member, management-intruding, shareholders. Conversely, younger family members advocated conversion to the corporate form because of the urgent need for more capital to compete with foreign challenger British American Tobacco. Eventually, the family advocates of corporatization won out, but in form only. The family firm was duly transformed into a joint stock company, but with the objecting patriarch embedded as "permanent president" and the new "shareholders" given no voice whatsoever in electing the new board of directors or the appointment of executive managers. When that openly declared structure was challenged by the government on the attempt to register the new firm, the family simply amended their initial governmental filing to obscure the ongoing lack of separation of (family) ownership and management and thus the family firm's continued operation as, in essence, a family partnership now decorated with the addition of deeply disenfranchised, non-family-member, dormant partners.[8]

Chinese scholars report that on the eve of the 1949 Communist Revolution there were approximately 1.3 million enterprises in China, of which only 10,000 were deemed "companies," the rest being either sole proprietorships or partnerships, and even 11 percent of the registered "companies" being unlimited liability companies, or effectively general partnerships. By 1956, there were over half a billion "private" investors in enterprises in the PRC, with 53.8 percent of those investments directed at partnerships and 38 percent in sole proprietorships.[9] Clearly, as the PRC entered two decades of political and economic turmoil from 1957 to 1976 with the Anti-Rightist Movement, the Great Leap Forward (and the resulting Great Famine) and the Great Proletarian Cultural Revolution (GPCR), there were abundant partnership-like establishments governing non-governmental (and likely governmental) investment, even in the absence of a legal basis or indeed a supporting legal system.

With the end of the GPCR and the death of Mao Zedong in 1976 came significant policy changes, and thus hopes for a new "commodity economy," economic revitalization, and renewed or different strategies for capital formation outside of the "state" sector. Nonetheless, in this early period after the death of Mao, political sensitivities remained paramount, and thus the idea or rhetoric of "private" corporations, partnerships, or investment was obscured, and certainly did not feature in new domestic regulatory

---

[8] See Cochran (1980: 96–102).
[9] See Fang (1989: 47).

initiatives or policy experiments.[10] So, starting in the early 1980s China saw the creation of a number of new enterprise vehicles similar in general terms to the organic partnership form, but which avoided any formal connection with a still disfavored private economy. They thus had to be anchored in then-acceptable policies and/or policy pronouncements only rarely reduced to formal administrative regulation, including: "cooperative operations organizations" (*hezuo jingying zuzhi*), "new economic association structures" (*xin jingji lianheti*), "commune members' joint enterprises" (*sheyuan lianying qiye*), "joint households enterprises" (*lianhu qiye*), etc. As domestic economic reform progressed in the early and mid-1980s, however, many of these establishments were absorbed under or channeled into the concept of "joint operation" (*lianying*) or "joint operation enterprises" (*lianying qiye*) addressed explicitly in the 1986 General Principles of the Civil Law of the PRC (GPCL), effective in 1987.[11] Whatever the defects of the GPCL, and they are many, the three short articles of that statute describing in summary terms the phenomenon of non-state, semi-autonomous, "joint operation" enterprises—and in particular the article authorizing joint operation between enterprises or enterprises and functional unit legal persons (*shiye danwei*) without the establishment of a separate legal person and joint and several unlimited liability for investors—represent the first attempt in the history of the PRC to describe the organic partnership form, just as the provision permitting joint operation via a newly established, and separate from the investors, legal person (with the implication of limited liability) is the true precursor in law of what have become China's corporate establishments.

China's "Reform and Opening to the Outside World" program and the related "legal construction" initiative starting in 1979, the introduction of direct foreign investment pursuant to a separate receiving legal system for PRC-domiciled foreign-invested enterprises (FIEs), reform and "corporatization" of SOEs, the establishment of domestic equity capital markets in 1990–91, the declaration of a "modern enterprise system" in the early 1990s, and PRC issuers' first accessing of the capital markets abroad, all served as a preface to the PRC's first post-1949 corporate law statute—the 1994 PRC Company Law (since generally amended in 2005 and more specifically in 2014, for what is referred to as the 2006 PRC Company Law). Just three years after 1994, the PRC promulgated a law for the business organization not addressed in the 1994 PRC Company Law—the partnership.

---

[10] Distinct, of course, from explicitly law-based initiatives designed to attract foreign direct investment via legally authorized Sino-foreign equity joint ventures and Sino-foreign cooperatives joint ventures starting from 1979, all of which served as precursors for the same systems offered more than a decade later for domestic investment and capital formation.

[11] See GPCL, arts. 51–3 (dividing "joint operation" into: joint operation via new/separate legal persons with independent legal competence (and with the implication of limited liability for investors) (art. 51); joint operation without establishment of a new/separate legal person where the investors bear joint and several unlimited liability (art. 52); and joint operation pursuant to contract where the contract parties bear unlimited liability severally and not jointly (art. 53)). Critically, under the GPCL "joint operation" was not permitted for individuals (natural persons), keeping all such proto-partnership activity within the purview of state-owned or collectively-owned economic activity. And joint operation enterprises there were in abundance from the early 1980s and after the PRC State Council's 1980 Provisional Regulations for the Promotion of Economic Association policy pronouncement, for example more than 26,000 nationwide in 1984. See Fang (1989, 60).

The 1997 PRC Partnership Enterprise Law (1997 PEL), even more than its slightly older cousin the 1994 PRC Company Law, stands as an important job done very badly.[12] The 1997 PEL assuredly provided the first ever legal basis in modern China for the partnership form, and thus an attempted elaboration of the legal person and non-legal person "joint operation" between enterprises or units allowance in the GPCL (and a 1988 PRC Supreme People's Court opinion elaborating the GPCL) from a decade before. It was very much, however, a business regulation-oriented statute, providing a number of apparently mandatory or immutable rules, with little room for what many consider the essence of partnership—contractual self-ordering, or contracting out of statutory default rules, in each case via a partnership agreement. In the context of late-1990s-reform China, the 1997 PEL provided an important new legal basis for the following:

- no minimum capitalization requirement for partnership establishments;
- allowance for capital contributions to the partnership by cash, in-kind, leasehold rights, intellectual property rights, other property rights, etc., and even labor service rights (and without a public or private valuation requirement, thus leaving valuation (or not) to agreement between the partners);
- joint management by all partners, or appointment of a sub-group of partners as managing partners (with other partners not permitted involvement in management), subject to an immutable unanimity requirement for certain decisions stipulated in the statute;
- agreed profit sharing, not tied to partners' respective capital contributions (with the same agreed profit-sharing ratio applicable to distribution of the residual upon liquidation of the partnership);
- joint and several, unlimited, liability for partners in the partnership;
- contribution liability among partners where one partner has bound the partnership without due authorization; and
- the embryo of partnership fiduciary duties of loyalty.

At the same time, the 1997 PEL suffered from a number of serious deficiencies, including:

- lack of clarity as to whether natural persons could be investors in a PRC-domiciled partnership (with the strong implication that such investors would be permitted, confirmed quickly in SAIC registration practice);
- various prohibitions on contractual deviation from what might be understood as penalty default norms, e.g., partner unanimity on certain decisions, distribution of the residual in liquidation pursuant to profit sharing, etc.;
- failure to stipulate legal personality (or not) of PRC partnerships (notwithstanding a clear requirement of registration of the partnership, making for a strong implication of legal personality under then-applicable Chinese legal norms);
- failure to provide for a limited partnership form (notwithstanding the implication in the 1997 PEL that where managing partners are designated, non-managing partners have no management rights);

---

[12] See Clarke, Howson and Qiao (1997).

- lack of clarity on the power of partners, or indeed any appointed managing partner(s), to bind the partnership;
- failure to authorize partnership investment in other legal entities, or state whether such investment is prohibited;
- failure to address the possibility of foreign-domiciled or foreign natural person investment in PRC-domiciled partnerships, and the characterization of the resulting partnerships vis-à-vis the pre-existing Sino-foreign cooperative joint venture form; and
- confusion regarding pass-through treatment for income tax.

By far the most problematic dysfunction in the 1997 PEL statutory initiative, and the reason why Chinese investors did not flock to the newly legalized form before passage of the 2006 PRC Partnership Enterprise Law (2006 PEL), was rather basic confusion on double-taxation of partnership investors. The 1997 PEL merely held that PRC-domiciled partnerships would pay all taxes "in accordance with the law." While this construction confirmed that PRC partnerships registered with the SAIC (and thus likely also with independent legal personality) would pay turnover taxes such as the PRC value-add tax and business tax, it remained silent on the question of whether such partnerships would pay tax on their own income as a separate entity (with subsequent income taxation on partners' income from the partnership), or if such partnerships would enjoy pass-through treatment. In the late 1990s, the PRC State Taxation Administration's (STA's) Domestic Enterprise Income Tax Department openly stated that a PRC partnership, as an entity with independent accounting and deriving income from business operations, should be treated as an independent taxpayer with taxable income taxed at 33 percent under then-applicable enterprise income tax rates. The corollary to that characterization, that partners would then be taxed on distributions from the partnership to the partners, whether under China's enterprise income tax or personal income tax, was also confirmed by the STA.[13] This was at stark variance with the pass-through treatment then afforded the GPCL-authorized legal person and non-legal person "joint operation" enterprises established by legal persons described above, which were only taxed once, at the "joint operation" level, with tax-free distributions to the legal person participants therein. Perhaps this very basic confusion was a major reason for the relatively few formal partnership establishments in the PRC to 2006, or only 127,804 registered partnerships nationwide as of the end of 2005.[14]

3. PARTNERSHIP LAW IN CONTEMPORARY CHINA

With the passage of the 2006 PEL, there is now a well-articulated and far more coherent formal partnership law and taxation regime in the PRC. The new-found clarity of the 2006 statute and related enactments did not contribute appreciably to a real increase in formal domestic partnership formations in China, but conversely did enable increased capital commitments to partnership-governed projects, as indicated in Table 23.1.

---

[13] *Ibid.*, 32.
[14] SAIC (2006).

Table 23.1 PRC—Partnership registrations and registered capital—2005 and 2011

Year	Registered Partnerships	Registered Capital
2005	127,804	RMB 6,290,685
2011	138,375	RMB 14,631,555

SAIC (2006, 2012). One reason for the more than doubling of registered capital in just five years is that starting in 2008 the SAIC has accounted for subscribed-for registered capital (rather than invested capital) in its statistical survey of partnership formations.

The question for China going forward will be the extent to which PRC legislative and regulatory institutions have the technical competence to further enable the partnership form, and/or whether related state enforcement institutions, judicial or administrative, have the competence to construe and enforce such formal partnership norms in a technically consistent, predictable, and even-handed way. As alluded to below, there is now significant pressure from foreign private equity funds to establish functioning partnership form-based investment funds (using RMB yuan investment) in China, which may prove a driver for these developments.

Under the 2006 PEL and subsequent enactments, there is a legal basis for three basic partnership forms in the PRC, and an allowance for foreign-domiciled (legal or natural) partners, as follows:

- the "general[15] partnership" (*putong hehuoqiye*) (analogous to a general partnership under U.S. state law);
- the "limited partnership" (*youxian hehuo qiye*) (analogous to a limited partnership under U.S. state law, but with no more than 50 partners permitted);
- the "special general partnership" (*teshude putong hehuoqiye*) (analogous to a limited liability partnership in U.S. state law); and
- the foreign-invested general or limited partnership.

Key aspects of the three primary forms above are as follows (for the remainder of this chapter, the relevant 2006 PEL article(s) are in parentheses following):

- The general partnership is not an independent legal person (even though it is subject to a registration requirement), formed by two or more natural persons, legal persons, and other organizations (2, 14), where partners have joint and several unlimited liability for the obligations of the partnership (2, 39), and all of the partners have equal rights to manage partnership operations unless agreed otherwise in the partnership agreement.
- The limited partnership (60–84) must have more than two and fewer than 50 partners, with at least one of the partners serving as the General Partner (GP) (61, 75)

---

[15] The sense of the Chinese language appellation "*putong*" is closer to the English language terms "regular," "normal" or even "everyday"; the English language word "general" is used in this chapter because the underling form is close to the Anglo-American "general partnership" form.

Table 23.2 PRC—Total partnerships, limited partnerships and special general partnerships (LLP) registrations—2010–11

Year	Total Partnerships	Limited Partnerships	Special General Partnerships
2010	127,073	3,132	666
2011	138,375	10,165	NA

that manages the partnership and with unlimited liability (2), while the limited partners (LPs) have liability limited up to their subscribed-for capital contribution (2) and cannot be involved in management of the partnership or act as an agent for the limited partnership with third parties (and, if they do, then may be subject to unlimited liability with respect to limited partnership obligations).[16]

- The special general partnership (55–59), a species of the general partnership, may only be used in stipulated professional sectors (lawyers, accountants, engineers, etc.) (55, 107), and the partners have joint and several, but limited (to the extent of their share of partnership property), liability with respect to the obligations of the special general partnership arising from the "intentional (*guyi*) or serious (*zhongda*) wrongful acts (*guoshi*)" of other partners (with those other partners having unlimited or unlimited joint and several liability for the obligations of the partnership); all of the partners in a special general partnerships have unlimited joint and several liability with respect to the debts and obligations of the special partnership not arising from "intentional or serious wrongful acts" (presumably of other partners, although the statute does not indicate that) (57).

China's SAIC does not consistently publish nationwide data on the limited partnership or special general partnership establishments, but one indication from 2010 to 2011[17] shows a significant increase in at least limited partnership establishments nationwide (see Table 23.2).

Personnel at the provincial-level SAIC for one of the PRC's most economically dynamic southern provinces (which does not benefit from the QFLP pilot initiative described immediately below, meaning all recorded limited partnership establishments are domestically promoted) reported privately to the author new partnership registrations between 2007 and 2013 in that province as shown in Table 23.3.

The picture with respect to the foreign-invested form, and not simply the relationship between a foreign-invested partnership and the pre-existing Sino-foreign CJV structure, especially those without legal person status or limited liability for partners/investors,[18] is

---

[16] For an extremely detailed, clause-by-clause comparison of the limited partnership form established in the 2006 PEL and US state law limited partnership laws and forms, see Wu and Geu (2007).
[17] SAIC (2011, 2012).
[18] China might have had the same problem with respect to foreign investment in legal person limited liability companies under the 1994 and 2006 Company Laws, but did not because of Articles 18 and 218 of the 1994 and 2006 Company Law enactments, respectively, which allow for application of Company Law norms which do not conflict with pre-existing FIE law and regulation norms applicable to such legal person foreign invested limited liability companies. Likewise, a

Table 23.3 PRC—One Province—general partnerships, limited partnerships and special general partnership (LLP) registrations—2007–13

Year	General Partnerships	Limited Partnerships	Special General Partnerships
2007	22	0	0
2008	18	0	0
2009	32	0	0
2010	60	0	0
2011	74	0	0
2012	37	0	0
2013	23	3	1

less clear. Pursuant to 2006 PEL (108) authorization, China's State Council first issued regulations permitting foreign investment in domestic partnerships in December of 2009, and the SAIC followed up with measures governing the registration of such partnerships in January 2010. For seasoned foreign investors, the most significant aspects of the State Council and SAIC rules were: (i) permission for foreign-domiciled legal persons, foreign-citizen natural persons, and China-domiciled investment-oriented FIEs (including foreign-invested partnership enterprises) investment in a China-domiciled partnership; (ii) the ability to make capital contributions in foreign currency and, under certain conditions, RMB; and (iii) the absence of any continuing role for the PRC Ministry of Commerce (MofCom) in approving the resulting establishment of a foreign-invested partnership prior to registration with the SAIC (contrary to more than three decades of foreign investment review and approval by MofCom and its predecessors), even though the foreign-invested partnership was to comply with sectoral restrictions and prohibitions pertaining to the business scope of the partnership.

The picture became even murkier in 2011 with the start of sub-national pilot programs in Shanghai (January), Beijing (February), Tianjin (October), and Chongqing (May, but without any specific measures promulgated, instead the initiative resulting from "contracts" signed between foreign fund promoters and the foreign affairs department of the municipal government), allowing the establishment in those jurisdictions of QFLPs, essentially PRC-domiciled limited partnerships with a foreign, or foreign-invested, GP contributing up to 5 percent of partnership capital in foreign currency (immediately converted into RMB), and domestic LPs funding the bulk of the passive equity in RMB. The purpose behind these pilot programs was to allow foreign private equity giants like Blackstone, Carlyle, and Texas Pacific Group to raise RMB investment funds for in-country investments, while—initially, at least—holding out the implication that such funds were neither "foreign" nor "foreign-invested," such that fund investments would not be governed by the long-standing MofCom-led foreign investment and approval system, or the PRC's Industrial Catalogue Governing Foreign Direct Investment in the

---

January 1995 regulation promulgated by the MofCom precursor simply authorized foreign investment in PRC companies limited by shares, leaving the PRC Company Law to govern most every other issue for the resulting foreign invested companies limited by shares.

PRC (Industrial Catalogue) (which forbids or constrains "foreign" investment in certain sectors), or even the web of foreign exchange conversion and remittance rules pertaining to traditional foreign direct investment. Although the likes of Blackstone, Carlyle, Texas Pacific Group, JP Morgan, and DT Capital immediately gained approvals for such QFLP establishments, the newly approved funds found it difficult to make any real investments in the PRC from their new RMB investment fund platforms for a host of reasons, only some related to uncertainties about the partnership form itself.

Then in late April 2012 the PRC's National Development and Reform Commission (NDRC) seriously dampened enthusiasm for the pilot program with a "response" to the Shanghai Commerce Commission indicating that the Blackstone-raised fund, Pudong-domiciled Shanghai Blackstone Equity Investment Partnership, L.P., would be understood as a "foreign" investor notwithstanding that only 5 percent of its capitalization came from a foreign exchange-providing foreign entity, and that 95 percent of its capitalization was in RMB and sourced from wholly Chinese LPs domiciled inside the PRC. The implication of this response was that foreign-promoted QFLPs with a foreign, or foreign-invested, GP would be subject to the sectoral and ownership constraints of the Industrial Catalogue, precisely the rules it was hoped the QFLP platform would avoid, even if the NDRC persisted in excluding MofCom from examination and approval jurisdiction over the establishment of such funds.[19] For the largest international private equity investment fund players, there was no solution to this newly revealed dilemma by ignoring the NDRC's interpretation and relying upon more pliant local government approvals—private equity funds established in the PRC with capitalization in excess of US$ 500 million must register with the NDRC, and any failure to comply with that requirement will block the ability to get investment from the largest RMB investor of all, the National Social Security Fund.

In the aftermath of the April 2012 response from the NDRC regarding characterization of Blackstone's Shanghai QFLP, there has been some discussion of allowing for a RMB-QFLP (RQFLP), based on a similar expansion of China's qualified foreign institutional investor (QFII) program for foreign investment in the domestic Chinese capital markets (which permitted the Hong Kong subsidiaries of PRC securities firms to use RMB investment from Hong Kong investors), which would allow the foreign GP of a QFLP to capitalize its China-domiciled limited partnership investment fund with RMB available offshore (i.e., Hong Kong). While there has been talk about allowing such RQFLPs, no fund organizers can be sure ex ante that the switch in funding by the investment funds' foreign or foreign-invested GPs from foreign currency to RMB would cure the inconvenient characterization already made by the NDRC. Accordingly, to this author's knowledge there have been no QFLP approvals or establishments to date. What seems most important in the present context is the degree to which the limited partnership form, under PRC

---

[19] See, for example, "*Fagaiwei jieding waizigufen QFLP tingzhi 'guomindaiyu'?*" ["Will the NRDC Determination of the Foreign Private Equity QFLP Terminate 'National Treatment'?"], East Money, May 8, 2012, available at http://fund.eastmoney.com/news/1593.20120508204486932.html, and Zhang Yi, Du Xionghui & Hu Xia, "*Fagaiwei guanyu waishangtouziqiye zuowei putong hehuoren de renminbi jijin de dafu*" ["The NRDC Reply on RMB Funds with Foreign Investment Enterprises as General Partners"], Sina.com, Aug. 21, 2012, available at http://blog.sina.com.cn/s/blog_9c680dbb01012fdb.html.

law, is being pushed by the most powerful and sophisticated foreign private equity fund management operations. Regardless of whether or not that push is well considered by these apparently sophisticated entities, it will certainly have a direct effect on the increasing acceptance and use of the partnership form generally, and the limited partnership specifically, by China's purely indigenous entrepreneurs.

4. CRITICAL ASPECTS OF PRC PARTNERSHIP LAW

Owing to space constraints, it is not possible to provide in this chapter a full exposition of how the 2006 PEL frames China's contemporary partnership form. However, there is space to describe some of the highlights of the statutory structure, especially those which are different from Anglo-American partnership norms or those which have attracted analysis by the Chinese courts in private law disputes.

Participants and the Private Economy; Capital Contributions

None of wholly state-owned companies (a sub-form of the limited liability company (LLC) authorized under the PRC Company Law), SOEs, listed companies, public welfare social units or social organizations can invest in a partnership enterprise (3). Perhaps most interesting here is the inclusion of listed companies, tacit admission that most listed companies in the PRC are in fact corporatized SOEs, which should not be allowed to divert value into what is deemed to be the preserve of the (or a more) private economy. Partners in general partnerships and special general partnerships may contribute cash, in-kind, intellectual property rights, granted land use rights, labor services or other property and interests to the capital of a partnership; LPs in limited partnerships may not contribute labor services (16, 64).

Business Scope

As with all other, traditional, business enterprises in the PRC, all partnerships are limited to a specific "business scope" permitted generally under PRC law and regulation, and as specified or approved at the time of partnership registration with the SAIC (9).

Legal Personality and SAIC Registration; Agency and Liability Implications

All PRC partnership enterprises must gain a registration with the SAIC before commencing business activities. However, this registration does not equate to the assumption of "legal person" (*faren*) status, or determine whether or not some of the partners enjoy limited liability. Indeed, there is no mention of such "legal person" status, or not, for any of the partnership forms authorized under the 2006 PEL. In Chinese law terms then, a partnership is not a formal separate legal person, but is instead a registered business made up of natural and legal person investors/partners with confirmed "pass-through" income taxation treatment (i.e., no taxation at the partnership level, only at the level of the partners). Accordingly, and again in Chinese law terms, when a registered partnership assumes a legal obligation, in reality the obligation is assumed by all of the partners as principals being bound by a signatory person or entity acting as an authorized or statutory agent. Importantly, any change to the governing partnership agreement, the business scope of the partnership, or even the make-up of the partners identified in a current filing, must be the subject of an application to the SAIC for amended registration. It remains unclear exactly what partnership exists, or who the partners are, in a partnership that has only submitted an application for amended registration but not completed the amended registration. For instance, if partner X—pursuant to unanimous approval of all other partners—sells and receives full consideration for its interest in an SAIC-registered general partnership to buyer A at T1, and the partnership submits its registration amendment application to the SAIC at T2 looking to T3 and an amended registration, yet the partnership incurs a large liability after T2 and before T3, who has unlimited joint and several liability, partner X or buyer A?

Default Rules, Immutable Rules and Contracting Out

In contrast to the 1997 PEL and a good deal of PRC economic and commercial law and regulation, the 2006 PEL proclaims the freedom of partners to contract into their own arrangements (5), and thus casts many more of the statute's rules as default, rather than mandatory or immutable, norms. This can be seen in the many examples throughout the statute whereby partners are authorized to agree on their own disposition of an issue, or where there are default rules accompanied by an explicit invitation to contract out of them. Such examples include provisions regarding: the valuation and timing of capital contributions (16, 19, 65); remedies for breach of the partnership agreement (18); unanimous partnership approval for, or right of first refusal granted to remaining partners upon, transfer of partnership interests (22, 23); appointment of managing partner(s) in a general partnership (26); voting power in general partnerships (30); general partnership decisions requiring partner unanimity (31); prohibitions on related party transactions (32); profit distributions and the bearing of losses (33, 54); admission of new partners in a general partnership (43); establishment of a not at-will general partnership (45); general partnership partner expulsion (49); disqualification of certain heirs to decedent partners (50); return of capital to partners withdrawing from general partnerships (52); compensation or return allocation for GPs in limited partnerships (67); distributions to LPs in limited partnerships (69); related party transactions and competitive business activities by LPs (70, 71); hypothecation of an LP interest (72); and partner approval for conversion from general partnership to limited partnership or vice versa (82). While the philosophy embodied in these structures may be assumed or not surprising for the Anglo-American legal system observer, they constitute a very significant shift of profound importance in the Chinese political, commercial, and legal situation.

Management

Partners in general partnerships have equal management rights, but the partnership may by the partnership agreement or resolution of all the partners appoint one or more partners to manage the affairs of the general partnership (26), which authority can be withdrawn by the appointing partners (29). In the event of such a designation, the non-designated partners in a general partnership no longer have the right to manage partnership affairs (27).

At limited partnerships, the GP manages the partnership (2), while the LPs cannot be involved in management of the partnership or act as an agent for the limited partnership with third parties (and, if they do, then the LPs may be subject to unlimited, joint and several, liability with respect to limited partnership obligations).

Partnership Interest Transferability

Any transfer of a general partnership interest to a new investor must be approved by all of the other partners, unless otherwise agreed in the partnership agreement, while a transfer to another existing general partner need merely be notified to the other partners (22). On a proposed external transfer, the non-transferring partners have a right of first refusal on the sale (except as set forth in the partnership agreement) (23). For limited partnerships, LPs may transfer their LP interest without prior approval and on 30 days' notice to the other partners (73), provided, however, that if a creditor seeks to take an LP's interest in a limited partnership in satisfaction of the LP's debt to the creditor, the LP must notify all of the other partners and give them a right of first refusal on the transfer to the creditor (74).

Agency Power

In general partnerships and special general partnerships, the partnership may by the partnership agreement or resolution of all the partners appoint a partner to represent the general partnership (26). Officers of a partnership who act outside of partnership-authorized authority are liable for compensatory damages to the partnership (35). Where a partner acts outside of its scope of actual authority, and a partnership is harmed, then the partner is liable for compensatory damages (90). At limited partnerships, LPs are not permitted to act as agents for the partnership enterprise (68), but if they do, then third parties are entitled to reasonably rely upon such apparent authority and the agreement will be binding upon the entire limited partnership (75). Where an LP has so acted without actual authority, and the limited partnership is harmed, then the LP is liable for compensatory damages (76).

Limited Liability

General partnerships are liable for partnership debts with all partnership property (38), and partners of general partnerships have unlimited joint and several liability for all partnership debts not paid when due (39), with new partners in general partnerships having the same joint and several liability for partnership obligations incurred prior to their entry (44) and withdrawing partners the same for partnership obligations incurred before their withdrawal (53), but with a right of contribution between partners based upon agreed sharing of losses (33, 40). Asset partitioning is declared, such that creditors of a partner for debts not related to the partnership may not offset those partner obligations against the debt such creditors owe to the partnership (nor may the creditor exercise the debtor's partnership rights in satisfaction of the partner debts) (41). General partnerships must have the Chinese characters for "general partnership" included in their registered name (15), no doubt to distinguish them from other enterprise establishments with investor limited liability. Where a general partnership is converted into a limited partnership, the partners continue to have unlimited joint and several liability for the obligations of the partnership created before it was changed into a limited partnership (84).

At the special general partnership, partners have joint and several, but limited (to the extent of their share of partnership property), liability with respect to the obligations of the special general partnership arising from the "intentional (*guyi*) or serious (*zhongda*) wrongful acts (*guoshi*)" of other partners (with those other partners having unlimited or unlimited joint and several liability for the obligations of the partnership); all of the partners in special general partnerships have unlimited joint and several liability with respect to the debts and obligations of the special partnership not arising from such "intentional or serious wrongful acts" (57).

At the limited partnership, the GP(s) has (have) unlimited liability, while the LPs have liability limited up to their subscribed-for capital contribution (2), with new LPs enjoying limited liability for partnership obligations incurred prior to their entry as an LP (77). Limited partnerships must have the Chinese characters for "limited partnership" in their registered name (62). Limited partnerships that are converted into general partnerships create unlimited joint and several liability for the partners, even for obligations incurred at the time such partners were LPs (83).

Fiduciary Duties and Fiduciary Litigation

Under the 2006 PEL, there is no explicit declaration of fiduciary duties in the partnership context. This is distinct from what occurred in the corporate law sphere, with the insertion of explicit fiduciary duties for orthodox fiduciaries (directors, officers and supervisory board members) in the wholesale re-write of China's Company Law.[20] Instead, the 2006 PEL includes only the following fiduciary duties-related principles:

- A managing general partner or a GP must report regularly to the other partners on partnership activities, business and finances, etc. (28).
- Partners in general partnerships are prohibited from carrying on competing businesses (32) (an obligation which cannot be altered by agreement), while LPs may be involved in competing businesses (unless restricted by agreement) (71).
- Partners in general partnerships may not engage in related party transactions with the partnership (32) (unless permitted by the partnership agreement), while LPs in limited partnerships may engage in related party transactions (unless restricted by agreement) (70).
- Partners in general partnerships may not engage in activities which harm the interests of the partnership enterprise (32) (which obligation may not be altered by contract).
- A partner may be expelled from a partnership by unanimous resolution of the partnership when such partner has caused losses for the partnership because of an

---

[20] See Howson (2008).

"intentional or serious wrongful act,"[21] performed an improper (*bu zhengdang*) act in conducting partnership affairs, or for other reasons stipulated in the partnership agreement (49) (which might include fiduciary breaches).
- A damages remedy where a partner or an officer of the partnership illegally misappropriates a partnership benefit or partnership property for its own interest sounding in compensation for harm visited on the partnership and return to the partnership of unjust enrichment (96).
- A damages remedy for breach of the 2006 PEL prohibitions on related party transactions and competitive businesses, sounding in compensation for harm visited on the partnership or the partners and return to the partnership of unjust enrichment (99).
- The ability of partnership liquidators to bring litigation or pursue arbitration on behalf of the partnership in liquidation (which might conceivably include something like a derivative claim against a single partner for breaching its fiduciary duties or the derivative-type claim granted to LPs in limited partnerships and described below) (87, 67).

Importantly, the obligations of appointed managing partners in general partnerships to report to the partners, and of all partners in general partnerships not to engage in activities which harm the interests of the partnership, are immutable and may not be altered by agreement. In addition, in those general partnerships where the partners have appointed one or more partners to manage the partnership business, the remaining partners have the power to "supervise" or "monitor" (*jiandu*) the managing partner(s) (27).

For limited partnerships the 2006 PEL provides—by negative implication—for something akin to an LP's derivative action where the GP does not undertake its duties. Article 67 of the statute prohibits LPs from involvement in management of a limited partnership. However, the action whereby "in the event a GP neglects the exercise of its rights and powers, an LP brings a lawsuit in [the LP's] own name to direct the undertaking of such rights and powers or in the interests of the limited partnership" is one of eight enumerated actions given safe harbor protection, i.e., it does not constitute impermissible involvement in limited partnership affairs.[22] This then is meant to be something similar to the LP's derivative action available under the U.S.'s Uniform Limited Partnership Act,[23] only distinct because the PRC action is clearly not "derivative" as the claim accrues to the plaintiff LP directly, not the limited partnership.

Income Taxation

All partnerships formed and registered under the 2006 PEL, whether or not registered as PRC legal persons, are "pass-through" entities for the purposes of income taxation (6). Each partner, whether natural person or legal person, reports its own allocable share

---

[21] As noted above, the same linguistic formulation/standard which triggers unlimited joint and several liability for certain partners in the special general partnership form (57).
[22] See 2006 PEL, art. 68(vii).
[23] In its most recent iteration, see Revised Uniform Limited Partnership Act (2001), §1002-5.

406   *Partnerships, LLCs and alternative forms of business organizations*

of gain and loss derived from the partnership on its own tax filing, as taxable business income is defined as total revenue from the partnership net of (allocable) costs, expenses, and losses incurred. Accordingly, registered PRC partnerships are not taxed at the partnership level, and thus income taxation is levied on the partners' business income only pursuant to the PRC Enterprise Income Tax if the partner is an enterprise legal person (25%) or the PRC Individual Income Tax if the partner is a natural person (5–35% on business profits, 5% on the first RMB 15,000, 10% on the next RMB 15,000, 20% on the next RMB 30,000, 30% on the next RMB 40,000, and 35% on income exceeding RMB 100,000).[24] As noted above, this is a significant and very welcome change from the income tax treatment visited upon partnerships formed and registered under the 1997 PEL.

5. FORMAL PARTNERSHIPS, OTHER ALTERNATIVE BUSINESS FORMS, PARTNERSHIP LAW, AND THE CHINESE COURTS

The PRC partnership form has now existed, in law, since 1997. While the form's attractiveness for investors and relevance for judicial institutions certainly benefited from the wholesale statutory revision of 2006 detailed in this chapter, partnerships do not figure as prominently in the Chinese courts as PRC-domiciled companies (established based upon statutory enactments dating from the same period (1992–94 for PRC companies)).[25] That is not to say, however, that there is any lack of cases concerning the partnership form in the Chinese courts. The author is currently embarked on a project which entails the review of more than a thousand post-2006 judicial opinions (most involving at least two levels of decision, and even some adjudicated by the PRC's Supreme People's Court on final re-hearing) where partnership law or the partnership form are central to the case decision. Given the nature of this volume, it suffices here to highlight in a preliminary manner some of the most interesting or indicative issues encountered so far.

First, one is struck by the truly nationwide incidence of purposeful and deemed partnership formations and partnership law disputes, regardless of region, proximity to the more developed coastal areas of China, level of urbanization, or degree of commercial sophistication and capital markets development. Importantly, however, this does not seem to mean that Chinese commercial actors are entering into formal partnerships or registering the same with the SAIC ex ante (as clearly indicated by the registration data set forth above). Instead, this fact indicates a second major hallmark of China's partnership project, with great significance for the PRC's 30-year legal construction program: the way in which judicial institutions are actively construing non-registered, non-partnership, non-law-based, arrangements as legal partnerships, or pursuant to deemed partnership principles, ex post. Indeed, the overwhelming majority of case opinions reviewed so

---

[24]   See the 2013 Deloitte summary, TAXATION AND INVESTMENT IN CHINA 2013— REACH, RELEVANCE AND RELIABILITY, *available at* www2.deloitte.com/content/dam/Deloitte/global/Documents/Tax/dttl-tax-chinaguide-2013.pdf.

[25]   See, for example, Howson (2010) (corporate law cases in the Shanghai court system 1992–2008) and Clarke and Howson (2012) (corporate derivative actions in the PRC courts from the early 1990s to 2011).

far hinge upon private claims-triggered ex post identification by a judicial institution of a non-registered or non-partnership-registered business organization or contractual arrangement as a "partnership" (*hehuo qiye*) or "partner relationship" (*hehuo guanxi*) as a legal fact determinative of issues important to firm participants and third parties acting in good faith, such as: the existence of a "capital" contribution or an "equity" stake (for return of same on liquidation, or as the basis for profit sharing during the life of the enterprise); governance rights and responsibilities (including agency powers) regarding the entity; property rights in assets (including intellectual property rights); equity interest transfer approval rights and rights of first refusal; personal, joint and several, liability for the obligations of the deemed partnership; priority of third-party claims as against the partnership assets or the partners' assets; the disposition of post-dissolution (and de-registration) claims, etc.

A 2014 PRC Supreme People's Court opinion[26] provides one example of how the Chinese judiciary is operating in the adjudicated partnership sphere. In 2002, the plaintiff entered into an "agreement" with a "jointly operated" (*lianban*) coal mine, whereby the plaintiff was ceded a 10 percent "equity" interest (*guquan*) in the mine business in exchange for "handling" land use rights issues. For several years the plaintiff demanded 10 percent profit distributions from the mine operation, to no avail. In mid-2009, the jointly operated mine's registration was cancelled, and the mine operation was merged with a second mine enterprise with four "partners" who explicitly assumed all assets and obligations of the original mine. Plaintiff brought suit for a declaration that the 2002 "agreement" was valid and that he had a 10 percent equity interest in the original mine business, and an order that he be paid dividends for his 10 percent interest in the original mine, and then a 6 percent interest in the post-2009 assuming partnership. Finally, plaintiff asked for a ruling that the four partners of the assuming partnership be jointly and severally liable for the adjudicated obligations of that partnership entity. The PRC Supreme People's Court overturned two confused lower-level (Intermediate People's Court and provincial Higher People's Court) judgments, and remanded the case back to the initial trial court level to determine: (i) the validity of the plaintiff's 2002 "agreement" with the original mine operation, and the existence of a 10 percent "equity" interest in that enterprise; and (ii) the extent to which the second partnership succeeded to the obligations of the original mine operation partnership. Most importantly in the context of this chapter, the Supreme People's Court decided that the original mine operation was a "partnership" by operation of law (based upon a reading of the original agreement between the mine promoters, and notwithstanding registration of the business with the SAIC as something else), that the 2002 agreement between plaintiff and the deemed partnership put the plaintiff into a "legal partnership relationship" (*hehuo falü guanxi*) with the pre-existing partners of the original partnership, and that such partners would have continuing joint and several liability for the obligations of the partnership—deemed by default a "general partnership"—even after dissolution and formal de-registration (citing Article 91 of the 2006 PEL). So, in this one

---

[26] Su Qi v. Li Zhanfei et al. (Yulin City Intermediate People's Court (2012)((2012) *yuzhongfaminchuzi* 00034); Shanxi Higher People's Court (2013) ((2013) *shanminerzhongzi* 00001), Supreme People's Court (2013) ((2013) *minjiazi* 1948), remanded Supreme People's Court (2014) ((2014) *mintizi* 20).

example, we see China's highest court adjudicating the existence of a legal "partnership" pursuant to equitable principles and in the face of a contrary legal registration, creating a property right (the plaintiff's interest in the capital account and claim on profit distributions), and then enforcing significant, statute-based, obligations (personal, unlimited, joint and several liability of partners for partnership obligations even after partnership dissolution) arising from that entirely equitable legal characterization.

For students of the Chinese legal system, it is fascinating to understand how much-maligned PRC judicial institutions plow forward with such partnership characterizations (and application of statutory or apparently universal partnership law principles) in the absence of a deemed partnership agreement (written or oral) or formal partnership registration, and indeed in the face of formal registration of the venture as another kind of business entity (whether LLC, collectively owned enterprise, stock cooperative enterprise, sole proprietor enterprise, etc.), which would have offered a more conservative judicial bureaucracy ample excuse to dismiss all claims based upon the lack of necessary requirements (a written partnership agreement, registration with the SAIC, etc.) Indeed, in some cases PRC judicial institutions base their determination of partnership status not on any identity of the partnership statute, but instead on the 1986 GPCL, which increasingly functions as a commercial and civil code "lite" for judicial decision-makers in this sector and others (e.g., tort claims).

Third, it is important to note what does not appear in the case opinions involving registered or deemed partnership arrangements reviewed to date. There is a pronounced lack of cases involving fiduciary duties between partners (including duty of loyalty type claims), much less between the partners and the partnership. Perhaps ironically, in the fiduciary duties realm the Chinese courts have been busy adjudicating formal corporations—usually PRC LLCs—under (usually universal, rarely statutory) partnership principles, for instance where they apply partnership law principles to close corporations, reading out the very existence of a corporation or corporate law, or where they reject a corporate derivative action arising from an LLC establishment, explicitly or implicitly urging the plaintiffs to lodge a direct, partnership law-based, claim against their co-"shareholders" in the LLC (recognizing it as, effectively, a corporatized partnership).[27] There is also no evidence whatsoever of claims based in the LP's direct right to sue a limited partnership GP in the interest of the limited partnership described above. One 2011 academic study of this formal mechanism was unable to find even one example of this kind of claim as of January of that year.[28] It is unclear whether this lack of LP claims against GPs in limited partnerships arises from the rarity of limited partnership establishments in the PRC, passivity and litigation adversity among LPs, lack of sophistication or rights consciousness among such LPs, competence deficiencies in the courts, familiar collective action problems at work (especially when cost-shifting mechanisms are disfavored generally in China),[29] or some other related factor. What is clear is that the 2006 PEL Article 68(vii) invitation to use fiduciary litigation in the context which best lends itself to such claims

---

[27] See, for example, the many cases between 1997 and 2008 discussed in Howson (2010: 359 fn 190, 362–3), and Clarke and Howson (2012: 252–3) regarding the rejection of "corporate" derivative claims.

[28] See Lin (2011: 210 fn 40).

[29] See Clarke and Howson (2012: 258–60, 287–8, and 292–3).

(where there is real separation of ownership and management and potential information asymmetries) has not been taken up. There also appears to be very little litigation in the PRC regarding partial or full limited liability protection given to certain partners in the special general partnership or the limited partnership forms, whether by partners seeking such protections, or creditors seeking to pierce such limitations. As with the comparison between litigation concerning corporate law and partnership law matters generally, this is not the case with respect to limited liability granted to shareholders in the PRC corporate establishments.[30]

There is also no evidence whatsoever of any litigation concerning foreign-invested partnerships, or FIEs generally or Chinese-foreign cooperative joint ventures (CJVs) specifically made subject to PRC partnership law norms. There are several possible reasons for this, including the very novelty of such foreign-invested partnership enterprise establishments in China (and the fact that they have made few investments with the money they have raised), or—as in the orthodox FIE context—the exclusive selection of arbitration for the resolution of disputes among partners or regarding such partnerships. Whatever the reason for this absence, it does indicate that foreign fund promoters of China-domiciled QFLPs or RQFLPs are establishing such partnerships based upon non-PRC "market" practice and legal/jurisprudential assumptions, with scant regard for Chinese statutory principles or understanding of partnership law adjudication.

Finally, and perhaps surprisingly, initial research has not encountered many situations where adjudication is stymied by overtly political factors. This is probably because partnerships in the PRC, since inception, have been the domain of non-SOE activity (as reflected in the 2006 PEL's Article 3 prohibition against SOE involvement in partnerships). The only exception identified so far is the relatively common situation where private individuals claim some kind of property right (equity, dividends, or post-dissolution return of capital) in a purported partnership that has arisen from what was originally a collectively owned enterprise.[31] In these cases, the judicial bureaucracy defers to other state organs to sort out who can claim real value from the transformation of an ideologically acceptable and explicitly "public" form (the collective) into a "private" enterprise (the partnership).

Given the prevalence of ex post judicial intervention creating and describing partnership arrangements, and the relative paucity of ex ante partnership agreements much less formal SAIC registrations of partnerships pursuant to the 2006 PEL, it is safe to say that participants in China's private economy are not affirmatively selecting or contracting into the rights, obligations and constraints of statutory or assumed partnership law. This is distinct from behavior seen in the PRC's formal corporate law sphere, where the same investors are selecting, and registering, a corporate form ex ante, although it is

---

[30] See, for example, Huang (2012).
[31] See, for example, the two opinions reported at Zhang and Tang (2013: 104–7), Beijing Haidian District People's Court (2005) ((2005) *haiminzhuzi* 13814), on appeal, Beijing No. 1 Intermediate People's Court (2005) ((2005) *yizhongminzhongzi* 12371) (plaintiff sues for equity interest and unpaid dividends arising from participation in a reorganized collective between a Beijing Municipal government company and a Beijing economic cooperation society (*jingji hezuoshe*) originally established in 1953, Beijing Intermediate People's Court holds that the decision is for government administrative authorities to sort out and not within the jurisdiction of "civil litigation" by the courts).

impossible to determine the extent to which such actors understand the legal implications of this choice (other than the long-term possibility of an exit into the domestic or even international public capital markets). So, observers are left with an environment whereby PRC judicial institutions are increasingly responsive to, and supportive of, the implied partnership law assumptions apparently held by China's private parties already joined or joining together in a business enterprise. Because China's judicial system does not operate on common law principles, and opinions have no precedential value (but instead some "guidance" value at least in the vertical silos that are the provincial Higher People's Court systems), there is little sense that such judicial intervention to vindicate private assumptions is well advertised or even understood by similarly placed investors or judicial officials.

6. CONCLUSION

In the longer view of Chinese history and looking back to the final years of China's last imperial dynasty at the start of the 20th century, we can say that the partnership form first concretized in a 1904 Qing dynasty statute has now been resurrected in law on the Chinese mainland. In the shorter history of post-1949 Communist China, we see a partnership form that was ideologically renovated and legalized in the late 1990s concurrent with an unprecedented program of legal system construction and movement away from a centrally controlled, planned, economy, and then appropriately modernized in 2006. Notwithstanding this, the rapid transitions in China's political, economic, legal, and property rights systems over the past three decades—and resulting instabilities—have left the nation with an abundance of legal and non-law-based, non-corporate, enterprise forms, which forms continue as vehicles for capital aggregation and business governance for a very substantial part of the truly "private" economy. For this reason alone—and even as the globe marvels at the world's largest IPOs launched by China's newly "corporatized" SOEs established pursuant to a modern Company Law and regulated by a surprisingly competent securities regulator—a comprehension of how the partnership form functions in modern China is of critical importance for an understanding of the PRC's productive economy. For legal system analysts, research on partnership formation and partnership adjudication in China has perhaps even greater significance. For it is in this arena observers may witness and analyze the most basic, and abundant, engagement between mostly "private" contract and property rights and expectations, the law, and judicial institutions permitted to work in an area with the lowest degree of state or Communist Party involvement in economic transactions and devoid of diverting political and/or social control implications (as in the criminal law sphere). Yet, the truth remains that these are early days for contemporary China's experience with a resurrected, legalized, partnership vehicle. Suffice to say at this point that China's law-based partnerships will continue to grow in volume and utility over the coming decades, and probably regardless of pressure from foreign fund promoters to establish ill-understood investment vehicles for the Chinese market. That growth in turn will continue to spur basic and salutary development in China's judiciary, as the only state institution positioned to vindicate the negotiated ex ante presumptions of China's growing corps of "private" capital providers.

REFERENCES

Chao, Howard and Yang Xiaoping (1985), *Private Enterprise in China: The Developing Law of Collective Enterprises*, 19 Int'l L. 1215 (1985)

Clarke, Donald C. (2005), *How Do We Know When an Enterprise Exists? Unanswerable Questions and Legal Polycentricity in China*, 19 Colum. J. Asian L. 51 (2005–6)

Clarke, Donald C. and Nicholas Calcina Howson (2012), *Pathway to Minority Shareholder Protection: Derivative Actions in the People's Republic of China*, in THE DERIVATIVE ACTION IN ASIA: A COMPARATIVE AND FUNCTIONAL APPROACH 243 (Dan W. Puchniak, Harald Baum & Michael Ewing-Chow eds., 2012)

Clarke, Donald C., Nicholas Calcina Howson, and Qiao Gangliang (1997), *China's New Partnership Law*, 24 China Bus. Rev. 30 (July–Aug. 1997)

Cochran, Sherman (1980) BIG BUSINESS IN CHINA: SINO-FOREIGN RIVALRY IN THE CIGARETTE INDUSTRY, 1890–1930 (1980)

Fang, Liufang (1989), *Chinese Partnership*, 52 Law and Contemporary Problems 44 (Summer 1989)

Howson, Nicholas Calcina (2008), *The Doctrine That Dared Not Speak Its Name—Anglo-American Fiduciary Duties in China's 2005 Company Law and Case Law Intimations of Prior Convergence*, in TRANSFORMING CORPORATE GOVERNANCE IN EAST ASIA 193 (Hideki Kanda, Kon-Sik Kim & Curtis Milhaupt eds., 2008)

Howson, Nicholas Calcina (2010), *Corporate Autonomy in the Shanghai People's Courts, 1992–2008: Judicial Autonomy in a Contemporary Authoritarian State*, 5 Penn. E. Asian L. Rev. 303 (2010)

Huang, Hui (2012), *Piercing the Corporate Veil in China: Where Is It Now and Where Is It Heading?*, 60 Am. J. Comp. L. 743

Kirby, William C. (1995), *China Unincorporated: Company Law and Business Enterprise in Twentieth Century China*, 54 J. of Asian. Stud. 43 (1995)

Lin, Lin (2011), *Limited Partners' Derivative Action: Problems and Prospects in the Private Equity Market of China*, 2 Hong Kong L.J. 517 (2011)

Lin, Lin (2013), *The Evolution of Partnerships in China from the Perspective of Asset Partitioning*, 18 Stan. J.L. Bus. & Fin. 216 (2013)

Ruskola, Teemu (2000), *Conceptualizing Corporations and Kinship: Comparative Law and Development Theory in a Chinese Perspective*, 52 Stan. L. Rev. 1599 (2000)

SAIC (year), ZHONGGUO GONGSHANG XINGZHENG GUANLI NIANJIAN (nian) [CHINA ADMINISTRATION OF INDUSTRY AND COMMERCE ANNUAL SURVEY (year)] (SAIC, Year)

Wu, Yong and Thomas Earl Geu (2007), *The New PRC Limited Partnership Enterprise Law and the Limited Partnership Law of the United States: A Selective Analytical Comparison*, 25 Pacific Basin L.J. 133 (2007)

Zelin, Madeleine (2009), *The Firm in Early Modern China*, 71 J. of Econ. Behavior & Org. 623 (2009)

Zhang, Haibin and Tang Qinglin (eds.), QIYE JIUFEN [ENTERPRISE DISPUTES] (2013)

24. Alternatives to capital-oriented corporations under Russian law
Vladimir Orlov

1. INTRODUCTION

For the purpose of this chapter with respect to the Russian business law, the term "corporation" is intended to mean a capital-based company with profit-oriented activity, generally known as a public (joint stock) company. Contrary to this, the recently updated Russian business legislation has adopted the term "corporation" to mean any association under civil law, recognized as juristic person,[1] for which I prefer to use the term "corporate entity." The primary purpose of the chapter is to introduce the legal forms of business activity that are distinct from capital-oriented corporations because of the personal participation of owners—that is, partnerships, cooperatives, and limited liability companies. They ought to be properly distinguished from capital-based or joint stock companies or capital-oriented corporations.

A common feature for the legal forms, which are the main subject of this chapter, is the presence of a personal element in them. In particular, the general partnership[2] can be characterized as based on purely personal relations, which presupposes a personal participation in its activities and decision-making. This feature is also characteristic of the limited partnership,[3] which requires the participation of a silent partner. He participates in the partnership only by his contribution to the joint capital, and, consequently, this does not change the character of the partnership itself, because only the general partners participate properly in the activities and the management of it. In turn, in the limited liability company,[4] which is based on membership interests, it can be regarded

---

[1] The placement of all the forms of collective business activity under the status of juristic person, which has recently occurred in Russian law, reflects its traditionally prescriptive nature. This means a strong belief in the omnipotence of the legisprudential, law-based solutions, which is reflected in the dominance of statute law. Together with the overemphasized role of the state, the legal-positivistic approach, where statute law (in the form of written legal source) is identified with law, has been dominant in Russian law during its modern and contemporary history. The question is whether Russian law ought to be based on practical reasonability, instead of conceptual consistency, obviously oriented to the algorythmization of the legal regulation of entrepreneurial activity. For more on the essentials of Russian law, see Orlov (2011): 1–5 and the material cited therein.

[2] In continental law, its analogue is *société en nom collectif* in France and *offene Handelsgesellschaft* in Germany.

[3] In continental law, its analogue is *société en commandite* in France and *Kommanditgesellschaft* in Germany.

[4] The limited liability company is a kind of an intermediary form between a partnership and joint stock company, in particular, non-public joint stock company. It is an analogue of *société à responsabilité limitée* known in French law and *Gesellschaft mit beschränkter Haftung* in German law.

that the personal nature and capital-based corporativeness are combined, because it is in the interests of the participant who has made the capital contribution to participate personally in the activity and decision-making of the company.[5] Also a production cooperative is an association of persons for which, in particular, personal labor participation is characteristic.[6] Personal labor participation is also required for employee-owned enterprises, which could be regarded as an attempt at the unification of capital and labor. In Russian law, there are also other corporate law forms for business activities based on personal involvement, which are not presented in this chapter, such as, for instance, a business (limited liability) partnership that is regarded as an intermediate form between the partnership and the limited liability company.[7] Russian law is also acquainted with contractual forms of joint entrepreneurial activities like simple partnership and its recently introduced modification—that is, the investment partnership, which is an intermediate form between the limited partnership and the simple partnership.[8] They also are not handled in this chapter.

2. GENERAL RULES

The legal regulation of entrepreneurial activities in Russia is comprised of the enterprise and company norms which are contained, particularly, in the provisions on juristic persons of the Civil Code (Articles 48–123), which is the main civil law source in Russia,[9] and other legal normative acts enacted in accordance with it.

---

[5] It is specific for the limited liability company that the right of its participant to transfer his membership interest to third persons could be limited by the charter. In such a case, however, he may withdraw from the company.

[6] It is a modern modification of a traditional Russian *artel*, association of workers, sometimes mixed with partnership. Initially, the *artel* was the traditional association of peasants, usually from the same rural commune, who worked or sought work together away from the village. In the Law on Labor Artels (Закон о трудовых артелях) of 1902, labor *artels* were defined as partnerships founded for performance of specific work or production as well as for provision of services through personal work of the participants at their expense and by their collective guarantee. For more on this subject *see*, for instance, Zelnik (1971): 21 and Drozdova (2009): 8–14. In the Soviet Economy, cooperatives in the form of collective farms, or *kolhoz*, played an important role. The same concerned production cooperatives until the "modernization" reforms of Khrushchev strove for a "light communist" future at the end of 1950s, when the production cooperatives were absorbed into the state sector, and almost any kind of self-initiative entrepreneurial activity was officially criminalized. However, in the 1980s, cooperatives had a renaissance by giving impulse to the expansion of private entrepreneurship in Russia.

[7] It is an analogue of the limited liability partnership known at common law.

[8] Business (limited liability) partnership and investment partnership are presented in Orlov (2014).

[9] The present Civil Code, composed of four parts (1994, 1996, 2001, and 2006; last amended by Law no 42-FZ of March 8, 2015), contains all the important civil law rules. As to praxis and doctrine, they are not (at least officially) regarded as legal sources in Russian law. There are, however, signs that the decisions of supreme judicial bodies are being recognized as legal sources. For more on this subject, *see*, for instance, Orlov (2011): 1–5. In turn, the recent amendments to the provisions of the first part of the Civil Code on juristic persons are found, for instance, at http://base.consultant.ru/cons/cgi/online.cgi?req=doc;base=LAW;n=162608 and www.rg.ru/2014/05/07/gkrf-dok.html

The concept of juristic person (legal entity) is essential in the civil law regulation of entrepreneurship in Russian law. The juristic person is defined in the Civil Code as an organization which has solitary (separate) property and which is liable for its obligations concomitant to this property, and may in its own name acquire civil law rights and obligations, as well as bear duties and be a plaintiff or defendant in court. The juristic person must be registered in the unified state register for juristic persons (the Register) in the legal form provided for by the Civil Code (Article 48).[10]

The legal forms of juristic persons practicing entrepreneurial activities[11] are listed exhaustively in the Civil Code. According to the recently amended provisions of the Civil Code, juristic persons in Russian law are distinguished into corporate and unitary entities as well as into commercial and non-commercial (non-profit) organizations. Commercial corporate entities include (general and limited) partnerships, business (limited liability) partnerships and companies as well as production cooperatives and farms. In turn, companies are distinguished into (public and non-public) joint stock companies and limited liability companies. The main purpose of commercial organizations is to practice enterprise activity, and their goal is deriving profits (Article 50), whereas the enterprise activity of the non-profit organizations, such as consumer cooperatives, societal organizations, and foundations, must be connected with the objects of their primary activities.[12]

Limited liability companies, partnerships, production cooperatives, and employee-owned enterprises presented in this chapter are governed by the general provisions of the Civil Code concerning those as juristic persons, corporate entities, and commercial organizations. These provisions include the rules on:

- legal capacity, participants, and their rights and duties as well as foundation, reorganization, and liquidation of juristic persons, and liability rules concerning them;
- administration in corporate entity;
- capital contributions to companies and partnerships; and
- companies' corporate agreements.

These rules are introduced before the presentation of the concrete subjects of this chapter.

Legal Capacity of Juristic Persons

The norms on legal capacity of the juristic person are incorporated expressly into the Civil Code (Article 49). According to the general rule, the juristic person enjoys (may

---

[both last accessed August 8, 2014] (in Russian). *See also* Overview of the amendments to Chapter Four of the Russian Civil Code, www.ey.com/Publication/vwLUAssets/EY-Legal-Alert-30-May-2014-Eng/$FILE/EY-Legal-Alert-30-May-2014-Eng.pdf [last accessed August 8, 2014] (in English).

[10] Noteworthy is the fact that only *de jure* legal persons are recognized in Russian law. *See* Osakwe (2008): 337.

[11] Entrepreneurship (business activity) may be practiced in Russia by forming or without forming a juristic person (legal entity), but in both cases it requires registration. According to the Civil Code, if a physical person intends to be engaged into entrepreneurship without forming a juristic person, he is obliged to be registered as an individual entrepreneur (sole trader) (Article 23.1).

[12] For more on this subject, *see* Sergeev (2009): 197–203, and particularly on non-commercial organizations Belyayev (2004): 390–405.

have) the civil rights (and makes legal acts, transactions) which correspond to the purposes (objects) of its activity provided in its constituent document. So, special legal (act) capacity is a general principle in Russian law. However, if the objects (purposes) of activity are definitely restricted in the rules of the company,[13] the legal act (transaction) effected by its representative in contradiction to (exceeding the limits of) it may be recognized by the court as invalid (Article 173).[14] On the other hand, commercial organizations, with the exception of unitary enterprises and other (types of) organizations provided for by the law, enjoy general legal capacity (powers) in Russia: they are not obliged to stipulate in their constituent documents the object of their activity.[15] Thus, they may enjoy those civil rights that are indispensable for the performance of any kinds of activity not prohibited by the law (Article 49.1). However, this rule is regarded as an exception to the general principle (of special legal capacity). Some kinds of activity may require in Russia, according to the Civil Code (Article 49.1.3), a special permit (license), and a legal act (transaction) made without a necessary permit is invalid (voidable). On the other hand, it is provided in the Civil Code that all restrictions concerning juristic persons must be based on the law.

The legal capacity of a juristic person arises, under the Civil Code, at the time the data concerning the foundation of the juristic person are entered into the Register and terminates from the moment the data concerning it is entered into the Register (Article 49.3).

Participants

According to the Civil Code, the founders as well as participants of a partnership can only be private entrepreneurs and commercial organizations (e.g. partnerships and companies). In turn, the founders (participants) of a company can in principle be any physical persons or other juristic persons as well as public law subjects; these may also participate as silent (limited) partners (investors) in a limited partnership. A person (private entrepreneur or commercial organization) has the right to be the participant of only one partnership and the general partner of only one limited partnership (Articles 69.2 and 82.3). A company may also be established in Russia by one (any) person, but a one-man (single company) is not allowed to be in another company as its sole participant, unless otherwise provided for by the law (Articles 66.2, 88.2, and 98.6). The participation of certain physical persons in partnerships and companies may be prohibited or limited by the law[16] (Article 66.6).

Foundation

The constituent (founding) document of juristic persons is, under the Civil Code (Article 52), the charter (Rules), except for partnerships the activities of which are based

---

[13] As stated in Russian judicial practice, this means a closed list of the activities in which the enterprise is allowed to participate. See Stepanov (2010): 95.
[14] Provided that the other party in the transaction knew or ought to have known of such restrictions.
[15] Enterprises are obliged to indicate their fields of activities in the application for registration, which shall be entered in the Register under the corresponding codes of fields of activity. However, these data are not regarded as restricting the legal capacity. See Tikhomirov (2009): 37.
[16] Such restrictions concern public servants in Russia. See Tikhomirov (2009): 91–4.

on the foundation agreement. The charter, confirmed by the founders of the enterprise, is a local normative act validated by registration, which specifies the legal status of the established (incorporated) enterprise, and is binding for not only the established enterprise (and its founders) but also third parties. The constituent document should also meet the general requirements established by law; this means that the name of the juristic person or its trade or firm name,[17] the place of its location (site), the procedure for managing, and other information specifically required by the law for juristic persons of the corresponding form must be indicated in the constituent document (Article 52.2). If the founders include stipulations on the objects (purposes) of the enterprise activity in the constituent document, the enterprise is regarded as enjoying the special legal (act) capacity, as stated above. The founders could use officially approved standard charters for state registration of their juristic person.

Capital Contribution

Under the Civil Code (Article 66^1), the capital contribution to both the company and partnership is to be money assets, things, shares (membership interests) in companies and state and municipal bonds. Exclusive and other intellectual property rights as well as license rights subject to evaluation in money also can be contributed, unless otherwise provided for by the law. The law or charter may provide that certain kinds of property not be considered as capital contribution. The minimum amount of the charter capital of a company is determined in the company laws; in the case of a limited liability company, it is, according to the Limited Liability Company (LLC) law, not less than 10,000 roubles (Article 14.1). Three-fourths of the charter capital of a company must be paid by the date of its registration, and the unpaid portion must be paid within one year, unless otherwise is provided for by the company laws (Article 66^2).

Corporate Agreement

According to the Civil Code (Article 67^2), participants (members, shareholders) in a company or a part of them have the right to enter into an agreement (between them, and also with third parties) on the exercise of their participation rights or a corporate agreement (operating or shareholders' agreement). In accordance with it, they undertake to practice and/or refrain from practicing their rights in a determinate way, including:

- voting at general meetings;
- the performance as agreed of the other actions relating to the governance of the company;
- the acquirement and disposal of shares at the price determined by the agreement or where conditions determined by the agreement occur; and
- refraining from the alienation of shares before the occurrence of determinate conditions.

---

[17] Which is subject to the intellectual property law regulation provided by the norms of the Civil Code (Articles 1473–6).

However, a corporate agreement may not contain an obligation of its participant to vote in accordance with the directions of the governing bodies and determine the structure and competence of the governing bodies. Non-observance of this requirement causes the invalidity of the agreement (Article 67^2.2). The corporate agreement must be concluded in written form by drawing up a single document signed by the parties (Article 67^2.3). The participants must inform the company of the conclusion of the corporate agreement (Article 67^2.4). However, its content is confidential or not subject to disclosure, unless otherwise provided for by the law.

A corporate agreement is intended primarily to be binding on its participants, *inter partes*. According to the Civil Code (Article 67^2.6), a violation of the agreement could be considered as grounds for invalidating the decisions of the company on the claim of its participant, provided that the agreement covered at the moment of the decision all the participants of the company. However, the invalidity of the decision of the company does not concern, per se, the consequent transactions concluded with third persons by it. A contract violating the provisions of the corporate agreement may be recognized by a court as invalid on the claim of the participant on the condition that his counterparty knew or should have known about the restrictions imposed by the agreement. The Civil Code expressly prohibits the parties to the corporate agreement from referring to its invalidity because it is contradictory to the provisions of the charter of the company (Article 67^2.7).

Rights and Duties

Participants (members, shareholders etc.) in a corporate entity have, according to the Civil Code, the right to:

- participate in the administration of the entity, except for the silent partner in a limited partnership (Article 84.2);
- get information about the activity of the company including accounting books and other documentation in the cases and order provided by the law and charter;
- complain against the entity's decisions inflicting civil law consequences in the cases and order provided by the law;
- demand in the name of the entity (according to Article 182.1) for compensation of damages caused to it (under Article 53.1);
- contest in the name of the entity (according to Article 182.1) the transactions concluded by this on the grounds provided for in the rules on the consequences of the improper execution of authorization of the Civil Code (Article 174) and corporate laws as well as demand the application of such consequences and of consequences of the invalidity of null transactions; and
- other rights established by the law or constituent document.

The general duty of the participant is, under the Civil Code (Article 65^2.4):

- to take part in the formation of the entity's property in the amount and order established by the Civil Code, other law or the charter;
- to maintain secrecy;

- to participate, if necessary, in the decision-making concerning vitally important issues;
- to refrain from actions obviously causing damage to the entity as well as essentially impeding the achieving of the objectives the entity is established for;
- other duties established by the law or constituent document.

Administration in Corporate Entity

According to the Civil Code (Article 65^3), the supreme governing body of the corporate entity is the general meeting of its participants, except for production cooperatives and non-commercial organizations with more than 100 participants where some other collective representative body, for instance the assembly or conference, could act as the supreme authority. Unless otherwise provided for by the Civil Code or other law, the issues which are within the exclusive authority of the supreme governing body of the corporate entity include:

- the determination of the priority directions for the activity and the principles for formation and use of property of the entity;
- the approval of the charter and its amendments;
- the determination of the order for entry and dismissal of participants except for the cases established by the law;
- the formation of the other bodies of the entity and early termination of their powers and
- the approval of annual reports, bookkeeping balance sheets, as well as
- decisions on the establishment of or participating in other juristic persons and on the establishment of branch and representative office, unless such matters fall under the charter in accordance with the law to the authority of the other collegial bodies;
- decisions on the reorganization and liquidation of the entity, and
- the election or the appointment of the audit body, as well as
- other issues determined by the law or constituent documents.

A corporate entity must have a (one or several) one-person executive body (the director, the director general, the president), and it may be also a juristic person. The executive power of the entity may rest, in the cases provided by the law or charter, with a collegiate executive body (the board, directorate). The law or charter may provide additionally under the Civil Code (Article $65^3.4$) for the foundation of a collegiate governing body for controlling the executive bodies.

Liability Rule

The person who by force of the law or of the juristic person's constituent document comes out on its behalf is expected, according to the Civil Code, to act in the interests of the juristic person it represents in good faith and reasonably (Article 53.3). In case of non-observance of these as well as the customary requirements, the representative of the juristic person is obliged, upon the demand of the juristic person, or the founders (the participants) acting on behalf of this, to compensate the damages caused by his fault. The same liability is extended also to the persons who may determine the actions of the juristic person, as well as to the members of the collegiate executive body, except for those who voted against the adoption of the decision or did not take part in the voting concerning the issue. The Civil Code expressly provides that an agreement on the restriction or elimination of the liability presented here is null and void (Article 53^1).

Reorganization and Liquidation

The general rules on reorganization and liquidation of the juristic person are contained in Articles 57–65 of the Civil Code. According to this (Articles 57 and 61), the reorganization and liquidation of the juristic person is possible. It could be effected by the decision of its founders (participants) or the body authorized to do this by the constituent document. The reorganization may be carried out in those cases provided for by the law in the form of a merger (with another juristic person), accession[18] (to another juristic person), division (into many juristic persons), spin-off (separation of a part), or transformation (into another form of juristic person). The law allows the reorganization with the participation of two or more juristic persons, even if they are of different forms, provided that such reorganization is permitted by the law (Article 57.1). However, the reorganization of partnerships and companies into non-commercial organization as well as into (state or municipal) unitary enterprises is not allowed (Article 68.3). In those cases provided for by the law, the reorganization of the juristic person, subjected to the application of competition law, through its division or separation, or liquidation of it, could be executed by the decision of the authorized state body or by the decision of a court (Articles 57.2 and 61.2). In turn, the merger, accession, or transformation of the juristic person could be effected only upon the consent of the authorized state body (Article 57.3).

According to the Civil Code, in the merger, all the rights and duties of the absorbing juristic persons are to pass to the new juristic person, whereas in the accession the rights and duties of the juristic persons are to pass to the existing juristic person with the termination of the absorbed juristic persons. In turn, in the division the reorganizing juristic person is terminated, but remains if only a part of it is separated off. As to the transformation (into another form of juristic person), the rights and duties of the reorganizing juristic person towards other persons (but not towards the participants, which are subject to the reorganization) remain intact (Article 58).

The juristic person is obliged, under the Civil Code (Article 60), after the decision to reorganize is adopted (by its participants or authorized body), (within three days) to inform in writing the registration body on the beginning of the reorganization procedure. After the registration of the reorganization, the reorganizing juristic person must publish notice of the reorganization twice (once per month) in the State Register publication. The law may also require the notification of creditors about the reorganization.

A creditor of the reorganizing juristic person has the right to demand from it by judicial procedure the performance at an earlier date, and, if this is impossible, the termination of any obligation arising with it before the publishing of the first notice, and compensation for damages connected therewith, unless otherwise provided for by the law or agreed

---

[18] Acquisition, affiliation.

between the reorganizing juristic person and the creditor, or where the performance of the obligation is not sufficiently secured (Article 60.2). The obligations of the reorganizing juristic person to its creditors may be secured by pledge, in which case the creditors may not demand additional securities for the performance. The new juristic person(s) and the reorganized juristic person, as well as the persons who may actually determine the actions of the reorganized juristic persons, the members of their collegiate executive bodies and their representatives, are to bear solidary (joint and several) liability on the obligations of the reorganized juristic person, where the demands of its creditors are not satisfied due their fault (Article 60.3).

The decision on the reorganization of the juristic person may be recognized, in accordance with the Civil Code, by a court as invalid (Article 60^1). However, such a decision is not considered be a ground for the liquidation of the new juristic person and the invalidation of its transactions. The persons who fraudulently promoted the invalidated decision[19] are to compensate solidarily for the damages caused to the participant of the invalidly reorganized juristic person who voted against the adoption of the decision on the reorganization or did not take part in the voting concerning the issue, and to its creditors. Solidary liability is imposed also on the juristic persons established by the decision in question. The participant of the reorganized corporate entity, who voted against the adoption of the decision on the reorganization or did not take part in the voting concerning the issue, may demand in a court that the reorganization be considered as ineffective. As a result of the recognition of the reorganization as ineffective, the legal situation prior to the reorganization in issue is to be restored with the corresponding entries in the state register. However, the transactions of the reorganized juristic person remain in force, and the executed payments are to be considered as duly performed, with respect to good faith counterparties and creditors (Article 60^2).

A juristic person is regarded, according to the Civil Code (Article 57.4), as reorganized from the moment of the registration of the reorganized juristic person(s) and in the case of the accession from the moment of the registration of the termination of the absorbed juristic person.

A juristic person is to be liquidated under the Civil Code (Article 61.2) by the decision of its founders (participants) or of the juristic person's body authorized for this by the constituent documents, as well as where the term for which it has been created is expired, or the goal for the purpose of which it has been established is achieved. Liquidation will also take place where, on the demand of the authorized state or municipal body, the court recognizes the registration of the juristic person as invalid because of violations of law or other legal normative acts committed in its establishment, unless these violations cannot be rectified (have an irremediable nature). A juristic person is to be liquidated also by court decision where an activity is practiced without a proper permit (license) or membership, or where such activity is prohibited by the law or contradictory to the Constitution, or as a result of repeated or gross violations of the law or of other legal (normative) acts (Article 61.3). The grounds for the liquidation can also be the insolvency (bankruptcy) of

---

[19] And if the decision was adopted by the collegiate executive body, those liable are its members who voted for it.

the juristic person (Article 61.3).[20] Liquidation of the juristic person means that its rights and duties do not pass to any other person (Article 61.1) in general succession.[21]

Under the Civil Code (Article 62), the decision on the liquidation of the juristic person must be notified to the state registration body, which duly makes a corresponding entry of such. A liquidation commission must also be appointed, and the order and term of the liquidation procedure laid down; the management of the juristic person's affairs passes to the liquidation commission. Information on the liquidation and the order and term for possible claims to be filed by the creditors are to be published; the term for the filing of the claims of creditors is to be at least two months from the publication date. Those creditors which are identified are to be notified in written form. The next stages in the liquidation procedure are the compilation of an intermediary liquidation balance, the organization of the sale of the juristic person's assets at a public auction (if the monetary means are insufficient), the payment of debts to the creditors in accordance with the established order of priority (Article 64), the compilation of the liquidation balance, and the registration of the liquidation. However, if the assets of the liquidating juristic person are insufficient to satisfy all the creditors' claims, it is subject to the liquidation proceedings through bankruptcy (Article 62.4), and in the lack of assets to cover the expenses for the liquidation proceedings, the juristic person is to be deleted from the state register (Article 62.6). The juristic person is to be regarded as liquidated and its obligations (debts) terminated after the corresponding entries are made in the state register (Article 63.9).

3. LIMITED LIABILITY COMPANY[22]

The main legal source regulating the establishment, activities, and termination of limited liability companies in Russia is the LLC law. The norms of the LLC law are based on the company law norms of the first part of the Civil Code, and they form the main part of the regulation concerning limited liability companies.

A limited liability company is, under the Civil Code (Article 87) and the LLC law (Article 2), a company established by one or several persons, the charter capital of which is divided into (ideal) shares (parts) or membership interests or members' ownership interests.[23] Under the LLC law, a limited liability company is liable for its obligations by its assets, but not answerable for the obligations of its members (Article 3). The constituent document of a limited liability company is the charter.

The members of a limited liability company can be, according to the Civil Code (Article 88) and the LLC law (Article 7), both physical and juristic persons, the number of which is limited by the law to 50. If it is exceeded, the company must be transformed into

---

[20] However, according to Article 64^2 of the Civil Code, an enterprise which has not submitted taxation documents and executed any operation through its bank account for 12 months is deemed actually to have finished its activities and is to be excluded as non-existent from the register.

[21] This does not exclude the transfer of some rights and duties of the liquidated enterprise by singular succession. *See* Sergeev (2009): 225.

[22] For more on this subject, *see* Orlov (2011): 71–82 and Tikhomirov (2010).

[23] Shares of a limited liability company, contrary to a joint stock company, are not security papers transferable per se.

a joint stock company in the course of a year, or liquidated in a court procedure. A limited liability company may be established by one person and it may exist as a single company. It is the minimum requirement, since the LLC law (Article 26.2) excludes the existence of a memberless company; the single as well as the last member is not allowed to withdraw from the company. Furthermore, a limited liability company may not include under the LLC law another company consisting of a sole person as a single member (Article 7.2).

The charter capital of a limited liability company must comprise the nominal value of the member's interests and not be less than the amount established by the Civil Code (Article 90.1) and LLC law (Article 14.1).[24] The size of the interest is defined as a percentage or portion of the charter capital. The actual value of an interest is also defined in the LLC law by reference to the value of the net assets of the company (Article 14.2).

The charter capital of a limited liability company may be increased, according to the LLC law (Articles 17–19), after it has been paid in full through assets of the company, additional contributions of members (which may be obligatory) or contributions of new members, unless this is prohibited by the charter. According to the LLC law, the charter capital can also be decreased by reducing the nominal value of the interests of all the members of the company and/or by redeeming the interests belonging to the company. A decrease of the charter capital is obligatory if the value of net assets of the company proves to be less than its charter capital at the end of the financial year (after the end of the second financial year); but if in this case the value of net assets proves to be less than the amount of the minimum charter capital specified in the law, the company must be liquidated. Alternatively to the decrease of charter capital, the company may increase the value of its net assets (Articles 20 and 30.4).

The membership interest in the charter capital or part thereof can be transferred (and consequently participation in the company ended), according to the Civil Code (Article 93) and the LLC law (Article 21), to another person through legal transaction or succession or some other legal ground. The sale or some other alienation of the interest or part thereof (that is paid) to another member or other members may require, if it is provided by the charter, the consent of the other members of the company, whereas in case of transfer to a third person or third persons, this can be forbidden by the charter. In these cases, other participants have the pre-emptive right to acquire the interest or part of it, and the charter may provide the fixed price for the interest as well as the order of the pre-emptive acquisition (Article 21.4). The charter can contain provisions that the company also have the pre-emptive right where the members have not used their pre-emptive right. As to the succession of membership interests (to the heirs and legal successors of juristic persons), the consent of the other members of the company may be required under the charter (Article 21.8). Such consent is explicitly required for the transfer of the membership through sale at a public auction (Article 21.8).

A member of a limited liability company has the right to withdraw from the company through alienation of his interest to the company, if this is provided for by the charter, according to the Civil Code (Article 94) and the LLC law (Article 26). It is also provided by the LLC law that a member of a limited liability company who violates his

---

[24] The minimum amount of the charter capital of a limited liability company shall be, according to the LLC law, not less than 10,000 roubles (Article 14.1).

duties or hinders activities of the company may be expelled from it through the court by the demand of the other members holding jointly more than 10 percent of the shares (Article 10).

The minimum requirement for a limited liability company is a two-level system of governing bodies consisting of the general meeting and the executive body. However, the charter may provide additionally under the LLC law (Article 32.2) for the foundation of a council of directors (supervisory council).

4. GENERAL AND LIMITED PARTNERSHIP[25]

The only legal source that regulates the establishment, activities, and liquidation of general and limited partnerships is the Civil Code with its Articles 69–86.

General (full) partnership is defined, under the Civil Code (Article 69), as a commercial organization (partnership) the participants of which (general partners) are engaged, in conformity with the agreement signed between them, in business activities on behalf of the partnership and bear liability for its obligations with their property, however subsidiary. According to the Civil Code, partners in a general partnership (the number of which must be no fewer than two) may be individual entrepreneurs and (or) commercial organizations (companies, partnerships, production cooperatives, and unitary enterprises); a person has the right to be the participant of only one general partnership (Articles 66.4 and 69.2). The partners participate in the activities of the partnership personally and by their capital contributions,[26] and they are prohibited from competing with the partnership (Article 73). Thus, the relations between the partners are based on personal confidence.[27]

Management in the general partnership is to be carried out, under the Civil Code (Article 71), by mutual agreement of all the partners, or it is based on the principle of consensus, but the constituent agreement may also indicate the cases when the majority decision is sufficient in decision-making. Every partner has one vote, but the constituent agreement may include other rules. Partners also have the right to operate on behalf of the partnership, unless the constituent agreement provides that this must be done jointly or by one of them, in which case other partners must have a power of attorney to conclude any transaction in the name of the partnership. The management rights granted to one or several partners may be terminated by the court on the demand of another (or other) partner, provided there are serious grounds for this, such as a gross violation of the duties or incapability to provide sensitive management[28] (Article 72.2).

The liability of the partners for the obligations of the partnership is very large, and it is joint (solidary) with the result that each of the partners will be liable for the deals (transactions) of another partner. Furthermore, a partner who is not its founder would also be responsible for the obligations which arose before his admittance to the partnership. A

---

[25] For more on this subject, *see* Sergeev (2009): 236–64, Popondopulo (2009): 115–21, and Butler (2009): 499–502.
[26] According to the Civil Code (Article 73.1), partners have the duty to participate in the activities of the partnership in accordance with the constituent agreement.
[27] Popondopulo (2009): 118.
[28] Popondopulo (2009): 116–17 and Sergeev (2009): 240.

partner who has withdrawn from the partnership will also be liable for the partnership's obligations that have arisen before the moment of his retirement in the course of two years (from the date of the approval of the last accounting report). The agreement of the partners on the restriction or elimination of such liability shall be insignificant (null and void)[29] (Article 75).

A partner has the right, with the consent of the rest of the partners, to transfer his share in the joint capital to another partner or to a third person (Article 79) or withdraw from the partnership. On the other hand, the partners have the right, according to the Civil Code (Article 76.2) to demand through the court that a certain partner be expelled (excluded) from the partnership in conformity with their unanimous decision in the event of serious grounds (the gross violation of duties or incapability of providing sensitive management). The withdrawal of a partner would cause the liquidation of the general partnership, unless it is stipulated by the constituent agreement or an agreement signed between the rest of the partners that the partnership should continue its activity (Article 76.1). However, if in consequence of the changes of the partnership only one partner is left in it, he has the right, in the course of six months, to transform such a partnership into a company (joint stock company or limited liability company) (Article 81).

A limited (special) or commandite (*in commendam*) partnership is defined under the Civil Code (Article 82) as a partnership in which, alongside the general partners (who have the status of the partner of the general partnership), there is (are) also one or several participants-investors (silent partners, commanditaires). The silent partner may be any physical or juristic person, with the exception of general partners. The number of silent partners is not to exceed 20; otherwise, it is to be transformed into a company or liquidated (Article 82.3). The limited partnership is subject to the application of the rules on the general partnership, as far as these do not contradict the special rules of the Civil Code on the limited partnership (Article 82.5). These rules concern above all the status of the silent partner and the special arrangements consequent on it. The relations between the general partners, as well as between the silent partners and the general partners, are based on personal confidence.[30]

The only duty of the silent partner is, according to the Civil Code, to make an investment (his contribution) into the joint capital[31] (Article 85.1). He bears the risk of losses in connection with the partnership's activity to the amount of his investment, but does not take part in the performance of the partnership's business activity. Thus, the participation of the silent partner in the limited partnership is limited to an investment (contribution) into the joint capital, the purpose of which is to secure the financing of the partnership's activity; the fact of his making the investment ought to be confirmed by the participation certificate (Article 85.1). The silent partner can make, for instance, a deposit agreement with the partnership; it can be also some other participation agreement but not the constituent agreement. Since the silent partner participates in the relationship with the

---

[29] *See* Sergeev (2009): 245–6.
[30] *See* Popondopulo (2009): 120.
[31] Thus, by conveying his contribution into the partnership, the silent partner entrusts himself, in fact, to the general partners.

partnership, but not with the partners, the amendments to the constituent agreement of the partnership without corresponding changes into the participation agreement (certificate) are ineffective in respect of the silent partner.[32] Furthermore, since the silent partner does not participate in the management of the partnership, he does not have the right to dispute the actions of the general partners involved in the management of the partnership (Article 84.2); however, this does not concern cases of misuse.[33]

A limited partnership must be liquidated, under the Civil Code (Article 86), in the event that all the silent partners have retired from it; it may also be transformed into a general partnership. The rules on the liquidation of the general partnership concern also the limited partnership, but this may continue operation if at least one general partner and one silent partner are left in it (Article 86.1). In the event of liquidation of the limited partnership, including its bankruptcy, the silent partner has the preferential right before the general partners to retrieve his investments from the property of the partnership (Article 86.2).[34]

5. PRODUCTION COOPERATIVES[35]

The foundation and activities of production cooperatives are regulated, in addition to the general rules, by the special provisions of the Civil Code (Articles 106^{1-6}), which are specified in the norms of the Law on Production Cooperatives 1996 (PC Law).

A production cooperative is defined in the Civil Code (Article 106^1) as a voluntary association of citizens on the basis of membership for joint production or other economic activities,[36] and which requires their personal labor and other participation together with the property share contributions of its members (participants). The law and charter of a production cooperative may provide for participation of juristic persons in its activity. However, participation of physical persons with their personal labor in the production cooperative is characteristic of this form. The number of participants (members) in a cooperative must be not less than five (Article 106^2.4). Members bear subsidiary liability for the obligations of the cooperative within the limits and according to the procedure established by the law and charter.

Membership in a cooperative is realized through the rights to participate in the administration and take part in the distribution of profit derived from the work of members. Participation in the activities of the cooperative is obligatory for all its members, and it may take the form of work or financial contribution.[37] According to the PC Law (Article 7.3), the number of the non-working members may not exceed 25 percent of those who participate through personal work in the cooperative. The members have the right

---

[32] For more on this subject, *see* Sergeev (2009): 250–54.
[33] *Ibid*: 262.
[34] For more on this subject, *see ibid*: 262–4.
[35] For more on this subject, *see ibid*: 264–75, Popondopulo (2009): 150–55, and Butler (2009): 503–5.
[36] Including production, processing, and sale of industrial, agricultural, and other products, performance of work, trade, consumer services, and provision of other services.
[37] Popondopulo (2009): 151.

to take part in managing the cooperative, and each member has one vote at its general meeting according to the Civil Code (Article 106^4.3).

Profits of a cooperative are to be distributed, under the Civil Code, among its members in accordance with their personal labor and/or other participation and the amount of the share contributions (Article 106^3.4). It should be noted that the part of the profit distributable proportionally to the share contributions may not, according to the PC Law (Article 12.2), exceed 50 percent of the total profit due to be distributed.

According to the Civil Code, a cooperative member has the right to withdraw from the cooperative. He may also be expelled from it in case of non-performance or improper performance of his duties. In these cases, the cooperative must pay him the value of his share or property equivalent to it. Moreover, a cooperative member has the right to transfer his share or part of it to another cooperative member unless otherwise provided by law and the cooperative articles (Article 106^5).

6. EMPLOYEE-OWNED ENTERPRISE[38]

Employee-owned Joint Stock Companies or Enterprises (EOE) are subject to the regulation provided by the Law on Peculiarities of the Legal Status of Employee-owned Joint Stock Companies (People's Enterprises) 1998 (EOE Law) and the norms of the Civil Code and Joint Stock Company Law, which are to be applied to non-public (former closed) joint stock companies.

An employee-owned company may be founded, according to the EOE Law, only by means of reorganization of an existing enterprise. This may be any commercial organization, except unitary enterprises and public joint stock companies, where employees possess less than 49 percent of shares (Article 2.1). The foundation of an employee-owned company requires, under the EOE Law (Article 2.4), the consent of three-fourths of the participants and all of the employees of the reorganizing organization, where the participants who voted against the adoption of the decision concerning the reorganization may demand the redemption of their shares (Article 2.3). Where these conditions are met, the participants and the employees who became the shareholders are to conclude the foundation agreement (Article 2.5); however, it is regarded not as a proper constituent document. As the constituent document of any company, the law provides only the charter. The charter must contain, among other things, the provisions on the maximum amount of the shares (size of the membership interest) that is allowed to be in possession of the non-employees in total, as well as a single employee (maximum 5 percent) (Articles 3.4 and 6.1).

According to the EOE Law, in the employee-owned company, the number of shareholders is not to exceed 5,000 (Article 9.4), and the minimum number of employees is not to be less than 51 (Article 9.1), among which the maximum share of non-shareholders ought to be 10 percent of all employees (Article 9.2). Moreover, the employees are to have in their possession more than 75 percent of shares (Article 4.2). Furthermore, the status of a shareholder in an employee-owned company is directly connected with working in the

---

[38] For more on this subject, *see* Sergeev (2009): 300–302 and Butler (2009): 494.

company—dividends are to be paid to the shareholder in proportion to his labor contribution. Moreover, the company is obliged to redeem the shares of an employee shareholder who has resigned, whereas the shareholder who has resigned is obliged to sell them to the company or to the other shareholders.

Special rules of the EOE Law concern also decision-making in the company where, in particular, the status of employees is safeguarded. The non-shareholders may participate in the general meeting (with consultative vote) and even, in certain cases, be represented in the supervisory council, if this is established. In respect of the main part of the issues that are under the exclusive authority of the general meeting, each shareholder has one vote in the general meeting (Article 10).

7. CONCLUSION

Enterprises considered as alternatives to capital-oriented corporations in Russia are exhaustively listed in the law. They include generally used traditional forms like limited liability companies, general and limited partnerships, and cooperatives as well as employee-owned enterprises. All these enterprises are recognized as juristic persons and, in accordance with the recent (mainly necessary and reasonable) amendments to the Civil Code, as commercial corporate entities or corporations subjected to general and special civil law rules. The introduction of the concept of corporation, which is a kind of hybrid of continental and common law concepts, seems linguistically problematic. Moreover, in practice, the provision of general rules paralleled with special rules regulating large public companies and small enterprises is of doubtful reasonableness, taking into account that the provision of simple and flexible rules is important in regulation of small enterprises. Contrary to large companies, these may not be able to afford to maintain sophisticated legal expertise for distinguishing and implementing properly the rules regulating their activities. Thus, despite all proclaimed attempts to reach similarity with Western business law, Russian law still preserves its specific features. It continues to be the law for lawyers, where conceptual (legal dogmatic) considerations prevent a pragmatic approach to legal regulation of enterprise activities. And, in respect of small enterprises based on personal involvement, the prescriptive nature of Russian business law has even been enhanced.

REFERENCES

Belyayev, K.P., Некоммерческие организации в системе юридических лиц [*Non-commercial Organizations in the System of Juristic Persons*] (Moscow: Statut 2004).
Butler, William E., Russian Law (Oxford University Press 2009).
Drozdova, N.P., "Russian Artel Revisited through the Lens of the New Institutional Economic" (Working Paper, Graduate School of Management, St. Petersburg State University 2009) available at www.gsom.spbu.ru/files/upload/niim/publishing/papers/2009/wp_drozdova.pdf (last accessed August 11, 2014).
Orlov, Vladimir, Entrepreneurship in Russia (Finnish Lawyers' Publishing 1999).
Orlov, Vladimir, Introduction to Business Law in Russia (Ashgate 2011).
Orlov, Vladimir, "New Legal Forms of Collective Investments in Russia," *Journal of Business Law*, 3, 207–27 (2014).
Osakwe, Christopher, Russian Civil Code (Moscow: Wolters Kluwer 2008).
Popondopulo, V.F. (ed), Коммерческое (предпринимательское) право, Том I [*Commercial (Entrepreneurial) Law, Volume I*] (Moscow: Prospekt 2009).

Sergeev, A.P. (ed), Гражданское право [Civil Law] 1 (Moscow: TK Velbi 2009).
Stepanov, S.A. (ed), Комментарий к гражданскому кодексу Российской Федерации [Commentary to the Civil Code of the Russian Federation] (Moscow: Prospekt 2010).
Tikhomirov, M.Yu. (ed), Комментарий к Федеральному закону об акционерных обществах [Commentary to the Federal Law on Joint Stock Societies] (Moskva: Izd. Tikhomirova 2009).
Tikhomirov, M.Yu (ed), Комментарий к Федеральному закону об обществах с ограниченной ответственностью [Commentary to the Federal Law on Limited Liability Societies] (Moscow: Izd. Tikhomirova 2010).
Zelnik, Reginald E., Labor and Society in Tsarist Russia: The Factory Workers of St. Petersburg, 1855–1870 (Stanford University Press 1971).

25. The advent of the LLP in India
Afra Afsharipour

1. INTRODUCTION

Around the world, unincorporated business associations have evolved to play a significant role in economic life. In the United States, for example, the limited liability company form is now often preferred by entrepreneurs and at times by even more established businesses. Countries around Europe have begun to introduce new forms of business associations to compete with the corporate form to better meet the needs of small and medium businesses and professional associations. Similarly, alternative entity forms have begun to make inroads in other parts of the world.

In 2008, India, one of the world's largest economies, passed a ground-breaking law to allow for the Limited Liability Partnership. The Indian LLP Act was the first major introduction of a new business form in India in over 50 years. While the partnership and corporate forms (i.e. companies under the Indian Companies Act) have long flourished in India, both forms have presented challenges for certain Indian businesses. For example, as the Indian government recently noted in a 2014 report, about 95 percent of firms in India are micro, small and medium enterprises, but less than 2 percent of these firms are corporations given the high compliance costs associated with the Indian Companies Act.

Like India's other business and financial law reform efforts in the 1990s and 2000s, the introduction of the LLP form is tied to India's rapid economic growth in the 1990s. Economic liberalization policies, which began to be implemented in the early 1990s, have led to the development of many new institutions and legal regimes. These new institutions, and the transformation of existing institutions, began numerous law reform projects to encourage foreign direct investment in Indian firms, to increase the competitiveness of Indian businesses around the world, and to manage the increasing competition faced by Indian businesses at home.

The Indian Ministry of Corporate Affairs (MCA)[1] has described the impetus for the LLP Act as the desire to develop a business association form that could better meet the needs of entrepreneurs and professionals with respect to liability exposure, regulatory compliance costs, and growth. In India, the Companies Act and securities regulations impose significant mandatory requirements on Indian corporations. So it is not surprising that freedom of contract was a driving force behind the adoption of the LLP form in India. As the MCA stated:

---

[1] The MCA (which until 2007 was known as the Ministry of Company Affairs) is charged with administering much of business law in India, including developing regulations to implement business law legislation such as the Companies Act 2013, the Companies Act 1956, the Limited Liability Partnership Act 2008, the Competition Act 2002, and the Partnership Act 1932. Ministry of Corporate Affairs, Government of India, About MCA, www.mca.gov.in/MinistryV2/about_mca.html (last visited April 17, 2015).

With the growth of the Indian economy, the role played by its entrepreneurs as well as its technical and professional manpower has been acknowledged internationally. It is felt opportune that entrepreneurship, knowledge and risk capital combine to provide a further impetus to India's economic growth. In this background, a need has been felt for a new corporate form that would provide an alternative to the traditional partnership, with unlimited personal liability on the one hand, and, the statute-based governance structure of the limited liability company [i.e. the corporation] on the other, in order to enable professional expertise and entrepreneurial initiative to combine, organize and operate in [a] flexible, innovative and efficient manner.[2]

This chapter examines the history and trajectory of India's 2008 LLP Act. It seeks to understand the genesis of the LLP form in India. Not only did India model its new LLP on the non-corporate forms developed in the United States, the United Kingdom, and Singapore, but the reasons that led to the creation of the LLP in India mirror those articulated for the development of alternative entity forms in these other countries. These reasons are not exclusive to India, and may foreshadow the rise of alternative forms in other emerging economies. After examining the history of the LLP form in India, this chapter identifies and discusses the salient features of the Indian LLP form in order to lay the foundations for a broader discussion about the implications and potential of India's LLP structure.

2. LEGISLATIVE HISTORY OF INDIA'S LLP ACT

Over the past two decades, the Indian government has convened a number of committees, largely made up of leading industrialists and government officials, to consider amendment and modernization of Indian business law. In the realm of corporate governance, for example, since the late 1990s, the Securities and Exchange Board of India (SEBI), the primary regulatory authority for India's capital markets, has convened a number of committees to help formulate corporate governance standards for publicly listed Indian companies. Many of these standards were inspired by corporate governance reforms around the world, and in particular by the corporate governance transformations that took place in the United States and the United Kingdom. Similarly, beginning in 2002, the MCA worked through a multi-committee process in order to amend the Companies Act 1956.[3] After years of debate and several failed starts, in 2013 India enacted the new Companies Act 2013 overhauling the entire company law regime in the country.

The process for enacting India's LLP Act took a similar route. The first discussion of an LLP law took place in the late 1990s. In 1997 the Expert Committee on Development of Small Sector Enterprises headed by Dr. Abid Hussain, a noted Indian civil servant

---

[2] STANDING COMMITTEE ON FINANCE (2007–2008), FOURTEENTH LOK SABHA, MINISTRY OF CORPORATE AFFAIRS, *The Limited Liability Partnership Bill, 2006—Fifty-Eighth Report* 124 (Nov. 27, 2007).

[3] For much of India's post-independence history, the Companies Act 1956 provided the general legal framework for companies in India, governing the incorporation, functioning, and winding up of Indian companies. The Companies Act 2013 replaces the 1956 Act, although not all of the provisions of the 2013 Act have been notified as of Spring 2015 and therefore some provisions of the 1956 Act continue to apply. Ministry of Corporate Affairs, Government of India, Acts & Rules, Companies Act 2013, www.mca.gov.in/MinistryV2/companiesact.html (last visited March 30, 2015).

and diplomat, recommended new legislation to allow for the creation of LLPs. The Abid Hussain committee's recommendations lingered without much action until a comprehensive report issued by the Naresh Chandra Committee in 2003. Discussion of the LLP form was again raised in 2005 in a report by the J.J. Irani Committee. Similar to the Chandra Committee, the Irani Committee recommended the adoption of the LLP structure as a new form of business association. These recommendations were followed by the MCA, which in late 2005 issued a concept paper supporting adoption of an LLP law. On December 7, 2006 the Cabinet approved the LLP Bill. However, a final Bill was not approved until 2008.

The sections below delve into this process in more detail, examining the reasons articulated by various government committees for recommending adoption of the LLP form, as well as the models used for the Indian LLP structure.

The Chandra Committee Pushes for Enactment of an LLP Law

The development of the LLP as a new business association form was first raised by the Abid Hussain committee in 1997. Nevertheless, there was little follow-up by the Indian government. A more full-scale discussion of legislation regarding an LLP form was revived several years later when the MCA formed the Naresh Chandra Committee II on Regulation of Private Companies and Partnership in 2003. Chaired by Shri Naresh Chandra, a former Cabinet secretary, the committee was charged with undertaking a wide-ranging examination of the legal regime then applicable to private companies and partnerships, with a particular focus on how to streamline legal risks and regulatory compliance costs for certain partnerships and small private companies. The Committee also included Mr. Shardul Shroff, Managing Partner of Amarchand & Mangaldas & Suresh A Shroff & Co, India's largest law firm, who appears to have presented draft legislation on LLPs to the government following discussion by the Chandra Committee.

The Naresh Chandra Committee Report on Regulation of Private Companies and Partnership (2003) recommended comprehensive LLP legislation to be introduced in Indian law. The Chandra Report discussed the genesis of the LLP form in the United Kingdom and the United States, and the advantages that the LLP structure could provide for Indian businesses. The Chandra Committee focused on two rationales to advocate for the LLP form: (i) the risks tied to unlimited liability, a central feature of the traditional partnership form; and (ii) limitations on partnerships' growth under the Indian Partnership Act 1932.

The Chandra Committee asserted that joint and several liability in traditional partnerships was the primary reason behind the lack of growth of professional partnerships in India. According to the committee, an increasingly competitive and litigious business environment made unlimited liability risky, especially given that since economic liberalization Indian professionals had begun to regularly transact with and represent multinational clients. The committee noted that "in order to encourage Indian professionals to participate in the international business community without apprehension of being subject to excessive liability, the need for having a legal structure like the LLP is self-evident."[4]

---

[4] MINISTRY OF FINANCE & COMPANY AFFAIRS, DEPARTMENT OF COMPANY AFFAIRS, GOVERNMENT OF INDIA (July 8, 2003), REPORT OF THE COMMITTEE ON REGULATION OF PRIVATE COMPANIES AND PARTNERSHIP (NARESH CHANDRA COMMITTEE, PART II).

While the Chandra Committee's assertions about the dangers that unlimited personal liability posed for the growth of professional partnerships in India could certainly be the case, there was little evidence offered by the committee to back up these assertions. The committee raised cautionary tales from the United States experience to address the dangers of liability in the partnership form, but similar tales from the Indian experience were missing. This may be due to the fact that actual finding of liability can take years under the Indian judicial system, which is often characterized by staggering delays in adjudication.

The Chandra Committee noted that aside from daunting liability, Indian partnership law impeded the ability of Indian professionals to meet the challenges posed by international competition. As the committee explained, the Indian Partnership Act 1932 impedes the growth of professional firms because it limits general partnerships to 20 partners. According to the Chandra Committee, this restriction on size would "prevent the growth of professional firms to the large entities operating on an international scale" so that "Indian professionals may well get excluded from taking their rightful place in the international community, that their skills otherwise entitle them to."[5] The committee further supported its recommendation for an LLP Act by referencing the need to meet competitive pressures arising from the development of the LLP structure in the United States and the United Kingdom, stating: "Since LLPs are now accepted non-corporate entities in developed countries like the USA and UK, it is appropriate to enhance the global competitiveness of our professional firms by ensuring that India's company law is flexible enough to provide mechanisms and instruments which foster growth of large professional firms."[6]

The Committee argued that it was essential for Indian law to recognize a new form—a hybrid between a company and partnership. The Committee argued that LLPs would provide flexibility (i.e. freedom for owners to adopt their preferred internal organization) while limiting liability to encourage professionals to enter the international business community. Limited liability companies (i.e. corporations) were recognized by law under the Companies Act, and according to the Committee, there was no reason that professional partnerships (e.g., lawyers, accountants, doctors, company secretaries, engineers, etc.) should not be afforded a similar choice when choosing a legal entity.

The Chandra Committee drew from experiences outside of India to bolster its recommendations. In arguing for a limited liability structure, the Chandra Committee recounted the United Kingdom and the United States experiences in developing the LLP structure. The committee recounted as one of the pitfalls of general partnership law the struggles of US law firms which became insolvent in the 1990s due to malpractice suits connected to the Savings and Loan crisis. As the committee noted, not only did the firms become insolvent, but given the basic principles of partnership law, the firms' partners were personally liable for the partnership's obligations. The committee then described the initial development of the LLP structure in Texas and its rapid adoption in other US states.[7]

---

[5] Id.
[6] Id.
[7] The Chandra Committee's report even briefly described nuances in LLP law in the United States, including, for example a discussion of differences in LLP liability regimes in Texas and

The committee also recounted the UK experience in adopting an LLP law in the early 2000s due to concerns expressed by partners in major accounting firms who lobbied for the ability to limit individual partners' liability.

The Report also included recommendations for the Act's applicability. The Committee argued that in the first instance, the LLP law should only cover firms providing professional services rather than trade or manufacturing firms for two reasons. First, professional firms were precluded from practicing under any other legal entity because of the specific regulatory requirements of each industry (e.g., law, medicine, accounting, engineering). Trading and manufacturing firms, however, were not so limited and could incorporate as private limited or public companies under the Companies Act. Second, the Chandra Committee reasoned that limiting coverage to professional partnerships minimized the inherent risk in testing new waters, provided a platform to evaluate the advantages and disadvantages of the Act, and provided a basis to consider expanding the Act to small-scale trade or manufacturing firms in the future.

J.J. Irani Committee Report on Company Law (May 2005)

In December 2004, the MCA convened the J.J. Irani Expert Committee on Company Law to help evaluate the Companies Act 1956 in the face of India's growing economy. The committee was led by J.J. Irani, a director of Tata Sons, Ltd., the primary shareholder in the large business conglomerate, the Tata Group. The Irani Committee viewed its task as recommending changes to Indian business law with the aim of "making India globally competitive in attracting investments from abroad."[8]

Like the Chandra Committee Report, the 2005 J.J. Irani Committee Report on Company Law recommended the adoption of a separate LLP law. Citing the potential growth of the Indian service sector, the Irani Committee emphasized that laws governing professional partnerships should be flexible. Unlike the Chandra Committee, however, the Irani Committee also recommended that the LLP form should be considered for small enterprises not seeking access to capital markets through listing on the stock exchange. The Irani Committee recommendations appeared to at least contemplate foreign direct investment (FDI) in entrepreneurial projects carried out through the LLP model, encouraging entrepreneurs to explore business ventures with foreign investment and collaboration. The Irani Committee reasoned that extending the LLP to small enterprises would enable these businesses to enter into joint ventures and agreements that would maximize access to technology, harness business synergies, and better enable businesses to compete globally. Finally, the Irani Committee recommended that the LLP concept be addressed separately from the Companies Act.

Delaware. The committee also noted that Delaware permits foreign LLPs, which the Committee said would be unwelcome "by any body of professionals in India."

[8] J.J. IRANI COMM. REPORT ON COMPANY LAW 19 (May 2005), *available at* www.primedirec tors.com/pdf/JJ%20Irani%20Report-MCA.pdf (listing the following regulated professionals as examples: "Company Secretaries, Chartered Accountants, Cost Accountants, Lawyers, Architects, Engineers, Doctors, etc.").

MCA Concept Paper on LLPs (November 2005)

In response to the recommendations of the Chandra and Irani Committees, in November 2005 the MCA released a concept paper on LLPs. The MCA concept paper was widely disseminated for public comment and provided the basis for the LLP Bill which would later be introduced into Parliament.

The MCA noted that recommendations of the Chandra and Irani Committees provided the impetus for the concept paper and potential LLP Bill. According to the concept paper, introduction of the LLP structure into Indian law would fill a gap between business firms such as sole proprietorships/partnerships, which are generally unregulated, and limited liability companies governed by the Companies Act 1956. Like the Chandra and Irani Committees, the MCA paper argued that the LLP structure "would foster the growth of the services sector" and "provide a platform for small and medium enterprises, and professional firms ... to conduct their business/profession efficiently which would in turn increase their global competitiveness."[9]

The MCA asserted that unlimited liability for partners in general partnerships had become a significant concern in light of increasing litigation for professional negligence, the size of claims, and risk to partners' personal assets. The concept paper stated that partners' unlimited liability was the "chief reason" why Indian professional partnership firms had not grown to successfully compete internationally. The MCA reasoned that LLPs would be an alternative corporate business vehicle that could address some of these concerns—allowing an unlimited number of partners the flexibility to adopt whatever form of internal organization to which the partners agreed, while limiting liability to partners' capital contributions.

The concept paper was comprised of 16 chapters and five schedules. Notably, Chapters II and III (Applicability and Incorporation) did not reflect the Chandra Committee's recommendation to limit the LLP structure to professional partnerships. Instead, with little explanation, the concept paper recommended that to form an LLP, there must be at least two people who are associated "for carrying on a lawful business with a view to profit."

MCA's Draft Bill

On December 15, 2006, the then Minister of Company Affairs, Shri Prem Chand Guptam, introduced the Limited Liability Partnership (LLP) Bill 2006, in the Rajya Sabha (the Upper House of the Parliament of India). The MCA described the LLP structure as "an agreement based business structure, which combines the flexibility of partnership in internal management with [the] limited liability advantage of a company."[10] Similar to the impetus for the LLP Bill, which was expressed by the various MCA committees, the government described the motivations behind the introduction of the Bill as follows:

---

[9] MINISTRY OF CORPORATE AFFAIRS, GOVERNMENT OF INDIA (November 2005), *Concept Paper on Limited Liability Partnerships*, available at www.taxindiaonline.com/RC2/pdfdocs/Concept_Paper_LLP.pdf.

[10] PRESS INFORMATION BUREAU, GOVERNMENT OF INDIA (Dec. 15, 2006), *Limited Liability Partnership Bill Introduced*, available at pib.nic.in/archieve/others/2006/dec06/r2006121530.pdf.

With the increasing role of [the] services sector in the national economy and a growing diversity in the range of services being offered, a need is increasingly being felt for a new corporate form that would enable professional expertise and entrepreneurial initiative to combine, organize and operate in an innovative and efficient manner. This need has also been recognised for businesses which may require a framework that provides flexibility suited to requirements of service, knowledge and technology based enterprises, without imposing on them detailed legal and procedural requirements intended for large widely held companies. Internationally, the LLP structure has emerged as a form of business organisation that is common to but not limited to entities offering professional services.[11]

The Bill was thereafter referred to the Lok Sabha Parliamentary Standing Committee on Finance for its examination. The committee's review process included gathering input from various industry and professional bodies that had long been involved in the development of Indian business law, including the Institute of Chartered Accountants of India (ICAI), the Institute of Company Secretaries of India (ICSI), the Federation of Indian Chambers of Commerce and Industries (FICCI), the Confederation of Indian Industries (CII), and Associated Chambers of Commerce and Industry of India (ASSOCHAM). According to the Standing Committee all of these various industry groups supported the introduction of the LLP Act.

The Standing Committee on Finance, chaired by Ananth Kumar, a veteran member of the Indian Parliament, released a detailed report on the LLP Bill (2006) in November 2007. The Standing Committee's report covered the general development of the Bill and the role of various government committees, including the Chandra and Irani Committees, in advocating for the LLP structure. It also clearly referenced LLP legislation from other countries, including the United States, the United Kingdom, and Singapore, stating that in such countries the development of LLP law has "proved to be of immense use to professionals and small enterprises."[12]

The Committee described the LLP as a hybrid form of business structure whereby partners would be shielded from unlimited personal liability while enjoying the flexibility of contractual freedom in organizing their internal governance. Accordingly, the Standing Committee report listed the perceived advantages of the LLP, as follows: (1) organizational flexibility vis-à-vis the LLP agreement; (2) granting LLP partners the advantage of combining into a body corporate form that is a separate legal entity with perpetual succession, leading to growth of professional expertise and entrepreneurial initiative in a flexible, innovative, and efficient manner; (3) partners will not rely on the LLP statute to determine the internal working arrangements of an LLP; (4) easy modification of the LLP agreement to suit each LLP's business model, risk, and rewards profile; (5) LLPs' suitability to various service enterprises given that services and enterprises change and evolve over time (i.e., service sectors expected to grow over time include: hospitality, tourism, IT, human resource development, creative and decorative art, etc.); (6) venture capital and technology-based enterprises would find the LLP structure particularly useful; (7) allowing two enterprises to combine to enhance

---

[11] MINISTRY OF CORPORATE AFFAIRS, GOVERNMENT OF INDIA (2007), *Annual Report 2006–2007*, available at www.mca.gov.in/Ministry/annual_reports/annualreport2007/Eng/CHAPTER1.pdf.

[12] STANDING COMMITTEE ON FINANCE ON THE LIMITED LIABILITY PARTNERSHIP BILL, 2006 (NOV. 27, 2007), FOURTEENTH LOK SABHA, FIFTY-EIGHTH REPORT 2.

synergies; and (8) small enterprises would find flexibility and ease of compliance in the LLP structure.

The Committee made numerous recommendations for amending the 2006 LLP Bill. For example, the committee recommended that the Act include a provision for vesting property on conversion of an entity (e.g., a private company converting to an LLP) to enable stakeholders to avoid stamp duty, i.e. a tax collected by the Indian government upon the sale and purchase of certain types of property. This recommendation had arisen due to input from industry advocates who argued for easy conversion of existing business associations into the LLP structure, similar to the regime provided for in the United Kingdom.

The Committee's report also addressed the interplay of other regulatory regimes in India with the LLP legislation and the need to harmonize the LLP Bill with other economic legislation, such as the Foreign Direct Investment (FDI) Guidelines. The Committee correctly noted that in order to realize the goals of the LLP Bill "statutory notice in other enactments need[s] to be taken of entities availing the LLP form. This would require consequential amendments in statutes regulating any specific profession, trade or activity such as Advocates Act and in other enactments such as the Income Tax Act for taxation purposes."[13] The Committee's report focused on limitations imposed on the legal profession by the Advocates Act, advocating for changes to provide flexibility for law firms to convert to an LLP form. The Committee similarly advocated for flexibility in the taxation of LLPs, arguing that industry advocates had somewhat conflicting views on the tax treatment of LLCs. The Committee, in line with the recommendations of the MCA, urged that entrepreneurs should have flexibility in choosing a tax structure that is efficient for their business and that "it should be ensured that the taxation regime is such that Indian LLPs do not suffer any discrimination or disadvantage in competition with foreign LLPs."[14]

Passage of the Final Bill

In response to the Standing Committee's report, the MCA reintroduced a revised LLP Bill in 2008. The revised Bill accepted the vast bulk of the Standing Committee's recommended changes. At least one factor behind the Bill's proposal and passage was the government's desire for the LLP format "to help the domestic industry compete with international firms [once] the legal and accounting professions are opened up eventually."[15] As discussed above, the MCA strongly supported the Bill, making statements such as "LLP, as proposed in the Bill, is a new corporate form that enables professional expertise and entrepreneurial initiative to combine, organize and operate in an innovative and efficient manner."[16]

---

[13] *Id.*
[14] *Id.*
[15] *Revised Bill Enters Rajya Sabha*, The Economic Times (Oct. 22, 2008), http://articles.economictimes.indiatimes.com/2008-10-22/news/28439984_1_llp-format-limited-liability-partnership-chartered-accountants.
[16] Sangeeta Singh, *Limited Liability Partnership Bill Introduced in Parliament*, LiveMint (Oct. 21, 2008), www.livemint.com/Politics/NB8fTh11JaPbZGyW5LDHOK/Limited-Liability-Partnership-Bill-introduced-in-Parliament.html.

The Bill was also welcomed by Indian industry leaders who hoped that the passage of the LLP Bill would allow domestic Indian service providers, like accounting firms, to compete with large global operations which provide a variety of services to clients. "LLP will encourage experts specializing in different fields—for instance, company law, accounting, capital markets, marketing, and so on—to come together and provide solutions to customers in a risk-free environment," said Preeti Malhotra, former president of the ICSI.[17] Speaking on specific advantages of the Act (e.g., partnerships may have only 20 partners, whereas the LLP Act imposes no limit on number of partners), Lalit Bhasin, a law firm partner, stated: "This will allow law firms to expand as we will be able to have more than 20 partners and, at the same time, not be bound by the complications of the Companies Act."[18]

On December 12, 2008, Parliament passed the LLP Bill (2008), and the President approved the Act on January 7, 2009. The Act was published in the official Gazette of India on January 9, 2009, with effect from March 31, 2009. The official title of the legislation is the Limited Liability Partnership Act 2008.

After passage of the LLP Act, it appeared that the LLP structure would quickly take hold. The first LLP was established on April 2, 2009, only a few days after the Act became effective. In a little over a year, almost 2,500 LLPs were registered in India.[19] And in January of 2014 alone, 800 new LLPs were registered in India.[20] Nevertheless, as described in Section 4 below, the LLP structure has fallen short of its goal of fostering flexibility and innovation, which could help Indian professionals and entrepreneurs bolster India's economic growth.

3. WHAT DOES THE LLP ACT PROVIDE?

While a comprehensive review of the LLP Act is outside the scope of this short chapter, it is useful to provide an overview of the highlights of the Act. These highlights help demonstrate the extent to which the drafters of the Act attempted to differentiate the LLP from the partnership and corporate structures already available in India, and the extent to which the Indian LLP Act used the UK, US and Singapore LLP legislation as models.

Nature and Organization of the LLP

With respect to the establishment of an LLP as a separate legal entity, the Indian LLP model drew quite heavily from the UK LLP Act (2000), and to some extent, the Singapore

---

[17] *Id.*
[18] *Id.*
[19] Rajiv K. Luthra, *LLP a New Buzzword in the Corporate World*, THE ECONOMIC TIMES (Oct. 10, 2010), *available at* http://articles.economictimes.indiatimes.com/2010-10-10/news/27627116_1_limited-liability-partnership-business-structure-llp.
[20] *On An Average 265 New Companies Got Registered Every Day in January*, THE ECONOMIC TIMES (Feb. 9, 2014), *available at* http://articles.economictimes.indiatimes.com/2014-02-09/news/47168732_1_companies-act-six-decade-old-companies-entities.

LLP Act (2005).[21] Unlike US LLPs, which are based primarily in partnership law, UK LLPs are corporate bodies with legal personality separate from their members, and are subject to certain aspects of company law. The UK grants LLPs greater organizational flexibility than corporations. Similarly, an LLP in Singapore is a separate legal entity under the Limited Liability Partnerships Act 2005.

As in the UK model, the word "partnership" in the Indian LLP Act is somewhat inaccurate since the LLP as an entity is a separate business association from the partners. Under the Indian Partnership Act 1932, a general partnership has no legal existence separate from the partners who constitute it. An LLP, however, is "a body corporate formed and incorporated" under Chapter III of the LLP Act and is a "separate legal entity" together with all the incidents of separate legal personality (e.g., perpetual succession, capacity to sue and be sued, capacity to own and otherwise deal with property, and common seal). Under the LLP Act, as a separate entity, the existence, rights, or liabilities of the LLP are not affected by a change in the partners.

Unlike Indian general partnerships in which the number of partners is limited to 20 and foreign nationals may not serve as partners, an LLP may be formed by any two or more individuals or corporate bodies, subject to certain disqualifications (e.g., mental incapacity, insolvency, etc.).[22] A "body corporate" eligible to be a partner in an LLP includes a company under the Companies Act, a foreign company, or another LLP, whether incorporated in India or abroad. In order to form the LLP, the founding partners must subscribe their names to an incorporation document, which must be filed with the Registrar having jurisdiction over the place where the registered office is to be situated. The incorporation document has to be accompanied by a declaration of compliance with all legal and regulatory stipulations by a professional engaged in the formation of the LLP and by persons subscribing their names to the incorporation document. The incorporation document has to be in the prescribed form and include basic information such as the name of the LLP, its proposed business, the address of the registered office, and the names and addresses of the proposed designated partners of the LLP.

The Act introduces the concept of "designated partners," who are in their position, functions, and powers akin to the directors of a company. An LLP must designate at least two "designated partners," who must be individuals and at least one of whom must be an Indian resident. Where an LLP is constituted of one or more corporate entities as partners, any individual nominee of such entities would be eligible to act as a designated partner. In an LLP having only foreign corporate entities as partners, the foreign partners would have to appoint individual nominees to act as designated partners and at least one of the nominees would necessarily have to be an Indian resident. There appears to be, however, no stipulation of citizenship as an eligibility norm for a person to be nominated as a designated partner.

---

[21] On LLPs in the UK, see Berry, Chapter 21.
[22] Every LLP must, at all times, maintain a minimum of two partners—whether individuals or bodies corporate. If the number of partners dips below two, and the LLP continues with one partner for six months or more (and the individual has knowledge that he is carrying on the business alone), that individual partner will be personally liable for the LLP's obligations. See Ch. II § 5-7, LLP Act.

Freedom of Contract: The LLP Agreement

Alternative forms in other parts of the world, including the United States, rely on private contracting and contractual freedom to provide flexibility to the members of firm in addressing their governance goals. As scholars have noted, "[u]ncorporations are characterized by their reliance on contracts," while much of corporate law has mandatory dimensions particularly with respect to internal governance matters.[23] Thus, unlike the Companies Act, the Indian LLP Act allows for many of the rules underlying the relationship between the partners and the LLP and between the partners themselves to be governed by an LLP agreement.

To provide organizational flexibility, the LLP Act provides a great deal of autonomy to the LLP and its partners in matters of organization and structuring. The relationship between the partners and the LLP and between the partners inter se, including any admission to and withdrawal from the LLP, is primarily governed by the LLP agreement entered into between the partners. Thus, as in partnerships, LLPs in India can organize their internal structure based on a negotiated contractual agreement. While it is commonly recommended that partners enter into a written LLP agreement, there is no legal obligation to do so. In the event that an LLP agreement is not entered into, the mutual rights of partners and the relationship of the Partners and the LLP are governed by the rules contained in the First Schedule to the Act.

Agency and Liability

Unlike under the Indian Partnership Act, which provides that a partner is an agent of the firm and also other partners for the purpose of the business of the firm, under the LLP Act every partner of an LLP is an agent of the LLP but not of the other partners. In addition, an LLP is not bound by any actions of a partner in dealing with a person if the partner has no authority in fact and the third party knows that such partner has no authority or does not believe the partner to be a partner of the LLP.

A primary goal of the LLP model is to limit exposure of partners to liability. One of the key differences between partnerships and LLPs in India is that in an LLP a partner is not personally liable directly or indirectly for obligations of the LLP solely by reason of being a partner of the LLP. However, a partner is personally liable for his own wrongful acts or omissions, but will not be personally liable for the wrongful acts or omissions of any other partner of the LLP. An LLP is liable if a partner of the LLP is liable to another person for wrongful acts or omissions in the course of the business of the LLP or with its authority. But, the obligation of the LLP is solely the obligation of the LLP (whether contract or otherwise) and the LLP's liabilities must be met out of the LLP's property. In case of fraud, the liability of the partner who acted with intent to defraud, and of the LLP if the act was committed with the knowledge and authority of the LLP, is unlimited.

---

[23] RIBSTEIN, LARRY E. (2009), THE RISE OF THE UNCORPORATION (Oxford University Press) 6.

Fiduciary Duties

Under the Act, the rights and duties of the partners are to be governed by the LLP agreement. In the absence of an LLP agreement, Schedule I to the Act provides the following with respect to the fiduciary duties of partners:

— Each partner must render true accounts and full information of all things affecting the limited liability partnership to any partner or his legal representatives.
— If a partner, without the consent of the LLP, carries on any business of the same nature as and competing with the LLP, he must account for and pay over to the LLP all profits made by him in that business.
— Every partner must account to the LLP for any benefit derived by him without the consent of the LLP from any transaction concerning the LLP, or from any use by him of the property, name or any business connection of the LLP.

Beyond this legislative description, Indian courts have yet to decide the scope, if any, of the fiduciary duties of LLP members.

Disclosure Obligations and Powers of the Government

Unlike a traditional partnership, where there is no requirement for any financial disclosures to the Registrar of Companies, an LLP must make, though to a more limited extent than the disclosures required for corporations, certain financial disclosures to the Registrar. There are also obligations to prepare an annual Statement of Account and Solvency, to have its accounts audited, and to file an annual return. The annual Statement of Account and Solvency and the annual return are public records and are available for public inspection at the office of the Registrar.

The Act was meant to maximize organizational flexibility and empower partners to enter into an LLP agreement, while at the same time ensuring transparency and regulation to prevent LLPs from defrauding creditors. The Act imposes severe penalties for contravention of the Act, including loss of LLP status (e.g., Registrar may strike an offending LLP off the register of companies), criminal prosecution, fines, and imprisonment. The LLP Act also provides for comprehensive investigation mechanisms, such as empowering the Registrar to request information before incorporation, and empowering the central government to appoint inspectors to inquire into an LLP's affairs.

Cessation of Partnership Interests and Winding Up of the LLP

The interest of a partner in an LLP may cease in accordance with the LLP agreement. In the absence of an LLP agreement, a person can cease to be a partner by providing 30 days' prior notice to the other partners of his or her intention to resign. A partner's interest in the LLP may also cease due to the partner's death, insanity, or insolvency, or by dissolution of the LLP. Subject to the provisions in the LLP agreement, upon withdrawal (referred to as cessation under the LLP Act), a partner is entitled to the partner's capital contribution and accumulated profits determined to the date of withdrawal and is liable for any accumulated losses at the time of withdrawal. Within 30 days of a partner's withdrawal, the LLP must file a notice with the Registrar informing it of the withdrawal. Failure to file such notice can expose the LLP and its designated partners to criminal liability under the Act. If a departing partner believes that the LLP may not undertake this filing, the departing partner may personally file a notice of withdrawal with the Registrar.

Similar to the Singapore LLP Act, an Indian LLP may be wound up by either voluntary action or by an order of the National Company Law Tribunal ("the Tribunal"). The LLP Act provides a host of grounds for wind up, many of which are similar to grounds for wind up in the case of Indian companies under the Companies Act. Such grounds include financial insolvency, voluntary winding up, continuing for more than six months as a single-partner LLP, acting against the sovereignty, integrity, or security of India, or failure to file a Statement of Account and Solvency. In addition the Tribunal has the power to wind up the LLP on the ground that "it is just and equitable" to do so. In 2010 the MCA adopted the LLP (Winding up and Dissolution) Rules, 2010 to govern the wind up of an LLP.

Taxes

As noted above, the Parliamentary Standing Committee on Finance recommended partnership-like pass-through status for LLP tax purposes. Several months after passage of the LLP Act, the 2009 Finance Bill, later passed in 2010, brought LLP taxation in line with taxation of general partnerships. An LLP, like a partnership firm, will pay tax on its profits after deduction of business expenditure, salaries, and interest paid to partners. Partners will then be taxed on their salary and interest receipts, whereas their shares in profits are exempt. Every partner of the LLP is jointly and severally liable for the payment of any tax due from the LLP, which cannot be recovered unless the partner proves that the non-recovery cannot be attributed to any gross neglect, misfeasance, or breach of duty on his or her part in relation to the affairs of the LLP.

4. EARLY AND CONTINUING UNCERTAINTIES FACING THE INDIAN LLP STRUCTURE

Despite the initial fanfare, the LLP structure has met with significant challenges. The two most prominent of these challenges, the ability of law firms to register as LLPs and FDI into LLPs, were predicted by the Standing Committee on Finance in its 2007 review of the LLP Bill. The sections below explore both of these ongoing challenges in more detail.

The LLP Structure in the Law Firm Setting

The LLP Act's legislative history as well as the statute itself enables professional associations, including law firms, to incorporate as LLPs, so long as there are two partners carrying on a business with a view to profit who have satisfied formalities and technical requirements. The Chandra Committee and the Irani Committee, as well as the MCA concept paper, had envisioned that service providers, such as law firms, would benefit from the ability to organize as an LLP and would flock to the LLP form in order to compete both nationally and internationally.

Nevertheless, years after the LLP Act's passage in 2008, law firms are still unsure about whether they may organize as LLPs. In 2011, the Bar Council of Delhi[24] sent warning letters to law firms converting from partnerships to LLPs, causing at least one firm to shut down its LLP entity. Subsequent reports indicated that the Chairman of the Bar Council may have sent the letters prematurely, but the incident illustrated general confusion generated by the law. Since then, the Bar Council has failed to clarify its stance on whether incorporation as an LLP violates the Bar Council's Rules of Professional Conduct. When Jyoti Sagar (founder and former managing partner of J. Sagar Associates, one of India's leading law firms) exited JSA in 2013, one report discussed how JSA's equity partners had reached the statutory limit (20). The firm avoided the model of running the firm as several partnerships (so-called "valve partners" or "parallel partnerships") in order to share wealth between offices and partners; one way that other law firms have skirted the partnership limit. Instead, JSA used an "equivalent-to-equity" partner position outside of the 20 equity partners. Sagar stated that the only real solution would be to allow the LLP structure for law firms: "The Bar Council of India has not yet taken a view whether LLP firms can practice law . . . It looks like it is not a high priority issue for them as of now."[25] Nevertheless, there has been little movement on this issue as of early 2015.

Foreign Direct Investment into LLPs

One of the reasons for the passage of the LLP Act was the hope that small and medium enterprises in India could form as LLPs rather than as companies under the Companies Act. Industry leaders and government officials argued that the LLP structure would allow small and medium enterprises to avoid the regulatory costs of being an incorporated entity while still attracting investors. Despite these hopes, significant uncertainty and restrictions in many different areas of Indian law has made FDI into LLPs unpalatable.

After passage of the LLP Act in 2009, the Department of Industrial Policy & Promotion (DIPP) first issued a 2010 discussion paper to consider whether and the extent to which FDI should be permitted into LLPs. In 2011 the Cabinet Committee on Economic Affairs approved FDI in LLPs with prior approval of the Foreign Investment Promotion Board (FIPB). These changes were not immediately incorporated into the Foreign Exchange Management Act (the statute governing foreign investments in India) leading to much uncertainty among foreign investors with respect to investments in LLPs. Despite this uncertainty, the Reserve Bank of India (RBI) delayed notifying[26] detailed regulations to incorporate provisions relating to FDI in LLPs until March of 2014. Moreover, the RBI's regulations provide for rather restrictive conditions with respect to FDI in LLPs.

---

[24] The Advocates Act 1961 is the governing legislation for the legal profession in India. The Advocates Act provides for the constitution of the Bar Council of India and bar councils for the states. In addition, the Bar Council of India's rules set out standards of professional conduct, available at http://lawmin.nic.in/la/subord/bci_index.htm.

[25] Ganz, Kian (Mar. 15, 2013), *JSA Founder Jyoti Sagar Exit Interview: From 100% Equity to Zero, the Chips are Now Down*, LEGALLY INDIA, www.legallyindia.com/201303153519/Interviews/jsa-founder-jyoti-sagar-exit-interview.

[26] To be effective and enforceable in India, a law or regulation must be notified (i.e. published) by the appropriate government ministry in the Official Gazette of India.

DIPP's press note permitting FDI in LLPs included substantial limitations on such FDI. DIPP's 2011 FDI conditions included the requirement that investment would be subject to government approval.[27] Moreover, DIPP limited FDI to LLPs operating in sectors or activities where 100 percent FDI is allowed, with no FDI-linked performance conditions (e.g., "nonbanking finance companies," or township, housing, infrastructure, or construction development). Thus, LLPs operating in sectors where less than 100 percent FDI is permitted or sectors which require prior regulatory approval, including sectors where any FDI-linked performance conditions are attached, cannot accept FDI. In addition, LLPs with FDI are not allowed to operate in several business lines, including agricultural/plantation activity, print media, and real estate. Indian companies with FDI would be permitted to make downstream investments in LLPs only if both the company and the LLP operated in sectors where 100 percent FDI is allowed, with no FDI-linked performance conditions. However, LLPs with FDI would not be eligible to make downstream investments. Foreign capital could only be in the form of cash consideration, received by inward remittance through normal banking channels or by debit to NRE/FCNR (Nonresident External/Foreign Currency Nonresident) accounts maintained with an authorized dealer or bank. Foreign Institutional Investors (FII) and Foreign Venture Capital Investors (FVCIs) would not be permitted to invest in LLPs. In addition, LLPs cannot resort to any external commercial borrowings; in other words, they cannot borrow in foreign currency.

Almost three years after DIPP's approval of FDI in LLPs, on March 13, 2014, the RBI issued a notification amending the Foreign Exchange Management Regulations, 2000 (FEMA 20, regulating foreign transfers and issuance of securities) to include LLPs within the purview of the regulations.[28] The amendment is applicable with retrospective effect from May 20, 2011, the date of DIPP's press note permitting FDI in LLPs subject to certain conditions.[29] The RBI's April 2014 amendment provides significant clarification regarding FDI in Indian LLPs, as well as continuing to impose the same restrictions imposed by DIPP on such FDI. As in the DIPP press note, the RBI rules continue to limit the LLPs eligible to accept FDI to those in sectors where 100 percent FDI under the automatic route is allowed with FDI-linked performance conditions. They also continue to impose DIPP's rules governing downstream investments. Under the RBI rules, any direct or indirect foreign investment will require government (i.e. FIPB) approval. The RBI rules also restrict persons eligible to invest in LLPs to exclude citizens/entities of Pakistan/Bangladesh; SEBI-registered FIIs, FCVIs, Qualified Foreign Investors, and Foreign Portfolio Investors. The rules impose significant pricing and payment requirements, as well as reporting requirements on LLPs which accept FDI. Overall, while the RBI rules provide much-needed clarification regarding FDI in LLPs, the conditions for doing so remain quite restrictive.

---

[27] GOV'T OF INDIA, MINISTRY OF COMMERCE & INDUSTRY, DEPARTMENT OF INDUSTRIAL POLICY AND PROMOTION, *Press Note No. 1 (2011 Series)* 1, (May 20, 2011), *available at* www.dipp.gov.in/English/acts_rules/Press_Notes/pn1_2011.pdf.

[28] *Foreign Direct Investment in Limited Liability Partnerships in India* 1, SAMVAD PARTNERS (Apr. 21, 2014), *available at*: www.samvadpartners.com/wp-content/uploads/2014/04 Samvad-Partners_ Note-on-FEMA-Amendment-on-FDI-in-LLPs-April-21-2014.pdf.

[29] RESERVE BANK OF INDIA, *Foreign Direct Investment in Limited Liability Partnership* (Apr. 16, 2014), *available at* www.rbi.org.in/scripts/NotificationUser aspx?Id=8844&Mode=0.

International private equity and venture capital investors have been a significant source of India's FDI inflows. Despite their exuberance for investing in Indian companies, private equity and venture capital investors have been reluctant to invest in LLPs due to initial limitations on their exit options. In India, rather than engaging in the leveraged buyout structure often used in the West, private equity and venture capital firms primarily engage in minority investments in promoter-controlled firms. Accordingly, these investors often negotiate for several alternative exit mechanisms when making their investment decisions. These mechanisms include offloading their investment stake in an initial public offering, a buyback by the company of the investor's stake or a put option against the company's promoters. Prior to November of 2013, however, LLPs were not permitted to list on stock exchanges, removing an IPO as a potential exit strategy. This further decreased the attractiveness of FDI in LLPs, at least in the earlier stages of the law's implementation.

Following loud complaints in the wake of India's economic downturn in the late 2010s, in November 2013, SEBI allowed LLPs membership and listing on its stock exchange.[30] As of August 2014, it does not appear that any LLPs have taken advantage of SEBI's new rules allowing LLPs to list on the stock exchange.

Overall, while the LLP form was initially heralded as a potential attractive target for FDI, the Indian government has been quite cautious in allowing FDI into LLPs.

5. CONCLUSION

An understanding of the development of the LLP form in India should help both deepen our understanding of law reform in India and contribute to the larger global debate on the development of alternative entities. This analysis can prove useful to both policymakers and academics seeking to introduce new alternative forms. While the LLP form is a welcome development in India, it is by no means without challenges and uncertainties. Given these uncertainties, even firms that could take advantage of the LLP form have thus far eschewed, or have needed to avoid, the Indian LLP structure. The Indian LLP experience demonstrates that without institutional reforms, including a more comprehensive legislative reform process, and buy-in from powerful constituencies, the success of a new business form may remain on shaky ground.

BIBLIOGRAPHY

Afsharipour, Afra (2009), *Corporate Governance Convergence: Lessons from the Indian Experience*, 29 Nw. J. Int'l L. & Bus. 335.

Afsharipour, Afra (2010), *The Promise and Challenges of India's Corporate Governance Reforms*, 1 Indian J.L. & Econ. 33.

Afsharipour, Afra (July 2013), *The Indian Private Equity Model*, Nat'l Stock Exch. of India (NSE Working Paper WP/8/2013), *available at* www.nseindia.com/research/content/res_WorkingPaper8.pdf.

Bromberg, Alan A. & Larry E. Ribstein (2009), Bromberg & Ribstein on LLPs, RUPA, and ULPA § 1.01.

---

[30] *See* Securities Contracts (Regulation) Amendment Rules, 2013 (amending Securities Contracts Regulations Rules, 1957) § 8(6), Securities & Exchange Board of India, *available at* www.sebi.gov.in/cms/sebi_data/attachdocs/1399433501593.pdf.

Chaudhry, Sharmendra (2010), *Limited Liability Partnership in India*, available at http://papers.ssrn.com/sol3/papers.cfm?abstract_id=1708215.
Dawar, Kartik (Nov. 11, 2010), *Limited Liability Partnership: An Emerging Concept in India*, Indo-Am. Chamber of Comm., http://iaccindia.wordpress.com/2010/11/11/limited-liability-partnership-an-emerging-concept-in-india.
Freedman, Judith (2001), *Limited Liability Partnerships in the United Kingdom—Do They Have A Role for Small Firms?*, 26 J. Corp. L. 897.
Galanter, Marc S. (2009), *"To the Listed Field . . . ": The Myth of Litigious India*, 1 Jindal Global L. Rev. 65.
Ganz, Kian (Dec. 9, 2011), *Law Firms Still Unsure About LLPs*, LiveMint, www.livemint.com/Politics/VXBB3O5b4m8YsXdFWNTCrJ/Law-firms-still-unsure-about-LLPs.html.
Ganz, Kian (Mar. 15, 2013), *JSA Founder Jyoti Sagar Exit Interview: From 100% Equity to Zero, the Chips are Now Down*, Legally India, www.legallyindia.com/201303153519/Interviews/jsa-founder-jyoti-sagar-exit-interview.
Hamilton, Robert W. (1995), *Registered Limited Liability Partnerships: Present at the Birth (Nearly)*, 66 U. Colo. L. Rev. 1065.
Jamshed J. Irani et al., Expert Committee on Company Law (2005), Report of the Expert Committee to Advise the Government on the New Company Law 3.
Kashyap, Amit Kumar & Deepak Kashyap (2010), *Limited Liability Partnership as Advantage to Small Business: Indian Scenario* 14, available at http://papers.ssrn.com/sol3/papers.cfm?abstract_id=1545766.
McCahery, Joseph A., Erik P.M. Vermeulen & Priyanka Priydershini (March 2013), *A Primer on the Uncorporation* 12 (European Corporate Governance Institute Working Paper No. 198), available at http://papers.ssrn.com/sol3/papers.cfm?abstract_id=2200783.
Ministry of Commerce & Industry, Department of Industrial Policy and Promotion (May 20, 2011), *Press Note No. 1 (2011 Series)* 1, available at www.dipp.gov.in/English/acts_rules/Press_Notes/pn1_2011.pdf.
Ministry of Company Affairs, Government of India (November 2005), *Concept Paper on Limited Liability Partnerships*, available at www.taxindiaonline.com/RC2/pdfdocs/Concept_Paper_LLP.pdf.
Ministry of Company Affairs, Government of India (2007), *Annual Report 2006–2007*, available at www.mca.gov.in/Ministry/annual_reports/annualreport2007/Eng/CHAPTER1.pdf.
Ministry of Corporate Affairs, Government of India (Jan. 7, 2009), *Explanatory Memorandum to Concept Limited Liability Partnership Rules in Relation to Establishment of Place of Business in India by Foreign LLPs*, available at www.mca.gov.in/Ministry/latestnews/CLLP_7jan2009.pdf.
Ministry of Corporate Affairs, Government of India (March 30, 2010), Limited Liability Partnership (Winding up and Dissolution) Rules, 2010, Gazette of India, Extraordinary Part II, section (3)(i), available at www.mca.gov.in/Ministry/pdf/llp_winding_up_rules_corrected.pdf.
Ministry of Corporate Affairs, Government of India (2014), *Annual Report 2013–2014*, available at www.mca.gov.in/Ministry/pdf/annualreport_2013_2014.pdf.
Ministry of Finance, Department of Economic Affairs (Oct. 24, 2013), Securities Contracts (Regulation) Amendment Rules, 2013 § 2 (amending Securities Contracts (Regulation) Rules, 1957), Gazette of India, Extraordinary, section (3)(i), available at www.egazette.nic.in/WriteReadData/2013/156790.pdf.
Ministry of Finance & Company Affairs, Department of Company Affairs, Government of India (July 8, 2003), Report of the Committee on Regulation of Private Companies and Partnership (Naresh Chandra Committee, Part II).
Press Information Bureau, Government of India (Dec. 15, 2006), *Limited Liability Partnership Bill Introduced*, available at pib.nic.in/archieve/others/2006/dec06/r2006121530.pdf.
Reserve Bank of India (Apr. 16, 2014), Foreign Direct Investment (FDI) in Limited Liability Partnership (LLP), A.P. (DIR Series) Circular No. 123, available at www.rbi.org.in/scripts/NotificationUser.aspx?Id=8844&Mode=0.
Ribstein, Larry E. (2009), The Rise of the Uncorporation (Oxford University Press).
Sachdeva, Amit M. & Yamini Mahajan (2009), *Indian Limited Liability Partnership Law: Some Concepts and Concerns*, available at http://papers.ssrn.com/sol3/papers.cfm?abstract_id=1557002.
Sachdeva, Amit M. & Sachin Sachdeva (2009), *The Indian LLP Law: Some Concerns for Lawyers and Chartered Accountants*, 92 SEBI & Corp. L. 6, 1.
Sai, Kranti Prakash (Apr. 10, 2010), *Limited Liability in India: A General Analysis*, available at http://papers.ssrn.com/sol3/papers.cfm?abstract_id=1587770.
Samvad Partners (Apr. 21, 2014), *Foreign Direct Investment in Limited Liability Partnerships in India*, www.samvadpartners.com/wp-content/uploads/2014/04/Samvad-Partners_Note-on-FEMA-Amendment-on-FDI-in-LLPs-April-21-2014.pdf.
Sen, Nivedita & Neha Mathen (2011), *Decoding the New Business Vehicle of India: The Limited Liability Partnership*, 4 Nat'l U. Jurid. Sci. L. Rev., 669, available at www.nujslawreview.org/pdf/articles/2011_4/nivedita-sen-neha-mathen.pdf.
Sharma, Raghav (2007), *Limited Liability Partnerships in India*, available at http://papers.ssrn.com/sol3/papers.cfm?abstract_id=1291854.

Singh, Sangeeta (Oct. 21, 2008), *Limited Liability Partnership Bill Introduced in Parliament*, LiveMint, www.livemint.com/Politics/NB8fTh11JaPbZGyW5LDHOK/Limited-Liability-Partnership-Bill-introduced-in-Parliament.html.

Standing Committee on Finance on the Limited Liability Partnership Bill, 2006 (Nov. 27, 2007), Fourteenth Lok Sabha, Fifty-Eighth Report.

Stover, Fallany O. & Susan Pace Hamill (1999), *The LLC Versus LLP Conundrum: Advice for Businesses Contemplating the Choice*, 50 Ala. L. Rev. 813.

The Econ. Times (Dec. 6, 2007), *Panel Proposes Key Changes in Limited Liability Partnership Bill*, http://articles.economictimes.indiatimes.com/2007-12-06/news/27680499_1_llp-bill-limited-liability-partnership-llp-act.

The Econ. Times (Sept. 15, 2008), *India to Soon Have Its Global Brand of CAs, Thanks to LLP*, http://articles.economictimes.indiatimes.com/2008-09-15/news/27717723_1_limited-liability-partnership-llp-bill-global-brand.

The Econ. Times (Oct. 22, 2008), *Revised Bill Enters the Rajya Sabha*, http://articles.economictimes.indiatimes.com/2008-10-22/news/28439984_1_llp-format-limited-liability-partnership-chartered-accountants.

The Econ. Times (Nov. 27, 2013), *Sebi Allows Limited Liability Partnerships to Get Stock Exchange Membership*, http://articles.economictimes.indiatimes.com/2013-11-27/news/44520032_1_limited-liability-partnerships-corporate-business-vehicle-securities-contracts.

The Econ. Times (Feb. 9, 2014), *On An Average 265 New Companies Got Registered Every Day in January*, http://articles.economictimes.indiatimes.com/2014-02-09/news/47168732_1_companies-act-six-decade-old-companies-entities.

The Econ. Times (Feb. 20, 2014), *Private Companies, Limited Liability Partnership Firms Can't Use 'National' in Names: Government*, http://articles.economictimes.indiatimes.com/2014-02-20/news/47527257_1_names-new-companies-act-rocs.

The Limited Liability Partnership Act, 2008, No. 6 of 2009, India Code (2014).

The Partnership Act, 2931, No. 9 of 1932, India Code (2014).

Vanvari, Girish (Jul. 28, 2013), *The Lack of Clarity on Foreign Direct Investment Has Left Entrepreneurs Unsure About Forming Limited Liability Partnership Firms*, Hindu BusinessLine, www.thehindubusinessline.com/features/taxation-and-accounts/starting-trouble-for-llp-business-model/article4960236.ece.

26. The evolution of non-corporate forms of business in Taiwan—introducing the LLP as an alternative business form
Andrew Jen-Guang Lin

1. INTRODUCTION

There are several forms of business associations that can be found in Taiwan. The most popular form is the company, particularly the limited liability company and the company limited by shares. As for non-corporate forms of business, most are partnerships and sole proprietorships. Several forms of unincorporated business associations, such as Massachusetts Trusts and limited liability partnerships (LLPs), are not yet available in Taiwan. With the continuing and collaborative efforts in studying alternative forms of business association, a Bill entitled "Limited Liability Partnership Act" was proposed by the Ministry of Economic Affairs and introduced to the Legislative Yuan. Although this Bill has not been passed because several issues remain to be solved, since the LLP has been adopted in many jurisdictions including common law and civil law countries, it is expected that the LLP will be an alternative form of unincorporated business association in Taiwan in the near future.*

Taiwan's Company Act allows the incorporation of four types of companies, i.e., (1) unlimited liability companies, (2) limited liability companies, (3) unlimited liability companies with limited liability shareholders, and (4) companies limited by shares (corporations).[1] As of June 2014, the total number of companies was 630,040 with paid-in capital of NT$21,156 billion (US$705.2 billion).[2] Among the 630,040 companies, the total number of limited liability companies was 469,252 with paid-in capital of NT$2,234 billion (US$74.46 billion).[3] Most limited liability companies are family-owned and small- and-medium enterprises (SMEs).[4] Corporations are the second most numerous type of

---

* As this book was in the final stages of going to press, the Legislative Yuan on June 8, 2015 approved the Limited Liability Partnership Act discussed in this chapter. The legislation awaits the President's signature.

[1] *See* Taiwan Company Act, §2.

[2] *See* Department of Statistics, Ministry of Economic Affairs (MOEA), Company Registration—Number of Registered Companies and Paid-in Capital (June 2014) [hereinafter Company Registration 201406], available at www.moea.gov.tw/Mns/dos/content/ContentLink. aspx?menu_id=6849 (last visited Aug. 11, 2014). The exchange rates in June 2014 were between US$1 to NT$30.102 on June 4 and US$1 to NT$29.915 on June 30 according to the records of the Central Bank of Taiwan.

[3] *See* Company Registration 201406.

[4] According to §2 of the Company Act prior to the amendment on November 12, 2001, the number of shareholders of a limited liability company is restricted to a range between 5 and 21. Beginning from November 12, 2001, the Company Act recognizes that a limited liability company can be a one-man company.

company. There were 156,261 corporations with paid-in capital of NT$18,792 billion (US$626.4 billion).[5] To register as a corporation, the minimum requirement is to have as few as one institutional shareholder or a minimum of two individual shareholders. Among the four types of companies, only corporations can issue shares and debentures. The other two types of company are less important because the total number of unlimited companies was 22 and there were only 11 unlimited liability companies with limited liability shareholders (as of June 2014).

A foreign company must obtain a certificate of recognition from the Ministry of Economic Affairs, the competent authority, before it can transact business in Taiwan.[6] As of June 2014, there were 4,494 foreign companies recognized to trade in Taiwan with operating capital of NT$129 billion (US$4.3 billion) and 4,173 representative offices.[7]

In addition to the four types of company that have separate legal personality from their shareholders, there are also non-corporate forms of business in which individuals are responsible for the debts of the business. Similar to other countries, the traditional and most common non-corporate forms of business in Taiwan are sole proprietorships and partnerships.[8] As of the end of June 2014, there were 158,609,864 businesses registered with paid-in capital of NT$216 million (US$7.2 million).[9]

2. GENERAL PRINCIPLES OF THE LAW OF PARTNERSHIPS UNDER THE CIVIL CODE

General Principles

There are two types of partnerships under Taiwan's Civil Code—"general partnerships" and "silent partnerships."[10] A partnership does not have a legal personality. Partnership is a contract governing the duties and rights of two or more people intending to contribute money, assets, or labor and manage the enterprise together.[11] The law of partnerships has the nature of collectivity or a group.[12] Therefore, in interpreting the law of partnerships, the concept and rules of "legal person" under the Civil Code or the corporate law

---

[5] *See* Company Registration 201406.
[6] *See* Taiwan Company Act, §371.
[7] *See* Company Registration 201406. A foreign company may file recordation with the competent authority and set up a representative office in Taiwan. Taiwan Company Act, §386.
[8] *See* Business Registration Act, §2.
[9] *See* Department of Statistics, Ministry of Economic Affairs (MOEA), Business Registration—Number of Registered Businesses and Paid-in Capital (June 2014) [hereinafter Business Registration 201406], available at www.moea.gov.tw/Mns/dos/content/ContentLink.aspx?menu_id=6849 (last visited Aug. 11, 2014).
[10] *See* Civil Code, Part II, Chapter 2, Section 18 Partnership (§§667–699) and Section 19 Silent Partnership (§§700–709).
[11] *See* Civil Code, §667, para. 1.
[12] Some scholars have observed that common law and various legal doctrines have in different ways expressly or implicitly recognized that group or "distinct group" is a nature of the partnership. For discussion regarding the legal nature of partnership, *see e.g.*, Paula J. Dalley, *To Whom It May Concern: Fiduciary Duties and Business Associations*, 26 Del. J. Corp. L. 515, 530–538.

will sometimes be referred to.[13] In addition, a partnership contains the characteristics of bilateral contract, continuing contract, groupness contract.[14] Although a writing is not necessary, a partnership is usually created in writing when forming a business because the partnership contract needs to be lodged with the competent authority.[15] However, it is necessary to note that a partnership under the Civil Code can be created for profit or not for profit.[16] In this chapter, the discussion is limited to partnership for profit or business partnership. The general principles of the law of partnerships will be introduced in the following sections and followed with discussions of the contemporary issues arising from the application of the partnership law.

In order to do business, a business partnership must file with the local city or county government according to the Business Registration Act, Business Registration Enforcement Act, and Rules Governing the Application of Business Registration.[17] For example, in order to do business in Taipei City, partners or their agent can file the application for registration of the partnership as a business in the Taipei City Office of Commerce either in person or electronically. As of the end of July 2014, there were a total of 55,261 sole proprietorships and partnership enterprises registered with Taipei City Office of Commerce. Among them, 52,802 enterprises are sole proprietorships and only 2,267 are partnerships.[18] Obviously, the businesses in the form of partnerships are far fewer than the number of proprietorships. One of the major reasons that partnership is not a popular form of business is that a partner is not only responsible for his own management, but also is jointly and severally liable for the debts incurred by other partners for their management.[19] However, the Business Registration Act deals only with the registration and relevant administration matters. The legal effect of the partnership contract, including the rights, obligations, and duties arising from the relationship, is governed by the Civil Code and the partnership contract itself if not in contravention of the law.

Since partnership is a contract, partners may agree with one another on most of the contents as they wish. For example, partners may in the partnership contract permit partners to receive remuneration,[20] impose a duty to contribute additional capital,[21]

---

[13] *See* Qiu Congzhi (邱聰智), Xinding Zhaifa Gelun (Xia) (新訂債法各論(下)) (Particular Kinds of Obligations), at 5 (2008).
[14] *See* Lin Chenger (林誠二), Minfa Zhaipian Gelun (Xia) (民法債編各論(下)) (Civil Code Particular Kinds of Obligations), at 6–10 (2013).
[15] *See* Business Registration Act, §9.
[16] *See* Qiu Congzhi, *supra* note 13, at 13.
[17] Business Registration Act, §4; Business Registration Enforcement Act, §3; Rules Governing the Application of Business Registration, §5.
[18] The statistical number was obtained from Taipei City Office of Commerce via telephone interview with Miss Liu on Aug. 13, 2014 at 1:42 pm Taipei time. Currently, the publicly available information regarding business registration contains monthly new establishment registration, amendment registration, and termination registration only.
[19] *See* Civil Code, §681. Although the Civil Code sets forth that a partner is jointly liable for the obligation of the partnership, the obligation of partnership arises from the management of all partners.
[20] The default rule is that a partner cannot request remuneration. However, the partnership contract may expressly state that partners can receive remuneration. *See* Civil Code, §678, para. 2.
[21] The default rule is that partners do not have an obligation to contribute more capital beyond the originally agreed amount. *See* Civil Code, §669.

designate a specific partner or partners to manage the partnership affairs, etc.[22] Although the Civil Code allows partners flexibility in arranging how the affairs and business of the partnership are to be managed, in order to protect partners and for the interest of counter-parties trading with partners, the law also sets forth many rules to regulate the internal and external relationships of a partnership. For example, because the partnership does not have a legal personality separate from individual partners, the law provides that contributions of the partners and properties of the partnership are held in common by all partners to prevent disputes arising from the ownership of the property of the partnership.[23] Moreover, there is a restriction on the resignation and removal of a partner or partners authorized by contract or resolution to manage the partnership affairs.[24] A partner authorized to manage the partnership affairs cannot resign unless there is a proper cause. On the other hand, the partner authorized to manage the partnership affairs cannot be removed either without unanimous consent of all of the other partners.

The Law of General Partnerships

Partnership, or general partnership, is one of the 27 types of contracts that can be found in Chapter Two of the Civil Code. There are 33 provisions (§§667–699) governing partnerships. As stipulated in the first provision, Article 667, a partnership is a contract between two or more people promising to contribute the capital and manage the enterprise together. Since it is a contract, parties to the contract have the freedom to arrange the rights, obligations, and interrelationship among themselves. Though the partnership enterprise itself does not have legal personality, it may have its own properties in practice and for accounting purposes. Moreover, it is recognized that the partnership enterprise has the capacity to be a party in the litigation for the convenience of resolving a dispute arising from the partnership.[25] Because of the partnership's nature as an unincorporated association, for the protection of persons dealing with the partnership, the Civil Code imposes legal effects on certain aspects that cannot be arranged or modified by the partnership agreement. The typical example is the supplemental joint and several liability of a partner for the debt of the partnership enterprise if its assets are insufficient to cover its liabilities.[26]

The law of partnership under the Civil Code can be observed from the following aspects: (1) creation of partnership enterprise, (2) compulsory legal effects of partnership, (3) partnership autonomy, and (4) liquidation and winding-up of partnership.

Creation of partnership enterprise
Partnership enterprise can be for profit or not for profit. The law of partnership under the Civil Code applies to both commercial partnership enterprises and

---

[22] The default rule is that the affairs of the partnership shall be managed by all partners in common. *See* Civil Code, §671.
[23] *See* Civil Code, §668.
[24] *See* Civil Code, §674.
[25] The Supreme Court has held that a partnership can be treated as an unincorporated association and can be a party to litigation according to the Taiwan Code of Civil Procedure. *See* Zuigao Fayuan 56-Tai-Shang 1609 Civil Judgment (Taiwan Supreme Ct. Oct. 24, 2012).
[26] *See* Civil Code, §681.

non-profit partnership enterprises. A commercial partnership must register with the local competent authority before it can begin to trade. However, registration is not a condition to determine the existence of the partnership.[27] The formation of the partnership contract is the determining factor. Registration is a prerequisite for a partnership to begin doing business. Compared with a corporation, a partnership enterprise is a form of business that shows a strong alignment between the ownership and the management.[28]

A commercial partnership must register the following information: (1) the name of the partnership, (2) the organization of the business, (3) the nature of the business, (4) the capital of the business, (5) the address of the business, (6) the information on and the amount of capital contributed by the responsible person of the partnership, (7) the information and contributed capital of each of the partners, and (8) a copy of the partnership contract.[29] A commercial partnership has its own name, address, organization, capital, and responsible person, representative, or administrator who is separate from the partners.[30] These factors make partnership an unincorporated association. According to Section 40 of the Taiwan Code of Civil Procedure, an unincorporated association has the capacity to be a party to litigation, as plaintiff or defendant. Therefore, partnership has the capacity to be a party in litigation.[31]

Although a partnership has the capacity to be a party in litigation, it does not have legal personality and does not have legal capacity as a juridical person under the substantive law. Therefore, a partnership cannot legally be a party to a contract. Such a contract will be deemed void because one of the contractual parties is legally non-existent. However, although the partnership is named as a party to the contract, the contract is not 100 percent invalid. The Supreme Court has upheld the validity of a contract when one of the parties is a partnership enterprise if the representative of the partnership has legally signed the contract and all other elements of a contract have also met the requirements of contract law.[32] Another Supreme Court decision has declared that an unincorporated association would be protected if there was an interest that needed to be protected and

---

[27] The Supreme Court has pointed out that registration of a commercial partnership enterprise is for the purpose of administration. Absence of registration would not affect the determination of the existence of the partnership. *See* QIU Zhe Qian et al. v. LIN Jin et al., 1975 Chinese (Taiwan), Zuigao Fayuan 64-Tai-Shang 1122 Civil Judgment (Supreme Ct. May 23, 1975).

[28] Ta-Ying Liaow (廖大穎), *Company and Unincorporated Business Organization*, (in Chinese) NCHU Law Review, No. 4, at 7 (Nov. 2008).

[29] *See* Business Registration Act, §9.

[30] The responsible person of a commercial partnership must be a partner and contribute capital to the partnership.

[31] Some scholars have taken the view that in order to effectively resolve the dispute, the counter-party may choose to sue the partnership and one or more partners at the same time. *See* Shen Kun-Ling, Sheji Fei Faren Tuanti Zhi Dangshiren Shige Ji Susong Dandang (*The Qualified Standing and Litigation Undertaking of Unincorporated Association*), 141 TAIWAN L.J. 29, 34–39 (2009). In contrast, one scholar has expressed a different opinion that partners shall be listed as the party in a litigation since partnership does not have legal capacity and the contributions and other property of partnership are held in common by all partners. *See* YANG SHU WEN, COMMON CLASS NOTES ON CODE OF CIVIL PROCEDURE, Vol. 1, 66–67 (Sept. 2008).

[32] *See* YE Song Ren et al. v. KMT, 2011 Chinese (Taiwan), Zuigao Fayuan 100-Tai-Shang 484 Civil Judgment (Supreme Ct. Mar. 31, 2011).

such unincorporated association had its own name, organization, and will, and it had used the business name to do business for years and was known to the public.[33] The Supreme Court held that although the unincorporated association does not have legal capacity, the juridical acts of an unincorporated association cannot be denied merely because of lack of legal capacity.[34]

It is important to note that a partnership contract in which partners simply promise to contribute the capital and manage the enterprise together without stipulating other matters is sufficient to make the contract enforceable. According to Article 667 of the Civil Code, this is the definition of a partnership contract. If there are any disputes arising from the partnership affairs, the Civil Code has provided most of the rules. Moreover, Article 1 of the Civil Code sets forth the general principle governing civil matters that law, custom, and jurisprudence will be applied in order to resolve the civil dispute.

Compulsory legal effects of partnership
A partnership contract allows partners to arrange their rights and obligations among themselves and between partners and the partnership enterprise. When doing business with the partnership enterprise, one is either trading with the partnership enterprise or trading with individual partners. The party dealing with partners or the representative of the partnership will not be able to know every detail of the internal arrangement among partners. Therefore, the Civil Code sets forth certain compulsory rules regarding the legal effect of the external relationship between the partnership, partners, and the creditors of the partnership enterprise. Although most rights and obligations of partners can be arranged through the covenants of the partnership contract, certain internal relationships must comply with the Civil Code.

Assets of the partnership The assets of the partnership are not just the gathering of contributed capital and other properties of partners. In reality, for the convenience of management of partnership affairs and trading, the partnership enterprise usually has its own assets separate from those of individual partners. The partnership enterprise can use its name to open a bank account. Moreover, commercial partnerships also need to register with the tax bureau. Although currently only partners pay income tax, from January 1, 2016, both the partnership enterprise and partners will be required to pay income tax separately according to the amended rules set forth in Article 71 of the Income Tax Act.[35]

---

[33] See YU You Ren Cultural and Educational Foundation v. LI Qi et al., 2002 Chinese (Taiwan), Zuigao Fayuan 91-Tai-Shang 1030 Civil Judgment (Supreme Ct. May 30, 2002).
[34] Id.
[35] Article 71 of the current Income Tax Act requires the partnership enterprise to file the Annual Income Tax Return by the end of May every year but it need not calculate and pay the amount of income tax. Such income tax is classified as "income from profit-seeking" and is calculated into the consolidated income of the individual partner according to the profit-sharing ratio stated in the partnership contract; that individual partner will file a Personal Consolidated Income Tax Return and pay income tax to the local tax collection authority. Taiwan Income Tax Act, §71, para. 2. Article 71 of the Income Tax Act was amended on June 4, 2014. According to the new rule, a partnership enterprise shall calculate the total payable income tax by deducting the unused withholding tax from 50% of the amount of income tax payable for the whole year. This amount is the income tax payable by the partnership enterprise. The gross profit-seeking-income of the partnership enter-

The fact that the partnership has the capacity to be a party in litigation, to open its own bank account, to have its own accounting books, and to pay income tax may somehow confuse people as to whether the partnership enterprise in reality has the legal ownership of the assets. We must therefore clarify that owning a bank account and litigation capacity, etc., are all for the convenience of the management and operation of the partnership enterprise and to resolve disputes arising from partnership affairs. Regarding the legal ownership of the assets of the partnership, the basic principle is that the contributed capital and other property of the partnership are held in common by all partners.[36]

The Supreme Court has held that though the real property of the partnership was registered under the name of some of the partners, showing the ownership of each registered partner will not affect the legal effect that assets of the partnership are held in common by all partners.[37] An individual partner does not have the right to sell the registered proportion of ownership of the real property.

The law of partnership observes the necessity of allowing the existence of partnership assets separate from the assets of an individual partner. The law specifically prohibits the request of an individual partner for the partition and analysis of the partnership assets until the partnership goes into liquidation.[38] The purpose of this prohibition is to affirm that partnership assets are held in common by all partners and to ensure that partnership affairs will not easily be disturbed. This rule is a reflection of the general principle governing the rights of persons who have created a relationship in common according to Article 827 of the Civil Code. By the same token, a partner, as the owner-in-common, cannot request the partition of the thing held in common for the duration of the relationship in common.[39] Moreover, for the protection of the partnership assets, the debtor of the partnership cannot offset his debt owed to the partnership with the claim against the partner.[40]

Duty of care A partner has a duty of care when managing the partnership affairs. The Civil Code varies the standard of care based on whether such partner receives compensation.[41] If a partner does not receive compensation, he shall exercise such care as he would in dealing with his own affairs. The standard of care will be raised to that of a good administrator if he receives compensation. The standard of care cannot be modified by the partnership contract. These two standards are well established under Taiwanese civil law and commercial law.

Resignation and removal of partner The Law of Mandate, from Article 537 to Article 546, applies *mutatis mutandis* to partners dealing with partnership affairs.[42] However,

---

prise deducting the amount of income tax paid by the partnership will become income from profit-seeking. Each partner will calculate his own income and file a Personal Consolidated Income Tax Return. See Taiwan Income Tax Act, §71, para. 2 (effective on Jan. 1, 2016).

[36] See Civil Code, §668.
[37] See Zuigao Fayuan 98-Tai-Shang 76 Civil Judgment (Supreme Ct. Jan. 15, 2009).
[38] See Civil Code, §682, para. 1. See also, Qiu Congzhi, *supra* note 13, at 34.
[39] See Civil Code, §829.
[40] See Civil Code, §682, para. 2.
[41] See Civil Code, §672.
[42] See Civil Code, §680.

unlike in the relationship of principal and mandatory (agent), the partner in charge of the partnership affairs, either by agreement or by resolution, does not have the right to resign at will.[43] To resign, the managing partner must show proper cause and submit the resignation to other partners. If some of the partners are not satisfied with the managing partner, other partners cannot remove the managing partner at will unless the removal proposal is approved by the partners unanimously.[44] When the law of partnership was enacted, the law maker perceived the different relationships and scenarios and made the rules governing the resignation and removal of managing partners different from those applied to the resignation and removal of the mandatory under the Law of Mandate.

Right to inspect partnership affairs The partners may in the partnership contract or by resolution designate or authorize one or more partners to manage the partnership affairs. Without such agreement or resolution, the partnership affairs shall be managed by all partners together unless they are ordinary affairs that every partner has the authority to deal with.[45] In order to manage the partnership affairs, the managing partner for a specific affair or for all affairs can access information of the partnership. However, other non-managing partners may not be able to access the same information as the managing partner. Because partners hold the partnership assets in common and are jointly liable for the deficit, it is important that non-managing partners enjoy equal access to the partnership information and not be deprived of such right. The law, therefore, grants the right of inspection of the partnership affairs, condition of assets, and accounting books to non-managing partners and prohibits the depriving of such right by contract.[46]

Representation and mandate When dealing with partnership affairs with other persons, it is important that the partner has the managerial power and can represent other partners from the legal aspect or represent the partnership enterprise from the practical aspect. There are at least two types of persons who have the right of representation when dealing with partnership affairs—the registered responsible person and other managing partners. A commercial partnership is required to register the responsible partner, either called a representative or administrator, when filing registration with the local government according to the Business Registration Act. This partner shall have the representation power because of the registration. In addition to the registered responsible partner, other partners while managing partnership affairs according to agreement or resolution shall also have the representation power to represent other partners.[47]

Although a partnership has the characteristic of a group, it is not a juridical person. Because of lack of legal personality, a partnership is legally non-existent. Therefore, when a managing partner deals with the partnership affairs, he legally represents all other partners as indicated in Article 679 of the Civil Code and practically represents the partnership that we believe is invisibly existent. In addition to the issue of representation, the law makers found the similarities between mandate (agency) and partnership. The

---

[43] *See* Civil Code, §674, para. 1.
[44] *See* Civil Code, §674, para. 2.
[45] *See* Civil Code, §671.
[46] *See* Civil Code, §675.
[47] *See* Civil Code, §679.

Civil Code sets forth that most of the provisions concerning mandate shall apply *mutatis mutandis* to the managing of the partnership affairs by partners.[48] Therefore, to some extent, when the managing partner deals with partnership affairs, he is considered as the mandatory (agent) and the rest of the partners are considered as the principal. Except for the removal and resignation of the managing partner where different rules are applied, most of the provisions of the Law of Mandate apply to the dealing of partnership affairs by partners.

Partner's supplementary joint liability Because the partnership enterprise has assets separate from partners, the money of the partnership is first used to repay the debt arising from the partnership affairs. However, if there are insufficient funds to repay the debt, the law imposes supplementary joint liability on partners. In other words, partners are jointly liable to creditors of partnership affairs only for the deficit.[49] When the creditor brings a lawsuit, he will name the partnership, its responsible person, and all partners as defendants in order to meet the requirement of standing to sue or be sued.[50] Moreover, if the creditor intends to sue partners as jointly liable for the debt arising from partnership affairs, the creditor will have to sue all partners, not some of the partners, and prove that the fund of the partnership is insufficient to repay the debt.[51]

An interesting scenario arises when a creditor of the partnership is one of the partners. How can he successfully claim his rights as a creditor when partnership assets are not sufficient to pay him? The partner is a creditor but also one of the partners that bear the supplementary joint liability. According to Article 274 of the Civil Code, if one of the joint debtors has extinguished the debt because of "merger," other debtors are also released from the debt obligation. The Supreme Court has denied the right of the partner,

---

[48] *See* Civil Code, §680. Examples of the provisions of mandate applying to partnership are the way to deal with the affairs commissioned (partnership affairs), reporting obligation of the mandatory (managing partner), duty to deliver money and things received as a result of dealing of the affairs commissioned, and the liability of the mandatory to the principal for the damages arising from the negligence of the mandatory in dealing with the affairs commissioned. *See* Civil Code, §§537–539, 540, 541, 544.

[49] *See* Civil Code, §681.

[50] In one case plaintiff subcontractor Yingcheng Paint sued defendant for payment of the painting work. The Supreme Court remanded the case asking the High Court to clarify whether plaintiff was a partnership or a proprietorship. If plaintiff is a partnership, all partners must be named as plaintiff to satisfy the standing requirement. The Supreme Court held that "partnership assets are owned by all partners in common. Partnership does not have independent personality. If the litigation is relating to the partnership affairs, in addition to naming the managing partner who represents the partnership as plaintiff or defendant, all partners shall also be named as plaintiff or defendant so that the requirement of standing to sue or be sued is satisfied." Taiyuan Construction Corporation v. Yingcheng Paint, 2003 Chinese (Taiwan), Zuigao Fayuan 92-Tai-Shang 1350 Civil Judgment (Supreme Ct. June 26, 2003). *See also* YANG Jianhuang et al. v. CHANG Bangji, 1993 Chinese (Taiwan), Zuigao Fayuan 82-Tai-Shang 3238 Civil Judgment (Supreme Ct. Dec. 31, 1993).

[51] The Supreme Court held that without proving the insufficiency of partnership assets to pay damages to plaintiffs, it would not be allowed to sue some of the partners (not all partners) as jointly liable for the damages arising from the partnership affairs. (Parties' name not disclosed), 1997 Chinese (Taiwan), Zuigao Fayuan 86-Tai-Shang 1432 Civil Judgment (Supreme Ct. May 8, 1997).

the creditor, to sue all partners as jointly liable for the money he paid for the partnership.[52] For this situation, it becomes the internal relationship among partners and the law regarding the internal relationship of joint-debtors shall apply. Therefore, according to Article 281 of the Civil Code, instead of suing all partners, the creditor (partner) should sue other partners for reimbursement of what he has paid exceeding his proportionate share of the debts of the partnership, plus interest from the date of release.[53]

Transfer of share, introduction of new partner, and withdrawal from partnership Transfer of shares to a non-partner is prohibited unless approved unanimously by all partners.[54] This will lead to a similar effect as the introduction of a new partner, which under the law also requires the approval of all partners.[55] It is important to note that after a partner withdraws from the partnership, the law requires that a partner continue to be liable for the debt of the partnership incurred before his withdrawal.[56] Although withdrawal from partnership is an official termination of the relationship between the withdrawing partner and other partners, to protect the creditors of the partnership, the withdrawing partner will continue to be liable for the existing debt. In contrast, a newly joining partner bears the same liability as all other partners, including liability for obligations incurred before he becomes a partner.[57]

Another issue is regarding a partner's withdrawal from a partnership and its legal consequence. A partner may voluntarily withdraw from a partnership if the duration of the partnership is not fixed or one partner's lifetime is used as the duration. The withdrawing partner must notify other partners two months prior to his withdrawal, and the timing of his withdrawal must not be harmful to the partnership.[58] However, even if the duration of a partnership is fixed, a partner may still withdraw from the partnership if there are significant reasons due to circumstances for which he is not to blame.

Partnership autonomy
In addition to the above discussed compulsory rules, partners do have the freedom to arrange their internal affairs. The law has set the default legal effects on the following matters but grants partners freedom to make their own rules regarding profit and loss sharing, duty to contribute additional capital, resolution of partnership affairs, and the right to manage and deal with partnership affairs.

With regard to profit and loss sharing, partners are free to decide the profit-sharing ratio. There could be different factors affecting the determination of the ratio, such as contribution of capital, evaluation of performance, or value creation to the partnership,

---

[52] *See* (Parties' name not disclosed), 2004 Chinese (Taiwan), Zuigao Fayuan 93-Tai-Shang 2487 Civil Judgment (Supreme Ct. Dec. 10, 2004).
[53] In this case, each partner has to reimburse the creditor (partner) according to the profit-sharing ratio stated in the partnership agreement or the proportion of the capital contributed by each partner. *See* Civil Code, §677.
[54] *See* Civil Code, §683.
[55] *See* Civil Code, §691, para. 1.
[56] *See* Civil Code, §690.
[57] *See* Civil Code, §691, para. 2.
[58] *See* Civil Code, §686, paras. 1 and 2.

but it is an autonomy matter that partners can agree upon and set the ratio in the partnership contract. However, if the profit- and loss-sharing ratio is not stated in the contract, the default rule is that the proportion of the capital contributed by each partner will be the profit- and loss-sharing ratio.[59] Those who contribute to the capital by means of labor may share the profit but will not share the loss unless it is stated otherwise.[60] The partner may claim reimbursement of expenses incurred dealing with partnership affairs. However, unless otherwise stated in the contract, partners may not claim remuneration for dealing with partnership affairs.[61]

Regarding the contribution of additional capital, partners do not have such a duty unless stated in the contract. Even when the partnership suffers losses, partners do not have the obligation to make up the deficiency.[62] The partners bear supplementary joint liability when the creditor claims the payment and the partnership assets are not sufficient to pay its debt.

How the partnership affairs are managed and decided is completely determinable by the partners. Nevertheless, if a partnership contract is created but does not state clearly how the resolution is decided and who can deal with the affairs, the default rule is that all partners will deal with the affairs in common except for the ordinary affairs that each partner can deal with alone. A partnership resolution shall be passed by unanimous consent of all partners unless different methods of resolution are designated in the contract.[63] Although partners may designate methods of partnership resolution other than unanimous consent, the minimum voting requirement for modification of the partnership contract or a change of partnership enterprise is that such resolution must obtain approval from at least two-thirds of partners.[64]

Dissolution and winding-up of partnership
The final part of the rules regards the dissolution and winding-up of a partnership. This part of the rules is very straightforward because most partnership contracts when created neglect to include the provisions governing the procedure to liquidate and wind up partnership affairs. Therefore, the law sets forth rules governing how liquidators are appointed, how liquidators deal with and resolve the affairs, the priorities of creditors and partners against the partnership assets, and how remaining assets are distributed to partners, without giving freedom to partners to arrange in different ways.

The partnership can be dissolved because of the occurrence of one of the following situations: (1) the period of the existence of the partnership has expired; (2) all partners have agreed to dissolve; or (3) the object of the partnership has been achieved or cannot be achieved.[65] If partners continue to deal with partnership affairs after the expiration date, the partnership will be deemed to continue to exist without expiration date.[66] Once

---

[59] See Civil Code, §677, para. 1.
[60] See Civil Code, §677, para. 3.
[61] See Civil Code, §678, para. 2.
[62] See Civil Code, §669.
[63] See Civil Code, §670, para. 1.
[64] See Civil Code, §670, para. 3.
[65] See Civil Code, §692.
[66] See Civil Code, §693.

the partnership has decided to dissolve, a liquidator or liquidators will be appointed to liquidate the partnership assets and wind up the business. All partners become liquidators in the liquidation procedure. Alternatively, partners may appoint liquidators with approval of majority partners.

In liquidation, the partnership assets will be used to pay off the debt. For the debt that has not matured or is subject to litigation, the liquidators will set aside and reserve a sufficient amount of money for that purpose. If there are remaining assets after paying off the partnership debt, the assets will first be distributed to partners according to the contributed capital of each partner, and any remaining assets will be distributed to partners according to the profit-sharing ratio.[67]

The Law of Silent Partnerships

A "silent partnership" (SP) is defined as a contract in which one of the parties agrees to contribute to the capital of an enterprise managed by other parties and to share the loss and profit of that enterprise.[68] Therefore, a silent partner does not have the right or obligation to deal with the business of the SP and it is purely a profit- and loss-sharing agreement for the silent partner. More specifically, the only loss the silent partner will share is limited to the capital he or she contributed to the SP, and the contract made between the active partner and third party will not create any legal obligation on the silent partner.[69] Because this is the major difference between the partnership and the SP, except for those expressly set forth for the SP, most provisions under the law of partnership are applied *mutatis mutandis* to the SP.[70] Similar to other types of business association, the silent partner who does not participate in management of the business may inspect the records and investigate the business and financial status at the end of each operating year, and may inspect and investigate anytime if there is significant reason and approval by the court.[71]

3. CONTEMPORARY ISSUES OF THE LAW OF PARTNERSHIP

Accounting Firm's Liability for Misleading Financial Reports

Taiwan's Securities and Exchange Act (TSEA) and Certified Public Accountant Act (CPA Act) impose civil and criminal liabilities on the certified public accountant (CPA) who commits any misconduct, or violates or neglects any required professional duties while performing his or her duties as a CPA and causes damage because of a fraudulent financial report disclosed by a publicly traded corporation.[72] The TSEA also expressly

---

[67] *See* Civil Code, §§697, para. 2, 698, 699.
[68] *See* Civil Code, §700.
[69] *See* Civil Code, §§703, 704.
[70] *See* Civil Code, §701.
[71] *See* Civil Code, §706.
[72] *See* Taiwan Securities and Exchange Act, §20-1, para. 3; Certified Public Account Act, §§41, 42.

imposes liability on the CPA who signs the prospectus.[73] Moreover, the competent authority may impose sanctions on the CPA who makes mistakes in the process of auditing and attesting the financial report.[74] There is no doubt that the CPA is liable for negligence to anyone to whom he owes a duty of care and to investors who suffer damage because of the fraudulent financial report and auditing report. The issue is whether the accounting firm is also liable for the negligence or wrongdoing of the CPA associated with the accounting firm.

In practice, there are several fraudulent financial report cases involving accounting firms that were in the form of joint CPA firms. The Securities and Futures Investors Protection Center (SFIPC), a non-profit organization, usually represents investors and brings class actions in its own name as the plaintiff to sue the wrongdoers, including the accountants and the accounting firm.[75] Formerly, the Statements of Auditing Standards No. 18 (now repealed) imposed a duty on the CPA regarding the quality control of the auditing affairs. It did not impose a duty of quality control on the accounting firm. Both the TSEA and the CPA Act are quiet on the issue of whether the joint CPA firm is also responsible when the accountants are held liable for damage caused by the their auditing work and auditing report included in the fraudulent financial report.[76] The Statements of Auditing Standards No. 46 was promulgated to replace Accounting Standards No. 18 to require accounting firms to establish quality control systems to set up policy and procedures regarding quality control of audit affairs, including leadership responsibility, engagement performance and monitoring, etc. Additionally, in order to protect the interests of relevant parties, the CPA Act also prohibits the accounting firm from including any exculpatory provision to exempt any partner from joint and several liability set forth under Article 681 of the Civil Code, which imposes supplementary joint liability on partners.[77] Based on the above law and regulation, the question remains whether the law of partnership under the Civil Code will be applied to this type of case so that both the accounting firm and the other partners can be held accountable for the negligence of auditing CPAs.

The issue has arisen mainly because of the existence of different forms of accounting firms. Before 2007, accounting firms could be in one of the following three forms: (1) single-person CPA firm, (2) shared-office CPA firm, or (3) joint CPA firm.[78] Among these three types of accounting firms, the joint CPA firm is considered as a partnership. According to the "Regulations Governing Approval of Certified Public Accountants to Audit and Attest to the Financial Reports of Public Companies," only qualified joint CPA firms can audit and attest the financial reports of public companies.[79] Because of

---

[73] See TSEA, §32.
[74] See TSEA, §37, para. 3.
[75] See Securities and Futures Investors Protection Act, §28.
[76] No. 18 of the Statements of Auditing Standards, published by the Accounting Research and Development Foundation, was repealed partly because it causes confusion in litigation regarding the responsibility and liability of the accounting firm. No. 18 was replaced by No. 46 of the Statements of Auditing Standards, promulgated on December 16, 2008.
[77] See Certified Public Account Act, §22, para. 2.
[78] See Certified Public Account Act, §15.
[79] See Regulations Governing Approval of Certified Public Accountants to Audit and Attest to the Financial Reports of Public Companies, §§2 and 4.

this controversy, in December 2007 the CPA Act was overhauled and a new form of accounting firm, the "incorporated CPA firm," was introduced; relevant regulations were also amended to allow both joint CPA firms and incorporated CPA firms to audit and attest the financial reports of public companies.[80] It is hoped that this will solve the problems. However, accountants are not interested in incorporating accounting firms mainly because of tax concerns and the restriction on the transfer of shareholding. To completely solve the controversies, it is suggested that the limited liability partnership can be introduced as an alternative solution. We will discuss the proposed LLP Act later in this chapter.

Cases Regarding the Liability of a Joint CPA Firm

For the first two cases, the SFIPC sued the CPAs who conducted the auditing work of listed companies, the joint CPA firm, and more than 100 accountants who were partners of the same accounting firm as jointly and severally liable for the damages caused by the negligence of the auditing CPAs. In these two cases, the accounting firms together with the auditing CPAs settled the case with the SFIPC.[81] The court's opinion on whether the accounting firm is jointly liable for the negligence of auditing CPAs was in favor of the accounting firm before October 24, 2012. For example, in the case of Cheng I Food Co., Ltd., the Taipei District Court and the Taiwan High Court accepted the accounting firm's allegation and opined that auditing of a financial report is expert and independent work, and if the auditing CPA is willfully or negligently conducting the work, he or she shall be personally liable for the damages incurred and the accounting firm is not jointly and severally liable for such damages.[82] This case was appealed to the Supreme Court.

The Supreme Court overruled the decision of the High Court and held that the accounting firm was liable.[83] The Supreme Court reasoned that the accounting firm in this case was in the form of a partnership and, by reference to Article 28 of the Civil Code, the accounting firm resembles a legal person and should be responsible for the tortious conduct of it representatives. The Supreme Court applied several provisions of the law of partnership of the Civil Code. For example, the property owned by the accounting firm is separate from the partners.[84] The CPAs, partners, are representatives of other partners when performing the partnership affairs.[85] The Civil Code also sets the rules regarding

---

[80] A new version of the CPA Act containing 81 articles was enacted on December 26, 2007. *See* Presidential Order No. Hua-Zong-I-Yi-09600175591.

[81] Interview with the Mr. Jung-Hung Lin, Deputy-Director of Legal Affairs Department of the SFIPC on Aug. 20, 2014, 05:10 pm.

[82] *See* SFIPC (representing investors) v. Zheng Feng Joint CPA Firm (CLOAK & Co., CPAs) et al., 2006 CHINESE (TAIWAN), Taipei Defang Fayuan 87-Chong-Su 1347 Civil Judgment (Taiwan Taipei District Ct. Nov. 30, 2006); SFIPC (representing investors) v. Zhang Cui Lian et al., 2011 CHINESE (TAIWAN), Gaodeng Fayuan 96-Jin-Shang 1 Civil Judgment (Taiwan High Ct. Sept. 28, 2011).

[83] *See* SFIPC (representing investors) v. Zheng Feng Joint CPA Firm (CLOCK & Co., CPAs) et al., 2012 CHINESE (TAIWAN), Zuigao Fayuan 101-Tai-Shang 1695 Civil Judgment (Taiwan Supreme Ct. Oct. 24, 2012).

[84] *See* Civil Code, §668.

[85] *See* Civil Code, §679.

The evolution of non-corporate forms of business in Taiwan 461

the dissolution and liquidation of the partnership. By referring to these provisions, the Supreme Court intended to say that though the partnership itself does not have legal personality, the accounting firm in the form of the partnership not only reflects the partnership agreement, but also exhibits the nature of a group so that the operation of the accounting firm resembles a legal person. Article 28 of the Civil Code makes a legal person jointly liable for the wrongdoing of its directors or other persons authorized to represent the legal person in the course of performing their duties. Therefore, the Supreme Court applied Article 28 of the Civil Code by analogy to the accounting firm and held the accounting firm jointly and severally liable with the CPAs who were found liable in performing the auditing work.[86]

Since the Supreme Court's decision on October 24, 2012, the High Court has consistently held that the joint accounting firm is jointly liable with the CPAs who are held liable for their auditing work.[87] Although these two cases are still pending at the Supreme Court, it is perceived that the High Court has followed the opinion of the Supreme Court to hold the accounting firms jointly liable. This also reflects the concerns from the accounting firms that there is a need for an LLP as the form of accounting firms.

4. PROPOSED LIMITED PARTNERSHIP ACT

Background of the Proposal

Taiwan's businesses are mainly in the form of the limited company, corporation, sole proprietorship, and partnership. As noted earlier in this chapter, use of the partnership form by businesses is limited mainly because of the unlimited liability of partners. Will the government introduce or develop new forms of business? The answer is that there must be a need and demand for a new form of business. There are at least two businesses, accounting firms and venture capitalists, expressing the need to introduce new forms of business into Taiwan, particularly the limited partnership and the limited liability partnership.[88]

The venture capital regime was introduced into Taiwan in the early 1980s. As of August 2014, there were 186 venture capital companies still operating according to the Taiwan Venture Capital Association.[89] As required by law, all of the venture capital businesses are in the form of the corporation.[90] According to a research report, several concerns

---

[86] The case was remanded to the High Court. The accounting firm and CPAs settled the case with the plaintiffs.

[87] *See e.g.*, SFIPC (Class Action) v. Gongyi Guoji et al., 2013 CHINESE (TAIWAN), Gaodeng Fayuan 101-Jin-Shang 7 Civil Judgment (Taiwan High Ct. Sept. 04, 2013); SFIPC (Class Action) v. Gongchuan Dianzi (Well Communication Corp.) et al., 2013 CHINESE (TAIWAN), Gaodeng Fayuan 101-Jin-Shang 5 Civil Judgment (Taiwan High Ct. Apr. 15, 2013).

[88] Wang Wen-Yu, Fei Gongsi Zujhih De Sinfajhan (非公司組織的新發展—從合夥到有限合夥)(*New Development of Unincorporated Organization: from partnership to limited partnership*), ACCOUNTING RESEARCH MONTHLY, No. 300, at 125 (Nov. 2010).

[89] Statistical number retrieved from website of Taiwan Venture Capital Association, at www.tvca.org.tw/tvc_condition.php# (last visited Aug. 10, 2014).

[90] *See* Rules Regarding the Administration of Venture Capital Enterprises, §3, promulgated by Ministry of Finance on Nov. 24, 1983 (the rules were repealed on June 4, 2001 and replaced by the

462 *Partnerships, LLCs and alternative forms of business organizations*

have been raised because of the requirement that venture capital must be in the form of the corporation.[91] The first concern is that venture capital in the form of the corporation means the contribution must be in the form of paid-in capital, which makes it more difficult to exit the market because it must follow the statutory and complicated procedures of dissolution and liquidation.[92] The other concern is that the organizational structure and operation must comply with the Company Act, including capital requirements and dividend rules. Although some of the requirements have been revised, such as the abolishment of minimum capital requirement in April 2009, the requirements of the Company Act are still inflexible and not suitable for venture capital business.[93] Some venture capitalists hesitate to establish a venture capital enterprise in Taiwan mainly because the current law requires that venture capital businesses must be in the form of a corporation and a limited partnership or a limited liability partnership is not an option. Of course, a partnership is not welcome by venture capitalists because of the fear of unlimited liability. In order to promote venture capital enterprises, the government received the message and decided to enact the limited partnership law.[94]

Limited partnership was mentioned in the Legislative Yuan in 2004 when the securities investment trust law was reviewed.[95] In 2005, when the Legislative Yuan reviewed the government budget for the fiscal year of 2005, it was the first time that the Cabinet's Council for Economic Planning and Development decided to study and introduce the limited partnership regime.[96] In March 2005, the Minister of Economic Affairs in the Legislative Yuan revealed the intention to create a limited partnership regime to be used by venture capital enterprises, law firms, and accounting firms.[97] A Limited Partnership Act Bill was proposed by the Ministry of Economic Affairs, approved by the Executive Yuan and sent to the Legislative Yuan for legislation in July 2007.[98] The Legislative Yuan decided to send the Bill to the Economic and Energy Committee for review, but it did not go through.[99] The Executive Yuan resent the Bill to the Legislative Yuan in January

---

"Regulations Governing the Application of Venture Capital Company after the Promulgation of the Regulations Governing the Scope of Venture Capital Enterprises" (創業投資事業範圍與輔導辦法施行後創業投資公司申設辦法) [hereinafter VC Regulation]. According to the current law, Article 3 of the VC Regulation and the official application form, a venture capital business must be a corporation.

[91] See Xuehui Ye et al. (Lee and Li Attorneys-at-Law), A Research on Limited Partnership Law [Research Project of the Council for Economic Planning and Development (merged into National Development Council on Jan. 22, 2014)] [hereinafter LP Research 2004] (Dec. 2004).

[92] See LP Research 2004 at 2.

[93] Id.

[94] See generally, Wang Jhih-Cheng, Fei Gongsi Chihye Zujhih Fajhih Jhih Jhankai (非公司企業組織法制之展開) (*The Development of Unincorporated Enterprise Organization Regime: to advocate the limited partnership law*), Taiwan Law Journal, No. 128, at 32–33 (May 2009).

[95] The dialogue between legislators and the competent authority representative reflects that limited partnership is still new and not a familiar regime in Taiwan. See Legislative Yuan Gazette, vol. 93, no. 22 (3356 Book II), at 320 (Apr. 28, 2004).

[96] See Legislative Yuan Gazette, vol. 93, no. 45 (3379 Book II), at 73 (Nov. 22, 2004).

[97] See Legislative Yuan Gazette, vol. 94, no. 13 (3395 Book II), at 6 (Mar. 30, 2005).

[98] The Executive Yuan approved the Limited Liability Act Bill on June 26, 2007 at the 3047th Meeting and decided to send it to the Legislative Yuan. See Executive Yuan Gazette, Vol. 13, No. 126 (July 5, 2007).

[99] See Legislative Yuan Gazette, vol. 96, no. 64 (3587), at 200 (Oct. 16, 2007).

2008.[100] The Legislative Yuan decided to send the Bill to the Economic Committee for review, but the Executive Yuan withdrew the Bill for the reason that it was "not compatible with current policy."[101] Recently, when discussing the development of the cultural and creative industry and the organization of law firms, the government was pushed to enact the Limited Partnership Act and the Executive Yuan is reviewing the Bill.[102]

Comparison of "Limited Partnership" with "Silent Partnership" and "Unlimited Company" with "Limited Liability Shareholder"

When the idea to introduce the limited partnership as a new form of business into Taiwan was proposed, there were different voices on whether it was indeed necessary to enact such a new law. Those objecting to the adoption of a limited partnership regime did so mainly because Taiwan already has two similar regimes, i.e., the SP set forth in the Civil Code and the unlimited company with limited liability shareholders set forth in the Company Act. Moreover, some are skeptical as to how the limited partnership, a legal regime derived from the common law system, can fit into Taiwan's civil law system. Before we discuss the proposed new regime, it will be helpful to compare the proposed limited partnership with Taiwan's existing two other similar regimes. There are three major characteristics that make these different forms of business distinguishable: legal personality of the business, limited liability of the members or partners, and flexibility to arrange the internal affairs. Moreover, though the wording in the proposed Limited Partnership Act may be modified during the legislation process, the basic concept and legal effect of this law are similar across the border.

Proposed Limited Partnership versus Silent Partnership under the Civil Code versus Unlimited Company with Limited Liability Shareholders under the Company Act

The major difference is that the proposed limited partnership (LP) and unlimited company with limited liability shareholders (UCLLS) each have legal personality separate from their partners or shareholders, while the SP is created by a contract without legal personality. Therefore, both the LP and UCLLS have legal capacity and can register real property under the name of the business enterprise. In contrast, the SP does not have legal capacity and cannot register property under the name of the SP enterprise. However, there are some instances where the SP can become a party. For example, an SP has litigation capacity as the plaintiff or defendant. An SP is subject to business tax and income tax and can open its own bank account.

In all three forms of business, the members are composed of at least one with limited liability and one with joint or unlimited liability. The business affairs are all managed by the members who bear joint or unlimited liability, while other members with limited liability do not participate in management. In terms of flexibility to arrange the internal

---

[100] The Executive Yuan decided to resend the LPA Bill to the Legislative Yuan on Jan. 30, 2008 at the 3078th Meeting. *See* Executive Yuan Gazette, vol. 14, no. 26 (Feb. 12, 2008).
[101] Legislative Yuan Gazette, vol. 97, no. 48 (3659 Book II), at 330 (Oct. 4, 2008).
[102] *See* Legislative Yuan Gazette, vol. 103, no. 11 (4120), at 282–83 (Jan. 28, 2014); Legislative Yuan Gazette, vol. 103, no. 22 (4131), at 186–87 (Apr. 18, 2014).

affairs, both the LP and the SP enjoy more flexibility than the UCLLS because the law provides more room for the LP and the SP to arrange the internal relations via partnership contract, while the UCLLS must comply with the rules set forth in the Company Act. For example, by complying with the Company Act procedure, the liquidation of the UCLLS takes longer than the liquidation of the LP or the SP.

We already know the benefit of a business form with legal personality. It provides convenience for the business to use its own name to contract or conduct other legal activities with other parties. Although LPs and SPs share many similarities, such as the partnership affairs are managed by a general partner or active partners while limited liability partners and silent partners bear only limited liability, the SP does not have legal personality and cannot conduct many juridical acts. If this is crucial, the question turns to whether the UCLLS can be used or the Company Act regarding the UCLLS can be amended without enacting a new Limited Partnership Act. In other words, because both the UCLLS and the LP have legal personality and share some similarities, there will be no need to have the LP law in Taiwan unless we can find some significant differences between these two forms of business.

There are actually some significant differences between the LP and the UCLLS. First, the Company Act sets forth most of the legal effects of the internal relationship of the UCLLS, while the LP law generally gives much more freedom to use the LP agreement to tailor the internal relationship. The UCLLS allows less flexibility to arrange its internal relationship via articles of incorporation. Moreover, the amendment of the articles must obtain consensus approval from all shareholders, and this makes it more inflexible.

The second major difference is regarding the qualification to be a general partner, particularly regarding whether a company can become the general partner in an LP. In most jurisdictions, the LP law does not prohibit a company from becoming a general partner.[103] This will be an issue in Taiwan. Currently, according to the Company Act, a company is prohibited from becoming an unlimited liability shareholder or a partner because a company bearing unlimited liability would involve too much investment risk.[104] It is illegal for a company to become an unlimited liability shareholder of the UCLLS. If the LP regime is to be introduced, the Company Act must be amended to allow a company to become a general partner of an LP.

Thirdly, though a general partner bears supplementary joint and several liability, the qualification of a general partner in an LP can be very flexible. For example, Delaware law does not require a person to contribute to the LP to become a general partner, and the LP agreement may allow the general partner to share the profits of the LP at the same time it waives the general partner's obligation to subscribe to the LP interest.[105] In contrast, the UCLLS does not have such flexibility. Of course, all general partners must execute the certificate of LP, including the name, business, and address of each general partner, and file with the competent authority.[106]

Based on the above discussion, several aspects make the LP and the UCLLS different forms of business. Because the UCLLS is a corporate form rarely used in Taiwan, one

---

[103] *See, e.g.*, Del. Code tit. 6, §§17-101(14), 17-401(a) (2014).
[104] *See* Taiwan Company Act, §13.
[105] *See* Del. Code tit. 6, §17-401(a) (2014).
[106] *Cf.* Del. Code tit. 6, §17-201(a) (2014).

alternative may be to amend the Company Act's UCLLS provisions to make the regime the same as the LP law. However, this may result in creating a new form of company with similar function as the LP but different from the original UCLLS. I believe that different forms of business provide businessmen an opportunity to choose the most appropriate form for their business, for their internal relationship, and for their individual liability toward the creditors of the enterprise. However, the competent authority and the law maker must also take into consideration the cost and effect of creating and maintaining a form of business. There are very few regimes in other countries similar to Taiwan's UCLLS. In contrast, the LP has been widely used in most jurisdictions. To amend the UCLLS provisions may not be workable because there are 11 UCLLSs still operating.[107] Moreover from the internationalization point of view, to adopt a globally recognized and widely used LP regime may be more plausible. Therefore, this chapter suggests Taiwan's competent authority and legislators carefully consider introducing the LP regime into Taiwan.

Major Content of the Proposed Limited Partnership Act

The following discussion is based on the most recent version sent to the Legislative Yuan, drafted by the Ministry of Economic Affairs (MOEA) and approved by the Executive Yuan in 2008. This proposed Limited Partnership Act (PLPA 2008), containing 42 provisions, introduces a new form of business modeled after the Anglo-American legal systems. Particularly mentioned in the PLPA 2008 are the Delaware Limited Partnership Act and the UK Limited Partnership Act.

Currently, the competent authority of the Company Act and the Business Registration Act is the MOEA. Since limited liability is considered as a form of business, it is agreed that the MOEA is suitable to be the competent authority of the PLPA 2008. In Taiwan, although the legislators have the right to propose bills for legislation, it is a common practice that the relevant government agency, the competent authority, or prospective competent authority, submits the proposed Bill to the Legislative Yuan, the congress in Taiwan, for legislation. Although the future version of the Limited Partnership Act may contain different provisions, the main frame of the PLPA 2008 will remain the same. The major features of the PLPA 2008 are discussed below.

Definition, responsible person, and representative of limited partnership
The PLPA 2008 first defines "limited partnership" as a form of business for profit that has legal personality upon registration with competent authority.[108] An LP is composed of at least one unlimited liability partner (general partner) who bears unlimited liability and one limited liability partner who is responsible for the amount of capital he or she agrees to contribute to the LP.[109] In registration, besides the name, the business, residence,

---

[107] There were only 11 UCLLSs as of July 2014. Department of Statistics, Ministry of Finance, Company Registration Information (July 2014).
[108] See PLPA 2008, §3, para. 1.
[109] The PLPA 2008 permits a juridical person to be either a limited liability partner or an unlimited liability partner. See PLPA 2008, §§5 and 6. In order to become an unlimited liability partner of a limited partnership, a limited company must obtain consensus approval from shareholders and

capital, and duration of the LP, information regarding partners, such as contributions of capital and type of liability, and the representative of the LP must be provided in the application.[110] The representative of the LP is elected by majority general partners.[111]

It is important to note that both Taiwan's Company Act and the PLPA 2008 use the term "responsible person," which includes not only directors and general partners, but also managers, supervisors, liquidators, and temporary administrators.[112] The purpose of using "responsible person" is to impose a fiduciary duty of loyalty and a duty of care on the responsible person and thereby include a broader scope of persons than just directors and general partners.[113]

Contribution, return of capital, withdrawal, and transfer of limited partnership interest
Regarding the contribution of capital, different rules apply to different types of partners. General partners have more flexibility to choose type of contribution, such as cash, non-cash assets, credit, and labor. In contrast, the role of a limited liability partner is that of a pure investor who is not involved in management of LP affairs. Therefore, the contribution from limited liability partners is limited to cash and other assets.[114] Once partners have contributed, the capital of the LP cannot be returned to partners unless the obligation of the LP has been discharged or the money for repaying the obligation of the LP has been lodged with the lodgment office of the courthouse.[115] Regarding the transfer of an LP interest, a limited liability partner may transfer the LP interest according to the LP agreement or with approval from all general partners, while a general partner must obtain approval from all the other partners.[116]

It is also important to spell out the rules regarding the addition of new partners and withdrawal from the partnership. The addition of a limited liability partner is subject to approval from all general partners, while the addition of a general partner requires approval from all partners.[117] The PLPA 2008 sets forth two types of withdrawal, i.e., statutory withdrawal and voluntary withdrawal. Statutory withdrawal is when certain events, such as death, dissolution, or exclusion from partnership by more than two-thirds of unlimited liability partners, occur.[118] The occurrence of any of these events will result in withdrawal from the partnership. A partner may also apply to withdraw from the partnership if approved by a majority of the partners.[119]

In case of withdrawal, a general partner will be held continuously liable for the debt of the LP. However, unlike the law of partnership under the Civil Code, a newly joined

---

a company limited by shares must obtain a special resolution from shareholders. *See* PLPA 2008, §6, para. 2.

[110] *See* PLPA 2008, §8.
[111] *See* PLPA 2008, §19, para. 1.
[112] *See* Taiwan Company Act, §8; PLPA 2008, §3, para. 2.
[113] *See* Taiwan Company Act, §23 (fiduciary duty of corporate responsible persons); PLPA 2008, §22 (fiduciary duty of limited partnership). Many jurisdictions focus on directors and general partners.
[114] *See* PLPA 2008, §13.
[115] *See* PLPA 2008, §17; *cf.* UK Limited Partnership Act, Section 4(3).
[116] *See* PLPA 2008, §18.
[117] *See* PLPA 2008, §32.
[118] *See* PLPA 2008, §33.
[119] *See* PLPA 2008, §34.

general partner will not be held liable for the obligation that is incurred before he joins the LP under the PLPA 2008.[120] This rule mainly reflects the new policy in the Uniform Limited Partnership Act 2001 adopted by the National Conference Commissioners on Uniform State Laws, which modifies the liability of the general partner.[121]

Management, duties, and liabilities
In addition to the separate roles of general partners in charge of management of LP affairs and limited liability partners as investors, the focus of the law is on the duties of responsible persons and conflict of interest transactions. The PLPA 2008 provides a huge range of freedom for partners to arrange how the LP is to be managed by setting their rules in the LP agreement. The law also provides supplemental rules if the LP agreement is quiet in several important aspects. For example, the LP affairs shall be conducted by resolution of a majority of the general partners if the LP agreement does not specify how the LP affairs are managed.[122]

It was mentioned earlier that the PLPA 2008 imposes fiduciary duties of care and loyalty on responsible persons. It expressly imposes civil liability on responsible persons who breach the duties. Moreover, similar to the tortious liability of a corporation imposed by the Company Act, the PLPA 2008 imposes joint and several liability on the responsible person and the LP for the damage caused by the responsible person while dealing with the LP affairs.[123]

The PLPA 2008 also regulates the transactions between the representative and the LP. The proposed rule prohibits the representative from representing the LP and himself at the same time. In that situation, another person shall be elected by the majority of other general partners, or if there is only one general partner, by a majority of limited liability partners among them.[124] The PLPA 2008 does not mention whether a transaction between the representative or other general partner and the LP must be approved by a higher voting requirement. It also contains no rule governing whether a general partner shall vote in case of conflict of interest. I believe this must be included in the future LP Bill for the protection of other partners' interests.

Issues Surrounding the Proposed Bill

Although some of the issues have been discussed in the previous sections, major issues surrounding the PLPA 2008 will be identified and summarized here. The first issue is regarding the legal personality of the LP. The PLPA 2008 clearly stated that the LP has legal personality, and one of the major reasons that the MOEA submitted the PLPA 2008 was to distinguish the LP from the SP, which does not have legal personality. Some are still skeptical as to whether it is necessary to create the LP for this purpose. Would this new form of LP be confused with partnership or SP? If the registration of the LP is similar to a partnership or SP, it may cause more confusion. Partnership and LP regimes co-exist in

---

[120] *Cf.* Civil Code, §691.
[121] *See* Uniform Limited Partnership Act 2001 (ULPA), §404.
[122] *See* PLPA 2008, §21.
[123] *See* PLPA 2008, §23; Taiwan Company Act, §23, para. 2.
[124] *See* PLPA 2008, §24.

many jurisdictions. Though there are certain similarities, an LP does have different rules from those of partnership or SP in addition to legal personality. Particularly for venture capitalists, current partnership or SP regimes are not fit for their needs.

This chapter suggests a different thought regarding the legal personality of the LP: Is it possible to have a new type of legal personality that is stronger than that of the unincorporated group but is weaker than that of a company? The reason for this is not necessarily to create a new form of legal personality but to focus on whether we should treat an LP similarly to a company or an unincorporated group. For the protection of the third parties dealing with the LP or creditors of the LP, should the scope of legal capacity of the LP be different from that of a company? What should be the adequate level of supervision from the government in addition to the registration and filing requirements?

The second issue is regarding the nature of the LP. Should an LP be incorporated as a corporate juridical person for profit, or for both profit and non-for-profit? Should Taiwan introduce the LP regime as a new form of business or as a form suitable for broader purposes? The answer from the PLPA 2008 is that an LP is a corporate legal person for profit after incorporation.[125] However, this definition may create arguments as to whether a law firm or accounting firm is established for profit. This issue may not be an issue in the United States or other jurisdictions, but it is an issue in Taiwan. For example, when the Certified Public Accountants Act was amended to create a corporate form of accounting firm, it was not called an "accounting company" but a "juridical person accounting firm." The major reason is that a company is a for-profit corporate legal person according to Article 1 of the Company Act. Although no one can deny that an accounting firm, a law firm, and even a hospital makes money, the government just cannot announce that these entities are created for profit. Therefore, if the proposed Bill identifies that an LP is for profit, it will be arguable that a law firm, accounting firm, or a hospital or clinic can incorporate as an LP.

The third issue is regarding the qualification of the general partner of the LP. One of the major concerns is whether a company can become a general partner of the LP. If so, is there any conflict with the current corporate law policy? The PLPA 2008 has three provisions governing the qualification of a general partner. It first sets forth circumstances to disqualify a person from being a general partner. For example, if a person has been sentenced to one year or more in prison because of committing a crime of fraud, breach of trust, or embezzlement, he is disqualified from being a general partner if the time lapsed after having served the full term of sentence is less than two years.[126] Those circumstances of disqualification mainly apply to an individual rather than a juridical person. The PLPA 2008 then stipulates that a juridical person can be a general partner of an LP and requires the juridical person to designate an individual to execute the LP affairs.[127] Currently, the policy under Article 13 of the Company Act is that a company is prohibited from being a partner of a partnership or an unlimited liability shareholder. To harmonize, the PLPA 2008 clearly sets forth an exemption permitting a company to be the general partner of an LP. It first provides that the restriction of Article 13 of the Company Act does not

---

[125] See PLPA 2008, §3, para. 1.
[126] See PLPA 2008, §4.
[127] See PLPA 2008, §5, para. 3.

apply.[128] It then requires a company to obtain approval from shareholders to be eligible.[129] Although the PLPA 2008 has removed the obstacle and set forth a safeguard to protect investors, I post my concerns here for further consideration. First, is it appropriate for a publicly traded company to become a general partner and bear unlimited liability? Second, is it more appropriate for the competent authority to reconsider the policy that a company is prohibited from bearing unlimited liability because of the investment in a partnership, LP, or unlimited company? If the worry still exists, there should be more reasons to justify why a company can be a general partner in an LP but still is prohibited from being a general partner in an SP or a general partnership.

Taxation is another concern. A reason to employ the LP is that its legal personality will facilitate transactions with others. However, it is hoped that the LP itself does not need to pay tax but instead leaves it for individual partners to pay tax. The tax authority is more conservative on this issue because the LP does have legal personality and therefore there is no reason why it should be exempted from corporate tax. This will be a difficult issue for the government to confront.

5. CONCLUSION

Limited liability companies and companies limited by shares are the two most commonly used corporate forms of business. For unincorporated forms of business, similar to other jurisdictions, sole proprietorships and partnerships are used most frequently. There are two types of partnerships according to the Civil Code, i.e., the general partnership and the SP. The SP is rarely used.

For a partnership, the Civil Code sets forth two sets of rules. One is the compulsory rules that cannot be changed by partnership agreement. For instance, the Civil Code imposes unlimited joint and several liability on partners or general partners of an SP. However, it must be emphasized that Article 681 of the Civil Code imposes the joint liability as supplementary joint liability, which means that an individual partner is liable only when the partnership assets are insufficient to pay its debt. The creditors have to seek payment or to recover damages from the partnership enterprise before they can ask individual partners to be responsible. The Supreme Court of Taiwan has long recognized the litigation capacity of a partnership enterprise as an unincorporated group or non-juridical body according to Article 40 of the Taiwan Code of Civil Procedure. Creditors usually will sue the partnership enterprise and list all partners as defendants. Without proving that the partnership enterprise has insufficient funds to pay its debt, creditors cannot sue partners without suing the partnership enterprise.

There also are compulsory rules regarding the internal relationships of the partnership. For example, Article 668 of the Civil Code defines the ownership of partnership assets. Although in practice a partnership's assets can be distinguished from the assets of partners, the Civil Code establishes that the ownership of partnership assets is ownership-in-common (i.e., all partnership assets are held in common by all partners). Another example

---

[128] *See* PLPA 2008, §6, para. 1.
[129] *See* PLPA 2008, §6, para. 2.

is Article 667 of the Civil Code, which requires the assessment of a non-cash contribution in order to determine the value of capital contributed by a partner. Other compulsory rules address the duty and standard of care of a partner, the resignation and removal of a partner in charge of the partnership affairs, the right of a non-executive partner to inspect the financial status and books of the partnership, the transfer of partnership interests (shares), the right of a partner's creditor against the partnership, removal of a partner and addition of a new partner, and dissolution and liquidation.

The other set of rules set forth in the Civil Code allows partners to arrange their internal relationships but also provides default rules in case the partnership agreement is silent on one or more aspects. These non-compulsory rules cover the obligation of a partner to contribute additional capital, the power and procedure to deal with partnership affairs, voting power, distribution of profits, profit-sharing and cost-sharing ratios, and compensation of partners.

There have been voices from within the business industry asking the government to introduce the LP as a new form for businesses.[130] The form would be particularly well suited for venture capitalists. Venture capital firms are usually structured as LPs or LLCs in the United States, and this tradition and practice have built up a custom that is familiar to the venture capitalists. Though there is a demand for legislation, there still are some issues and concerns that have not been resolved since the MOEA first introduced the LP Bill to the Legislative Yuan in 2004. Among the issues discussed above, the tax concern could be one of the most difficult issues to resolve to the satisfaction of both the tax authority and the venture capitalists.

---

[130] *See e.g.*, Liu Shao-Liang (劉紹樑), Youxian Hehuo Fa Caoan Qianque Linmen Yijiao (有限合夥法草案欠缺臨門一腳) (*A Need to Push Limited Partnership Bill*), Taiwan Banker, at 22–27 (July 2014).

27. Brazilian alternatives to the corporate form of organization

André Antunes Soares de Camargo

1. INTRODUCTION

Before doing business in any country, business people need to have some understanding of the local environment, including economic, cultural, and legal aspects. Investors need to have information, confidence, and at least a basic idea of the hurdles and risks of doing business in a different scenario. In addition, each jurisdiction presents a list of options to accommodate business projects providing different pros and cons depending on many different factors.

Doing business in Brazil is no different from any other country. An interested investor needs to consider many options and alternatives before making an investment decision. The aim of this chapter is to provide a broad view of the Brazilian alternatives to the corporate form of organization. This task is challenging, we can already advance, since the number of corporations in Brazil is extremely low in comparison with other business association forms.[1] Therefore, I will be presenting to the reader the choices of most Brazilian and foreign investors in the following pages.

This chapter is structured in the following manner. After this brief introduction, I will discuss the main characteristics of doing business in Brazil, a necessary step before venturing into the local environment. Then I will analyze the most important contractual forms that an investor may consider as a first move into the Brazilian market, which I believe is a relevant way to learn more closely the specific hurdles and opportunities with a local party. Subsequently, I will discuss the main business association forms under

---

[1] Data are limited, except as to the number of publicly held corporations. According to the Brazilian Securities and Exchange Commission (*Comissão de Valores Mobiliários*—"CVM"), by the end of 2013 there were just 647 publicly held corporations in Brazil (www.cvm.gov.br/port/relgest/Relatorio_Anual_CVM_2013.pdf, accessed on 10.04.2014). It is common sense among Brazilian lawyers and scholars that a corporation (*sociedade anônima*) in Brazil, either closely or publicly held, is expensive, both to incorporate and to comply with all existing corporate rules set forth by the Brazilian Law of Corporations (Law n. 6,404, of December 15, 1976, as amended—"LSA"). Brazilian corporations need to have at least two officers, and there are mandatory rules for having corporate decisions published in newspapers (more disclosure than other business forms), as well as corporate books to be organized and always updated. Brazilian publicly held corporations need to follow several listing requirements as far as corporate governance principles are concerned (equality, transparency, accountability, and corporate responsibility). The list of these companies can be found at www.bmfbovespa.com.br/Cias-Listadas/Empresas-Listadas/BuscaEmpresaListada.aspx?idioma=pt-br, accessed on 10.04.2014. It is also recommended to search through a new official website from the Brazilian federal government to assist new entrepreneurs in Brazil, with detailed guidelines about doing business in Brazil in Portuguese, Spanish, and English as well (www.portaldoempreendedor.gov.br/, accessed on 10.12.2014).

Brazilian laws and consider investor options in establishing a different and separate legal entity, which leads to different rules (rights and obligations) and possible reduction of autonomy but synergy gains as well. Before reaching my conclusions, I will present the main changes that two Bills of Law currently under discussion by the Brazilian Congress will possibly cause to this subject matter.

2. DOING BUSINESS IN BRAZIL

There are two relevant issues to be considered before investing in Brazil: taxation and bureaucracy. Both of them will certainly influence the choice of the business form that an investor will choose. Although there is a strong reaction against the problems associated with these two issues, it is extremely important to conduct a tax planning analysis to decide which alternative (e.g. direct investment, joint venturing, creating a business association with a local partner, or using an investment fund vehicle) is preferable.

The Brazilian tax system is complex, and there is not much room for aggressive tax planning since the Brazilian tax authorities are currently imposing the so-called "business purpose test" for the analysis of tax avoidance or reduction schemes, in addition to the worldwide lawfulness requirement.[2] The cross-reference tax systems do actually work efficiently in Brazil as well. Also because of the complexity of the system (e.g. federal, state, and local taxes may apply for the activity, revenue, and profits of a legal entity), investors in Brazil do actually spend considerable money, human resources, and time to comply with all tax rules and to file the necessary forms.

The taxation and bureaucracy hurdles are confirmed by the Brazil analysis in a highly regarded study carried out by the World Bank.[3] As an example, to start a business in Brazil requires compliance with no fewer than 13 procedures, which can take more than 100 days altogether. Moreover, in order to comply with all Brazilian tax rules, it takes approximately 2,600 hours and a total tax rate of around 68.3 percent of the entire business revenue. Agreeing or not with the methodology of such study, the comparative view of Brazil with other countries leads us to the preliminary conclusion that taxation and bureaucracy are the two primary concerns of an investor. Having these issues in mind, the choice of the business form will certainly be more adequate and efficient according to the overall business strategy.

---

[2] In Brazil, tax planning is legal if the following criteria are observed: (a) there is a business purpose; (b) the essence of the planning corresponds to the form of its legal instruments; and (c) such planning is not a misrepresentation/simulation. Inspired by the US jurisprudence and not clearly set forth in the Brazilian tax law (but developed by the Brazilian tax authorities), the business purpose test requires that any tax planning has to pursue an economic objective other than just tax reduction or avoidance. There is a clear analogy to the "abuse of right" idea prescribed in Article 187 CC (Civil Code), which provides that an illicit act is committed by someone who has a specific right and exercises it in a way that clearly exceeds the limits imposed by its economic or social objectives, good faith, and custom.

[3] See http://doingbusiness.org/data/exploreeconomies/brazil, accessed on 10.04.2014.

Contractual Forms

Brazil has a civil law system derived from the Roman-Continental European legal tradition, that is to say, its most important sources of law come from statutes and rules enacted by the legislative power. Basically, in order to enter into any contract according to the Brazilian laws one has to follow the rules and principles set forth by the Brazilian Civil Code of 2002 (Law n. 10.406, of January 10, 2002—"CC"), a federal statute that is enforceable in the entire country. The rules for business contracts are prescribed in Articles 412 to 886 CC.

Court decisions are just studied and interpreted for argumentation purposes, with the only exception being the so-called *súmulas vinculantes* exceptionally approved by the Brazilian Supreme Court (*Supremo Tribunal Federal*), which gives binding effects on decisions handed down by lower courts. The work of legal scholars is also important in the interpretation of many legal institutes, mainly those with broad and undetermined concepts that will only be completely understood on a case-by-case basis. The role of uses and practices (custom) is not as important as in common-law systems, but they are normally considered in court disputes where the statutory or contractual rules either do not exist or there is an interpretation gap in the case.

Although there are multiple alternatives to build a contractual relationship,[4] the four most common contractual structures in Brazil preferred by local investors, but especially foreign ones, are the following: collaboration contracts, *aliança*, business groups, and investment funds.

Collaboration contracts

"Collaboration contracts" are those structures that fall between doing business directly (exchange contracts) and establishing a relationship of partners, splitting results (e.g. profits) and sharing decision power as a rule. In other words, a collaboration contract would be a long-lasting relationship between two separate and independent business entities or individuals. It creates a mutual dependence and influence, especially because of the considerable high specific investments that may be required to support the ongoing contractual relationship. Since a foreign investor does not know the new local business environment, it is very common to start with a collaboration contract with a local entity or individual, and then decide to move on to a business association form that will probably be more long-lasting and stable in the future.[5]

Examples of these collaboration contracts are: (a) *comissão* (Articles 693 to 709 CC); (b) *agência e distribuição* (Articles 710 to 721 CC); (c) *franquia* (Law n. 8,955, of December 15, 1994—franchising); (d) *consórcio* (Articles 278 and 279 LSA); (e) *arrendamento mercantil* (Laws n. 6.099, of September 12, 1974, 11.649, of April 4, 2008, as amended—leasing); (f) *concessão comercial* (Law n. 6.728, of November 29, 1979, as

---

[4] According to Article 425 CC, it is permitted to enter into non-typical contracts, provided that the general rules of this Code are observed.

[5] Business association forms in Brazil have more mandatory legal rules, leaving less discretion for the parties to organize their contractual relationship. Collaborative contracts, on the other hand, are more open to case-by-case rules designed by the parties, considering that their effects on third parties are lower than the ones by regular business association forms.

amended—automobile distribution). For each of these collaboration contracts there is a specific legal regime mandatory by law, completed by the terms and conditions detailed in each contractual instrument.

Aliança

Aliança is a growing alternative contractual structure in Brazil, mainly for important projects with the participation of large companies making significant investments. While it is not a contract prescribed or regulated by law, projects requiring high investment, especially for infrastructure, normally need complex arrangements among parties with solid reputations. These contracts are normally long, carefully drafted and negotiated with a multidisciplinary team involving specialized lawyers and experts from many areas. They typically include detailed and sophisticated dispute resolution procedures.

Aliança was first used in Brazil in the 1990s, especially in oil, gas, and home construction projects, for which the participation of many companies with different expertise was necessary. It is a private cooperation model among companies that remain independent but share technology and other resources to develop a project. Clearly needing corporate governance mechanisms to keep it operational, this model aims at circumventing traditional formalities, bureaucracies, and mandatory rules that are imposed on other contractual forms in Brazil, focusing instead on mutual trust and risk sharing, expertise, control, and effort sharing among its participants.

Business groups

Creating and participating in a business group in Brazil is very common. Business activity in Brazil is normally conducted by legal entities that are part of business groups for many historical, cultural, and legal reasons. Grouping is a long-lasting tradition in Brazil, and it is rare to see a single-unit legal entity that manages to succeed in a determined field. Grouping in Brazil is incentivized by law (mainly tax law), and there is a broad freedom to carry on the so-called related-party transactions inside Brazilian business groups.

Inspired by German and US laws on the subject matter, grouping in Brazil is a natural result of the commercial relationships among companies that combine resources or efforts to pursue their activities at the same time they preserve their separate legal existences. In Brazil, there are two different types of groups: contractual (*de direito*) or factual (*de fato*) groups. While the first ones are ruled by Articles 265 to 277 LSA, they are formally created by a contact (*convenção grupal*), by means of which companies comprising a business group may pursue a common objective. There is a joint administrative unit in practice, and the governing instrument is registered with the Registry of Commerce.

Grupos de fato, in turn, do not require any formal contact among their participants, which just maintain corporate relationships, such as control or relevant equity participation of one legal entity in another. There are just a few mandatory rules that need to be followed, mainly on information that must be disclosed in the financial documents (investments in controlling and controlled companies—Article 243 LSA), on accounting, and on the liability of management and the controlling company for losses that may take place in the event that one company is favored over another in the same business group, therefore causing harm to minority shareholders or creditors (these related-party transactions need to have equal terms and conditions or adequate compensation payment—Article 245 LSA).

Investment funds

Finally, the use of investment funds is extremely interesting and common in Brazil. According to the Comissão de Valores Mobiliários—CVM (the Securities Commission of Brazil), in 2013 there were 14,278 registered investment funds in Brazil with almost BRL 2.5 trillion as net assets to manage.[6] The use of this alternative has been increasing in recent years, and it is very common to see the participation of at least one investment fund in most recent local and cross-border M&A transactions. The CVM Rule n. 409/2004, as amended, sets forth rules for the setting up, managing, functioning, and disclosure of information by Brazilian investment funds.

Investment funds are valuable instruments for channeling resources by investors that seek stable returns with liquidity and minimum risk. They are mechanisms organized for obtaining and investing funds in the financing market without the need of a bank to intermediate. They offer a collective form of investment with several tax incentives mainly for individuals. Investment funds in Brazil do not have a separate legal existence (no separate assets), and therefore all assets pertain to the investors. Nowadays, there are several different investment funds depending upon the kind of the investment or the incentives for the development of a certain economic sector.[7]

Business Association Forms

According to Article 44 CC, private legal entities in Brazil may take the following forms: (a) *associação*; (b) *sociedades*; (c) *fundações*; (d) *organizações religiosas* (religious organizations); (e) *partidos politicos* (political parties); or (f) *empresas individuais de responsabilidade limitadas* ("EIRELI"). While the others have to be not-for-profit organizations, *sociedades* and EIRELIs may distribute profits to their partners and are the forms relevant to the discussion in this chapter.

Sociedade

The *sociedade* is the most important legal entity in Brazil to carry on a for-profit business activity capable of distributing profits to its stockholders. One needs at least two individuals and/or other legal entities to form a *sociedade*. There are two main categories of *sociedades* in Brazil: those without separate legal existences (*sociedade em comum* and *sociedade em conta de participação*) and those with separate legal existences (*simples*, *em nome coletivo*, *em comandita simples*, *em comandita por ações*, *cooperativa*, and, finally, the most preferred one in Brazil: *sociedade limitada*).

The *sociedade em comum* (CC Articles 986 to 990) deals with situations in which the corporate documents of any other *sociedade* have not yet been registered. In this case, the legal relationship exists between the partners, and the common assets destined for such business are already subject to claims for possible debts with third parties. After these assets are seized, the personal assets of these partners would be claimed to pay such a

---

[6] See www.cvm.gov.br/port/relgest/Relatorio_Anual_CVM_2013.pdf, accessed on 10.04.2014.

[7] Examples of investment funds in Brazil: (a) Real estate (*Fundo de Investimento Imobiliário*); (b) Credit rights (*Fundo de Investimento em Direitos Creditórios*); (c) Equity (*Fundo de Investimento em Participações*); and (d) Emerging Companies (*Fundo de Investimento em Empresas Emergentes*).

debt, which is much better than a 100 percent direct liability, which would be incurred in a direct investment.

In the *sociedade em conta de participação* (CC Articles 991 to 996), the business activity is solely carried on by one of the partners (*ostensivo*) in its own name and at its own risk, and the other party (*participante*) does not appear to third parties, but may participate in the distribution of profits. Similar to a limited partner under U.S. law, this "participant" partner may not take part in the relationships with third parties, otherwise it may be held jointly liable for the company's debts. This *sociedade* is very common in some markets, such as in real estate construction and in hotel/flat renting, and is legal under Brazilian law, provided that specific accounting and tax rules are fully observed by all parties involved.

Although they all have a separate legal existence, it is not worth devoting much space to *sociedades simples* (Articles 997 to 1038 CC), *em nome coletivo* (Articles 1039 to 1044 CC), *comandita simples* (Articles 1045 to 1051 CC), or *comandita por ações* (Articles 280 to 284 LSA), since they are extremely rare (if there are any nowadays) for many reasons. They either do not provide the partners with limited liability, which is a great risk that is normally not accepted by investors, require a 100 percent quorum for most business decisions, or bring different types of investors, one of which is jointly liable for business debts. That is to say, they are not interesting at all, especially in comparison with the other business association forms available in accordance with the Brazilian law.

The *sociedade cooperativa*, in turn, is regulated both by Articles 1093 to 1096 CC and by Law n. 5.764, of December 16, 1971. Businesses in this form may not distribute profits (just repayment of commercial contracts made on behalf of the partners), may have capital or not, may set a minimum number of partners, may limit the amount of the quotas that each partner can hold, do not allow the transfer of the quotas to third parties other than the other partners even *post mortem*, follow a "one share, one vote" principle regardless of the amount of the capital held, may render services to their partners (e.g. marketing, distribution, training), and do not divide reserves among the partners in the event of a company's dissolution. This association form is normally used in rural areas, and it actually is a venture to help promote the businesses of the partners themselves as a "marketing engine" for these individual business individuals or small legal entities.

Finally, the most preferred business association form in Brazil is the *sociedade limitada* ("LTDA") (Articles 1052 to 1087 CC). The LTDA represents the majority of the business forms in Brazil for many reasons. First of all, it allows limited liability of its partners, provided that all capital is paid in (otherwise, all partners are jointly liable for the payment of the remaining capital, but always limited to the total amount of the capital). Secondly, the LTDA may be chosen by small, medium-sized, and large businesses, with not so many mandatory rules imposed by the Brazilian laws. That is, there is a considerable freedom to design the company organization and procedures depending on the stage of the business to be developed. In addition, there is no need to pay in any capital initially, and partners may simply subscribe to capital and pay it at a later date. Only one individual is necessary to manage a LTDA, and he or she may be one of the partners as well. There are not so many formal procedures to carry on business decisions, such as to call for and to have meetings among the partners, or to have financial statements published for third parties, which reduces the routine expenses of this business association form.

On the other hand, a LTDA is not recommended over a corporation (*sociedade anônima*) in case there is a need for investments through capital markets or issuance of private securities, such as debentures. These are investment alternatives just available to corporations in Brazil. Moreover, a LTDA does not allow the partners to have different kinds of investors (capital, services, or even preferred rights in addition to the regular financial rights for profits, for example). In addition to that, there is not as much freedom for partners' side agreements as is allowed for shareholders' agreements in corporations (Article 118 LSA). A very important rule to be considered in a LTDA is the one requiring a quorum of 75 percent to implement most of the decisions that will cause an amendment to the Articles of Association of the LTDA (Article 1076, I CC), creating barriers, for example, for many capital structures such as three partners of equal equity holdings, or even two partners with a distribution of quotas other than on a 75 percent–25 percent basis, causing the need for a unanimous decision in most cases.

EIRELI

EIRELI (created by Law n. 12.441, of July 11, 2011) may only be set up by a sole individual having to pay in advance minimum capital in the amount equivalent to 100 times the Brazilian federal minimum wage. The individual may be an owner of only one EIRELI. The public policy behind this alternative was to bring individuals from informality into an option that brings limited liability, separation of assets and risks, and for which a second partner (normally not a real participating one) would not be necessary. Before EIRELI, the only way to have a structure owned by a single individual was through the very exceptional use of the corporation form (Articles 251 to 253 LSA) or a temporary 180-day *sociedade* (Article 1033, IV CC). However, this noble idea has not yet achieved its goals for many reasons, mainly because of the high initial capital required.

3. CURRENT DISCUSSIONS

There currently are two Bills being discussed by the Brazilian Congress that may cause some changes to the options discussed above. Both of them include the idea of reinstating a commercial code (this time based more on principles than rules), which was partially revoked by the CC in 2002 (the former Commercial Code was enacted in 1850). Regardless of the need or not for a separate commercial code to regulate business association forms in Brazil, it is important to present some of the ongoing discussions on the subject matter.

The first Bill, Bill of Law n. 1,572/2011, initiated by the Brazilian House of Representatives, sets forth in Article 122 that a for-profit business activity may choose among the following forms: (a) *sociedade anônima*; (b) *sociedade limitada*; (c) *sociedade em nome coletivo*; (d) *sociedade em comandita simples*; and (e) *sociedade em comandita por ações*. The current *sociedade simples* would then disappear, as would the *sociedade em comum*, the latter replaced by the *sociedade regular* (Articles 132 to 137), which may have activities even before its Articles of Association are registered with the competent public registry.

One of the main changes that this Bill seeks is a reduction of the quorum of the LTDA from the current 75 percent threshold to a 50 percent +1 vote, which used to be the rule before the CC. Most Brazilian business people and legal practitioners favor this change. There is also an idea to allow the LTDA to have preferred quotas and to be able to issue private securities, such as debentures, which would enable it to attract more investments without converting to a *sociedade anônima*. Another objective of this Bill is to reduce the daily formalities (and, of course, the expenses) of running an LTDA. Lastly, the Bill tries to regulate the dissolution process of an LTDA, which may be provoked either by a dissenting partner or because of an exclusion, and provides details on the calculation of the payments to be made. This Bill, however, has longer and more detailed rules than the CC, which would obviously lead to several discussions among congressional representatives and corporate law experts. The main question is: will these changes actually make the LTDA form more attractive to investors?

The second proposed piece of legislation is Bill of Law n. 487/2013, proposed by the Brazilian Senate. According to its Article 184, there would be only four different business association forms in Brazil, namely: (a) *sociedade limitada*; (b) *sociedade anônima*; (c) *sociedade em nome coletivo*; and (d) *sociedade em conta de participação*. This Bill is very similar to the previous one, except for its more detailed regulation of each topic. One important difference is one of the subspecies of LTDAs that is created, the *sociedade de profissão intelectual*, to which the partners would be able to contribute services rather than just capital. As set forth in Articles 324 to 335, this business association form would only be used by partners engaged in professional practices, always respecting specific norms of each profession, and could not be used to carry on any activities besides those allowed by the professional association. This alternative may have just one partner or more, provided that any partner must be certified to carry on such profession by the respective association. The partners would be jointly liable for the company's debts.

4. CONCLUSIONS

It is reasonable to conclude that Brazil is currently trying to improve its business environment in many ways. Besides the attempt to reduce corruption in Brazil (e.g. Law n. 12.846, of August 1, 2013—the Brazilian Anticorruption Act), reduce bureaucracy (there are several projects trying to remove the hurdles to setting up, operating, and dissolving legal entities), and organize the tax laws and other laws related to business activities,[8] Brazil offers a number of good and safe alternatives to the corporate form of organization.

LTDAs and investment funds are the preferred forms today and will probably continue as such in the near future. Although a comparative view, which is proposed by the brief comments made in this chapter, does not seek to discourage investors from trusting in corporations or other business association forms, the Brazilian legal rules create many incentives to choose the LTDA, at least as a starting form for newcomers. Corporations in Brazil would only be recommended if there are several partners that will have a need

---

[8] Another important discussion is how to apply the "piercing the corporate veil doctrine" in Brazil as set forth in Article 50 CC (among other rules spread throughout Brazilian law). There are several cases in Brazil in which this doctrine is not correctly applied by the judiciary, creating an additional risk for doing business mainly through an LTDA. There are several Bills of law currently under discussion by the Brazilian Congress trying to regulate such a theory, which has important but aggressive effects in practice. E.g. Bill of Law n. 3.401, of 2008; Articles 77 to 79 Bill of Law n. 8,046, of 2010, both initiated by the Brazilian House of Representatives.

for a more stable structure with corporate governance rules that are mandatory by law, as well as a need for capital from capital markets or private placements.

It is also important to follow the discussions of both the previously mentioned Bills of law, since they may cause some important changes that likely will affect this analysis. The cost-benefit analysis that is mandatory in a business plan may be altered depending on the changes that may take place.

Notwithstanding the hurdles of doing business in Brazil, I am sure that many opportunities are on the table for any local and foreign investor interested in an emerging market full of possibilities. And choosing the adequate form is a very relevant preparatory step.

BIBLIOGRAPHY

Borba, José Eduardo Tavares (2012), Direito Societário, 13th edition, Ed. Renovar, Rio de Janeiro, Brazil.
Britcham Brasil (2005), Doing Business in Brazil, The British Chamber of Commerce and Industry in Brazil, São Paulo, Brazil.
Enei, José Virgílio Lopes (2007), Project finance, Ed. Saraiva, São Paulo, Brazil.
Franco, Beatriz, Kalansky, Daniel, Soares, Bianca & Vella, Rodrigo V. (ed.) (2008), International Business Transactions with Brazil, Juris Publishing, Inc., New York, USA.
Freitas, Ricardo de Santos (2006), Natureza jurídica dos fundos de investimento, Ed. Quartier Latin, São Paulo, Brazil.
Gonçalves Neto, Alfredo de Assis (2012), Direito de Empresa, 4th edition, Ed. Revista dos Tribunais, São Paulo, Brazil.
Grego, Marco Aurélio (2011), Planejamento tributário, 3rd edition, Ed. Dialética, São Paulo, Brazil.
Lamy Filho, Alfredo and Pedreira, José Luiz Bulhões (coord.) (2009), Direito das Companhias, Ed. Forense, Rio de Janeiro, Brazil.
Martins de Carvalho, Mário Tavernard (2012), Regime jurídico dos fundos de investimentos, Ed. Quartier Latin, São Paulo, Brazil.
Verçosa, Haroldo Malheiros Duclerc (2014), Direito Comercial—Sociedades—Vol. 2—Teoria Geral das Sociedades—As sociedades em espécie do Código Civil, 3rd edition, Ed. Revista dos Tribunais, São Paulo, Brazil.

Index

Abrams, H. 156
accounting, capital account *see* capital accounts in limited liability companies and partnerships, basic capital account accounting
accounting firm's liability for misleading financial reports, Taiwan 458–60
Adams, E. 292, 293, 365
Afsharipour, A. 429–46
agency
   external, and binding the firm *see* common-law perspectives on binding the firm, and external agency
   and liability, India 439
   power, China 403
Aizawa, T. 376
Albert, S. 365
Alchian, A. 48
Alexander, G. 279
Alexander, K. 368, 369
alternative entities *see* individual countries; limited liability headings; partnerships
Altman, P. 11, 23, 24
Anderson, E. 45
"apparent authority" doctrine 84, 87–8, 91
Ashforth, B. 45, 46
asset protection limited liability companies, attacking 129–44
   affirmative asset partitioning 129–30
   bankrupt member's rights 134
   bankruptcy law 133–6, 144
   charging order in non-business and single-owner LLCs 130–31
   charging order in original partnership context 129–30
   charging orders and transferee rights 129–33
   contract rights 134
   corporate salary payments to principal shareholders as disguised and non-deductible dividends 132
   creative enforcement of charging orders 132
   family LLCs and fraudulent transfer law 136
   fraudulent transfer law 136–7, 144
   fraudulent transfer law, transfer occurring before debt 137
   levying on entire membership interest 133
   management rights 131
   personal performance exception and bankruptcy 135–6
   statutory reform and choice of law 144
   turnover orders 132
   voting powers 134
asset protection limited liability companies, attacking, reverse veil piercing 137–43
   asset transfers from owner to company 139–40
   charging order remedy 139–40, 141–2
   control and stakeholder equities 142–3
   fraud and creditor knowledge 140–42
   inadequate capitalization 142
   involuntary creditors 141
   non-debtor members and property protection 143
   normal piercing grounds 138
   shareholder or member's debt, corporation or LLC liability for 138–9
   veil piercing overview 137–8
assets
   and estimated depreciation 171–2
   "marked to market" 172, 177
   securitization, business trusts 275
   Taiwan partnerships 452–3
Axberg, R. 280–95
Ayres, I. 49, 50, 386

Babson, E. 255
Bainbridge, S. 108, 110
Baker, D. 171
Baldwin, S. 148
Bankman, J. 159
bankruptcy
   counterparty financial distress *see* counterparty limited liability company's financial distress, mitigating impact, bankruptcy
   law, asset protection 133–6, 144
   member's rights 134
   UK partnership options 371
   see also liquidations
Banks, R. 359, 364
bargaining
   close corporations, Japan 377–8
   complementarities between legal forms, Japan 385–6, 387

481

limitations, Delaware contractual freedom, end of unlimited 12
Bartlett, R. 387
Barzuza, M. 264
Becerra, M. 369
Belyayev, K. 414
benefit corporations
  and social enterprise law *see* state laboratories and social enterprise law, benefit corporations and benefit limited liability companies
  statutes 305
Berle, A. 16, 24
Berry, E. 357–73, 438
Bhattacharyya, S. 377
Bishop, C. 83, 85, 86, 88, 89, 93, 253, 263, 320, 322
Blackett-Ord, M. 359
Blair, M. 49
Blumberg, P. 100, 110
Borden, B. 147–67
Bork, D. 47, 49
Boxx, K. 47
Boyd, C. 107
Brakman Reiser, D. 255, 256
Branson, D. 41, 55–69, 339
Brazil, alternatives to corporate form of organization 471–9
  Aliança contracts (projects requiring high investment) 474
  bureaucracy problems 472
  business association forms 475–7
  business groups, contractual and factual 474
  "business purpose test" and tax avoidance analysis 472
  Civil Code 473
  collaboration contracts 473–4
  Commercial Code, current discussions 477–8
  contractual forms 473–5
  dissenters and exclusions 478
  EIRELI (sole individual corporation structure) 477
  investment funds 475, 476–8
  liabilities in *sociedade* 475–6
  private legal entities 475–7
  profit distribution 475–6
  sociedade 475–7
  sociedade limitada (LTDA) 476–8
  taxation 472
Brewer, C. 227–51, 253
Bromberg, A. 101, 214
Bruner, C. 264
Brunson, S. 162
Bugg-Levine, A. 261
Burdick, F. 74

Busch, D. 81
business organization law and family law 46–9
business registration, Taiwan 449, 450–51, 454
business termination constraints, UK 362–3
business trusts 268–79
  Britain to Massachusetts 269–70
  common law to statutory trusts 270–73
  Delaware business trust statute 271–2
  Employee Retirement Income Security Act (ERISA) 276
  future research 278–9
  Investment Company Act 271
  liability of limited liability entities 103
  Massachusetts trusts, advantages of 270, 273
  origins 269–73
  personal liability limitations 272
  Securities and Exchange Commission (SEC) study 271
  as separate legal entity 272
  as special purpose entity (SPE) 275
  Trust Indenture Act 274
  trustees' fiduciary duties of good faith and fair dealing 272
  UK Bubble Act 269
business trusts, modern 273–8
  asset securitization 275
  pension and mutual funds 276–7
  pooled asset management 276–7
  pooled asset management, asset partitioning 277
  pooled asset management, as Maryland corporations 277
  property holding 274–5
  risk management 275–6
  tax advantages 277–8
Butler, W. 423, 425, 426
buyouts
  capital accounts in limited liability companies and partnerships 173–5, 178
  see also mergers

Callison, W. 70–80, 129, 216, 253, 254, 255, 256, 257, 258, 260, 263
Camargo, A. 471–9
Canada
  partnership tax system 161–3
  U.S.-Canada tax treaty amendments 163–5
capital accounts in limited liability companies and partnerships 168–86
  balance sheet and basic accounting principles 169
  owners' individual capital accounts 169
capital accounts in limited liability companies and partnerships, basic capital account accounting 170–75, 176, 178

assets and estimated depreciation 171–2
assets "marked to market" 172, 177
basic maintenance 170–75, 182
cash transactions 170–71
current distributions 175, 178
current versus liquidating distributions and buyouts, confusion over 174–5
equity accounts, mixture of contents 170–72, 175
liquidation of business 173–4, 182
liquidations and buyouts 173–5
loss sharing 173–4
misunderstandings and unintended consequences 173–5
negative account shock to service partner 173–4, 182–3
noncash assets and transfers 171–2
opposite-signed capital accounts 173–4
primacy of intent 170
services contributed by owner 172, 174
capital accounts in limited liability companies and partnerships, federal income tax significance 180–85
"at risk" rules 181
clarity in agreements, lack of 184–5
disregarded allocation, reallocation of 181–2
drafting challenges and strategies 184
"forced" allocation provisions 184
origins of binding tax rules 180–81
owner's interest in firm, in accordance with 183–4
"passive loss" rules 181
"qualified income offset" 183
safe harbor regulations 182–3
Section 704(b) and ways to defend tax allocations among owners 180, 181–4
special allocations rules 180–81
Subchapter K 180
substantial economic effect and strict capital account observance 181, 182–3
capital accounts in limited liability companies and partnerships, statutory default rules 175–80
buyout provisions (RUPA) 178
Delaware Limited Liability Company Act 180
distributions before dissolution 179
limited liability companies 179
liquidating distributions and RUPA's capital account reconciliation requirement 177–8
partnership liquidations 177
partnerships 175–8
Revised Uniform Limited Liability Company Act (RULLCA) 179

Revised Uniform Partnership Act (RUPA) maintenance rules 176–7
set aside conditions 177
and small businesses 177
capital-oriented corporations, Russian alternatives *see* Russia, alternatives to capital-oriented corporations
care, fiduciary duty *see* fiduciary duty of care
Carey, S. 150
Carney, W. 149
Cary, W. 259
Case, M. 48
Cauble, E. 160
charging orders, asset protection limited liability companies 129–33, 139–40, 141–2
charitable uses
low-profit limited liability companies (L3Cs), "charitable or education purposes" 258
nonprofit *see* nonprofit and charitable uses of limited liability companies
Chernoff, D. 253
Child, J. 365
China, partnerships and partnership law 390–411
agency power 403
business scope 401, 402
contemporary China 396–401
contracting out 402
court cases 406–10
court cases, political factors, lack of 409
critical aspects 401–6
Cultural Revolution 393–4
damages remedies 405
default rules 402
definition 390
double-taxation of partnership investors 396
duty of loyalty 408
economic reform 394
FDI introduction and conditions 394, 399–400
fiduciary duties and fiduciary litigation 404–5, 408
foreign private equity funds 397, 400
foreign-invested partnership 398–401, 409
general partnership 397, 399, 401, 403–5, 408
General Principles of the Civil Law of the PRC (GPCL) 394, 395, 396, 408
history and evolution 392–6
immutable rules 402
joint operation enterprises 394
legal "partnership" adjudication 407–8
legal personality and SAIC registration 401–2
limited liability 403–4

limited partnership 397–8, 399, 401, 403, 404, 405, 408
liquidations 395, 405
management rights 402–3, 405
National Social Security Fund 400
partnership interest transferability 403
partnership registrations and registered capital 396–7
post-1904 extra-legal partnership norms 393
PRC Company Law 394, 398–9, 404
PRC National Development and Reform Commission (NDRC) 400
PRC Partnership Enterprise Law 395, 401–6, 408–9
PRC Partnership Enterprise Law, deficiencies 395–6
PRC State Administration of Industry and Commerce (SAIC) 395, 396, 398, 399, 401–2, 408, 409
pre-legalization partnership forms 392–3
private economy and capital contributions 401
profit distribution 407–8
qualified foreign institutional investor (QFII) program 400
Qualified Foreign Limited Partnership (QFLP) pilot initiative 392, 398, 399–401, 409
Reform and Opening to the Outside World program 394
special general partnership 398, 399, 401, 403, 404, 409
Su Qi v. Li Zhanfei 407–8
sub-national pilot programs 399–400
taxation 396, 401, 405–6
Chrisman, R. 14, 18, 147
Clark, R. 138
Clark, W. 254, 255
Clarke, D. 391, 395, 406, 408
Cleveland, S. 339, 340, 341
Cochran, S. 393
Collins, M. 243
common law
  business entity governance 199
  business trusts 270–73
  counteracting arrest of 310
  liability of limited liability entities 105–6, 108–9
common-law perspectives on binding the firm, and external agency 81–96
  "apparent authority" doctrine 84, 87–8, 91
  Delaware LLC statute 86, 88–9, 93–5
  delegation permission 94–5
  formal statutory reforms 90–93
  freedom of contract principle 89–90
  general partnership 82–3, 86
  inherent agency power 85–6
  limited liability company 86–90
  manager-managed LLC 87, 91, 92
  member-managed LLC 91, 92
  non-partner agents 84–5
  non-statutory solutions 93–5
  North Carolina statute 92–3
  operating agreements, impact of restrictions on authority in 87–90, 92
  partnership authority 82–3
  partnership positional power 83–5, 87, 90–92
  potential solutions 90–95
  Revised Uniform Limited Liability Company Act (RULLCA) 90–91, 93
  self-dealing transactions 92
  stickiness problems 93
  tax classification for LLCs as partnerships 86
  third parties dealing with a partner 82–3, 84, 87–9, 91, 92–3
  Uniform Partnership Act 82–3, 84–5, 86, 87
compensation
  corporate executives excessive pay packages, concerns over, Delaware 340
  corporate salary payments to principal shareholders as disguised and non-deductible dividends 132
  taxation 158–9
  wage claims of employees' liabilities 111–12
competition concerns, India, limited liability partnerships 432, 434, 436–7
Conaway, A. 104
conflict of interest
  Delaware, reintroduction of fiduciary concepts 65, 68
  Japan, limited liability companies legislative policy 377–8, 384, 385
  resolution, Delaware freedom of contract 30–31, 36
Conti, L. 202
contract drafting *see* drafting
contract rights, asset protection limited liability companies 134
contractual duty, Delaware, reintroduction of fiduciary concepts 55–6, 59–60, 65–7
contractual freedom
  for corporations, lack of, Delaware 28–9
  problems, Uniform Limited Liability Company Act (ULLCA) 316–17
contractual freedom, end of unlimited, and alternative entities, Delaware 11–27
  bargaining limitations 12
  contract evaluation concerns 12–13

corporate opportunity doctrine, limiting
    risks posed by 14–15
corporate statutory requirements
    comparison 14–15
cost concerns of redrafting 17
Delaware General Corporation Law
    (DGCL) 14, 15, 16–17, 21, 22, 25
drafting problems 12–13
duty of loyalty as protection to passive
    investors in corporations and
    partnerships 12, 13, 19
efficiency and fairness balance 16–17
entity managers and investors, establishment
    of purely contractual relationship 15–16
equitable principles 13, 16
fiduciary duties 15–17, 19
governing instruments' investors 11–12
language and contractual prose difficulties
    12–13, 16, 17, 19, 24, 27
managerial discretion 12
motivations for creating alternative entities
    14–17
Special Approval mechanism 12
standard fiduciary defaults, need for 13
tax minimization aims and pass-through tax
    treatment 14, 17
waivers of all fiduciary duties 12
contractual freedom, end of unlimited,
    and alternative entities, Delaware,
    market standard for conflict-of-interest
    transactions 18–27
contractual duties, owed by and to whom
    20
director and investor liabilities 22, 25–6
duty of good faith and fair dealing 25–6
familiarity illusion and surface-level
    standardization 18–19
governing fiduciaries and veil piercing
    patterns 21–4
gross negligence and indemnification
    provisions 21
indemnification and exculpation provisions
    20–21
independent directors' status 22–3
investor detriments 26–7
liability in subjective bad faith 19–21, 23–4
monetary damages liability and duty of care
    breach 23–4, 25, 27
publicly traded master limited partnerships
    (MLPs) 18–19
self-dealing transaction as fair to
    corporation 19
self-interest considerations 24–5, 26
contractual freedom and family business 40–51
    arm's-length deals, problems with 43, 45

business organization law and family law
    46–9
contract law and adequate protection 42
contractarian framework 41–2, 43
contractual challenges 45–7
divorce law implications 46, 47–8
equitable principles 43–4
implied covenant of good faith and fair
    dealing 41
judicial monitoring, importance of 42, 44,
    49
limited liability companies, attraction of 40,
    42–3
mergers and equitable principles 43–4
operating agreement creation 43
opportunism concerns 41, 42, 43–4
overlapping doctrine 46–7
overlapping values 45–6, 47
parties' expectations, protection of 47–9
private ordering principles 48–9
relational aspects 42, 45–6
small-business investors 40
and social identity theory 45–6
status and control concerns 46
succession law 47
see also small businesses
contractual "gap fillers", Delaware 347, 348–9
convergence of unincorporated entity law,
    casual 319–35
    ABA Revised Prototype LLC Act 330
    casual, use of term 319
    efficient uniformity, concerns over 322–3
    governmental/admin provisions 324, 325,
        327
    and interstate business transactions 321
    limited liability company internal affairs 324,
        325, 327
    name requirements 327, 333–4
    NCCUSL, advice to committees on
        organizational laws 330, 332
    NCCUSL model acts and uniformity
        320–23, 326–7
    NCCUSL, and state participation in
        drafting of uniform statutes 321–2
    NCCUSL, and Uniform Limited Liability
        Company Act (ULLCA) 326
    organizational laws, importance of keeping
        current 329–30
    third party provisions 322, 324, 325, 326–7,
        332–3
    uniformity, arguments against 322–3
    uniformity framework 319, 320–23
    uniformity, reasons for 320–22
convergence of unincorporated entity law,
    casual, RULLCA

and "bad" case law, concerns about borrowing 331
certificate of formation requirement 332
consistency concerns 332
and consistency with states' other unincorporated entity statutes 331
and cost savings created by convergence 331–2
dispute resolution concerns 333
state decisions, reasons for convergence 329–32
state decisions on use or variation from 328–34
state powers, concerns over maintenance of 333
state-specific variation from 324–6, 327
and states' ability to cross-reference with other states 331
and states' concerns about being left behind 330
use of familiar terminology 321, 322, 330
convergence of unincorporated entity law, casual, state LLC law 323–34
LLC Act committee members' interviews, and reasons for state adoptions and variations 328–34
reasons for convergence with RULLCA 329–32
reasons for divergence from RULLCA 332–4
research study data 324–8
Cooney, K. 260
Corbin, A. 60
corporate law and freedom of contract, fundamental changes *see* fundamental changes in limited liability companies, path divergence and convergence, corporate law and freedom of contract
corporate managers *see* management
corporate opportunity doctrine, limiting risks posed by, Delaware 14–15
corporations as separate legal entities 100
counterparty limited liability company's financial distress, mitigating impact 116–28
key issues 117–26
operating agreement as executory contract 120–21
planning, importance of 116–17
series LLC (multiple businesses under a common organizational umbrella) 126–8
series LLC (multiple businesses under a common organizational umbrella), assets and liabilities, substantive consolidation analysis 127–8

counterparty limited liability company's financial distress, mitigating impact, bankruptcy
court enforcing prepetition contractual agreements between creditor and LLC 122–3
creditor blocking 119
creditor enforcing a charging order in 123–4
creditor filing involuntary bankruptcy against LLC 120
creditor pursuing non-debtor parties 124
language in operating agreement 118–19
LLC filing for 117–19
member's bankruptcy affecting LLC and LLC's creditors 124–6
Countryman, V. 120, 121
Crane, J. 148, 149
Crespi, G. 138
Cross, M. 371
Cuff, T. 152

Dagan, H. 43
Daines, R. 259–60
Dalley, P. 448
damages
monetary liability and duty of care breach, Delaware 23–4, 25, 27
remedies, China 405
Dammann, J. 323
Dawson, S. 127
Dean, S. 159, 256
Deards, E. 358
default duties, uncertainty surrounding, judicial power expansion in Delaware 343
default rules
argument (opt-in/opt-out of fiduciary duty), Delaware 56, 57, 59–60, 64–5, 66–7
capital accounts *see* capital accounts in limited liability companies and partnerships, statutory default rules
China, partnerships and partnership law 402
separation/non-separation of ownership and management, Japan 376–7
Delaware
ad hoc harmonization 306, 309
business trust statute 271–2
contractual freedom, end of unlimited *see* contractual freedom, end of unlimited, and alternative entities, Delaware
freedom of contract *see* freedom of contract for alternative entities in Delaware, reality of

judicial power expansion *see* judicial power expansion in Delaware
jurisdictional competition for corporation charters 260, 261–2, 263–4
LLC law 180, 194–5, 198–200
LLC statute, common-law perspectives on binding the firm 86, 88–9, 93–5
Series, liability of limited liability entities 104
Delaware, alternative entities, and reintroduction of fiduciary concepts 55–69
  agreement drafting 64–7
  conflict of interests 65, 68
  contractual duty 55–6, 59–60, 65–7
  contractual provisions superseding implied covenant 63
  default rules argument (opt-in/opt-out of fiduciary duty) 56, 57, 59–60, 64–5, 66–7
  Delaware Limited Liability Company Act 57–8, 60
  directors' personal liability 57–8, 68
  elimination of fiduciary duties 57–9, 64–5
  hedge funds 64–5, 67
  judicial attitudes 58–9
  loyalty breaches and litigation costs 58
  Master Limited Partnerships (MLPs) 64–5, 67
  mergers and deal protection measures 56–7
  Paramount Communications v. QVC Network 55, 56–7
  revenues and profits generation 60
Delaware, alternative entities, and reintroduction of fiduciary concepts, good faith and fair dealing contract 56, 58, 59, 60–62
  agreement drafting 64–7
  conduct breaching and not breaching 61–2
  exercise of discretion 64
  interpretation of 62–4
delegation permission, common-law perspectives on binding the firm 94–5
DeMott, D. 81–96
Demsetz, H. 48, 148
Dewan, S. 234
DiMatteo, L. 43
disclosure
  and filing requirements, UK 370
  obligations, India 440
dispute resolution
  concerns, convergence of unincorporated entity law 333
  and decision on duty of care, unincorporated entity 219–21
  harmonization 309
  Taiwan Code 453
dissenters' rights 256, 259
dissolution
  distributions before 179
  fundamental changes in limited liability companies 195–6, 197–8
  unincorporated entity *see* unincorporated entity, care and loyalty after dissociation from or dissolution
  and winding-up of partnership, Taiwan 457–8, 461
  see also withdrawal procedure
Djelic, M. 368
Dodd, E. 269
Donn, A. 99–115
drafting
  contract drafting improvements, Delaware 345–6
  contract redrafting concerns, Delaware 12–13, 17
  legislative drafting choices 201–2
  unincorporated entity *see* unincorporated entity, care and loyalty after dissociation from or dissolution, drafting, need for careful
  see also language
Drake, D. 45
Drozdova, N. 413
Dubler, A. 47
Dunn, W. 270
duties *see* fiduciary duties

Easterbrook, F. 79, 148, 369
education programs 310
Egashira, K. 375
Eisenberg, M. 48
Elliott, A. 156
Ely, B. 127
Emerson, J. 261
employee-owned enterprise, Russia 426–7
Empson, L. 368
entrepreneurs
  foreign direct investment in entrepreneurial projects, India 433, 442–4
  and sweat equity scheme, Japan 378, 379, 380
  and vesting scheme, Japan 383
equity
  accounts, mixture of contents 170–72, 175
  claims, and freedom of contract, Delaware 30
  foreign private equity funds, China 397, 400
  holder voting rights, Delaware 31–3, 38

exit options
  Japan *see* Japan, limited liability companies legislative policy, exit options
  see also withdrawal procedure
expulsion options, law firm as industry model 282

family firms
  bargaining position, Japan 377, 379, 382, 386–7
  and contractual freedom *see* contractual freedom and family business
  exit options, Japan 382, 386–7
  fiduciary duties, Japan 384, 386
  and fraudulent transfer law 136
  see also small businesses
Fang, L. 392, 393, 394
Farnsworth, E. 18
Feetham, N. 104
Fenton, W. 271
fiduciary concepts, Delaware reintroduction *see* Delaware, alternative entities, and reintroduction of fiduciary concepts
fiduciary duty
  China 404–5, 408
  and contractual freedom, Delaware 15–17, 19
  India 440
  Japan *see* Japan, limited liability companies legislative policy, fiduciary duties
  partners during and after dissolution and winding up of partnership 216–18
  partners resigning and remaining after partner's withdrawal 212–16
  UK partnership options 366–7
fiduciary duty of care
  contractual freedom, Delaware 23–4, 25, 27
  Japan 383–4, 386, 387
  Taiwan 453, 467
  UK partnership options 366–7
  unincorporated entity *see* unincorporated entity, care and loyalty after dissociation from or dissolution
fiduciary duty of good faith
  corporate law and freedom of contract 199–200
  Delaware 25–6, 31–9, 41, 56, 58, 59, 60–62, 337, 338, 340, 344, 345, 347–9
  UK partnership options 366
fiduciary duty of loyalty
  breach of, Delaware 33–4
  China, partnerships and partnership law 408
  Japan 383–4, 386, 387
  as protection to passive investors, Delaware 12, 13, 19

Taiwan 467
unincorporated entity *see* unincorporated entity, care and loyalty after dissociation from or dissolution
Field, H. 159
financial distress *see* counterparty limited liability companies financial distress, mitigating impact
Finch, V. 358
Fisch, J. 339, 340, 341, 350, 352
Fischel, D. 79, 148, 369
Fisher, S. 292
Flannigan, R. 268, 274
Fleischer, V. 159
flexible purpose corporation (FPC) statute 256, 257, 258–9, 262
Folk, E. 16
foreign direct investment 394, 399–400, 433, 442–4
foreign private equity funds, China 397, 400
foreign-invested partnership, China 398–401, 409
Frankel, T. 270–71, 272
Freedman, J. 358, 359
freedom of contract
  common-law perspectives 89–90
  and corporate law *see* fundamental changes in limited liability companies, path divergence and convergence, corporate law and freedom of contract
  India 429–30, 435, 439
  Japan 376, 379, 383–4, 387
  nonprofit and charitable uses of limited liability companies 231
freedom of contract for alternative entities in Delaware, reality of 28–39
  breach of fiduciary duty of loyalty 33–4
  conflict of interest resolution 30–31, 36
  contractual freedom for corporations, lack of 28–9
  Delaware Limited Liability Company Act 29, 31, 35–6, 37–8
  enforceability of operating agreement precluding judicial dissolution 30
  equity claims 30
  equity holder voting rights 31–3, 38
  good faith negotiations 31–9
  hedges, use of 29–32
  implied covenant of good faith and fair dealing 34–6
  judicial dissolution access 29–30
  management majority written consent without prior notice 33
  maximum effect concept 29
  merger cases 32–3

narrow construction of an agreement 33–4
"Special Approval" consideration 36
Friedman, H. 40
Frost, S. 82, 89, 90, 91–2
fundamental changes in limited liability companies, path divergence and convergence 189–205
  buyouts of member interests as non-dissolution remedy 196
  dissolutions 195–6
  dissolutions, state variations 196
  legislative drafting choices 201–2
  legislative drafting choices, "junction box" statutes 201–2
  organizational documents, amendments to 191–2
  Revised Prototype Limited Liability Company Act (RPLLCA) 190, 191, 193, 195–6, 198
  Revised Uniform Limited Liability Company Act (RULLCA) 190, 191, 192–3, 195–6
  Revised Uniform Partnership Act (RUPA) 196, 198
  series LLC 190–91
  vested property rights 200–201
  vested property rights, state differences 200
fundamental changes in limited liability companies, path divergence and convergence, corporate law and freedom of contract 197–200
  contractual relations of the partners 198–9
  customization of fiduciary duties 199–200
  Delaware law 198–200
  dissolution schemes 197–8
  good faith and fair dealing 199–200
  statutory and common law elements of business entity governance 199
  unanimous consent, move away from 197, 200–201
fundamental changes in limited liability companies, path divergence and convergence, mergers, conversions and domestications 192–5
  corporatization of fundamental change rules 194–5
  Delaware's LLC law 194–5
  state variations 193–4
  unanimous member consent requirements 194
fundamental policy changes, and harmonization 315–16

Ganz, K. 442
Garcia, J. 184

Gazur, W. 305–6
general partnerships
  China 397, 399, 401, 403–5, 408
  common-law perspectives 82–3, 86
  India 432, 438
  law firm as industry model 290, 291, 292
  liability of limited liability entities 101
  Russia 412, 423–4
  special general partnership, China 398, 399, 401, 403, 404, 409
  Taiwan 450–58, 464, 468–9
  UK 357–8, 360, 361, 363, 366, 367, 368, 370
Gerson, C. 184
Gertner, R. 49, 50, 386
Geu, T. 204, 220, 398
Gevurtz, F. 88, 129–44, 352
Gilbert, W. 99
Gillers, S. 293
Gilson, R. 49, 339
Goforth, C. 291, 321, 322, 331
Goldberg, D. 159
Golub, T. 184
good faith, fiduciary duty see fiduciary duty of good faith
Gould, J. 271
Gravelle, J. 227, 228
Grayson, T. 269
Greenbaum, A. 293
Griffiths, A. 365, 369
Groshoff, D. 254
Grossman, N. 319–35
Gryta, T. 157
Gulati, G. 48
Gupta, A. 162

Haden, E. 156
Halloran, M. 378, 382, 383
Halpern, P. 275, 278
Hamilton, R. 21
Hanks, J. 100
Hanna, C. 155
Hansmann, H. 148, 272, 277, 279, 369
Haren, S. 359
Harman, T. 271
harmonization, rationalization and uniformity 299–318
  ad hoc harmonization (Delaware) 306, 309
  alternative approaches to harmonization 305–8
  "benefit corporation" statutes 305
  benefits and drawbacks of harmonization 308–11
  characteristics, eliminating idiosyncratic differences 309, 310

characteristics of organization 299, 300–301, 307, 309, 310, 311–14
common law, counteracting arrest of 310
common terminology for common characteristics 314
contractual freedom problems and Uniform Limited Liability Company Act (ULLCA) 316–17
corporate concept of voting 315
dispute resolution 309
education programs 310
external characteristics 300, 301, 303, 312
form of organization 299–300, 303, 304, 306–8, 309, 310, 311–12
fundamental policy changes 315–16
future amendment effectiveness 309
Harmonization of Business Entity Acts (NCCUSL Harmonization Project) 302, 314–16, 317, 318
harmonization Characteristics 302–3
harmonization definition 302
harmonization evaluation 308–18
inter-form transactions 302, 306, 307–8
internal characteristics 301, 313, 316, 317
judicial interpretation, scarcity of 310
"Junction Box" harmonization (Colorado and META) 306–8
language conformity 306, 309
LLC creation and Organic statute modification 306–8
LLP legislation adoption 304
Model Entity Transactions Act (META) 302
Model Registered Agents Act (MRAA) 302
names as characteristics 302–3
non-policy-driven distinctions, elimination of 309–10
nuances of meaning, concerns over 311
over-harmonization dangers 314–18
partnership formation characteristics 313
plumbing Characteristics 302, 310
rationalization benefits and drawbacks 311–13
rationalization combination problems 314–16
rationalization definition 303
rationalization, differences from harmonization 313
regressive legislation dangers 317–18
special interest groups and uniformity pursuit 304–5
state statutes 299, 300, 301, 302, 303, 304, 306–8
third party rights and expectations 303
Uniform Partnership Act (UPA) 299
uniformity pursuit 304–5

uniformity pursuit, benefits and drawbacks 313–14
unintended statutory inconsistencies between corresponding characteristics 310
Harner, M. 116–28
Hart, J. 207
Hasen, D. 149
Haynsworth, H. 305
Heminway, J. 189–205, 303
Hiller, A. 127
Hillman, R. 208, 283, 284, 288, 291, 366
Hirsch, A. 50
Hobbs, P. 148
Hoffman, D. 107
Hopkins, J. 253
Horton, B. 12, 18–19, 344, 345, 346
Horwitz, M. 148
Howson, N. 390–411
Huang, H. 409
Hwang, E. 253
hybrid entities
  company/partnership suggestion, India 432, 435
  taxation 161–5

India, limited liability partnerships 429–46
  adjudication delays 432
  Advocates Act 436, 442
  agency and liability 439
  Bar Council's Rules of Professional Conduct, concerns over violation of 442
  "body corporate" eligibility to be a partner 438
  cessation of partnership interests 440–41
  Chandra Committee for enactment of LLP law 431–3, 434, 435, 441
  Companies Act 429, 430, 432, 433, 438
  company/partnership hybrid suggestion 432, 435
  designated partners 438
  disclosure obligations and powers of government 440
  economic liberalization effects 429–30, 431
  fiduciary duties 440
  foreign direct investment in entrepreneurial projects 433, 442–4
  freedom of contract 429–30, 435, 439
  general partnerships 432, 438
  harmonization with other economic legislation 436
  Indian Partnership Act 432, 438, 439
  international competition concerns 432, 434, 436–7

international private equity and venture
    capital investors 444
Irani Committee Report on Company Law
    433, 434, 435, 441
law firm setting 441–2
legislative history 430–37
Limited Liability Partnership Act provisions
    437–41
Limited Liability Partnership Act provisions,
    UK and Singapore LLP Acts,
    similarities to 437–8, 441
MCA (Ministry of Corporate Affairs)
    429–30
MCA (Ministry of Corporate Affairs)
    Concept Paper on LLPs 434, 441
MCA (Ministry of Corporate Affairs) Draft
    Bill 434–6
MCA (Ministry of Corporate Affairs),
    passage of Final Bill 436–7
organizational flexibility 439
parallel partnerships 442
partner numbers 437, 438, 442
partnership, understanding of 438
personal liability 439
regulatory requirements of professional
    firms 433
Securities and Exchange Board of India
    (SEBI) 430, 444
service sector growth 433, 434, 437
small enterprises 433, 434, 436,
    442–4
taxation 436, 441
uncertainties facing 441–4
unlimited personal liability concerns 431–2,
    435
US and UK comparisons 432–3
vesting of property on conversion of an
    entity 436
insolvency *see* bankruptcy
interest transfers among existing partners and
    members, *Achaian v. Leemon Family* case
    70–80
    entire ownership interest consideration
        72–3
    operating agreement 71–4
    partnership tax classification 72
    statutory default rules 71–2
    voting rights 73
interest transfers among existing partners and
    members, *Achaian v. Leemon Family* case,
    "pick-your-partner" (PYP) rule 70, 72–3,
    74–8
    application 79–80
    historical background 74–5
    in limited liability companies 77–8
    in limited partnerships 76–7
    and Uniform Partnership Act 75–6
Ivey-Crickenberger, J. 116–28

Jackson, J. 148, 149, 153
Japan, limited liability companies legislative
    policy 374–89, 375, 376–7
    bargaining positions of close corporations
        377–8
    Companies Act 376, 379, 380–81
    complementarities between legal forms
        385–7
    complementarities between legal forms,
        bargaining situations 385–6, 387
    conflicts of interest 377–8
    default rule of separation/non-separation of
        ownership and management 376–7
    entrepreneurs and sweat equity scheme 378,
        379, 380
    entrepreneurs and vesting scheme 383
    family firms, bargaining position 377, 379,
        382, 386–7
    freedom of contract 376, 379
    human capital in exchange for membership
        rights 379, 380
    joint-venture corporations and shareholder
        agreements 380
    legal forms of business organizations 375–6
    Limited Liability Partnership (LLP) 375–6
    order-made membership rights 378–80
    partnership-type firms 377–8, 379–80, 382,
        387
    Stock Company 375
    Stock Company/LLC comparison 376–7,
        378–9
    taxation 376
    venture capital-backed firms, bargaining
        position 378, 379, 380, 382–3, 387
    voting rights 378–9
Japan, limited liability companies legislative
    policy, exit options 378, 380–83
    family firms 382, 386–7
    mandatory withdrawal rights 382–3
    partnership-type firms 382, 387
    shareholders and transfer of stock 381–2
    squeeze-out, reducing risk of 386
    Stock Companies vs. LLCs 380–82, 383, 387
    transfer of membership rights 381
    US comparison 380
    venture capital-backed firms 382–3, 387
Japan, limited liability companies legislative
    policy, fiduciary duties 378, 383–5
    conflicts of interest 384, 385
    costs and benefits of contracting around 386
    directors and officers 383

duty of care and duty of loyalty 383–4, 386, 387
family firms 384, 386
freedom of contract 383–4, 387
gap-filling role 386
and opportunistic behavior 385, 386
partnership-type firms 384–5, 386, 387
self-dealing transactions 384
Stock Companies vs. LLCs 383–4, 387
US comparison 383–4
venture capital-backed firms 385, 386, 387
Jensen, M. 138
Johnson, E. 161, 164
joint ventures
China 394
nonprofit and charitable uses of limited liability companies 238–40
Russia 421
shareholder agreements, Japan 380
Jones, G. 104
Jones, S. 269, 277
judicial exceptions to liability shield 107–10
judicial interpretation, scarcity of, and harmonization 310
judicial monitoring, importance of, contractual freedom and family business 42, 44, 49
judicial power expansion in Delaware 336–53
cash versus stock consideration and *Revlon* question 338, 339
"conclusive presumption" cases 348, 349
confidential arbitrations 351
contract drafting improvements 345–6
contractual "gap fillers" 347, 348–9
corporate charters, attracting 340
corporate criminal malfeasance concerns 340
corporate executives excessive pay packages, concerns over 340
default duties, uncertainty surrounding 343
dictum's emergent role in alternative entity jurisprudence 341–9
dictum's emergent role in alternative entity jurisprudence, guidance function 341–4
dictum's emergent role in alternative entity jurisprudence, regulatory function 344–6
dictum's emergent role in alternative entity jurisprudence, responsiveness function 340, 346–9
dictum's judicial empowerment element 349–52
dictum's recognised role in corporate jurisprudence 336–41
dictum's recognised role in corporate jurisprudence, corporate law 337–8
dictum's recognised role in corporate jurisprudence, guidance function 339
dictum's recognised role in corporate jurisprudence, regulatory power 339
dictum's unintended consequences 340–41
dictum's valuable functions, recognition of 340–41
directors' oversight obligations 337
extra-judicial engagement with business law practitioners 349
fiduciary duty of good faith and fair dealing 337, 338, 340, 344, 345, 347–9
frauds statute and LLC agreements 341, 342
future behavior of corporate actors, and *dictum* use 339
future developments, foreshadowing 343–4
future doctrinal changes and *dictum* use 339
limited rights afforded in the alternative entities, concerns over 346–7
mergers and acquisitions 339
overreach by drafters of publicly traded alternative entity governing agreements, caution against 347
partnership agreements and elimination of fiduciary duties 342
regulatory efficiency and *dictum* use 339
"special approval" provisions for publicly traded alternative entities 344–5, 346, 349
state constitution amendments 350
state courts' control over business law 351
state statute involvement 351
"transcript opinions" to address emergent and unresolved legal questions 349–50
vulnerabilities of public investors, addressing 347
"junction box" statutes 201–2, 306–8
jurisdictional competition for corporation charters *see under* state laboratories and social enterprise law

Kahan, M. 18, 260, 339
Kamar, E. 260, 263, 339
Kean, W. 92
Keatinge, R. 106, 107, 299–318
Kessler, R. 305
King, T. 156
Kirby, W. 392
Klausner, M. 18
Kleinberger, D. 83, 85, 86, 88, 89, 93, 149, 253, 263, 320, 322
Knutson, R. 157
Kobayashi, B. 260, 313, 322, 326–7, 333, 352
Koriya, D. 376
Kraakman, R. 277, 279, 369

L3Cs (low-profit limited liability companies) *see under* state laboratories and social enterprise law
Labouchere, H. 369
Lafontaine, F. 377
Lang, R. 252, 253
Langbein, J. 268, 274, 275, 276, 277, 279
language
  conformity, and harmonization 306, 309, 311, 314
  and contractual prose difficulties, Delaware 12–13, 16, 17, 19, 24, 27
  in operating agreement, bankruptcy 118–19
  use of familiar terminology, convergence of unincorporated entity law 321, 322, 330
  see also drafting
Lansberg, I. 46
Larson, J. 171
Laster, J. 11–27, 41, 44, 344, 345, 348, 350, 351, 386, 387
law firm as industry model for entity choice and management 280–95
  business model evolution 292–4
  centralized management 286
  corporate formality concerns 286
  entity selection trends 291–2
  ethics rules 281–4
  expulsion options 282
  fees regulation 282–3
  general partnerships 290, 291, 292
  global law firm, future of 294
  historical entities 288–9
  law firm ownership volatility 283
  lawyer exclusivity in ownership 282–4
  lease obligations 284
  liability 285, 288, 289
  limited liability company 291–2
  limited liability partnership (LLP) 290–91, 292
  management considerations and Model Rules 281–3
  management and control considerations in partnerships 285–6
  Model Rule 5.4 282, 292–3
  modern entity forms 290–91
  multidisciplinary practice 292–3
  multijurisdictional practice, future of 293–4
  non-competition clauses 283–4
  non-equity partner, emergence of 287–8
  operation considerations 285–8
  organizational framework or policy statement 281–2
  professional corporation 290, 291
  profits and compensation 286–7, 288
  protection for economic interests 284
  regulatory requirements 281–5
  relationships between lawyers and non-lawyers 282, 292–3
  safeguards 289
  sale of law practices 283
  shareholder dividends 286, 290
  sole proprietorship 290
  state by state licensing and geographic boundaries 293–4
  state regulation 284–5
  tax benefits 289, 290, 291, 292
  two-tier partnership structure 287–8
  Uniform Partnership Act (UPA) and Revised Uniform Partnership Act (RUPA) 289
  Verein structure and global law firms 294
Lawrence, S. 242
legal personality
  and capacity restrictions, Taiwan 451–2, 454–5
  and SAIC registration, China 401–2
  Taiwan 464, 467–8
  UK partnership options 361–3
legislative drafting *see* drafting
Lewis, W. 86, 148
liability
  joint certified public accountant (CPA), cases, Taiwan 460–61
  law firm as industry model 285, 288, 289
  limited *see* limited liability headings
  personal *see* personal liability
  protection, nonprofit and charitable uses of limited liability companies 231, 232
liability of limited liability entities 99–115
  business trusts 103
  capital contribution deficiencies 106
  common law of agency 105–6
  corporate income tax treatment 99
  corporate parent of a general partner 109–10
  corporations as separate legal entities 100
  Delaware Series 104
  direct liability imposed on owners or affiliates by other statutes 110–13
  direct liability for own acts or omissions 105
  donative trusts 103
  employment laws 110–11
  environmental laws 112
  exceptions 105–7
  federal common law of piercing 108–9
  Federal Volunteer Protection Act 104
  full shield states 102
  general partnerships 101
  general principles 100–104
  interim distributions 106–7

judicially created exceptions to liability shield 107–10
lawyer's right to protection 103
limited liability companies 100–101, 104, 105–6, 108, 112
limited liability limited partnerships 102
limited liability partnerships 102, 105, 106
limited partnerships 101, 104
pension funding 113
personal trusts 103
piercing the corporate veil 107–9, 110
professional entities 103
"responsible person" tax statutes 112
Revised Uniform Limited Partnership Act (RULPA) and "safe harbor" list of activities 101
Revised Uniform Unincorporated Nonprofit Association Act (RUUNA) 103–4
single business enterprise doctrine 110
statutory trusts 103
"substantive consolidation" 108–9
successor liability 109
trust funds 112
Uniform Trust Code 103
unincorporated nonprofit associations 103–4
voluntary personal liability 106
wage claims of employees' liabilities 111–12
wrongful liquidation distributions 107
Lidstone, H. 257
Lifshitz, S. 48
Lille, G. 161, 164
limited liability companies
  attraction of, family business 40, 42–3
  capital accounts *see* capital accounts in limited liability companies and partnerships
  common-law perspectives 86–90
  counterparty's financial distress *see* counterparty limited liability companies financial distress, mitigating impact
  fundamental changes *see* fundamental changes in limited liability companies, path divergence and convergence
  Japan *see* Japan, limited liability companies legislative policy
  law firm as industry model 291–2
  liability *see* liability of limited liability entities
  low-profit (L3Cs) *see under* state laboratories and social enterprise law
  nonprofit and charitable uses *see* nonprofit and charitable uses of limited liability companies
  and organic statute modification 306–8
  "pick-your-partner" (PYP) rule 77–8

Russia 412–13, 416, 421–3
series 126–8, 190–91
single member 159–60, 231–6
Taiwan, evolution of non-corporate forms of business 447
unincorporated entity law *see* convergence of unincorporated entity law, casual, state LLC law
limited liability limited partnerships 102
limited liability partnerships
  India *see* India, limited liability partnerships
  Japan 375–6
  law firm as industry model 290–91, 292
  legislation adoption and harmonization 304
  liability of limited liability entities 102, 105, 106
  UK partnership options 358–9, 360, 361, 362–3, 364–5, 366–9, 370
limited partnerships
  China 397–8, 399, 401, 403, 404, 405, 408
  liability of limited liability entities 101, 104, 346–7
  master limited partnerships (MLPs) 18–19
  "pick-your-partner" (PYP) rule 76–7
  Russia 412, 424–5
  UK partnership options 358, 360, 361, 365, 366, 367, 368, 370
  see also partnerships
Lin, A. 447–70
Lin, C. 449
Lin, L. 392, 408
Lins, G. 271
Lipton, R. 156
liquidations
  and capital accounts 173–5, 177–8, 182
  China 395, 405
  Russia 419–21
  Taiwan 453, 458, 461
  wrongful distributions 107
  see also bankruptcy
Liu, S. 470
Loewenstein, M. 28–39, 255, 305, 311
Long, W. 46–7
Lord, R. 60
low-profit limited liability companies (L3Cs) *see under* state laboratories and social enterprise law
loyalty, fiduciary duty *see* fiduciary duty of loyalty
Lubaroff, M. 11, 23, 24
Luthra, R. 437

McCarthy, E. 156
McCray, R. 236
Macey, J. 48, 107, 110, 114, 262, 263

Macgregor, L. 81
Machell, J. 363
McKee, W. 181
McLoughlin, M. 127
McMeel, G. 85
McNally, E. 349
Mallen, R. 285
management
   China, partnerships and partnership law 402–3, 405
   common-law perspectives 87, 91, 92
   discretion, and contractual freedom 12
   freedom of contract and majority written consent without prior notice 33
   and interest group theory 263
   law firm as industry model *see* law firm as industry model for entity choice and management
   rights, and asset protection 131
   Russia, general partnership 423
   Taiwan, business affairs 463–4, 467
   Taiwan, partnership affairs 454–5, 457
   UK partnership options 365–7
Manesh, M. 12, 17, 19, 21, 260, 262, 336–53
Manning, B. 100
market standard for conflict-of-interest transactions *see* contractual freedom, end of unlimited, and alternative entities, Delaware, market standard for conflict-of-interest transactions
Marks, G. 202
Marsico, N. 127
Martin, C. 365
Martin Rhodes, A. 280–95
master limited partnerships (MLPs) 18–19
Matheson, J. 107
Mattei, U. 277, 279
Mazie, E. 271
Means, B. 40–51
Meckling, W. 148
members
   expulsion/exclusion, UK partnership options 362–3
   member-managed limited liability company, common-law perspectives 91, 92
   member-managed limited liability company, unincorporated entity 210–11
   membership limitations, lack of, nonprofit and charitable uses of limited liability companies 231
   withdrawal, Russia 422–3, 426
mergers
   contractual freedom and family business 43–4
   deal protection measures, Delaware 56–7
   freedom of contract for alternative entities in Delaware 32–3
   fundamental changes *see* fundamental changes in limited liability companies, path divergence and convergence, mergers, conversions and domestications
   judicial power expansion in Delaware 339
   Russia 419
   see also buyouts
Merrill, T. 279
Miller, C. 248
Miller, G. 208, 262, 263
Miller, P. 276, 278
Miller, S. 12, 15, 42, 43, 199
Millon, D. 107
Minnigh, E. 253
Mitts, J. 107, 110, 114
Moll, F. 41, 43
Monroe, A. 149, 150, 151, 152, 154, 180
Morgenson, G. 346
Morse, S. 159
Murray, J. 252–67

NCCUSL (National Conference of Commissioners on Uniform State Laws) *see under* convergence of unincorporated entity law, casual
Nedelsky, J. 46
non-equity partner, emergence of, law firm as industry model 287–8
non-partner agents 84–5
non-policy-driven distinctions, elimination of 309–10
non-statutory solutions, common-law perspectives 93–5
nonprofit and charitable uses of limited liability companies 227–51
   charitable private foundations 228, 229
   controlled "subsidiaries" 230–31
   donor uses for LLCs 247–8
   donor uses for LLCs, anonymity measures 248
   employment taxes 228–9, 234–5
   federal excise taxes 229
   federal income tax law and tax exemptions 227, 228–9
   grantmaking foundations 228
   mutual benefit nonprofit corporations 229–30
   "nondistribution constraint" 230, 232
   operating foundations 228
   public benefit nonprofit corporations 229–30
   public charities 228

state law and prevalence of nonprofit corporations 229–31
state law and prevalence of nonprofit corporations, tax exemption under federal law 230
tax-deductible charitable contributions 230, 232, 233, 234, 235
nonprofit and charitable uses of limited liability companies, charitable subsidiary and affiliated LLCs 231–40
charitable contributions vehicle 234
development of adjacent land as rental property 232
election to be treated as corporation for tax purposes, reasons for 234
employment tax requirement 234–5
federal unrelated business income tax (UBIT) 233–4, 238
freedom of contract 231
liability protection 231, 232
membership limitations, lack of 231
nonprofit/for-profit joint ventures and ancillary joint ventures 238–40
nonprofit/for-profit joint ventures and ancillary joint ventures, membership interest "substantial" or "insubstantial" part of its activities and assets 239
nonprofit/for-profit joint ventures and ancillary joint ventures, passive investments 239
private foundation grants 232
regarded but tax-exempt LLCs 236–7
single-member LLCs, disregarded 231–6
tax treatment, malleable 231
taxpayer entitlement to charitable contribution deduction 235–6
"veil piercing" arguments made by claimants against parent organizations 235
nonprofit and charitable uses of limited liability companies, strictly for-profit but charitably used LLCs 240–47
benefit LLCs 245–7
impact investing and for-profit social enterprise 243–4
low profit limited liability company (L3C) 244–5
low-income housing and new markets tax credit LLCs 240–41
program-related investments (PRIs) by private foundations and LLCs 241–3
program-related investments (PRIs) by private foundations and LLCs, "expenditure responsibility" rules 242
program-related investments (PRIs) by private foundations and LLCs, limited technical guidance 242–3
Norli, O. 275, 278

O'Connor, B. 185
Oesterle, D. 42, 305–6
Oh, P. 99, 107, 108, 268–79
O'Hara, E. 259
O'Neal, F. 40, 41
opportunism concerns
contractual freedom and family business 41, 42, 43–4
corporate opportunity doctrine, limiting risks posed by, Delaware 14–15
Japan 385, 386
Orlov, V. 412–28
Orts, E. 81

Palmer, F. 361, 362
Parsons, D. 31, 63, 340, 345, 346, 348
partnerships
agreements and elimination of fiduciary duties, Delaware 342
authority, common-law perspectives 82–3
"body corporate" eligibility, India 438
capital accounts *see* capital accounts in limited liability companies and partnerships
cessation of interests, India 440–41
China *see* China, partnerships and partnership law
company/partnership hybrid suggestion, India 432, 435
formation characteristics 313
interest transferability, China 403
interest transfers *see* interest transfers among existing partners and members, *Achaian v. Leemon Family* case
legal capacity, Russia 415
limited *see* limited partnerships
limited liability *see* limited liability partnerships
parallel partnerships, India 442
partner numbers, India 437, 438, 442
partnership-type firms, Japan 377–8, 379–80, 382, 387
positional power, common-law perspectives 83–5, 87, 90–92
registrations and registered capital, China 396–7
silent 424–5, 458
Taiwan *see* Taiwan, evolution of non-corporate forms of business, partnerships law under Civil Code

taxation *see under* taxation
UK *see* UK partnership options
"passive loss" rules, capital accounts 181
pension funding 113, 276–7
personal labor participation, Russia 413
personal liability
  directors 57–8, 68
  India, limited liability partnerships 439
  UK partnership options 358, 366, 368–70
  voluntary 106
  see also liability headings
personal performance exception and bankruptcy 135–6
personal trusts 103
"pick-your-partner" (PYP) rule *see* interest transfers among existing partners and members, "pick-your-partner" (PYP) rule
piercing the corporate veil *see* veil piercing
Platt, C. 143
Plerhoples, A. 256
plumbing characteristics, harmonization, rationalization and uniformity 302, 310
Polsky, G. 149, 150, 151, 152
Pomeroy, C. 133
Popondopulo, V. 423, 424, 425
Posner, E. 331
Prentice, R. 304–5
Presser, S. 107, 108
price discrimination concerns 260–62
private equity, India 444
production cooperative, Russia 413, 418, 425–6
profit sharing
  China 407–8
  law firm as industry model 286–7, 288
  Russia 426
  Taiwan 456–7
  UK partnership options 365, 370
property holding, business trusts, modern 274–5
property information used for private gain 213, 221
public benefit corporations (PBCs) 257, 258, 262, 263

Qiu, C. 448, 449, 453
"qualified income offset", capital accounts 183
Quinn, B. 351

Ragazzo, R. 43
Rawhouser, H. 262
Reiss, D. 158
representation restrictions, Taiwan 454–5, 467
Reyes, F. 149

Ribstein, L. 42, 43, 81, 82, 84, 89, 101, 107, 137, 144, 149, 214, 259, 260, 313, 316, 322, 326–7, 333, 352, 360, 365, 439
Richmond, D. 287
risk management, business trusts, modern 275–6
Roberts, E. 305
Rock, E. 339
Romano, R. 252, 259, 260, 264, 330
Rosen, K. 47
Rosin, G. 148
Rowley, S. 74
RPLLCA (Revised Prototype Limited Liability Company Act), fundamental changes in limited liability companies 190, 191, 193, 195–6, 198, 211
Rubin, B. 156
RULLCA (Revised Uniform Limited Liability Company Act)
  capital accounts 179
  common-law perspectives 90–91, 93
  convergence of unincorporated entity law *see* convergence of unincorporated entity law, casual
  fundamental changes in limited liability companies 190, 191, 192–3, 195–6
  unincorporated entity 210–11, 212
RUPA (Revised Uniform Partnership Act)
  buyout provisions, capital accounts 178
  fundamental changes in limited liability companies 196, 198
  maintenance rules, capital accounts 176–7
  unincorporated entity 209–10, 212
Ruskola, T. 392
Russia, alternatives to capital-oriented corporations 412–28
  administration in corporate entity 418
  capital contribution 416
  capital transfer in general partnership 424
  charter capital of limited liability company 422
  constituent (founding) document of juristic persons 415–16
  corporate agreement 416–17
  corporation definition 412
  employee-owned enterprise 426–7
  executive power 418
  general partnership 412, 423–4
  invalid decisions on reorganization 420
  joint stock company 421
  juristic person (legal entity), legal capacity 414–15
  liability of partners in general partnership 423–4
  liability rule 418–19

limited liability company 412–13, 416, 421–3
limited partnership 412, 424–5
liquidation of limited partnership 425
management in general partnership 423
management of production cooperative 426
member withdrawal from limited liability company 422–3
member withdrawal from production cooperative 426
membership interest in charter capital of limited liability company 422
mergers 419
partnership participants, legal capacity 415
personal labor participation 413
production cooperative 413, 418, 425–6
profit distribution of production cooperative 426
reorganization and liquidation of juristic person 419–21
rights and duties 417–18
shareholders in employee-owned enterprise 426–7
silent partner in limited partnership 424–5
solidary liability 420
voting rights 417, 420, 427
voting rights in employee-owned enterprise 427
withdrawal of partner in general partnership 424
Rutledge, T. 91–2, 206–23, 311, 341

safe harbor regulations 151–2, 182–3
salaries *see* compensation
Saltuk, Y. 261
Sargent, M. 219
Savitt, W. 339, 340, 341, 350, 352
Schneider, S. 185
Schündeln, M. 323
Schwarcz, S. 268, 274, 275, 276
Schwidetzky, W. 219
Seavoy, R. 269
self-dealing transactions 19, 92, 384
Sergeev, A. 414, 423, 424, 425, 426
series limited liability companies 126–8, 190–91
see also limited liability companies
service sector growth, India 433, 434, 437
shareholders
  corporate salary payments to principal shareholders as disguised and non-deductible dividends 132
  debt, corporation or LLC liability for 138–9
  dividends, law firm as industry model 286, 290
  in employee-owned enterprise, Russia 426–7

share transfer to new partner, Taiwan 456
and transfer of stock, Japan 381–2
see also voting
Shen, K. 451
Sherlock, M. 227, 228
Sherman, J. 47
Shishido, Z. 374–89
silent partnerships 424–5, 458
Simmons, D. 155
Simmons, O. 264
Simpson, J. 294
Singapore, Limited Liability Partnership Act, similarity to India 437–8, 441
Singer, J. 48
Singh, S. 436
single business enterprise doctrine 110
single member limited liability companies 159–60, 231–6
see also limited liability companies
Sissel, S. 46–7
Sitkoff, R. 47, 48–9, 268, 270, 271, 272, 273, 277, 278, 279
small businesses
  and capital accounts 177
  India 433, 434, 436, 442–4
  taxation 156–7, 158–9
  see also family firms
Smith, H. 279
social enterprise law *see* state laboratories and social enterprise law
social identity theory, contractual freedom and family business 45–6
sole proprietorship 290, 448
"special approval" provisions 12, 36, 344–5, 346, 349
special general partnership, China law 398, 399, 401, 403, 404, 409
special interest groups and uniformity pursuit 304–5
state laboratories and social enterprise law 252–67
  corporate managers and interest group theory 263
  flexible purpose corporation (FPC) statute 256, 257, 258–9, 262
  flexible purpose corporations and social purpose corporations 256
  "impact investing" 261
  interest group theory and benefits 262–3
  jurisdictional competition for corporation charters 259–61
  jurisdictional competition for corporation charters, Delaware pre-eminence 260, 261–2, 263–4
  jurisdictional competition for corporation

Index

charters, race to the bottom/race to the bottom theories 259–60
jurisdictional positioning 261–2
lawyers and business people and interest group theory 263
low-profit limited liability companies (L3Cs) 252–4, 258–9, 262, 263
low-profit limited liability companies (L3Cs), "charitable or education purposes" 258
low-profit limited liability companies (L3Cs), statutes passed 253–4
low-profit limited liability companies (L3Cs), suggested reforms 253
price discrimination concerns 260–62
profit concerns 253
Program Related Investments (PRIs) and L3Cs 252–3
public benefit corporations (PBCs) 257, 258, 262, 263
social enterprise law iterations and innovations 257–9
social enterprise law iterations and innovations, entity conversion requirements 259
social enterprise law iterations and innovations, and L3Cs 258–9
social enterprise law iterations and innovations, Model Benefit Corporation Legislation 258–9, 260, 263
social purpose (SPC) statute 256, 257, 258, 262
Socially Responsible Investing (SRI) 261
state politicians and interest group theory 262–3
state laboratories and social enterprise law, benefit corporations and benefit limited liability companies 254–6
benefit corporation law, benefit reporting requirements 255–6, 257, 258
benefit corporation law and increased accountability and transparency 254–6
benefit corporation purpose clause 254
Benefit Corporation White Paper (Proponent White Paper) 254–5
Benefit Corporation White Paper (Proponent White Paper), criticism of 255
benefit corporations and "general public benefit purpose", criticism of 255, 256, 258, 260
dissenters' rights 256, 259
statutory default rules, capital accounts
   see capital accounts in limited liability companies and partnerships, statutory default rules
statutory inconsistencies, and harmonization 310
statutory trusts 103
Steele, M. 32–3, 59–60, 339, 340, 349, 384, 386
Stein, R. 304
stock companies, Japan 375, 376–7, 378–9, 380–82, 383–4, 387
Stout, L. 49
Strine, L. 11–27, 28, 30–31, 34, 41, 44, 58, 59–60, 254, 256, 342, 344, 350, 386, 387
"substantive consolidation" liability 108–9
Sullivan, J. 137
Sullivan, M. 216

Taiwan, evolution of non-corporate forms of business 447–70
Company Act 447, 462, 463, 464, 466, 468–9
corporations (companies limited by shares) 447–8
foreign companies 448
limited liability companies 447
Limited Liability Partnership Act 447
QIU Zhe Qian et al. v. LIN Jin 451
sole proprietorships 448
Taiyuan Construction Corporation v. Yingcheng Paint 455
unlimited liability companies 447, 462
unlimited liability companies with limited liability shareholders 447
Yu You Ren Cultural and Educational Foundation v. LI Qi 452
Taiwan, evolution of non-corporate forms of business, Limited Partnership Act, proposed 461–9
addition of limited liability partner 466–7
contribution and return of capital 466
definition, responsible person, and representative 465–6
fiduciary duties of care and loyalty 467
general partner qualification 464, 468–9
legal personality 464, 467–8
limited partnership/silent partnership comparison 463–5
major content 465–7
management of business affairs 463–4, 467
representation restrictions 467
taxation 463, 469
transfer of limited partnership interest 466
unlimited company/limited liability shareholder comparison 463–5
venture capital regime 461–2
withdrawal from partnership 466–7

Taiwan, evolution of non-corporate forms of business, partnerships law under Civil Code 448–58
   accounting firm's liability for misleading financial reports 458–60
   assets of partnership 452–3
   business registration 449, 450–51, 454
   compulsory legal effects 452–6
   contemporary issues 458–61
   contribution of additional capital 457
   dispute resolution 453
   dissolution and winding-up of partnership 457–8, 461
   duty of care 453
   enterprise creation 450–52
   general partnerships 450–58
   incorporated certified public accountant (CPA) 460
   internal and external relationships, regulation of 450
   "legal person" concept 448
   legal personality and capacity restrictions 451–2, 454–5
   liability of joint certified public accountant (CPA), cases regarding 460–61
   liquidations 453, 458, 461
   management of partnership affairs 454–5, 457
   new partner introduction 456
   partner's supplementary joint liability 455–6
   partnership autonomy 456–7
   partnership contract 449–50, 452
   profit and loss sharing 456–7
   representation and mandate 454–5
   resignation and removal of partners 450, 453–4
   right to inspect partnership affairs 454
   share transfer to new partner 456
   silent partnerships 458
   taxation 452–3
   withdrawal from partnership 456
Talley, E. 15
Tang, Q. 391, 409
taxation
   aggregate versus entity taxation 148–9, 151, 152, 153, 154–5, 159
   allocation of tax items 149–52
   allocation of tax items, governance problems 151
   alternative forms of business organization 147–67
   business trusts 277–8
   Canada partnership tax system 161–3
   Canada partnership tax system, U.S.-Canada tax treaty amendments 163–5
   capital-intensive partnerships and tax allocations 150
   China, double-taxation of partnership investors 396
   China, partnerships and partnership law 396, 401, 405–6
   classification for LLCs as partnerships 86
   compensation payments 158–9
   contribution and distribution rules 153–5
   corporations and entity-level tax 147, 149
   depreciation deductions and tax allocations 150, 151
   distribution waterfall and tax allocations 150–51, 157
   elective classification rules 158–60
   employment tax planning 158–9
   federal income tax significance *see* capital accounts in limited liability companies and partnerships, federal income tax significance
   hybrid entities 161–5
   "income-stripping" arrangements and hybrid entities 162–3
   India, limited liability partnerships 436, 441
   Japan, limited liability companies legislative policy 376
   minimization aims and pass-through tax treatment 14, 17
   non-U.S. entities 160
   nonprofit and charitable uses of limited liability companies 227–38
   partners' interest in a partnership, shortcomings of test for 151
   partnership liabilities, effects of 155–6
   partnership and LLC taxation overview 147–56
   partnership tax classification 72
   partnership tax law 147
   partnership taxation, election out and inapplicability of 158–60
   pre-contribution gain or loss 157
   publicly traded partnerships 160
   real estate investment trusts (REITs) 157, 158
   real estate mortgage investment conduits (REMICs) 157–8
   regulated investment companies (RICs) 158
   "responsible person" tax statutes 112
   safe harbor requirements 151–2
   single member LLCs 159–60
   small business corporations (S corporations) as entity-minus regime 156–7, 158–9
   "special allocations" 149–50
   start-ups 159

substantial economic effect, two-part test 151–2
Taiwan 452–3, 463, 469
tax benefits, law firm as industry model 289, 290, 291, 292
tax-free disguised sales of property 155
tax-free formations and dissolutions 154–5
terminology problems 152
transfers of partnership property and interest in partnerships 152–3
UK partnership options 364, 371
Taylor, W. 162
third parties
  contracts, UK partnership options 361–2
  convergence of unincorporated entity law 322, 324, 325, 326–7, 332–3
  dealing with a partner, common-law perspectives 82–3, 84, 87–9, 91, 92–3
  protection, UK partnership options 369
  rights and expectations, and harmonization 303
Thomas, W. 236
Thompson, R. 40, 41, 42
Tikhomirov, M. 415
"transcript opinions", judicial power expansion in Delaware 349–50
transfer of partnership interests 129–33, 152–3, 466
trust funds, liability of limited liability entities 112
trusts, business *see* business trusts
Tsoflias, P. 104
Tyler, J. 340

UK
  Bubble Act 269
  limited liability partnerships, similarities to India 432–3, 437–8, 441
UK, cases
  Burland v. Earle 362
  Castledine v. RSM Bentley Jennison 360
  Clyde & Co v. Bates van Winkelhof 364
  Coward v. Phaistos Ltd 360
  Cowell v Quilter Goodison 364
  Daniels v. Daniels 342
  Drake v. Harvey 360
  Eaton v. Caulfield 362–3, 368
  Ebrahimi v. Westbourne Galleries 363
  Ellis v. Joseph Ellis & Co 364
  F&C Alternative Investments (Holdings) v. Barthelemy (No 2) 367
  Foss v. Harbottle 362
  Gilford Motor Co Ltd v Horne 369
  Hurst v. Bryk 363
  Ilott v. Williams 360
  Khan v. Miah 360
  M Young Legal Associates v. Zahid 367
  Mullins v. Laughton 363
  O'Neill v. Phillips 362, 363
  Reinhard v. Ondra 364–5
  Ross Harper & Murphy v. Banks 366–7
  Smith v. Croft (No 1) 362
  Tann v. Herrington 366
  Tiffin v. Lester Aldridge 364
  Winsor v. Schroeder 366
UK partnership options 357–73
  agreements, lack/scarcity of 360–61
  Bills of Sale Act and floating charges to secure loans 367–8
  business "carried on" extent 359–60
  business termination constraints 362–3
  company law and LLPs 358–9
  derivative claims, regulation of 362
  disclosure and filing requirements 370
  duty of care 366–7
  duty of good faith 366
  employment status 364–5
  exclusion of right to petition 363
  fiduciary duties 366–7
  finances 365, 367–8, 370
  general partnerships 357–8, 360, 361, 363, 366, 367, 368, 370
  insolvency 371
  integrated management and ownership, benefits of 365–6
  liability 358, 366, 368–70
  limited liability partnerships (LLPs) 358–9, 360, 361, 362–3, 364–5, 366–9, 370
  limited partnerships 358, 360, 361, 365, 366, 367, 368, 370
  management rights and responsibilities 365–7
  members' expulsion/exclusion 362–3
  model agreement 361
  partner/member agreements 360–61
  Partnership Act 358, 361–2
  partnership formation 359–60
  personal liability concerns 358, 366, 368–70
  "persons", understanding of 359
  profit sharing 365, 370
  proper plaintiff principle 362
  registration proof 360
  risk of fraudulent behavior, reducing 369–70
  separate legal personality and continuity 361–3
  separate legal personality and continuity, disadvantages of 362–3
  taxation of members 364, 371
  third party contracts 361–2

third party protection 369
unlimited liability risk 369
uniformity *see* harmonization, rationalization and uniformity
unincorporated entity, care and loyalty after dissociation from or dissolution 206–23
"member-managed" LLC 210–11
"opportunity" for venture withdrawal 212
Revised Prototype Limited Liability Company Act (RPLLCA) 211
Revised Uniform Limited Liability Company Act (RULLCA) 210–11, 212
Revised Uniform Partnership Act (RUPA) 209–10, 212
Uniform Partnership Act (UPA) 209, 212
unincorporated entity, care and loyalty after dissociation from or dissolution, case law 212–21
Bluestein v. Davis 213–14
Cass JV v. Host International 219, 221
dispute resolution and decision on duty of care 219–21
fiduciary duties of partners during and after dissolution and winding up of partnership 216–18
fiduciary duties of resigning and remaining partners after a partner's withdrawal 212–16
Fouchek v. Janicek 212–13
Frates v. Nichols 216–17
Hooper v. Yoder 217–18
Lund v. Albrecht 214–15
Meinhard v. Salmon 208–9, 215, 218–19, 378
modification of statutory default rules 219
Monin v. Monin 218
Newburger, Loeb & Co. v. Gross 215, 222
partner dissociated from partnership in violation of controlling agreement 213–14
partnership fiduciary duties of utmost good faith, fairness and loyalty 215–16
property information used for private gain 213, 221
strained relations between the partners and fiduciary duties 214–15
term and undertaking partnerships 218–19
unincorporated entity, care and loyalty after dissociation from or dissolution, drafting, need for careful 221–2
confidentiality requirements 221–2
gains from exploitation of venture assets 221–2
non-solicitation obligation 222
operating provisions as to fiduciary obligations 221

purpose clause 221
time factors 222
unincorporated entity law *see* convergence of unincorporated entity law, casual
unincorporated nonprofit associations 103–4
unlimited company/limited liability shareholder comparison, Taiwan 463–5
unlimited liability companies, Taiwan 447, 462
unlimited liability risk, UK partnership options 369
unlimited personal liability concerns, India 431–2, 435
UPA (Uniform Partnership Act)
common-law perspectives on binding the firm 82–3, 84–5, 86, 87
harmonization, rationalization and uniformity 299
and interest transfers among existing partners and members 75–6
law firm as industry model 289
unincorporated entity 209, 212
US
business trusts *see* business trusts
capital accounts *see* capital accounts in limited liability companies and partnerships
common-law perspectives on binding the firm *see* common-law perspectives on binding the firm, and external agency
comparison, India, limited liability partnerships 432–3
comparison, Japan, limited liability companies 383–4
contractual freedom and family business *see* contractual freedom and family business
convergence of unincorporated entity law *see* convergence of unincorporated entity law, casual
Delaware *see* Delaware headings
Employee Retirement Income Security Act (ERISA) 276
Federal Volunteer Protection Act 104
harmonization, rationalization and uniformity *see* harmonization, rationalization and uniformity
interest transfers among existing partners and members *see* interest transfers among existing partners and members, *Achaian v. Leemon Family* case
Investment Company Act 271
Model Entity Transactions Act (META) 302
Model Registered Agents Act (MRAA) 302
RPLLCA (Revised Prototype Limited Liability Company Act), fundamental

changes in limited liability companies 190, 191, 193, 195–6, 198, 211
RULLCA *see* RULLCA (Revised Uniform Limited Liability Company Act)
RUPA *see* RUPA (Revised Uniform Partnership Act)
RUUNA (Revised Uniform Unincorporated Nonprofit Association Act) 103–4
Securities Exchange Act 13
state laboratories and social enterprise law *see* state laboratories and social enterprise law
taxation *see* taxation
UPA *see* UPA (Uniform Partnership Act)
U.S.-Canada tax treaty amendments 163–5
US, cases
In re 210 West Liberty Holdings 118
In re A-Z Electronics 117, 118
Achaian v. Leemon Family see interest transfers among existing partners and members, *Achaian v. Leemon Family* case
Albert v. Alex Brown Mgmt Servs. 25
In re Albright 135–6
Allen v. Encore Energy Partners 32, 65, 67, 347
Allied Capital Corp. v. GC-SUN Holdings 26
In re Atlas Energy Resources 20, 23, 33, 345
Ault v. Brady 73
Auriga Capital Corp. v. Gatz Props. 25, 26, 58–9, 62, 304
In re Avalon Hotel Partners 117–18
B.A.S.S. Group v. Coastal Supply Co. 94
In re Bay Club Partners 119
Bay Ctr. Apartments Owner v. Emery Bay PKI 24, 344
Bluestein v. Davis 213–14
Boilermakers v. Chevron 351
Braswell v Ryan Investments Ltd 141
Brickwell Partners v. Wise 23–4, 30–31
Brinckerhoff v. Enbridge Energy Co. 19–20, 345, 348
In re Caremark 337–8, 339, 340
Cass JV v. Host International 219, 221
In re Catron 121
Chambers v. Kay 283
Cohen v. Lord, Day & Lord 283–4
In re DB Capital Holdings 119–20, 122
In re Delta Starr Broadcasting 118
In re Desmond 126
In re East End Dev. 118–19
Elf Atochem N. Am. v. Jaffari 11, 71
In re Encore Energy Partners LP Unitholder Litigation 22, 31–2, 35, 345, 346–7, 348
Feeley v. NHAOCG 99, 200, 304, 344

Firmani v. Firmani 136
Fliegler v. Lawrence 68
Forsythe v. ESC Fund Mgmt Co. 25, 345
Fouchek v. Janicek 212–13
Frates v. Nichols 216–17
In re Frye 122
In re Garcia 125, 126
In re Garrison-Ashburn 124, 125
Gatz Props. v. Auriga Capital Corp. 200, 304, 342–3
Gelfman v. Weeden Investors 25, 344, 346
Gerber v. EPE Holdings 22, 35–8, 66–7, 345, 347, 348–9
Gotham Partners v. Hallwood Realty Partners 20, 23, 25, 57, 109, 342, 343, 344
In re Green Power Kenansville 119, 122
In re H & W Food Mart 117, 118
Hooper v. Yoder 217–18
Howard v. Babcock 284
Huatuco v. Satellite Healthcare 29–30, 199
In re Hyde Park P'ship 126
Jack J. Morris Assocs. v. Mispillion Street Partners 93–4
Kahn v. Icahn 24
Kahn v. Lynch Communications 338, 339, 340
Kahn v. M&F Worldwide 338, 339, 340
In re Keeler 123
In re Klingerman 124, 125
Litchfield Asset Management Corp. v. Howell 139
Lonergan v. EPE Holdings 345, 348
In re Lull 125–6
Lund v. Albrecht 214–15
Meinhard v. Salmon 208–9, 215, 218–19, 378
Milford Power Co. v. PDC Milford Power 72, 125
Miller v. American Real Estate Partners 33–4
Monin v. Monin 218
Monroe v. Berger 123–4
Nemec v. Shrader 26, 347, 348
Newburger, Loeb & Co. v. Gross 215, 222
Norton v. K-Sea Transp. Partners 25, 346
Olmstead v. FTC 133, 135
Olson v. Halvorsen 11, 341, 342
Oram Sylvania v. Townsend Ventures 63
Paige Capital Mgmt. v. Lerner Master Fund 20–21, 344
Paramount Communications v. QVC Network 55, 56–7
In re Phillips 108, 117
Pierre v. Comm'r 235–6
R & R Capital v. Buck & Doe Run Valley Farms 30, 39, 55, 199

In re Raiton 123
RERI Holdings I 235–6
Revlon 56–7, 254, 338, 339, 351
Schnell v. Chris-Craft Indus. 16, 33, 34, 68
Shuttleworth, Ruloff & Giordano v. Nutter 284
Sonet v. Timber Co. 32, 342
Stewart v. Bolthouse Holdco 62
In re Trans World Airlines 122, 123
In re Tristar Esperanza Props. 123
Twin Bridges Ltd. Partnership v. Draper 33, 38
In re USACafes 22, 23, 343–4
VGS v. Castiel 32, 33, 38, 41, 43–4
In re Walt Disney Co. Derivative Litig. 26, 337, 339, 340
Weinberger v. UOP 19, 337, 338, 339
Winshall v. Viacom 35, 63–4
Wood v. Baum 57

Varley, M. 369
veil piercing
  liability of limited liability entities 107–9, 110
  nonprofit and charitable uses of limited liability companies 235
  patterns, and contractual freedom 21–4
  reverse *see* asset protection limited liability companies, attacking, reverse veil piercing
venture capital-backed firms
  Japan 378, 379, 380, 382–3, 385, 386, 387
  Taiwan 461–2
Vermeulen, E. 149
Verret, J. 339, 340, 349
Vestal, A. 253, 360
vested property rights 200–201, 383, 436
voluntary sector *see* nonprofit and charitable uses of limited liability companies
voting

corporate concept, and harmonization 315
equity holder rights, and freedom of contract 31–3, 38
rights, Russia 417, 420, 427
see also shareholders
Vranka, L. 254, 255

Walker, D. 257
Wang, J. 462
Wang, W. 461
Warren, E. 270
Weidner, D. 42, 168–86
Westaway, K. 262
Whittaker, J. 363
Williston, S. 60–61, 62, 148
Winship, V. 350
Winter, R. 259
withdrawal procedure
  Japan *see* Japan, limited liability companies legislative policy, exit options
  Russia 422–3, 424, 426
  Taiwan 450, 453–4, 456, 466–7
  see also dissolution
Wood, A. 253
Wu, Y. 398

Yablon, C. 261, 264
Yang, J. 455
Yang, S. 451
Ye, S. 451
Ye, X. 462
Yin, G. 159
Yockey, J. 255

Zall, B. 248
Zelin, M. 392
Zelnik, R. 413
Zhang, H. 391, 409
Zhang, Y. 400